Computers in the Human Context

Also by Tom Forester

The Labour Party and the Working Class (1976)
The Microelectronics Revolution (ed.) (1980)
The Information Technology Revolution (ed.) (1985)
High-Tech Society (1987)
The Materials Revolution (ed.) (1988)

Computers in the Human Context

Information Technology, Productivity, and People

Edited and introduced by
TOM FORESTER

The MIT Press
Cambridge, Massachusetts

First MIT Press edition, 1989

Copyright © Basil Blackwell 1989

Library of Congress Cataloging-in-Publication Data
Computers in the human context : information
  technology, productivity, and people/
  edited and introduced by Tom Forester.
    p. cm.
  Bibliography: p.
  Includes index.

  ISBN 0-262-06124-4.
  ISBN 0-262-56050-X (pbk.)
  1. Computers and civilization. 2. Information technology—Social aspects. I. Forester, Tom.
QA76.9.C66C659   1989
303.4'834—dc19   89-2331
                                                                              CIP

Printed and bound in Great Britain

Contents

Preface

Over $300 billion a year is now spent world-wide on computers and communications hardware and software, but it's doubtful whether more than 300 researchers around the world are studying the impact of all this spending on the economy and society at large. We are in the midst of an information technology (IT) revolution, but the human, organizational and social factors shaping this revolution have been scarcely analyzed and they are as yet imperfectly understood. We know a lot about the technical capabilities of computers, but comparatively little about their social consequences and possibilities.

The contributors to this book have been brought together to help rectify this imbalance and in so doing they ask some fundamental questions: questions about the productivity payoff so far from the enormous capital investment in IT; questions about the employment impact of IT; questions about the changes to the quality of our domestic and working lives; questions about the desirability of having computers involved in more and more societal and govern-mental tasks; questions about the unforeseen side-effects of the IT revolution, like computer crime and workplace surveillance; and questions about the distribution of wealth, power and information in our future high-tech society. The impact of IT is explored, illustrated and analyzed at different social levels – at the level of the individual, at the level of organizations, at the level of national economies and at the global level – in an effort to make sense of the complex interrelationship between IT and society.

The emerging consensus seems to be that the productivity payoff from IT is slow in coming and that it may be some years before we see the real economic and social benefits feeding through. Robots do not as yet run factories and the most flexible manufacturing system produced to date remains the human operator. In offices and other paper-using organizations, expensive automated systems have not always been a success: one researcher suggests that the most effective form of communication between people is not electronic mail, but human speech. To many people, "artificial intelligence" seems little nearer to becoming a reality than it was 33 years ago when the term was first used. Despite numerous predictions to the contrary, not many people are working from home (or shopping or banking from home) in the "electronic cottage" and the computer revolution in the classroom has been slow to materialize. Fanciful notions such as the imminent arrival of "teledemocracy" or push-button voting are rarely heard these days. In short, the euphoria that followed the arrival of the microchip in the 1970s and the accompanying utopian scenarios have been dispaced by a calmer, more rational assessment of the future with IT.

In particular, it is becoming increasingly apparent that what decides the difference between success and failure in the implementation of IT systems is the human factor. It is people who have to operate the new systems and it is people who have to change their work and leisure habits to accommodate them. Computers alter the pattern of social relationships in organizations and in turn their use is affected by prevailing ideologies and social relationships within organizations. Together, these human and social factors normally combine to delay the pace of change or influence its direction.

From the studies reported here, it is clear that many companies and institutions using IT are not using IT effectively because they have ignored or underestimated the importance of the human factor. Systems which do not utilize human abilities or do not take into account human needs risk becoming financial and social-psychological disasters. We will not, it seems, make a success of the IT revolution until we learn to design human-centered systems.

This book is an update of my earlier anthologies published by Basil Blackwell and MIT Press, *The Microelectronics Revolution* (1980) and *The Information Technology Revolution* (1985). At the same time, it develops some of the arguments touched upon in my recent book, *High-Tech Society* (1987), which has just been published in Japan. The "human context" theme and the more critical – some would say "debunking" – tone emerged from my reading of the latest research and thinking on the subject of computers and society, which I believe is adequately reflected in this volume. All the 43 pieces reproduced here were published in the period 1984–8. The contents have been further modified in the light of my experience teaching two courses ("Information: the Human Context" and "Information, Technology, and the Future") on the Informatics degree program in the School of Computing and Information Technology at Griffith University.

For their helpful advice, comments and other assistance, I wish to thank Professor Geoff Dromey and colleagues at the School of CIT, Griffith University; Michael Marien, editor of the World Future Society's *Future Survey*; and many of the authors included here who have been very cooperative and helpful, in particular Ian Miles, John Bessant, Rick Long, Rob Kling, Larry Hirschhorn, Langdon Winner, David Bolter, Melvin Kranzberg, Brian Winston, James Beniger, Ben Shneiderman, Steve Smith, and Tim Warner.

Tom Forester

Acknowledgments

The editor and the publishers are grateful to the following:

Addison-Wesley Publishing Company, for Ben Shneiderman, "Designing the User Interface," reprinted from *Designing the User Interface,* © 1987, Addison-Wesley Publishing Co., Inc., Reading, MA; pp. v–vi and pp. 4–18 text only. Reprinted with permission.

American Scientist, for Kenneth R. Foster, "The VDT Debate," reprinted from *American Scientist,* vol. 74, March–April 1986. Reprinted with permission.

The Atlantic, for Justine De Lacy, "The Sexy Computer," reprinted from *The Atlantic,* July 1987. Reprinted with permission.

Beech Tree Publishing, for Marie Jahoda, "Artificial Intelligence: An Outsider's Perspective," reprinted from *Science and Public Policy,* December 1986; and S. L. Smith, "Information Technology: Taylorisation or Human-Centred Office Systems?" *Science and Public Policy,* June 1987 (retitled: "Information Technology in Banks: Taylorization or Human-centered Systems?"). Reprinted with permission.

The British Psychological Society, for David J. Oborne, "Ergonomics and Information Technology," reprinted from Frank Blackler and David Oborne (eds), *Information Technology and People,* BPS Books, Leicester, UK and MIT Press, Cambridge, MA, 1987. Reprinted with permission.

Business Week, for John Hoerr, Michael A. Pollock, and David E. Whiteside, "Management Discovers the Human Side of Automation," reprinted from *Business Week,* September 29, 1986 and Catherine L. Harris et al., "Office Automation: Making It Pay Off," reprinted from *Business Week,* October 12, 1987. Reprinted by special permission, copyright © 1986, 1987 by McGraw-Hill, Inc.

Butterworth Scientific Ltd, for William E. Halal, "Beyond Left Versus Right" (retitled "The New Capitalism"), reprinted from *Futures*, June 1985; and Tom Forester, "The Myth of the Electronic Cottage," reprinted from *Futures*, June 1988. Reprinted with permission.

Elsevier Science Publishing Company, for Richard H. Franke, "Technological Revolution and Productivity Decline: Computer Introduction in the Financial Industry" (retitled: "Technological Revolution and Productivity Decline: The Case of US Banks"), reprinted from *Technological Forecasting and Social Change*, vol. 31, 1987, pp. 143–54. Copyright © 1987, Elsevier Science Publishing Co., 52 Vanderbilt Ave., New York NY 10017.

Fortune, for William Bowen, "The Puny Payoff from Office Computers," reprinted from *Fortune*, May 26, 1986. Copyright © 1986 Time Inc. All rights reserved.

Harper's Magazine, for Steven Levy, "A Spreadsheet Way of Knowledge," reprinted from the November 1984 issue by special permission. Copyright © 1984 by *Harper's Magazine*. All rights reserved.

Harvard Business Review, for Roger Miller and Marcel Côté, "Growing the Next Silicon Valley," reprinted from *Harvard Business Review*, July–August 1985 and Beau Sheil, "Thinking about Artificial Intelligence," reprinted from *Harvard Business Review*, July–August 1987. Copyright © 1985, 1987 by the President and Fellows of Harvard College All rights reserved.

Harvard University Press, for James R. Beniger, "The Evolution of Control," reprinted by permission of the publishers from *The Control Revolution: Technological and Economic Origins of the Information Society*, by James R. Beniger, Cambridge, MA, Harvard University Press. Copyright © 1986 by the President and Fellows of Harvard College.

Kluwer Academic Publishers for Langdon Winner, "Myth Information: Romantic Politics in the Information Age," reprinted from Carl Mitcham and Alois Huning (eds), *Philosophy and Technology II: Information Technology and Computers in Theory and Practice*. Copyright © 1986 Kluwer Academic Publishers, Dordrecht, Holland.

National Academy Press, for Melvin Kranzberg, "The Information Age," reprinted from Bruce R. Guile (ed.), *Information Technologies and Social Transformation*, National Academy Press, Washington, DC, 1985. Reprinted with permission.

Oxford University Press, for Robert Schware and Ziauddin Choudhury, "Aid Agencies and Information Technology Development" (retitled: "The Role of IT in Third World Development"), reprinted from *Information Technology for Development*, June/July 1988. Reprinted with permission.

Pergamon Press, for Keith Hearnden, "Computer Crime: Multi-million Pound Problem" (retitled: "Computer Criminals are Human, Too"), reprinted from *Long Range Planning*, vol. 19 (5), October 1986. Reprinted with permission.

Plenum Publishing Corporation, for Elisabeth Gerver, "Computers and Gender," reprinted from Elisabeth Gerver, *Humanizing Technology*, Plenum Press, London and New York, 1985. Reprinted with permission.

Routledge and Kegan Paul, for Brian Winston, "The Illusion of Revolution," reprinted from Brian Winston, *Misunderstanding Media*, Routledge and Kegan Paul, London and Harvard University Press, Cambridge, MA, 1986. Reprinted with permission.

Sage Publications, for F. Christopher Arterton, "Teledemocracy Reconsidered," reprinted from F. Christopher Arterton, *Teledemocracy: Can Technology Protect Democracy?*, pp. 18–24, 53–5, 184–190 and 204. Copyright © 1987 by the Roosevelt Center for American Policy Studies. Reprinted by permission of Sage Publications, Inc.

Scientific American, for James Brian Quinn, Jordan J. Baruch, and Penny Cushman Paquette, "Technology in Services", reprinted from *Scientific American*, vol. 257 (6), December 1987. Reprinted with permission. Copyright © 1987 Scientific American, Inc. All rights reserved.

Sloan Management Review, for Timothy N. Warner, "Information Technology as a Competitive Burden," reprinted from *Sloan Management Review*, vol. 29 (1), Fall 1987, by permission of the publisher. Copyright © 1987 by the Sloan Management Review Association. All rights reserved.

Technology Review, for Stephen S. Cohen and John Zysman, "Manufacturing Matters: The Myth of the Post-Industrial Economy," reprinted from *Technology Review*, February–March 1987; Hubert and Stuart Dreyfus, "Why Computers May Never Think Like People," January 1986; Alison B. Bass, "Computers in the Classroom," April 1987; Harley Shaiken, "The Automated Factory: The View From the Shop Floor" (retitled: "The Automated Factory: Vision and Reality"), January 1985; Edward J. Malecki, "Hope or Hyperbole? High Tech and Economic Development" (retitled: "High Tech and Economic Development: Hope or Hype?"), October 1987; John Shattuck and Muriel Morisey Spence, "The Dangers of Information Control," April 1988; Anne W. Branscomb, "Who Owns Creativity?" May–June 1988; Gary T. Marx and Sanford Sherizen, "Monitoring on the Job," November–December 1986; Antonio José J. Botelho, "Brazil's Independent Computer Strategy," May–June 1987; and Frank Barnaby, "How The Next War Will Be Fought," October 1986. All reprinted with permission from *Technology Review*. Copyright © 1985, 1986, 1987, 1988.

UNESCO Institute for Education, for Donald P. Ely and Tjeerd Plomp, "The Promises of Education Technology: A Reassessment," reprinted from *International Review of Education*, vol. 32 (3), 1986. Reprinted with permission.

University of North Carolina Press, for Jay David Bolter, "The Computer as a Defining Technology," reprinted from *Turing's Man: Western Culture in the Computer Age*, by J. David · Bolter. Copyright © 1984 The University of North Carolina Press. Reprinted with permission.

Editor's Introduction: Making Sense of IT

Clearly, something very important is happening to society with the influx of IT, but we don't as yet fully understand what it is. It is generally agreed that the computer is probably the most important technological innovation this century and that information technology (IT) is a pervasive technology at least as important as electricity or steam power. Information processing has always been an essential element of human consciousness and information processing technologies such as smoke signals and flags have played a major role in all past societies. Since the Industrial Revolution, societies have become infinitely more complex. This has created a need for more and more information to be processed – and the development of more efficient information processing technologies.

The revolutionary importance of IT stems from the fact that decreases in the cost and size of computers have been accompanied by increases in their power, speed and sophistication. The digitization of information has in addition brought about the convergence of voice, image and data and of the electronics, telecommunications and computing industries based upon them.[1] It is further accepted that the arrival of IT has created a new technological "paradigm" for companies and other institutions for two reasons: first, they ignore IT at their peril because IT creates a new "best practice" or set of ground rules – the use of IT has rapidly become accepted as the new "common sense"; second, IT calls for dramatic changes in organizational structures, from the smallest firm to the largest government bureaucracy, although as we shall see the choice of systems is not determined but is open to social negotiation.

Conceptual frameworks

There is considerable disagreement as to whether we are witnessing a new industrial "revolution" on a par with the Industrial Revolution in late eighteenth-century Britain – or whether IT is just another example of steady technological evolution. Immediately this raises the question of what constitutes a "revolution" and in particular whether major clusters of technological innovation like IT must be accompanied by a wholesale social transformation for them to qualify as a full-blown "revolution." This debate in turn is a reflection of the much broader, long-standing debates among historians about the extent to which the Industrial Revolution itself was a "revolution"; among philosophers of science about the possible existence of "paradigm" shifts (fundamental breaks with the prevailing view of the world); among sociologists about the process of social development (including the possible rise of new classes like scientists and technologists or "technocrats"); and among economists about the path of economic development (including the possible existence of economic cycles or "long waves"). Social scientists in general are still trying to understand the dialectical relationship between technology and society and indeed the nature of society itself.

Of particular importance is the interrelationship between technology and society. Just as philosophers talk about "free will" and "determinism" and economists debate the relative merits of "demand-pull" and "technology-push" theories of innovation and economic development, so too sociologists argue about the merits of "technological determinism" versus "social shaping," or human choice within a sociocultural context. In other words, is our future being determined by technology or are we to some extent free to choose and shape the future?

There are many different types of technological determinism. There is "soft" determinism and "hard" determinism and a continuum of positions in between. There is the determinism that sees technology as the *cause* of social change and the determinism that sees technology as a *consequence* of social change (cf. "technology-push" and "demand-pull"). There is the type of determinism that sees technological development as following an inevitable, fixed course and the determinism that sees a particular technology like IT as having a uniformity of "impact."[2] But broadly speaking a major distinction can be made between writers on the basis of the relative importance they attribute to technology itself on the one hand and to human choice or sociocultural values on the other. This tends to come across clearly in their writings as does the oft-mentioned distinction between "optimists" and "pessimists."[3] Not surprisingly, technological determinists tend also to be pessimists while "human choice" supporters tend to be optimists, but this is not always the case.

The contrasting of optimists versus pessimists, technological determinism versus human choice, and revolution versus evolution are useful though somewhat simplistic devices which we use to clarify the different positions taken. In a further effort to shed light on these differences of viewpoint, some writers have found it helpful to distinguish between two or three "perspectives" or schools of thought which social scientists bring to the problem of IT and society. Barry Jones, for example, makes a distinction between those who see the coming of IT and associated changes as a fundamental break with the past or a "radical discontinuity" amounting to a "paradigm shift" on the one hand and those on the other hand who see what's happening to society now as merely another case of "traditional incrementalism" or steady, evolutionary change which does *not* mark a major break with the past.[4] Jones himself sees the industrial era we have experienced since the Industrial Revolution as being superseded by the current "Age of Discontinuity" leading to a "Post-Service Society."

Miles et al. distinguish three perspectives on IT: the "continuist," the "transformationist," and the "structuralist."[5] Continuists see recent developments in IT as merely the current stage in a long-term process of incremental change in information processing technology. The rate of diffusion will be slow and society will remain essentially unchanged. IT promises "more of the same." Transformationists, on the other hand, see IT as a truly revolutionary technology which will be accompanied by revolutionary changes to society. Adoption of IT will be swift and the transformation of society on a par with the transition from agricultural to industrial societies is already evident. Nothing will be the same again as we become a new type of society – the most popular labels for this society being "Post-industrial Society" and "Information Society." Thirdly, structuralists steer a middle course, arguing that IT *is* a revolutionary technology, but it is one which can be accommodated within the existing structure of industrial society. Unlike the transformationists, structuralists argue that IT has the capacity to reshape many institutions of industrial society, but not to totally transform them. Unlike the continuists, structuralists say the changes in the next few decades cannot be extrapolated from the past. IT has created new technological and organizational paradigms that offer social choices not available before. This classification roughly corresponds to the "evolutionary," "revolutionary" and "restructuring of industrial society" perspectives identified earlier by John Bessant et al.[6]

Of course, any three-fold typology cannot do justice to the infinite variety of positions on the relationship between IT and society which, as we have seen, also embrace different degrees and types of "determinism" and of "optimism" or "pessimism." But there is one important group of thinkers, who, though in a sense are "continuists," perhaps merit a category to themselves. "Heretics" such as Herbert Marcuse, Joe Weizenbaum, Herbert Schiller, Theodore Roszak, Langdon Winner and Frank Webster and Kevin Robins pour scorn on all the talk of "revolutions" and generally see no good at all coming out of IT, which is viewed primarily as an ideological weapon in the hands of corporate leaders and capitalist governments. IT is seen as increasing the power of the transnational corporations over organized labor and individuals; as strengthening mechanisms of social control by governments and their agencies through increased electronic surveillance; as generating yet more pap for the masses in the form of cable TV, satellite TV and videotex-based "infotainment"; and as widening the already obscene gap between the developed nations and the Third World. The vast increase in information processing capacity has also led to a positively dangerous situation of "information overload" or "infoglut" in many organizations, which increases the likelihood of major systems failures like Three Mile Island, Chernobyl and the *Challenger* space shuttle disaster – and could even lead in future to an "accidental" Third World War. Moreover, the very idea of trying to make machines to rival the human brain is anathema to the heretics, who see "artificial intelligence" as both an unrealizable and an improper goal.

Important contributions

Writers included in this volume have been chosen both for the importance of their work, its relevance to our chosen theme and because they represent the different schools of thought in the ongoing debate about the "impact" of IT on society we have just outlined. Melvin Kranzberg* sets himself the task of comparing and contrasting IT with the Industrial Revolution. He points out that the Industrial Revolution not only involved an explosion of technical innovation, it also marked "a truly revolutionary transformation of society because it changed where and how people worked, lived, thought, played and prayed."[7] In other words, a true revolution, according to Kranzberg, involves both economic/technological and

*Denotes authors represented in this volume.

sociocultural changes of the first order – or changes to the base and superstructure of society. Kranzberg argues that recent developments in IT do indeed constitute a technological revolution, but it will be some time before we see the full social effects. Some are already apparent, but there will be unintended effects and, he says, the same information technology will have quite different impacts when introduced into different sociocultural settings. Kranzberg is generally optimistic about the prospects of what he calls the "Information Age" and he is open-minded and non-deterministic about the future. He concludes: "While it [the Information Age] might be evolutionary, in the sense that all the changes and benefits will not appear overnight, it will be revolutionary in its effects upon society."[8]

James Beniger,* on the other hand, sees IT merely as part of an ongoing "control revolution" dating from the nineteenth century. This "essential social dynamic" of our age originated, he says, in a fundamental "crisis of control" generated by the Industrial Revolution.[9] That revolution resulted in a speeding-up of society's underlying materials processing system, causing many control problems in the areas of manufacturing and distribution (keeping track of stock, railway wagons, etc.). Early responses to this crisis were technological innovations like the telegraph, the rationalization of information and the development of bureaucracy – all of which were designed to improve information flows. Since 1945, the development of new information processing technologies such as the computer, better telecommunications and new mass media have assumed central importance in the continuing control crisis. Thus, he concludes, "microprocessing and computing technology, contrary to currently fashionable opinion, do not represent a new force only recently unleashed on an unprepared society but merely the most recent installment in the continuing development of the Control Revolution."[10] While not appearing to be unduly optimistic or pessimistic about the future, Beniger clearly sees new technologies like IT as being a consequence rather than a cause of social change – a case of demand-pull rather than technology-push.

In contrast J. David Bolter* is convinced that the computer is the new "defining technology" of our era. "A defining technology defines or redefines man's role in relation to nature," he says. While "the technology of any age provides an attractive window through which thinkers can view both their physical and metaphysical worlds . . . only a few devices or crafts in any age deserve to be called defining technologies . . ." The computer qualifies in the same way that the potter's wheel, clocks, and steam engines were the defining technologies of previous eras: it is changing the way we think about ourselves and the world around us. Thus the computer is used as a metaphor for the human brain: "By promising (or threatening) to replace man, the computer is giving us a new definition of man, as an 'information processor,' and of nature, as 'information to be processed'. . . By making a machine think as a man, man recreates himself, defines himself as a machine."[11] No short summary can do justice to Bolter's thesis, but generally speaking he tends toward both determinism and optimism, and the view that IT is a genuinely revolutionary technology. In terms of Miles et al.'s typology, Bolter would appear to be the more "transformationist" while Kranzberg is probably on balance a "structuralist" and Beniger an obvious "continuist."

Representing the heretics, Langdon Winner* has little time for the grand notions and apocalyptic visions of Bolter and other well-known transformationists like Daniel Bell and Alvin Toffler. Winner denounces the "computer romantics" and all the talk about the "revolutionary" promise of IT, claiming that the word itself has been degraded. He ridicules as "flights of utopian fancy" suggestions that IT will lead to a cultural renaissance, the elimination of drudgery and the development of a genuine participatory democracy. He sees the political implications of IT as particularly important: "Current developments in the information age suggest an increase in power by those who already had a great deal of power, an enhanced centralization of control by those already prepared for control, an augmentation of wealth by the already wealthy . . . if there is to be a computer revolution, the best guess would be that it would have a distinctly conservative character."[12]

It thus becomes obvious to Winner that all the "revolutionary" hype surrounding IT is a self-serving ideology promoted by those who stand to gain most from increased sales of, and the increased use of, computers. Although pessimistic in many respects, Winner is not a determinist and believes there is still time to change the course of the IT revolution so that it better reflects human needs and brings about improvements rather than a deterioration in the quality of life. But he acknowledges that "the occasions for reflection, debate and public choice are extremely rare indeed. The important decisions are left in private hands inspired by narrowly focused economic motives."[13]

Whither post-industrial society?

Apart from the onslaught by the heretics, the transformationists have also taken a beating of late from new arguments and evidence which amount to a full-frontal assault on the widely accepted notion that we are moving toward a "post-industrial" society – other popular societal labels being the "information society," the "knowledge society" and the "leisure society" (although as Beniger shows, these are just a few examples of the many social transformations proposed in recent years).

Stephen Cohen and John Zysman* totally reject the notion of post-industrial society. They argue forcefully that the United States does not have a post-industrial economy, nor is it ever likely to have one – and, what's more, it had better not try to acquire one. First, they suggest that the conventional view that sees a service-based or knowledge-based "post-industrial" society as the next stage up in social development from societies based on agriculture and industry simply does not stand up. For example, manufacturing in the United States has in fact maintained its share of GNP (if not employment) over the past 40 years and industrial output contributes about as much to the US economy as the whole of the service sector if you omit construction. To talk of being in a "post-industrial" phase because of the decline in manufacturing employment is therefore misleading. By the same token, since only 3 percent of employment is on farms, we might just as well call ourselves a "post-agricultural" society (except that US farm output regularly sets new records). The view of social development that sees "inevitable" stages of progression and that sees a smooth transition from traditional "sunset" industries to high-tech "sunrise" industries may be comforting to non-interventionists and it may have captured the fancy of many, but it is a myth. Post-industrial politics, in the form of increased power for the technocrats, hasn't appeared either. "The transition we are experiencing," say Cohen and Zysman, "is not one of industry into services, but from one kind of industrial society to another."[15]

Consequently, suggestions that the United States should accept "deindustrialization" and "give up" on manufacturing and concentrate on services (popular at one time in US government and business circles) is dangerously misleading because the linkages between "manufacturing" and "service sector" jobs are strong. Indeed, manufacturing supports many jobs in the service sector and the US cannot succeed or indeed survive as a world power without being successful in manufacturing. Shifting production overseas, particularly of IT goods, will be followed by the migration of R&D facilities and will lead to the "hollowing-out" of US industry, which will further damage the US economy. Yet US industry and even traditional sectors like farming and construction need the very latest in high-tech equipment if they are to remain internationally competitive. Cohen and Zysman therefore conclude that a superficially attractive but nevertheless incorrect "transformationist" view of the development of society has led to the wrong policy positions being adopted by the US government and business – and indeed threatens the economic future of the United States. As a corollary, it should be pointed out that the "deindustrialization" thesis took a further knock with the dramatic revival of US manufacturing industry (helped by a weakened dollar) in the period 1987–8.[16]

A quite different perspective on the service sector is provided by James Brian Quinn, Jordan J. Baruch, and Penny Cushman Paquette.* Their key finding is that many service industries are every bit as large-scale, as capital-intensive and as thoroughly grounded in technology as are the manufacturing industries: "This means that a US economy dominated by services can continue to support real increases in income and wealth for a very prolonged period."[17] The new technologies are affecting the service industries greatly – in some cases, entirely restructuring them – and the beneficial consequences are radiating right through the economy. What's more, they say, most of the economic growth, the opportunities for entrepreneurship and the applications of IT will arise in the services sector in the next two decades, as has been the case in the past 20 years. The real danger is that important people – especially those in government – will misunderstand the importance of the services sector and will mistakenly attempt to shore up certain troubled manufacturing areas at great corporate and national cost.

The notion that society under the influence of new information processing technologies is developing into an "information society" or a "knowledge society" has been around for a while. Way back in 1962, Fritz Machlup published his landmark book *The Production and Distribution of Knowledge in the United States*, which drew attention to the high proportion of the workforce employed in the "knowledge" or "information" industries. This fact was popularized by, for example, *Scientific American*, who published a special issue on "Information" in September 1966, following the announcement of "The Electronic Revolution" in *The American Scholar*, Spring 1966 issue. By 1974, the American Academy of Political and Social Science, in a special issue edited by Don Lamberton, felt confident enough to proclaim "The Information Revolution." But more importantly, it was Machlup's work, among others, which influenced Daniel Bell to write his seminal work *The Coming of Post-Industrial Society*, published in 1973, which became something of a bestseller (although Bell later switched allegiances to the concept of the "Information Society"). Others, notably Marc Porat, updated and developed Machlup's work in the 1970s.[18]

But recent work by Michael Rubin and Mary Huber has provided a severe jolt for theorists of the "information" or "knowledge" society. Machlup had reported that the "knowledge" sector of the US economy – education, R&D, communications, information services, etc. – already accounted for 29 percent of US GNP in 1958. Dramatic predictions of future growth in the knowledge industry were made at the time and new theories of social development were propounded as a result. Yet Rubin and Huber show that the knowledge sector as conceived by Machlup had only grown to 34 percent of US GNP by 1980.[19] What is more, its rate of growth had been slipping since 1972 to roughly that of the rest of the economy. Growth of the "knowledge" sector from 29 percent to 34 percent in more than two decades is interesting but it is hardly sensational. Machlup's original work was one of the key props underpinning a number of economic and social theories: Rubin and Huber appear to have kicked it away.

Finally, recent US data have cast doubt on the once-popular notion that we are moving toward a "leisure" society in which all employees work much shorter hours and many people simply won't need to work at all. In the idealized "leisure" society, leisure will be the main focus of people's lives, the leisure industries will be big business and a whole army of analysts and counsellors will be employed to help teach people how to best enjoy their new-found leisure time. The only problem with this scenario is that it is not coming about: in fact, according to US Bureau of Labor Statistics figures, the exact opposite seems to be happening. Over the past decade or so, the trend has been for employees to work as hard if not harder than ever. About three-quarters of US wage and salary earners put in at least a 40 hour week in 1985 – a percentage that was little changed from the early 1970s. The proportion holding down two jobs actually increased from 4.9 percent in 1980 to 5.4 percent of the workforce in 1985. People also seem to be putting in a lot of work at home (about 8 million say they do at least 8 hours), more are taking part-time or temporary jobs and absenteeism (down to 4.7 percent in 1985) is at its lowest since the early 1970s. A recent Harris Poll concluded that leisure time for Americans had dropped 8.5 hours a week between 1973 and 1985, while other polls (including Department of Labor surveys) show that most US employees would still prefer longer hours and higher incomes to more leisure and less pay.[20] Obviously, inflationary pressures, falling real incomes and the shakeout in manufacturing lie behind the trend to longer hours and harder work, but this apparent negation of the accepted wisdom that we are moving towards some kind of "leisure" society is certainly worth noting.

The long and the short of IT

In a further attempt to make sense of the IT revolution, some writers have found it helpful to distinguish between the long run and the short run. Richard H. Franke,* for example, has taken a detailed look at the use of IT in the first sector of the economy to adopt computers back in the late 1950s, the financial industry. By 1980, he says, half of all US bank capital expenditure other than for buildings was for computers and ancillary equipment. After a complex analysis, Franke concluded that the increased use of computers in the financial sector had initially led to both a *decrease* in capital productivity and a *fall* in profitability, as users struggled to make the new systems work. Vastly increased expenditure on IT was not matched by increases in output or labor productivity. While integrating people and organizations into a new way of working can be costly, he says, the huge capital outlay on computing equipment was the main financial burden. However, 30 years or so on from the introduction of computers in the financial industry, it is possible, says Franke, to detect signs at last of an improvement in capital productivity.

Making a direct comparison with the Industrial Revolution, Franke argues that this "second technological transformation" brought about by IT is following a similar path. A cluster of new technologies, including the coal-fired steam engine, were introduced in the 1770s, but it was not until the 1820s, he says, before the economy and society saw the benefits in terms of increased output, productivity and income. Likewise, it will take time before the benefits of IT are realized: "According to this assessment, it will be early in the 21st century when the accumulated experience in producing and using the equipment of the second technological revolution leads to more effective utilization of human and capital resources and to major increases in output."[21]

Coming at the problem from the different angle of media historian, Brian Winston* seeks to demonstrate how human and social factors have consistently delayed major technological and communication "revolutions." It has taken much longer than popularly imagined, he says, for society to assimilate innovations such as the TV and the telephone. As with the computer, TVs and telephones were initially acclaimed as remarkable, "revolutionary" technologies, but their penetration rate was surprisingly slow and their dissemination to the masses was delayed, chiefly by the Establishment who feared their potential for the radical disruption of the existing social structure: "the history of the technologies of information reveals a gradual, uncataclysmic progress. No telecommunications technology of itself or in aggregate suggests revolutionary development. On the contrary, each of them can be seen as a technological response to certain social relations which, at least in the West, have remained basically unchanged during the entire industrial period."[22]

In the light of this analysis, Winston says that there is little or no reason to link the epithet "revolution" to the epithet "information." This is the fallacy of technological determinism: just because something has been invented, he says, it cannot be assumed that it will be widely used. The IT "revolution" has already produced a crop of technological innovations like videodisks, interactive TV and videotex, which have been market failures. Moreover, he says, personal computers will only play a minor role in most people's lives (chiefly as a replacement for the typewriter); cinemas will survive; home shopping and banking will not take off; and, thanks to cable and satellite TV, the quality of TV programming will get worse and worse. Furthermore, it is misleading to claim that there has been an information "explosion" in the world and that the pace of technological and social change has speeded up. The proponents of the IT "revolution" have made so much noise, he says, that "alternative readings are all but drowned out." Emphasizing his "continuist" stance, Winston writes: "it is my contention that far from a revolution we have business, *and I mean business*, as usual" (my emphasis).[23]

A professor of computer science, Rob Kling,* has made a similar point about the rate of diffusion of computers. He, too, questions whether the computer revolution is quite as "revolutionary" as some people have made out and says there will be no overnight trans-formation of society: "It is common to view technologies as potent forces which foster rapid social change, but the most significant technologies are diffused through modern societies over several decades. Automobiles, telephones, electricity, central heating, television and birth control did not act as independent, powerful forces in the USA. They were shaped and fitted so that the larger social order was not radically uprooted."[24]

Likewise, from the studies carried out by Kling and his University of California colleagues, "There is evidence that computerization develops similarly within public agencies. It is also likely that EFT technologies and instructional computing will be similarly absorbed over several decades." In the short run, says Kling, value conflicts will delay or alter the course of computing developments. This is because computing developments are not socially neutral or value-free, but rather because they acquire ideological and political dimensions. The direction of social change is not therefore predetermined since IT has no uniformity of impact and so much is still open to social choice. According to Kling's analysis, about the only thing we can say with certainty at present is that computerization will result in far-reaching social changes: quite what those changes will be will only become clearer in the long run.

The IT story so far

We have already said that not enough research is being done to monitor the social impact of IT. We need to know more about what's happening on the ground, so to speak – in the homes where we live, in the schools which our children attend, in the factories, offices, banks, shops, hospitals and laboratories where we work. But from the research that *has* been done, it is possible to draw some tentative conclusions. These are that the productivity payoff from IT so far has been disappointing, to say the least; that the impact of IT on employment levels has been less dramatic than almost everyone expected; that the impact of IT on the quality of worklife has not necessarily been deleterious; and that human (psychological, social, organizational) factors have played a key role in slowing the rate or altering the direction of social change. This in turn leads to the need to develop more human-centered systems. I will illustrate the argument here with reference to the IT story so far in homes, factories, and offices.

Let's start with the "Factory of the Future." As long ago as the 1920s and 1930s, visionaries were proclaiming the dawn of the automatic factory. In the 1950s, the writings of Norbert Weiner and John Diebold created a new wave of interest in factory automation. But the enabling technology did not exist at the right price and it was not until the arrival of the microchip in the 1970s that people started to talk seriously again about the factory of the future in our lifetime. Upbeat predictions were made about completely unmanned, automated factories being the norm by 1995. It seemed that nothing could stop the march of the robots and FMS (flexible manufacturing systems) on to the factory floor. Millions of blue-collar workers, it was said, would "soon" lose their jobs to robots and other high-tech gadgetry.

But the robot revolution didn't really happen, progress with FMS has been very slow and plans to create CIM (computer-integrated manufacturing) have been scaled right back. Ten years ago, some reputable analysts were confidently predicting 250,000 robots in US factories by 1990. By 1988, less than 30,000 had been installed (compared, incidentally, with about 120,000 in Japan). US sales of robots slumped in the period 1985–7, especially after GM cut back on robot purchases, and some US robot manufacturers went out of business. Pioneer robot maker Unimation was in deep trouble and GE pulled out of robot manufacture altogether. Only about 200 fully fledged flexible manufacturing systems are up and running worldwide, still fewer are in regular commercial use and less than 10 percent have made the expected return on investment. As Tim Warner* shows, some of these "showcase" installations, like the John Deere farm equipment factory at Waterloo, Iowa, appear to have been complete disasters. Progress toward CIM has been hampered by the high cost and the failure of manufacturers to agree on a common software language like MAP (manufacturing automation protocol), which could help link up all the "islands" of automation in plants into one integrated system.

The reasons for this state of affairs are not hard to find: people got carried away with the utopian visions of automated factories, overlooking the high cost of high tech and the enormous complexity of factory operations. Robots were absurdly over-hyped: it was conveniently ignored that they are both much more expensive and less flexible than humans. As one commentator put it: "Contrary to the early hype, it rarely makes business sense simply to replace a human worker with a robot and expect the machine to pay for itself in saved labor costs."[25] FMS more often than not has been used as a solution to a production design or materials management problem which should not have existed in the first place. Much can be achieved by improving quality and product or inventory flow without resorting to this expensive high-tech "fix." Managers have found that direct human labor is a more cost-effective, flexible tool than FMS: as Ken Jones of the Ontario Centre for Advanced Manufacturing in Canada has pointed out, many have come to appreciate that "full realization of CIM would require the encoding of all related human intelligence for computer management decisions. Anything less would be less effective and flexible than human powers of decision . . ."[26] So rather than pressing on toward CIM, many companies are now simply upgrading their factory operations with improved production methods, just-in-time (JIT) inventory control and more imaginative management, often involving the creation of a more cooperative work climate. Massive spending on IT without accompanying changes in work design is now rare. IT is, of course, being applied more and more – but a total machine takeover in factories no longer seems to be the goal. Rather, it is a common sense *partnership* between machine and man.

The delayed arrival of the "Office of the Future" is now an old story. Back in the late 1970s, it was widely believed that the wholly automated, "paperless" office was just around the corner. Companies like Exxon, Xerox and Wang poured millions of dollars into developing integrated office automation systems. Theorists explained how we were poised on the threshold of a new *kind* of office – one more suited to the "information" age rather than the "industrial" age. But by the early 1980s it was clear that an office "revolution" of the type envisaged simply had not happened. The expensive, integrated systems had generally failed to sell and users of the systems that had sold were not happy with their performance. Far from going "paperless," US offices were consuming more and more paper, according to market researchers.[27] One UK consultant advised clients to stop trying to communicate by computer and to try speaking to each other instead: human speech, he wrily observed, was a "competitive alternative" to IT. But the main factors making for slow progress with office automation were the colossal expense of the new systems; management resistance to change; the lack of demonstrable increases in productivity; shortages of suitable software; a lack of agreement on standards; and manufacturers pursuing technological cul-de-sacs which further exacerbated the problem of incompatibilty.

What happened instead, of course, was that people started taking their newly acquired personal computers into their offices, often using them initially in a fairly modest way. IBM spotted the trend and in 1981 launched its own PC,which was to spearhead IBM's attack on the office automation market. Helped by the availability of new business software packages like the best-selling VisiCalc, Lotus's 1-2-3 and Ashton-Tate's dBase III, personal computers rapidly became the basic building blocks of the office of the future – rather than the expensive, integrated systems. IBM's PC was a huge success and a great number of "IBM-compatible" or IBM "clone" makers were attracted into the market. One company, Compaq, was so successful in selling IBM clones that it rapidly became the fastest-growing US company *ever*.

Despite these sales successes, official figures still indicated that white-collar productivity was no higher in the mid-1980s than it was in the late 1960s.[28] Measuring white-collar productivity is very tricky at the best of times, but in so far as it *can* be measured, the evidence suggests that IT as yet has had little beneficial effect. Paul A. Strassman, for example, in his book *Information Pay-Off*, found no clear link between high IT spending and management effectiveness. William Bowen* cites analysts like Morgan Stanley's Stephen Roach who say that the productivity payoff from IT in offices is hard to detect. Catherine L. Harris,* on the other hand, has assembled some impressive success stories, but her main message is that office automation is a necessary but not a *sufficient* condition for success: investment in IT must be accompanied by changes in work practices if it is to be effective. Unless management fully understands the work process, and sets clear goals and communicates these to the workforce, much expenditure will be wasted. Even when new systems are successfully implemented in a technical sense, patience is required before the real payoff is achieved. In the short term, productivity will very likely fall rather than rise. It takes time for people to adapt to new ways of working and to learn how to use new equipment to the greatest effect.

A predicted increase in home-based activities is an enduring theme in the literature on the impact of computers on society. "Electronic cottage" visionaries like Alvin Toffler forecast some time ago a rapid growth in working at home and the increased consumption of IT-based services, which together would amount to a revolutionary change in lifestyles. The general idea was that the Industrial Revolution had taken people out of their homes – the IT revolution would enable them to return. Now a new wave of theorists like Ian Miles* are making equally bullish statements about the impact of "home informatics" gadgetry in the home environment. In my piece in this book, I attempt to show that home working, home shopping, home banking and home information services have not taken off as predicted with the aid of IT, largely because of human factors. I argue that writers have consistently underestimated the *psychological* problems of working at home and that consumers have by and large not found new IT-based services to be cheaper, usable or useful – nor do they fulfill their psychological needs. I conclude that any increase in home-based activity is likely to be gradual and the vast majority of homes will *not* become the focus of new economic activity – thus making comparisons with cottage industry prior to the Industrial Revolution difficult to sustain.

The world of work

Fears that the adoption of IT would lead rapidly to massive technological unemployment have not been realized. In the late 1970s, the linking of the microchip to job losses became something of a cliché with many commentators. In continental Europe, the chip even became known for a while as the "job destroyer" and a number of quasi-official government reports warned of potentially huge job losses and impending social catastrophe. But although unemployment has risen to historically high levels in most OECD countries (largely due to the shakeout in manufacturing), the public debate about "chips and jobs" has gone off the boil. This is not to say that IT is not seen to be eroding job opportunities; rather, it is that the rate of adoption of IT and thus the impact of IT on employment levels has been much slower than expected. Managers have also learned not to measure – or to proclaim from the rooftops – success with new IT installations in terms of "how many people have been got rid of."

"Optimists" and "pessimists" continue to offer very different prognoses for the employment impact of IT. For example, in a recent report commissioned by the US National Academy of Science (*Technology and Employment*, National Academy Press, Washington, DC, 1987), Richard Cyert and David Mowery reiterate the familiar, orthodox argument that IT ultimately creates more jobs than it destroys through higher productivity, the creation of greater wealth and thus more jobs and prosperity for all in the long run. The main problem with US industry, they say, is not that it is adopting IT but that it is not adopting IT fast enough to keep pace with rival nations. On the other hand, we have detailed forecasts from David R. Howell on the impact of robots on blue-collar employment in the United States and from J. David Roessner on the impact of office automation on clerical employment in the United States, both of which point to fairly alarming reductions in demand for these two categories of labor.[29] But these studies were completed before the recent slowdown in office and factory automation became apparent. It also has to be said that similar forecasts over recent years have not had a good track record; employment reductions that do take place are nearly always achieved through "natural" attrition; and many companies also have a tremendous ability to hoard labor – for example, a recent study by Ann Daniel of the University of New South Wales found that British law firms had *increased* staff numbers since they began using computers.

Fears that IT would "de-skill" employees and generally degrade the quality of worklife have also been assuaged somewhat by recent developments. Again in the 1970s, writers like Harry Braverman, Howard Rosenbrock, and Mike Cooley made great play with the argument that every effort to introduce new technology was an attempt to take away workers' skills so that they would be more easily controlled and exploited. This view is shared by Harley Shaiken,* who argues that the new jobs created by IT are often every bit as tedious, high-paced and stressful as old assembly-line jobs. Shaiken says that the decision-making power of machine operators has been taken away by employers who are now looking for less-skilled machine "minders." Managers are obsessed, he says, with the desire to exert tighter control over production by transferring skill from people to less troublesome machines. Shaiken's approach has received support from a number of quarters, notably a 1987 Office of Technology Assessment (OTA) report to the US Congress (*The Electronic Supervisor: New Technology, New Tensions*) which described some companies studied as "electronic sweatshops" in which employees slogged through boring repetitive tasks, their work progress constantly monitored by IT equipment.[30]

A contrary view is put by Larry Hirschhorn,* who argues that new electronic IT is just as prone to error and failure as old mechanical technology – and it is more complex. Consequently, this *increases* the dependence of organizations on their skilled workers, and not the opposite: "Robots can't run factories," he writes. "The common notion that computers eliminate the need for human skill and judgment is wrong . . . the new cybernetic machines create new sources of error and failure with which only skilled workers, ready to learn and adapt to new production conditions, can contend . . . they [the workers] must be able to survey and understand the entire production process so that they are ready to respond to the unpredictable mishap."[31] However, Hirschhorn is at pains to point out that he is only describing a *potential* state of affairs and that the new technology alone cannot determine work and organization design, which are shaped by social and political interests: "The new technologies do not constrain social life and reduce everything to a formula. On the contrary, they demand that we develop a culture of learning, an appreciation of emergent phenomena, an understanding of tacit knowledge, a feeling for interpersonal processes, and an appreciation of our organisational design choices."[32]

Human-centered systems

From the foregoing, it is clear that human factors have played a very important role in the IT story so far – an unexpected role that was greatly underestimated by most commentators ten years ago. Now, as John Hoerr et al.* point out, companies are rediscovering that people and not machines are their most valuable resource and that they can best improve their competitive performance by getting humans and technology working together in harmony. US managers are realizing what the Japanese figured out years ago: that you can have the best gee-whiz technology in the world, but you need to get the people side of the equation right if you want to get the most out of it. Thus the introduction of new Japanese-style management techniques in the United States, such as "quality circles" and "teamwork" and the beginnings of a shift in the West's industrial relations paradigm from "control" to "commitment."[33]

The rationale for getting the human side of automation right is that it is (a) more efficient and therefore more profitable for employers and (b) that it is better for the psychological well-being of the employees involved and by implication, society as a whole. In his study of UK banks, Steve Smith* shows that automation in the financial industry on Tayloristic lines has not been very successful in either economic or social terms – producing sub-optimal financial outcomes, disrupting work systems and alienating the workforce from bank work and from each other. In particular: "Technologists have under-estimated the value and importance of skill, knowledge, flexibility and career . . . contrary to scientific management, efficiency actually improves and control is made easier if the 'labor process' is as coherent as possible. There should be a presumption in favour of skills, pride in the job, staff flexibility, apprentice-based careers and intuitive knowledge."[34]

The task therefore is to develop more human-centered systems. Following Hirschhorn, the human-centered approach may be conceived as one which seeks to retain and enhance human skills, control, and discretion, rather than taking them away from the operator as Taylorist orthodoxy dictates. Instead of splitting jobs into innumerable minor tasks, the human-centered approach would give workers more knowledge of, and responsibility for, the entire production process. With workers being re-skilled rather than de-skilled, this would, for example, reduce what Jay Galbraith called "task uncertainty" in organizations, resulting in the need for fewer managers and less information processing capacity. Human-centered systems therefore make both economic and social sense and they are particularly suited to the IT era. Calling for their more widespread utilization involves both a rejection of technological determinism and the adoption of a fairly optimistic view of the future with IT.

Notes

1   Tom Forester, *High-Tech Society: The Story of the Information Technology Revolution* (Basil Blackwell, Oxford and MIT Press, Cambridge, MA, 1987), pp. 1, 83–6; James Beniger, *The Control Revolution: Technological and Economic Origins of the Information Society* (Harvard University Press, Cambridge, MA, 1986), pp. 25–6. In view of the importance accorded to digitization by Beniger and others, it is perhaps surprising that we don't talk about the "digital revolution" rather than the IT revolution.

2   John Bessant et al., *IT Futures: What Current Forecasting Literature Says About the Social Impact of Information Technology* (NEDO Books, HMSO, London, 1985), pp. 4–5. For good coverage of the autonomous technology debate, see Larry Hickman and Azizah Al-Hibri (eds), *Technology and Human Affairs* (C. V. Mosby, St Louis, MO, 1981).

3   See, for example, Michael Marien, "Some Questions for the Information Society," in Tom Forester (ed.), *The Information Technology Revolution* (Basil Blackwell, Oxford, and MIT Press, Cambridge, MA, 1985); Christopher Rowe, *People and Chips: The Human Implications of Information Technology* (Paradigm Publishing, London, 1986).

4   Barry Jones, *Sleepers, Wake! Technology and the Future of Work* (Oxford University Press, Sydney, Australia, 1982), pp. 11–45 and *Australia as a Post-Industrial Society: Radical Discontinuity or Traditional Incrementalism?* (Occasional Paper No. 2, Commission for the Future, Melbourne, Australia, 1985).

5   Ian Miles, Howard Rush, John Bessant et al., *IT Horizons* (Edward Elgar, Aldershot, UK, 1988).

6   Bessant et al., *IT Futures*, pp. 12–13.

7   Melvin Kranzberg, "The Information Age: Evolution or Revolution?" in Bruce R. Guile (ed.), *Information Technologies and Social Transformation* (National Academy Press, Washington, DC, 1985), p. 37.

8   Ibid., p. 52.

9   Beniger, *The Control Revolution*, pp. 6–7.

10 Ibid., p. 435.

11 J. David Bolter, *Turing's Man: Western Culture in the Computer Age* (University of North Carolina Press, 1984 and Penguin, London and New York, 1986), pp. 10–13.

12 Langdon Winner, "Myth Information: Romantic Politics in the Computer Revolution," in Carl Mitcham and Alois Huning (eds), *Philosophy and Technology II* (D. Reidel Publishing Company, Netherlands, 1986), p. 277.

13 Ibid., p. 287.

14 Stephen S. Cohen and John Zysman, *Manufacturing Matters: The Myth of the Post-Industrial Economy* (Basic Books, New York, 1987).

15 Ibid., p. 260.

16 See successive reports in the business press, e.g. "The Smokestacks Steam Again," *Fortune*, December 21, 1987; and "Made in the USA," *Business Week*, February 29, 1988.

17 James Brian Quinn, Jordon J. Baruch and Penny Cushman Paquette, "Technology in Services," *Scientific American*, vol. 257 (6), December 1987, p. 24.

18 Fritz Machlup, *The Production and Distribution of Knowledge in the United States* (Princeton University Press, Princeton, NJ, 1962); Donald M. Lamberton (ed.), "The Information Revolution," *The Annals of the American Academy of Political and Social Science*, vol. 412, March 1974; Daniel Bell, *The Coming of Post-Industrial Society* (Basic Books, New York, 1973) and "The Social Framework of the Information Society," in Tom Forester (ed.), *The Microelectronics Revolution* (Basil Blackwell, Oxford, 1980 and MIT Press, Cambridge, MA, 1981), pp. 500–50; Marc Uri Porat, *The Information Economy* (US Department of Commerce, Washington, DC, 1977).

19 Michael R. Rubin and Mary T. Huber, *The Knowledge Industry in the United States 1960–1980* (Princeton University Press, Princeton, NJ, 1986).

20 George C. Church, "The Work Ethic Lives!" *Time*, September 7, 1987; "Americans Are Still Having A Love Affair With Work," *Business Week*, January 18, 1988.

21 Richard H. Franke, "Technological Revolution and Productivity Decline: Computer Introduction in the Financial Industry," *Technological Forecasting and Social Change*, vol. 31 (1987), p. 152.

22 Brian Winston, *Misunderstanding Media* (Harvard University Press, Cambridge, MA, 1986), p. 1.

23 Ibid., p. 2.

24 Rob Kling, "Value Conflicts in Computing Developments," *Telecommunications Policy*, March 1983. See also Kling interview, "Assessing Computer Technology," *Orange County Register*, December 25, 1987, p. B2.

25 Herb Brody, "US Robot Makers Try to Bounce Back," *High Technology Business*, October 1987. See also "Factory Automation Reconsidered," special report in *High Technology*, October 1986; Gordon Bock, "Limping Along In Robot Land," *Time*, July 13, 1987.

26 Ted Davis, "Manufacturers Revise Their Strategy On Factory Automation," *The Globe and Mail*, Toronto, July 4, 1987, p. B7. See also Ralph E. Winter, "Upgrading of Factories Replaces the Concept of Total Automation," *The Wall Street Journal*, November 30, 1987.

27 For a more recent report, see Edward Tenner, "The Revenge of Paper," *The New York Times*, March 5, 1988, p. 29.

28 Catherine L. Harris et al., "Office Automation: Making It Pay Off," *Business Week*, October 12, 1987; William Bowen, "The Puny Payoff From Office Computers," *Fortune*, May 26, 1986; J. Daniel Couger, "E Pluribus Computum," *Harvard Business Review*, September–October 1986.

29 David R. Howell, "The Future Employment Impacts of Industrial Robots," *Technological Forecasting and Social Change*, vol. 28, 1985, pp. 297–310; J. David Roessner, "Forecasting the Impact of Office Automation on Clerical Employment, 1985–2000," *Technological Forecasting and Social Change*, vol. 28, 1985, pp. 203–16.

30 A noteworthy article along these lines is Curt Suplee, "The Electronic Sweatshop," *The Washington Post*, Outlook Section, January 3, 1988, p. B1.

31 Larry Hirschhorn, *Beyond Mechanization: Work and Technology in a Postindustrial Age* (MIT Press, Cambridge, MA, 1984), pp. 1–2.

32 Ibid., p. 169.

33 See, for example, Richard E. Walton, "From Control to Commitment in the Workplace," *Harvard Business Review*, March–April 1985.

34 S. L. Smith, "Information Technology: Taylorisation or Human-Centred Office Systems?" *Science and Public Policy*, June 1987, p. 166.

Part One: Computers and Society

1   IT as Revolution

The Information Age

Melvin Kranzberg

This scene-setting article contains some shrewd observations and a wealth of insight into the historical relationship between technology and society. The author sets himself the task of comparing the IT revolution with the technological and social changes associated with the Industrial Revolution. Broadly speaking, he concludes that IT will be equally revolutionary in its impact on society, although there are qualifications. Melvin Kranzberg is the Callaway Professor of the History of Technology at Georgia Institute of Technology and this paper first appeared in Bruce R. Guile (ed.), Information Technologies and Social Transformation *(National Academy Press, Washington, DC, 1985).*

Every time we pick up a newspaper or a journal or listen to the news we learn about new technological developments heralding major sociotechnical changes: "Microelectronics Revolution," "Post-industrial Society," "Computer Revolution," "Automation Age," and so on. Since all of these involve the accumulation, manipulation, and retrieval of data by computerized electronic devices and their application to many facets of human life, it is no wonder that the headlines shout that computer developments are transforming industry and society to produce a new "Information Age."

Is this transformation evolutionary or revolutionary? After all, most technologies are evolutionary in the sense that they derive from prior developments. The steam engine did not emerge full-blown out of James Watt's brain, but was based upon Thomas Newcomen's engine, which in turn rested on still earlier attempts. Similarly, Gutenberg's invention of printing derived from a whole series of previous innovations – paper, block printing, inks, and movable type – which he put together in a new way. Indeed, virtually every major technological innovation can be shown to have been the outcome of evolutionary advance, in that historians can trace the elements comprising them far back in time.

Computers, the basis of the Information Age, find their origins in earlier devices, such as the ancient abacus, the seventeenth-century calculators of Pascal, the work of Charles Babbage in the nineteenth century, and Herman Hollerith's development of punched-card operations for the US Census in the 1890s.[1]

Even though such technologies evolve over a long period of time, they can have revolutionary technical and social impacts even during the process of reaching full development and application. However, history indicates that changes in individual technologies do not by themselves have revolutionary sociocultural effects. Thus the medieval improvements in power sources – the introduction of the windmill and the waterwheel on a wide scale – did not produce a "revolution" because they remained based in a small-scale agrarian society. Most people continued to live in rural villages with farming as their chief occupation; hence there were no major changes in where and how people lived and worked.

Not until the eighteenth century did a whole series of technological innovations come together to produce the classical Industrial Revolution. Although popular opinion credits Watt's steam engine with starting industrialization, many of its elements, such as power-driven machinery, the factory organization of work, and specialization of labor, had already begun in the textile industry long before Watt.[2] Concomitant changes were occurring in mining and metallurgy, and transportation was being improved by the development of canals and roadways. Furthermore, the foundation of a national banking system and extension of joint-stock companies helped provide the capital and financial requirements for technical investment and commercial growth. The point is that a single major technical advance does not in itself constitute a technological revolution. There must be other and related technical advances plus major changes occurring in the political-economic-social-cultural context of the times.

Nevertheless, scholars delight in labeling an era by its most advanced technology, even when that technology is at first very limited in its application. For example, even though the "Age of Steam" is said to have begun with James Watt, for almost a century after Watt's engine more aggregate power was generated in Britain by waterpower than by steam; and it took nearly 100 years after Fulton's creation of the "Steam-boat Era" before sailing vessels disappeared from oceanic commerce.

Similarly, the Wright Brothers at the beginning of this century began the "Era of Flight," but then it was postponed for another 25 years until Lindbergh's famous solo flight from New York to Paris; yet the "Aviation Age" really did not take off until after World War II. In similar fashion, the "Space Age" was said to have dawned with Sputnik, but more than a quarter of a century has elapsed since then, and we have scarcely begun to exploit space. That is indeed a long day's dawning!

Obviously, a single technological feat, no matter how much attention is showered upon it, does not by itself constitute a complete technological transformation. Indeed, one of the characteristics of a true technological revolution is that a great many innovations take place at about the same time. Their coming together creates a synergistic, indeed, explosive, impact upon the production of goods and services.

But technology does not occur in a vacuum. Instead, it takes place in a social matrix and interacts with society. Thus, despite the evolutionary nature of its individual technical components, the British Industrial Revolution marked a truly revolutionary transformation of society because it changed where and how people worked, lived, thought, played, and prayed.

For millennia, agriculture had been the chief source of production. The home-and-hearth was the center of work, education, social relationships, recreation, and, indeed, all life. The Industrial Revolution changed all that.

With the Industrial Revolution the factory became the workplace, and the city became the dwelling place. Family relationships changed as the father left home each day to earn wages in a factory while the mother stayed home with the children; other new social patterns emerged in the crowded cities, while some traditional institutions, such as the Church, saw their hold on people's lives weakened in the urban environment. Technological and societal changes interacted, overturning old patterns of living, thinking, and working, and creating new institutional systems and cultural values.

Using the classical Industrial Revolution of the eighteenth and nineteenth centuries as our criterion, we learn that an industrial revolution consists of two chief elements: (1) a series of fundamental technical changes in the production and distribution of goods accompanied by – sometimes caused by, sometimes reflecting, but in any event, interconnected with – (2) a series of social and cultural changes of the first magnitude. Both elements must be present; a series of technological changes alone would not constitute an industrial revolution, nor would sociocultural changes without concomitant technological developments produce a new industrial era.[3]

To see if the much-heralded, incoming Information Age is truly a revolutionary phenomenon, let us analyze both the technological and sociocultural changes in the classical Industrial Revolution and see if parallel transformations are occurring today.

The classical Industrial Revolution

Looking at the main technical features of the classical Industrial Revolution, we find:

- The use of new basic materials, chiefly iron and steel.
- New energy sources, deriving from new prime movers and fuels, such as coal and the steam engine, and, later, electricity, petroleum, and the internal-combustion engine.
- Mechanical inventions, such as the spinning jenny, the power loom, and machine tools, which increased production with a smaller expenditure of human energy.
- The centralized organization of work in the factory system, which entailed the further division of labor and specialization of function, and these, together with improved machines, making possible interchangeable parts and mass production.[4]
- The quickening of transportation and communication through the steamship, the steam locomotive, the automobile, and eventually the airplane; and in communications, the telegraph, telephone, and radio.
- The development of a science of technology.[5]

In the nonindustrial technological sphere, agricultural improvements embodying many of the same technical changes made possible the provision of food for a larger population. All these technological developments involved larger use of natural resources, increased efficiency, and the low-cost, mass production and distribution of food, manufactured goods, and accompanying services.[6]

Not so incidentally, all these technical advances also involved information. After all, technology is a form of knowledge – knowledge of how to make and do things – which is why we sometimes refer to it as "know-how." Technology implies hands and minds working together to produce more efficient machines, processes, products, and services. All of these require the application of new and better information or at least the bringing together of old items of information in a new and different way. Thus, the industrial transformation of the eighteenth and nineteenth centuries was based upon the application of new and better information to improve traditional methods and machines and, in the process, to create new products and services. And their synergistic interaction accelerated the pace of change.

While political revolutions occur rather quickly – or at least can sometimes be assigned definite dates – sociocultural revolutions, involving deep-seated changes in the ways in which people work, think, and live, require somewhat more time for their effects to manifest themselves. Nevertheless, they too are revolutionary in their impact.

We can see this in the nontechnical elements – the economic-social-political-cultural transformations – that accompanied and became part of the classical Industrial Revolution:

- the decline of land as the chief source of wealth in the face of the immense wealth created by industrial production;
- political changes reflecting this shift in economic power, as well as new state policies corresponding to the needs of an industrialized, rather than agrarian, society; and
- sweeping demographic and social changes, including the growth of cities, the development of working-class movements (indeed, the birth of a whole new social class, the urban factory proletariat), and the emergence of new patterns of authority within the family and at work.[7]

There were other broad cultural transformations. Workers were forced to acquire new and distinctive skills, and their relation to their work shifted; instead of being craftsmen working with hand tools, workers became machine operators, subject to factory discipline. Also, there were major psychological changes in people's confidence in their power over nature, and, of course, in hedonistic satisfaction. For industrialization made possible a torrent of material goods, which ultimately brought about a higher standard of living. Advances in agriculture, combined with progress in medical knowledge and public health measures, meant that hunger began to disappear as a major threat in the industrially advanced nations. People lived longer – and better, in terms of material goods.

This was indeed a revolution, because it transformed individual lives and society. And it was an Industrial Revolution because the development of industrial technology provided the basis for the sociocultural changes.

A current technological revolution?

Are the technological and the sociocultural changes occurring in relation to today's advances in computers of sufficient magnitude to hail ours as a revolutionary "Information Age?"

Certainly the technical foundation has been built, including a change in basic materials.[8] Let us remember that the introduction of new technologies does not always mean the complete demise of older technologies, especially in the case of materials. After all, wood continued to be a major material source even when the Age of Steel developed. While today's improvements in materials – composites, plastics, synthetic fibers, sophisticated ceramics, and the introduction of new alloys and lighter metals – do not mean that iron and steel are outmoded any more than the coming of the Age of Steel meant that wood ceased being used, these do represent a transformation in and an augmentation of materials resources affecting many other technical changes. Furthermore, the development of these new materials is roughly concomitant with the emergence of computer-aided design and manufacture. There is a synergy between technological developments as new materials find use in improving the operating effectiveness of the computers used to control manufacturing of the materials and manufacturing processes that work with the new materials.

In terms of energy, with the exception of hydroelectricity, the nineteenth century brought almost total reliance on fossil fuels. Within our own times, the fear that finite fossil fuels will eventually be exhausted has been somewhat alleviated by the possibility of almost limitless energy through exploitation of the power within the atom – although certain problems remain associated therewith. Also, greater emphasis is being placed upon conservation, synthetic fuels, renewable sources of energy, and greater and more efficient use of solar power. So although recurrent "energy crises" might come about through political and economic forces, we possess the requisite technical knowledge and potential to produce an abundance of energy in different forms. This represents a truly revolutionary technological advance over the fossil fuel era.

However, current changes in production mechanisms follow a somewhat different, yet nevertheless revolutionary, pattern than those of the past. The Industrial Revolution introduced power machinery and centralized production by multitudes of factory workers, and the early twentieth century further rationalized this process with Henry Ford's moving assembly line and Frederick W. Taylor's Scientific Management. But nowadays, computerized information devices form the heart – rather, the eyes, hands, and mind – of the machine and allow for completely automated machinery, robots. Instead of a machine operator, the human worker becomes a machine supervisor, overseeing a multitude of dials while the robotized machine – the steel-collar worker – does the actual work and replaces many blue-collar workers. Robots can perform dangerous operations, relieving humans from tasks that pose a threat to health and safety. They can also perform the monotonous and routine tasks which, some people claim, had made factory workers into machines [9] The older mechanical devices had taken the burden off man's back; computerized devices also take the burden off man's mind.

In transportation too, information devices play a major role. Sophisticated jet engines – highly dependent upon electronic control and monitoring – have enabled airplanes to grow larger and speedier, replacing long-haul railroad and steamship passenger transportation. Also, we have completed the first voyages of exploration and are beginning to utilize space in new ways. These aerospace developments are linked with the microminiaturization of computerized information devices and are, indeed, dependent upon them. Still another example of the ubiquity of these revolutionary information devices is their application to the workings of automobiles and trucks performing very earthly tasks.

Communications too are being transformed, with satellite transmission of instantaneous information from all parts of the world. But that is only the most spectacular demonstration of how communication expertise has increased apace. Indeed, revolutionary advances in the flow, storage, manipulation, and retrieval of information, resulting from the improvements in computers, rightly entitle the future to be known as the Information Age.

These contemporary major technical changes – in materials, fuels and prime movers, machinery, the organization of work, transportation, and communication – all involve more knowledge and more information. Our industrial and agricultural technologies are increasingly reliant upon the newfound and enlarged technical capacity given us by computerized information devices.

As long as computers relied on vacuum tubes and were bulky, balky, and expensive, they had only a minor impact on industrial processes and structure. However, with the invention of transistors and their refinement into today's microchips, computers became omnipresent; their power was greatly multiplied, and they found many applications beyond computational number-crunching. It is this application of computerized information to all facets of life and technology that makes it the centerpiece of the new technological revolution.[10]

The computer has repercussions far beyond the field of information and computer science narrowly conceived. Civil, mechanical, textile, metallurgical, chemical, ceramic, and, of course, electrical engineering also make full use of our new informational capacity and expertise. The old slide rule hanging from the belt of the engineering student has given way to the pocket computer. Increasingly at every engineering institution in the country, the students have access to desk computers wired into larger computer systems. Indeed, computer literacy is no longer a monopoly of a small group of technical experts; instead it is being taught at the elementary school level, and it is fast becoming a necessary adjunct to liberal arts education, with personal computers becoming a ubiquitous item in educated households.

Just as the old Industrial Revolution transformed agriculture as well as industry, so today there have been revolutionary improvements in agricultural production. Less than 3 percent of the American population now lives on farms, and one American farm worker now produces enough food to feed 84 people. This is because agriculture itself has become thoroughly industrialized in methods and scale of production; like industry, it is being computerized in the breeding and feeding of livestock and poultry and in the growing of crops. Furthermore, the development of genetic technology to improve varieties of vegetables, fruit, and grain, to say nothing of livestock, rests upon biotechnological advances,[11] which in turn rely upon enhanced computer capabilities, as do new chemical fertilizers and pesticides. Agricultural technology is thus one of the chief beneficiaries of and contributors to the new Information Age.

The R&D laboratory, which grew out of the German chemical industry in the latter part of the nineteenth century, helped create a science of technology – or engineering science – and that is reflected in the education and practices of today's engineers.[12] Research and development, which has become characteristic of all technologically advanced industry, has, of course, been enhanced by our heightened informational capabilities. As a result our scientific/technical knowledge increases apace.

In brief, the Information Age has indeed revolutionized the technical elements of industrial society. But does it have similar revolutionary implications for nontechnical institutions, values, and society as a whole?

A current societal revolution?

Let us look at some of the nontechnical changes that are occurring, partly as a result of the technological changes but also causing the advance of technology because of the synergistic relationship between technology and society. We can see that revolutionary changes are occurring in the pattern of industrial society, just as it marked a vast transformation from the preceding agrarian society.

Certainly, formidable economic changes are taking place which depart greatly from nineteenth-century industrial concentration. Although financial concentration is now occurring on an unprecedented scale, the economics and production technology of the older Industrial Revolution, which favored the consolidation of production, are now giving way to decentralized facilities – and on an international scale.

Henry Ford's River Rouge plant represented the peak of the older development: raw materials went in one end, and finished automobiles came out the other end. It was a marvel for its time, and people came from all over the world to see the wonders of "Fordismus." But no one ever built another River Rouge; instead, it was discovered to be more efficient and economical to disperse production facilities. Today's greater reliance upon more sophisticated materials and technologies reinforces the tendency toward dispersion – with, of course, profound impact upon the former centers of America's smokestack industries.

Similarly, when the first electronic computers were introduced some decades ago, their complexity, size, and expense seemed to dictate that the computerized information would perforce be concentrated and hence be susceptible to control by relatively few individuals. Indeed, this appeared to lend substance to George Orwell's vision of *1984* when all information – and hence all thought – would be controlled by "Big Brother." However, the introduction of the transistor and the development of the microchip allowed for ·the miniaturization of computing devices, so that today's small, hand-held computer can rival the past giants in information capacity and activity. As the young hackers at CalTech showed when they took over control of the scoreboard at the 1983 Rose Bowl game, the problem is no longer that Big Brother is watching you, but that "Little Brother" is messing up his program.

As a result, while the dispersion of information capabilities makes impossible the centralized control of information and the power implied therein, new problems regarding the secrecy of data, the patentability of software, and a whole host of new sociolegal problems confront us. We are still engaged in the process of discovering these new problems, and seeing if the old legal maxims still apply or whether we must work out new legal mechanisms to ensure a proper balance between private rights and the needs of the public.

Just as microcomputers make possible the diffusion as well as the centralization of information control, so industrialization, which had begun first on a regional, then on a national basis, is today being internationalized. Advancing technologies have made feasible the creation of new production centers, having different resource advantages, throughout the world. Partly this is due to the geographical dispersion of natural resources; today's sophisticated technology frequently requires exotic materials not available in the United States, so that we are no longer a self-sufficient nation producing all we need for our own uses and exporting to others. We even find it practical to import relatively commonplace energy supplies such as oil. Another resource advantage is lower labor costs, especially since some advanced manufacturing techniques, including those of assembling electronic devices themselves, oftentimes require only low skill levels on the part of production-line workers. The result is an internationalization of production of revolutionary dimensions, the implications of which are still not clearly discerned. However, it has led to a debate on "industrial policy" dealing with new mechanisms in order to provide training and gainful employment to those thrown out of work by automated manufacturing processes or by the transfer of production abroad.[13]

Yet, while employment in traditional industries declines, the statistics on the total number of employed people in the United States continue to mount. For, while computerized production technology allows us to produce a cascade of material goods with fewer workers, there has been an enlargement of the service sector of the economy. As a result, for the past 30 years more people have been employed in the service trades than in factory production, and the service sector continues to grow.

One reason is the enlargement of administrative and clerical activities, many of which derive from the heightened productive capability offered by automated devices and the consequent enhancement of service activities. Information automation in the office is proceeding apace,[14] and we historians, while having 20/20 hindsight, do not possess 20/20 foresight about its social impact.

Other writers, however, apparently possess a clearer vision of the future. For example, Alvin Toffler points out that computers will enable information workers to do their work at home, being tied in with central computers at the office.[15] Yes, it is indeed possible for more people to work at home. But the fact is that, with very few exceptions in certain occupations, such as editing and writing and the piece-rate processing of insurance forms and the like, that is simply not happening on a wide scale. The reason is that, as the ancient philosophers pointed out, man is a social and political animal. People like to congregate together; they derive intellectual stimulus and social satisfaction from personal contacts. The workplace is not only a spot for making a living but is also the site of the social interchange that is apparently a hallmark of our human species.[16] So, just because computers might offer us certain capabilities, this does not mean that we would want to take advantage of them, nor does it mean that they would necessarily be advantageous for the social interchange that, in the vast majority of cases, is essential for individual fulfillment.

Besides, Toffler neglects the fact that new technologies do not immediately and completely replace older forms. Instead, as we can see from the example of the classical Industrial Revolution, old technologies do not immediately die, nor do they quickly fade away. Instead, the new technologies are superimposed upon them and in many cases are used to augment the older capabilities.

My own guess is that we will be in the midst of the "Second-and-a-Half Wave" for a long time before we reach Toffler's "Third Wave," by which time the futurist scholars will already be talking about a "Fourth Wave."

Nevertheless, we can already foresee some possible changes in political and economic power. The old Industrial Revolution shifted political and economic power from the landed nobility, whose ownership of the land was the key to power and wealth in an almost totally agrarian society, to the industrialists. In England the new factory owners allied themselves with the old landed nobility to control the political apparatus. Yet at the same time the factory system, by concentrating workers, enabled them to organize and obtain considerable economic clout, not as individuals, but as a group. Then the enfranchisement of the workers in the industrially advanced states gave them a share in political power. In brief, industrialization carried with it political and social democratization – and the Information Age, by facilitating widespread communication, might conceivably fortify democratic political control in the advanced industrial nations.

Although we cannot be sure of that, we can be certain that governments will continue to be involved in economic policy and hence in technological activities. The nineteenth-century myth of *laissez-faire* blinded us to the fact that governments did in reality play a major role in developing the industrial economy: through tariffs to protect infant industries and by building or financing roads, bridges, and other elements of the transportation network and infrastructure. Indeed, the needs of a coordinated transportation system led not only to the adoption of a standard gauge for railroads but also to standard time zones. Furthermore, the increasing complexity of technology made governments encourage the development of measurement standards, such as for screw threads, and then safety standards. Today's sophisticated information technology has required further government action, often on an international scale, to assign radio frequencies and thereby allow for a freer flow of communications. In addition, the widespread use of more powerful chemicals and the fears of water and atmospheric pollution require governmental policing of safety standards in many industries.

Added to the technological need for governmental action is a growing public awareness of technology's importance to society, now and in the future, and hence the desire for some measure of public control. Partly this is an outgrowth of a rising level of education, itself made possible through previous technological advance. As the Industrial Revolution began producing enough goods so that young children no longer had to be in the workforce, they could be sent to school. Besides, the increasingly complex nature of technological devices required an educated workforce.

As a result, we can trace the democratization of education throughout the nineteenth and twentieth centuries in the industrially advanced nations as a function of technological growth and complexity. At first elementary education became compulsory, then secondary education, and in the twentieth century America pledged itself to give equal access to higher education to all its citizens (sometimes irrespective of their ability to take advantage of it).

The new Information Age requires even more complex and sophisticated technology, so there is need for a still higher degree of specialized technical skills – including social skills as well as manipulative ones. Educational responses to the needs of the Information Age are already being discussed and fought over throughout the educational establishment – including, and perhaps especially, among engineering educators.

Still another revolutionary social change has been abetted by the new Information Age: the entrance of women into the workforce in unparalleled numbers. Before the onset of industrialization, women worked alongside the menfolk in the fields and in the home handcraft production of the times. With the rise of the factory system and its regimen of disciplined work and hours, men became the breadwinners, while the women remained at home and were responsible for homemaking and child rearing.

However, machine technology has advanced to the point that brute strength is no longer a special asset, so women no longer labor under any physical disability. Machines do not know or care whether the hands that guide them are those of a man or a woman – or, for that matter, whether they are white, black, blue, purple, or green. As a result, advancing technology means that racial and gender distinctions scarcely matter in the actual production process – although, for social and cultural reasons such distinctions unfortunately persist in many parts of the world.

Women possess the physical stamina, intellectual qualities, and moral virtues that make them the equals of men in an Information Society where burdensome physical work has been taken over by machines. Hence, we are in the midst of a social revolution – some call it a sexual revolution – that is closely linked with the technical advances which have given women technical equality with men, even though they may not yet have acquired the social and political power that goes with their technical equality, to say nothing of wage equality.

Office automation will not only affect the clerical work that was the domain of women for almost the entire past century. Rather, it will extend to all aspects of production and distribution, since it allows for close monitoring of production processes as well as clerical tasks of billing and the like. Furthermore, it can give top managers fingertip access to information formerly supplied them by the middle managerial group. Here again, we cannot foretell with exactitude what will happen, but there will undoubtedly be further rationalization in the office procedures inherited from an earlier age, while the information user in the office will have more direct contact with the production process itself.

What is equally interesting to social historians and cultural anthropologists is that many of the revolutionary information devices will be incorporated into the mechanisms of our daily lives without our being aware of them. Already microchips are being used in the thermostats for our home heating and air conditioning systems and in the ignition and carburation systems of our automobiles. But we will still set our thermostat at 70°, without awareness that the microchip is increasing the energy efficiency of our heating and air conditioning systems; and we will step on the gas or on the brakes without realizing that the microchip enables us to achieve better control of the automobile.

Of much greater significance than simply catering to our creature comforts are those major social changes occurring as an outgrowth of advancing information technology which will have a powerful effect upon our country's and the world's future. Among the most important are demographic changes resulting from public health, medical, and nutritional advances deriving from sophisticated computerized research in health technologies. As a result, people are living longer – and this is already changing the character of American society.

But there is a reverse side to this demographic coin, namely, rapidly exploding populations in the developing nations, where more than half the people are under 15 years of age. As a result, there are demands for technological development to meet the material needs of the world's growing population. At the same time there are apparently conflicting demands that this be done without plundering the earth of its resources or damaging the environment. In other words, the Information Age must stimulate technological growth to meet these demands and do so by new kinds of technical applications that will maintain the productivity and salubrity of our planet for future generations.

Finally, we come to the psychological changes, both social and individual, effected by technological changes. Until the Industrial Revolution people had always been fearful that the vagaries of nature would deprive them of life's necessities. With the plethora of material goods and foods made available through the technological advances of the nineteenth century, people were able to keep hunger at bay, and indeed overcome many of the hardships inflicted by nature through centralized heating and air conditioning systems, electrical lighting, and the like.

Not surprisingly, the world's fairs of the past century emphasized the great accomplishments of science and technology. The notion that human technical abilities would enable us to accomplish anything we attempted was given further credence some 20 years ago when man first set foot on the moon. Here was the culmination of the Scientific Revolution of the seventeenth century and the Industrial Revolution of the eighteenth and nineteenth centuries, the actual fulfillment of one of man's most ancient myths and dreams. It is no wonder that we could be accused of the old Greek sin of hubris, inordinate pride.

Paradoxically, however, at almost the very same time, we began discovering that many of our previous technological triumphs were despoiling the environment and that our military technology posed a threat to the continuation of life on our planet.

As a result, the new Information Age has brought with it a somewhat more equivocal view of the human relationship to nature. Instead of man's being the master of nature, it is now realized that man is a part of nature and that our future depends upon a fuller recognition of both nature's and humanity's capabilities and limitations.

But, that does not necessarily mean that doomsday is forthcoming, nor need it deprive us of hope. Unlike earlier ages when human technical capacities were prescribed by the availability of certain natural resources, limited in the forms of energy that might be applied, and constrained to do and to make things in the same way as their ancestors had done, our new technology provides us with many different ways of attacking problems. We now have many and growing options in regard to the materials that we wish to employ, the energy sources that we intend to utilize, and the ways in which we go about producing and distributing food, goods, and services. Because the scientific technology of the incoming Information Age offers us manifold choices, we can make decisions about the future course of society with due concern for conservation of natural resources, the preservation of the environment, and the well-being of our fellow man now and in the future.

Technology and cultural lag

However, just because we have the ability to do new and wonderful things with our technology does not necessarily mean that we will actually do so. Many years ago the great sociologist William Fielding Ogburn postulated the concept of "cultural lag" in terms of human response to technical capabilities.[17] He pointed out that the technologies developed in the preceding century gave mankind the opportunity to bring about a new and better social system, allowing the vast quantity of material goods being turned out by an advancing technology to redound to the benefit to all of mankind, rather than being confined to a narrow few. However, he also stated that cultural systems and human institutions – governmental, legal, and the like – tend to lag in responding to new opportunities offered by these technical innovations.

Lewis Mumford's analysis, some 50 years ago, of the relations between technology and culture seemed to reinforce Ogburn's thesis.[18] He claimed that the latest technical innovations were still being employed to further the aims and goals of the earlier industrial transformation based upon the exploitation of nature and of human beings. In other words, while our technology might enable us to make a better world for all, it was being employed in the service of institutions and values belonging to an older and more selfish age, one that considered neither humanity nor the natural world.

The analyses of both Ogburn and Mumford were provocative when initially stated, but they appear simplistic in light of what actually happened. True, our new technology gives us capabilities to do many wonderful things, but we often continue to employ them in the service of institutions and values belonging to an older age. Mumford hoped our bright new technologies would point the way to a brave new world founded upon social justice and a concern for nature. Ogburn too felt that technology could better humanity's lot, and he deplored the "cultural lag" that prevented it from doing so. Both men implied that technology could do wonderful things for mankind, but things went wrong when we did not allow it to do so.

True, but what they forgot is that technology is a quintessential human activity, so it bears the contradictions – the "goods" and "bads" – to be found in all complex human activities. It is designed for human use, but that means it is also subject to human misuse and abuse. If technology were the sole determinant of human actions, our current world might be a much better – and certainly a different – place.

Here is an example of how an advance made possible by technology – international goodwill through better communications and more contact among different peoples throughout the world – bogs down under the "cultural lag" afforded by nontechnical factors that take precedence over technical capabilities. Electronic messages can flow across the globe in a fraction of a second, irrespective of the political boundaries; hence the technical element of modern communication is indifferent to national boundaries. Similarly, there are no technical barriers to prevent airplanes from transcending national borders. In other words, modern communication and transportation have made nationalism technologically obsolete; however, any glance at the headlines convinces us that while nationalism might be technically obsolete, it still remains one of the most powerful forces affecting the future of mankind.

Evolution and revolution

Acknowledgment of this and similar facts has led me to reformulate the concepts of my predecessors who pioneered in analyzing the interactions between technical and sociocultural elements and has led me to formulate "Kranzberg's First Law." Kranzberg's First Law reads as follows: Technology is neither good nor bad, nor is it neutral.

By that I mean that technology's interactions with both the social and cultural milieus sometimes lead to developments that are far removed from the original goals of the technical elements themselves. For example, Henry Ford thought of his motorcar as a means to cheapen transportation and make personalized transport available to the masses. It did that of course, but it also did much more than that, transforming where and how we work, play, live, shop, eat, sleep, and – for those of you who remember rumble seats – even where we made love.

In accordance with Kranzberg's First Law, the Information Age will have similar and unanticipated impacts, as the computer goes far beyond the task of number-crunching and instantaneous communication of data. The variety of functions that computers serve suggests that their consequences will be mixed, unevenly distributed, and diffused, assimilated, and modified at uneven rates. Hence, we still cannot foresee exactly what some of the consequences will be, any more than the prophets at the turn of this century could foretell that the automobile would lead to the suburbanization of American society, provide the prototype for the mass production of all kinds of material goods, do away with the old distinction between city and country dweller, and, with its related industries, help produce the richest society in the world's history.

Furthermore, as a corollary to Kranzberg's First Law, the same technology can have quite different results when introduced into a different cultural setting. Thus, some technologies developed in advanced industrial countries have quite different effects when introduced into some developing nations. Because technology functions in a sociocultural matrix and depends upon an infrastructure that includes the educational level of the population, its political and economic institutions, and its value system (including religious beliefs), it can produce markedly different results when it interacts with a culture that differs from our Western industrial society.

The point I am trying to make is that this new Information Age presents mankind with many different possibilities. But because people differ historically in their cultural and social institutions throughout the world, the new technology can have quite different results when applied in differing sociocultural settings. Besides, the technology itself is still evolving, and hence might interact with our values, institutions, and attitudes along quite different lines than expected.

Even so, the historical record gives us some cause for optimism. The technical advances of the Information Age, if they follow the pattern of previous technical changes, could provide us with more goods and services, increase material well-being, and help do away with poverty and misery throughout the globe. And by giving us greater knowledge of the human, social, and environmental consequences of our technical options through the new informational tools available for technology assessment and impact analysis, the Information Age might help us avoid catastrophic assaults upon nature and upon our fellow human beings. For computer technology – along with its associated cluster of increasingly sophisticated analytic software, simulation models, and data bases – permits more complex analyses than have been previously possible in the social sciences. Indeed, the more information people have about nature, technology, and society, the more it might not only enable them to improve their living standards but also to do away with hatred and fanaticism – although we cannot be sure of that.

One thing we do know. Despite the many defects we can find in highly industrialized societies, including our own, the fact is that the most technologically advanced nations are the ones that have abandoned cruel and unusual punishments; have provided social welfare and medical services for all segments of society; have allowed for the greatest measure of racial, religious, and sexual equality; and have, in large measure, provided for freedom and a humane life for all.

The Information Age promises to carry those hopes for the good life even further. While it might be evolutionary, in the sense that all the changes and benefits will not appear overnight, it will be revolutionary in its effects upon our society.

Notes

1 Although it was written before some recent, major developments, Jeremy Bernstein, *The Analytical Engine: Computers – Past, Present, and Future* (Random House, New York, 1964) provides a good popular account of computer history. See also Nancy Stern and Robert Stern, *Computers in Society* (Prentice-Hall, Englewood Cliffs, NJ, 1983). The *Annals of the History of Computing*, published by the American Federation of Information Processing Societies, contains articles about the recent as well as the "ancient history" of computers.

2 Terry S. Reynolds, "Medieval Roots of the Industrial Revolution," *Scientific American*, vol. 251 (1), July 1984, pp. 122–30.

3 Melvin Kranzberg, "Prerequisites for Industrialization," in Kranzberg and Carol W. Pursell,

Technology in Western Civilization, 2 vols (Oxford University Press, New York, 1967), vol. 1, chap 13.

4   Although Britain was the birthplace of the Industrial Revolution, these developments were carried further in the "American System of Manufactures." See Otto Mayr and Robert C. Post (eds), *Yankee Enterprise: The Rise of the American System of Manufactures* (Smithsonian Press, Washington, DC, 1981); and David A. Hounshell, *From the American System to Mass Production, 1800–1932: The Development of Manufacturing Technology in the United States* (Johns Hopkins University Press, Baltimore, MD, 1984).

5   A major article on this topic is Edwin T. Layton, "Mirror-image Twins: The Communities of Science and Technology in 19th-century America," *Technology and Culture*, vol. 12, October 1971, pp. 562–80.

6   Standard accounts of the Industrial Revolution include David Landes, *The Unbound Prometheus: Technical Change and Industrial Development in Western Europe from 1750 to the Present* (Cambridge University Press, London, 1969); and T. S. Ashton, *The Industrial Revolution, 1760–1970* (Oxford University Press, Oxford, 1943).

7   See E. P. Thompson, *The Making of the English Working Class* (Random House Pantheon Books, New York, 1963); and Raymond Williams, *The Long Revolution* (Columbia University Press, New York, 1961).

8   Melvin Kranzberg and Cyril Stanley Smith, "Materials in History and Society," *Materials Science and Engineering*, vol. 37 (1), January 1979, pp. 1–39; National Academy of Engineering, *Cutting Edge Technologies* (National Academy Press, Washington, DC, 1983), part III; Philip H. Abelson, "Materials Science and Engineering," *Science*, vol. 225 (4675), (November 9, 1984), p. 613.

9   Larry Hirschhorn, *Beyond Mechanization Work and Technology in a Postindustrial Age* (MIT Press, Cambridge, MA, 1984).

10   See Tom Forester (ed.), *The Microelectronics Revolution: The Complete Guide to the New Technology and Its Impact on Society* (MIT Press, Cambridge, MA, 1981).

11   Charles J. Arntzen, "Biotechnology and Agricultural Research for Crop Improvement," NAE, *Cutting Edge Technologies*, pp. 52–61.

12   Melvin Kranzberg, "The Wedding of Science and Technology: A Very Modern Marriage," in John Nicholas Burnett (ed.), *Technology and Science: Important Distinctions for Liberal Arts Colleges* (Davidson College, Davidson, NC, 1984), pp. 27–37.

13   A good summation of the issues involved is provided in Bruce Babbitt, "The States and the Reindustrialization of America," *Issues in Science and Technology* vol. 1 (i), Fall 1984, pp. 84–93. Works featured in the debate include Lester C. Thurow, *The Zero-Sum Society: Distribution and the Possibilities for Economic Change* (Basic Books, New York, 1980); Bennett Harrison and Barry Bluestone, *The Deindustrialization of America: Plant Closings, Community Abandonment, and the Dismantling of Basic Industry* (Basic Books, New York, 1982); and Robert B. Reich, *The Next American Frontier* (Times Books, New York, 1983).

14   J. David Roessner et al., *Impact of Office Automation on Office Workers*, 4 vols, US Department of Labor R&E Grant/Contract No. 21-13-82-13 (Tech Research Institute, Atlanta, CA, 1983); Vincent E. Giuliano, "The Mechanization of Office Work," *Scientific American* vol. 247 (3), September 1982, pp. 148–64.

15   Alvin Toffler, *The Third Wave* (Morrow, New York, 1980). Similar optimism about the future role of information technology is to be found in John Diebold, *Making the Future Work: Unleashing Our Powers of Innovation for the Decades Ahead* (Simon and Schuster, New York, 1984).

16   Sherry Turkle, *The Second Self: Computers and the Human Spirit* (Simon and Schuster, New York, 1984) provides an interesting discussion of this point.

17   William Fielding Ogburn, *On Culture and Social Change: Selected Papers*, edited by Otis Dudley Duncan (University of Chicago Press, Chicago, 1964).

18   Lewis Mumford, *Technics and Civilization* (Harcourt, Brace and World, New York, 1934).

The Computer as a Defining Technology

Jay David Bolter

One of the more notable books to appear on the subject of computers and society in recent years is Jay David Bolter's Turing's Man: Western Culture in the Computer Age *(University of North Carolina Press, 1984 and Penguin Books, 1986). Here we reproduce the introductory chapter in which Bolter outlines his thesis that computers are the new "defining technology" of our times. Not only is IT having a revolutionary impact on society, argues Bolter, but it is actually redefining humanity's role in relation to nature – that is, changing the way we view ourselves. Bolter is Assistant Professor of Classics at the University of North Carolina.*

We live in spectacular but very uncertain times. In some ways, the prospects for the future have never been more exciting: they include great advances in the physical sciences, the freeing of men and women from all dangerous and dreary work through automation, and the exploration of outer space. At the same time, the social and economic problems of the near future are staggering – enormous overpopulation, the scarcity of resources, and the deterioration of the environment. Many ages in the past have shown great promise while facing great difficulties, yet our age is perhaps unique in that its problems and its promise come from the same source, from the extraordinary achievements of science and technology. Other factors have remained constant. Men and women are no more greedy, violent, compassionate, wise, or foolish than before, but they find themselves in command of a technology that greatly enhances their capacity to express these all-too-human qualities. Technology enables them to reshape nature to conform to their needs, as far as possible to make nature over in their image.

But it is a flawed image. Mankind is indeed both good and evil, and it is to be expected that human technology will sometimes harm nature rather than improve it. Until recently, however, our technical skills were so feeble in comparison with the natural forces of climate and chemistry that we could not seriously affect our environment for good or ill, except over millennia. High technology promises to give us a new power over nature, both our own nature and that of our planet, so that the very future of civilization now depends upon our intelligent use of high technology.

There are many elements in our technological future, but the key, I think most will agree, is our burgeoning electronic technology. By focusing upon it, I hope to suggest possibilities and limitations that apply to the whole of our technological world. This essay is not a primer on computer programming, nor does it provide a thorough technical explanation of how computers work. It is instead a study of the impact that electronic logic machines are having upon our culture. It does not concern the immediate economic and political impact, although these are interesting in their own right. It does concern a subtler effect that is more difficult to describe but in the long run perhaps more important: a change in the way men and women in the electronic age think about themselves and the world around them.

It is true that the most visible results of technological change are economic. Automation – the Europeans call it "rationalization" – is altering every traditional industry, bringing increased production but also threatening jobs. The trend will likely continue in the coming decades, as microelectronics permits machines and machine tools to become "smart" – to be programmed for several related tasks rather than the rigid repetition of one task. The file clerk's job is already in danger; for nearly three decades computers have been processing inventories, billing customers, and providing endless reports for major corporations, and minicomputers are now doing the same for smaller businesses. Whether all this information processing necessarily improves efficiency is not the question. Most large companies claim that they can no longer handle the volume of their business without electronic equipment.

This might now be said of Western society in general. Because there are so many people, demanding so many services from both the government and the private sector, computers have become indispensable. Critics of the computer age see dangerous consequences of this dependency. The social atmosphere in which we work and live is being poisoned by these new machines. The opportunities for human beings to respond humanely toward one another are lost when each is treated not as an individual with a unique history and unique problems but as an identification number to which is attached a vector of quantified data. As our society moves toward the conviction that there is nothing important in the human condition that cannot be quantified and fed as data into a digital computer, the positive qualities of Western humanism may well be lost.

Are the critics right? Does the computer threaten the values of a humane society? Electronic technology is not yet well enough understood to evaluate properly its potential for good or ill. Surely we do not explain how electronics is changing our society simply by pointing to its widespread economic impact. Merely to rehearse the number of jobs lost to automation, the number of bank transactions conducted electronically, or the amount of money invested in computers by corporations is to commit the same error that is charged to the computer itself – to mistake a quantitative analysis for a qualitative one. The economic background is important because the business world has financed the frenetic pace at which electronic technology has developed over the past thirty years, and today the large majority of machines are devoted to such mundane purposes as controlling inventories and preparing invoices.

Economic conditions have only served to make computers commonplace and therefore potentially influential: what is allowing them to realize this potential is not merely their numbers but their peculiar qualities as machines. The same was true of the automobile and the telephone. Until there were millions of cars on the road, they could not change the character of American society: allow the middle class new physical and social mobility, give writers a new, largely negative symbol of the American technological spirit, and so on. Before the telephone was common, it could not serve as a means of distance-annihilating communication for the millions and again for authors as a peculiar symbol of isolation and distance between men. The economic conditions simply enabled these devices to express qualities that were latent in them from the moment the first prototypes were tinkered together.

So it is with the computer, with the difference that the electronic technology has not yet reached the maturity that the revolutions in communications and transport achieved in America in the 1920s. Computers affect the lives of all members of North American and European society, but so far largely at secondhand. Banks use them to keep our accounts, the government to calculate our taxes and to take the census, but these expensive and arcane machines have remained out of personal reach, in the possession of organizations with the capital needed to buy them and the personnel to operate them. Most laymen have never been in the same room with a computer (except for electronic games and the ubiquitous pocket calculator). This will surely change when powerful microprocessors become available to the middle class at prices that make them increasingly attractive, first as toys and then as amenities of modern life. When computers too are counted in the millions, rather than the tens of thousands, they will manifest their full impact upon our society. In a matter of years, most educated people will be using computers in their work, and this is far more important than the fact that home computers will serve as entertainment centers or menu-planners.

We have already reached the stage in which physicists and chemists and many biologists call upon electronic logic to measure their experiments and to help interpret results, statistically or through models. Sociologists and economists cannot do without computers. Humanists, scholars, and creative writers have as yet little use for these machines. This too will change, rather rapidly, as they realize that at least text editing by computer is far easier than working with pens, paper, or typewriters. Even now, the publishing industry understands the advantages of electronically controlled photocomposition. Further in the future, we may well expect libraries of information, literary as well as scientific, to be stored on electric media and made available by computer. Whether literature, philosophy, or the study of history could ever be quantified and made into input for a program is not the question. Humanists as well as scientists will employ computers, simply because these devices will be a principal medium of communication for the educated community of Europe and North America. The philosophy and fiction of the next hundred years will be written at the keyboard of a computer terminal, edited by a program, and printed under electronic control – if indeed such works are printed at all, for they may simply be stored on magnetic disk and called up electronically by the reader. In the long run, the humanist will not be able to ignore the medium with which he too will work daily: it will shape his thought in subtle ways, suggest possibilities, and impose limitations, as does any other medium of communication.

Think of a woodcut or painting of a scholastic monk living in the late Middle Ages. We see the man dressed in a habit and crowded with his precious books into a small cell, and perhaps through the window we catch a glimpse of the grounds of his monastery. He sits or stands at a high inclined desk with one or two large volumes before him; perhaps he is composing a treatise or laboriously copying a manuscript. He works by candlelight or daylight, and on the wall behind him there hangs an astrolabe or a compass for geometry. It is not hard to imagine that every element in such a picture has its bearing upon the metaphysical as well as the everyday thinking of a medieval or Renaissance schoolman. The habit and the cell itself represent the social conditions under which scholastic thought flourished: their bearing is obvious. The stylus and indeed the alphabet with which he writes, the parchment he uses, the fact that he must work from manuscripts rather than printed books, the precious authority of the few works he possesses, the absence of reliable electric light, the quality of the scientific and other instruments at his disposal – all these elements too have an influence on his work. One picture cannot fully characterize a way of life, yet if we could step into one such cell, handle the books and tools, or walk around the grounds of a functioning monastery before the Reformation and the invention of printing, we would clearly be in a better position to understand the summae, biblical commentaries, treatises on logic, and collections of letters that have come down to us. In the same way, the ancient mosaic or wall painting of a Roman poet, reclining in his garden and composing to a literate slave, who takes down the lines on a wax tablet or roll of papyrus, has much to tell us about ancient literary and philosophical thinking and the particular genres that served to express that thinking.

The next archetypal picture will be a photograph of a scientist or philosopher seated at a computer terminal: in front of him will be a television screen displaying the words as he types. The room will be low-lit, because the words and diagrams on the screen will themselves be illuminated, and sparsely furnished, because most of the references and working tools will be in the computer itself. Memory devices will hold experimental results or literary texts; programs will copy texts and present results in legible formats. The blinking cursor on the screen, far more convenient than the medieval copyist's stylus, will erase errors; editing programs will be more responsive and careful than the scribe who took down the lines of the ancient poet. The scientist or philosopher who works with such electronic tools will think in different ways from those who have worked at ordinary desks with paper and pencil, with stylus and parchment, or with papyrus. He will choose different problems and be satisfied with different solutions.

The computer as a defining technology

In the past, even a major new technology of materials or power has seldom done away with its predecessor entirely. Instead one technology relegates another to subservience, to tasks at which the new technology is either inappropriate or uneconomical. The invention of iron did not eliminate bronze tools, which were cheaper and easier to make, nor did effective windmills and waterwheels eliminate the use of harnessed animals, since there was no convenient way to pull a cart over land with wind or water power. The steam engine, the internal combustion engine, and now the nuclear reactor are unlikely to replace the workman using nothing more sophisticated than a dolly to get a heavy load up a short flight of stairs. We still rely today upon skills and discoveries (fire, farming, mining) that are thousands of years old; electronics is not the technology most important to our survival or prosperity. In that sense the Neolithic invention of agriculture has never been rivaled. We depend today upon a small number of farmers using high technology to feed us and so free us to ponder the significance of computers or anything else.

Computers perform no work themselves; they direct work. The technology of "command and control," as Norbert Wiener has aptly named it, is of little value without something to control, generally other machines whose function is to perform work. For example, the essence of the American space shuttle is the computers that control almost every phase of its operation.

But unless the powerful rocket engines provide the expected thrust, there is no mission for the computers to control. The computer leaves intact many older technologies, particularly the technologies of power, and yet it puts them in a new perspective. With the appearance of a truly subtle machine like the computer, the old power machines (steam, gas, or rocket engines) lose something of their prestige. Power machines are no longer agents on their own, subject only to direct human intervention; now they must submit to the hegemony of the computer that coordinates their effects.

As a calculating engine, a machine that controls machines, the computer does occupy a special place in our cultural landscape. It is the technology that more than any other defines our age. Our generation perfected the computer, and we are intrigued by possibilities as yet only half-realized. Ruthlessly practical and efficient, the computer remains something fantastic. Its performance astonishes even the engineers who build it, just as the clock must have astonished craftsmen in the fourteenth century and the power of the steam engine even the rugged entrepreneurs of the nineteenth century. For us today, the computer constantly threatens to break out of the tiny corner of human affairs (scientific measurement and business accounting) that it was built to occupy, to contribute instead to a general redefinition of certain basic relationships: the relationship of science to technology, of knowledge to technical power, and, in the broadest sense, of mankind to the world of nature.

This process of redefinition is not new. Technology has always exercised such an influence; it has always served both as a bridge and a barrier between men and their natural environment. The ability to make and use tools and the subtle capacity to communicate through language have allowed men to live more comfortably in the world, but these achievements have also impressed upon them their separation from nature.

Men and women throughout history have asked how it is that they and their culture (their technology in the largest sense) transcend nature, what makes them characteristically human and not merely animal. For the Greeks, a cardinal human quality was the ability to establish the political and social order embodied in a city-state; men at their best could set collective goals, make laws, and obey them, and none of these could be achieved by animals in a state of nature. Their city-state was a feat of social technology. In the Middle Ages, the accomplishments of technology were perhaps more physical than social, but the use of inanimate sources of power, wind and water, fostered a new view of mankind versus the forces of nature. The discoveries of the Renaissance and the Industrial Revolution moved men closer to nature in some respects and separated them even more radically in others. Continued emphasis on exploring and manipulating the physical world led to a deeper appreciation of the world's resources. Yet the desire to master nature – to harness her more efficient sources of power in steam and fossil fuels and to mine her metals for synthetic purposes – grew steadily throughout this period. When Darwin showed convincingly that man was an animal like any other, he shattered once and for all the barrier that separated men from the rest of nature in the Greek and medieval chains of being. Yet nineteenth-century engineers with their railroads and still more twentieth-century physicists with their atomic bombs seemed less natural than ever before, less under the control of either nature or a personal deity and more responsible for their own misjudgments.

Continually redrawing the line that divides nature and culture, men have always been inclined to explain the former in terms of the latter, to examine the world of nature through the lens of their own created human environment. So Greek philosophers used analogies from the crafts of pottery and woodworking to explain the creation of the universe; the stars, the planets, the earth, and its living inhabitants. In the same way, the weight-driven clock invented in the Middle Ages provided a new metaphor for both the regular movements of heavenly bodies and the beautifully intricate bodies of animals, whereas the widespread use of the steam engine in the nineteenth century brought to mind a different, more brutal aspect of the natural world. It is certainly not true that changing technology is solely responsible for mankind's changing views of nature, but clearly the technology of any age provides an attractive window through which thinkers can view both their physical and metaphysical worlds.

Technology has had this influence even upon philosophers, like Plato, who generally disdain human craftsmanship and see it as a poor reflection of a greater nonhuman reality. And even in Christian theology and poetry, the pleasures of heaven could only be described as grand versions of the tainted pleasures men know on earth, and the tortures of hell were earthly tortures intensified. Almost every sort of philosopher, theologian, or poet has needed an analogy on the human scale to clarify his or her ideas. Speaking of creation as the imposition of order upon the natural world, he or she generally assumes a creator as well, and this creator is a craftsman or technologist.

It is in this context that I propose to examine electronic technology. The computer is the contemporary analog of the clocks and steam engines of the previous six centuries; it is as important to us as the potter's wheel was to the ancient world. It is not that we cannot live without computers, but that we will be different people because we live with them. All techniques and devices have the potential to become defining technologies because all to some degree redefine our relationship to nature. In fact, only a few devices or crafts in any age deserve to be called defining technologies. In the ancient world, carpentry and masonry were about as important as spinning and pottery, and yet poets and philosophers found the latter two far more suggestive. In medieval Europe, crop rotation and the moldboard plough had a greater economic and social impact than the early clockwork mechanisms. Yet not many philosophers and theologians compared the world to a lentil bean. Certain skills and inventions have moved easily out of the agora into the Academy, out of the textile mill into the salon, or out of the industrial research park into the university classroom.

The vision of particular philosophers and poets is important to such a transference. Descartes and his followers helped to make the clock a defining technology in Western Europe. Certainly the first poet to elaborate the myth of the Fates who spin the thread of life helped to make textiles a defining technology for ancient Greece. But there must be something in the nature of the technology itself, so that its shape, its materials, its modes of operation appeal to the mind as well as to the hand of their age – for example, the pleasing rotary motion of the spindle or the autonomy and intricacy of the pendulum clock.

Such qualities combine with the social and economic importance of the device to make people think. Very often a device will take on a metaphoric significance and be compared in art and philosophy to some part of the animate or inanimate world. Plato compared the created universe to a spindle. Descartes thought of animals as clockwork mechanisms, and scientists in the nineteenth century and early twentieth centuries have regularly compared the universe to a heat engine that is slowly squandering its fuel. Today the computer is constantly serving as a metaphor for the human mind or brain: psychologists speak of the input and output, sometimes even the hardware and software, of the brain; linguists treat human language as if it were a programming code; and everyone speaks of making computers "think."

A defining technology develops links, metaphorical or otherwise, with a culture's science, philosophy, or literature; it is always available to serve as a metaphor, example, model, or symbol. A defining technology resembles a magnifying glass, which collects and focuses seemingly disparate ideas in a culture into one bright, sometimes piercing ray. Technology does not call forth major cultural changes by itself, but it does bring ideas into a new focus by explaining or exemplifying them in new ways to larger audiences. Descartes's notion of a mechanistic world that obeyed the laws of mathematics was clear, accessible, and therefore powerful because his contemporaries lived with clocks and gears. So today electronic technology gives a more catholic appeal to a number of trends in twentieth-century thought, particularly the notions of mathematical logic, structural linguistics, and behavioral psychology. Separately these trends were minor upheavals in the history of ideas; taken together, they become a major revision in our thinking.

Turing's man

In the development of the computer, theory preceded practice. The manifesto of the new electronic order of things was a paper ("On Computable Numbers") published by the mathematician and logician A. M. Turing in 1936. Turing set out the nature and theoretical limitations of logic machines before a single fully programmable computer had been built. What Turing provided was a symbolic description, revealing only the logical structure and saying nothing about the realization of that structure (in relays, vacuum tubes, or transistors). A Turing machine, as his description came to be called, exists only on paper as a set of specifications, but no computer built in the intervening half century has surpassed these specifications; all have at most the computing power of Turing machines. Turing is equally well known for a very different kind of paper; in 1950 he published "Computing Machinery and Intelligence." His 1936 work was a forbidding forest of symbols and theorems, accessible only to specialists. This later paper was a popular polemic, in which Turing stated his conviction that computers were capable of imitating human intelligence perfectly and that indeed they would do so by the year 2000. This paper too has served as a manifesto for a group of computer specialists dedicated to realizing Turing's claim by creating what they call "artificial intelligence," a computer that thinks.

Put aside for the moment the question of whether the computer can ever rival human intelligence. The important point is that Turing, a brilliant logician and a sober contributor to the advance of electronic technology, believed it would and that many have followed him in that belief. The explanation is partly enthusiasm for a new invention. In 1950 the computer was just beginning to bring vast areas of science and business under its technological aegis. These machines were clearly taking up the duties of command and control that had always been assumed by human operators. Who could say then where the applications of electronic command and control might end? Was it not natural to believe that the machine would in time eliminate the human operator altogether? Inventors, like explorers, have a right to extravagant claims. Edison had said that the record player would revolutionize education; the same claim was made for radio and, of course, television.

I think, however, that Turing's claim has had a greater significance. Turing was not simply exaggerating the service his machine could perform. (Does a machine that imitates human beings perform any useful service at all? We are not running short of human beings.) He was instead explaining the meaning of the computer for our age. A defining technology defines or redefines man's role in relation to nature. By promising (or threatening) to replace man, the computer is giving us a new definition of man, as an "information processor," and of nature, as "information to be processed."

I call those who accept this view of man and nature Turing's men. I include in this group many who reject Turing's extreme prediction of an artificial intelligence by the year 2000. We are all liable to become Turing's men, if our work with the computer is intimate and prolonged and we come to think and speak in terms suggested by the machine. When the cognitive psychologist begins to study the mind's "algorithm for searching long-term memory," he has become Turing's man. So has the economist who draws up input–output diagrams of the nation's business, the sociologist who engages in "quantitative history," and the humanist who prepares a "key-word-in-context" concordance.

Turing's man is the most complete integration of humanity and technology, of artificer and artifact, in the history of the Western cultures. With him the tendency, implicit in all eras, to think "through" one's contemporary technology is carried to an extreme; for him the computer reflects, indeed imitates, the crucial human capacity of rational thinking. Here is the essence of Turing's belief in artificial intelligence. By making a machine think as a man, man recreates himself, defines himself as a machine. The scheme of making a human being through technology belongs to thousands of years of mythology and alchemy, but Turing and his followers have given it a new twist. In Greek mythology, in the story of Pygmalion and Galatea, the artifact, the perfect ivory statue, came to life to join its human creator. In the seventeenth and eighteenth centuries, some followers of Descartes first suggested crossing in the other direction, arguing, with La Mettrie, that men were no more than clockwork mechanisms. Men and women of the electronic age, with their desire to sweep along in the direction of technical change, are more sanguine than ever about becoming one with their electronic homunculus. They are indeed remaking themselves in the image of their technology, and it is their very zeal, their headlong rush, and their refusal to admit any reservation that calls forth such a violent reaction from their detractors. Why, the critics ask, are technologists so eager to throw away their freedom, dignity, and humanity for the sake of innovation?

Should we be repelled by the notion of man as computer? Not until we better understand what it means for man to be a computer. Why on the face of it should we be more upset by this notion than by the Cartesian view that man is a clock or the ancient view that he is a clay vessel animated by a divine breath? We need to know how Turing's man differs from that of Descartes or Plato, how the computer differs conceptually and symbolically from a clock or a clay pot. And to do this, we must isolate the precise qualities of computers and programming, hardware and software, that have the magnifying effect mentioned earlier – bringing ideas from philosophy and science into a new focus.

IT: You Ain't Seen Nothing Yet

Michael Marien

In a paper specially written for this volume, the editor of Future Survey *identifies no less than 60 major impacts of IT – both positive and negative – which have been proposed by recent writers. Whilst providing an authoritative overview of the latest literature on IT and society, Marien makes the obvious yet often-overlooked point that the best and the worst of IT is yet to come. The IT Revolution is still in its early stages and nobody knows what might happen in the next 20 years. A future-oriented perspective is therefore essential, rather than too much emphasis on "impacts so far."*

What are the impacts of information technology? Does it all add up to a revolution or a mere evolution? Overall, is it a good development for society and human beings, or a bad one? And what can we do about it?

This is a very broad set of questions. And it is an important one, that should be continually addressed by a broad range of people in their roles as students, workers, and citizens.

The brief introductory overview presented here does not seek to take one side or another in the ongoing debate, but to urge an appreciation of the magnitude of the "IT impacts" question, and to suggest a broad framework to approach it.

Too few people, in my opinion, take a serious interest in basic IT-related questions, which are as fundamental as anything having to do with "national security," the future development of any society, and the quality of our lives. Those who do address the questions of IT impacts often do so from a present-oriented perspective of today's technologies, and the impacts are viewed only in one sector of society.

To fully address the IT impacts question, one must ask: *Which information technologies, at what point in time, are affecting what components of which countries, both for better and for worse?*

A plethora of IT, running wild

One must first ask, Which information technologies? The computer immediately comes to mind, and assessing the impacts of computers is no small task, especially because they are taking many forms, ranging from supercomputers,[1] to robots[2] to smart cards.[3] But there is often a tendency to equate IT with computers alone, rather than looking at the whole range of new and improved tools for producing and distributing information. Recent and prospective changes of both modest and awesome proportions have .not only taken place as regards computers, but also as concerns broadcasting via satellites, fiberoptic cable networks, mobile telephones, cable TV, videocassettes, and compact disks. Some of the less glamorous and unheralded technologies, such as VCRs[4] and facsimile machines,[5] may eventually prove to be very significant for human affairs, for better and/or for worse. So keep your eye on all technologies great and small, especially because two heretofore modestly evolutionary elements could be combined into something revolutionary. The most notable prospect in this regard is the integration of computers and communications as proposed by Koji Kobayashi, Chairman and CEO of Japan's NEC Corporation.[6] The resulting global infrastructure, featuring an "automatic interpretation telephone system," is not a utopian fantasy, but a project that NEC is working on and hopes to realize – and profit from – by the year 2000.

This leads to the second part of the basic "IT impacts" question. One should not only look at a broad range of technologies, but extend the time frame to escape imprisonment in the present. Too many critiques are confined to today's technology, which is rapidly becoming yesterday's.

To use the phrase of computer entrepreneur Adam Osborne, information technology is "running wild."[7] He exaggerates, of course, as many in the computer/IT area do in making their heady forecasts of dazzling things to come. But Osborne is quite correct in one simple but often overlooked factor: the IT story is unfolding, and there is little or nothing that can control or stop any aspect of the global industry. To the contrary, the industry is widely supported by both academia and government as a source of jobs, intellectual curiosity, national prestige, and economic hegemony.[8] Never mind what is produced; we are seen as "at war" in the global economy, and any country that shirks from battle will be left behind.[9]

So if today's technology seems somewhat less than revolutionary, as notably argued by Brian Winston,[10] that does not necessarily mean that one or more revolutions, for better and/or for worse, are just over the horizon. For example, IBM boasts that the new 1-million-bit memory chip of 1985, will become a 16-million-bit chip, and then on to a 64-million-bit chip and a 256-million-bit chip.[11] The vice president of IBM forecasts that "The progress in computing systems will continue – perhaps exponentially and certainly unabated – for at least the next 10 or 15 years."[12] Rex Malik views the shift towards the information society as just beginning to gather speed, and calls it an "exponential cascade."[13] And Stewart Brand, after reviewing various new IT thrusts being cooked up at MIT's Media Lab, concludes that the wired world is like "a teenager with a new car, taking dumb risks, finding new freedoms."[14] In other words, to employ two vernacular phrases for emphasis, "it ain't over 'til it's over" – and there is no end in sight – and, in so far as impacts, it is most likely that "you ain't seen nothing yet."

What impacts and where?

The key to understanding IT impacts is where you look, and how. There are plenty of places where one can find exuberant successes and unabated happiness. And, if one looks, one can also find unabated failures and ominous threats. This distinction may seem simplistic, but the literature is rife with one-sided optimists and pessimists, the technophiles (generally physical scientists and computer specialists with a professional or a commercial interest in IT) and the technophobes (generally non-technical outsiders in the social sciences and humanities).

Most assessments are confined to a single sector of society (manufacturing, health, education, offices), a single class of workers (professional/managerial or low-level), and a single nation.

To open horizons, I shall list and partially document 60 actual or potential impacts of various information technologies (largely computers), grouped in seven basic categories, and roughly assessed as positive (+), negative (−), or mixed or ambiguous (+ / −). This list is adapted from a longer and fully documented listing, "125 Impacts of New Information Technologies."[15]

1 International relations

+ Improved Soviet communications favoring *glasnost, perestroika*, and US–USSR relations.[16]

+ Aid to Third World development.

+ Automatic language translation to create closer ties (see n. 6).

+ / − International financial services enhance world trade, but make the international financial system increasingly vulnerable.

+ / − Large transnational corporations enabled, reinforcing power of rich over poor, but perhaps a force for world peace.

+ / − Stock trading globalized and accelerated.

+ / − Power leaking out of sovereign nation-states.

− Possible military false alert leading to release of nuclear weapons and possible nuclear war.

− Increased rich–poor gap between nations.

− Threat to cultural autonomy in Third World.

2 Government

+ New computer models and software for better decision-making in complex situations.[17]

+ Better-informed and more democratized legislative bodies.

+ Tax collection facilitated.

+ Auto traffic monitoring to enable road use fees (being tested in Hong Kong).

+ Potential to enhance citizen participation.

− Dossier society integrating personal files into national data bases and threatening privacy.[18]

− Pollution of public communication; shriveled discourse.[19]

3 Crime and justice

+ Electronic identification of fingerprints and voiceprints for foolproof ID.

+ Electronic devices to monitor parolees and nonviolent offenders.

+ Potential of robots as prison and security guards.

+ Potential to ease caseload in courts.

+ / – National comprehensive criminal history system (also see dossier society, n. 18).
+ / – Better surveillance technologies and property protection.
–   Computer crime more costly than physical bank robbery.

4   Economy and work

+   Productivity gains; better models for decisions.
+   Lower inventories ("just-in-time" manufacturing).
+   Consumer use to assist in purchasing.
+   Potential of robots to do hazardous and boring work.
+   Potential to do work at home (not yet realized; see Forester essay in this volume).
+ / – Decentralization of organizations enabled – but also more centralization?
+ / – Job displacement – but also job creation?
–   "Gods and Clods": work divided into smart jobs and dumb jobs, as middle managers disappear.[20]
–   Monitoring of employees invades privacy.
–   Conspicuous consumption of computers leads to waste and abuse.

5   Health and health care

+ Computer assistance in diagnosis and cost analysis.
+ IT to handle increased demand for health information.[21]
+ Potential of smart card health records to carry medical history.
+ Preparation of patient-specific educational materials.
+ Computer as home health advisor for physical and mental health.
– Occupational illness in computer industry.
– Computerphobia, VDT effects, technostress.[22]

6   Education and knowledge

+ Facilitation of research.
+ Facilitation of library acquisitions and borrowing.[23]
+ Potential for individual tutoring and improved learning.
+ Mind extension: expert systems for everyone.
+ Mass storage of information on compact disks.
+ Knowledge of earth enhanced; monitoring of remote areas enabled; mapmaking greatly improved.
+ Use of computers in design and for artistic creations.
– Potential displacement of teachers.
– Growing division between information haves and have-nots.
– Infoglut: information overload resulting in fragmentation and narrow perspectives.[24]
– Blind faith in computer capabilities; quantitative criteria become more important than wisdom.
– Referencing becomes more ambiguous due to modification of electrified historical record.
– Computerized photo composites create dangerous deceptions.[25]

7   *The Individual*

+ Humanized users: friendly machines liberate people and amplify the brain.
- Human–machine interaction as dehumanizing and isolating.
- Potential robot species (*silico sapiens*) superior to *homo sapiens*.[26]
- Infoglut leading to boredom, meaninglessness.
- Sense of time accelerated and jumbled.[27]
- No sense of place: new structure of societal interaction not based on locality.[28]

This listing is by no means complete in space and especially in time. Twenty years from now, it may seem naïve both in the threats and promises listed, and in the numerous omissions which perhaps will only be clear by then. But it is a start in suggesting a more comprehensive space/time assessment.

Even at the present moment, more impacts can doubtlessly be added to the list simply by reading the contributions in this volume. Some impacts could justifiably be removed from the list because of their triviality or duplication. And the reader is encouraged to argue with the (+) and (–) designations, or weight certain impacts as especially important.

As it stands, the positive impacts in this list outnumber the negative impacts by a ratio of almost 3 to 2. But if one looks at the really important impacts, the negatives outweigh the positives. In rough summary, many of the positive impacts add up to a better capability to understand and manage a complex world. This is offset by the potentials of computer crime and a dossier society, the aggravation of rich–poor differences between nations and social classes, the pollution and fragmentation of discourse by infoglut, and the distortion of human time and space (the last two items in the above listing). As a crowning irony, this brief exercise advocating assessment of IT in time and space ends on the note that the most important IT impacts may very well be on our experience of time and space itself!

What can we do?

Studying the impacts of IT on society is an unfolding realm of challenging intellectual inquiry which is far from receiving its due. Universities have a variety of courses in literary and art criticism to help us understand artistic creations. And universities have many courses and programs that encourage human creation in technology, notably the so-called computer sciences. What is missing is a balance in the intellectual regimen that encourages any serious reflection on the present and prospective consequences of technology (notably, information technologies), and how we can manage our plethora of new tools to the benefit of all, or at least the greatest number.[29] We thus need more and better technology assessment by governments, greatly improved dissemination of these findings, and a more balanced liberal education that prepares students for life in the technology-drenched world of the twenty-first century. Even these actions, if fully realized, will result only in some effective social control and government legislation. It is the best we can hope for.

My position staked out here (benefiting from access to an early draft of the editor's Introduction to this volume), can be described as a "human choice pessimist," somewhat in the tradition of the late René Dubois, who called himself a "despairing optimist." From a broad time/space view of technology, IT is viewed as both cause and consequence of social change. IT is also seen as both "continuist" and "transformationist." Indeed, the broadest view is simply that IT is a major facet of the high-tech multi-revolution,[30] which in turn is part of our Era of Multiple Transformations. The question of whether technology is cause or consequence may be relatively minor, and a distraction from the need to study all ongoing and prospective transformations. We must and can try to understand our emerging world, and shape it as best as we can. At least in the near future, our capability and willingness to do so is so underdeveloped that we will invariably respond with too little, too late.

Notes

1 Sidney Karin and Norris Parker Smith, *The Supercomputer Era* (Harcourt Brace Jovanovich, Boston, 1987).

2 Joseph Deken, *Silico Sapiens: The Fundamentals and Future of Robots* (Bantam New Age Books, New York, 1986). Robotics is described here as the final step in computer evolution, the ultimate computer form of independent action.

3 Robert McIvor, "Smart Cards," *Scientific American*, November, 1985. See also "Smart Cards," *High Technology*, July 1986; "Smart Cards Get Smarter," *High Technology Business*, September 1987.

4 Gladys D. Ganley and Oswald H. Ganley, *Global Political Fallout: The First Decade of the VCR, 1976–1985* (Ablex Publishing Co., Norwood NJ, 1987). The authors conclude that the use of VCRs, still in its infancy, will have an "important, perhaps critical, global political impact . . . in the perhaps not-too-distant future."

5 Calvin Sims, "Coast-to-Coast in 20 Seconds: Fax Machines Alter Business," *The New York Times*, May 6, 1988, p. 1.

6 Koji Kobayashi, *Computers and Communications: A Vision of C&C* (MIT Press, Cambridge MA, 1986).

7 Adam Osborne, *Running Wild: The Next Industrial Revolution* (Osborne/McGraw-Hill, Berkeley, CA, 1979).

8 Kenneth Flamm, *Targeting the Computer: Government Support and International Competition* (The Brookings Institution, Washington, DC, 1987).

9 David H. Brandin and Michael A. Harrison, *The Technology War: A Case for Competitiveness* (Wiley-Interscience, New York, 1987).

10 Brian Winston, *Misunderstanding Media* (Harvard University Press, Cambridge, MA, 1986).

11 "The 4-Million-Bit Chip and Great Memories of the Future" (advertisement), *The New York Times*, March 20, 1987, p. D4.

12 Abraham Peled, "The Next Computer Revolution," *Scientific American*, October 1987.

13 Rex Malik, "Beyond the Exponential Cascade: On the Reduction of Complexity," *InterMedia*, March 1986.

14 Stewart Brand, *The Media Lab: Inventing the Future at MIT* (Viking, New York, 1987).

15 Michael Marien, *Future Survey Annual 1986: A Guide to the Recent Literature of Trends, Forecasts, and Policy Proposals* (World Future Society, Bethesda, MD, 1987), Appendix 1, pp. 185–6.

16 Wilson P. Dizard and S. Blake Swensrud, *Gorbachev's Information Revolution: Controlling Glasnost in a New Electronic Era* (Westview Press, Boulder, CO, 1987). The authors cautiously note that the massive upgrading of communications that is planned will not necessarily relax totalitarian controls.

17 Gerald O. Barney and Sheryl Wilkins, *Managing a Nation: The Software Source Book* (Global Studies Center, Arlington, VA, 1986). See also Donella H. Meadows and J. M. Robinson, *The Electronic Oracle: Computer Models and Social Decisions* (Wiley, New York, 1985).

18 Kenneth C. Laudon, *Dossier Society: Value Choices in the Design of National Information Systems* (Columbia University Press, New York, 1986).

19 Neil Postman, *Amusing Ourselves to Death: Public Discourse in the Age of Show Business* (Viking, New York, 1985). The principal IT culprit here is television and its pervasive influence in our culture.

20 James N. Danziger and Kenneth L. Kraemer, *People and Computers: The Impacts of Computing on End Users in Organizations* (Columbia University Press, New York, 1986). A thorough study of more than 2,500 managers, professionals, and bureaucrats, finding considerable differences in impacts, though on balance the benefits surpass the negative effects.

21 G. Octo Barnett, "The Application of Computer-Based Medical-Record Systems in Ambulatory Practice," *The New England Journal of Medicine*, June 21, 1984. Barnett asserts that the need for radically improved computer management and the growing demand for health-related information, rather than the power of the computer, is the driving force introducing computer technology into medicine.

22 Craig Brod, *Technostress: The Human Cost of the Computer Revolution* (Addison-Wesley, Reading, MA, 1984).

23 For example, the smallish public library in the suburban/rural community of 5,000 where I live in Upstate New York has recently acquired a computer link to the central county library. The previous time to acquire a book from "downtown" was usually more than a week; now it is two days.

24 Orrin E. Klapp, *Overload and Boredom: Essays on the Quality of Life in the Information Society* (Greenwood Press, Westport, CT, 1986).

25 Fred Ritchin, "Photography's New Bag of Tricks," *The New York Times Magazine*, November 4, 1984.

26 Deken, *Silico Sapiens*.

27 Michael Young, *The Metronomic Society: Natural Rhythms and Human Timetables* (Harvard University Press, Cambridge, MA, May 1988), on the increasing scarcity of time in our social evolution. In *Time Wars: The Primary Conflict in Human History* (Henry Holt and Co., New York, 1987), Jeremy Rifkin heatedly argues that computers are accelerating the tempo of modern life. In "The Re Decade" (*Esquire*, March 1986) *Washington Post* TV critic Tom Shales entitles the 1980s as a by-product of the communications revolution: a decade of recycle, recall, retrieve, reprocess, and rerun.

28 Manuel Castells (ed.), *High Technology, Space, and Society* (Sage Publications: Beverly Hills, CA, 1985). See also Joshua Meyrowitz, *No Sense of Place: The Impact of Electronic Media on Social Behavior* (Oxford University Press, New York, 1985).

29 Edward Wenk, Jr, *Tradeoffs: Imperatives of Choice in a High-Tech World* (Johns Hopkins University Press, Baltimore, MD, 1986). See also Mark A. Boroush, Kan Chen, and Alexander N. Christakis (eds), *Technology Assessment: Creative Futures* (North-Holland, New York, 1980).

30 Michael Marien, "Hope, Fear, and Technology: Changing Prospects in the 1980s," *Vital Speeches of the Day*, December 15, 1984. Describes four ongoing/potential technological transformations. I have subsequently employed the phrase "high-tech multi-transformation."

2 IT as Evolution

The Evolution of Control

James R. Beniger

Another book to cause a stir in recent years is Jim Beniger's The Control Revolution: Technological and Economic Origins of the Information Society *(Harvard University Press,
Cambridge, MA, 1986). Here we reprint the first chapter, in which Beniger summarizes his
argument that IT is merely the latest instalment in a much longer-running show – the Control
Revolution. From this perspective, the information society is seen as part of the continuing response
to a "crisis of control" generated way back at the time of the Industrial Revolution. James Beniger
is Associate Professor at the Annenberg School of Communications, University of Southern
California, Los Angeles.*

One tragedy of the human condition is that each of us lives and dies with little hint of even the
most profound transformations of our society and our species that play themselves out in some
small part through our own existence. When the earliest *Homo sapiens* encountered *Homo
erectus*, or whatever species was our immediate forebear, it is unlikely that the two saw in their
differences a major turning point in the development of our race. If they did, this knowledge
did not survive to be recorded, at least not in the ancient writings now extant. Indeed, some
fifty thousand years passed before Darwin and Wallace rediscovered the secret – proof of the
difficulty of grasping even the most essential dynamics of our lives and our society.

Much the same conclusion could be drawn from any of a succession of revolutionary societal
transformations: the cultivation of plants and the domestication of animals, the growth of
permanent settlements, the development of metal tools and writing, urbanization, the
invention of wheeled vehicles and the plow, the rise of market economies, social classes, a
world commerce. The origins and early histories of these and many other developments of
comparable significance went unnoticed or at least unrecorded by contemporary observers.
Today we are hard pressed to associate specific dates, places, or names with many major
societal transformations, even though similar details abound for much lesser events and trends
that occurred at the same times.

This condition holds for even that most significant of modern societal transformations, the
so-called Industrial Revolution. Although it is generally conceded to have begun by the mid-

eighteenth century, at least in England, the idea of its revolutionary impact does not appear until the 1830s in pioneering histories like those of Wade (1833) and Blanqui (1837). Widespread acceptance by historians that the Industrial Revolution constituted a major transformation of society did not come until Arnold Toynbee, Sr, popularized the term in a series of public lectures in 1881 (Toynbee, 1884). This was well over a century after the changes he described had first begun to gain momentum in his native England and at least a generation after the more important ones are now generally considered to have run their course. Although several earlier observers had described one or another of the same changes, few before Toynbee had begun to reflect upon the more profound transformation that signaled the end – after some ten thousand years – of predominantly agricultural society.

Two explanations of this chronic inability to grasp even the most essential dynamics of an age come readily to mind. First, important transformations of society rarely result from single discrete events, despite the best efforts of later historians to associate the changes with such events. Human society seems rather to evolve largely through changes so gradual as to be all but imperceptible, at least compared to the generational cycles of the individuals through whose lives they unfold. Second, contemporaries of major societal transformations are frequently distracted by events and trends more dramatic in immediate impact but less lasting in significance. Few who lived through the early 1940s were unaware that the world was at war, for example, but the much less noticed scientific and technological byproducts of the conflict are more likely to lend their names to the era, whether it comes to be remembered as the Nuclear Age, the Computer Age, or the Space Age.

Regardless of how we explain the recurrent failure of past generations to appreciate the major societal transformations of their own eras, we might expect that their record would at least chasten students of contemporary social change. In fact, just the opposite appears to be the case. Much as if historical myopia could somehow be overcome by confronting the problem head-on, a steadily mounting number of social scientists, popular writers, and critics have discovered that one or another revolutionary societal transformation is now in progress. The succession of such transformations identified since the late 1950s includes the rise of a new social class (Djilas, 1957; Gouldner, 1979), a meritocracy (Young, 1958), post-capitalist society (Dahrendorf, 1959), a global village (McLuhan, 1964), the new industrial state (Galbraith, 1967), a scientific-technological revolution (Richta, 1967; Daglish, 1972; Prague Academy, 1973), a technetronic era (Brzezinski, 1970), post-industrial society (Touraine, 1971; Bell, 1973), an information economy (Porat, 1977), and the micro millennium (Evans, 1979), to name only a few. A more complete catalog of these and similar transformations, listed by year of first exposition in a major work, is given in table 2.1.

The writer who first identified each of the transformations listed in table 2.1 usually found the brunt of the change to be – coincidentally enough – either in progress or imminent. One best-seller, for example, surveys the sweep of human history, notes the central importance of the agricultural and industrial revolutions, and then finds in contemporary society the seeds of a third revolution – the impending "Third Wave":

Humanity faces a quantum leap forward. It faces the deepest social upheaval and creative restructuring of all time. Without clearly recognizing it, we are engaged in building a remarkable new civilization from the ground up. This is the meaning of the Third Wave . . . It is likely that the Third Wave will sweep across history and complete itself in a few decades. We, who happen to share the planet at this explosive moment, will therefore feel the full impact of the Third Wave in our own lifetimes. Tearing our families apart,

Table 2.1 Modern societal transformations identified since 1950

Year	Transformation	Sources
1950	Lonely crowd	Riesman, 1950
	Posthistoric man	Seidenberg, 1950
1953	Organizational revolution	Boulding, 1953
1956	Organization man	Whyte, 1956
1957	New social class	Djilas, 1957; Gouldner, 1979
1958	Meritocracy	Young, 1958
1959	Educational revolution	Drucker, 1959
	Post-capitalist society	Dahrendorf, 1959
1960	End of ideology	Bell, 1960
	Post-maturity economy	Rostow, 1960
1961	Industrial society	Aron, 1961; 1966
1962	Computer revolution	Berkeley, 1962; Tomeski, 1970; Hawkes, 1971
	Knowledge economy	Machlup, 1962; 1980; Drucker, 1969
1963	New working class	Mallet, 1963; Gintis, 1970; Gallie, 1978
	Post-bourgeois society	Lichtheim, 1963
1964	Global village	McLuhan, 1964
	Managerial capitalism	Marris, 1964
	One-dimensional man	Marcuse, 1964
	Post-civilized era	Boulding, 1964
	Service class society	Dahrendorf, 1964
	Technological society	Ellul, 1964
1967	New industrial state	Galbraith, 1967
	Scientific-technological revolution	Richta, 1967; Daglish, 1972; Prague Academy, 1973
1968	Dual economy	Averitt, 1968
	Neocapitalism	Gorz, 1968
	Post-modern society	Etzioni, 1968; Breed, 1971
	Technocracy	Meynaud, 1968
	Unprepared society	Michael, 1968
1969	Age of discontinuity	Drucker, 1969
	Post-collectivist society	Beer, 1969
	Post-ideological society	Feuer, 1969
1970	Computerized society	Martin and Norman, 1970
	Personal society	Halmos, 1970
	Post-economic society	Kahn, 1970
	Post-liberal age	Vickers, 1970
	Prefigurative culture	Mead, 1970
	Technetronic era	Brzezinski, 1970
1971	Age of information	Helvey, 1971
	Compunications	Oettinger, 1971

Table 2.1 cont.

Year	Transformation	Sources
1971	Post-industrial society	Touraine, 1971; Bell, 1973
	Self-guiding society	Breed, 1971
	Superindustrial society	Toffler, 1971
1972	Limits to growth	Meadows, 1972; Cole 1973
	Post-traditional society	Eisenstadt, 1972
	World without borders	Brown, 1972
1973	New service society	Lewis, 1973
	Stalled society	Crozier, 1973
1974	Consumer vanguard	Gartner and Riessman, 1974
	Information revolution	Lamberton, 1974
1975	Communications age	Phillips, 1975
	Mediacracy	Phillips, 1975
	Third industrial revolution	Stine, 1975; Stonier, 1979
1976	Industrial-technological society	Ionescu, 1976
	Megacorp	Eichner, 1976
1977	Electronics revolution	Evans, 1977
	Information economy	Porat, 1977
1978	Anticipatory democracy	Bezold, 1978
	Network nation	Hiltz and Turoff, 1978
	Republic of technology	Boorstin, 1978
	Telematic society	Nora and Minc, 1978; Martin, 1981
	Wired society	Martin, 1978
1979	Collapse of work	Jenkins and Sherman, 1979
	Computer age	Dertouzos and Moses, 1979
	Credential society	Collins, 1979
	Micro millennium	Evans, 1979
1980	Micro revolution	Large, 1980, 1984; Laurie, 1981
	Microelectronics revolution	Forester, 1980
	Third wave	Toffler, 1980
1981	Information society	Martin and Butler, 1981
	Network marketplace	Dordick, 1981
1982	Communications revolution	Williams, 1982
	Information age	Dizard, 1982
1983	Computer state	Burnham, 1983
	Gene age	Sylvester and Klotz, 1983
1984	Second industrial divide	Piore and Sabel, 1984

rocking our economy, paralyzing our political systems, shattering our values, the Third Wave affects everyone. (Toffler, 1980, p. 26)

Even less breathless assessments of contemporary change have been no less optimistic about the prospect of placing developing events and trends in the broadest historical context. Daniel Bell, for example, after acknowledging the counter-evidence of Toynbee and the Industrial Revolution, nevertheless concludes, "Today, with our greater sensitivity to social consequences and to the future . . . we are more alert to the possible imports of technological and organizational change, and this is all to the good" (1980, pp. x–xi).

The number of major societal transformations listed in table 2.1 indicates that Bell appears to be correct; we do seem more alert than previous generations to the possible importance of change. The wide variety of transformations identified, however, suggests that, like the generations before us, we may be preoccupied with specific and possibly ephemeral events and trends, at the risk of overlooking what only many years from now will be seen as the fundamental dynamic of our age.

Because the failures of past generations bespeak the difficulties of overcoming this problem, the temptation is great not to try. This reluctance might be overcome if we recognize that understanding ourselves in our own particular moment in history will enable us to shape and guide that history. As Bell goes on to say, "to the extent that we are sensitive [to the possible importance of technological and social change], we can try to estimate the consequences and decide which policies we should choose, consonant with the values we have, in order to shape, accept, or even reject the alternative futures that are available to us" (1980, p. xi)

Much the same purpose motivates – and I hope justifies – the pages that follow. In them I argue, like many of the writers whose names appear in table 2.1, that society is currently experiencing a revolutionary transformation on a global scale. Unlike most of the other writers, however, I do not conclude that the crest of change is either recent, current, or imminent. Instead, I trace the causes of change back to the middle and late nineteenth century, to a set of problems – in effect a crisis of control – generated by the industrial revolution in manufacturing and transportation. The response to this crisis, at least in technological innovation and restructuring of the economy, occurred most rapidly around the turn of the century and amounted to nothing less, I argue, than a revolution in societal control.

The Control Revolution

Few turn-of-the-century observers understood even isolated aspects of the societal transformation – what I shall call the "Control Revolution" – then gathering momentum in the United States, England, France, and Germany. Notable among those who did was Max Weber (1864–1920), the German sociologist and political economist who directed social analysis to the most important control technology of his age: bureaucracy. Although bureaucracy had developed several times independently in ancient civilizations, Weber was the first to see it as the critical new machinery – new, at least, in its generality and pervasiveness – for control of the societal forces unleashed by the Industrial Revolution.

For a half-century after Weber's initial analysis bureaucracy continued to reign as the single most important technology of the Control Revolution. After World War II, however, generalized control began to shift slowly to computer technology. If social change has seemed to accelerate in recent years (as argued, for example, by Toffler, 1971), this has been due in large part to a spate of new information-processing, communication, and control technologies like the computer, most notably the microprocessors that have proliferated since the early 1970s. Such technologies are more properly seen, however, not as causes but as consequences of societal change, as natural extensions of the Control Revolution already in progress for more than a century.

Revolution, a term borrowed from astronomy, first appeared in political discourse in seventeenth-century England, where it described the restoration of a previous form of government. Not until the French Revolution did the word acquire its currently popular and opposite meaning, that of abrupt and often violent change. As used here in Control Revolution, the term is intended to have both of these opposite connotations.

Beginning most noticeably in the United States in the late nineteenth century, the Control Revolution was certainly a dramatic if not abrupt discontinuity in technological advance. Indeed, even the word *revolution* seems barely adequate to describe the development, within the span of a single lifetime, of virtually all of the basic communication technologies still in use a century later: photography and telegraphy (1830s), rotary power printing (1840s), the typewriter (1860s), transatlantic cable (1866), telephone (1876), motion pictures (1894), wireless telegraphy (1895), magnetic tape recording (1899), radio (1906), and television (1923).

Along with these rapid changes in mass media and telecommunications technologies, the Control Revolution also represented the beginning of a restoration – although with increasing centralization – of the economic and political control that was lost at more local levels of society during the Industrial Revolution. Before this time, control of government and markets had depended on personal relationships and face-to-face interactions; now control came to be reestablished by means of bureaucratic organization, the new infrastructures of transportation and telecommunications, and system-wide communication via the new mass media. By both of the opposite definitions of *revolution,* therefore, the new societal transformations – rapid innovation in information and control technology, to regain control of functions once contained at much lower and more diffuse levels of society – constituted a true revolution in societal control.

Here the word *control* represents its most general definition, purposive influence toward a predetermined goal. Most dictionary definitions imply these same two essential elements: *influence* of one agent over another, meaning that the former causes changes in the behavior of the latter; and *purpose,* in the sense that influence is directed toward some prior goal of the controlling agent. If the definition used here differs at all from colloquial ones, it is only because many people reserve the word *control* for its more determinate manifestations, what I shall call "strong control." Dictionaries, for example, often include in their definitions of control concepts like direction, guidance, regulation, command, and domination, approximate synonyms of *influence* that vary mainly in increasing determination. As a more general concept, however, *control* encompasses the entire range from absolute control to the weakest and most probabilistic form, that is, any purposive influence on behavior, *however slight.* Economists say that television advertising serves to control specific demand, for example, and political scientists say that direct mail campaigns can help to control issue-voting, even though only a small fraction of the intended audience may be influenced in either case.

Inseparable from the concept of control are the twin activities of information processing and reciprocal communication, complementary factors in any form of control. Information processing is essential to all purposive activity, which is by definition goal-directed and must therefore involve the continual comparison of current states to future goals, a basic problem of information processing. So integral to control is this comparison of inputs to stored programs that the word *control* itself derives from the medieval Latin verb *contrarotulare*, to compare something "against the rolls," the cylinders of paper that served as official records in ancient times.

Simultaneously with the comparison of inputs to goals, two-way interaction between controller and controlled must also occur, not only to communicate influence from the former to the latter, but also to communicate back the results of this action (hence the term *feedback* for this reciprocal flow of information back to a controller). So central is communication to the process of control that the two have become the joint subject of the modern science of cybernetics, defined by one of its founders as "the entire field of control and communication theory, whether in the machine or in the animal" (Wiener, 1948, p. 11). Similarly, the pioneers of mathematical communication theory have defined the object of their study as purposive control in the broadest sense: communication, according to Shannon and Weaver (1949, pp. 3–5), includes "all of the procedures by which one mind may affect another"; they note that "communication either affects conduct or is without any discernible and probable effect at all."

Because both the activities of information processing and communication are inseparable components of the control function, a society's ability to maintain control – at all levels from interpersonal to international relations – will be directly proportional to the development of its information technologies. Here the term *technology* is intended not in the narrow sense of practical or applied science but in the more general sense of any intentional extension of a natural process, that is, of the processing of matter, energy, and information that characterizes all living systems. Respiration is a wholly natural life function, for example, and is therefore not a technology; the human ability to breathe under water, by contrast, implies some techno-logical extension. Similarly, voting is one general technology for achieving collective decisions in the control of social aggregates; the Australian ballot is a particular innovation in this technology.

Technology may therefore be considered as roughly equivalent to that which can be done, excluding only those capabilities that occur naturally in living systems. This distinction is usually although not always clear. One ambiguous case is language, which may have developed at least in part through purposive innovation but which now appears to be a mostly innate capability of the human brain. The brain itself represents another ambiguous case: it probably developed in interaction with purposive tool use and may therefore be included among human technologies.

Because technology defines the limits on what a society *can* do, technological innovation might be expected to be a major impetus to social change in the Control Revolution no less than in the earlier societal transformations accorded the status of revolutions. The Neolithic Revolution, for example, which brought the first permanent settlements, owed its origin to the refinement of stone tools and the domestication of plants and animals. The Commercial Revolution, following exploration of Africa, Asia, and the New World, resulted directly from technical improvements in seafaring and navigational equipment. The Industrial Revolution, which eventually brought the nineteenth-century crisis of control, began a century earlier with greatly increased use of coal and steam power and a spate of new machinery for the manufacture of cotton textiles. Like these earlier revolutions in matter and energy processing, the Control Revolution resulted from innovation at a most fundamental level of technology – that of information processing.

Information processing may be more difficult to appreciate than matter or energy processing because information is epiphenomenal: it derives from the *organization* of the material world on which it is wholly dependent for its existence. Despite being in this way a higher order or derivative of matter and energy, information is no less critical to society. All living systems must process matter and energy to maintain themselves counter to entropy, the universal tendency of organization toward breakdown and randomization. Because control is necessary for such processing, and information, as we have seen, is essential to control, both information processing and communication, in so far as they distinguish living systems from the inorganic universe, might be said to define life itself – except for a few recent artifacts of our own species.

Each new technological innovation extends the processes that sustain life, thereby increasing the need for control and hence for improved control technology. This explains why technology appears autonomously to beget technology in general (Winner, 1977), and why, as argued here, innovations in matter and energy processing create the need for further innovation in information-processing and communication technologies. Because technological innovation is increasingly a collective, cumulative effort, one whose results must be taught and diffused, it also generates an increased need for technologies of information storage and retrieval – as well as for their elaboration in systems of technical education and communication – quite independently of the particular need for control.

As in the earlier revolutions in matter and energy technologies, the nineteenth-century revolution in information technology was predicated on, if not directly caused by, social changes associated with earlier innovations. Just as the Commercial Revolution depended on capital and labor freed by advanced agriculture, for example, and the Industrial Revolution presupposed a commercial system for capital allocations and the distribution of goods, the most recent technological revolution developed in response to problems arising out of advanced industrialization – an ever-mounting crisis of control.

Crisis of control

The later Industrial Revolution constituted, in effect, a consolidation of earlier technological revolutions and the resulting transformations of society. Especially during the late nineteenth and early twentieth centuries industrialization extended to progressively earlier technological revolutions: manufacturing, energy production, transportation, agriculture – the last a transformation of what had once been seen as the extreme opposite of industrial production. In each area industrialization meant heavy infusions of capital for the exploitation of fossil fuels, wage labor, and machine technology and resulted in larger and more complex systems – systems characterized by increasing differentiation and interdependence at all levels.

One of the earliest and most astute observers of this phenomenon was Emile Durkheim (1858–1917), the great French sociologist who examined many of its social ramifications in his *Division of Labor in Society* (1893). As Durkheim noted, industrialization tends to break down the barriers to transportation and communication that isolate local markets (what he called the "segmental" type), thereby extending distribution of goods and services to national and even global markets (the "organized" type). This, in turn, disrupts the market equilibrium under which production is regulated by means of direct communication between producer and consumer:

Insofar as the segmental type is strongly marked, there are nearly as many economic markets as there are different segments. Consequently, each of them is very limited. Producers, being near consumers, can easily reckon the extent of the needs to be satisfied. Equilibrium is established without any trouble and production regulates itself. On the contrary, as the organized type develops, the fusion of different segments draws the markets together into one which embraces almost all society . . . The result is that each industry produces for consumers spread over the whole surface of the country or even of the entire world. Contact is then no longer sufficient. The producer can no longer embrace the market in a glance, nor even in thought. He can no longer see limits, since it is, so to speak, limitless. Accordingly, production becomes unbridled and unregulated. It can only trust to chance . . . From this come the crises which periodically disturb economic functions. (1893, pp. 369–70)

What Durkheim describes here is nothing less than a crisis of control at the most aggregate level of a national system – a level that had had little practical relevance before the mass production and distribution of factory goods. Resolution of the crisis demanded new means of communication, as Durkheim perceived, to control an economy shifting from local segmented markets to higher levels of organization – what might be seen as the growing "systemness" of society. This capacity to communicate and process information is one component of what structural-functionalists following Durkheim have called the problem of *integration*, the growing need for coordination of functions that accompanies differentiation and specialization in any system.

Increasingly confounding the need for integration of the structural division of labor were corresponding increases in commodity flows through the system – flows driven by steam-powered factory production and mass distribution via national rail networks. Never before had the processing of material flows threatened to exceed, in both volume and speed, the capacity of technology to contain them. For centuries most goods had moved with the speed of draft animals down roadway and canal, weather permitting. This infrastructure, controlled by small organizations of only a few hierarchial levels, supported even national economies. Suddenly – owing to the harnessing of steam power – goods could be moved at the full speed of industrial production, night and day and under virtually any conditions, not only from town to town but across entire continents and around the world.

To do this, however, required an increasingly complex system of manufacturers and distributors, central and branch offices, transportation lines and terminals, containers and cars. Even the logistics of nineteenth-century armies, then the most difficult problem in processing and control, came to be dwarfed in complexity by the material economy just emerging as Durkheim worked on his famous study.

What Durkheim described as a crisis of control on the societal level he also managed to relate to the level of individual psychology. Here he found a more personal but directly related problem, what he called *anomie*, the breakdown of norms governing individual and group behavior. Anomie is an "abnormal" and even "pathological" result, according to Durkheim (1893, p. 353), an exception to his more general finding that increasing division of labor directly increases normative integration and, with it, social solidarity. As Durkheim argued, anomie results not from the structural division of labor into what he called distinct societal "organs" but rather from the breakdown in communication among these increasingly isolated sectors, so that individuals employed in them lose sight of the larger purpose of their separate efforts:

> The state of anomie is impossible wherever solidary organs are sufficiently in contact or sufficiently prolonged. In effect, being continguous, they are quickly warned, in each circumstance, of the need which they have of one another, and, consequently, they have a lively and continuous sentiment of their mutual dependence . . . But, on the contrary, if some opaque environment is interposed, then only stimuli of a certain intensity can be communicated from one organ to another. Relations, being rare, are not repeated enough to be determined; each time there ensues new grouping. The lines of passage taken by the streams of movement cannot deepen because the streams themselves are too intermittent. If some rules do come to constitute them, they are, however, general and vague. (1893, pp. 368–9)

Like the problem of economic integration, anomie also resulted – in Durkheim's view – from inadequate means of communication. Both problems were thus manifestations, at opposite extremes of aggregation, of the nineteenth-century control crisis.

Unlike Durkheim's analysis, which was largely confined to the extremes of individual and society, this book will concentrate on intervening levels, especially on technology and its role in the processing of matter, energy, and information – what might be called the *material economy* (as opposed to the abstract ones that seem to captivate most modern economists). Chapter 6 includes separate sections on the production, distribution, and consumption of goods and services in the industrializing economy of the United States in the nineteenth century and on the new information-processing and communication technologies – just emerging during Durkheim's lifetime – that served to control the increasing volume and speed of these activities. We will find that, just as the problem of control threatened to reach crisis proportions late in the century, a series of new technological and social solutions began to contain the problem. This was the opening stage of the Control Revolution.

Rationalization and bureaucracy

Foremost among all the technological solutions to the crisis of control – in that it served to control most other technologies – was the rapid growth of formal bureaucracy first analyzed by Max Weber at the turn of the century. Bureaucratic organization was not new to Weber's time, as we have noted; bureaucracies had arisen in the first nation-states with centralized administrations, most significantly in Mesopotamia and ancient Egypt, and had reached a high level of sophistication in the pre-industrial empires of Rome, China, and Byzantium. Indeed, bureaucratic organization tends to appear wherever a collective activity needs to be coordinated by several people toward explicit and impersonal goals, that is, to be *controlled*. Bureaucracy has served as the generalized means to control any large social system in most institutional areas and in most cultures since the emergence of such systems by about 3000 BC.

Because of the venerable history and pervasiveness of bureaucracy, historians have tended to overlook its role in the late nineteenth century as a major new control technology. Nevertheless, bureaucratic administration did not begin to achieve anything approximating its modern form until the late Industrial Revolution. As late as the 1830s, for example, the Bank of the United States, then the nation's largest and most complex institution with 22 branch offices and profits 50 times those of the largest mercantile house, was managed by just three people: Nicholas Biddle and two assistants (Redlich, 1951, pp. 113–24). In 1831 President Andrew Jackson and 665 other civilians ran all three branches of the federal government in Washington, an increase of 63 employees over the previous ten years. The Post Office Department, for example, had been administered for 30 years as the personal domain of two brothers, Albert and Phineas Bradley (Pred, 1973, ch. 3). Fifty years later, in the aftermath of rapid industrialization, Washington's bureaucracy included some 13,000 civilian employees, more than double the total – already swelled by the American Civil War – only ten years earlier (US Bureau of the Census, 1975, p. 1103).

Further evidence that bureaucracy developed in response to the Industrial Revolution is the timing of concern about bureaucratization as a pressing social problem. The word *bureaucracy* did not even appear in English until the early nineteenth century, yet within a generation it became a major topic of political and philosophical discussion. As early as 1837, for example, John Stuart Mill wrote of a "vast network of administrative tyranny . . . that system of *bureaucracy*, which leaves no free agent in all France, except the man at Paris who pulls the wires" (Burchfield, 1972, p. 391); a decade later Mill warned more generally of the "inexpediency of concentrating in a dominant bureaucracy . . . all power of organized action . . . in the community" (1848, p. 529). Thomas Carlyle, in his *Latter-Day Pamphlets* published two years later, complained of "the Continental nuisance called 'Bureaucracy' " (1850, p. 121). The word *bureaucratic* had also appeared by the 1830s, followed by *bureaucrat* in the 1840s and *bureaucratize* by the 1890s.

That bureaucracy is in essence a control technology was first established by Weber, most notably in his *Economy and Society* (1922). Weber included among the defining characteristics of bureaucracy several important aspects of any control system: impersonal orientation of structure to the information that it processes, usually identified as "cases," with a pre-determined formal set of rules governing all decisions and responses. Any tendency to humanize this bureaucratic machinery, Weber argued, would be minimized through clear-cut division of labor and definition of responsibilities, hierarchical authority, and specialized decision and communication functions. The stability and permanence of bureaucracy, he noted, are assured through regular promotion of career employees based on objective criteria like seniority.

Weber identified another related control technology, what he called *rationalization*. Although the term has a variety of meanings, both in Weber's writings and in the elaborations of his work by others, most definitions are subsumed by one essential idea: control can be increased not only by increasing the capability to process information but also by decreasing the amount of information to be processed. The former approach to control was realized in Weber's day through bureaucratization and today increasingly through computerization; the latter approach was then realized through rationalization, what computer scientists now call *preprocessing*. Rationalization must therefore be seen, following Weber, as a complement to bureaucratization, one that served control in his day much as the preprocessing of information prior to its processing by computer serves control today.

Perhaps most pervasive of all rationalization is the increasing tendency of modern society to regulate interpersonal relationships in terms of a formal set of impersonal and objective criteria. The early technocrat Claude Henri Comte de Saint-Simon (1760–1825), who lived through only the first stages of industrialization, saw such rationalization as a move "from the government of men to the administration of things" (Taylor, 1975, pt 3). The reason why people can be governed more readily *qua* things is that the amount of information about them that needs to be processed is thereby greatly reduced and hence the degree of control – for any constant capacity to process information – is greatly enhanced. By means of rationalization, therefore, it is possible to maintain large-scale, complex social systems that would be overwhelmed by a rising tide of information they could not process were it necessary to govern by the particularistic considerations of family and kin that characterize preindustrial societies.

In short, rationalization might be defined as the destruction or ignoring of information in order to facilitate its processing. This, too, has a direct analog in living systems, as we shall see in the next chapter. One example from within bureaucracy is the development of standardized paper forms. This might at first seem a contradiction, in that the proliferation of paperwork is usually associated with a growth in information to be processed, not with its reduction. Imagine how much more processing would be required, however, if each new case were recorded in an unstructured way, including every nuance and in full detail, rather than by checking boxes, filling blanks, or in some other way reducing the burdens of the bureaucratic system to only the limited range of formal, objective, and impersonal information required by standardized forms.

Equally important to the rationalization of industrial society, at the most macro level, were the division of North America into five standardized time zones in 1883 and the establishment the following year of the Greenwich meridian and International Date Line, which organized world time into twenty-four zones. What was formerly a problem of information overload and hence control for railroads and other organizations that sustained the social system at its most macro level was solved by simply ignoring much of the information, namely that solar time is different at each node of a transportation or communication system. A more convincing demonstration of the power of rationalization or preprocessing as a control technology would be difficult to imagine.

So commonplace has such preprocessing become that today we dismiss the alternative – that each node in a system might keep a slightly different time – as hopelessly cumbersome and primitive. With the continued proliferation of distributed computing, ironically enough, it might soon become feasible to return to a system based on local solar time, thereby shifting control from preprocessing back to processing – where it resided for centuries of human history until steam power pushed transportation beyond the pace of the sun across the sky.

New control technology

The rapid development of rationalization and bureaucracy in the middle and late nineteenth century led to a succession of dramatic new information-processing and communication technologies. These innovations served to contain the control crisis of industrial society in what can be treated as three distinct areas of economic activity: production, distribution, and consumption of goods and services.

Control of production was facilitated by the continuing organization and preprocessing of industrial operations. Machinery itself came increasingly to be controlled by two new information-processing technologies: closed-loop feedback devices like James Watt's steam governor (1788) and preprogrammed open-loop controllers like those of the Jacquard loom (1801). By

1890 Herman Hollerith had extended Jacquard's punch cards to tabulation of US census data. This information-processing technology survives to this day – if just barely – owing largely to the corporation to which Hollerith's innovation gave life, International Business Machines (IBM). Further rationalization and control of production advanced through an accumulation of other industrial innovations: interchangeable parts (after 1800), integration of production within factories (1820s and 1830s), the development of modern accounting techniques (1850s and 1860s), professional managers (1860s and 1870s), continuous-process production (late 1870s and early 1880s), the "scientific management" of Frederick Winslow Taylor (1911), Henry Ford's modern assembly line (after 1913), and statistical quality control (1920s), among many others.

The resulting flood of mass-produced goods demanded comparable innovation in control of a second area of the economy: distribution. Growing infrastructures of transportation, including rail networks, steamship lines, and urban traction systems, depended for control on a corresponding infrastructure of information processing and telecommunications. Within fifteen years after the opening of the pioneering Baltimore and Ohio Railroad in 1830, for example, Samuel F. B. Morse – with a congressional appropriation of $30,000 – had linked Baltimore to Washington, DC, by means of a telegraph. Eight years later, in 1852, 13,000 miles of railroad and 23,000 miles of telegraph line were in operation (Thompson, 1947; US Bureau of the Census, 1975, p. 731), and the two infrastructures continued to coevolve in a web of distribution and control that progressively bound the entire continent. In the words of business historian Alfred Chandler, "the railroad permitted a rapid increase in the speed and decrease in the cost of long-distance, written communication, while the invention of the telegraph created an even greater transformation by making possible almost instantaneous communication at great distances. The railroad and the telegraph marched across the continent in unison . . . The telegraph companies used the railroad for their rights-of-way, and the railroad used the services of the telegraph to coordinate the flow of trains and traffic" (1977, p. 195).

This coevolution of the railroad and telegraph systems fostered the development of another communication infrastructure for control of mass distribution and consumption: the postal system. Aided by the introduction in 1847 of the first federal postage stamp, itself an important innovation in control of the national system of distribution, the total distance mail moved more than doubled in the dozen years between Morse's first telegraph and 1857, when it reached 75 million miles – almost a third covered by rail (Chandler, 1977, p. 195). Commercialization of the telephone in the 1880s, and especially the development of long-distance lines in the 1890s, added a third component to the national infrastructure of telecommunications.

Controlled by means of this infrastructure, an organizational system rapidly emerged for the distribution of mass production to national and world markets. Important innovations in the rationalization and control of this system included the commodity dealer and standardized grading of commodities (1850s), the department store, chain store, and wholesale jobber (1860s), monitoring of movements of inventory or "stock turn" (by 1870), the mail-order house (1870s), machine packaging (1890s), franchising (by 1911 the standard means of distributing automobiles), and the supermarket and mail-order chain (1920s). After World War I the instability in national and world markets that Durkheim had noted a quarter-century earlier came to be gradually controlled, largely because of the new telecommunications infrastructure and the reorganization of distribution on a societal scale.

Mass production and distribution cannot be completely controlled, however, without control of a third area of the economy: demand and consumption. Such control requires a means to communicate information about goods and services to national audiences in order to stimulate or reinforce demand for these products; at the same time, it requires a means to gather information on the preferences and behavior of this audience – reciprocal feedback to the controller from the controlled (although the consumer might justifiably see these relationships as reversed).

The mechanism for communicating information to a national audience of consumers developed with the first truly mass medium: power-driven, multiple-rotary printing and mass mailing by rail. At the outset of the Industrial Revolution, most printing was still done on wooden handpresses – using flat plates tightened by means of screws – that differed little from the one Gutenberg had used three centuries earlier. Steam power was first successfully applied to printing in Germany in 1810; by 1827 it was possible to print up to 2,500 pages in an hour. In 1893 the New York *World* printed 96,000 eight-page copies every hour – a 300-fold increase in speed in just 70 years

The postal system, in addition to effecting and controlling distribution, also served, through bulk mailings of mass-produced publications, as a new medium of mass communication. By 1887 Montgomery Ward mailed throughout the continent a 540-page catalog listing more than 24,000 items. Circulation of the Sears and Roebuck catalog increased from 318,000 in 1897 (the first year for which figures are available) to more than 1 million in 1904, 2 million in 1905, 3 million in 1907, and 7 million by the late 1920s. In 1927 alone, Sears mailed 10 million circular letters, 15 million general catalogs (spring and fall editions), 23 million sales catalogs, plus other special catalogs – a total mailing of 75 million (Boorstin, 1973, p. 128) or approximately one piece for every adult in the United States.

Throughout the late nineteenth and early twentieth centuries uncounted entrepreneurs and inventors struggled to extend the technologies of communication to mass audiences. Alexander Graham Bell, who patented the telephone in 1876, originally thought that his invention might be used as a broadcast medium to pipe public speeches, music, and news into private homes. Such systems were indeed begun in several countries – the one in Budapest had 6,000 subscribers by the turn of the century and continued to operate through World War I (Briggs, 1977). More extensive application of telephony to mass communication was undoubtedly stifled by the rapid development of broadcast media beginning with Guglielmo Marconi's demonstration of long-wave telegraphy in 1895. Transatlantic wireless communication followed in 1901, public radio broadcasting in 1906, and commercial radio by 1920; even television broadcasting, a medium not popular until after World War II, had begun by 1923.

Many other communication technologies that we do not today associate with advertising were tried out early in the Control Revolution as means to influence the consumption of mass audiences. Popular books like the novels of Charles Dickens contained special advertising sections. Mass telephone systems in Britain and Hungary carried advertisements interspersed among music and news. The phonograph, patented by Thomas Edison in 1877 and greatly improved by the 1890s in Hans Berliner's "gramophone," became another means by which a sponsor's message could be distributed to households: "Nobody would refuse," the United States Gramophone Company claimed, "to listen to a fine song or concert piece or an oration – even if it is interrupted by a modest remark, 'Tartar's Baking Powder is Best' " (Abbot and Rider, 1957, p. 387). With the development by Edison of the "motion picture" after 1891, advertising had a new medium, first in the kinetoscope (1893) and cinematograph (1895), which sponsors located in busy public places, and then in the 1900s in films projected in "movie houses." Although advertisers were initially wary of broadcasting because audiences could not be easily identified, by 1930 sponsors were spending $60 million annually on radio in the United States alone (Boorstin, 1973, p. 392).

These mass media were not sufficient to effect true control, however, without a means of feedback from potential consumers to advertisers, thereby restoring to the emerging national and world markets what Durkheim had seen as an essential relationship of the earlier segmental markets: communication from consumer to producer to assure that the latter "can easily reckon the extent of the needs to be satisfied" (1893, p. 369). Simultaneously with the development of mass communication by the turn of the century came what might be called *mass feedback* technologies: market research (the idea first appeared as "commercial research" in 1911), including questionnaire surveys of magazine readership, the Audit Bureau of Circulation (1914), house-to-house interviewing (1916), attitudinal and opinion surveys (a US bibliography lists nearly 3,000 by 1928), a Census of Distribution (1929), large-scale statistical sampling theory (1930), indices of retail sales (1933), A. C. Nielsen's audimeter monitoring of broadcast audiences (1935), and statistical-sample surveys like the Gallup Poll (1936), to mention just a few of the many new technologies for monitoring consumer behavior.

Although most of the new information technologies originated in the private sector, where they were used to control production, distribution, and consumption of goods and services, their potential for controlling systems at the national and world level was not overlooked by government. Since at least the Roman Empire, where an extensive road system proved equally suited for moving either commerce or troops, communications infrastructures have served to control both economy and polity. As corporate bureaucracy came to control increasingly wider markets by the turn of this century, its power was increasingly checked by a parallel growth in state bureaucracy. Both bureaucracies found useful what Bell has called "intellectual technology":

The major intellectual and sociological problems of the post-industrial society are . . . those of "organized complexity" – the management of large-scale systems, with large numbers of interacting variables, which have to be coordinated to achieve specific goals . . . An *intellectual technology* is the substitution of algorithms (problem-solving rules) for intuitive judgments. These algorithms may be embodied in an automatic machine or a computer program or a set of instructions based on some statistical or mathematical formula; the statistical and logical techniques that are used in dealing with "organized complexity" are efforts to formalize a set of decision rules. (1973, pp. 29–30)

Seen in this way, intellectual technology is another manifestation of bureaucratic rationality, an extension of what Saint-Simon described as a shift from the government of men to the administration of things, that is, a further move to administration based not on intuitive judgments but on logical and statistical rules and algorithms. Although Bell sees intellectual technology as arising after 1940, state bureaucracies had begun earlier in this century to appropriate many key elements: central economic planning (Soviet Union after 1920), the state fiscal policies of Lord Keynes (late 1920s), national income accounting (after 1933), econometrics (mid-1930s), input–output analysis (after 1936), linear programming and statistical decision theory (late 1930s), and operations research and systems analysis (early in World War II).

In the modern state the latest technologics of mass communication, persuasion, and market research are also used to stimulate and control demand for governmental services. The US government, for example, currently spends about $150 million a year on advertising, which places it among the top 30 advertisers in the country; were the approximately 70 percent of its ads that are presented free as a public service also included, it would rank second – just behind Proctor and Gamble (Porat, 1977, p. 137). Increasing business and governmental use of control technologies and their recent proliferation in forms like data services and home computers for use by consumers have become dominant features of the Control Revolution.

The information society

One major result of the Control Revolution had been the emergence of the so-called information society. The concept dates from the late 1950s and the pioneering work of an economist, Fritz Machlup, who first measured that sector of the US economy associated with what he called "the production and distribution of knowledge" (Machlup, 1962). Under this classification Machlup grouped 30 industries into five major categories: education, research and development, communications media, information machines (like computers), and information services (finance, insurance, real estate). He then estimated from national accounts data for 1958 (the most recent year available) that the information sector accounted for 29 percent of gross national product (GNP) and 31 percent of the labor force. He also estimated that between 1947 and 1958 the information sector had expanded at a compound growth rate double that of GNP. In sum, it appeared that the United States was rapidly becoming an "information society."

Over the intervening 20 years several other analyses have substantiated and updated the original estimates of Machlup (1980, pp. xxvi–xxviii): Burck (1964) calculated that the information sector had reached 33 percent of GNP by 1963; Marschak (1968) predicted that the sector would approach 40 percent of GNP in the 1970s. By far the most ambitious effort to date has been the innovative work of Marc Uri Porat for the Office of Telecommunications in the US Department of Commerce (1977). In 1967, according to Porat, information activities (defined differently from those of Machlup) accounted for 46.2 percent of GNP – 25.1 percent in a "primary information" sector (which produces information goods and services as final output) and 21.1 percent in a "secondary information" sector (the bureaucracies of noninformation enterprises).

The impact of the information society is perhaps best captured by trends in labor force composition. As can be seen in figure 2.1 and the corresponding data in table 2.2, at the end of the eighteenth century the US labor force was concentrated overwhelmingly in agriculture, the location of nearly 90 percent of its workers. The majority of US labor continued to work in this sector until about 1850, and agriculture remained the largest single sector until the first decade of the twentieth century. Rapidly emerging, meanwhile, was a new industrial sector, one that continuously employed at least a quarter of US workers between the 1840s and 1970s, reaching a peak of about 40 percent during World War II. Today, only some 40 years later, the

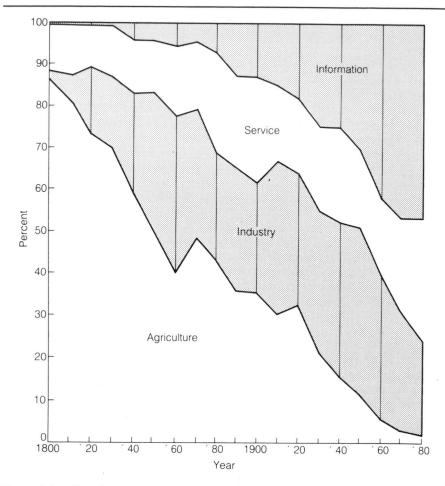

Figure 2.1   US civilian labor force by four sectors, 1800–1980.

industrial sector is close to half that percentage and declining steadily; it might well fall below 15 percent in the next decade. Meanwhile, the information sector, by 1960 already larger (at more than 40 percent) than industry had ever been, today approaches half of the US labor force.

At least in the timing of this new sector's rise and development, the data in figure 2.1 and table 2.2 are compatible with the hypothesis that the information society emerged in response to the nineteenth-century crisis of control. When the first railroads were built in the early 1830s, the information sector employed considerably less than 1 percent of the US labor force; by the end of the decade it employed more than 4 percent. Not until the rapid bureau-cratization of the 1870s and 1880s, the period that marked the consolidation of control, did the

Table 2.2   US experienced civilian labor force by four sectors, 1800–1980

Year	Agricultural	Industrial	Service	Information	Total labor force (in millions)
	Sector's percent of total				
1800	87.2	1.4	11.3	0.2	1.5
1810	81.0	6.5	12.2	0.3	2.2
1820	73.0	16.0	10.7	0.4	3.0
1830	69.7	17.6	12.2	0.4	3.7
1840	58.8	24.4	12.7	4.1	5.2
1850	49.5	33.8	12.5	4.2	7.4
1860	40.6	37.0	16.6	5.8	8.3
1870	47.0	32.0	16.2	4.8	12.5
1880	43.7	25.2	24.6	6.5	17.4
1890	37.2	28.1	22.3	12.4	22.8
1900	35.3	26.8	25.1	12.8	29.2
1910	31.1	36.3	17.7	14.9	39.8
1920	32.5	32.0	17.8	17.7	L45.3
1930	20.4	35.3	19.8	24.5	51.1
1940	15.4	37.2	22.5	24.9	53.6
1950	11.9	38.3	19.0	30.8	57.8
1960	6.0	34.8	17.2	42.0	67.8
1970	3.1	28.6	21.9	46.4	80.1
1980	2.1	22.5	28.8	46.6	95.8

Sources: Data for 1800–50 are estimated from Lebergott (1964) with missing data interpolated from Fabricant (1949); data for 1860–1970 are taken directly from Porat (1977); data for 1980 are based on US Bureau of Labor Statistics projections (Bell, 1979, p. 185).

percentage employed in the information sector more than double to about one-eighth of the civilian workforce. With the exception of these two great discontinuities, one occurring with the advent of railroads and the crisis of control in the 1830s, the other accompanying the consolidation of control in the 1870s and especially the 1880s, the information sector has grown steadily but only modestly over the past two centuries.

Temporal correlation alone, of course, does not prove causation. With the exception of the two discontinuities, however, growth in the information sector has tended to be most rapid in periods of economic upturn, most notably in the post-war booms of the 1920s and 1950s, as can be seen in table 2.2. Significantly, the two periods of discontinuity were punctuated by economic depressions, the first by the Panic of 1837, the second by financial crisis in Europe and the Panic of 1873. In other words, the technological origins of both the control crisis and the consolidation of control occurred in periods when the information sector would not have been expected on other economic grounds to have expanded rapidly if at all. There is therefore no reason to reject the hypothesis that the information society developed as a result of the crisis of control created by railroads and other steam-powered transportation in the 1840s.

A wholly new stage in the development of the information society has arisen, since the early 1970s, from the continuing proliferation of microprocessing technology. Most important in social implications has been the progressive convergence of all information technologies –

mass media, telecommunications, and computing – in a single infrastructure of control at the most macro level. A 1978 report commissioned by the President of France – an instant best-seller in that country and abroad – likened the growing interconnection of information-processing, communication, and control technologies throughout the world to an alteration in "the entire nervous system of social organization" (Nora and Minc, 1978, p. 3). The same report introduced the neologism *telematics* for this most recent stage of the information society, although similar words had been suggested earlier – for example, *compunications* (for "computing + communications") by Anthony Oettinger and his colleagues at Harvard's Program on Information Resources Policy (Oettinger, 1971; Berman and Oettinger, 1975; Oettinger, Berman, and Read, 1977).

Crucial to telematics, compunications, or whatever word comes to be used for this convergence of information-processing and communications technologies is increasing digitalization: coding into discontinuous values – usually two-valued or binary – of what even a few years ago would have been an analog signal varying continuously in time, whether a telephone conversation, a radio broadcast, or a television picture. Because most modern computers process digital information, the progressive digitalization of mass media and telecommunications content begins to blur earlier distinctions between the communication of information and its processing (as implied by the term *compunications*), as well as between people and machines. Digitalization makes communication from persons to machines, between machines, and even from machines to persons as easy as it is between persons. Also blurred are the distinctions among information types: numbers, words, pictures, and sounds, and eventually tastes, odors, and possibly even sensations, all might one day be stored, processed, and communicated in the same digital form.

In this way digitalization promises to transform currently diverse forms of information into a generalized medium for processing and exchange by the social system, much as, centuries ago, the institution of common currencies and exchange rates began to transform local markets into a single world economy. We might therefore expect the implications of digitalization to be as profound for macrosociology as the institution of money was for macroeconomics. Indeed, digitalized electronic systems have already begun to replace money itself in many informational functions, only the most recent stage in a growing systemness of world society dating back at least to the Commercial Revolution of the fifteenth century.

Societal dynamics reconsidered

Despite the chronic historical myopia that characterizes the human condition as documented in the opening pages of this article, it is unlikely that the more astute observers of our era would fail to glimpse – however dimly – even a single aspect of its essential social dynamic. For this reason the ability of a conceptual framework to subsume social changes noted by previous observers might be taken as one criterion for judging its claim to portray a more fundamental societal transformation. The various transformations identified by contemporary observers as listed in table 2.1 can be readily subsumed by the major implications of the Control Revolution: the growing importance of information technology, as in Richta's scientific-technological revolution (1967) or Brzezinski's technetronic era (1970); the parallel growth of an information economy (Machlup, 1962, 1980; Porat, 1977) and its growing control by business and the state (Galbraith, 1967); the organizational basis of this control (Boulding,

1953; Whyte, 1956) and its implications for social structure, whether a meritocracy (Young, 1958) or a new social class (Djilas, 1957; Gouldner, 1979); the centrality of information processing and communication, as in McLuhan's global village (1964), Phillips's communications age (1975), or Evans's micromillennium (1979); the information basis of postindustrial society (Touraine, 1971; Bell, 1973); and the growing importance of information and knowledge in modern culture (Mead, 1970).

In short, the argument that motivates our investigation of the nineteenth-century crisis of control and the resulting Control Revolution is that particular attention to the material aspects of information processing, communication, and control makes possible the synthesis of a large proportion of the literature on contemporary social change.

References

Abbot, Waldo and Rider, Richard L. (1957), *Handbook of Broadcasting: The Fundamentals of Radio and Television*, 4th edn, New York: McGraw-Hill.

Aron, Raymond (1961), *18 Lectures on Industrial Society*, trans. M. K. Bottomore, London: Weidenfeld and Nicolson (1967).

Aron, Raymond (1966), *The Industrial Society: Three Essays on Ideology and Development*, New York: Simon and Schuster, Clarion (1967).

Averitt, Robert T. (1968), *The Dual Economy: The Economics of American Industry Structure*, New York: Norton.

Beer, Samuel H. (1969), *British Politics in the Collectivist Age*, rev. edn, New York: Random House, Vintage.

Bell, Daniel (1960), *The End of Ideology: On the Exhaustion of Political Ideas in the Fifties*, New York: Free Press, rev. edn 1965.

Bell, Daniel (1973), *The Coming of Post-Industrial Society: A Venture in Social Forecasting*, New York: Basic Books.

Bell, Daniel (1979), "The social framework of the information society," in Michael L. Dertouzos and Joel Moses (eds), *The Computer Age: A Twenty-year View*, Cambridge, MA: MIT Press, pp. 163–211.

Bell, Daniel (1980), "Introduction," in Simon Nora and Alain Minc, *The Computerization of Society: A Report to the President of France*, Cambridge, MA: MIT Press, pp. vii-xvi.

Berkeley, Edmund Callis (1962), *The Computer Revolution*, Garden City, NY: Doubleday.

Berman, Paul J. and Oettinger, Anthony G. (1975), *The Medium and the Telephone: The Politics of Information Resources*, Working Paper 75-8 (December 15), Cambridge, MA: Harvard University Program on Information Technologies and Public Policy.

Bezold, Clement (ed.) (1978), *Anticipatory Democracy: People in the Politics of the Future*, New York: Random House, Vintage.

Blanqui, Jérôme Adolphe (1837), *History of Political Economy in Europe*, trans. Emily J. Leonard, New York: G. P. Putnam's Sons, 1880.

Boorstin, Daniel J. (1973), *The Americans The Democratic Experience*, New York: Random House, Vintage.

Boorstin, Daniel J. (1978), *The Republic of Technology: Reflections on Our Future Community*, New York: Harper and Row.

Boulding, Kenneth E. (1953), *The Organizational Revolution: A Study in the Ethics of Economic Organization*, New York: Harper.

Boulding, Kenneth E. (1964), *The Meaning of the Twentieth Century: The Great Transition*, New York: Harper and Row.

Breed, Warren (1971), *The Self-Guiding Society*, New York: Free Press.

Briggs, Asa (1977), "The Pleasure Telephone: a chapter in the prehistory of the media," in Ithiel de Sol Pool (ed.), *The Social Impact of the Telephone*, Cambridge, MA: MIT Press, pp. 40–65.

Brown, Lester R. (1972), *World Without Borders*, New York: Random House.

Brzezinski, Zbigniew (1970), *Between Two Ages: America's Role in the Technetronic Era*, New York: Viking Press.

Burchfield, R. W. (ed.) (1972), *A Supplement to the Oxford English Dictionary*, vol. 1, Oxford: Oxford University Press, Clarendon.

Burnham, David (1983), *The Rise of the Computer State*, New York: Random House.

Carlyle, Thomas (1850), *Latter-Day Pamphlets*. New York: Charles Scribner's Sons, 1898.

Chandler, Alfred D., Jr (1977), *The Visible Hand: The Managerial Revolution in American Business*, Cambridge, MA: Belknap Press of Harvard University Press.

Cole, H. S. D., Freeman, Christopher, Jahoda, Marie, et al. (eds) (1973), *Models of Doom: A Critique of the Limits to Growth*, New York: Universe Books.

Collins, Randall (1979), *The Credential Society: An Historical Sociology of Education and Stratification*, New York: Academic.

Daglish, Robert (ed.) (1972), *The Scientific and Technological Revolution: Social Effects and Prospects*, Moscow: Progress Publishers.

Dahrendorf, Ralf (1959), *Class and Class Conflict in an Industrial Society*, Stanford, CA: Stanford University Press.

Dahrendorf, Ralf (1964), "Recent changes in the class structure of European societies," in Stephen R. Graubard (ed.), *A New Europe?*, Boston: Houghton Mifflin.

Dertouzos, Michael L. and Moses, Joel (eds) (1979), *The Computer Age: A Twenty-Year View*, Cambridge, MA: MIT Press.

Dizard, Wilson P., Jr (1982), *The Coming Information Age: An Overview of Technology, Economics, and Politics*, New York: Longman.

Djilas, Milovan (1957), *The New Class: An Analysis of the Communist System*, New York: Praeger.

Dordick, Herbert S., Bradley, Helen G., and Nanus, Burt (1981), *The Emerging Network Marketplace*, Norwood, NJ: Ablex.

Drucker, Peter F. (1959), *Landmarks of Tomorrow*, New York: Harper and Row.

Drucker, Peter F. (1969), *The Age of Discontinuity*, New York: Harper and Row.

Durkheim, Emile (1893), *The Division of Labor in Society*, trans. George Simpson, New York: Free Press, 1933.

Eichner, Alfred S. (1976), *The Megacorp and Oligopoly: The Micro Foundations of Macro Dynamics*, Cambridge: Cambridge University Press.

Eisenstadt, Shmuel N. (ed.) (1972), *Post-Traditional Societies*, New York: Norton.

Ellul, Jacques (1964), *The Technological Society*, trans. John Wilkinson, New York: Knopf.

Etzioni, Amitai (1968), *The Active Society: A Theory of Societal and Political Processes*, New York: Free Press.

Evans, Christopher (1979), *The Micro Millennium*, New York: Washington Square/Pocket Books.

Evans, Lawrence B. (1977), "Impact of the electronics revolution on industrial process control," *Science*, 195 (March 18), pp. 1146–51.

Fabricant, Solomon (1949), "The changing industrial distribution of gainful workers: some comments on the American decennial statistics for 1820–1940," *Studies in Income and Wealth*, vol. 11, New York: National Bureau of Economic Research.

Feuer, Lewis S. (1969), *Marx and the Intellectuals: A Set of Post-Ideological Essays*, Garden City, NY: Anchor Books.

Forester, Tom (ed.) (1980), *The Microelectronics Revolution*, Cambridge, MA: MIT Press.

Galbraith, J. K. (1967), *The New Industrial State*, Boston: Houghton Mifflin, 3rd rev. edn, 1978.

Gallie, Duncan (1978), *In Search of the New Working Class*, Cambridge: Cambridge University Press.

Gartner, Alan and Riessman, Frank (1974), *The Service Society and the Consumer Vanguard*, New York: Harper and Row.

Gintis, Herbert (1970), "The new working class and revolutionary youth," *Continuum*, 8 (1, 2), pp. 151–2.

Gorz, André (1968), *Strategy for Labor*, Boston, MA: Beacon Press.

Gouldner, Alvin W. (1979), *The Future of Intellectuals and the Rise of the New Class*, New York: Seabury Press, Continuum.

Halmos, Paul (1970), *The Personal Society*, London: Constable.
Hawkes, Nigel (1971), *The Computer Revolution*, New York: Dutton.
Heaton, Herbert (1948), *Economic History of Europe*, rev. edn, New York: Harper.
Helvey, T. C. (1971), *The Age of Information: An Interdisciplinary Survey of Cybernetics*, Englewood Cliffs, NJ: Educational Technology Publications.
Hiltz, Starr Roxanne and Turoff, Murray (1978), *The Network Nation: Human Communication via Computer*, Reading, Mass.: Addison-Wesley.
Ionescu, Ghita (ed.) (1976), *The Political Thought of Saint-Simon*, Oxford: Oxford University Press.
Jenkins, Clive and Sherman, Barrie (1979), *The Collapse of Work*, London: Eyre Methuen.
Kahn, Herman (1970), *Forces for Change in the Final Third of the Twentieth Century*, Croton-on-Hudson, NY: Hudson Institute.
Lamberton, Donald M. (ed.) (1974), *The Information Revolution*, Annals of the American Academy of Political and Social Science, vol. 412, Philadelphia: American Academy of Political and Social Science.
Large, Peter (1980), *The Micro Revolution*, London: Fontana.
Large, Peter (1984), *The Micro Revolution Revisited*, Totowa, NJ: Rowman and Allanheld.
Laurie, Peter (1981), *The Micro Revolution: Living with Computers*, New York: Universe Books.
Lebergott, Stanley (1964), *Manpower in Economic Growth: The American Record since 1800*, New York: McGraw-Hill.
Lewis, Russell (1973), *The New Service Society*, London: Longman.
Lichtheim, George (1963), *The New Europe: Today and Tomorrow*, New York: Praeger.
Machlup, Fritz (1962), *The Production and Distribution of Knowledge in the United States*, Princeton, NJ: Princeton University Press.
Machlup, Fritz (1980), *Knowledge: Its Creation, Distribution, and Economic Significance*, vol. 1, Princeton, NJ: Princeton University Press.
McLuhan, Marshall (1964), *Understanding Media: The Extensions of Man*, New York: McGraw-Hill.
Mallet, Serge (1963), *La Nouvelle Classe Ouvrière*, Paris: Editions du Seuil.
Marcuse, Herbert (1964), *One-Dimensional Man: Studies in the Ideology of Advanced Industrial Society*, Boston, MA: Beacon Press.
Marris, Robin (1964), *The Economic Theory of Managerial Capitalism*, New York: Free Press.
Marschak, Jacob (1968), "Economics of inquiring, communicating, and deciding," *American Economic Review*, 58(2), pp. 1–8.
Martin, James (1978), *The Wired Society*, Englewood Cliffs, NJ: Prentice-Hall.
Martin, James (1981), *The Telematic Society: A Challenge for Tomorrow*, Englewood Cliffs, NJ: Prentice-Hall.
Martin, James and Butler, David (1981), *Viewdata and the Information Society*, Englewood Cliffs, NJ: Prentice-Hall.
Mead, Margaret (1970), *Culture and Commitment: A Study of the Generation Gap*, New York: Doubleday, Natural History Press.
Meadows, Donella H., Meadows, Dennis L, Randers, Jorgen et al. (1972), *Limits to Growth: A Report for the Club of Rome's Project on the Predicament of Mankind*, New York: Universe Books.
Meynaud, Jean (1968), *Technocracy*, trans. Paul Barnes, London: Faber and Faber.
Michael, Donald N. (1968), *The Unprepared Society: Planning for a Precarious Future*, New York: Harper and Row, Colophon.
Mill, John Stuart (1848), *Principles of Political Economy, with Some of their Applications to Social Philosophy*, 2 vols, Boston, MA: Little, Brown.
Oettinger, Anthony G. (1962), "Retiring computer pioneer – Howard Aiken," *Communications of the ACM*, 5(6), pp. 298–9.
Oettinger, Anthony G. (1971), "Communications in the national decision-making process," in Martin Greenberger (ed.), *Computers, Communications, and the Public Interest*, Baltimore, MD: Johns Hopkins University Press, pp. 78–114.
Oettinger, Anthony G., Berman, Paul J. and Read, William H. (1977), *High and Low Politics: Information Resources for the 80's*, Cambridge, MA: Ballinger.

Phillips, Kevin P. (1975), *Mediacracy: American Parties and Politics in the Communications Age*, Garden City, NY: Doubleday.

Piaget, Jean (1970), *Structuralism*, trans. Chaninah Maschler. New York: Basic.

Porat, Marc Uri (1977), *The Information Economy: Definition and Measurement*, Washington, DC: Office of Telecommunications, US Department of Commerce.

Prague Academy (1973), *Man, Science, and Technology: A Marxist Analysis of the Scientific Technological Revolution*, Prague: Academia Prague.

Pred, Allan R. (1973), *Urban Growth and the Circulation of Information: The United States System of Cities, 1790–1840*, Cambridge, MA: Harvard University Press.

Redlich, Fritz (1951), *The Molding of American Banking, Men and Ideas*, New York: Johnson Reprint Corporation, 1968.

Richta, Radovan (ed.) (1967), *Civilization at the Crossroads: Social and Human Implications of the Scientific and Technological Revolution*, White Plains, NY: International Arts and Sciences Press.

Riesman, David (1950), *The Lonely Crowd: A Study of the Changing American Character*, with Reuel Denney and Nathan Glazer, New Haven, CT: Yale University Press.

Rostow, Walt W. (1960), *The Stages of Economic Growth*, Cambridge: Cambridge University Press.

Seidenberg, Roderick (1950), *Posthistoric Man: An Inquiry*, Chapel Hill: University of North Carolina Press.

Shannon, Claude E. and Weaver, Warren (1949), *The Mathematical Theory of Communication*, Urbana: University of Illinois Press.

Stine, G. Harry (1975), *The Third Industrial Revolution*, New York: G. P. Putnam's Sons.

Stonier, Tom (1979), "The Third Industrial Revolution – microprocessors and robots," in *Microprocessors and Robots: Effects of Modern Technology on Workers*, Vienna: International Metalworkers' Federation.

Sylvester, Edward J. and Klotz, Lynn C. (1983), *The Gene Age: Genetic Engineering and the Next Industrial Revolution*, New York: Scribner's.

Taylor, Keith (ed.) (1975), *Henri Saint-Simon (1760–1825): Selected Writings on Science, Industry, and Social Organization*, New York: Holmes and Meier.

Thompson, Robert Luther (1947), *Wiring a Continent: The History of the Telegraph Industry in the United States, 1832–1866*, Princeton, NJ: Princeton University Press.

Toffler, Alvin (1971), *Future Shock*, New York: Bantam Books.

Toffler, Alvin (1980), *The Third Wave*, New York: William Morrow.

Tomeski, Edward Alexander (1970), *The Computer Revolution: The Executive and the New Information Technology*, New York: Macmillan.

Touraine, Alain (1971), *The Post-Industrial Society*, New York: Random House.

Toynbee, Arnold (1884), *Lectures on the Industrial Revolution of the Eighteenth Century in England*, London: Longmans, Green, 1920.

US Bureau of the Census (1975), *Historical Statistics of the United States, Colonial Times to 1970*, 2 vols, Washington, DC: US Government Printing Office.

Vickers, Geoffrey (1970), *Freedom in a Rocking Boat: Changing Values in an Unstable Society*, London: Allen Lane, Penguin.

Wade, John (1833), *History of the Middle and Working Classes*, London: E. Wilson, 3rd edn, 1835.

Weber, Max (1905), *The Protestant Ethic and the Spirit of Capitalism*, trans. Talcott Parsons, New York: Scribner's, 1958.

Weber, Max (1922), *Economy and Society: An Outline of Interpretive Sociology*, 3 vols, ed. Guenther Roth and Claus Wittich, New York: Bedminster Press, 1968.

Whyte, William H., Jr (1956), *The Organization Man*, New York: Simon and Schuster.

Wiener, Norbert (1948), *Cybernetics: or Control and Communication in the Animal and the Machine*, Cambridge, MA: MIT Press, 1961.

Williams, Frederick (1982), *The Communications Revolution*, Beverly Hills, CA: Sage.

Winner, Langdon (1977), *Autonomous Technology: Technics-out-of-Control as a Theme in Political Thought*, Cambridge, MA: MIT Press.

Young, Michael (1958), *The Rise of the Meritocracy 1870–2033: An Essay on Education and Equality*, Harmondsworth, UK: Penguin, 1961.

The Illusion of Revolution

Brian Winston

Taking the debunking of IT one stage further, Brian Winston says that the so-called information "revolution" is an illusion and a misunderstanding. In this excerpt from his book, Misunderstanding Media *(Routledge and Kegan Paul, London and Harvard University Press, Cambridge, MA, 1986), Winston recalls the early history of another "revolutionary" device, television, and shows how its diffusion into households was delayed by social and political factors. He remains deeply skeptical about the impact of new communications technologies, especially in the home. Brian Winston is Dean of the School of Communications at Pennsylvania State University.*

My intention is to attempt to demonstrate why there is little or no reason to join the epithet "revolution" to the epithet "information." This purpose is perhaps best symbolized by the fact that although every word on this page has been in the clutches of various computers, from my personal word processor to the publisher's more elaborate devices, what you hold in your hands is a user-friendly, portable, randomly accessible retrieval device half a millennium old and of a design elegance unmatched by any of the vaunted machines of the "information revolution" – a book.

The persistence of books, and the ironies of books about the "information revolution," are too glibly ignored. This glibness can be attributed to a general lack of historical sense, for the "information revolution" exists only as a consequence of far-reaching misunderstandings about electronic media, their development, diffusion and present forms. I shall be exactly concerned with these matters; and it will be a central thesis that the history of the technologies of information reveals a gradual, uncataclysmic progress. No telecommunications technology of itself or in aggregate suggests revolutionary development. On the contrary, each of them can be seen as a technological response to certain social relations which, at least in the West, have remained basically unchanged during the entire industrial period; the technology, far from being a disruptive force, actually reflects the comparative stasis of these relations.

The devices in question range from the telegraph, and its immediate non-electronic predecessors, to holography. Included are computers – macro, micro, personal and pocket – cameras, xerography, telephones and videophones, satellites and videotape, radio and other electromagnetic/photokinetic distribution systems including fiberoptics, Polaroid, photographic printing processes (and the developments in the press that preceded them) and, above all, television – in short, the range of machines which, it is now claimed, has reached such a critical mass that not only are deep, radical alterations in our society being effected but even our very sensoria are changed under the impact, to make us new women and men.

Received opinion is that a combination of developments has brought us to this revolutionary point. The by-now-ancient telephone wire has had its capacity increased to accommodate the most complex of electrical signals, those encoding visual information, in great numbers. The communications satellite has created an elegant worldwide method of communication, equally capable of carrying "broadband" audiovisual signals. The computer has rendered vast amounts of information accessible in wholly new ways. And finally, various other methods of duplication and storage have been developed to allow us to copy instantly visual and audiovisual messages into a number of media. Joining the computer to the telephone and both to satellites creates a McLuhanesque patchwork of electronic nerves stretching down into every last household, linking them together into the global village. And our window on to the village square is the television cathode ray tube.

Such noise and hubbub have the proponents of this "revolution" made that alternative readings are all but drowned out. However, it is my contention that far from a revolution we have business, and I mean business, as usual. All of the following could be just as viable a set of predictions as those promising revolutionary "world boxes," "wired cities," "electronic cottages," and all sorts of "future shocks."

- Entertainment-led cable television, that is cable systems relying on traditional television broadcasting forms, will have discernible effects only in situations where free-air broadcasting widely delivers poor signals (as in the United States) or where the population at large prefers signals originating in a neighboring nation to its own (as in Canada).
- The free transnational propagation of audiovisual signals elsewhere will be contained by both governmental action and public (non) response.
- Entertainment channels, whether delivered by cable or by other means, will probably never exceed one dozen – as the slow process of shakeout in the United States is revealing.
- Videocassette recorders are *the* crucial device to expand entertainment television. They will have the most significant effect on all current and proposed systems for the mass distribution of audiovisual signals, including cable.
- All new means of distribution and expansion of service will not produce new content for television. (Expanding television to include replications of bourgeois "high culture" in societies where such coverage has hitherto not been much seen does not, self-evidently, create new content.) A more varied range of distribution systems (including the "bicycling" of videocassettes) will exist without national audiovisual establishments being essentially changed.
- Subteens may, for a time, give up dancing together and substitute the watching of videos for audiorecords. This, in effect a dance (or rather nondance) style, will pass as all such do. Music videos will develop via an increasing reliance on narrative forms.
- Flat screen, component television will replace current receivers. Big screen projection television will not – unless accompanied by the wholesale remodelling of the housing stock to make bigger rooms. People will not walk about watching personal TV screens either, for fear of bumping into each other or getting run over.

- Videotext devices, whether two-way interactive or not, will never replace print except in very limited situations.
- Interactive services will be provided, in so far as they are required, by updating the basic telephone to broadband capacity using waveguides and fiberoptic technologies, rather than by the laying down of alternative national systems. Containing the power of the telephone company over these expanded services will pose a major problem.
- Narrowband interactive services (burglar and fire alarms, metering, etc.) will be provided, in so far as they are needed, by this updating rather than by entertainment-led cable television systems. The telephone will gain in intelligence and scope. It will never become a 'videophone'.
- Interactive television uses will not include shopping (except perhaps of a limited mail-order type), schooling, political decision-making by the entire electorate or by any substantial proportion thereof or any other "global village" use. In fact, interactive television will meld into the intelligent telephone.
- Videodisks, except for laser-based systems which will be used only in training or archival situations (and might therefore be uneconomic of themselves), are doomed to oblivion – and are already well on their way there.
- Videodisks masquerading as audiorecordings will offer the recording industry its only hope of destroying the public's ability inexpensively to copy their product.
- Light-sensitive polymers will render nitrate-based film stocks obsolete but, except for still photography processes, will fail to compete with electronics. Thus videocameras will replace 8mm film cameras as the primary tool of personalized audiovisual image creation. Home videos will be as important (and unimportant) as home movies are.
- Professional film use will inexorably be replaced by electronic systems except at the final stage of theatrical print preparation. Cinemas will, like theaters, opera houses and concert halls, survive.
- The personal computer will be an essential of the academy and businesses however small. It will also find a variety of professional uses. But the basic structure and functions of the academy, business and the professions will remain unaltered.
- Home computing will prove to be a fad – albeit a widespread and probably quite persistent one – like railroad modelling or philately. The central thrust of home computing will continue to be games and this play will constitute the dominant fad within the fad, although in more affluent homes the computer might replace the typewriter.
- Computer literacy will function like driving instruction, only be less complex. It will be limited to understanding the operation of extremely user-friendly computers with cheap, prepared software for word processing, book-keeping, graphics and data-base management – by definition, no major feat.
- The marketing of previously free information via databases will result in people learning to live without that information. Effective databases will be limited to professional situations with the result that the home computer will remain a largely isolated device.
- Holography, true stereoscopicy, is, given this culture's addiction to realism, a necessity. It will therefore be marketed. And it will have as much and no more effect than any other advance (including film, radio and television) has done.

(In parenthesis it can be added that medicine will contribute evidence as overwhelming as that connecting smoking to cancer as to the (physically) deleterious effect of the television screen and with parallel limited effects on behaviour. The evidence is already being gathered. The US National Institute for Occupational Safety and Health found that in the United Airlines office in San Francisco, an environment with a high density of VDTs (visual display terminals, known in the UK as VDUs – visual display units, i.e. televisions), half of 48 pregnancies between 1979 and 1984 had ended in miscarriages, birth defects or other abnormalities. Working with VDTs can also increase risk of seizure in epileptics, according to the British Health and Safety Executive. The HSE also found facial dermatitis occurred in VDT work environments with low humidity.[1] The Newspaper Guild commissioned a study from the Mount Sinai School of Medicine in New York in which 1,100 VDT workers in six locales were monitored for six months. Increased eye and radiation problems were found. The clincher is that the American Electronics Association (who make the things) testified before the Congress in 1984 that there was no evidence as to the deleterious effects of television. Their spokesman said: "Regulation of VDTs on any health and safety basis is unwarranted."[2])

Business, media, alienation, nuclear families, right-wing governments, technologically induced health hazards, traffic jams, deep-fried food, dating – all as usual. No revolution – just "the constant revolutionising of production, uninterrupted disturbance of all social conditions, ever-lasting uncertainty and agitation," as the *Communist Manifesto* puts it – in effect, a continuation of the developments of the last two centuries.

The justification for the above provocations is to be found in what follows. The "information revolution" is said to depend on the chip, the bird, the wire, and the screen. In order to make the case against the "revolution" a pattern of change must be demonstrated which would hold good for the histories of these dominant devices – computer, satellite, telephone and television – and sustain the predictions listed above. Television is crucial in all of this – a paradigm of how telecommunications technologies develop, of their supposed radical impact as they are diffused through society, of their revolutionary potential. We shall begin with television.

A kind of a glow

A quarter of a century ago, when the television set first became firmly established in the living rooms of the West, considered opinion was that our civilization had taken a further turn for the worse. The age of television ("chewing-gum for the eyes" was a 1950s phrase) was yet another tread in the staircase of that civilization's decline.[3] Those McLuhan was to call "the elders of the tribe" saw the warp and weft of social life under threat. "There is now a vast crowd that is a permanent audience waiting to be amused, cash customers screaming for this money's worth, all fixed in a consumer attitude. They look on more and more and join in less and less."[4] As we slumped before the electronic Cyclops it was clear that the end was drawing ever nigh.

In the quarter of a century that has followed these initial reactions, considered opinion – informed, intelligent, well-educated, middle-class opinion – has changed little. The elders of the tribe and their cohorts, the guardians of public morality and the taste-making lackeys of the haute bourgeoisie, always respond thus to every new, popular mode of communication. As Raymond Williams has pointed out, they are always wrong: wrong about

Shakespeare in the 1590s, about Austen in the 1810s; wrong, it might be added, about circuses and quilts, vaudeville and narrowboat decoration, Marvel Comics and Hollywood, jazz and brass bands.

One central reason why all this huffing and puffing has been utterly misplaced is that television, particularly, is no subversive demon. High-minded critics have worried endlessly about the circumstances and social consequences of viewing, never, beyond an obsession with sex and violence, taking cognizance of what was viewed; how traditional, hidebound and safe, how tied to the past were the new medium's programme forms and contents. Television's function has been to reinforce the central value system of the society it serves and the dominant mode it has used has been primarily dramatic.

Take mode. Television adopted, from film, a system of representing reality which is extremely naturalistic. Actors needed to learn almost nothing for work in the electronic studio that they had not already learned for the big screen; in turn, the rules governing the presentation of personality used there were imported with little change from the stage. Television, film and stage in the West are a seamless web, unlike the various different traditions of performance in the East, each with its own elaborate presentation code – and what is true of acting is equally true of setting, lighting, directing. The very fact that studios have multiple cameras, four being the norm, is a tribute to the need to emulate, live and therefore instantaneously, the rules of special and temporal continuity created by the classic discontinuous and noninstantaneous shooting of the film camera.

The charge that television has rotted society by the imposition of ersatz and debased entertainment forms is not sustainable. Every television form has an honorable and lengthy history. At best the new medium has privileged some forms, giving them considerable vibrancy – the short dramatic piece, the one-act play or extended sketch, now situation comedies, would be a good example. But in many other areas – variety and the whole range of "classical performance" arts for instance – the television does little but preserve previous theatrical modes in aspic. Even in the programming types which thrive on the small screen tradition looms very large. Almost every single-set situation comedy obeys realistic *theatrical* conventions, including the downstage sofa and the canted side walls of the set. What takes place on that sofa owes much to either Aristophanes or Menander, performances utterly obedient to the conventions of Greek comedy either old or new. And in general all of television is as time-honored. It has created no new story-forms; its narrative structures, fictional and nonfictional alike, are dominated, like all others in this culture whatever the medium, by puzzles and the slow revelation of solutions, the liquidation of the audience's initial lack of knowledge about the story being told.

The drama intrudes into everything television does. It makes all of life dramatic, obeying an injunction in our culture which says that this is the price of our attention. Television, just as the radio and the movies before it, has failed to escape from the culturally imposed imperatives of conflict in its coverage of sports and news, religion and dance, children and the weather. Conflict and deviancy are the mainstays of its documentaries.

Its presentational codes in these nonfiction areas, too, reflect a close understanding of the past. The setting for current (or public) affairs television, often a cross between the contemporary sitting room and an airport departure lounge, also reference the schoolroom, with a magic movie screen behind the presenter in place of the blackboard. Television knows that in our culture, from medieval magistrates' benches and clerical pulpits on, authority hides its knees.

Newscasters do the same. The rank and file are ranked and filed on unenclosed chairs. And it is a mark of the common touch for talk show hosts and hostesses to be similarly exposed.

And what is the dominant image of non-fiction television? A person addressing the camera – newscaster to correspondent to reporter to expert. The vaunted visual imperative to which television newspeople claim to be in thrall does not amount, on close examination, to much. When the head is replaced (although its voice never stops) by other visual material, the film or tape, the still photograph or dynamic computer graphic symbolize as much as illustrate the subject. Shots of the exteriors of the sites of power, courts, parliaments and white houses, stand for politics. Industry is workers at assembly line or factory gate. Trade is shots of the docks. Inflation is bank clerks and supermarket shelves. Defense is old film of weapons being tested. War is distant puffs of smoke or horrific corpses. The weather is seen through the blizzard-swept screen of the camera-car. The pictures, unless of sporting events, press conferences, hostage situations or fires, are all of aftermaths. Deviate from these norms and a Pulitzer prize is the certain reward.

Instead of the newspaper, we have a photogenic journalist reading the newspaper. Instead of the stage, we have the studio, set and lit like the stage. Instead of the fairground booth, we have the game show. Instead of the opera or the sporting event we have the outside (or, as the American terminology more accurately and aptly has it, the remote) broadcast replicating the event. Instead of the Tories of Oxfordshire spending, in 1745, £40,000 to unseat the Whigs, we have the Democrats spending millions of dollars on commercials to dislodge the Republicans.[5]

The mode is traditional and the function essentially conservative although, since we live in complex and contradictory societies, that conservatism is often masked by conflicting inconsistencies. But in setting a social agenda for an otherwise atomized society – giving people something to talk to each other about, reinforcing the ways in which they see the world – an overall conservative tendency, as evidence by its forms, is also the mark of television's central function.

Television's deeper purposes are concealed, even, in the main, from those who work within the industry it has spawned, behind the transparency of its mode of representation. Our taste for realistic presentation has resulted in almost all production being unperceived by the audience. The scene within is unaffected by any interferences on the part of the professionals creating the message. They are the glaziers who, having situated and meticulously cleaned the pane of glass, can now leave the viewer wondering if it is really in place. This transparency is crucial. It is what allows newspeople and their audiences to confuse a certain type of ideological production with objectivity. It removes any underlying notion of effectiveness from the idea of entertainment, allowing audiences to receive everything from law-and-order dramas to the daily wash of the soap operas as being without social meaning.

The world created parallels our own in detail but it is also a world, even at its most serious, curiously unbeset by many of our quotidian concerns – the need to work, the divisions of class and race, the strain of alienation.

The agenda set by television for society is a propaganda agenda of the very best, most convincing type. It does not preclude problems. It highlights them, concentrates on them even, only to displace them – in fictional and nonfictional modes alike – from real consideration into the realm of melodrama. The television world is largely a world of two dominant groups – the fictional rich and/or criminal and the nonfictional poor and their rulers. It is a world of minute surface detail underpinned by a hidden and simplistic account of the complex ideology that governs the way we live our lives. It is the world of entertainment, where a show that is really a show keeps you in (rather than sending you out) with a kind of a glow. So television has become what, in 1953, NBC-TV network chief "Pat" Weaver hoped it would become – "the shining center of the home."[6]

Despite all attempts at creating "moral panics" because of the medium's supposedly baleful influences (and without prejudice to the reality of those influences), television has fitted into our lives exactly because it is so much a product of our culture and poses so little threat to it. It also fitted in because, contrary to common belief but like almost all the other devices we shall be discussing, it was a very long time coming. Telecommunications in general, and television as the example *par excellence*, do not suddenly descend upon us. 1984 was not only the year of Orwell's fictional nightmare, in which interactive television – in its most repressive surveillance mode – plays such a prominent role; it was also the year, in reality, in which television celebrated its first century.

The first television century

Early in January of 1884, Paul Nipkow, a Berlin science student, filed patents for an "electric telescope". He had, over that previous Christmas, placed a small disk perforated with a spiral of holes between a lens and an element of selenium which was inserted into an electrical circuit. It had been known for a decade that selenium, when exposed to light, would vary any electrical current passed through it in response to the intensity of the light. In this selenium was not unlike other substances, such as carbon, which varied in their resistance to current when exposed to pressure. The effects of the pressures exerted by the human voice on an element of carbon in an electrical circuit had been incorporated into a device seven years previously. It was called a telephone. The principle of transforming sound pressure into a modulated electrical signal was, and still is, its heart. The same principle, but now of transforming light into a modulated electrical current, was at the heart of Nipkow's telescope.

When Nipkow spun his disk, he scanned the image before the lens, breaking it down into a series of varying light impulses. These, as they hit the selenium plate, created variable resistance in the circuit. At the other end of the circuit, the process could be reversed. The electric current could be reconstituted into a series of light waves which, when passed through an exactly synchronous spinning disk, would reconstruct the picture. This could then be viewed through an eyepiece.

After another year's work Nipkow filed a master patent for television. Although he had established a viable system of "scanning" with the disk, he then did nothing more. The rest is silence.

It could not have been that he had no real concept of what he was about. Since the phenomenon of selenium had been announced in 1873 and the telephone patented in 1876, the search for "seeing by electricity" had been going on. The science informing that search dated back to the isolation of selenium in 1818. Photoelectricity, the creation of electricity through the operation of light, had been observed in 1839. In 1877, exploiting selenium, a French lawyer Senlecq had described a *telectroscope*, adapting the telephone to create a facsimile apparatus. (These had existed in various forms for telegraphy since 1843 and in 1847 a *copying telegraph* using a scanning technique had been introduced.[7] Phototelegraphy begins with a device, developed by the Abbé Caselli and introduced in 1862, which could transmit *daguerreotypes* or a facsimile of the sender's handwriting. With the support of Napoleon III, Caselli established a number of commercial stations, but the slowness of the system prevented him from mounting a real challenge to Morse.[8])

Senlecq reported: "The picture is, therefore, reproduced almost instantaneously; . . . we can obtain a picture, of a fugitive nature, it is true, but yet so vivid that the impression on the retina does not fade."[9] It is unlikely that Senlecq's electrically driven pencil would have created the half-tones necessary to duplicate a photographic effect. He did, however, suggest a scanning system, involving moving the selenium across the ground-glass screen of a *camera obscura*.

Senlecq's announcement stirred professional electricians all over the old and new world. For the next few decades schemes were put forward of one sort or another – even the great Alexander Graham Bell reportedly deposited plans for a television system at the Smithsonian in 1880. The usual arguments as to who suggested what, when, proliferate. A selenium camera is credited to an American, Carey, in 1875, although he did not publish until 1879. Probably most of these devices remained unbuilt, but an Englishman, Bidwell, adapted a common laboratory device to demonstrate the possibilities of picture transmission by selenium in 1881. He used it in that year to obtain a still image on chemically treated paper, and his machinery still exists in the London Science Museum.

Nipkow was in a not inconsiderable company. Even more were to be inspired by him and experiments with mechanical scanning persisted well into this century. John Logie Baird, a showman as much as a scientist who kept up British popular interest in television in the 1920s, was still using mechanical scanning a decade later. His pioneering demonstration of April 1925 – and the work of Charles F. Jenkins (another independent inventor), publicly revealed in America in June of the same year – both used mechanical scanning systems. CBS demonstrated a color television in the 1940s which used spinning disks.

In the early period it was not the fallibility of the mechanical scanning principle that held up progress, although viable systems of synchronization for camera and receiver were hard to develop, but rather the low sensitivity of selenium.

A separate strand, in the realm of pure science, comes into play at the turn of the twentieth century. In 1897 J. J. Thomson discovered the electron, thus explaining, among much else, that what was happening in photoelectric emission was the liberation of electrons from the atoms of the substance through the action of the light. In that same year an electron beam or cathode ray tube was developed. Between 1904 and 1906 Fleming and De Forest built the first electron vacuum tubes (or valves), devices which can be used to amplify signals. In 1907 a Russian scientist, B. L. Rozing, applied for a patent – "A Method of Transmitting Images Over A Distance" – in which he proposed electrical instead of mechanical methods for scanning an image. He took the cathode ray tube, by then a common laboratory device in the form of an oscilloscope, and adapted it so that it could be used to scan a scene. On 9 May 1911 he had got so far as to transmit over a distance "a distinct image . . . consisting of four luminous bands."[10] Rozing's scanning electron beam at the transmission end was joined, in a suggestion by the distinguished British scientist Campbell Swinton in 1908, by a similar beam at the receiving end. Campbell Swinton also described a different theoretical basis for modulating the electrons in the camera tube. He built no devices.

By the First World War the photoelectric quality of substances with greater sensitivity than selenium was being used, notably potassium. After the war Vladimir Zworykin, a student of Rozing's, now in America and working first for Westinghouse and then for RCA, developed an effective camera tube along the lines suggested by Campbell Swinton. It used within it a plate sensitized with silver and cesium. As a stream of electrons was fired at the plate in a zigzag pattern, its direction controlled by electromagnets, a sequential variation in the current was created at the anode, the positive terminal of the tube, behind the plate. This information then modulated a carrier wave for transmission by either cable or wireless into the receiver. At the home end the process was reversed. The internal signal plate of the camera became the phosphor-treated front end of the tube, the screen. The electron beam, again generated by a cathode and controlled by electromagnets, was modulated by the incoming wave. These variations were translated by the scanning electron dot into variations in intensity which became, through the phosphors, perceptible to the human eye.

The scanning system produced by the zigzagging dot was one which created the image sequentially, line by line, just as Nipkow's spinning disk had done. In the British version of this electronic camera, built by EMI, the pattern or raster was to scan the picture area twice, every even line in one 25th of a second and every odd line in the next 25th of a second. This way a sufficiently fast rate of change (50 a second in effect) was created from frame to frame for the physiological requirements of critical fusion fequency (CFF), the point at which the eye ceases to see discrete pictures, to operate. Achieving this sort of speed was necessary because a single scan in a 25th of a second gave a flickering impression. Film projectors with double or treble blades in their shutters effectively reveal each image twice or thrice at a rate of anything from 32 to 72 times per second.[11] The interlaced raster achieved the same range of CFF for the electronic image. The American version, because of the different characteristics of American electrical supply, scanned at a 30th of a second.

Other electronic cameras were developed on slightly different principles which ultimately failed to compete with RCA's in the studio. Of these the most significant is one built by Philo T. Farnsworth and patented in 1927, which produced better images than the earliest Zworykin camera tubes and continued to out-perform them well into the 1930s, when transmitting films.

In 1929 Baird had begun a series of experiments for the BBC using low-definition mechanical systems. By 1932 the BBC took over the enterprise. Two years later the Postmaster General appointed a committee to consider the development of television and "advise on the general merits of the several systems" then available.[12] The BBC was entrusted with the experiment. Baird's company had by now refined mechanical scanning to give 240 lines and, to consolidate its strengths, it produced (using a system created in Germany the previous year) a film camera with a rapid developing tank underneath it. In effect the camera could expose the scene and then develop and fix the film in about 60 seconds. This was then placed in the telecine device, and scanned mechanically at a 25th of a second. The EMI camera was placed in competition with this device. It effectively scanned at twice the Baird rate and also had the further advantage of producing 405 lines instantaneously. Yet the two technologies were closer than might be supposed from this.

Sir Archibald Gill, a member of the 1934 committee, recalls the case was not quite open-and-shut. The Baird system did indeed, even with the line and frame disadvantage, produce a slightly better picture than the EMI system when transmitting film.[13] And, as film transmission was held by all experts in every country to be vital as a major source of television images, this was no small advantage.

The world's second long-running public television service had been inaugurated from studios in Alexandra Palace, London on 2 November 1936 using both systems. The Germans were actually first with a public – as opposed to an experimental – system using technology comparable to both Baird's and EMI's for the Berlin Olympics that summer. The network reached to five German cities and the service, as in Britain, was continued until the war.

The committee supervising the British run-off gave it until February 1937 before opting for EMI. Not only was the stability of the all-electronic picture superior, but the complexities of the intermediate film stage in studio-based originations counted against Baird. Beyond that, mechanical scanning was reaching the end of the road, while electronic systems were obviously capable of much refinement. Clearly the future was with the electronic camera.

But, paradoxically, in America the progress of these same devices was subject to various delays. The technological development was subjected to intra-industry argument and government regulation. Low-definition experimentation had commenced with the granting of a licence, by the Federal Radio Commission (FRC), to Charles Jenkins, Baird's opposite number, in 1927. In 1929 22 more stations were licensed and between 20 and 40 a year were operating experimentally until 1944. The great corporations in the field and the Federal Communications Commission (the FCC, successor, in 1934, to the FRC), in various combinations, fought about everything during the 1930s: the system, the number of lines, the place on the radio frequency spectrum. The FCC declared that RCA should not be allowed to go ahead with a viable 441 line system in 1938 because it would freeze technical standards at this level; yet the BBC had been publicly running virtually the same system with fewer lines (405) for over a year. By 1939 Philco was using 605 lines. Despite this the US standard of 525 lines, one 30th of a second per frame, and the VHF part of the spectrum was finally agreed in 1941.

A further delay then occurred because of the war, no more receivers being built from exactly the year in which the go-ahead came. Following the war, the FCC again intervened to slow the granting of licences for stations, with a consequential brake on the selling of sets. Between 1946 and 1950 the number of stations licensed increased from 30 to 109 and the number of sets from 5,000 to just under 10 million. In the next five years, stations jumped to 573 and sets to nearly 33 million. And between 1955 and 1960 another 80 stations and 36½ million sets finally made America into the earth's first televisual nation.[14]

This then is how the beast television came amongst us. For those living through the explosive expansion of the television universe in America and northern Europe during the 1950s, forgetting the flickering demonstrations of the previous decades, it might well have seemed that a gadget on the frontiers of science had been turned loose with little thought as to its overall social effect. But, as this brief retelling of what ought to be a familiar story reveals, the pace of the development was quite leisurely, for the 'explosion' followed at least two decades of careful preparation. The pace of these events cannot be accounted for by the progress of technology alone. Zworykin, when he patented the first effective electronic camera in 1923, had no new tools and little more theory than did his teacher Rozing. During the 1930s, the most significant developments were all to do with subsidiary circuits improving the performance of the tubes. Everything else had been to hand since, at least, the last part of the previous decade.

To understand this history in terms of the technology alone, the stance of the technological determinist, is inadequate. Information revolutionists, in predicting the future, take exactly such a technologically determined view. If the technology makes it possible, they seem to be saying, then it will happen (normally, most of them seem to add, through the beneficence of the market). But as even this cursory glance reveals, this was not the pattern with television. The technology could have been made more widely available sooner, even in Germany and the UK; the factors delaying it were not limited to technology. In America in the late 1930s they were not technological at all. Such external factors persist, an inevitable concomitant of technology being produced by, with and for a society.

More than this, beneath the confusions of the chronological history of television a pattern, a sequence of phases which the technology went through on its journey from the realm of pure science to everybody's living room, can be discerned.

Notes

1 *The Times*, April 24, 1984, p. 16.
2 UPI, *The Daily Freeman* (Kingston, New York), March 16, 1984, p. 4.
3 R. T. Tripp (comp.), *The International Thesaurus of Quotations* (Penguin Books, Harmondsworth, UK, 1976), p. 564.
4 J. B. Priestley, *Thoughts in the Wilderness* (1957), quoted in Tripp, *Thesaurus of Quotations*.
5 R. Porter, *English Society in the Eighteenth Century* (Penguin Books, Harmondsworth, UK, 1982), p. 124.
6 My understanding of the earliest period of American television (from whence comes this ambition of Weaver's) is largely conditioned by William Boddy's "From Golden Age to Vast Waste Land: The Struggles Over Market Power and Dramatic Formats in 1950s Television," an NYU Doctoral Dissertation, 1984.
7 R. W. Hubbell, *4,000 Years of Television* (Putnam, New York, 1942), p. 55.
8 S. Handel, *The Electronic Revolution* (Penguin Books, Harmondsworth, UK, 1967), p. 128.
9 G. R. M. Garratt and A. H. Mumford, "The History of Television," *Proceedings of the Institution of Electrical Engineers*, vol. 99, pt IIIA, 1952, in G. Shiers (ed.), *Technical Development of Television* (Amo Press, New York, 1977), p. 26.
10 P. K. Gorokhov, "History of Modern Television," *Radiotekhnika*, translated as *Radio Engineering*, (New York, 1961), in Shiers, *Development of Television*, p. 75.
11 B. Nichols and S. J. Lederman, "Flicker and Motion in Film," in T. de Lauretis and S. Heath (eds), *The Cinematic Apparatus* (St Martin's Press, New York, 1980), pp. 97ff.
12 Garratt and Mumford, "History of Television," p. 38.
13 Ibid., p. 41.
14 C. H. Owen, "Television Broadcasting." *Proceedings of the Institute of Radio Engineers*, vol. 50, May, 1962, in Shiers, *Development of Television*, p. 820.

Mythinformation in the High-tech Era

Langdon Winner

For a full-frontal assault on the notion of an IT "revolution", Langdon Winner's now-famous piece on "Mythinformation" would be hard to beat. This full-length version, reprinted from the author's book of essays, The Whale and the Reactor: A Search for Limits in the Age of High Technology *(University of Chicago Press, Chicago, 1986), denounces the computer "romantics" and "utopians" who see IT as an answer to our problems. All the talk about IT being "revolutionary" is just so much hype generated by those who profit by selling computers, he says. Langdon Winner is Associate Professor of Political Science at Rensselaer Polytechnic Institute, Troy, New York.*

> Computer power to the people is essential to the realization of a future in which most citizens are informed about, and interested and involved in, the processes of government.
>
> J. C. R. Licklider

In nineteenth-century Europe a recurring ceremonial gesture signaled the progress of popular uprisings. At the point at which it seemed that forces of disruption in the streets were sufficiently powerful to overthrow monarchical authority, a prominent rebel leader would go to the parliament or city hall to "proclaim the republic." This was an indication to friend and foe alike that a revolution was prepared to take its work seriously, to seize power and begin governing in a way that guaranteed political representation to all the people. Subsequent events, of course, did not always match these grand hopes; on occasion the revolutionaries were thwarted in their ambitions and reactionary governments regained control. Nevertheless, what a glorious moment when the republic was declared! Here, if only briefly, was the promise of a new order – an age of equality, justice, and emancipation of humankind.

A somewhat similar gesture has become a standard feature in contemporary writings on computers and society. In countless books, magazine articles, and media specials some intrepid soul steps forth to proclaim "the revolution." Often it is called simply "the computer revolution"; my brief inspection of a library catalogue revealed three books with exactly that title published since 1962.[1] Other popular variants include the "information revolution," "microelectronics revolution," and "network revolution." But whatever its label, the message is usually the same. The use of computers and advanced communications technologies is producing a sweeping set of transformations in every corner of social life. An informal consensus among computer scientists, social scientists, and journalists affirms the term "revolution" as the concept best suited to describe these events. "We are all very privileged," a noted computer scientist declares, "to be in this great Information Revolution in which the computer is going to affect us very profoundly, probably more so than the Industrial Revolution."[2] A well-known sociologist writes, "This revolution in the organization and processing of information and knowledge, in which the computer plays a central role, has as its context the development of what I have called the post-industrial society."[3] At frequent intervals during the past dozen years, garish cover stories in *Time* and *Newsweek* have repeated this story, climaxed by *Time's* selection of the computer as its "Man of the Year" for 1982.

Of course, the same society now said to be undergoing a computer revolution has long since gotten used to "revolutions" in laundry detergents, underarm deodorants, floor waxes, and other consumer products. Exhausted in Madison Avenue advertising slogans, the image has lost much of its punch. Those who employ it to talk about computers and society, however, appear to be making much more serious claims. They offer a powerful metaphor, one that invites us to compare the kind of disruptions seen in political revolutions to the changes we see happening around computer information systems. Let us take that invitation seriously and see where it leads.

A metaphor explored

Suppose that we were looking at a revolution in a Third World country, the revolution of the Sandinistas in Nicaragua, for example. We would want to begin by studying the fundamental goals of the revolution. Is this a movement truly committed to social justice? Does it seek to uphold a valid ideal of human freedom? Does it aspire to a system of democratic rule? Answers to those questions would help us decide whether or not this is a revolution worthy of our endorsement. By the same token, we would want to ask about the means the revolutionaries had chosen to pursue their goals. Having succeeded in armed struggle, how will they manage violence and military force once they gain control? A reasonable person would also want to learn something of the structure of institutional authority that the revolution will try to create. Will there be frequent, open elections? What systems of decision-making, administration, and law enforcement will be put to work? Coming to terms with its proposed ends and means, a sympathetic observer could then watch the revolution unfold, noticing whether or not it remained true to its professed purposes and how well it succeeded in its reforms.

Most dedicated revolutionaries of the modern age have been willing to supply coherent public answers to questions of this sort. It is not unreasonable to expect, therefore, that something like these issues must have engaged those who so eagerly use the metaphor "revolution" to describe and celebrate the advent of computerization. Unfortunately, this is not the case. Books, articles, and media specials aimed at a popular audience are usually content to depict the dazzling magnitude of technical innovations and social effects. Written as if by some universally accepted format, such accounts describe scores of new computer products and processes, announce the enormous dollar value of the growing computer and communications industry, survey the expanding uses of computers in offices, factories, schools, and homes, and offer good news from research and development laboratories about the great promise of the next generation of computing devices. Along with this one reads of the many "impacts" that computerization is going to have on every sphere of life. Professionals in widely separate fields – doctors, lawyers, corporate managers, and scientists – comment on the changes computers have brought to their work. Home consumers give testimonials explaining how personal computers are helping educate their children, prepare their income tax forms, and file their recipes. On occasion, this generally happy story will include reports on people left unemployed in occupations undermined by automation. Almost always, following this formula, there will be an obligatory sentence or two of criticism of the computer culture solicited from a technically qualified spokesman, an attempt to add balance to an otherwise totally sanguine outlook.

Unfortunately, the prevalence of such superficial, unreflective descriptions and forecasts about computerization cannot be attributed solely to hasty journalism. Some of the most prestigious journals of the scientific community echo the claim that a revolution is in the works.[4] A well-known computer scientist has announced unabashedly that "revolution, transformation and salvation are all to be carried out."[5] It is true that more serious approaches to the study of computers and society can be found in scholarly publications. A number of social scientists, computer scientists, and philosophers have begun to explore important issues about how computerization works and what developments, positive and negative, it is likely to bring to society.[6] But such careful, critical studies are by no means the ones most influential in shaping public attitudes about the world of microelectronics. An editor at a New York publishing house stated the norm, "People want to know what's new with computer technology. They don't want to know what could go wrong."[7]

It seems all but impossible for computer enthusiasts to examine critically the *ends* that might guide the world-shaking developments they anticipate. They employ the metaphor of revolution for one purpose only – to suggest a drastic upheaval, one that people ought to welcome as good news. It never occurs to them to investigate the idea or its meaning any further.

One might suppose, for example, that a revolution of this type would involve a significant shift in the locus of power; after all, that is exactly what one expects in revolutions of a political kind. Is something similar going to happen in this instance?

One might also ask whether or not this revolution will be strongly committed, as revolutions often are, to a particular set of social ideals. If so, what are the ideals that matter? Where can we see them argued?

To mention revolution also brings to mind the relationships of different social classes. Will the computer revolution bring about the victory of one class over another? Will it be the occasion for a realignment of class loyalties?

In the busy world of computer science, computer engineering, and computer marketing such questions seldom come up. Those actively engaged in promoting the transformation – hardware and software engineers, managers of microelectronics firms, computer salesmen, and the like – are busy pursuing their own ends: profits, market share, handsome salaries, the intrinsic joy of invention, the intellectual rewards of programming, and the pleasures of owning and using powerful machines. But the sheer dynamism of technical and economic activity in the computer industry evidently leaves its members little time to ponder the historical significance of their own activity. They must struggle to keep current, to be on the crest of the next wave as it breaks. As one member of Data General's Eagle computer project describes it, the prevailing spirit resembles a game of pinball. "You win one game, you get to play another. You win with this machine, you get to build the next."[8] The process has its own inertia.

Hence, one looks in vain to the movers and shakers in computer fields for the qualities of social and political insight that characterized revolutionaries of the past. Too busy. Cromwell, Jefferson, Robespierre, Lenin, and Mao were able to reflect upon the world historical events in which they played a role. Public pronouncements by the likes of Robert Noyce, Marvin Minsky, Edward Feigenbaum, and Steven Jobs show no similar wisdom about the transformations they so actively help to create. By and large the computer revolution is conspicuously silent about its own ends.

Good Console, Good Network, Good Computer

My concern for the political meaning of revolution in this setting may seem somewhat misleading, even perverse. A much better point of reference might be the technical "revolutions" and associated social upheavals of the past, the Industrial Revolution in particular. If the enthusiasts of computerization had readily taken up this comparison, studying earlier historical periods for similarities and differences in patterns of technological innovation, capital formation, employment, social change, and the like, then it would be clear that I had chosen the wrong application of this metaphor. But, in fact, no well-developed comparisons of that kind are to be found in the writings on the computer revolution. A consistently ahistorical viewpoint prevails. What one often finds emphasized, however, is a vision of drastically altered social and political conditions, a future upheld as both desirable and, in all likelihood, inevitable. Politics, in other words, is not a secondary concern for many computer enthusiasts; it is a crucial, albeit thoughtless, part of their message.

We are, according to a fairly standard account, moving into an age characterized by the overwhelming dominance of electronic information systems in all areas of human practice. Industrial society, which depended upon material production for its livelihood, is rapidly being supplanted by a society of information services that will enable people to satisfy their economic and social needs. What water- and steam-powered machines were to the industrial age, the computer will be to the era now dawning. Ever-expanding technical capacities in computation and communications will make possible a universal, instantaneous access to enormous quantities of valuable information. As these technologies become less and less expensive and more and more convenient, all the people of the world, not just the wealthy, will be able to use the wonderful services that information machines make available. Gradually, existing differences between rich and poor, advantaged and disadvantaged, will begin to evaporate. Widespread access to computers will produce a society more democratic, egalitarian, and richly diverse than any previously known. Because "knowledge is power," because electronic information will spread knowledge into every corner of world society, political influence will be much more widely shared. With the personal computer serving as the great equalizer, rule by centralized authority and social class dominance will gradually fade away. The marvelous promise of a "global village" will be fulfilled in a worldwide burst of human creativity.

A sampling from recent writings on the information society illustrates these grand expectations.

The world is entering a new period. The wealth of nations, which depended upon land, labor, and capital during its agricultural and industrial phases – depended upon natural resources, the accumulation of money, and even upon weaponry – will come in the future to depend upon information, knowledge and intelligence.[9]

The electronic revolution will not do away with work, but it does hold out some promises: Most boring jobs can be done by machines; lengthy commuting can be avoided; we can have enough leisure to follow interesting pursuits outside our work; environmental destruction can be avoided; the opportunities for personal creativity will be unlimited.[10]

Long lists of specific services spell out the utopian promise of this new age: interactive television, electronic funds transfer, computer-aided instruction, customized news service, electronic magazines, electronic mail, computer teleconferencing, on-line stock market and weather reports, computerized Yellow Pages, shopping via home computer, and so forth. All of it is supposed to add up to a cultural renaissance.

Whatever the limits to growth in other fields, there are no limits near in telecommunications and electronic technology. There are no limits near in the consumption of information, the growth of culture, or the development of the human mind.[11]

Computer-based communications can be used to make human lives richer and freer, by enabling persons to have access to vast stores of information, other "human resources," and opportunities for work and socializing on a more flexible, cheaper and convenient basis than ever before.[12]

When such systems become widespread, potentially intense communications networks among geographically dispersed persons will become actualized. We will become Network Nation, exchanging vast amounts of information and social and emotional communications with colleagues, friends and "strangers" who share similar interests, who are spread all over the nation.[13]

A rich diversity of subcultures will be fostered by computer-based communications systems. Social, political, technical changes will produce conditions likely to lead to the formation of groups with their own distinctive sets of values, activities, language and dress.[14]

According to this view, the computer revolution will, by its sheer momentum, eliminate many of the ills that have vexed political society since the beginning of time. Inequalities of wealth and privilege will gradually fade away. One writer predicts that computer networks will "offer major opportunities to disadvantaged groups to acquire the skills and social ties they need to become full members of society."[15] Another looks forward to "a revolutionary network where each node is equal in power to all others."[16] Information will become the dominant form of wealth. Because it can flow so quickly, so freely through computer networks, it will not, in this interpretation, cause the kinds of stratification associated with traditional forms of property. Obnoxious forms of social organization will also be replaced. "The computer will smash the pyramid," one best-selling book proclaims. "We created the hierarchical, pyramidal, managerial system because we needed it to keep track of people and things people did; with the computer to keep track, we can restructure our institutions horizontally."[17] Thus, the proliferation of electronic information will generate a leveling effect to surpass the dreams of history's great social reformers.

The same viewpoint holds that the prospects for participatory democracy have never been brighter. According to one group of social scientists, "The form of democracy found in the ancient Greek city-state, the Israeli kibbutz, and the New England town meeting, which gave every citizen the opportunity to directly participate in the political process, has become impractical in America's mass society. But this need not be the case. The technological means exist through which millions of people can enter into dialogue with one another and with their representatives, and can form the authentic consensus essential for democracy."[18]

Computer scientist J. C. R. Licklider of the Massachusetts Institute of Technology is one advocate especially hopeful about a revitalization of the democratic process. He looks forward to "an information environment that would give politics greater depth and dimension than it now has." Home computer consoles and television sets would be linked together in a massive network. "The political process would essentially be a giant teleconference, and a campaign would be a months-long series of communications among candidates, propagandists, commentators, political action groups and voters." An arrangement of this kind would, in his view, encourage a more open, comprehensive examination of both issues and candidates. "The information revolution," he exclaims, "is bringing with it a key that may open the door to a new era of involvement and participation. The key is the self-motivating exhilaration that accompanies truly effective interaction with information through a good console through a good network to a good computer."[19] It is, in short, a democracy of machines.

Taken as a whole, beliefs of this kind constitute what I would call mythinformation: the almost religious conviction that a widespread adoption of computers and communications systems along with easy access to electronic information will automatically produce a better world for human living. It is a peculiar form of enthusiasm that characterizes social fashions of the latter decades of the twentieth century. Many people who have grown cynical or discouraged about other aspects of social life are completely enthralled by the supposed redemptive qualities of computers and telecommunications. Writing of the "Fifth Generation" supercomputers, Japanese author Yoneji Masuda rhapsodically predicts "freedom for each of us to set individual goals of self-realization and then perhaps a worldwide religious renaissance, characterized not by a belief in a supernatural god, but rather by awe and humility in the presence of the collective human spirit and its wisdom, humanity living in a symbiotic tranquility with the planet we have found ourselves upon, regulated by a new set of global ethics."[20]

It is not uncommon for the advent of a new technology to provide an occasion for flights of utopian fancy. During the last two centuries the factory system, railroads, telephone, electricity, automobile, airplane, radio, television, and nuclear power have all figured prominently in the belief that a new and glorious age was about to begin. But even within the great tradition of optimistic technophilia, current dreams of a "computer age" stand out as exaggerated and unrealistic. Because they have such a broad appeal, because they overshadow other ways of looking at the matter, these notions deserve closer inspection.

The great equalizer

As is generally true of a myth, the story contains elements of truth. What were once industrial societies are being transformed into service economies, a trend that emerges as more material production shifts to developing countries where labor costs are low and business tax breaks lucrative. At the same time that industrialization takes hold in less-developed nations of the world, deindustrialization is gradually altering the economies of North America and Europe. Some of the service industries central to this pattern are ones that depend upon highly sophisticated computer and communications systems. But this does not mean that future employment possibilities will flow largely from the microelectronics industry and information services. A number of studies, including those of the US Bureau of Labor Statistics, suggest that the vast majority of new jobs will come in menial service occupations paying relatively low wages.[21] As robots and computer software absorb an increasing share of factory and office tasks, the "information society" will offer plenty of opportunities for janitors, hospital orderlies, and fast-food waiters.

The computer romantics are also correct in noting that computerization alters relationships of social power and control, although they misrepresent the direction this development is likely to take. Those who stand to benefit most obviously are large transnational business corporations. While their "global reach" does not arise solely from the application of information technologies, such organizations are uniquely situated to exploit the efficiency, productivity, command, and control the new electronics make available. Other notable beneficiaries of the systematic use of vast amounts of digitized information are public bureaucracies, intelligence agencies, and an ever-expanding military, organizations that would operate less effectively at their present scale were it not for the use of computer power. Ordinary people are, of course, strongly affected by the workings of these organizations and by the rapid spread of new electronic systems in banking, insurance, taxation, factory and office work, home entertainment, and the like. They are also counted upon to be eager buyers of hardware, software, and communications services as computer products reach the consumer market.

But where in all of this motion do we see increased democratization? Social equality? The dawn of a cultural renaissance? Current developments in the information age suggest an increase in power by those who already had a great deal of power, an enhanced centralization of control by those already prepared for control, an augmentation of wealth by the already wealthy. Far from demonstrating a revolution in patterns of social and political influence, empirical studies of computers and social change usually show powerful groups adapting computerized methods to retain control.[22] That is not surprising. Those best situated to take advantage of the power of a new technology are often those previously well situated by dint of wealth, social standing, and institutional position. Thus, if there is to be a computer revolution, the best guess is that it will have a distinctly conservative character.

Granted, such prominent trends could be altered. It is possible that a society strongly rooted in computer and telecommunications systems could be one in which participatory democracy, decentralized political control, and social equality are fully realized. Progress of that kind would have to occur as the result of that society's concerted efforts to overcome many difficult obstacles to achieve those ends. Computer enthusiasts, however, seldom propose deliberate action of that kind. Instead, they strongly suggest that the good society will be realized as a side effect, a spin-off from the vast proliferation of computing devices. There is evidently no need to try to shape the institutions of the information age in ways that maximize human freedom while placing limits upon concentrations of power.

For those willing to wait passively while the computer revolution takes its course, technological determinism ceases to be mere theory and becomes an ideal: a desire to embrace conditions brought on by technological change without judging them in advance. There is nothing new in this disposition. Computer romanticism is merely the latest version of the nineteenth- and twentieth-century faith we noted earlier, one that has always expected to generate freedom, democracy, and justice through sheer material abundance. Thus there is no need for serious inquiry into the appropriate design of new institutions or the distribution of rewards and burdens. As long as the economy is growing and the machinery in good working order, the rest will take care of itself. In previous versions of this homespun conviction, the abundant (and therefore democratic) society was manifest by a limitless supply of houses, appliances, and consumer goods.[23] Now "access to information" and "access to computers" have moved to the top of the list.

The political arguments of computer romantics draw upon a number of key assumptions: (1) people are bereft of information; (2) information is knowledge; (3) knowledge is power; and (4) increasing access to information enhances democracy and equalizes social power. Taken as separate assertions and in combination, these beliefs provide a woefully distorted picture of the role of electronic systems in social life.

Is it true that people face serious shortages of information? To read the literature on the computer revolution one would suppose this to be a problem on a par with the energy crisis of the 1970s. The persuasiveness of this notion borrows from our sense that literacy, education, knowledge, well-informed minds, and the widespread availability of tools of inquiry are unquestionable social goods, and that, in contrast, illiteracy, inadequate education, ignorance, and forced restrictions upon knowledge are among history's worst evils. Thus, it appears superficially plausible that a world rewired to connect human beings to vast data banks and communications systems would be a progressive step. Information shortage would be remedied in much the same way that developing a new fuel supply might solve an energy crisis.

Alas, the idea is entirely faulty. It mistakes sheer supply of information with an educated ability to gain knowledge and act effectively based on that knowledge. In many parts of the world that ability is sadly lacking. Even some highly developed societies still contain chronic inequalities in the distribution of good education and basic intellectual skills. The US Army, for instance, must now reject or dismiss a fairly high percentage of the young men and women it recruits because they simply cannot read military manuals. It is no doubt true of these recruits that they have a great deal of information about the world – information from their life experiences, schooling, the mass media, and so forth. What makes them "functionally illiterate" is that they have not learned to translate this information into a mastery of practical skills.

If the solution to problems of illiteracy and poor education were a question of information supply alone, then the best policy might be to increase the number of well-stocked libraries, making sure they were built in places where libraries do not presently exist. Of course, that would do little good in itself unless people are sufficiently well educated to use those libraries to broaden their knowledge and understanding. Computer enthusiasts however, are not noted for their calls to increase support of public libraries and schools. It is *electronic information* carried by *networks* they uphold as crucial. Here is a case in which an obsession with a particular kind of technology causes one to disregard what are obvious problems and clear remedies. While it is true that systems of computation and communications, intelligently structured and wisely applied, might help a society raise its standards of literacy, education, and general knowledgeability, to look to those instruments first while ignoring how to enlighten and invigorate a human mind is pure foolishness.

"As everybody knows, knowledge is power."[24] This is an attractive idea, but highly misleading. Of course, knowledge employed in particular circumstances can help one act effectively and in that sense enhance one's power. A citrus farmer's knowledge of frost conditions enables him/her to take steps to prevent damage to the crop. A candidate's knowledge of public opinion can be a powerful aid in an election campaign. But surely there is no automatic, positive link between knowledge and power, especially if that means power in a social or political sense. At times knowledge brings merely an enlightened impotence or paralysis. One may know exactly what to do but lack the wherewithal to act. Of the many conditions that affect the phenomenon of power, knowledge is but one and by no means the most important. Thus, in the history of ideas, arguments that expert knowledge ought to play a special role in politics – the philosopher-kings for Plato, the engineers for Veblen – have always been offered as something contrary to prevailing wisdom. To Plato and Veblen it was obvious that knowledge was *not* power, a situation they hoped to remedy.

An equally serious misconception among computer enthusiasts is the belief that democracy is first and foremost a matter of distributing information. As one particularly flamboyant manifesto exclaims: "There is an explosion of information dispersal in the technology and we think this information has to be shared. All great thinkers about democracy said that the key to democracy is access to information. And now we have a chance to get information into people's hands like never before."[25] Once again such assertions play on our belief that a democratic public ought to be open-minded and well informed. One of the great evils of totalitarian societies is that they dictate what people can know and impose secrecy to restrict freedom. But democracy is not founded solely (or even primarily) upon conditions that affect the availability of information. What distinguishes it from other political forms is a recognition that the people as a whole are capable of self-government and that they have a rightful claim to rule. As a consequence, political society ought to build institutions that allow or even encourage a great latitude of democratic participation. How far a society must go in making political authority and public roles available to ordinary people is a matter of dispute among political theorists. But no serious student of the question would give much credence to the idea that creating a universal gridwork to spread electronic information is, by itself, a democratizing step.

What, then, of the idea that "interaction with information through a good console, through a good network to a good computer" will promote a renewed sense of political involvement and participation? Readers who believe that assertion should contact me about some parcels of land my uncle has for sale in Florida. Relatively low levels of citizen participation prevail in some modern democracies, the United States, for example. There are many reasons for this, many ways a society might try to improve things. Perhaps opportunities to serve in public office or influence public policy are too limited; in that case, broaden the opportunities. Or perhaps choices placed before citizens are so pallid that boredom is a valid response; in that instance, improve the quality of those choices. But it is simply not reasonable to assume that enthusiasm for political activity will be stimulated solely by the introduction of sophisticated information machines.

The role that television plays in modern politics should suggest why this is so. Public participation in voting has steadily declined as television replaced the face-to-face politics of precincts and neighborhoods. Passive monitoring of electronic news and information allows citizens to feel involved while dampening the desire to take an active part. If people begin to rely upon computerized data bases and telecommunications as a primary means of exercising power, it is conceivable that genuine political knowledge based in first-hand experience would vanish altogether. The vitality of democratic politics depends upon people's willingness to act together in pursuit of their common ends. It requires that on occasion members of a community appear before each other in person, speak their minds, deliberate on paths of action, and decide what they will do.[26] This is considerably different from the model now upheld as a breakthrough for democracy: logging onto one's computer, receiving the latest information, and sending back an instantaneous digitized response.

A chapter from recent political history illustrates the strength of direct participation in contrast to the politics of electronic information. In 1981 and 1982 two groups of activists set about to do what they could to stop the international nuclear arms race. One of the groups, Ground Zero, chose to rely almost solely upon mass communications to convey its message to the public. Its leaders appeared on morning talk shows and evening news programs on all three major television networks. They followed up with a mass mail solicitation using addresses from a computerized data base. At the same time another group, the Nuclear Weapons Freeze Campaign, began by taking its proposal for a bilateral nuclear freeze to New England town meetings, places where active citizen participation is a long-standing tradition. Winning the endorsement of the idea from a great many town meetings, the Nuclear Freeze group expanded its drive by launching a series of state initiatives. Once again the key was a direct approach to people, this time through thousands of meetings, dinners, and parties held in homes across the country.

The effects of the two movements were strikingly different. After its initial publicity, Ground Zero was largely ignored. It had been an ephemeral exercise in media posturing. The Nuclear Freeze campaign, however, continued to gain influence in the form of increasing public support, successful ballot measures, and an ability to apply pressure upon political officials. Eventually, the latter group did begin to use computerized mailings, television appearances, and the like to advance its cause. But it never forgot the original source of its leverage: people working together for shared ends.

Of all the computer enthusiasts' political ideas, there is none more poignant than the faith that the computer is destined to become a potent equalizer in modern society. Support for this belief is found in the fact that small "personal" computers are becoming more and more powerful, less and less expensive, and ever more simple to use. Obnoxious tendencies associated with the enormous, costly, technically inaccessible computers of the recent past are soon to be overcome. As one writer explains, "The great forces of centralization that characterized mainframe and minicomputer design of that period have now been reversed." This means that "the puny device that sits innocuously on the desktop will, in fact, within a few years, contain enough computing power to become an effective equalizer."[27] Presumably, ordinary citizens equipped with microcomputers will be able to counter the influence of large, computer-based organizations.

Notions of this kind echo beliefs of eighteenth- and nineteenth-century revolutionaries that placing fire arms in the hands of the people was crucial to overthrowing entrenched authority. In the American Revolution, French Revolution, Paris Commune, and Russian Revolution the role of "the people armed" was central to the revolutionary program. As the military defeat of the Paris Commune made clear, however, the fact that the popular forces have guns may not be decisive. In a contest of force against force, the larger, more sophisticated, more ruthless, better equipped competitor often has the upper hand. Hence, the availability of low-cost computing power may move the baseline that defines electronic dimensions of social influence, but it does not necessarily alter the relative balance of power. Using a personal computer makes one no more powerful vis-à-vis, say, the National Security Agency than flying a hang glider establishes a person as a match for the US Air Force.

In sum, the political expectations of computer enthusiasts are seldom more than idle fantasy. Beliefs that widespread use of computers will cause hierarchies to crumble, inequality to tumble, participation to flourish, and centralized power to dissolve simply do not withstand close scrutiny. The formula information = knowledge = power = democracy lacks any real substance. At each point the mistake comes in the conviction that computerization will inevitably move society toward the good life. And no one will have to raise a finger.

Information and ideology

Despite its shortcomings as political theory, mythinformation is noteworthy as an expressive contemporary ideology. I use the term "ideology" here in a sense common in social science: a set of beliefs that expresses the needs and aspirations of a group, class, culture, or subculture. In this instance the needs and aspirations that matter most are those that stem from operational requirements of highly complex systems in an advanced technological society; the groups most directly involved are those who build, maintain, operate, improve, and market these systems. At a time in which almost all major components of our technological society have come to depend upon the application of large and small computers, it is not surprising that computerization has risen to ideological prominence, an expression of grand hopes and ideals.

What is the "information" so crucial in this odd belief system, the icon now so greatly cherished? We have seen enough to appreciate that the kind of information upheld is not knowledge in the ordinary sense of the term; nor is it understanding, enlightenment, critical thought, timeless wisdom, or the content of a well-educated mind. If one looks carefully at the writings of computer enthusiasts, one finds that information in a particular form and context is offered as a paradigm to inspire emulation. Enormous quantities of data, manipulated within various kinds of electronic media and used to facilitate the transactions of today's large, complex organizations is the model we are urged to embrace. In this context the sheer quantity of information presents a formidable challenge. Modern organizations are continually faced with overload, a flood of data that threatens to become unintelligible to them. Computers provide one way to confront that problem; speed conquers quantity. An equally serious challenge is created by the fact that the varieties of information most crucial to modern organizations are highly time specific. Data on stock market prices, airline traffic, weather conditions, international economic indicators, military intelligence, public opinion poll results, and the like are useful for very short periods of time. Systems that gather, organize, analyze, and utilize electronic data in these areas must be closely tuned to the very latest developments. If one is trading on fastpaced international markets, information about prices an hour old or even a few seconds old may have no value. Information is itself a perishable commodity.

Thus, what looked so puzzling in another context – the urgent "need" for information in a social world filled with many pressing human needs – now becomes transparent. It is, in the first instance, the need of complex human/machine systems threatened with debilitating uncertainties or even breakdown unless continually replenished with up-to-the-minute electronic information about their internal states and operating environments. Rapid information processing capabilities of modern computers and communications devices are a perfect match for such needs, a marriage made in technological heaven.

But is it sensible to transfer this model, as many evidently wish, to all parts of human life? Must activities, experiences, ideas, and ways of knowing that take a longer time to bear fruit adapt to the speedy processes of digitized information processing? Must education, the arts, politics, sports, home life, and all other forms of social practice be transformed to accommodate it? As one article on the coming of the home computer concludes, "running a household is actually like running a small business. You have to worry about inventory control – of household supplies – and budgeting for school tuition, housekeepers' salaries, and all the rest."[28] The writer argues that these complex, rapidly changing operations require a powerful information processing capacity to keep them functioning smoothly. One begins to wonder how everyday activities such as running a household were even possible before the advent of microelectronics. This is a case in which the computer is a solution frantically in search of a problem.

In the last analysis, the almost total silence about the ends of the "computer revolution" is filled by a conviction that information processing is something valuable in its own right. Faced with an information explosion that strains the capacities of traditional institutions, society will renovate its structure to accommodate computerized, automated systems in every area of concern. The efficient management of information is revealed as the *telos* of modern society, its greatest mission. It is that fact to which mythinformation adds glory and glitter. People must be convinced that the human burdens of an information age – unemployment, de-skilling, the disruption of many social patterns – are worth bearing. Once again, those who push the plow are told they ride a golden chariot.

Everywhere and nowhere

Having criticized a point of view, it remains for me to suggest what topics a serious study of computers and politics should pursue. The question is, of course, a very large one. If the long-term consequences of computerization are anything like the ones commonly predicted, they will require a rethinking of many fundamental conditions in social and political life. I will mention three areas of concern.

As people handle an increasing range of their daily activities through electronic instruments – mail, banking, shopping, entertainment, travel plans, and so forth – it becomes technically feasible to monitor these activities to a degree heretofore inconceivable. The availability of digitized footprints of social transactions affords opportunities that contain a menacing aspect. While there has been a great deal written about this problem, most of it deals with the "threat to privacy," the possibility that someone might gain access to information that violates the sanctity of one's personal life. As important as that issue certainly is, it by no means exhausts the potential evils created by electronic data banks and computer matching. The danger extends beyond the private sphere to affect the most basic of public freedoms.

Unless steps are taken to prevent it, we may develop systems capable of a perpetual, pervasive, apparently benign surveillance. Confronted with omnipresent, all-seeing data banks, the populace may find passivity and compliance the safest route, avoiding activities that once represented political liberty. As a badge of civic pride a citizen may announce, "I'm not involved in anything a computer would find the least bit interesting."

The evolution of this unhappy state of affairs does not necessarily depend upon the "misuse" of computer systems. The prospect we face is really much more insidious. An age rich in electronic information may achieve wonderful social conveniences at a cost of placing freedom, perhaps inadvertently, in a deep chill.

A thoroughly computerized world is also one bound to alter conditions of human sociability. The point of many applications of microelectronics, after all, is to eliminate social layers that were previously needed to get things done. Computerized bank tellers, for example, have largely done away with small, local branch banks, which were not only ways of doing business, but places where people met, talked, and socialized. The so-called electronic cottage industry, similarly, operates very well without the kinds of human interactions that once characterized office work. Despite greater efficiency, productivity, and convenience, innovations of this kind do away with the reasons people formerly had for being together, working together, acting together. Many practical activities once crucial to even a minimal sense of community life are rendered obsolete. One consequence of these developments is to pare away the kinds of face-to-face contact that once provided important buffers between individuals and organized power. To an increasing extent, people will become even more susceptible to the influence of employers, news media, advertisers, and national political leaders. Where will we find new institutions to balance and mediate such power?

Perhaps the most significant challenge posed by the linking of computers and telecommunications is the prospect that the basic structures of political order will be recast. Worldwide computer, satellite, and communication networks fulfill, in large part, the modern dream of conquering space and time. These systems make possible instantaneous action at any point on the globe without limits imposed by the specific location of the initiating actor. Human beings and human societies, however, have traditionally found their identities within spatial and temporal limits. They have lived, acted, and found meaning in a particular place at a particular time. Developments in microelectronics tend to dissolve these limits, thereby threatening the integrity of social and political forms that depend on them. Aristotle's observation that "man is a political animal" meant in its most literal sense that man is a *polis* animal, a creature naturally suited to live in a particular kind of community within a specific geographical setting, the city-state. Historical experience shows that it is possible for human beings to flourish in political units – kingdoms, empires, nation-states – larger than those the Greeks thought natural. But until recently the crucial conditions created by spatial boundaries of political societies were never in question.

That has changed. Methods pioneered by transnational corporations now make it possible for organizations of enormous size to manage their activities effectively across the surface of the planet. Business units that used to depend upon spatial proximity can now be integrated through complex electronic signals. If it seems convenient to shift operations from one area of the world to another far distant, it can be accomplished with a flick of a switch. Close an office in Sunnyvale; open an office in Singapore. In the recent past corporations have had to demonstrate at least some semblance of commitment to geographically based communities; their public relations often stressed the fact that they were "good neighbors." But in an age in which organizations are located everywhere and nowhere, this commitment easily evaporates. A transnational corporation can play fast and loose with everyone, including the country that is ostensibly its "home." Towns, cities, regions, and whole nations are forced to swallow their pride and negotiate for favors. In that process, political authority is gradually redefined.

Computerization resembles other vast, but largely unconscious experiments in modern social and technological history, experiments of the kind noted in earlier chapters. Following a step-by-step process of instrumental improvements, societies create new institutions, new patterns of behavior, new sensibilities, new contexts for the exercise of power. Calling such changes "revolutionary," we tacitly acknowledge that these are matters that require reflection, possibly even strong public action to ensure that the outcomes are desirable. But the occasions for reflection, debate, and public choice are extremely rare indeed. The important decisions are left in private hands inspired by narrowly focussed economic motives. While many recognize that these decisions have profound consequences for our common life, few seem prepared to own up to that fact. Some observers forecast that "the computer revolution" will eventually be guided by new wonders in artificial intelligence. Its present course is influenced by something much more familiar: the absent mind.

Notes

1 See, for example, Edward Berkeley, *The Computer Revolution* (New York, Doubleday, 1962); Edward Tomeski, *The Computer Revolution: The Executive and the New Information Technology* (New York, Macmillan, 1970); and Nigel Hawkes, *The Computer Revolution* (New York, E. P. Dutton, 1972). See also Aaron Sloman, *The Computer Revolution in Philosophy* (Hassocks, UK, Harvester Press, 1978); Zenon Pylyshyn, *Perspectives on the Computer Revolution* (Englewood Cliffs, NJ, Prentice-Hall, 1970); Paul Stoneman, *Technological Diffusion and the Computer Revolution* (Cambridge, Cambridge University Press, 1976); and Ernest Braun and Stuart MacDonald, *Revolution in Miniature: The History and Impact of Semiconductor Electronics* (Cambridge, Cambridge University Press, 1978).

2 Michael L. Dertouzos in an interview on "The Today Show," National Broadcasting Company, August 8, 1983.

3 Daniel Bell, "The Social Framework of the Information Society," in *The Computer Age: A Twenty Year View*, Michael L. Dertouzos and Joel Moses (eds) (Cambridge, MA, MIT Press, 1980), p. 163.

4 See, for example, Philip H. Abelson, "The Revolution in Computers and Electronics," *Science*, 215, pp. 751–3.

5 Edward A. Feigenbaum and Pamela McCorduck, *The Fifth Generation: Artificial Intelligence and Japan's Computer Challenge to the World* (Reading, MA, Addison-Wesley, 1983), p. 8.

6 Among the important works of this kind are David Burnham, *The Rise of the Computer State* (New York, Random House, 1983); James N. Danziger et al., *Computers and Politics: High Technology in American Local Governments* (New York, Columbia University Press, 1982); Abbe Moshowitz, *The Conquest of Will: Information Processing in Human Affairs* (Reading, MA, Addison-Wesley, 1976); James Rule et al., *The Politics of Privacy* (New York, New American Library, 1980); and Joseph Weizenbaum, *Computer Power and Human Reason: From Judgment to Calculation* (San Francisco, W. H. Freeman, 1976).

7 Quoted in Jacques Vallee, *The Network Revolution: Confessions of a Computer Scientist* (Berkeley, CA, And/Or Press, 1982), p. 10.

8 Tracy Kidder, *Soul of a New Machine* (New York, Avon Books, 1982), p. 228.

9 Feigenbaum and McCorduck, *The Fifth Generation*, p. 14.

10 James Martin, *Telematic Society: A Challenge for Tomorrow* (Englewood Cliffs, NJ, Prentice-Hall, 1981), p. 172.

11 Ibid., p. 4.

12 Starr Roxanne Hiltz and Murray Turoff, *The Network Nation: Human Communication via Computer* (Reading, MA, Addison-Wesley, 1978), p. 489.

13 Ibid., p. xxix.

14 Ibid., p. 484.

15 Ibid., p. xxix.

16 *The Network Revolution*, p. 198.

17 John Naisbitt, *Megatrends: Ten New Directions Transforming Our Lives* (New York, Warner Books, 1984), p. 282.

18 Amitai Etzioni, Kenneth Laudon, and Sara Lipson, "Participating Technology: The Minerva Communications Tree," *Journal of Communications*, 25, Spring 1975, p. 64.

19 J. C. R. Licklider, "Computers and Government," in Dertouzos and Moses (eds), *The Computer Age*, pp. 114, 126.

20 Quoted in Feigenbaum and McCorduck, *The Fifth Generation*, p. 240.

21 *Occupational Outlook Handbook, 1982–1983*, US Bureau of Labor Statistics, Bulletin No. 2200, Superintendent of Documents, US Government Printing Office, Washington, DC. See also Gene I. Maeroff, "The Real Job Boom Is Likely to be Low-Tech," *New York Times*, September 4, 1983, 16E.

22 See, for example Danziger et al., *Computers and Politics*.

23 For a study of the utopia of consumer products in American democracy, see Jeffrey L. Meikle, *Twentieth Century Limited: Industrial Design in America, 1925–1939* (Philadelphia, Temple University Press, 1979). For other utopian dreams see Joseph J. Corn, *The Winged Gospel: America's Romance with Aviation, 1900–1950* (Oxford University Press, 1983); Joseph J. Corn and Brian Horrigan, *Yesterday's Tomorrows: Past Visions of America's Future* (New York, Summit Books, 1984); and Erik Barnow, *The Tube of Plenty* (Oxford, Oxford University Press, 1975).

24 Feigenbaum and McCorduck, *The Fifth Generation*, p. 8.

25 "The Philosophy of US," from the official program of The US Festival held in San Bernardino, California, September 4–7, 1982. The outdoor rock festival, sponsored by Steven Wozniak, co-inventor of the original Apple Computer, attracted an estimated half million people. Wozniak regaled the crowd with large-screen video presentations of his message, proclaiming a new age of community and democracy generated by the use of personal computers.

26 "*Power* corresponds to the human ability not just to act but to act in concert. Power is never the property of an individual; it belongs to a group and remains in existence only so long as the group keeps together," Hannah Arendt, *On Violence* (New York, Harcourt Brace and World, 1969), p. 44.

27 John Markoff, "A View of the Future: Micros Won't Matter," *Info-World*, October 31, 1983, p. 69.

28 Donald H. Dunn, "The Many Uses of the Personal Computer," *Business Week*, June 23, 1980, pp. 125–6.

3 The Future with IT

Manufacturing Matters: The Myth of the Post-industrial Economy

Stephen S. Cohen and John Zysman

In a powerful critique of the notion that society is moving inevitably into a "post-industrial" stage, in which "information" or "knowledge" is more important than materials, Cohen and Zysman argue that it is essential for the United States to retain its manufacturing base. Relying on the information or service sector to create new jobs and prosperity would be foolhardy. This article is adapted from the author's highly acclaimed book Manufacturing Matters: The Myth of the Post-industrial Economy *(Basic Books, New York, 1987) and is reprinted from* Technology Review, *February/March 1987. Stephen Cohen is Professor of Planning and John Zysman is Professor of Political Science at the University of California, Berkeley.*

Manufacturing matters mightily to the wealth and power of the United States and to our ability to sustain the open society we have come to take for granted. But this contention is a distinctly minority view in the United States today. In part this is due to the power of a central tenet of American economic thought: government policy should be indifferent to what makes up the gross national product.

This conventional view is supported by numerous authors in books, journal articles, op-ed pieces, and expert testimony. They point to the relentless decline in manufacturing employment – from 50 percent of all jobs in 1950 to 20 percent now – and the increase in service jobs, which now constitute about 70 percent of all employment. These figures underwrite the mainstream view that economic development is a never-ending shift from activities of the past up into newer, more profitable activities. The United States shifted from farming to industry. Now we are shifting from industry to services and high technology.

The lesson for government is clear: keep hands off. For example, in a 1985 report to the Congress on trade agreements, President Reagan set out the following framework for understanding a troubling trade imbalance. "The move from an industrial society toward a 'post-industrial' service economy has been one of the greatest changes to affect the developed world since the Industrial Revolution. The progression of an economy such as America's from agriculture to manufacturing to services is a natural change."

The New York Stock Exchange, in a recent report on trade, industrial change, and jobs, put it more pointedly: "A strong manufacturing sector is not a requisite for a prosperous economy."

Or, in the words of a *Forbes* editorial, "Instead of ringing in the decline of our economic power, a service-driven economy signals the most advanced stage of economic development. . . . Instead of following the Pied Piper of 'reindustrialization,' the US should be concentrating its efforts on strengthening its services."

In this view, America's loss of market share and employment in industries such as textiles, steel, apparel, autos, consumer electronics, machine tools, random-access memories, computer peripherals, and circuit boards is neither surprising nor bad. It is not a sign of failure but part of the price of success. The United States should be shedding sunset industries and moving on to services and high tech, the sunrise sectors. Such a change is part of an ever-evolving international division of labor from which everyone benefits.

This view is soothing in its message, calm in tone, confident in style, and readily buttressed by traditional economic theory. We believe it is also quite possibly wrong. At the heart of our argument is a notion we call "direct linkage:" many service jobs are tightly tied to manufacturing. Lose manufacturing and you will lose – not develop – those high-wage services. Nor is the relationship between high tech and manufacturing, like that between services and manufacturing, a simple case of evolutionary succession. High tech is intimately tied to manufacturing, not a free-floating laboratory activity.

Our argument takes issue – fundamentally – with the widely articulated view that a service-based, "post-industrial" economy is the natural successor to an industry-based economy, the next step up a short but steep staircase consisting of "stages of development." Because the traditional view justifies economic policies that risk the wealth and power of the United States, it is, for all its conventionality, a terribly radical guide for policy. If the United States wants to stay on top – or even high up – we can't just shift out of manufacturing and into services.

Nor can we establish a long-term preserve around traditional blue-collar jobs and outmoded plants. If the United States is to remain a wealthy and powerful economy, American manufacturing must automate, not emigrate. Moreover, it must automate in ways that build flexibility through the imaginative use of skilled labor. In a world in which technology migrates rapidly and financial services are global, the skills of our workforce and the talents of our managers together will be our central resource.

Linkages and wealth

Most celebrations of the shift from industry to services construct a parallel to the shift from agriculture to industry. According to that argument, the shift from low-productivity, low-paid farm labor to higher-productivity, hence higher-paid employment in industry is precisely what economic development is about. The same developmental movement, the same "creative destruction," is now being repeated in the shift out of industry and into services and high tech.

This view of economic history, although familiar and reassuring, is misleading. It confuses two separate transitions: a shift out of agricultural production and a shift *of labor* out of agriculture.

The first shift never occurred. US agricultural production did not go offshore or shrivel up.

To the embarrassment of those who view the cultivation of large quantities of soybeans, tomatoes, and corn as incompatible with a high-tech future, agriculture has sustained the highest long-term productivity of any sector of the economy. We automated agriculture; we did not send it offshore or shift out of it. As a result we developed massive quantities of high-value-added, high-paid jobs in related industries and services such as agricultural machinery and chemicals. These industries and services owe their development, scale, and survival to a broad and strong American agricultural sector.

Even the employment shift from agriculture merits a second look. The generally accepted figure for US agricultural employment is about 3 million, or 3 percent of the workforce. But this figure arbitrarily excludes many categories of employment. Are crop dusters and large-animal veterinarians employed in agriculture? The 3 million figure is blind to such important economic realities. If we ask what would have happened to employment (and wealth) if the United States had shifted out of agriculture instead of moving labor off the farm, we encounter the notion of linkage: the relationship of agricultural production to employment in tractor repair, ketchup making, and grape crushing.

The more advanced a production process, the longer and more complicated the linkages. Primitive farmers scratch the ground with sticks. They need very little from outside. Their productivity is also very low. Modern farmers head a long, elaborate chain of specialists, most of whom don't often set foot on the farm, yet all of whom are vital to its successful operation and directly depend on it.

Such linkage is not a new notion. But conventional economics does not like linkages to be used as evidence of some special economic importance for particular sectors. Linkage has no place in a discussion of a subject like why manufacturing matters, critics say. Their objection is not that linkages are dubious or rare, or impossible to demonstrate. Rather, it is that they are ubiquitous. In economics, everything is linked to everything else.

The linkages admitted in traditional economics are all of the same special kind: they are loose couplings. Each is a simple market relationship between a buyer and a seller, and each involves a traded good. The United States can, in principle at least, make cars or textiles with imported machines. We do it every day, though at a steadily shrinking volume. These are the loosest linkages imaginable.

There are, however, tighter linkages, such as those between agricultural production and the food-processing industry, which employs about 1.7 million Americans. Here the linkages are tight and concrete. Move the tomato farm offshore and you close the ketchup plant or move it offshore also. It is technically possible but economically difficult to mill sugar cane in a country far from the sugar fields, or to process tomatoes far from the tomato patch, or to dry grapes into raisins far from the vineyard. An economy like ours is based on an enormous number of such tight bonds. It is not simply a system of loose linkages like those that dominate the models from which conventional economics produces its conventional prescriptions.

It is extremely implausible that the United States would sustain a major agricultural-chemicals industry if it were not the world's largest and most advanced market for those products. It is not likely that we would have developed the world's largest agricultural-machinery industry in the absence of the world's largest agricultural sector. Were the wheat fields to vanish from the United States, the machinery makers would shrink and so would their suppliers of parts, computers, trucking, and janitorial services.

The Department of Agriculture provides estimates of agriculture-dependent employment, but they outrageously overstate the case by tracing the food and fiber chain up through textile mills and food stores. Their 1982 estimate was 28.4 million jobs dependent on agriculture. Using rather conservative assumptions, we found that 3 to 6 million jobs – in addition to the 3 million traditionally classified as agricultural – can be considered part of this sector.

Manufacturing linkages

If we turn from agriculture to industry – where direct employment is 21 million jobs – we find that even a remotely similar "linkage rate" would radically alter the place of manufacturing in the US economy. The employment of another 40, 50, or even 60 million Americans, half to three-quarters of whom are counted as service workers, depends directly upon manufacturing production. If manufacturing goes, those service jobs will go with it.

If we lose control and mastery of manufacturing production, the problem is not simply that we will be unable to replace the jobs lost with service jobs, or simply that those service jobs will pay less, or that the scale and speed of adjustment will shock the society – and polity – in potentially dangerous ways. It is that the high-paying service jobs that are directly linked to manufacturing will, after a few short rounds of industrial innovation, wither away, only to sprout out offshore.

Many service jobs that follow manufacturing, such as wholesaling, retailing, and advertising, would not be directly affected if manufacturing were ceded to offshore producers. The same sales effort is involved in selling a Toyota as in selling a Buick.

The services that are directly linked to manufacturing are concentrated in that relatively narrow band of services that precedes it. Examples of such activities include design and engineering services; payroll, inventory, and accounting services; finance and insurance; repair and maintenance of plant and machinery; training and recruitment; testing services and labs; industrial waste disposal; and the accountants, designers, publicists, payroll, transportation and communication firms who work for the engineering firms that design and service production equipment.

Two questions pose themselves. The first concerns the nature of the linkages. How can we go about determining how many jobs would vanish from the US economy if manufacturing were lost? The second involves scale: do services to manufacturing constitute a scale of employment sufficient to justify a new set of concerns, a rethinking of theory, and a recasting of policy?

The President's Report on the Trade Agreements Program provides an approximate answer for the second question: "25 percent of US GNP originates in services used as inputs by goods-producing industries – more than the value added to GNP by the manufacturing sector."

But charting how much of this service employment is tightly linked to manufacturing is difficult. It should be right at the top of the economics research agenda, so that it can get to the top of the policy debate. Unless it can be shown that the overwhelming bulk of those services are weakly linked to manufacturing, we must quickly reformulate the terms of that policy debate.

Some of those services that precede are so tightly linked to manufacturing that they are best understood as direct extensions of it. These would include truckers who specialize in shipping raw materials, components, and semi-finished goods. The US textile industry, for example, is a major employer of trucking services. The category of services tightly linked to manufacturing is real, and it is peopled. But unfortunately we do not yet know how big it is.

Is exporting services an answer?

If, indeed, many services are tied to manufacturing, can the United States significantly offset its trade deficit in merchandise by running a surplus in trade of services? Recent experience provides no reason for assuming – wishing is a better word – that the United States is better at exporting services than it is at exporting manufactured goods. The total volume of service trade is an order of magnitude less than trade in goods. Consequently, only a sudden multiplication of service exports could compensate for the present deterioration in traded goods.

There are a number of problems with counting on an expansion in American service exports. First, almost all the current trade surplus in services stems from interest on old loans abroad. These loans are not very bankable since Third World nations threaten to default. Indeed, our obligations to foreign countries now exceed theirs to us. The United States is a debtor nation.

Second, as with domestic services, large segments of trade in international services are directly tied to a strong and technologically advanced manufacturing sector.

Consider US exports of engineering services. These top-of-the-line services are knowledge-intensive and employ highly paid professionals who in turn purchase significant amounts of other services, including telecommunications, data processing, computer programming, and legal advice. Competitive advantage in engineering services depends upon mastery and control of the latest production technology by US producers. Not very long ago we exported such services in the steel industry. Then US steel producers fell behind in the design and operation of production technologies and facilities. When leadership in production changed hands, the flow of services for this industry also reversed. Now we import those services from our former customers in Europe and Japan, and might soon obtain them from Korea and Brazil.

Third, it is not only engineering services that go through this development cycle. Financial services – a sector in which the United States is said to have a strong competitive advantage – are often cited as an area where export earnings could offset deficits in the merchandise account in a big way. Financial services are high in knowledge and technology, and are supposedly located within the most advanced economy: ours.

But the situation in banking services may be less rosy than we like to think. There is no compelling reason to assume a special advantage for US banks compared with their competitors. Foreign banks are bigger, and they are growing faster than US banks. A recent listing of the world's largest banks included 23 Japanese banks, 44 European banks, and only 18 US banks.

US banks are not even particularly succeeding in holding on to their home market. For example, foreign banks are doing as well in California as foreign auto producers. Six of the ten largest banks in California are now foreign owned, up from two of ten five years ago. Foreign banks now account for about 40 percent of the big commercial loans – the high end of the business – made in New York and San Francisco. Service trade is not an alternative to trade in goods.

The high-tech link

Some analysts, such as Robert Z. Lawrence of the Brookings Institution, take comfort in the fact that high-technology exports have grown in importance for the United States. They see that as a sign of a healthy, normal development process. But the supposed US advantage in high-technology goods is also deeply misleading. It suggests less a distinctive international advantage than a deep incapacity to compete with our industrial partners even in more traditional sectors. A failure by American firms to remain competitive in manufacturing processes seems to underlie this weakness. Moreover, the US position in high-technology trade is quite narrow and fragile.

In the early 1980s the range of high-technology sectors from which a surplus was generated was actually quite narrow: aircraft, computers, and agricultural chemicals. The overall high-tech surplus disappeared by 1983, and in 1984 and 1985 high technology, too, ran a growing deficit. Moreover, a substantial portion of US high-tech exports are military goods, which indicates more about the character of America's strategic ties than about its industrial competitiveness. At a minimum, military sales reflect such factors as foreign policy far more than simple commercial calculus.

Like the service industries, much of high tech is tightly linked to traditional manufacturing. Most high-tech products are producer goods, not consumer items, despite the popularity of home computers and burglar alarms. They are bought to be used in the products of other industries (such as microprocessors in cars) or in production processes (such as robots, computers, and lasers). If American producers of autos, machine tools, telephones, and trousers don't buy American-made silicon chips, who will?

A second tie to manufacturing is even tighter. If high tech is to sustain a scale of activity sufficient to matter, America must control the production of those high-tech products it invents and designs – and it must do so in a direct and hands-on way. Unless R&D is closely tied to manufacturing – and to the innovation required to maintain competitiveness – it will lose its cutting edge. For example, by abandoning the production of televisions, the US electronics industry quickly lost the know-how to design, develop, refine, and competitively produce the VCR, the next generation of that product.

Defense: a footnote

Until now, we have treated military needs in parenthesis, as they are treated in conventional economics. However, it is not easy to make exceptions for something as big as the US military effort. Exceptions of that scale are never without consequences for the rest of the system.

A strong domestic manufacturing capability greatly reduces the costs of our defense effort. Diverse and leading-edge production of technologies such as semiconductors, computers, telecommunications, and machine tools makes the costs of advanced weaponry much lower than if we had to create an industrial structure exclusively for military use.

If US commercial semiconductor manufacturers, say, fall behind foreign competitors, the military might not even be able to produce the components for its own use. Domestic capability in critical links in the production chain – for example, mask-making, clean rooms, and design and production tools for semiconductors – could quickly disappear.

Such an erosion of our ability to produce critical technologies would massively reduce our strategic independence and diplomatic options. Whatever the ups and downs of military spending and the changes in defense strategies, our basic security is built on the assumption that the United States will maintain a permanent lead in a broad range of advanced industrial technologies. Loss of leading-edge capacity in chip making would quickly translate into a loss of diplomatic and strategic bargaining chips.

This argument suggests that commercial development often drives military capability. It is the reverse of the common notion that military needs drive commercial development. If the United States had to support the full weight of a vast arsenal economy, we would become vis à vis Japan not so different from the arsenal Soviet economy vis à vis that of the United States.

Manufacturing and wealth

Sometimes new notions capture the public fancy, resonate to some element of our experience, and color the way we see the world. The concept of a "post-industrial" society is such a notion. But it also obscures the precise nature of changes in the US economy and what they mean.

Things have changed: production workers go home cleaner; more and more workers leave offices rather than assembly lines. And the organization of society has changed along with the technologies of product and production.

But the relationship of changes in technology and society to changes in the fundamentals of economics – the process of creating wealth – is less clear. There is not yet, nor is there likely to be in the near future, a post-industrial economy. The division of labor has become infinitely more elaborate and the production process far less direct – involving ever more specialized services as well as goods and materials located far from the traditional scene of production. However, the key generator of wealth for this vastly expanded division of labor remains production. The United States is shifting not out of industry into services but from one kind of industrial economy to another.

Insisting that a shift to services or high technology is "natural" is irresponsible analysis and perverse policy. The competitiveness of the US economy – the ability to maintain high and rising wages – is not likely to be enhanced by abandoning production to others. Instead of ceding production, public policy should actively aim to convert low-productivity, low-wage, low-skill ·production processes into high-technology, high-skill, high-wage activities – whether they are included in the manufacturing unit itself or counted largely as service firms.

America's declining competitiveness is troubling precisely because emerging fundamental changes in production technologies and the extent and forms of international competition are likely to prove enduring. The international hierarchy of wealth and power is being reshuffled, and it is happening fast and now.

Technology in Services

James Brian Quinn, Jordan J. Baruch, and Penny Cushman Paquette

Taking the opposite view to Cohen and Zysman, Quinn et al. argue in this major study that many service industries are every bit as large-scale and technology-intensive as manufacturing. Indeed, most of the economic growth and most of the business opportunities over the next two decades will arise from the application of IT in the service sector. A US economy dominated by services, they say, can support real increases in income and wealth for years to come. Quinn and Paquette are at the Amos Tuck School of Business Administration, Dartmouth College, while Baruch is a consultant. Reprinted from Scientific American, *vol. 257 (6), December 1987.*

In the decades since World War II the provision of services has displaced manufacturing as the largest element in the economy of virtually all advanced nations. In the United States the service industries, broadly defined, now account for 71 percent (or $2,996 billion) of the gross national product and 75 percent (or 81.4 million) of all jobs. The services sector continues to grow, although there are signs that its rate of growth may be slowing. In contrast, total employment in manufacturing has declined slightly over the past 15 years; although manufacturing output has continued to grow in real terms, some traditional and highly visible industries, such as basic steel and automaking, have experienced pronounced declines in both output and employment.

For the past two centuries it has been new technologies in agriculture and manufacturing that have driven economic growth and created steady increases in US standards of living. What will be the long-term effect of technologies in the service industries? Can they have similar favorable consequences for the economy and for human welfare? To examine these questions we undertook a three-year study under the auspices of the National Academy of Engineering, with the support of the Bell & Howell Company, the Banker's Trust Company, the Royal Bank of Canada, Braxton Associates and the Bell Atlanticom Corporation.

This article is an early report on our findings. What may come as a surprise is the finding that many service industries are as large-scale, as capital-intensive and as thoroughly grounded in technology as manufacturing is. Our statistical data bases and case studies also demonstrate that new technologies can affect entire service industries intensely, and indeed restructure them, with consequences that radiate throughout the economy.

The technologies that are now transforming the service industries have profound implications for US manufacturing, economic stability and growth, for national and regional job markets and for the position of the United States in world politics and international competition. Perhaps more important for the future is the fact that technology, properly applied, can enhance productivity, quality and economic output in the services sector just as it has in manufacturing. This means that a US economy dominated by services can continue to support real increases in income and wealth for a very prolonged period.

What is meant by "services"? A clarification may help to dispel a number of misconceptions. Most authorities consider the services sector to include all economic activities whose output is not a physical product or construction, is generally consumed at the time it is produced and provides added value in forms (such as convenience, amusement, timeliness, comfort or health) that are essentially intangible concerns of its first purchaser. A raw material or manufactured product, in contrast, may retain its value when it is transported, stored or resold. The *Economist* has more simply defined services as "anything sold in trade that could not be dropped on your foot."

People alarmed at the growth of the services sector often caricature it as merely "making hamburgers" or "taking in laundry." Such services do fall within the broad definition, but so do activities that fulfill many much more basic needs: communications, transportation, finance, health care and education, to name only a few. Efficient and high-quality services are crucial not only to consumers but also to product manufacturers. Clearly an automobile manufacturer requires financial services to provide capital for its production facilities, communication and transportation services to coordinate and move its parts and finished products, and distribution and retail networks to present the products to consumers and to service them.

Why have services gained such importance in recent years? Steady productivity increases in manufacturing and agriculture – brought about largely by technology – have meant that it takes ever fewer hours of work to produce or buy a pound of food, an automobile, a piece of furniture or a home appliance. For example, in 1956 it took about 125 hours of work to buy a kitchen stove; in 1986 it took 41 hours. At the same time the demand for goods was capped somewhat: the average person can eat only so many pounds of food in a day and utilize only so many cars, sofas or washing machines. As the demand for individual products reached such constraints, the utility of other possible purchases, in the form of services, grew apace.

Growth in services, then, is a natural effect of increasing productivity in manufacturing, but constantly improving service technologies have also helped to shift economic activity towards services. They have expanded the versatility of existing services and made totally new types of services practical. Jet aircraft have radically improved the efficiency and convenience of long-distance travel and freight movements, opening entirely new markets and providing new options for siting production facilities. Revolutionary technologies for diagnosis and treatment have enlarged the dimensions of human health care. New methods for handling fragile, perishable or volatile goods have vastly extended the geographic horizons of international trade and the scope of its products. Electronic information and communication technologies have stimulated innovation in virtually all service areas – notably in retailing and wholesale trade, engineering design, financial services, communications and entertainment.

The burgeoning of the services sector disturbs many who hold a point of view – possibly first articulated by Adam Smith – that services are somehow less important than products on a scale of human needs. Perhaps in elemental societies it is true that production of food, shelter and clothing must at first take precedence over other demands. As soon as there is local self-sufficiency or a small surplus in a single product, however, any extra production has little value in the absence of storage, distribution and transportation systems for reaching new marketplaces – all service activities. In most emerging societies services such as health care, religion, banking, entertainment, trading, law and the arts quickly become more highly valued (high-priced or capable of generating great wealth) than basic production. And in affluent societies it is clear that a nation's wealth is measured as often by the level of its arts, education, public health and social services as by its sheer abundance of physical goods.

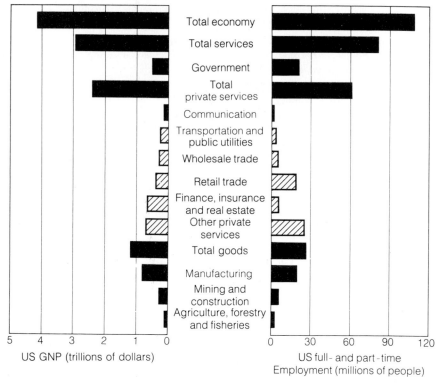

Figure 3.1   Scale of services sector is suggested by a comparison of the contribution to the gross national product (*left*) and employment (*right*) of service (*black*) and goods-producing (*shaded*) industries in 1986, according to national income accounts. Services have long surpassed manufacturing: now individual service sector categories rival manufacturing as a whole in size.

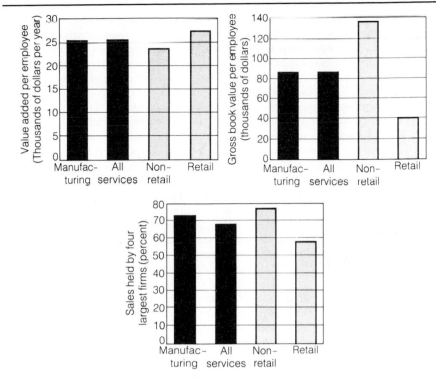

Figure 3.2 Stereotyped view of services as being labor-intensive and small in scale is challenged by the evidence. The level of value added per employee (*left*) in large service companies is comparable to that of similar manufacturing enterprises, suggesting that services need be no more labor-intensive than manufacturing. In this survey services equaled or exceeded manufacturing in capital intensity (*middle*) and in concentration (*right*), a measure of the dominance of companies large enough to invest in new technology. All three indicators suggest that service companies utilize technology in a major way. Data from the Profit Impact of Management Strategy (PIMS) data base of the Strategic Planning Institute were analyzed by Christopher E. Gagnon.

Even products themselves generally owe their value to the services they can deliver. An automobile delivers transportation and convenience services. A television set has value because it can present broadcast entertainment: another service. A computer diskette's primary value lies not in its plastic base and magnetic coating but in the software programs or data sets it stores: more services. Indeed, in many cases products and services are interchangeable. A home washing machine (a product) can substitute for the use of a laundromat (a service), a frozen dinner for a meal in a restaurant or CAD/CAM software for additional production equipment.

At its core the professed alarm about the growing dominance of the services sector may reflect a genuine doubt that services can sustain the increases in real income and personal wealth that have been hallmarks of the industrial era. There is serious concern that the kinds of productivity increases automation has wrought in manufacturing cannot be replicated in services. Continuous increases in productivity will be required if there is to be noninflationary growth in incomes; otherwise higher wages will only increase the relative amount of money competing for available goods or services.

Can technology boost productivity in services as it had in manufacturing? To evaluate the potential one must understand the structure of service industries today. For new technology to have high and favorable impact the industries receiving it generally must have the scale, capital intensity and technical sophistication to be able to apply technology effectively. Services, in the popular stereotype, are small-scale, labor-intensive, relatively unsophisticated undertakings that make few large equipment investments.

This stereotype may be valid for some household-service and retail activities, but it clearly does not hold for the communications, transportation, pipeline, health-care and electric-utility systems that make up much of the US services sector. Increasingly some other major service industries, including banking, entertainment, mass retailing, financial services, car rental and package or message delivery, are also investing heavily in technology.

Stephen Roach of Morgan Stanley and Company has found that total capital investment, in particular high-technology investment, per "information worker" has been rising rapidly since the mid-1960s and now exceeds that for workers in basic industrial activities. Similarly, in a sampling of 145 industries that were analyzed by Ronald E. Kutscher and Jerome A. Mark of the Bureau of Labor Statistics, nearly half of the 30 most capital-intensive industries were services. Our own analyses of the Strategic Planning Institute's Profit Impact of Management Strategy (PIMS) data base confirm these findings.

PIMS and Fortune 500 data also suggest that major service enterprises are comparable in relative size and profitability to major manufacturers. The large service companies clearly have the financial power to buy technology as it becomes available and needed. In fact, many of these companies now play a crucial role in the creation and diffusion of new technologies for both products and services. Citicorp, for example, helped to develop and introduce the first automated teller machines; the Federal Express Corporation made major innovations in package-sorting, -handling and -tracking equipment that other express companies and materials-handling concerns have now begun to duplicate.

Can technology adequately improve productivity in the services sector, however? Productivity in services is notoriously difficult to measure. For most services it is harder to identify a unit of output than it is in manufacturing, not only because there are no physical goods to count or weigh but also because output must be defined with reference to quality too, and that is even more ephemeral in services than in manufacturing. How, for example, does one evaluate the productivity of a medical procedure that may consume fewer resources or take less time than its predecessor but may subject the patient to greater pain or risk? Is the number of letters delivered per postal worker an effective measure of productivity if such "productivity" means that more letters are lost or delayed? One should be extremely cautious in interpreting aggregate productivity data about services.

Nevertheless, if a customer has a choice between a given service and a competing service or between the service and a product that performs the same function, the revenue the service brings to its producers (its "sales value") offers a much better indication of both the quantity and the quality of output. Comparing this sales value with inputs of labor or capital can often provide a reasonable measure of an individual service industry's productivity. Bureau of Labor Statistics data for the past 35 years suggest that some individual service industries (such as communications, utilities or wholesale trade) can sustain rates of productivity growth as high as those in manufacturing for extended periods. Although data on US services productivity growth from 1980 through 1985 are less encouraging in the aggregate, rates of productivity growth vary widely among individual service industries, just as they do in manufacturing. Some service industries have outperformed some manufacturing industries, and vice versa.

In a recent study of the British economy, Richard Barras of the Technical Change Centre in London has shown that services-sector productivity (measured as the real value of output per employee) grew at 2.9 percent per year between 1960 and 1981; manufacturing productivity, according to the same measure, grew by less than 1 percent per year. The data suggest there is no inherent reason individual service industries cannot keep up with – or outperform – individual product industries in productivity increases.

Investment in technology has also soared among service producers since 1975. Companies in financial services and wholesale trade, for example, have made large purchases of computers and communications equipment; providers of health care have invested heavily in new medical technologies and information systems. Such technologies have precipitated major structural changes and employment adjustments that, after a period of adaptation, should substantially boost both the quality of output and productivity.

Other structural changes brought about by service technologies are already apparent. In industry after industry we examined there were similar patterns of change. Typically, major new service technologies at first created new economies of scale, generally favoring an industry's larger enterprises. Middle-size service enterprises, unable to afford such technologies themselves, were often forced to merge into larger companies, identify a protected niche in the marketplace or go out of business. Increases in the scale and relative power of larger companies in transportation, financial services, health care and banking readily attest to such trends. At the same time, however, smaller companies often flourish because of the countervailing effects of new data-management and communications systems. They make it possible for small companies to serve remote areas or specialized niches on their own, or to link up in coalitions or networks sharing data and resources with larger enterprises.

Once they have been properly installed, the same technologies that created the new economies of scale often generate a secondary effect that might be called "economies of scope." Enterprises exploiting the new technologies find they can handle a much wider array of data, variety of services and range of customers than before without significant cost increases. Banks (Citicorp), airlines (American Airlines), retailers (Sears) and bank-travel services (American Express) have used newly installed information and distribution facilities to extend their presence into a broad range of new activities – in the case of Sears, for example, into insurance, real estate, brokerage activities, financial services and credit cards.

The recent history of the securities industry exemplifies both major effects of new service technologies. In the early 1970s the volume of shares being traded (then between 10 and 12 million shares daily) began to overwhelm the securities trading houses, which were still

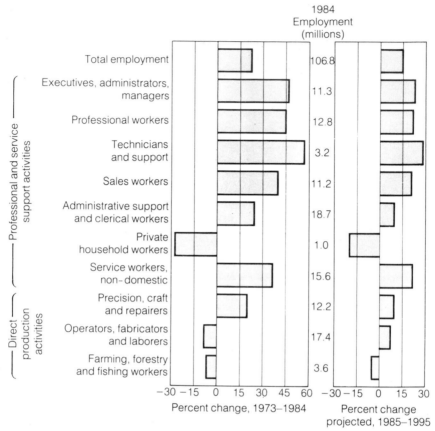

Figure 3.3   Job growth in various employment categories is shown for the decade ending in 1984 and projected for the decade ending in 1995. Service-related jobs have grown more rapidly than blue-collar production jobs; the more highly paid professional categories have accounted for much of that growth. Many service-related jobs are actually in manufacturing and have been responsible for much of the increase in output value in the goods-producing sector. The trends shown here are expected to continue. The data are from a study done by George T. Silvestri and John M. Lukasiewicz of the US Bureau of Labor Statistics.

handling and delivering each certificate physically. The major Wall Street firms formed what became the Depository Trust Company to collect and keep virtually all traded certificates under one roof and transfer their ownership electronically. The resulting technologies created new economies of scale for their sponsors but also forced many small and middle-size brokerage houses, which could not afford automation on their own, to merge or to affiliate with larger houses.

The surviving houses found that the in-house electronic systems they had developed for automated trading enabled them not only to cope with larger numbers of transactions (now more than 200 million per day) but also to provide novel specialized "products" and services (such as "cash management" accounts) for their customers. Since their installed electronics systems allowed these companies to present this greater variety of products at low additional cost (the essence of economies of scope), many of them started to decentralize again: to develop networks of affiliated local offices around the country to make the most of their new opportunities.

In the course of such restructurings, traditional industry boundaries have tended to blur or disappear. For example, as their new electronic technologies enabled the various financial institutions (banks, brokerage houses and insurance companies) to carry out easily functions traditionally reserved through regulation to their competitors, they began to seek new opportunities through deregulation. Soon consumers began to use financial-services houses quite interchangeably.

Similarly, airlines, hotels and tour operators have all begun to collaborate in selling vacation "packages" and replacing traditional middlemen by means of electronic technologies that make direct reservations and ticketing possible. Even the boundaries between public and private services are eroding, as town and local governments look to private companies for maintenance, health care, transportation, accounting and other functions they had long provided themselves.

What does growth and structural change in the services sector mean for employment and international trade? Perhaps the most pressing concern is jobs. Can the service industries provide both the quantity and the quality of jobs the US needs for continuous growth in its economy and in its base of human skills? In recent years services have provided the engine for employment expansion throughout the country: between 1976 and 1986 they accounted for 85 percent of the new jobs in the private sector. No state registered a decline in service jobs, whereas manufacturing jobs shifted markedly among regions, states and industries. Today every state has more service jobs than it has manufacturing, mining, construction and agricultural jobs combined.

But what kinds of jobs are being created? On the average, hourly wages are somewhat lower in services than in manufacturing. Some observers, including Barry Bluestone and Bennett Harrison in a recent report to Congress, suggest that most new jobs in the US economy have been in lower wage categories and that the number of workers in the middle-income brackets is declining. On the other hand, Neal Rosenthal of the Bureau of Labor Statistics has reported that during the decade from 1973 through 1982 (a period when service jobs represented a growing percentage of total employment) the number of middle-income jobs declined only slightly, whereas the number of lower-income jobs fell by a much larger amount.

The evidence on recent wage trends, then, is somewhat ambiguous. More important is the future. The relation of pay scales in services to those in manufacturing will depend in large part on how rapidly technology can improve productivity in each sector. The more productivity grows in either sector, the more latitude that sector will have for higher wages. Rapid productivity increases and demand for higher skills will probably continue to keep wages in individual service industries (such as transportation or public utilities, including communications) higher than in some manufacturing fields. Moreover, the wages and work conditions many future service jobs offer should easily surpass the conditions employees in distressed manufacturing industries would have to accept to keep their companies from relocating production overseas. In either event, developing the services sector could be a better way to sustain a high US standard of living than subsidizing certain outmoded manufacturing industries.

Services have a demonstrated advantage as a source of employment: they are far more resistant to recessions than goods-producing industries. In business cycles from 1948 through 1980, US services employment actually advanced at an average annual rate of 2.1 percent during economic contractions. In these same recessions employment in the goods-producing sector declined by an average of 8.3 percent. In Canada the picture has been much the same: services employment declined only during the deepest recessions.

If services really are in some sense less vital than manufactures, one would expect people to give up their services first during a recession, thereby eliminating jobs in the sector. Actually much consumer spending for services seems to be less discretionary than spending for products. Although people may go to movies, restaurants or hairdressers less often during recessions, they seem reluctant to give up their telephone, health-care, education, banking or utility services. Instead they tend to postpone expenditures for durable goods.

The demand for certain services may even grow during recessions; people may forsake driving for public transportation, for example. And continuing population growth during these periods tends to keep increasing the demand for such services as education, health care and fire and police protection.

Even when demand for services does decline temporarily, employment can remain relatively stable. Because a substantial fraction of the income of many service workers comes from part-time work, tips, commissions or profit sharing, income levels can contract more easily during recessions without comparable contraction of the workforce. In addition many service enterprises, unlike manufacturing industries, do not build up inventories when demand slows. Hence when demand reasserts itself, there is no pause in service rehiring, whereas product sales merely deplete old inventories.

In addition to reducing the depth of recessions and their impact on employment levels, the services sector helps to make them shorter. Stable employment in the service industries provides wages that preserve a large, continuing market for manufactured consumer goods. Moreover, service industries provide major markets for complex technological products. According to Roach, the useful life of capital equipment in service businesses tends to be shorter than it is in manufacturing. One reason is that services rely heavily on communications and computer technologies, in which rapid technological advances quickly lead to obsolescence. Consequently the replacement of capital equipment is usually more constant in services. Many service enterprises therefore continue to invest during recessions, enabling manufacturers of capital goods to recover more quickly as well.

The large and stable markets that service companies create for manufactured goods is only one of several strong linkages between manufacturing and the services sector. Some studies suggest that 80 percent of the communications technologies and information-management systems sold in the US in 1982 went to service enterprises. A comparable study in the UK showed that service businesses were the buyers of 70 percent of the computer systems sold there in 1984.

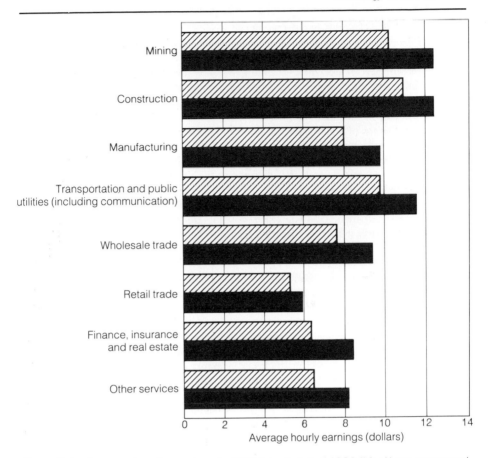

Figure 3.4 Average hourly earnings in 1981 (*shaded*) and 1986 (*black*) are compared for goods-producing industries and services. Average wages are higher in mining, construction, and manufacturing than in services, but some service industries wages equal or exceed those in manufacturing. The service industries paying the most tend to be ones in which the intensive application of technology has increased output value.

Similarly, manufacturing concerns are also major consumers of virtually all modern services. Manufacturing activities clearly depend heavily on communications, financing, transportation and waste-handling services, to name only a few essentials. Manufacturers also pay for their employees' health care, retirement and life insurance – either directly, through insurance policies or indirectly through wages. When new technologies help to provide such services more efficiently, they obviously lower manufacturers' costs for directly purchased services; to the extent that efficiencies in services lower employees' living costs, they can help to reduce wage demands.

Yet the interdependence of manufacturing and services is even more intricate. Services are not simply external adjuncts to the manufacturing process, bought to keep a factory going or to get goods to consumers; they are intimately embodied in the manufactured object itself. For the manufacturing sector as a whole (according to studies done by the Office of the US Trade Representative and the National Association of Accountants) service activities within the producing company itself create between 75 and 85 percent of all the value the average manufacturer adds in making its product.

This means that the price a product can command (whether it is a car, a processed food or a home appliance) reflects the product's content of raw materials and direct labor less than it does the characteristic, quality and availability of the product, which are created by research, product design, quality control and marketing. In industries such as automobiles or pharmaceuticals the cost of such services in a product can be from three to ten times its direct labor costs and can provide virtually all the perceived distinction between it and competitive products. Clearly, therefore, an important way for US manufacturers to improve their competitive position is to increase the effectiveness of their own internal service activities.

Computers, communications technologies and rapid-response inventory-control and distribution systems can also help manufacturers to exploit the expanding demand for differentiated and customized products. Affluent consumers increasingly want products that reflect their particular tastes, and they want immediate delivery rather than a wait of weeks or even months. Not surprisingly, both industrial and commercial customers also want a larger variety of products to be delivered more quickly and on a more precise schedule – a "just in time" approach, which can substantially lower inventory costs.

Ever more frequently, success in manufacturing requires not only flexible facilities for turning out a wide variety of products at low cost but also the capacity to acquire and respond to rapid feedback from the marketplace. The service technologies that make possible improved collection, analysis and transmittal of data about customer preferences have become crucial strategic weapons. For example, at the end of each day a national women's specialty retailer, Limited Stores, electronically gathers and aggregates that day's sales details (items, sizes, colors, styles and so on) from its entire network of stores. The information is converted into orders that are instantly transmitted to its manufacturer-suppliers all over the world. The orders specify precise deliveries, many of which depend on transpacific jumbo-jet flights – to defined distribution sites within a few days.

Today many of the factories supplying such large retail chains are in Asia or developing countries. Yet rising demand for faster response and more customized products offers potential advantages for US manufacturers. A domestic manufacturer with sensitive links between its own flexible production system and its distribution and customer networks should be able both to respond more quickly to the market and to enjoy lower transportation costs than foreign competitors.

In the case of heavy, bulky or complex products such as automobiles, it could even become impossible for overseas producers of the more standardized lines to compete here against responsive, well-integrated US manufacturing and retailing systems. As a case in point, the Honda Motor Company's decision to produce increasing numbers of cars in the US coincided with its introduction of a much wider variety of styles and options to the US market. Its US

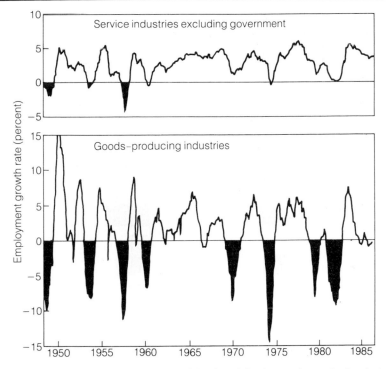

Figure 3.5 Service industry jobs are stabler than jobs in goods-producing industries. During four recessions between 1948 and 1961, employment in private services fell (*shaded areas*) an average of 1 percent; in goods-producing industries the average drop was 7.2 percent. During four recessions between 1969 and 1982, services employment actually rose an average of 1 percent; in goods-producing industries it dropped an average of 7.9 percent. Growth in services largely offset manufacturing declines, so that total nonfarm employment losses averaged only 1.6 percent in these last four recessions. Geoffrey H. Moore of the Columbia University Graduate School of Business did the study.

manufacturing base was essential for the other key element in this strategy: fast delivery of its full product range, which would have been impossible if Honda had continued to make cars only in Japan.

Many other foreign investors are also seeing the potential of more direct connections with US services. Technologies have made it possible for US service companies to grow to a scale where they are attractive acquisitions for foreign competitors. The same technologies enable the acquirers to manage worldwide service networks from their home bases. Total foreign investment in the United States has ballooned 46.7 percent since 1982, much of it in services, notably in the areas of communications, finance and distribution.

Service technologies are also causing another profound change in the worldwide competitive

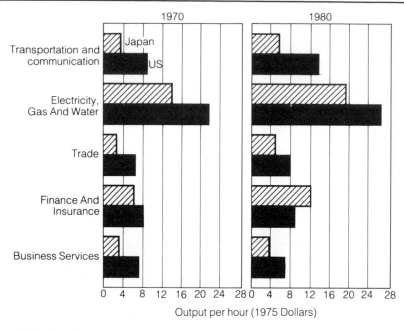

Figure 3.6 Productivity of US service industries, measured as the market value of output per hour of labor, has exceeded that of Japanese services except in finance and insurance. In addition to making service industries more competitive, service technologies reduce costs and improve quality in production, distribution, and sale of manufactures.

situation. Computer and communications technologies are rapidly integrating the world's financial centers into a single financial marketplace. The flow of money from country to country has become largely independent of the movement of goods or trade. Whereas world trade in goods and services amounts to only between $3 and $4 trillion per year, the financial transactions handled by just one intermediary, the Clearing House for International Payments, totaled $105 trillion in 1986, and transactions in early 1987 were proceeding at a rate of $200 trillion per year. Instead of following goods, these vast sums now flow toward the highest available real interest rates or toward safer, more stable economic and political conditions.

Hence the value of a nation's currency increasingly depends less on its position in international trade than on the fiscal or monetary policies of many governments and on banking decisions and other world events that affect foreign investment. In recent years exchange rates for the dollar against even stable currencies such as the yen, the mark or the Swiss franc have fluctuated by close to 50 percent, not so much because of trade choices as because of fiscal and monetary decisions. The effect of such fluctuations on the relative cost of a product being sold in international trade have become so great that they can dwarf the impact of a producer's internal productivity improvements or other managerial decisions. Even well-run Japanese companies find it difficult to compete when the price of the yen – and hence their production costs in Japan – can jump 43 percent in 18 months in relation to their competitors' costs or their customers' buying power.

On the other hand, most governments, banks and large companies now have much freer access to all the major money markets. As a result it is becoming increasingly difficult for a single nation to maintain exceptionally low domestic interest rates in order to stimulate economic development – a policy followed by the United States in earlier years and by Japan more recently. Today an artificially low interest rate simply drives capital out of the country in search of higher interest rates – and at the same time it attracts foreign borrowers, whose demand tends to drive the manipulated interest rate up again. As variations in the cost of capital among nations are decreased by these forces, countries burdened by higher labor and materials costs, such as the United States and Japan, will feel even greater pressure from foreign manufacturers.

In this environment innovation in services offers one of the few strategies for keeping the domestic economy competitive. First, higher productivity in services will lower the cost or increase the value of the large part of the GNP generated by the services sector. Second, more efficiently produced services will hold down the large component of each manufactured product's cost that reflects its services content. It is heartening to note that in most service industries US productivity is higher than Japan's, but innovative and aggressive efforts will be necessary in order to stay ahead.

Service technologies, then, may help to support US manufacturing against foreign incursions. Can they also enable services themselves to make a major contribution to the improvement of the US trade balance? It is worth noting that unlike merchandise, in which there has been a trade deficit in half of the past 26 years (it reached $146 billion in 1986), services have consistently shown a positive trade balance. Since 1981, however, the US advantage in services has become more tenuous. Indeed, data from the International Monetary Fund show that the US share of world service exports fell from 23.8 percent in 1970 to 19.2 percent in 1985.

What does it mean to export a service? Relatively few services are produced in one country and then sold (as a software program is) for its full value abroad. More typical is the example of a US bank's Middle Eastern branch participating in a large transaction there, or a US company providing overnight package deliveries overseas. Much of the income generated by such service exports goes into salaries and overheads abroad and remains in the foreign country. In the case of an automobile export, trade data reflect the car's wholesale sales value: export data on services often recognize only the fees or profits that can be repatriated to the home office.

Hence the volume of US international service transactions would have to expand enormously to eliminate the nation's huge merchandise trade deficit. A further complication is the fact that US Government trade-data recognize only about 40 categories of services (in contrast to some 10,000 merchandise items), so that the data may not capture many important service exports. Many observers now think the total volume of US services trade, both export and import, has been seriously understated. Attempting to improve on the official figures, the Office of Technology Assessment estimated that in 1984 the US exported between $69 and $91 billion in services and imported between $57 and $74 billion; the official figures were $43.8 and $41.5 billion respectively. Even interpreted optimistically, these figures still do not come close to covering current merchandise trade deficits.

In individual categories the US services-trade situation varies greatly. In some areas, such as public accounting, law, communications and international finance, US companies enjoy a strong position in the global market. Some individual US service companies, such as Citicorp, AT&T and Federal Express, enjoy economies of scale and scope that few international competitors can equal. Their aggressive application of proprietary technologies has forced domestic competitors to follow suit, thereby improving the comparative position of both their own industries and those they support in international trade. In other service industries, such as international air travel, the US has been faltering. The once dominant US carriers, Pan American and TWA, have done badly, whereas competitors such as Japan Air Lines, Swissair and Singapore Airlines have thrived.

The causes of such shifts are always complicated, but much of the credit for the foreign airlines' gains must go to their governments' strong support and their own long-term investment in equipment and exceptional attention to the quality of customer care on flights. Much thoughtful customer-oriented management and serious long-term investment in technology will be essential if US service enterprises are to forestall and defeat further competitive incursions into both their domestic and their international markets. With more than 70 percent of its total economy at stake, this is a battle the US cannot afford to lose.

Enlightened government policies can also help. US deregulation of services has already stimulated substantial restructuring and application of technology in US service industries, although this has sometimes been at the cost of extensive customer inconvenience. Perhaps in time the more open competition will prompt US service companies to avoid the complacency, concern with short-term gains, inattention to quality and emphasis on economies of scale (rather than on customers' concerns) that earlier undercut US competitiveness in manufacturing.

The fact is that deregulation itself has created a need for further social innovations. Already new requirements for product labeling, financial disclosure and self-reporting have been found to be necessary to replace, respectively, the direct regulation of some over-the-counter drugs, SEC registrations and detailed FAA approvals of airline routes and schedules. Future dynamics will undoubtedly call for even more imaginative solutions.

The overwhelming evidence is that the United States can bolster its standard of living, the stability of its job markets and some aspects of its international competitive position by developing its services sector effectively. That conclusion still leaves some nagging concerns, notably the sense that an economy dominated by services could weaken the United States in world affairs. There is no doubt that a drop in manufacturing and in raw-materials production beyond some point could decrease US flexibility and capabilities in defense and impair the nation's bargaining power in world affairs.

None the less, over the next two decades most of the nation's growth and many of its greatest opportunities for entrepreneurship and application of new technologies will arise in the services sector, as they have in the past 20 years. We should not fear an economy dominated by services, or deride it. Rather we should fear the possibility that we may misunderstand the services sector, underdevelop it or mismanage it, at the same time attempting to shore up certain troubled manufacturing areas at great corporate and national cost.

Selected Further Reading

These selective lists do not include books and articles excerpted in the text or referred to in the Editor's Introduction. Nor do they include items which appeared before 1984. For earlier publications, see the lists of further reading in *The Microelectronics Revolution* (1980), *The Information Technology Revolution* (1985) and *High-Tech Society* (1987). For the very latest publications, readers are advised to monitor the magazines and journals which figure prominently in the lists.

General overviews

Frank Blackler and David Oborne (eds), *Information Technology and People* (British Psychological Society, Leicester, 1987).
James N. Danziger, "Social Science and the Social Impacts of Computer Technology," *Social Science Quarterly*, vol. 66, 1985, pp. 3–21.
Ruth Finnegan, Graeme Salaman and Kenneth Thompson (eds), *Information Technology: Social Issues* (Hodder and Stoughton, Sevenoaks, UK, 1987).
Bruce R. Guile (ed.), *Information Technologies and Social Transformation* (National Academy Press, Washington, DC, 1985).
David Lyon, *The Information Society: Issues and Illusions* (Polity Press, Cambridge, UK and New York, 1988).
Carl Mitcham and Alois Huning (eds), *Philosophy and Technology II: Information Technology and Computers in Theory and Practice* (D. Reidel, Dordrecht, Netherlands, 1986).
Richard S. Rosenberg, *Computers and the Information Society* (Wiley, New York, 1986).
Christopher Rowe, *People and Chips: The Human Implications of Information Technology* (Paradigm Publishing, London, 1986).
Frederick Williams (ed.), *Measuring the Information Society* (Sage, Newbury Park, CA, 1988).

Optimists

"The Third Industrial Revolution," *Impact of Science on Society*, vol. 37 (2), 1987.
Edward Cornish (ed.), *The Computerized Society: Living and Working in an Electronic Age* (World Future Society, Bethesda, MD, 1985).

Akira Ishikawa, *Future Computer and Information Systems: The Uses of the Next Generation Computer and Information Systems* (Praeger, New York, 1986).

Pamela McCorduck, *The Universal Machine: Confessions of a Technological Optimist* (McGraw-Hill, New York, 1985).

James Martin, *Technology's Crucible: An Exploration of the Explosive Impact of Technology on Society During the Next Four Decades* (Prentice-Hall, Englewood Cliffs, NJ, 1987).

Joseph F. Traub (ed.), *Cohabiting with Computers* (William Kaufmann, Los Altos, CA, 1985).

Pessimists

Craig Brod, *Technostress: The Human Cost of the Computer Revolution* (Addison-Wesley, Reading, MA, 1984).

Orrin E. Klapp, *Overload and Boredom: Essays on the Quality of Life in the Information Society* (Greenwood Press, Westport, CT, 1986).

Jerry Mander, "Six Grave Doubts About Computers," *Whole Earth Review* (44), January, 1985.

Theodore Roszak, *The Cult of Information* (Pantheon Books, New York, 1986).

Herbert I. Schiller, *Information and the Crisis Economy* (Ablex, Norwood, NJ, 1984).

Jennifer Daryl Slack and Fred Fejes (eds), *The Ideology of the Information Age* (Ablex, Norwood, NJ, 1987).

Tony Solomonides and Les Levidow (eds), *Compulsive Technology: Computers as Culture* (Free Association Books, London, 1985).

Michael Traber (ed.), *The Myth of the Information Revolution: Social and Ethical Implications of Communication Technology* (Sage, Newbury Park, CA, 1986).

Frank Webster and Kevin Robins, *Information Technology: A Luddite Analysis* (Ablex, Norwood, NJ, 1986).

"Post-industrial Society"

Richard J. Badham, *Theories of Post-Industrial Society* (Croom Helm, Beckenham, UK, 1986).

Daniel Bell, "The World and the United States in 2013," *Daedalus*, vol. 116 (3), Summer 1987.

Selwyn Enzer, *Working Our Way to the Twenty-First Century*, Report F-60 (Center for Futures Research, University of Southern California, Los Angeles, CA, 1985).

Benjamin T. Hourani, "Towards the 21st Century: The Organization of Power in Post-industrial Society," *Science and Public Policy*, vol. 14 (4), August 1987.

Sar A. Levitan, "Beyond 'Trendy' Forecasts," *The Futurist*, November–December 1987.

Ian Miles, "The New Post-industrial State," *Futures*, vol. 17 (6), December 1985.

M. R. Rubin, "US Information Economy Matures," *Transnational Data and Communications Report*, June 1986.

A. J. Veal, *Leisure and the Future* (Allen and Unwin, London and Boston, MA, 1987).

Murray L. Weidenbaum, "The Business Landscape in 2001," *Across the Board*, vol. 23 (5), May 1986.

Recent Developments in IT

"Advanced Computing," special issue of *Scientific American*, vol. 257 (4), October 1987, including keynote article by Abraham Peled, "The Next Computer Revolution."

"Frontiers in Computers," special issue of *Science*, vol. 231 (4741), February 28, 1986.

"Parallelism," special issue of *Communications of the ACM*, vol. 29 (12), December 1986.

Yaser S. Abu-Mostafa and Demetri Psaltis, "Optical Neural Computers," *Scientific American*, vol. 256 (3), March 1987.

William F. Allman, "Designing Computers That Think the Way We Do," *Technology Review*, May–June, 1987.

C. David Chaffee, *The Rewiring of America* (Academic Press, New York, 1988).

Michael L. Dertouzos, "The Multiprocessor Revolution: Harnessing Computers Together," *Technology Review*, vol. 84 (2), February–March 1986.

Philip Elmer-DeWitt et al., "Fast and Smart: Designers Race to Build the Supercomputers of the Future," *Time*, March 28, 1988.

Jeff Hecht, *Understanding Fiber Optics* (Howard W. Sams, New York, 1987).

W. Daniel Hillis, "The Connection Machine," *Scientific American*, June 1987.

Sidney Karin and Norris Parker Smith, *The Supercomputer Era* (Harcourt Brace Jovanovich, New York, 1987).

Steven Lambert (ed.), *CD ROM: The New Papyrus* (Microsoft Press, Redmond, WA, 1986).

John S. Mayo, "New Developments in Computer and Communications Technologies," *Vital Speeches of the Day*, vol. 53 (16), June 1, 1987.

Jeremy Peckham, "When Machines Have Ears," *New Scientist*, December 4, 1986.

Part Two: Computers and People

4 Minds and Machines: The AI Debate

Why Computers May Never Think Like People

Hubert and Stuart Dreyfus

We begin with a powerful critique of "artificial intelligence" (AI), taken from the authors' book Mind Over Machine *(The Free Press, New York and Basil Blackwell, Oxford, 1986). In this excerpt, the Dreyfus brothers argue that AI has failed to live up to its promise and there is no evidence that it ever will. Computers can be useful tools in many ways, but they will never replace human intelligence and expertise, which is intuitive. Moreover, it would be positively dangerous to leave crucial military decisions to machines rather than humans, say the authors. Hubert Dreyfus is Professor of Philosophy and Stuart Dreyfus is Professor of Industrial Engineering at the University of California, Berkeley. This adaptation first appeared in* Technology Review, *January 1986.*

Scientists who stand at the forefront of artificial intelligence (AI) have long dreamed of autonomous "thinking" machines that are free of human control. And now they believe we are not far from realizing that dream. As Marvin Minsky, a well-known AI professor at MIT, recently put it: "Today our robots are like toys. They do only the simple things they're programmed to. But clearly they're about to cross the edgeless line past which they'll do the things we are programmed to."

Patrick Winston, Minsky's successor as head of the MIT AI Laboratory, agrees: "Just as the Wright Brothers at Kitty Hawk in 1903 were on the right track to the 747s of today, so artificial intelligence, with its attempt to formalize common-sense understanding, is on the way to fully intelligent machines."

Encouraged by such optimistic pronouncements, the US Department of Defense (DOD) is sinking millions of dollars into developing fully autonomous war machines that will respond to a crisis without human intervention. Business executives are investing in "expert" systems whose wisdom they hope will equal, if not surpass, that of their top managers. And AI entrepreneurs are talking of "intelligent systems" that will perform better than we can – in the home, in the classroom, and at work.

But no matter how many billions of dollars the Defense Department or any other agency invests in AI, there is almost no likelihood that scientists can develop machines capable of making intelligent decisions. After 25 years of research, AI has failed to live up to its promise, and there is no evidence that it ever will. In fact, machine intelligence will probably never replace human intelligence simply because we ourselves are not "thinking machines." Human beings have an intuitive intelligence that "reasoning" machines simply cannot match.

Military and civilian managers may see this obvious shortcoming and refrain from deploying such "logic" machines. However, once various groups have invested vast sums in developing these machines, the temptation to justify this expense by installing questionable AI technologies will be enormous. The dangers of turning over the battlefield completely to machines are obvious. But it would also be a mistake to replace skilled air-traffic controllers, seasoned business managers, and master teachers with computers that cannot come close to their level of expertise. Computers that "teach" and systems that render "expert" business decisions could eventually produce a generation of students and managers who have no faith in their own intuition and expertise.

We wish to stress that we are not Luddites. There are obvious tasks for which computers are appropriate and even indispensable. Computers are more deliberate, more precise, and less prone to exhaustion and error than the most conscientious human being. They can also store, modify, and tap vast files of data more quickly and accurately than humans can. Hence, they can be used as valuable tools in many areas. As word processors and telecommunication devices, for instance, computers are already changing our methods of writing and our notions of collaboration.

However, we believe that trying to capture more sophisticated skills within the realm of electronic circuits – skills involving not only calculation but also judgment – is a dangerously misguided effort and ultimately doomed to failure.

Acquiring human know-how

Most of us know how to ride a bicycle. Does that mean we can formulate specific rules to teach someone else how to do it? How would we explain the difference between the feeling of falling over and the sense of being slightly off-balance when turning? And do we really know, until the situation occurs, just what we would do in response to a certain wobbly feeling? No, we don't. Most of us are able to ride a bicycle because we possess something called "know-how," which we have acquired from practice and sometimes painful experience. That know-how is not accessible to us in the form of facts and rules. If it were, we could say we "know that" certain rules produce proficient bicycle riding.

There are innumerable other aspects of daily life that cannot be reduced to "knowing that." Such experiences involve "knowing how." For example, we know how to carry on an appropriate conversation with family, friends, and strangers in a wide variety of contexts – in the office, at a party, and on the street. We know how to walk. Yet the mechanics of walking on two legs are so complex that the best engineers cannot come close to reproducing them in artificial devices.

This kind of know-how is not innate, as is a bird's skill at building a nest. We have to learn it. Small children learn through trial and error, often by imitating those who are proficient. As adults acquire a skill through instruction and experience, they do not appear to leap suddenly from "knowing that" – a knowledge guided by rules – to experience-based know-how. Instead, people usually pass through five levels of skill: novice, advanced beginner, competent, proficient, and expert. Only when we understand this dynamic process can we ask how far the computer could reasonably progress.

During the novice stage, people learn facts relevant to a particular skill and rules for action that are based on those facts. For instance, car drivers learning to operate a stick shift are told at what speed to shift gears and at what distance – given a particular speed – to follow other cars. These rules ignore context, such as the density of traffic or the number of stops a driver has to make.

Similarly, novice chess players learn a formula for assigning pieces point values independent of their position. They learn the rule: "Always exchange your pieces for the opponent's if the total value of the pieces captured exceeds that of pieces lost." Novices generally do not know that they should violate this rule in certain situations.

After much experience in real situations, novices reach the advanced-beginner stage. Advanced-beginner drivers pay attention to situational elements, which cannot be defined objectively. For instance, they listen to engine sounds when shifting gears. They can also distinguish between the behavior of a distracted or drunken driver and that of the impatient but alert driver. Advanced-beginner chess players recognize and avoid overextended positions. They can also spot situational clues such as a weakened king's side or a strong pawn structure. In all these cases, experience is immeasurably more important than any form of verbal description.

Like the training wheels on a child's first bicycle, initial rules allow beginners to accumulate experience. But soon they must put the rules aside to proceed. For example, at the competent stage, drivers no longer merely follow rules; they drive with a goal in mind. If they wish to get from point A to point B very quickly, they choose their route with an eye to traffic but not much attention to passenger comfort. They follow other cars more closely than they are "supposed" to, enter traffic more daringly, and even break the law. Competent chess players may decide, after weighing alternatives, that they can attack their opponent's king. Removing pieces that defend the enemy king becomes their overriding objective, and to reach it these players will ignore the lessons they learned as beginners and accept some personal losses.

A crucial difference between beginners and more competent performers is their level of involvement. Novices and advanced beginners feel little responsibility for what they do because they are only applying learned rules; if they foul up, they blame the rules instead of themselves. But competent performers, who choose a goal and a plan for achieving it, feel responsible for the result of their choices. A successful outcome is deeply satisfying and leaves a vivid memory. Likewise, disasters are not easily forgotten.

The intuition of experts

The learner of a new skill makes conscious choices after reflecting on various options. Yet in our everyday behavior, this model of decision-making – the detached, deliberate, and sometimes agonizing selection among alternatives – is the exception rather than the rule. Proficient performers do not rely on detached deliberation in going about their tasks. Instead, memories of similar experiences in the past seem to trigger plans like those that worked before. Proficient performers recall whole situations from the past and apply them to the present without breaking them down into components or rules.

For instance, a boxer seems to recognize the moment to begin an attack not by following rules and combining various facts about his body's position and that of his opponent. Rather, the whole visual scene triggers the memory of similar earlier situations in which an attack was successful. The boxer is using his intuition, or know-how.

Intuition should not be confused with the re-enactment of childhood patterns or any of the other unconscious means by which human beings come to decisions. Nor is guessing what we mean by intuition. To guess is to reach a conclusion when one does not have enough knowledge or experience to do so. Intuition or know-how is the sort of ability that we use all the time as we go about our everyday tasks. Ironically, it is an ability that our tradition has acknowledged only in women and judged inferior to masculine rationality.

While using their intuition, proficient performers still find themselves thinking analytically about what to do. For instance, when proficient drivers approach a curve on a rainy day, they may intuitively realize they are going too fast. They then consciously decide whether to apply the brakes, remove their foot from the accelerator, or merely reduce pressure on the accelerator. Proficient marketing managers may intuitively realize that they should reposition a product. They may then begin to study the situation, taking great pride in the sophistication of their scientific analysis while overlooking their much more impressive talent – that of recognizing, without conscious thought, the simple existence of the problem.

The final skill level is that of expert. Experts generally know what to do because they have a mature and practised understanding. When deeply involved in coping with their environment, they do not see problems in some detached way and consciously work at solving them. The skills of experts have become so much a part of them that they need be no more aware of them than they are of their own bodies. Airplane pilots report that as novices they felt they were flying their planes, but as experienced pilots they simply experience flying itself. Grand masters of chess, engrossed in a game, are often oblivious to the fact that they are manipulating pieces on a board. Instead, they see themselves as participants in a world of opportunities, threats, strengths, weaknesses, hopes, and fears. When playing rapidly, they sidestep dangers as automatically as teenagers avoid missiles in a familiar video game.

One of us, Stuart, knows all too well the difference between expert and merely competent chess players; he is stuck at the competent level. He took up chess as an outlet for his analytic talent in mathematics, and most of the other players on his college team were also mathematicians. At some point, a few of his teammates who were not mathematicians began to play fast five- or ten-minute games of chess, and also began eagerly to replay the great games of the grand masters. But Stuart and his mathematical colleagues resisted because fast chess didn't give them the time to *figure out* what to do. They also felt that they could learn nothing from the grand master games, since the record of those games seldom if ever provided specific rules and principles.

Some of his teammates who played fast chess and studied grand master games absorbed a great deal of concrete experience and went on to become chess masters. Yet Stuart and his mathematical friends never got beyond the competent level. Students of math may predominate among chess enthusiasts, but a truck driver is as likely as a mathematician to be among the world's best players. Stuart says he is glad that his analytic approach to chess stymied his progress because it helped him to see that there is more to skill than reasoning.

When things are proceeding normally, experts do not solve problems by reasoning; they do what normally works. Expert air-traffic controllers do not watch blips on a screen and deduce what must be going on in the sky. Rather, they "see" planes when they look at their screens and they respond to what they see, not by using rules but as experience has taught them to. Skilled outfielders do not take the time to figure out where a ball is going. Unlike novices, they simply run to the right spot. In *The Brain*, Richard Restak quotes a Japanese martial artist as saying, "There can be no thought, because if there is thought, there is a time of thought and that means a flaw . . . If you take the time to think, 'I must use this or that technique', you will be struck while you are thinking."

We recently performed an experiment in which an international chess master, Julio Kaplan, had to add numbers at the rate of about one per second while playing five-second-a-move chess against a slightly weaker but master-level player. Even with his analytical mind apparently jammed by adding numbers, Kaplan more than held his own against the master in a series of games. Deprived of the time necessary to see problems or construct plans, Kaplan still produced fluid and coordinated play.

As adults acquire skills, what stands out is their progression *from* the analytic behavior of consciously following abstract rules *to* skilled behavior based on unconsciously recognizing new situations as similar to remembered ones. Conversely, small children initially understand only concrete examples and gradually learn abstract reasoning. Perhaps it is because this pattern in children is so well known that adult intelligence is so often misunderstood.

By now it is evident that there is more to intelligence than calculative rationality. In fact, experts who consciously reason things out tend to regress to the level of a novice or, at best, a competent performer. One expert pilot described an embarrassing incident that illustrates this point. Once he became an instructor, his only opportunity to fly the four-jet KC-135s at which he had once been expert was during the return flights he made after evaluating trainees. He was approaching the landing strip on one such flight when an engine failed. This is technically an emergency, but an experienced pilot will effortlessly compensate for the pull to one side. Being out of practice, our pilot thought about what to do and then overcompensated. He then consciously corrected himself, and the plane shuddered violently as he landed. Consciously using rules, he had regressed to flying like a beginner.

This is not to say that deliberative rationality has no role in intelligence. Tunnel vision can sometimes be avoided by a type of detached deliberation. Focussing on aspects of a situation that seem relatively unimportant allows another perspective to spring to mind. We once heard an Israeli fighter pilot recount how deliberative rationality may have saved his life by rescuing him from tunnel vision. Having just vanquished an expert opponent, he found himself taking on another member of the enemy squadron who seemed to be brilliantly eluding one masterful ploy after another. Things were looking bad until he stopped following his intuition and deliberated. He then realized that his opponent's surprising maneuvers were really the predictable, rule-following behavior of a beginner. This insight enabled him to vanquish the pilot.

Is intelligence based on facts?

Digital computers, which are basically complicated structures of simple on-off switches, were first used for scientific calculation. But by the end of the 1950s, researchers such as Allen Newell and Herbert Simon, working together at the Rand Corp., began to exploit the idea that computers could manipulate general symbols. They saw that one could use symbols to represent elementary facts about the world and rules to represent relationships between the facts. Computers could apply these rules and make logical inferences about the facts. For instance, a programmer might give a computer rules about how cannibals like to eat missionaries, and facts about how many cannibals and missionaries must be ferried across a river in one boat that carries only so many people. The computer could then figure out how many trips it would take to get both the cannibals and the missionaries safely across the river.

Newell and Simon believed that computers programmed with such facts and rules could, in principle, solve problems, recognize patterns, understand stories, and indeed do anything that an intelligent person could do. But they soon found that their programs were missing crucial aspects of problem-solving, such as the ability to separate relevant from irrelevant operations. As a result, the programs worked in only a very limited set of cases, such as in solving puzzles and proving theorems of logic.

In the late 1960s, researchers at MIT abandoned Newell and Simon's approach, which was based on imitating people's reports of how they solved problems, and began to work on any processing methods that could give computers intelligence. They recognized that to solve "real-world" problems the computer had to somehow simulate real-world understanding and intuition. In the introduction to *Semantic Information Processing*, a collection of his students' PhD theses, Marvin Minsky describes the heart of the MIT approach:

If we . . . ask . . . about the common everyday structures – that which a person needs to have ordinary common sense – we will find first a collection of indispensable categories, each rather complex: geometrical and mechanical properties of things and of space; uses and properties of a few thousand objects; hundreds of "facts" about hundreds of people; thousands of facts about tens of people; tens of facts about thousands of people; hundreds of facts about hundreds of organizations . . . I therefore feel that a machine will quite critically need to acquire on the order of a hundred thousand elements of knowledge in order to behave with reasonable sensibility in ordinary situations. A million, if properly organized, should be enough for a very great intelligence.

However, Minsky's students encountered the same problem that had plagued Newell and Simon: each program worked only in its restricted specialty and could not be applied to other problems. Nor did the programs have any semantics – that is, any understanding of what their symbols meant. For instance, Daniel Bobrow's STUDENT program, which was designed to understand and solve elementary algebraic story problems, interpreted the phrase "the number of times I went to the movies" as the product of the two variables "number of" and "I went to the movies." That's because, as far as the program knew, "times" was a multiplicative operator linking the two phrases.

The restricted, ad hoc character of such work is even more striking in a program called ELIZA, written by MIT computer science professor Joseph Weizenbaum. Weizenbaum set out to show just how much apparent intelligence one could get a computer to exhibit without giving it any real understanding at all. The result was a program that imitated a therapist using simple tricks such as turning statements into questions: it responded to "I'm feeling sad" with "Why are you feeling sad?". When the program couldn't find a stock response, it printed out statements such as "Tell me about your father." The remarkable thing was that people were so easily fooled by these tricks. Weizenbaum was appalled when some people divulged their deepest feelings to the computer and asked others to leave the room while they were using it.

One of us, Hubert, was eager to see a demonstration of the notorious program, and he was delighted when Weizenbaum invited him to sit at the console and interact with ELIZA. Hubert spoiled the fun, however. He unintentionally exposed how shallow the trickery really was by typing, "I'm feeling happy," and then correcting himself by typing, "No, elated." At that point, the program came back with the remark, "Don't be so negative." Why? Because it had been programmed to respond with that rebuke whenever there was a "no" in the input.

Microworlds versus the real world

It took about five years for the shallowness of Minsky's students' programs to become apparent. Meanwhile, Hubert published a book, *What Computers Can't Do*, which asserted that AI research had reached a dead end since it could not come up with a way to represent general common-sense understanding. But just as *What Computers Can't Do* went to press in 1970, Minsky and Seymour Papert, also a professor at MIT, developed a new approach to AI. If one could not deal systematically with common-sense knowledge all at once, they asked, then why not develop methods for dealing systematically with knowledge in isolated sub-worlds and build gradually from that?

Shortly after that, MIT researchers hailed a computer program by graduate student Terry Winograd as a "major advance" in getting computers to understand human language. The program, called SHRDLU, simulated on a TV screen a robot arm that could move a set of variously shaped blocks. The program allowed a person to engage in a dialogue with the computer, asking questions, making statements, and issuing commands within this simple world of movable blocks. The program relied on grammatical rules, semantics, and facts about blocks. As Winograd cautiously claimed, SHRDLU was a "computer program which 'understands' language in a limited domain."

Winograd achieved success in this restricted domain, or "microworld," because he chose a simple problem carefully. Minsky and Papert believed that by combining a large number of these microworlds, programmers could eventually give computers real-life understanding.

Unfortunately, this research confuses two domains, which we shall distinguish as "universe" and "world." A set of interrelated facts may constitute a "universe" such as the physical universe, but it does not constitute a "world" such as the world of business or theater. A "world" is an organized body of objects, purposes, skills, and practices that make sense only against a background of common human concerns. These "sub-worlds" are not isolable physical systems. Rather, they are specific elaborations of a whole, without which they could not exist.

If Minsky and Papert's microworlds *were* true sub-worlds, they would not have to be extended and combined to encompass the everyday world, because each one would already incorporate it. But since microworlds are only isolated, meaningless domains, they cannot be combined and extended to reflect everyday life. Because scientists failed to ask what a "world" is, another five-year period of AI research ended in stagnation.

Winograd himself soon gave up the attempt to generalize the techniques SHRDLU used. "The AI programs of the late sixties and early seventies are much too literal," he acknowledged in a report for the National Institute of Education. "They deal with meaning as if it were a structure to be built up of the bricks and mortar provided by the words."

From the late 1970s to the present, AI has been wrestling unsuccessfully with what is called the common-sense knowledge problem: how to store and gain access to all the facts human beings seem to know. This problem has kept AI from even beginning to fulfill the predictions Minsky and Simon made in the mid-1960s: that within 20 years computers would be able to do everything humans can.

Can computers cope with change?

If a machine is to interact intelligently with people, it has to be endowed with an understanding of human life. What we understand simply by virtue of being human – that insults make us angry, that moving physically forward is easier than moving backward – all this and much more would have to be programmed into the computer as facts and rules. As AI workers put it, they must give the computer our belief system. This, of course, presumes that human understanding is made up of beliefs that can be readily collected and stored as facts.

Even if we assume that this is possible, an immediate snag appears: we cannot program computers for context. For instance, we cannot program a computer to know simply that a car is going "too fast." The machine must be programmed in a way free of interpretation – we must stipulate that the car is going "20 miles an hour," for example. Also, computers know what to do only by reference to precise rules, such as "shift to second at 20 miles an hour." Computer programmers cannot use common-sense rules, such as "under normal conditions, shift to second at about 20 miles an hour."

Even if all the facts were stored in a context-free form, the computer still couldn't use them because it would be unable to draw on just the facts or rules that are relevant in each particular context. For example, a general rule of chess is that you should trade material when you're ahead in the value of the pieces on the board. However, you should not apply that rule if the opposing king is much more centrally located than yours, or when you are attacking the enemy king. And there are exceptions to each of these exceptions. It is virtually impossible to include all the possible exceptions in a program and do so in such a way that the computer knows which exception to use in which case.

In the real world, any system of rules has to be incomplete. The law, for instance, always strives for completeness but never achieves it. "Common law" helps, for it is based more on precedents than on a specific code. But the sheer number of lawyers in business tells us that it is impossible to develop a code of law so complete that all situations are unambiguously covered.

To explain our own actions and rules, humans must eventually fall back on everyday practices and simply say, "This is what one does." In the final analysis, all intelligent behavior must hark back to our sense of what we *are*. We can never explicitly formulate this in clear-cut rules and facts; therefore, we cannot program computers to possess that kind of know-how.

Nor can we program them to cope with changes in everyday situations. AI researchers have tried to develop computer programs that describe a normal sequence of events as they unfold. One such script, for instance, details what happens when someone goes to a restaurant. The problem is that so many unpredictable events can occur – one can receive an emergency telephone call or run into an acquaintance – that it's virtually impossible to predict how different people will respond. It all depends on what else is going on and what their specific purpose is. Are these people there to eat, to hobnob with friends, to answer phone calls, or to give the waiters a hard time? To make sense of behavior in restaurants, one has to understand not only what people typically do in eating establishments but why they do it. Thus, even if programmers could manage to list all that is *possibly* relevant in typical restaurant dining, computers could not use the information because they would have no understanding of what is *actually* relevant to specific customers.

Thinking with images, not words

Experimental psychologists have shown that people actually use images, not descriptions as computers do, to understand and respond to some situations. Humans often think by forming images and comparing them holistically. This process is quite different from the logical, step-by-step operations that logic machines perform.

For instance, human beings use images to predict how certain events will turn out. If people know that a small box is resting on a large box, they can imagine what would happen if the large box were moved. If they see that the small box is tied to a door, they can also imagine what would result if someone were to open the door. A computer, however, must be given a list of facts about boxes, such as their size, weight, and frictional coefficients, as well as information about how each is affected by various kinds of movements. Given enough precise information about boxes and strings, the computer can deduce whether the small box will move with the large one under certain conditions. People also reason things out in this explicit, step-by-step way – but only if they must think about relationships they have never seen and therefore cannot imagine.

At present, computers have difficulty recognizing images. True, they can store an image as a set of dots and then rotate the set of dots so that a human designer can see the object from any perspective. But to know what a scene depicts, a computer must be able to analyze it and recognize every object. Programming a computer to analyze a scene has turned out to be very difficult. Such programs require a great deal of computation, and they work only in special cases with objects whose characteristics the computer has been programmed to recognize in advance.

But that is just the beginning of the problem. The computer can make inferences only from lists of facts. It's as if to read a newspaper you had to spell out each word, find its meaning in the dictionary, and diagram every sentence, labeling all the parts of speech. Brains do not seem to decompose either language or images this way, but logic machines have no choice. They must break down images into the objects they contain – and then into descriptions of those objects' features – before drawing any conclusions. However, when a picture is converted into a description, much information is lost. In a family photo, for instance, one can see immediately which people are between, behind, and in front of which others. The programmer must list all these relationships for the computer, or the machine must go through the elaborate process of deducing these relationships each time the photo is used.

Some AI workers look for help from parallel processors, machines that can do many things at once and hence make millions of inferences per second. But this appeal misses the point: that human beings seem to be able to form and compare images in a way that cannot be captured by any number of procedures that operate on descriptions.

Take, for example, face recognition. People can not only form an image of a face, but they

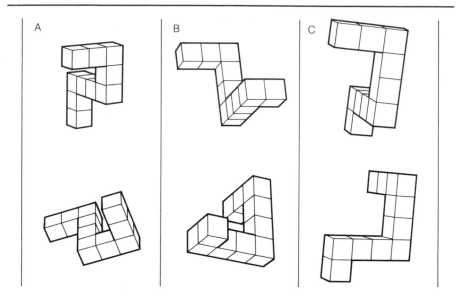

Figure 4.1   Psychologist Roger Shepard has shown that people actually use images, not words, to understand and respond to some situations. For instance, when asked to compare two figures, as in the examples above, people reported that they mentally rotate one of the figures to see if it matches the other. The figures shown in (A) are identical, as a clockwise rotation of this page by 80 degrees will prove. The figures in (B) are also identical but those in (C) are not, as no rotation can bring them into congruence. Like humans, computers can rotate images to check if one image can be superimposed on the other. However, computers do not see these figures as whole images. They have to break them down into lines, angles, and points to compare them.

can also see the similarity between one face and another. Sometimes the similarity will depend on specific shared features, such as blue eyes and heavy beards. A computer, if it has been programmed to abstract such features from a picture of a face, could recognize this sort of similarity.

However, a computer cannot recognize emotions such as anger in facial expressions, because we know of no way to break down anger into elementary symbols. Therefore, logic machines cannot see the similarity between two faces that are angry. Yet human beings can discern the similarity almost instantly.

Many AI theorists are convinced that human brains unconsciously perform a series of computations to perceive such subtleties. While no evidence for this mechanical model of the brain exists, these theorists take it for granted because it is the way people proceed when they are reflecting consciously. To such theorists, any alternative explanation appears mystical and therefore anti-scientific.

But there is another possibility. The brain, and therefore the mind, could still be explained in terms of something material. But it does not have to be an information processing machine.

Other physical systems can detect similarity without using any descriptions or rules at all. These systems are known as holograms.

Is the mind like a hologram?

An ordinary hologram works by taking a picture of an object using two beams of laser light, one of which is reflected off the object and one of which shines directly on to film. When the two beams meet, they create an interference pattern like that produced by the waves from several pebbles thrown into a pond. The light waves form a specific pattern of light and dark regions. A photographic plate records this interference pattern, thus storing a representation of the object.

In ordinary light, the plate just looks blurry, a uniform silvery gray. But if the right frequency of light is projected on to it, the recorded pattern of light and dark shapes the light into a replica of the object. This replica appears three-dimensional: we can view different sides of it as we change position.

What first attracted neuropsychologists to the hologram was that it really is holistic: any small piece of the blur on the photographic plate contains the whole scene. For example, if you cut one corner off a hologram of a table and shine a laser beam through what remains, you do not see an image of a table with a corner missing. The whole table is still there but with fuzzier edges.

Certain areas of the brain also have this property. When a piece is cut out, a person may lose nothing specific from vision, for example. Instead, that person may see everything less distinctly. Holograms have another mindlike property: they can be used for associative memory. If one uses a single hologram to record two different scenes and then bounces laser light off one of the scenes, an image of the other will appear.

In our view, the most important property of holograms is their ability to detect similarity. For example, if we made a hologram of this page and then made a hologram of one of the letters on the page, say the letter F, shining a light through the two holograms would reveal an astonishing effect: a black field with bright spots wherever the letter F occurs on the page. Moreover, the brightest spots would indicate the Fs with the greatest similarity to the F we used to make our hologram. Dimmer spots would appear where there are imperfect or slightly rotated versions of the F. Thus, a hologram can not only identify objects; it can also recognize similarity between them. Yet it employs no descriptions or rules.

The way a hologram can instantly pick out a specific letter on a page is reminiscent of the way people pick out a familiar face from a crowd. It is possible that we distinguish the familiar face from all the other faces by processing rules about objectively identifiable features. But we would have to examine each face in the crowd, detect its features, and compare them with lists of our acquaintances' features. It is much more plausible that our minds work on some variation of the holistic model. While the brain obviously does not contain lasers or use light beams, some scientists have suggested that neurons could process incoming stimuli using interference patterns like those of a hologram.

However, the human mind seems to have an ability that far transcends current holographic techniques: the remarkable ability to recognize whole meaningful patterns without decomposing them into features. Unlike holography, our mind can sometimes detect faces in a crowd that have expressions unlike any we have previously seen on those faces. We can also pick out familiar faces that have changed dramatically because of the growth of a beard or the ravages of time.

We take no stand on the question of whether the brain functions holographically. We simply want to make clear that the information processing computer is not the only physical system that can exhibit mindlike properties. Other devices may provide closer analogies to the way the mind actually works.

Given the above considerations, what level of skill can we expect logic machines to reach? Since we can program computers with thousands of rules combining hundreds of thousands of features, the machines can become what might be thought of as expert novices in any well-structured and well-understood domain. As long as digital computers' ability to recognize images and reason by analogy remains a vague promise, however, they will not be able to approach the way human beings cope with everyday reality. Despite their failure to capture everyday human understanding in computers, AI scientists have developed programs that seem to reproduce human expertise within a specific, isolated domain. The programs are called expert systems. In their narrow areas, such systems perform with impressive competence.

In his book on "Fifth Generation" computers, Edward Feigenbaum, a professor at Stanford, spells out the goal of expert systems: "In the kind of intelligent systems envisioned by the designers of the Fifth Generation, speed and processing power will be increased dramatically. But more important, the machines will have reasoning power: they will automatically engineer vast amounts of knowledge to serve whatever purpose human beings propose, from medical diagnosis to product design, from management decisions to education."

The knowledge engineers claim to have discovered that all a machine needs to behave like an expert in these restricted domains are some general rules and lots of very specific knowledge. But can these systems really be expert? If we agree with Feigenbaum that "almost all thinking that professionals do is done by reasoning," and that each expert builds up a "repertory of working rules of thumb," the answer is yes. Given their speed and precision, computers should be as good as or better than people at following rules for deducing conclusions. Therefore, to build an expert system, a programmer need only extract those rules and program them into a computer.

Just how expert are expert systems?

However, human experts seem to have trouble articulating the principles on which they allegedly act. For example, when Arthur Samuel at IBM decided to write a program for playing checkers in 1947, he tried to elicit "heuristic" rules from checkers masters. But nothing the experts told him allowed him to produce master play. So Samuel supplemented these rules with a program that relies blindly on its memory of past successes to improve its current performance. Basically, the program chooses what moves to make based on rules and a record of all past positions.

This checkers program is one of the best expert systems ever built. But it is no champion. Samuel says the program "is quite capable of beating any amateur player and can give better players a good contest." It did once defeat a state champion, but the champion turned around and defeated the program in six mail games. None the less, Samuel still believes that chess champions rely on heuristic rules. Like Feigenbaum, he simply thinks that the champions are poor at recollecting their compiled rules: "The experts do not know enough about the mental processes involved in playing the game."

INTERNIST-1 is an expert system highly touted for its ability to make diagnoses in internal medicine. Yet according to a recent evaluation of the program published in *The New England Journal of Medicine*, this program misdiagnosed 18 out of a total of 43 cases, while clinicians at Massachusetts General Hospital misdiagnosed 15. Panels of doctors who discussed each case misdiagnosed only 8. (Biopsies, surgery, and post-mortem autopsies were used to establish the correct diagnosis for each case.) The evaluators found that "the experienced clinician is vastly superior to INTERNIST-1, in the ability to consider the relative severity and independence of the different manifestations of disease and to understand the . . . evolution of the disease process." The journal also noted that this type of systematic evaluation was "virtually unique in the field of medical applications of artificial intelligence."

In every area of expertise, the story is the same: the computer can do better than the beginner and can even exhibit useful competence, but it cannot rival the very experts whose facts and supposed rules it is processing with incredible speed and accuracy.

Why? Because the expert is not following any rules! While a beginner makes inferences using rules and facts just like a computer, the expert intuitively sees what to do without applying rules. Experts must regress to the novice level to state the rules they still remember but no longer use. No amount of rules and facts can substitute for the know-how experts have gained from experience in tens of thousands of situations. We predict that in no domain in which people exhibit such holistic understanding can a system based on rules consistently do as well as experts. Are there any exceptions?

At first glance, at least one expert system seems to be as good as human specialists. Digital Equipment Corp. developed R1, now called XCON, to decide how to combine components of VAX computers to meet consumers' needs. However, the program performs as well as humans only because there are so many possible combinations that even experienced technical editors depend on rule-based methods of problem-solving and take about 10 minutes to work out even simple cases. It is no surprise, then, that this particular expert system can rival the best specialists.

Chess also seems to be an exception to our rule. Some chess programs, after all, have achieved master ratings by using "brute force." Designed for the world's most powerful computers, they are capable of examining about 10 million possible positions in choosing each move.

However, these programs have an Achilles' heel: they can see only about four moves ahead for each piece. So fairly good players, even those whose chess rating is somewhat lower than the computers, can win by using long-range strategies such as attacking the king side. When confronted by a player who knows its weakness, the computer is not a master-level player.

In every domain where know-how is required to make a judgment, computers cannot deliver expert performance, and it is highly unlikely that they ever will.

Those who are most acutely aware of the limitations of expert systems are best able to exploit their real capabilities. Sandra Cook, manager of the Financial Expert Systems Program at the consulting firm SRI International, is one of these enlightened practitioners. She cautions prospective clients that expert systems should not be expected to perform as well as human experts, nor should they be seen as simulations of human expert thinking.

Cook lists some reasonable conditions under which expert, or rather "competent," systems can be useful. For instance, such systems should be used for problems that can be satisfactorily solved by human experts at such a high level that somewhat inferior performance is still acceptable. Processing of business credit applications is a good example, because rules can be developed for this task and computers can follow them as well as and sometimes better than inexperienced humans. Of course, there are some exceptions to the rules, but a few mistakes are not disastrous. On the other hand, no one should expect expert systems to make stock-market predictions because human experts themselves cannot always make such predictions accurately.

Expert systems are also inappropriate for use on problems that change as events unfold. Advice from expert systems on how to control a nuclear reactor during a crisis would come too late to be of any use. Only human experts could make judgments quickly enough to influence events.

It is hard to believe some AI enthusiasts' claim that the companies who use expert systems dominate all competition. In fact, a company that relies too heavily on expert systems faces a genuine danger. Junior employees may come to see expertise as a function of the large knowledge bases and masses of rules on which these programs must rely. Such employees will fail to progress beyond the competent level of performance, and business managers may ultimately discover that their wells of true human expertise and wisdom have gone dry.

Computers in the classroom

Computers pose a similar threat in the classroom. Advertisements warn that a computer deficiency in the educational diet can seriously impair a child's intellectual growth. As a result, frightened parents spend thousands of dollars on home computers and clamor for schools to install them in the classroom. Critics have likened computer salespeople to the encyclopedia peddlers of a generation ago, who contrived to frighten insecure parents into spending hundreds of dollars for books that contributed little to their offsprings' education.

We feel that there is a proper place for computers in education. However, most of today's educational software is inappropriate, and many teachers now use computers in ways that may eventually produce detrimental results.

Perhaps the least controversial way computers can be used is as tools. Computers can sometimes replace teaching aids ranging from paintbrushes, typewriters, and chalkboards to lab demonstrations. Computer simulations, for instance, allow children to take an active and imaginative role in studying subjects that are difficult to bring into the classroom. Evolution is too slow, nuclear reactions are too fast, factories are too big, and much of chemistry is too dangerous to reproduce realistically. In the future, computer simulations of such events will surely become more common, helping students of all ages in all disciplines to develop their intuition. However, since actual skills can be learned only through experience, it seems only common sense to stick to the world of real objects. For instance, basic electricity should be taught with batteries and bulbs.

Relying too heavily on simulations has its pitfalls. First of all, the social consequences of decisions are often missing from simulations. Furthermore, the appeal of simulations could lead disciplines outside the sciences to stress their formal, analytic side at the expense of lessons based on informal, intuitive understanding. For example, political science departments may be tempted to emphasize mathematical models of elections and neglect the study of political philosophies that question the nature of the state and of power. In some economics departments, econometrics – which relies heavily on mathematical models – has already pushed aside study of the valuable lessons of economic history. The truth is that no one can assess the dynamic relationships that underlie election results or economies with anything like the accuracy of the laws of physics. Indeed, every election campaign or economic swing offers vivid reminders of how inaccurate predictions based on simulation models can be.

On balance, however, the use of the computer as a tool is relatively unproblematic. But that is not the case with today's efforts to employ the computer as tutor or tutee. Behind the idea that computers can aid, or even replace, teachers is the belief that teachers' understanding of the subject being taught and their profession consists of knowing facts and rules. In other words, the teacher's job is to convey specific facts and rules to students by drill and practice or by coaching.

Actually, if our minds were like computers, drill and practice would be completely unnecessary. The fact that even brilliant students need to practise when learning subtraction suggests that the human brain does not operate like a computer. Drill is required simply to fix the rule in human memory. Computers, by contrast, remember instantly and perfectly. Math students also have to learn that some features such as the physical size and orientation of numbers are irrelevant while others such as position are crucial. In this case, they must learn to "decontextualize," whereas computers have no context to worry about.

There is nothing wrong with using computers as drill sergeants. As with simulation, the only danger in this use stems from the temptation to overemphasize some skills at the expense of others. Mathematics might degenerate into addition and subtraction, English into spelling and punctuation, and history into dates and places.

AI enthusiasts believe that computers can play an even greater role in teaching. According to a 1984 report by the National Academy of Sciences, "Work in artificial intelligence and the cognitive sciences has set the stage for qualitatively new applications of technology to education."

Such claims should give us pause. Computers will not be first-rate teachers unless researchers can solve four basic problems: how to get machines to talk, to listen, to know, and to coach. "We speak as part of our humanness, instinctively, on the basis of past experience," wrote Patrick Suppes of Stanford University, one of the pioneers in computer-aided instruction, in a 1966 *Scientific American* article. "But to get a computer to talk appropriately, we need an explicit theory of talking."

Unfortunately, there is no such theory, and if our analysis of human intelligence is correct, there never will be. The same holds true for the problem of getting computers to listen. Continuous speech recognition seems to be a skill that resists decomposition into features and rules. What we hear does not always correspond to the features of the sound stream. Depending on the context and our expectations, we hear a stream of sound as "I scream," or "ice cream." We assign the space or pause in one of two places, although there is no pause in the sound stream. One expert came up with a sentence that illustrates the different ways we can hear the same stream of sound: "It isn't easy to wreck a nice beach." (Try reading that sentence out loud.)

Without the ability to coach, a computer could hardly substitute for an inexperienced teacher, let alone a Socrates. "Even if you can make the computer talk, listen, and adequately handle a large knowledge data base, we still need to develop an explicit theory of learning and instruction," Suppes writes. "In teaching a student, young or old, a given subject matter, a computer-based learning system can record anything the student does. It can know cognitively an enormous amount of information about the student. The problem is how to use this information wisely, skillfully, and efficiently to teach the student. This is something that the very best human tutors do well, even though they do not understand at all how they do it."

While he recognizes how formidable these obstacles are, Suppes persists in the hope that we can program computers to teach. However, in our view, expertise in teaching does not consist of knowing complicated rules for deciding what tips to give students, when to keep silent, when to intervene – although teachers may have learned such rules in graduate school. Rather, expert teachers learn from experience to draw intuitively and spontaneously on the common-sense knowledge and experience they share with their students to provide the tips and examples they need.

Since computers can successfully teach only novice or, at best, competent performance, they will only produce the sort of expert novices many feel our schools already graduate. Computer programs may actually prevent beginning students from passing beyond competent analysis to expertise. Instead of helping to improve education, computer-aided instruction could easily become part of the problem.

In the air force, for instance, instructors teach beginning pilots a rule for how to scan their instruments. However, when psychologists studied the eye movements of the instructors during simulated flight, the results showed that the instructors were not following the rule they were teaching. In fact, as far as the psychologists could determine, the instructors were not following any rules at all.

Now suppose that the instrument-scanning rule goes into a computer program. The computer monitors eye movements to make sure novices are applying the rule correctly. Eventually, the novices are ready, like the instructors, to abandon the rules and respond to whole situations they perceive as similar to others. At this point, there is nothing more for the computer to teach. If it is still used to check eye movements, it would prevent student pilots from making the transition to intuitive proficiency and expertise.

This is no mere bogeyman. Expert systems are already being developed to teach doctors the huge number of rules that programmers have "extracted" from experts in the medical domain. One can only hope that someone has the sense to disconnect doctors from the system as soon they reach the advanced-beginner stage.

Can children learn by programming?

The concept of using computers as tutees also assumes the information-processing model of the mind. Adherents of this view suppose that knowledge consists of using facts and rules, and that therefore students can acquire knowledge in the very act of programming. According to this theory, learning and learning to program are the same thing.

Seymour Papert is the most articulate exponent of this theory. He is taking his LOGO program into Boston schools to show that children will learn to think more rigorously if they teach a literal-minded but patient and agreeable student – the computer. In Papert's view, programming a computer will induce children to articulate their own program by naming the features they are selecting from their environment, and by making explicit the procedures they are using to relate these features to events. Says Papert: "I have invented ways to take educational advantage of the opportunities to master the art of *deliberately* thinking like a computer, according, for example, to the stereotype of a computer program that proceeds in a step-by-step, literal, mechanical fashion."

Papert's insistence that human know-how can be analyzed has deep roots in our "rationalistic" Western tradition. We can all probably remember a time in school when we knew something perfectly well but our teacher claimed that we didn't know it because we couldn't explain how we got the answer.

Even Nobel laureates face this sort of problem. Physicist Richard Feynman had trouble getting the scientific community to accept his theories because he could not explain how he got his answers. In his book *Disturbing the Universe*, physicist and colleague Freeman Dyson wrote.

The reason Dick's physics were so hard for the ordinary physicists to grasp was that he did not use equations . . . He had a physical picture of the way things happen, and the picture gave him the solutions directly with a minimum of calculation. It was no wonder that people who spent their lives solving equations were baffled by him. Their minds were analytical; his was pictorial.

While Papert tries to create a learning environment in which learners constantly face new problems and need to discover new rules, Timothy Gallwey, the author of *Inner Tennis*, encourages learners to achieve mastery by avoiding analytic thinking from the very start. He would like to create a learning environment in which there are no problems at all and so there is never any need for analytic reflection.

Our view lies in between. At any stage of learning, some problems may require rational, analytic thought. None the less, skill in any domain is measured by the performer's ability to act appropriately in situations that might once have been problems but are no longer problems and so do not require analytic reflection. The risk of Gallwey's method is that it leaves the expert without the tools to solve new problems. But the risk of Papert's approach is far greater: it would leave the learner a perpetual beginner by encouraging dependence on rules and analysis.

AI on the battlefield

The Department of Defense is pursuing a massive Strategic Computing Plan (SCP) to develop completely automomous land, sea, and air vehicles capable of complex, far-ranging reconnaissance and attack missions. SCP has already spent about $145 million and received approval to spend $150 million in fiscal 1986. To bolster support for this effort, the DOD's Defense Advanced Research Projects Agency (DARPA) points to important advances in

AI – expert systems with common sense and systems that can understand natural language. However, no such advances have occurred.

Likewise, computers are no more able today to deal intelligently with "uncertain data" than they were a few years ago when our computerized ballistic-missile warning system interpreted radar reflections from a rising moon as an enemy attack. In a report evaluating the SCP, the congressional Office of Technology Assessment cautioned, "Unlike the Manhattan Project or the Manned Moon Landing Mission, which were principally engineering problems, the success of the DARPA program requires basic scientific breakthroughs, neither the timing nor the nature of which can be predicted."

Even if the Defense Department invests billions of dollars in AI, there is almost no likelihood that this state of affairs will change. Yet once vast sums of money have been spent, there will be a great temptation to install questionable AI-based technologies in a variety of critical areas – from battle management to "data reduction" (figuring out what is really going on given noisy, contradictory data).

Military commanders now respond to a battlefield situation using common sense, experience, and whatever data are available. The frightening prospect of a fully computerized and autonomous defense system is that the expert's ability to use intuition will be replaced by merely competent decision-making. In a crisis, competence is just not good enough.

Furthermore, to justify its expenditures to the public, the military may feel compelled to encourage the civilian sector to adopt similar technologies. Full automation of air-traffic control systems and of skilled factory labor are both real possibilities.

Unless illusions concerning AI are dispelled, we are risking a future in which computers make crucial military and civilian decisions that are best left to human judgment. Knowledgeable AI practitioners have learned from bitter experience that the development of fully autonomous war machines is unlikely. We hope that military decision-makers or the politicians who fund them will see the light and save US taxpayers' money by terminating this crash program before it is too late.

The other side of the story

At this point the reader may reasonably ask: If computers used as logic machines cannot attain the skill level of expert human beings, and if the "Japanese challenge in fifth-generation systems" is a false gauntlet, then why doesn't the public know that? The answer is that AI researchers have a great deal at stake in making it appear that their science and its engineering offspring – expert systems – are on solid ground. They will do whatever is required to preserve this image.

When public television station KCSM in Silicon Valley wanted to do a program on AI to be aired nationally, Stanford AI expert John McCarthy was happy to take part. So was a representative of IntelliCorp, a company making expert systems that wished to air a promotional film. KCSM also invited one of us, Hubert, to provide a balanced perspective. After much negotiating, an evening was finally agreed upon for taping the discussion.

That evening the producer and technicians were standing by at the studio and Hubert had already arrived in San Mateo when word came that McCarthy would not show up because

Hubert was to be on the program. A fourth participant, expert-systems researcher Michael Genesereth of Stanford University, also backed out.

All of us were stunned. Representatives from public TV's NOVA science series and CBS news had already interviewed Hubert about AI, and he had recently appeared on a panel with Minsky, Papert, philosopher John Searle of Berkeley, and McCarthy himself at a meeting sponsored by the New York Academy of Sciences. Why not on KCSM? It seems the "experts" wanted to give the impression that they represented a successful science with marketable products and didn't want to answer any potentially embarrassing questions.

The shock tactic worked. The station's executive producer, Stewart Cheifet, rescheduled the taping with McCarthy as well as the demo from IntelliCorp, and he decided to drop the discussion with Hubert. The viewers were left with the impression that AI is a solid, ongoing science which, like physics, is hard at work solving its quite manageable current problems. The public's chance to hear both sides was lost and the myth of steady progress in AI was maintained. The real story remained to be told, and that is what we have tried to do here.

Artificial Intelligence: An Outsider's Perspective

Marie Jahoda

A slightly different account of the history and progress of AI is provided by the Emeritus Professor of Social Psychology at the University of Sussex. Writing as an "outsider," Jahoda argues that AI research should continue to be supported, although she doubts the value of trying to simulate such things as common sense. And like the Dreyfus brothers, she sees expert systems as tools rather than masters. This piece first appeared in the UK-based journal Science and Public Policy, *vol. 13 (6), December 1986.*

Artificial intelligence (AI) demonstrates the habitual state of every science – uncertainty and controversy – almost to the extreme. Few things are certain in this young and rapidly growing field and controversy within and without the AI community is sharp on major issues.

For several reasons it is a rash undertaking for an outsider to attempt an overview of the problems and promises of AI. Even though AI is by general agreement among its practitioners only about 30 years old, the relevant literature is already unmanageable in size. It relates to computer science, psychology, linguistics, philosphy, and logic.

Partly as a result of these wide ramifications, there is no agreement on a definition of this field. One outstanding expert, M. L. Minsky,[1] wrote in 1968 "artificial intelligence is the science of making machines do things that would require intelligence if done by men." Though at first appealing, this is both too wide (including simple calculators), and too narrow to encompass some current thought and work in AI.

In straightforward computational sequences, machines are clearly superior to humans in processing speed, but clearly deficient in common sense, intuition and relations to the external world. Beyond the difference between these two types of intelligence, some AI scientists now virtually equate intelligence with the total functioning of the human mind. So A. Sloman[2] writes: "not every intelligent robot will necessarily be emotional, only . . . have the ability [to be emotional] – and abilities are not always exercised."

As in all specialized fields, much of the AI literature consists of highly technical reports, beyond an outsider's capacity to understand. The intimidation that stems from this fact is intensified by the realization that some of the very best minds are engaged in AI, but do not agree with each other on some salient issues.

With such weighty obstacles confronting an outsider's overview, why try? The justification lies partly in the power experts have to influence the way of life of everybody. When G. Simons,[3] the Chief Editor of Britain's National Computing Centre in Manchester, can write "the emergence of computer life on Earth must be one of the half dozen or so most momentous events in the 2,000 million year history of terrestrial biology," the issues are clearly important (though this particular view of AI has been widely rejected within the AI community).

Even a cautious expert who does not hesitate to use the term "artificial intelligentsia" in a derogatory sense for those who make global claims, J. Weizenbaum,[4] Professor of Computer Science at MIT, accepts "the idea that a modern computer system is sufficiently complex and autonomous to warrant our talking about it as an organism" that "can be made to develop a sense of itself . . . a kind of self-consciousness."

Futhermore, AI raises very fundamental questions which have preoccupied in different contexts many human scientists in many fields. Whether or not one accepts its tentative and divergent answers, it offers a challenge to consider these questions once again.

In what follows, I shall first sketch AI's intellectual origins, and then outline its achievements to date as active workers in the field see them. Since the current preoccupations of AI researchers hardly explain the intense responses they can generate, I will then discuss some difficult questions which touch on people's world views. There then follows a presentation of the critique of AI from within the scientific community. The nature of AI's promise is then indicated. In conclusion, some policy issues are raised.

Beginnings

By the early 1950s some intellectual and technological developments had converged to make AI possible. Norbert Wiener's *Cybernetics*[5] had pointed to the similarity between control and communication processes in animals and some machines, both functioning adaptively with the help of feedback mechanisms. The thermostat, made familiar through household appliances, became the prototypical example for self-regulating systems in several fields.

Cybernetic concepts and ideas infiltrated psychology where a dramatic change in the dominant paradigm was quietly in the making, a change that is now called the cognitive revolution. Behaviorism had regarded the mind as a black box, not available for direct observation and hence excluded from a scientific psychology. Partly through the impact of cybernetics, which encouraged the modelling of internal processes, this narrow conception of psychology was undermined.

The term "cognitive" for the new paradigm is unfortunate, but by now unalterable; unfortunate because of its Aristotelean connotation, suggesting a sharp distinction between cognitive, affective and conative processes. *De facto* the new psychology deals with everything in the black box, since not only perceiving, reasoning, remembering and learning but also desire and emotion are processes predicated on some form of symbolic representation in the mind.

The point is important in considering AI which, notwithstanding its name, is concerned with the mind, not just with intelligence. According to Alan Newell,[6] "One of the world's deepest mysteries – the nature of the mind – is at the center of AI."

These intellectual developments were matched by the ever-increasing sophistication in the design of the digital computer and of programming languages. The crucial turning point here was the realization that computers were capable of more than "number crunching": computers were also competent manipulators of concepts and meaning.

The convergence of these developments gave rise to the birth of AI in a mood of over-whelming optimism. In 1958 H. A. Simon and A. Newell[7] wrote: "There are now in the world machines that think, that learn and that create. Moreover, their ability to do these things is going to increase rapidly until in the visible future – the range of problems they can handle will be coextensive with the range to which the human mind has been applied."

Not surprisingly not everybody shared this enthusiasm even then, let alone now. In any case, the early period of over-expectation is said by some writers in the field to have been followed by sober reappraisal, even pessimism. This is true for the UK where the SRC-commissioned Lighthill report,[8] combined with the general economic stringency, had its dampening effect.

It is not true for the mood in the United States where the early pioneers (McCarthy, Newell, Simon, Minsky, according to James Fleck[9]) are still leading the field with high expectations, even if "the visible future" has receded considerably; neither can it be true for Japan, whose Fifth Generation plan is based as much on developments in AI as on developments in computer architecture.

Even in the UK not all enthusiasm was quelled when Lighthill reported. It seems that there has been too much diversity of views and moods within the AI community all through its short history to identify clearly stages of development of the entire field. There were optimists and pessimists in the beginning as there are now, when some speak of an "AI winter"[10] while others remain undeterred by the increasing complexity of the issues they face.

Achievements

Mood and expectation are one thing; actual achievement is another. In March 1985 the inter-national journal *Artificial Intelligence* published comments from members of the AI community to whom the journal in celebration of its 25th birthday had sent a set of questions to assess the past, present and future of the field.[11]

One of the questions was about the achievements in AI. There was general agreement that the field has grown rapidly in terms of members, publications, publicity, funding and, in the United States,[12] commercial exploitation. There agreement stopped.

Several people felt that the last 10 years had not resulted in intellectual advance, even though the technology had progressed. After the early achievement "showing that computers could be programmed to *simulate* certain forms of human symbolic manipulations"[13] (emphasis added), no new breakthrough occurred.

The major stumbling block was the issue of human common sense which has defied computer simulation – at least so far. The enormous amount of tacit knowledge acquired through sense perception and language, and stored in the human brain, seems to some inimitable and beyond theoretical formulation.

There are other commentators who speak of progress, but the very nature of the advances mentioned clearly shows the enormous distance from earlier claims and from current journalistic talk of a new living species. Several experts declare that progress consisted in the realization that many problems in AI turned out to be much harder than they had anticipated, that they now had a better assessment of the nature and the dimensions of complexity, had learned how complex even "simple" perception, let alone thinking is.

Even when a specific advance is mentioned it is qualified as, for example, by John McCarthy,[14] one of the earliest pioneers in the field, who identifies the formalization of non-monotonic reasoning as an advance but adds in a pessimistic mood: "All the major problems of AI seem intractable."

There are exceptions mentioned by several people to this fairly general recognition of the relatively slow intellectual development of AI. Margaret Boden regards the theoretical analysis of the computational processes that constitute low-level (or low quality) vision as a significant advance with practical implications.

Several others mention expert systems and robotics. Both present one of the most engaging features of this new science. In contrast to some of the human sciences, AI avoids the pernicious separation of pure from applied science. However abstract and formal the theories, concepts and methods in the field may be, expert systems and robots deal with problems in the real world and it is the real world in which abstract theories must be tested and from which new theoretical conceptions arise.

Expert systems

Expert systems are limited to highly specific domains of human knowledge. They are constructed by making explicit and formalizing the existing knowledge of the best available human expert, including rules of thumb (heuristics), and forcing routinized, tacit knowledge into the open (thereby feeding back into the theoretical issue of how to deal with common sense).

Some such systems already exist. For example, systems for difficult differential medical diagnosis and for geological exploration are already in practical use. A highly successful example in commercial use by the Digital Equipment Corporation in the States is RI,[15] later rechristened XCON. Its language development had been supported by the US Defense Department.

The input to the system consists of the special requirements of a customer for a one-off piece of digital equipment. The diagrammatic output indicates the spatial relationships between components that satisfy these requirements, so that a technician can assemble the equipment. This complex feat is achieved by XCON on the basis of a memory of 420 components, each classified according to eight attributes, and of 480 rules. This system has already dealt with several hundred individual orders without recourse to human experts.

Other expert systems, such as DENDRAL for a highly specific chemical analysis, are already in use and have proved their worth. Because commercial or defense secrets may be involved, the number of expert systems actually in use is difficult to ascertain. Those that achieve publicity are occasionally reported in the AI literature with exaggerated claims.

For example, it was reported that PROSPECTOR, used for geological exploration, had saved a company $100 million; but in July 1985 three leading contributors to the PROSPECTOR team[16] protested against this false claim. "Prospector's success to-date has been scientific rather than economic." It has not yet been used for discovery, only for verifying already discovered deposits.

How do expert systems differ from the original mastermind or a book that could have been written with the same material? Programs can be relied upon not to forget any facts or inference rules that have been built into them and to consider jointly more data and rules than a human expert can juggle simultaneously. Humans are limited to "The magic number seven plus or minus two" (G. Miller[17]).

A book containing all the expert's knowledge usually proceeds linearly and thereby confronts the human user with the task of keeping all the information in mind. However, a few books, such as those for the identification of plants, have for a long time been organized in a manner that anticipated the principle underlying expert systems. Expert systems proceed stepwise in interaction with the user, who feeds in symptoms or data and is questioned by the program for additional input before an answer emerges that can be modified by probability estimates for various possible answers. An expert system is also easier to use than a book.

There is, then, some superiority in the expert system for fully understood, narrow domains compared to the human expert: it is more reliable; it can deal with more information simultaneously and it can respond to specific input in a concrete situation. In addition, there may be only one expert while a program could be multiplied.

Of course, it all depends on the quality of information put into the system in the first place. There remains a basic inferiority, however: the expert system cannot transcend its highly specific input; it cannot see analogies with other issues; cannot deal with unforeseen contingencies; cannot freely associate.

Robots

Today's robots, already widely used in several industrialized countries, are still much in need of more artificial intelligence, even though they have already benefited from research on low-level vision. Other improvements in the performance of robots are largely the result of progress in engineering where flexibility and movement over unstandardized territory present major problems. Both these features require something akin to sense perception and thus define some very difficult tasks for AI, such as shape recognition beyond the very limited tasks in industrial robotics; speech recognition; advanced visual and some kinesthetic sense.

Impressive though expert systems and robotics are, they appear to be technological applications of ideas that were around in AI's earlier history. They do not represent an intellectual breakthrough (perhaps with the exception of low-level vision). Rather, they function as a challenge to AI scientists to implement, if possible, their promises.

AI in the light of current achievements is indeed not yet a reality but an ambitious research program.[18] No machine now in existence is capable of passing the Turing test in its strong interpretation, that is, of responding to questions in a manner indistinguishable from that of a human being. In a weak interpretation of the Turing test some people claim that Colby's program PARRY, which simulates the responses of a paranoid person in an in-take interview (a first interview with a psychiatrist), has already succeeded because some psychiatrists were fooled by its transcribed output. However, Margaret Boden,[19] who has analyzed the strengths and weaknesses of this and many other programs, concludes "considered *qua* conversationalist, PARRY is a fraud."

Some difficult questions

The fact that AI has so far not produced programs that equal everyday human performance (though they may be superior in limited specialist areas) is, of course, no argument for saying that it cannot do so. Thirty years is, after all, a very short period in the development of a science. Whether or not it is possible in principle is a matter of sharp controversy in which convictions, values and biases are intermingled with good rational arguments on all sides.

This will be undoubtedly true in what follows as well. Where one stands in this controversy may have implications for funding policy; this makes retreat into the fact that all science proceeds into the unknown, less than helpful. So I shall attempt to discuss as rationally as possible some assumptions and issues underlying AI.

The basic assumption in AI is that mental processes are computational; they consist of manipulations of symbolic representations of stored material. Computer programs are *de facto* computational in that sense. That human mental processes are of that kind remains an assumption, but an exceedingly plausible one, commensurable with several diverse theoretical approaches in psychology. The implications of this assumption are far reaching. They offer an approach to a problem that no other psychology has so far tackled satisfactorily: the translation of mechanisms into meaning.

It is this plausibly assumed similarity in organizational structure between computers and human minds that gives rise to the most contentious question: are computers simulating human performance or are they identical with it? In its extreme form some who regard the performance as identical conclude that computers are alive, a new species on the planet.[20] This, however, involves a sleight of hand by using a definition of life based exclusively on functions of living organisms and ignoring DNA as the common basis of all known life.

Admittedly, all definitions are to some extent matters of convenience. In this particular case, however, convenience is stretched very far indeed. To argue, as some AI people do, that if and when living beings are discovered in some remote galaxy they may not be based on DNA, is not a very convincing defense of a definition of life that includes human artifacts. At present the claims that computers are a new form of life on this planet is pernicious in its effect on the intellectual standing of AI, changing a developing science into science fiction, though disguised by a respectable but misleading terminology.

This is not to deny the value of assuming a formal and abstract similarity between living and computerized processes. Such formal similarities exist between the structure of the universe and, reduced by an enormous order of magnitude, that of a single atom; but to regard them as identical in anything but abstract structural terms would be blatant nonsense.

In part, the AI terminology used by less extreme members of the community is responsible for such exaggerations. The vocabulary is often anthropomorphic, a practice that Margaret Boden[21] cogently defends: computers beat chess players, solve problems, learn from experience, search their memory, operate in a cautious mode, use rules of thumb heuristically, ask the user questions, provide answers, and so on. It would indeed be awkward to precede each of these terms by the word "simulate," and even then a difficult issue would remain.

To give an example used by Hofstadter[22] and elsewhere in the AI literature: while a simulated hurricane could not make people wet, what (if anything) is the difference between a "simulated" mathematical proof and the "real" thing? A "simulated" or a "real" inference from data? The answer must surely be: none in the outcome, even if the one is mediated by microchips and the other by the central nervous system.

There is in this recognition of identity in the results of computers and human abstract processes a new stance to the millenia-old Body/Mind problem which cannot be called either monistic – the mental is inseparable from the living brain – or dualistic – mind and brain are independent functions. AI implies dualism (of a non-metaphysical kind) to the extent that mental processes are regarded as independent from the brain; it implies monism because these processes must be materially incorporated in some "body."

Does this recognition of identity of outcome undermine the preceding strong argument against according possible computers of the future, which may be equipped with simulations of sense organs, the status of a living species? I believe not. Computational processes are abstractions even though applied to concrete issues. Human minds have the competence for such abstractions but life in its essence – birth, copulation and death – is above all biological.

AI critics

Religious people with faith in a Creator have no problem in rebutting major and minor claims in AI. A Jesuit priest with whom I discussed the issue dismissed it half-jokingly by saying that computers could never go to heaven. AI as an emerging science has been criticized within the scientific community; it is these criticisms which need scrutiny.

In 1972 the Science Research Council asked Sir James Lighthill to review the field for policy purposes. Because of the impact of the ensuing report,[23] which has been both praised and attacked with arguments that can still be heard, it is in order to consider it here.

The gist of the report is to divide the hard-to-define field of AI into three categories, two of them being assigned to other fields with clearer definitions, while the third is described as too unpromising to deserve support. Lighthill predicts and advocates "a slow but increasing . . . fission of the field of AI." Of the three categories, A, which stands for Advanced Automation, aims at practical application for industrial and military purposes. Lighthill sees closer affinities between category A and general computer science and control engineering than between it and the other categories.

The next component, C for Computer based Central Nervous System research, is described as essentially theoretical with close affinities to neurobiology and psychology. Category B (for Bridge between A and C, also (surprisingly) for Building Robots) is the one for which Lighthill sees no justification. Here he obviously has extreme formulations in mind (he refers to "another step in the general process of evolution") which have already been discussed and rejected in this article.

It is only fair, however, to add to this brief summary of the Lighthill report that, in a postscript, he acknowledged admiration for the human ingenuity involved in a piece of work in his category B: Terry Winograd's program, unpronounceably named SHRDLU. In Margaret Boden's description this enabled "a robot to answer questions, execute commands, and accept information in an interactive English dialogue with a human being."[24] However this was only as long as the human partner refrained from talking about the weather or anything else outside the program's severely limited knowledge base.

The AI community reacted by and large with dismay to the proposed administrative dismantling of their field which, they understandably feared, would undercut support for what they regarded as central to AI. The SRC published the report together with a critical rejoinder by Stuart Sutherland opposing the suggested fission, and three other briefer comments.

Those who argue against the split of the field can point to several factors which unite what Lighthill puts asunder. There is the common basic assumption of AI: complex processes are computational in that they consist of the manipulation of symbolic representations. There is the development and shared use of sophisticated programming languages. Above all there is the commonality of the specific aims of all AI workers wherever they are located, within industry or university.

On closer reading, the report itself reveals the artificiality of the proposed tripartite split, for the detailed objectives listed there for categories A and C overlap. Lighthill lists the following: visual and auditory pattern recognition, speech synthesis, machine translation, inductive generalization, problem-solving and learning. Whether these objectives are reached for the purpose of industrial application or the development of theoretical psychology or linguistics does not change the nature of these tasks, which define the current preoccupations of AI.

Much as one sympathizes with Lighthill's rejection of the extremist claims for AI, his strict separation of practical from theoretical work, his emphasis on material structures at the expense of concern with functions of the mind and his advocacy of fission are perhaps not in the best interest of promoting advances in his categories A and C. On the assumption that AI is indeed committed to the development of a theory of mind, a theory which is fed by and feeding into practical applications while it is emerging, Lighthill's recommendations must be questioned.

Further challenges

Another challenge, imbued by theoretical concerns, has more recently been presented to AI by the philosopher John R. Searle,[25] whose views have received wide currency in Britain through his Reith lectures. The essence of his attack, vividly communicated through his "Chinese room" thought experiment, is the denial of human-like faculties to artifacts because intentionality – the basic causal power in living organisms – is absent.

The argument hinges on the term "understanding," that is, the attribution of meaning to symbolic representations. Can a computer be said to understand Chinese if it is programmed to give appropriate Chinese answers to Chinese questions? Searle's answer is an emphatic "no," based on imagining a non-Chinese-speaking person trained to memorize mechanically Chinese questions and answers. By no stretch of the imagination could such a person be said to understand Chinese.

Searle's initial presentation of these ideas was published in 1980 together with critical commentaries by AI scientists, philosophers and psychologists. With some glee Searle pointed out that his critics disagreed with each other in their unsuccessful (according to him) refutation of his argument. It is indeed a strong argument against the possibility of linking artificial mechanisms to meaning, even if the manner of how the mechanisms in the brain perform this feat remains equally a mystery.

In 1985 A. Sloman[26] tried to end this inconclusive debate by arguing that Searle and his critics talked unwittingly about different interpretations of AI. He was attacking the idea that every mechanical performance should be regarded as a mental process. They were defending the notion that mental status should be accorded to mechanical processes only if they are based on a causally controlling program that leads to the internal manipulation of internal symbolic representations.

By Sloman's argument the non-Chinese-speaker must engage in some mental activity (memory search) in giving the right answer, as does the computer, even if both fall short of understanding Chinese. Sloman agrees that higher mental processes require as yet unachieved knowledge of mental architecture plus the construction of connectionist (parallel) computers, but he does not hesitate to expect computers in the future that will hope, fear, desire, and even hesitate at implausibility.

This debate harks back to the question: simulation or identity? – with the complication of cases where the difference between the two is hard to distinguish as, for example, with a mathematical proof.

Perhaps an outsider can be forgiven for an excursion into philosophy. There is a distinction between what is and how we think about it, that is between ontological assumptions and conceptual approaches. It seems to me that Searle and his critics, including Sloman, differ in their ontological assumptions; Searle's: only the brain produces intentionality; Sloman's: specifiable processes within a brain or some other material are intentional.

Perhaps the debate could proceed more fruitfully if ontological statements were deliberately excluded in favor of dealing with the question: what follows from conceptualizing program-produced and brain-produced processes in identical manner? The answer to this question has legal implications which will be briefly mentioned in the next section.

Intellectual and practical prospects

Within the AI community there is a widely shared expectation that the next ten years will bring slow but systematic progress in areas which are now already on the drawing board, as it were: three-dimensional shape recognition, natural language processing, and language translation are dominant in current work.

For these, and other types of processes conceptualized as mental, there exist various not very precise psychological theories and a considerable amount of empirical research. Any AI progress in these matters would certainly advance theories of the mind.

Since mind is involved in all human activities, a more adequate theorizing about its functioning has the potential of influencing the way we all apply our minds to personal, social, educational and intellectual issues. Whether this potential will be realized is, of course, another matter. As indicated above, ontological claims, exaggerated or not, are hardly conducive to legitimizing AI as long as that elusive commodity, common sense, exists in most people.

In any case, the theoretical concerns of AI are directed to very fundamental issues which other approaches have tackled without much success. What AI research will produce in the future cannot be predicted; what it has already achieved, such as the understanding of the complexities of vision or the development of programming languages, promises new insights into major intellectual issues and their application in a wide range of practical matters.

It should be noted that progress in some areas of AI is not necessarily dependent on the availability of Fifth Generation computer architecture, though it may be helped by it. In other areas, however, the development of computer technology and of theoretical progress are closely interlinked. This is so for robotics, which continues to produce tasks for AI while it already benefits from its so far modest achievements, and for the construction of expert systems, where the application of already available AI techniques promises useful results in the not too distant future.

The potential value of interactive expert systems is probably beyond doubt in a world where highly specialized expertise tends to be concentrated in very few human minds. This is especially so given that large numbers of people in many walks of life have to make decisions in areas in which knowledge exists, but is not easily accessible.

One example of an expert system that may soon be ready for general use in clinical diagnosis is MYCIN. Its knowledge base consists of 100 bacterial organisms, the symptoms they create and the drugs to which they respond. It contains rules, can ask for more information from the physician, distinguish degrees of uncertainty and explain its recommendations when asked.

A program for the identification of soy bean diseases is said to be already superior to human experts. There is little doubt that the UK Ministry of Defence already uses expert systems, but for obvious reasons nothing is known about them. Several commercial firms in the UK and many in the United States are engaged in the production of software for expert systems. All this indicates that the development of such systems will continue in future, though not without some difficulties.

The remarkable achievements in this area are the result of many man-years of work. Perhaps the most difficult task in the construction of an expert system is the debriefing of the human experts who unwittingly place great reliance on tacit knowledge, which, together with their explicit expertise, must be translated into the formalisms with which a machine can cope. There seems to be general agreement that the major hurdle in this field is the shortage of properly trained personnel, even in the United States, though they have already benefited by a brain-drain from the UK.

An indication of the time and effort required for the construction of an expert system lies in the publication in 1984 of a book of 700 pages by the MYCIN team. In this, the construction, assets and weaknesses of the system are discussed.[27] This is about a decade after the basic principles and aims of MYCIN became known in the AI community.

Since several specialists are involved in building an expert system, the system in the end has more knowledge than any individual, a fact that makes such systems potentially both powerful and dangerous. It is difficult to know who can be held responsible for the advice they offer.

In the medical, industrial, and, above all, the military field, the consequences of decision-making can be very far-reaching indeed, whether made by fallible unaided human judgment or by the fallible expert systems that J. A. Campbell[28] calls "idiots savants." Narayanan and Perrott[29] argue that computers can be regarded as persons and therefore can have legal rights and duties; others argue strongly against this line.

The legal issues are indeed complex, as a recent symposium on AI and legal responsibility at the 1985 International Congress of AI[30] demonstrated. There, members of the legal professions reminded the AI community of the power of the law to impose its definition of "person." A corporation, for example, is regarded as a legal person with rights and duties.

As case law on AI-related issues develops, some judges may accord computers or their programs the status of legal persons, perhaps as the best solution in cases where no human being can be identified as responsible. It is certainly not too soon for the AI community to consider these matters, even though at present most expert systems are based on interactive communications with human experts, who can, and must, use common sense, intuition, and their values in accepting or rejecting the program's advice, and who therefore might be expected to carry responsibility.

One can only hope that no major decisions will ever entirely depend on an expert system complying with its duties. As long as they remain tools, not masters, however, their potential utility is considerable, an opinion apparently shared by those members of the business community who, largely in the United States, are investing considerable sums in the production of expert systems. As indicated before, improvement of their performance will crucially depend on the progress made on the more general tasks that currently preoccupy all AI researchers.

Some policy questions

This article has touched on some matters apparently far removed from the concern of policy-makers. Yet it seems to me that some indication of the climate of thought surrounding this controversial new intellectual enterprise, of the nature of the arguments that attack or defend it, and of its wide-reaching philosophical implications forms a necessary background for decision-makers. Considering these issues has helped me to formulate some policy questions, even though I cannot answer them all.

- Should AI be supported? The answer here is a decided yes. AI is here to stay; it tackles important issues and engages some outstanding minds in the UK and abroad.
- Should such support be restricted to practical applications (expert systems, robotics, educational tools)? Here the answer is a qualified no. In AI, theoretical and practical concerns are in principle indivisible in their bearing on each other, even though they can be artificially divided. Every theoretical question in AI (such as what are the computational processes that enter into the production of a grammatical sentence?) is answered only if realized practically in a computer simulation, with obvious applications beyond the theoretical concerns of linguistics.

    On the other hand, however, the simulation of common sense, a theoretical concern of AI, would be so vast and costly an enterprise that its support even on the assumption that it could succeed seems unjustified, given that humans excel in it, certainly at present and probably in the future.
- What should be supported? To answer this question would require information not currently available on what members of the AI community are actually doing or planning to do. Such information could be collected through a systematic survey, based either on *Alvey News* or the list of British subscribers to *Artificial Intelligence*, or both. This suggestion is based on the assumption that a balance should be sought between

what AI people are interested in doing and what appears to be useful to a central funding body. Such a survey could simultaneously aim at collecting information on the actual costs of conducting AI research.

- Who should be supported? Apart from the overlap of this question with the previous one, this raises the question of centers of excellence versus a wider spread of resources. By and large, but not entirely, the answer is pre-empted by the availability or otherwise of very costly computing equipment. But not everybody with access to it does excellent work and some excellent work may be done without it.

There is now available a body of interrelated methods (citation indexes plus publication counts plus peer judgments plus trainee judgments) designed to establish the productivity of a scientific center. This could be applied to AI in this country for a systematic assessment.

- There remains a question which even an offer of unlimited funds could not answer decisively: what are the priorities within AI and what priority does AI have compared to other demands on limited resources? Much good work in AI helps decision-making, as do rational arguments and systematic information; in the end, however, nobody can remove from decision-makers the responsibility of relying on values, hunches, intuition, and common sense.

Notes

1 M. L. Minsky (ed.), *Semantic Information Processing* (MIT Press, Cambridge, MA, 1986).
2 A. Sloman, "Towards a Computational Theory of Mind," in M. Yazdani and A. Narayanan (eds), *Artificial Intelligence: Human Effects* (Ellis Harwood, Chichester, UK, 1984).
3 G. L. Simons, *Are Computers Alive?* (Harvester Press, Brighton, UK, 1983).
4 J. Weizenbaum, *Computer Power and Human Reason* (Pelican, London, 1984), pp. 209–10.
5 N. Wiener, *Cybernetics – Control and Communication in Animal and Machine* (Wiley, New York, 1948).
6 A. Newell in D. G. Bobrow and P. J. Hayes (eds), "Artificial Intelligence – Where are We?," *Artificial Intelligence*, vol. 25, 1985, p. 378.
7 H. A. Simon and A. Newell, quoted in Weizenbaum, *Computer Power*, p. 138.
8 J. Lighthill, "Artificial Intelligence: a General Survey," in *Artificial Intelligence: a Paper Symposium* (Science Research Council, London, 1973).
9 J. Fleck, 1982, "Development and Establishment in Artificial Intelligence," in N. H. Martins and R. Whitley (eds), *Scientific Establishments and Hierarchies: Sociology of the Sciences*, vol. VI.
10 R. C. Muller (ed.), "Impact 1984," SPL–Insight, mimeo, p. 3.
11 Bobrow and Hayes, "Artificial Intelligence."
12 P. H. Winston and K. A. Prendergast (eds), *The AI Business, The Commercial Uses of Artificial Intelligence* (MIT Press, Cambridge, MA, 1984).
13 Bobrow and Hayes, "Artificial Intelligence," p. 381.
14 J. McCarthy in Bobrow and Hayes, "Artificial Intelligence," p. 383.
15 J. McDermott, "R1: a Rule-based Configurer of Computer," *Artificial Intelligence*, vol. 19, September 1982, pp. 39–88.
16 R. O. Duda, P. E. Hart and R. Rebot, "Letter to the Editor," *Artificial Intelligence*, vol. 26 (3), July 1985.
17 G. A. Miller, "The Magic Number Seven, plus or minus Two: Some Limits on Our Capacity for Processing Information," *Psychology Review*, vol. 63, 1956.
18 A. M. Turing, "Computing Machinery and Intelligence," *Mind*, vol. LIX (236), 1950.
19 M. Boden, *Artificial Intelligence and Natural Man* (Harvester Press, Brighton, UK 1977), p. 106.

20   Simons, *Are Computers Alive?*

21   Boden, *Artificial Intelligence.*

22   D. R. Hofstadter, "A Coffeehouse Conversation," in D. R. Hofstadter and D. C. Dennett (eds), *The Mind's I* (Basic Books, New York, 1981).

23   Lighthill, "Artificial Intelligence: General Survey," p. 21.

24   Boden, *Artificial Intelligence*, p. 144ff.

25   J. R. Searle, "Minds, Brains and Programs," *The Behavioural and Brain Sciences*, vol. 3, 1980.

26   A. Sloman, "Strong Strong and Weak Strong AI," mimeo, Sussex University, 1985.

27   B. G. Buchanan and E. H. Shortliffe, *Rule-based Expert Systems: The MYCIN Experiments of the Stanford Heuristic Programming Project* (Addison-Wesley, Reading, MA, 1984). Reviewed in *Artificial Intelligence*, vol. 26 (3), July 1985.

28   J. A. Campbell, in Yazdani and Narayanan, *Artificial Intelligence: Human Effects.*

29   A. Narayanan and D. Perrott, in Yazdani and Narayan, *Artificial Intelligence: Human Effects.*

30   The sessions, chaired by Margaret Boden, were tape recorded; she kindly made the tapes available to me.

Thinking about Artificial Intelligence

Beau Sheil

Like Jahoda, Sheil is cautiously optimistic about the future of AI. Here, he discusses the practicalities of putting AI to work in business. In particular, he examines the possible uses of rule-based or "expert" systems, citing some relevant examples. Beau Sheil, an Australian, is Director of Artificial Intelligence at the Price Waterhouse Technology Center in Menlo Park, California. This piece first appeared in Harvard Business Review, *July–August 1987.*

According to some, artificial intelligence (AI) is on the verge of transforming the way we do business. Soon, we are told, "smart" computer programs will begin replacing doctors and lawyers, factory workers and managers. In the face of such hyperbole, it is hard to know whether to jump on the bandwagon or to dismiss the whole enterprise out of hand.

AI is indeed moving from the research lab into business, industrial, and professional applications. But it is still a long way from delivering on the more extravagant claims that some have made for it. And its integration into the daily operations of a large organization requires more subtlety than dreams of robot lawyers (or doctors, or accountants, or whomever else you'd just as soon be rid of in the flesh).

Yet, although many seemingly "obvious" applications of AI are unlikely ever to happen, there are some very effective and near-term ones that are so subtle they're apt to be overlooked. Knowing one from the other and recognizing the unique problems of deploying AI in a large organization are the keys to understanding the real potential of this new technology.

The uses of knowledge

Much of the confusion about the use of AI comes from our own largely unconscious beliefs about "intelligence." To a great extent, these beliefs reflect notions of general-purpose intellectual *power*, analogous to concepts like strength or speed. This is one reason journalistic accounts of AI often cover "supercomputer" technology as well as AI, even though the two fields have little in common.

Current AI technology, however, places much greater emphasis on the specific *knowledge* a particular task requires rather than on the computational power it demands. Thus an AI program to play chess is more likely to rely on a great deal of detailed knowledge about specific moves and situations than on an extremely fast processor armed with little more than the rules of the game.

How can a programmer capture and encode this knowledge? For very simple tasks like playing ticktacktoe, one way is to list every situation and its corresponding best move so that the machine can decide what to do at each step simply by looking up the appropriate move on the list. Alternatively, because the number of possibilities is very small, the program could generate every possible legal move at each step and select the best one (a course that requires generating all the possible responses). But for more complex tasks like playing chess, neither approach is feasible. In these cases, an AI system must represent the knowledge as some compromise between specific answers for every situation – of which there are always far too many – and general principles – whose application to any particular situation may be very unclear. (The insert "Rule-based Systems" on p. 160 explains one common way that knowledge is represented in many AI applications.)

The principal commercial appeal of these knowledge-based systems is that they can be used to program behavior that is very difficult to write down as a conventional program. In particular, the rule-based technology seems to be well suited to describing many routine diagnostic decisions made by professionals such as doctors or engineers. These decisions are far too complex to be exhaustively described by tables or rote procedures, yet they seem to be made, not by any analysis from first principles, but by the application of a large collection of rules of thumb that are well described by situation – action rules.

Even if one is unable to specify and automate some task completely using knowledge-based techniques, there is often substantial value to both the process of development and any partial solution.

Computer technology requires precision and detail. A precise, detailed description of the knowledge needed to carry out an important task can be of great value in and of itself. Often, only the people who actually do a task know exactly what is required to carry it out, and they rarely examine or articulate what they know. As a result, the systematic description of knowledge that AI technology requires will sometimes uncover alarming gaps and inconsistencies. But even if it doesn't, the description itself is a valuable distillation of a vast amount of an organization's experience. Capturing some part of this otherwise intangible asset so that it can be preserved in spite of personnel turnover, shared throughout the organization, and systematically extended is clearly worthwhile.

The value is most clear, of course, if the knowledge happens to be captured in a form that allows it to be applied mechanically, so that the task can be completely automated. More often, however, we cannot capture all of the knowledge used by a human decision-maker. Consequently, AI systems are often designed to help with only one component of a task, and the human user is left to interpret the output and buffer it from problems beyond its range.

This limited task focus is particularly important in systems designed for use by professionals. Since most professionals are expensive, expediting even minor components of their work can be a good investment. And since many professionals make decisions with far-reaching financial or other consequences, it is well worth improving the quality of those decisions by providing additional analysis or information or by auditing them against general guidelines to reduce the potential for expensive mistakes. On both dimensions, the leverage for a well-chosen AI application can be substantial. Tiny increases in a foreign currency trader's effectiveness, for example, could produce dramatic benefits.

Schlumberger's AI-based geological analysis systems show how this technology can leverage professionals' decision-making abilities in this way. Starting in 1980, Schlumberger began to develop AI systems for determining the probable value of oil wells, based on measurements taken during drilling. An elite group of petroleum geologists perform these analyses, and large sums of money ride on their decisions. There are rarely enough of these people, and training or recruiting more is very expensive. For all these reasons, Schlumberger wanted to use AI to automate this task.

Doing so remains a goal of Schlumberger's research. However, despite significant investments, truly expert performance has proved to be an elusive goal. The company has built systems that have the competence of junior geologists but so far has not produced a system that it can trust to make such important decisions autonomously.

Measured against the original goal, this result could be considered a failure. But the work has produced a variety of intelligent tools that can assist both expert geologists and less experienced trainees with aspects of their work – for example, the selection of numerical analysis software for a given problem. These AI tools are proving useful enough that the company has begun to deploy them to field sites throughout the world and expects such systems to permeate the organization over the next five years.

A little knowledge

AI's knowledge-based account of intelligence has some sobering implications. For example, if performance is determined primarily by how much you know rather than by inherent brainpower, it is clear that good performance will require a considerable amount of knowledge. Sometimes, the volume alone can be intimidating.

Consider, for example, the difference between the rules of chess, which take only a few pages, and the hundreds of books of analysis and commentary on the game. Expert chess players are familiar with most of this material. So to match a human chess expert, a knowledge-based chess program must "know" much of this material also.

The implication is simple: bulk alone will make acquiring and encoding the knowledge required to cover chess (or any other subject) a major problem. Consequently, it will be easier to build systems for highly specialized problems than for broad, general ones since the amount of knowledge required for a narrow problem is typically much smaller.

This sequence reverses human experience since people usually become expert only after they have acquired a broad, general competence. The problems involved in acquiring and encoding a broad range of knowledge are such, however, that most AI systems are highly specialized experts but have no basic capabilities in "their" fields. Thus we see programs that are expert on infectious diseases but know nothing of general medicine and systems that can diagnose faults in atomic power plants but are ignorant of freshman physics. The simpler, more general, problems are in fact *harder* to solve with existing AI techniques.

One reason is the immense importance of basic knowledge and common sense. Our ordinary interactions assume a great deal of shared knowledge about an enormous variety of topics. But when we judge a task's difficulty, we tend to forget that fact and focus only on the amount of information that must be *added* to our base of common knowledge. Thus we regard answering a telephone and taking messages as a simple task because it takes only a few sentences to tell another person how to do it. And we consider diagnosing infectious diseases to be very difficult because it takes a great deal of time and effort to learn how to do it. From any other perspective, however, telephone answering is clearly much more complicated because an almost unbounded number of topics and activities can be introduced in the course of a telephone conversation.   Dealing with them all requires an enormous breadth, if not depth, of knowledge. Disease diagnosis, in contrast, lives in a much more limited world of symptoms, causes, and treatments that can be more fully described with far less information.

This need for a wide range of commonsense knowledge has prompted some to put their hopes on some Manhattan-Project-like efforts to encode, once and for all, the basic knowledge found in, say, several encyclopedias. Unfortunately, this is difficult for exactly the reason it is desirable. To begin with, most of the material in an encyclopedia is designed for readers who already have the general knowledge that the project is trying to acquire – just as dictionaries are designed for those who already speak the languages whose words they describe. As a result, much of the material would be uninterpretable if it were encoded in isolation. However, determining a sequence that would present the material so that each element would be understandable in terms of those that went before is not just a difficult technical problem but also one of the enduring concerns of Western philosophy. This should engender a certain amount of humble caution, at least.

Moreover, even a child's encyclopedia contains much information that is difficult to capture with contemporary AI techniques. For example, understanding how we reason about physical

---

Rule-based systems

By far the most common method used to represent knowledge in contemporary AI applications is the rule-based, or "expert," system technology. This was first demonstrated in the MYCIN system for infectious disease diagnosis and treatment planning developed at Stanford University in the early 1970s. In a rule-based system, knowledge is represented as a collection of individual situation–action rules, each one of which captures a single inference, action, or contingency for a particular class of situations. For example, in a medical diagnosis system one might find a rule such as:

if the patient's blood pressure is dropping
and there is no external injury
then suspect internal bleeding.

Each such rule describes a single dependency between a small number of attributes of a complex situation. Because of this focus, each rule is fairly transparent and easily understood. Collections of such rules, however, when applied systematically by a fairly simple program, known as a rule interpreter, can produce surprisingly complex behavior. Furthermore, each rule can be used in several different ways. It not only indicates what action to take in certain types of situations but also allows the system to reason "backward" to decide what might cause certain things to happen. For example, the sequence above could be used to answer the question, "What might cause you to suspect internal bleeding?" Finally, by keeping a record of the rules used to solve a given problem, it is straightforward for the system to provide a simple explanation or justification for its actions or conclusions.

causality, about events over time, or with incomplete or uncertain information are only partially solved problems at best. AI theorists appreciate just how difficult these problems are and how they differ from the relatively well-understood situation – action rule technology. That is one reason AI theorists are generally unhappy with the naively optimistic coverage AI gets in the business press.

Our limited ability to capture knowledge in machine-usable form sharply constrains the kind of AI applications it is currently practical to build to those that focus on rather narrow domains of knowledge. As a result, these specialized systems will tend to find their natural use as assistants to human specialists, since the tasks these systems can carry out are unlikely to be of much use to someone who knows little about their field. Thus the earliest practical AI systems are likely to be used in applications that are quite esoteric from a human perspective, rather than in commonplace ones. In particular, at no time soon will we see any automated secretaries, general-purpose household robots, or mechanical general practitioners in law or medicine. We must look first to simpler, more specialized tasks.

Intelligent uses of "intelligent" machines

The consequences of an AI application having only a limited range of knowledge can be problematic in other ways. For openers, people's expectations of systems that have been described to them as "intelligent" are typically wildly unrealistic, but it is hard to provide them with more accurate ones. Part of the problem is simply a failure of language. Lacking any precise definition of what it means to be "intelligent," most people will conclude that an intelligent computer system will behave much as a person would. But this expectation is usually far off the mark, if only for pragmatic reasons such as the limits of the system's knowledge.

This type of misunderstanding is a familiar problem to those who design computer-based natural-language systems. Consider, for example, a system for extracting information from a data base. When a manager asks, "How much sales activity do we have in Minnesota?" the system can probably respond obligingly with a detailed report. But if a user asks the apparently similar question, "How much confidence do we have in these figures?" the system is very likely to be confused – even though any human who could answer the first question could respond intelligently to the second.

Of course, the programmer designing such a system can cushion the machine's response to questions that are out of bounds. But the root of the problem remains: What can users expect from a machine that bills itself as intelligent? Lacking a good answer, users are almost certain to generalize too broadly and to wander out of the machine's domain of competence. If the machine can detect this and confess its ignorance, the only consequence is the user's frustration at its seemingly capricious limits. But since "knowing what you don't know" is one of the subtlest mental skills, user and machine are likely to talk at cross-purposes for some time until the misunderstanding becomes clear.

This problem can have serious consequences when the application involves a critical decision. Most AI-based medical diagnostic systems, for example, are "smart" in very narrow fields of expertise but completely ignorant about everything else. So an expert system designed to diagnose heart disease is likely to make intelligent-sounding but completely misguided recommendations for a patient with a broken leg. The danger, of course, is that users will mistake the intelligent tone for real competence and act on the machine's advice.

Many of these problems with "intelligent" programs actually reflect a deep level of confusion in our own thinking about thinking. Marvin Minsky, one of the pioneers of artificial intelligence, once commented that intelligence is "an attribute people ascribe to mental behavior that they admire but do not understand." In other words, about the only thing that "intelligent" skills obviously have in common is our ignorance about how they are done.

Consider, for example, the procedure for long division. Small children view it as requiring a lot of intelligence. Adults only know better because they know the trick. Or think of the incredible range of skills we label "intelligent." It's clear why we think medical diagnosis requires intelligence – people must go to medical school to learn how to do it and only a few succeed. But speech comprehension is also classed as intelligent for a machine – even though people learn to understand spoken language at the age of two – because we don't know how to do it mechanically.

Conversely, the more we understand a problem, the faster it moves out of the realm of AI: we no longer need to postulate intelligence to explain it. Checkers, for example, is no longer a topic of AI research, because machines can now beat the most proficient humans. Chess, on the other hand, still eludes us: human chess masters defeat the best programs, and theorists are not altogether sure how far they can be improved.

The set of concerns that Minsky's comment captures highlights a key problem for an applied technology of AI: describing something as intelligent means that we don't fully understand it, and any technology that attempts to capture and automate something that we don't fully understand is inherently weak.

Putting AI to work

Although what we've been discussing may seem abstract, philosophical, and quite removed from practicality, it has very real implications for the senior manager who is considering using AI technology. What that person wants to know is whether the AI system is reliable. Will it perform to specifications? Will its answers always be right or, at the very least, defensible?

The problem is that no one is likely to be in any position to answer these questions satisfactorily. (We will set aside, without disputing it, the cynic's point of view that such questions are never answered satisfactorily for any large piece of software, for they are certainly *thought* to be, and that's what is important here.) No theory even in principle purports to predict what range of problems can be solved with a given set of knowledge. There is no way to check that all the knowledge is "correct" and no way to prove that the system has no significant gaps in its coverage.

Furthermore, as the system is described in more detail, the language of AI is apt to strike fear into the manager's heart. Operating managers are held accountable for a particular set of activities and are typically managed very tightly on a range of detailed targets, not to mention overall gross propriety. Is such a manager likely to put the company's future into the hands of an intelligent computer system that "makes guesses?" Will the manager trust a system for whose behavior there are only flimsy assurances couched in terms that translate, to a skeptical ear, as "flaky", "unreliable", and "unpredictable?" No. If the system is installed at all, it will be over that manager's dead body.

The fundamental issues for operational deployment are predictability and accountability. Naively constructed AI systems typically have neither. And even if predictable competence were not an issue, wouldn't any manager still hesitate before making intelligent systems responsible for major business decisions?

Consider the first patient who dies as a result of a bad diagnosis from a robotic doctor. Who will be held responsible? And how will that decision be made? We have a great many avenues for ascribing legal and ethical responsibility to people. Some of them extend to well-specified, well-understood machines. But even here there are problems when the decisions are highly consequential. For example, it is quite possible that we will never see commercial airliners flown entirely under computer control even if that technology becomes clearly superior – statistically – to human pilots. The reason is that although human pilots crash the occasional plane when trying to land in poor weather, their failures are understandable and thus, though regrettable, can be tolerated. When the mechanical pilot fails, however, even though it might do so much less frequently, it's likely to be by flying a plane into the side of a mountain in broad daylight. And this kind of inhuman failure we are unlikely to tolerate, whatever the long-run statistics say.

Operational solutions

If AI applications are to achieve widespread commercial use, these operational issues must be addressed. One approach is simply to give AI a low profile – to call the technology by a different name that removes the notion of intelligence with all its implicit problems. At least one Silicon Valley company, a producer of engineering workstations, has a corporate policy against using the term *artificial intelligence* when describing its products for just this reason.

A second approach is to concentrate on low-responsibility applications in which the consequences of errors are nil. Digital Equipment Corporation's XCON system, for example, configures VAX minicomputers to fill sales orders by using a knowledge base of rules that indicates which components can be used together. The occasional mistake can be rectified easily by an extra shipment of parts. The hitch, of course, is that most routine decision problems of this type can be solved with much simpler, less intelligent technology. After all, helping with highly consequential decisions is one of the principal economic justifications for turning to AI in the first place.

A third approach is to package AI technology as an assistant to rather than as the primary decision-maker. This approach uses AI technology to facilitate, support, or audit a human's decision process. It casts AI in a supportive and subordinate role that is not only a good match for the technology's uneven capabilities but also a good fit for the structure of existing organizations. There is a role that human assistants fill: they have some knowledge, they help but are expected to make occasional mistakes, and they assist a person who bears the responsibility for any mistakes. In many cases, a machine can play this role.

Schlumberger's geological analysis systems use AI in just this way. Another excellent example is the ONCOCIN system, developed by Edward Shortliffe and others at the Stanford

Medical School, which assists physicians in prescribing chemical treatment for cancer patients. Instead of assuming the obtrusive role of a would-be mechanical doctor, the ONCOCIN system stays in the background.

Most of the time, ONCOCIN appears to be nothing more than a sophisticated electronic forms system. The physician uses the display screen to fill out exact replicas of the paper forms normally used for recording symptoms and treatments. But behind the display screen is a full-blown expert system for cancer therapy. It watches the case history and looks for options the doctor may have overlooked. For a long time the doctor may be unaware of this backup assistance. But occasionally, the system will break in with additional information – noting, for example, that patients with this profile should receive alternate drugs or reduced doses or perhaps questioning the rationale for an unexpected treatment.

The benefit is that doctors get access to knowledge they otherwise might not have and are thereby called on to think through unconventional therapies. Doctors may reject the machine's advice, seek more information about it, or even ask for detailed explanation or citations. But it is always clear who is in charge.

Though writing an "assistant" system may sound easier than writing an "expert" one, both require the same underlying AI technology. In addition, because they must be easy to use and require some grace and tact in how they present advice, assistant systems actually demand even greater skills from system designers. Our society permits real geniuses to be quite incorrigible and extends the privilege to computer systems (like number crunchers) that so far outperform people that we tolerate their idiosyncracies. But assistant systems don't have such decisive advantages, so they must be more accommodating. Inconsiderate, unhelpful assistants get fired, after all.

AI systems technology

The need to tailor assistant AI systems so that they fit unobtrusively into a professional user's working environment presents a serious problem, as even conventional software finds this level of integration difficult. Indeed, this additional requirement might seem to escalate the difficulty of applying AI from the simply hard to the flatly impossible. Buried in AI technology, however, is an unsuspected strength that not only solves this problem but also turns the argument on its head.

Most of the large, well-known AI systems use a very different software technology from that employed in the rest of computing. AI's software technology evolved specifically to facilitate the development of large software systems for very poorly understood problems. The programming style that resulted is known as *exploratory programming* because the programmer explores a problem and develops a design for its solution as the program is being developed, rather than settling on a design first.

The deficiencies of this style are obvious – if one really does have the option of thinking everything through in advance. But just as it is wasteful to discover by building what you can discover by thinking, so is it wasteful to try to plan too far ahead in the face of great uncertainty. In that situation, the best approach is to build a few fragments to see if they give you enough information to reduce the uncertainty so that you can build others.

The technology of exploratory development has a number of components: programming languages that let you finesse many design details as long as possible, programming environments that provide both intelligent assistants to help manage the details of programming and a rich set of supporting utilities, and programming techniques that allow easy incremental growth. Together, they allow designers to build complex systems and to develop them rapidly in response to a changing set of demands.

Of course, it should be clear at once why AI is well suited to exploratory programming. After all, Minsky's characterization of intelligence suggests that a programmer who can develop precise specifications in advance isn't even doing AI. The surprise was the discovery, early in the commercial development of AI, that the difficulty of obtaining precise specifications was almost as pronounced for many non-AI applications as it was for AI itself. In particular, when it came to building highly customized interactive environments for professionals to use to manage their information needs, this experimental approach proved very effective.

John Seely Brown of Xerox's Palo Alto Research Center was the first to point out this enabling role of AI software technology. He observed that a goodly amount of the early commercial activity in AI was simply using the AI systems' development technology to prototype conventional applications quickly. The standard perception that AI was encumbered with its idiosyncratic software was, he argued, mistaken. In fact, the ability to provide highly customized, integrated applications software has turned out to be a major strength of AI technology.

Recently this argument has taken yet another turn with the incorporation of fragments of AI software technology, especially rule interpreters, into conventional software systems. The short-term value of this is clear. Rule-based programming is an effective way to arrive at a clear, concise, yet easily extended statement of the logic underlying many discrimination and classification tasks. Many data processing professionals find rule-based programming a great improvement over the often convoluted code used for these tasks in conventional data processing programs. As a result, we are seeing a wave of simple rule interpreters being added to existing data processing software, and some even claim that these rule interpreters are the "real" commercial technology of artificial intelligence. Eventually, these systems will be used to make such prosaic decisions as which sales forms to send a customer or what details of the tax code to represent.

The skeptic might ask how much real intelligence there is in such applications, especially given how weak the supporting rule systems are compared with the AI research systems that have inspired them. But there is little to be gained from such a concern. The simple rule-based interpreter is an effective technology for a wide class of simple, practical problems. The more sophisticated AI development environments provide much greater power where that is appropriate to the problem. Beyond them both loom the major issues of computational philosophy that continue to challenge the research science of AI. As long as we are realistic in our choice of weapons and refrain from proposing a popgun to slay a dragon, the skeptic should surely be satisfied.

5 Machines and Users

Designing the User Interface

Ben Shneiderman

There is growing recognition of the importance of the "interface" between human beings and computers. A fervent advocate of good interface design is Ben Shneiderman, whose book, Designing the User Interface *(Addison-Wesley, Reading, MA, 1987), is a standard text. In this excerpt, the author outlines the key steps in putting together a high-quality interactive system, taking into account the major human factors. Ben Shneiderman is Head of the Human–Computer Interaction Laboratory in the Department of Computer Science, University of Maryland.*

Frustration and anxiety are a part of daily life for many users of computerized information systems. They struggle to learn command languages or menu selection systems that are supposed to help them do their job. Some people encounter such serious cases of computer shock, terminal terror, or network neurosis that they avoid using computerized systems. These electronic-age maladies are growing more common; but help is on the way!

Researchers have shown that redesign of the human–computer interface can make a substantial difference in learning time, performance speed, error rates, and user satisfaction. Information and computer scientists have been testing design alternatives for their impact on these human performance measures. Commercial designers recognize that systems that are easier to use will have a competitive edge in information retrieval, office automation, and personal computing.

Programmers and quality assurance teams are becoming more cautious and paying greater attention to the implementation issues that guarantee high-quality user interfaces. Computer center managers are realizing that they must play an active role in ensuring that the software and hardware facilities provide high-quality service to their users.

In short, the diverse use of computers in homes, offices, factories, hospitals, electric power control centers, hotels, banks, and so on is stimulating widespread interest in human factors issues. Human engineering, which was seen as the paint put on at the end of a project, is now understood to be the steel frame on which the structure is built.

However, an awareness of the problems and a desire to do well are not sufficient. Designers, managers, and programmers must be willing to step forward and fight for the user. The enemies include inconsistent command languages, confusing operation sequences, chaotic display formats, inconsistent terminology, incomplete instructions, complex error recovery procedures, and misleading or threatening error messages.

I believe that progress in serving users will be rapid because as examples of excellence proliferate, users' expectations will rise. The designers, managers, and researchers who are dedicated to quality and to nurturing the user community will have the satisfaction of doing a good job and the appreciation of the users they serve.

The battle will not be won by angry argumentation over the "user friendliness" of competing systems or by biased claims that "my design is more natural than your design." Victory will come to people who take a disciplined, iterative, and empirical approach to the study of human performance in the use of interactive systems. More and more, system developers, maintainers, and managers are collecting performance data from users, distributing subjective satisfaction surveys, inviting users to participate in design teams, conducting repeated field trials for novel proposals, and using field study data to support organizational decision-making.

Marshall McLuhan observed that "the medium is the message." Designers send a message to the users by the design of interactive systems. In the past, the message was often an unfriendly and unpleasant one. I believe, however, that it is possible to send a much more positive message that conveys the genuine concern a designer has for the users. If the users feel competent in using the system, can easily correct errors, and can accomplish their tasks, then they will pass on the message of quality to the people they serve, to their colleagues, and to their friends and families. In this way, each designer has the possibility of making the world a little bit warmer, wiser, safer, and more compassionate.

New technologies provide remarkable, almost supernatural, powers to those who master them. Computer systems are a new technology in the early stages of dissemination and refinement. Great excitement now exists as designers provide remarkable functions in simple and elegant interactive systems. The opportunities for system builders and entrepreneurs are substantial since only a fraction of the potential functions and market has been explored.

Like early photography or automobiles, computers are available only to people who devote extensive effort to mastering the technology. Harnessing the computer's power is a task for designers who understand the technology and are sensitive to human capacities and needs.

Human performance in the use of computer and information systems will remain a rapidly expanding research and development topic in the coming decades. This interdisciplinary journey of discovery combines the experimental methods and intellectual framework of cognitive psychology with the powerful and widely used tools developed from computer science. Contributions also accrue from educational psychologists, instructional designers, graphic artists, technical writers, and traditional areas of human factors or ergonomics.

Applications developers who apply human factors principles and processes are producing exciting interactive systems. Provocative ideas emerge in the pages of the numerous computer magazines, the shelves of the proliferating computer stores, and the menus of the expanding computer networks.

There is a growing interest in the human factors issues of computer use with systems such as:

- text editors, word processors, and document formatters
- electronic mail and computer conferencing
- expert systems and science workstations

- electronic spreadsheets and decision support systems
- personal, home, and educational computing
- bibliographic and data base systems
- commercial systems, such as inventory, personnel, and reservations
- air-traffic and electric utility control
- programming environments and tools
- computer-assisted design and manufacturing
- art and entertainment.

Practitioners and researchers in many fields are making vital contributions. Academic and industrial experimenters and theorists in computer science, psychology, and human factors are studying cognitive theories and models of human performance; novice versus expert user differences; individual differences, such as cognitive style, personality, or gender; and experimental methodologies for evaluation.

Software designers and researchers are exploring:

- menu selection techniques
- command, parametric, and query languages
- use of graphics, animation, and color
- direct manipulation
- natural language facilities
- error handling, messages, and prevention
- screen formatting

Hardware developers and system builders are offering novel approaches to:

- keyboard design
- large, high resolution displays
- rapid response time
- fast display rates
- novel pointing devices
- speech input and output.

Developers with an orientation toward educational psychology, instructional design, and technical writing are coping with online tutorials, effective training and reference manuals, online manuals and assistance, classroom and individual training methods, and lectures versus experiential training. Sociologists, philosophers, policy-makers, and managers are dealing with organizational impact, computer anxiety, job redesign, retraining, work-at-home, and long-term societal changes.

This is an exciting time for developers of interactive computer systems. The hardware and software foundations for the bridges and tunnels have been built. Now, the roadway can be laid and the stripes painted to make way for the heavy traffic of eager users.

Primary design goals

Every designer wants to build a high quality interactive system that is admired by colleagues, celebrated by users, circulated widely, and frequently imitated. Appreciation comes, not from flamboyant promises or stylish advertising brochures, but from inherent quality features that are achieved by thoughtful planning, sensitivity to user needs, careful attention to detail in design and development, and diligent testing. Multiple design alternatives are raised for consideration, and the leading contenders subjected to further development and testing. Evaluation of designs refines the understanding of appropriateness for each choice.

Successful designers go beyond the vague notion of "user friendliness" and probe deeper than a checklist of subjective guidelines. They must have a thorough understanding of the diverse community of users and the tasks that must be accomplished. Moreover, they must have a deep commitment to serving the users.

Effective systems generate positive feelings of success, competence, and clarity in the user community. The users are not encumbered by the computer and can predict what happens with each of their actions. When an interactive system is well designed, it almost disappears, enabling the users to concentrate on their work or pleasure. Creating an environment in which tasks are carried out almost effortlessly, requires a great deal of hard work for the designer.

Proper functionality

The first step is to ascertain the necessary functionality – what tasks and subtasks must be carried out. The frequent tasks are easy to determine, but the occasional tasks, the exceptional tasks for emergency conditions, and the repair tasks to cope with errors in use of the system are more difficult to discover. Task analysis is central, because systems with inadequate functionality frustrate the user and are often rejected or underutilized. If the functionality is inadequate, it doesn't matter how well the human interface is designed. Excessive functionality is also a danger, and probably the more common mistake of designers, because the clutter and complexity make implementation, maintenance, learning, and usage more difficult.

A related issue is compatibility with other computer and noncomputer systems that the users may be using. Slight differences among systems can lead to annoying and dangerous errors. Gross differences among systems requires substantial retraining and burden the users. Incompatible storage formats, hardware, and software versions cause frustration and delay. Designers must decide whether the improvements they offer are enough to offset the disruption to the users.

Reliability, availability, security, and integrity

The second step is ensuring proper system reliability. The software architecture and hardware support must ensure high availability, ease of maintenance, and correct performance. If the system is not functioning or introduces errors, then it doesn't matter how well the human interface is designed. Attention must also be paid to ensuring privacy, security, and information integrity. Protection must be provided from unwarranted access, inadvertent destruction of data, or malicious tampering.

Schedules and budgets

The third step is to plan carefully to be on schedule and within budget. Delayed delivery or cost overruns can threaten a system because the confrontive political atmosphere in a company or the competitive market environment contains potentially overwhelming forces. If an in-house system is late, then other projects are affected, and the disruption may cause managers to choose an alternative. If a commercial system is too costly, customer resistance may emerge to prevent widespread acceptance, allowing competitors to capture the market.

Proper attention to human factors principles and testing often leads to reductions in the cost and time for development. A carefully tested design generates fewer changes during implementation and after release of new systems.

Human factors design goals

If adequate functionality has been chosen, reliability is ensured, and schedule plus budgetary planning is complete, then attention can be focused on the design and testing process. The multiple design alternatives must be evaluated for specific user communities and for specific benchmark sets of tasks. A clever design for one community of users may be inappropriate for another community. An efficient design for one class of tasks may be inefficient for another class.

The Library of Congress experience

The relativity of design played a central role in the evolution of information services at the Library of Congress. Two of the major uses of computer systems were cataloging new books and searching the online book catalog. Separate systems for these tasks were created that optimized the design for one task and made the complementary task difficult. It would be impossible to say which was better, because they were both fine systems, but serving different needs. It would be like asking whether the New York Philharmonic Orchestra was better than the New York Yankees baseball team.

The bibliographic search system, SCORPIO, was very successfully used by the staffs of the Library of Congress, the Congressional Research Service (CRS), and the Senate and House of Representatives. They could do bibliographic searching and used the same system to locate and read CRS reports, to view events recorded in the bill status system, and much more. The professional staff members took a three- to six-hour training course and then could use terminals in their office, where more experienced colleagues could help out with problems and where adequate consultants were usually available.

Then, in January 1981, the Library of Congress stopped entering new book information in the manual card catalogs, thus requiring the general public to use one of the 18 terminals in the main reading room to locate new books. For even a computer-knowledgeable individual, learning to use the commands, understanding the cataloging rules, and formulating a search strategy would be a challenging task. The reference librarians claimed that they could teach a willing adult the basic features in 15 minutes. But 15 minutes per patron would overwhelm the staff and, more importantly, most people are not interested in investing even 15 minutes in learning to use a computer system. Library patrons have work to do and often perceive the computer as an intrusion or interference with their work. The SCORPIO system that worked so well for one community of users was inappropriate for this new community.

The system designers revised the online messages to provide more supportive and constructive feedback, offered extensive online tutorial material, and began to explore the use of menu selection approaches for the novice users. In short, a new community of users demanded substantial redesign of the human interface.

Measurable human factors goals

Once a determination has been made of the user community and the benchmark set of tasks, then the human factors goals can be examined. For each user and each task, precise measurable objectives guide the designer, evaluator, purchaser, or manager. These five measurable human factors are central to evaluation:

- *Time to learn*. How long does it take for typical members of the target community to learn how to use the commands relevant to a set of tasks?
- *Speed of performance*. How long does it take to carry out the benchmark set of tasks?
- *Rate of errors by users*. How many and what kinds of errors are made in carrying out the benchmark set of tasks? Although time to make and correct errors might be incorporated into the speed of performance, error making is such a critical component of system usage that it deserves extensive study.
- *Subjective satisfaction*. How much did users like using aspects of the system? This can be ascertained by interview or written surveys that include satisfaction scales and space for free-form comments.
- *Retention over time*. How well do users maintain their knowledge after an hour, a day, or a week? Retention may be closely linked to time to learn; frequency of use plays an important role.

Every designer would like to succeed in every category, but there are often forced tradeoffs. If lengthy learning is permitted, then task performance speed may be reduced by use of complex abbreviations and shortcuts. If the rate of errors is to be kept extremely low, then speed of performance may have to be sacrificed. In some applications, subjective satisfaction may be the key determinant of success, while in others short learning times or rapid performance may be paramount. Project managers and designers must be aware of the tradeoffs and make their choices explicit and public. Requirements documents and marketing brochures should make clear which goals are primary.

After multiple design alternatives are raised, the leading possibilities should be reviewed by designers and users. Paper mock-ups are useful, but online prototype versions of the system create a more realistic environment for review. After extensive testing of design goals, the final design should be written down. The user manual and the technical reference manual can be written before the implementation to provide another review and perspective on the design. Then the implementation can be carried out; this should be a modest effort if the design is complete and precise. Finally, the acceptance test certifies that the delivered system meets the goals of the designers and customers.

Motivations for human factors in design

The enormous interest in human factors of interactive systems arises from the complementary recognition of how poorly designed many current systems are and the genuine desire to create elegant systems that effectively serve the users. This increased concern emanates from four primary sources: life-critical systems; industrial/commercial uses; office, home, and entertainment applications; and exploratory, creative, and expert systems.

Life-critical systems

Life-critical systems include air-traffic, nuclear reactor, or power utility control; medical intensive care or surgery; manned spacecraft; police or fire dispatch; and military operations. In these applications, high costs are expected, but they should yield high reliability and effectiveness. Lengthy training periods may be acceptable to obtain rapid, error-free performance. Subjective satisfaction is less of an issue because the users are well motivated and paid. Retention is obtained by frequent use of common functions and practice sessions for emergency actions.

Industrial/commercial uses

Typical industrial/commercial uses include banking, insurance, order entry, inventory management, airline, hotel, or car rental, utility billing, credit card management, and point-of-sales terminals. In these cases, costs shape many judgments; lower cost may be preferred even if there is some sacrifice in reliability. Operator training time is expensive, so ease of learning is important. The tradeoffs for speed of performance and error rates are decided by the total cost over the system's lifetime. Subjective satisfaction is of modest importance, and, again, retention is obtained by frequent use. Speed of performance becomes central for most of these applications because of the high volume of transactions. Trimming 10 percent off the mean transaction time means 10 percent fewer operators, 10 percent fewer terminal workstations, and possibly a 10 percent reduction in hardware costs. A 1982 study by a leading motel chain reported that a 1-second reduction in the 150-second mean time per reservation would save $40,000 per year.

Office, home, and entertainment applications

The rapid expansion of office, home, and entertainment applications is the third source of interest in human factors. Personal computing applications include word processing, automated teller machines, video games, educational packages, information retrieval, electronic mail, computer conferencing, and small business management. For these systems, ease of learning, low error rates, and subjective satisfaction are paramount because use is frequently discretionary and competition is fierce. If the users can't succeed quickly, they will abandon the use of a computer or try a competing package. In cases where use is intermittent, retention is important, so online assistance becomes very important.

Choosing the right functionality is difficult. Novices are best served by a constrained simple set of actions; but as experience increases, so does the desire for more functionality. A layered or level structured design is one approach to graceful evolution from novice to expert usage. As users gain competence, their desire for more rapid performance and extensive functionality grows. Low cost is important because of lively competition, but extensive design and testing can be amortized over the large number of users.

Exploratory, creative, and expert systems

An increasing fraction of computer use is to support human intellectual and creative enterprises. Electronic encyclopedias, database browsing, statistical hypothesis formation, business decision-making, and graphical presentation of scientific simulation results are examples of exploratory environments. Creative environments include writer's tool kits or workbenches, architecture or automobile design systems, artist or programmer workstations, and music composing systems. Expert systems aid knowledgeable users in medical diagnosis, financial decision-making, oil-well log data analysis, satellite orbit maneuvering, and military advising.

In these systems, the users may be knowledgeable in the task domain but novices in the underlying computer concepts. Their motivation is often high, but so are their expectations. Benchmark tasks are more difficult to describe because of the exploratory nature of these applications. Usage can range from occasional to frequent. In short, it is difficult to design and evaluate these systems.

Ergonomics and Information Technology

David J. Oborne

In a further plea on behalf of computer users, David J. Oborne says that much expensive IT equipment remains unused because it is virtually unusable. The answer, he says, is to get machines and users working together in harmony and he provides examples of ergonomics studies which have enabled systems to be designed which better suit their human operators. Oborne is Senior Lecturer in Psychology at the University College of Swansea, South Wales, and this piece comes from a notable recent collection edited by Frank Blackler and David Oborne, Information Technology and People *(British Psychological Society, Leicester, UK and MIT Press, Cambridge, MA, 1987).*

The problems arising from the application of new technology are not new. Ever since people first began to use tools to extend their own limited abilities – to help them to live and to expand their horizons – they have been confronted with the need to adapt both the facilities and them-selves to create harmonious working environments. Archaeological evidence appears to suggest, for example, that stone-age man spent considerable time and effort adapting pieces of flint to make usable killing, digging, and living implements. Even these hundreds of thousands of years ago, in designing their tools primitive people realized that to use the new technologies of the day with any degree of efficiency the tools needed to be designed and built to fit their own requirements; in this case their strength, dexterity, and other physical capacities.

Modern new technologies have advanced considerably since then. These days we are able to generate new tools and applications, rather than relying on nature's provisions. These days the new technologies are mass-produced rather than being built for an individual purpose and for an individual user.

Unfortunately, the very technological advances that have brought humanity from the caves and provided us with safety, comfort, and higher living standards have, in many respects, also brought with them the seeds of their own possible destruction. Since the introduction of mass-produced tools, over the centuries technological advances have not been matched with technological efficiency. Whenever new technology has been introduced – from bows and arrows towards the end of the last millenium to computers towards the end of the present one – the abilities required of the operators have generally been greater than the operators' abilities to perform. Only gradually, when people have learned to adapt themselves to the new technologies and when designers have learned to adapt their systems to the operators, have the new technologies been used with any efficiency. Unfortunately, by then the new technologies are no longer new. Other new technology is introduced and the cycle of inefficiency is continued.

This (hi)story has been, and still is being, repeated even with the new, information technologies that are presented to modern-day people. Systems are still being designed and built, controlling software is still being written, hardware is still being created, which, in the most part, requires from the operator more than the operator is able or willing to provide. Considerable evidence is available to support the argument that users' cognitive, perceptual, and motor abilities are often not sufficient to operate successfully these new, highly sophisticated pieces of information processing machinery. The result is, then, that the theoretical capabilities of these systems are not, in actual fact, realized. Substantial amounts of time, effort and money are being wasted simply because man and machine are not in harmony.

Ergonomics and information technology

The importance of considering further the human operator's role within a technological system was made explicit with the development of the new discipline of ergonomics (sometimes called human factors) during World War II and after. Although the need to regard human abilities as variables that could affect operator efficiency was certainly understood for many years beforehand, it was only with the emergence of this new concept – that *all* features of the system (behavioral, physical, and physiological) should be integrated and studied as a whole – that modern working situations began to be created in which people gained superiority over their environment. It was soon discovered, then, that by taking this comprehensive view of the working system – machine and operator working together and matching each other's abilities and requirements – efficiency could be increased to levels which were theoretically possible. (Oborne, 1982, 1985, provides examples of the extent to which costs have been reduced and efficiency increased through employing general ergonomics investigations.)

The central concept of ergonomics is the working system established between the machine and the operator. In terms of information technology systems, by linking "man" and "machine" in this way a relationship is created between these two components so that the computer presents information to the operator using its output mechanisms and via the operator's sensory apparatus to which a response is given. This time the operator uses his or her output apparatus – usually motor controlled – to present information via the computer's input systems. So, information is passed from the computer to the operator and back to the computer in a closed, information-control loop. Ergonomics' role is to investigate features of this loop and to make the information flow more efficient. Thus, aspects of the operator's performing behavior – sensory, cognitive, and motor abilities – are studied with the aim of discovering their strengths and limitations so that the system can be designed with these aspects in mind.

Ergonomics' role with the new technologies is to consider all aspects of the working relationship set up between the operator and the machine, in which, of course, the environment plays as important part. By gathering information concerning the strengths and weaknesses of the operator's perceptual, cognitive, and motor abilities, and the extent that these features interact with the environment and the task, ergonomics is able to provide design parameters for the working system. By adapting the machine to fit the operator and by designing the system to suit these parameters, work can be carried out with maximum efficiency, comfort, and safety.

Licklider (1960) emphasizes that, when applied to computers at least, this relationship can be described more as a symbiotic than as a "master–slave" relationship (in whichever direction one conceives the relationship to work). Thus, he suggests that each of the two components in the system – "operator" and "computer" – depends on the other to perform well. The relationship, then, is not simply one in which the computer works to extend the abilities of the operator; nor is it one in which the operator simply reacts to stimuli provided by the computer. In many respects, the relationship is one in which not only does the computer depend on the operator to survive (this is obvious, at least at present) but also, in some ways, the operator is now unable to be a viable performing entity without the computer's abilities.

Shackel (1985) has argued cogently that taking account of the ergonomics aspects of IT is bound to become increasingly important as the application and use of IT changes. Thus, when IT was being developed and its uses probed over the past two decades or so, users – often dedicated users – were generally willing to put up with poorly designed interfaces since they knew and understood the system and its foibles. For a viable present and future IT industry, however, the new technology needs to be accepted by the users of the applications in addition to the designers. Doctors, lawyers, educationalists, managers, clerks can now choose between available systems. These "end-users" are thus likely to become the individuals who will determine in the future whether or not a system or a piece of software will survive within a harsh economic climate.

Thus, to be successful, the IT industry must improve the usability of interactive systems, and to do so the understandable orientation of designers in the earlier years must now be completely reversed. "The last shall be first;" designing must *start* with the end user. Therefore the ergonomics aspects become paramount. (1985 p. 265)

Shackel also provides evidence for the economic impact of ergonomics. With personnel time and turnover these days costing more than the systems that they have to use, and the difference becoming greater, "actions to reduce the human cost and simplify the human interface to computers will have the greatest impact on growth."

This paper provides examples of some of the different areas in which ergonomics investigations have enabled new information technologies to be designed to suit the operator. It takes a selective view of the various aspects that ergonomics needs to consider to provide the relevant information for designers to design for usability. Because of the wealth of material to draw from and the limited space available some specific applications are not covered in detail – rather, the principles to be applied will be emphasized. Thus, neither speech input nor output is considered, nor the ergonomic problems surrounding new applications of IT in industry, such as flexible manufacturing systems or robotics.

Essentially, the approach is to consider the two sides of the information technology loop – presenting information from the machine to the user and vice versa. Within these two broad areas, evidence will be adduced to illustrate the need to consider the cognitive, perceptual and motor features of the user and the relationship of such data to designing various parts of the system.

Presenting visual information to the operator

Over the years, some considerable ergonomics work has been done to investigate many different features of display design. The thrust of such work can, essentially, be classified into two areas. First, aspects of the display's physical parameters: brightness, contrast, color, flicker, etc. and the extent to which these relate to the observer's abilities to see clearly the material presented. In the second area, work has been done to consider more the perceptual parameters of the material presented – character shape and size, display line spacing, character case, etc. Considerable amounts of data have arisen from such investigations and, since many of these results have been reported elsewhere (Cakir, 1980; Oborne, 1985), detailed consideration will not be given here. Reasonably firm design parameters are thus quite widely available, so that there is no real excuse for designers and manufacturers to produce display systems which are less than usable for most people. Unfortunately, evidence is available which suggests that many of the guidelines are not being taken notice of.

Given that there appears to be a mis-match between the amount of design data available and the extent to which these data are incorporated into display designs, it is pertinent to question the reasons for the mis-match. A possible answer lies in the relevance of the available data to present-day applications. Without considering their application, ergonomics studies of, for example, optimum character founts remain just that – studies of optimum character founts. They are not studies of optimum character founts for spreadsheet use, for example, in which the display consists of high-density groups of numbers, nor of optimum character founts for use with graphs, in which the display is essentially pictorial and the characters present supplementary information. They are not even studies of optimum character founts for different sized display areas: 80 column, 40 column, high resolution, low resolution screens, for example. It is accepted, therefore, that some of the laboratory studies published in the available literature address questions that may not be central either to those being asked by designers or to those being faced by end-users. In this respect Shackel's criticisms of IT designers who frequently disregard the end-user might also be applied to IT investigators.

To produce relevant design data for presenting material to the user it is likely that future studies will have to relate more to the end-user and to the end-use. What does the material represent? How should it be presented to emphasize its meaning? What does the user wish to obtain from the material? Within ergonomics the need for such questions is generally becoming accepted – particularly with studies of task classification, task requirements and different forms of investigative methods.

Task classification

The simple example given above relating to the design of character founts indicates the importance of understanding something about the types of task normally carried out using a VDT screen and computer system. Different tasks may require different actions from the operator and impose different types and levels of strain. Yamamoto (1985), for example, points out that there is quite a considerable difference between normal, non-computerized, office work and office work that involves computer operations. Thus, whereas the non-computerized office worker generally works at a self-paced rate (for example, reading the next document when he or she decides to pick it up), the computerized worker's pace is generally determined by the computer – a response generally generated another display and the computer is ready for another response. Clearly, then, different working practices may require different ergonomics considerations. Indeed, evidence that even the same task – for example, reading a page – may be performed in a different way using a vertical (computer screen) as opposed to a horizontal (paper) display (Wright and Lickorish, 1983) suggests that far more consideration needs to be placed on the tasks performed by the operator, rather than just on the design of the system itself.

To produce a classification of the many different types of work carried out using visual displays would be a considerable task. However, some start has been made, although this has been primarily in the area of investigating health complaints of VDT users. Very little work has been done in considering other ergonomic aspects of the systems.

Grandjean (1980) classifies VDT work into two main types: data entry and conversational. In the first, the operator spends the largest proportion of the time entering data without much interaction with the machine: word processing, spreadsheet work, statistical analyses, etc. In conversational work, however, more interaction occurs with some time spent waiting for responses from the computer. Different physical and cognitive loads, then, are placed on the operator. Interestingly, the different types of task produce different patterns of fatigue complaints, with the data entry processors reporting higher frequencies of postural problems.

Coe et al. (1980) also reported variations in the effects of different working patterns on operator complaints (and thus efficiency). They divided the type of work done into four categories. First, *input* work was similar to Grandjean's data entry work. Secondly, *creative* work which included tasks such as computer programming. Thirdly, *editing* tasks, which were similar to Grandjean's conversational category, in that continual interaction occurred with the systems. Finally, Coe et al. included a *question–answer* category in which the tasks were highly screen interactive and involved a great deal of dialogue between the screen and keyboard. Again, significant differences were obtained between the classes of users for fatigue and strain complaints.

Task requirements and information layout

Following from classification of the types of task to be carried out is attention to the requirements of those tasks – what they expect from the operator and what the operator is able to give. Again, ergonomics considerations are paramount in this respect, since they stress the matching of operator and system by designing the system to suit the operator rather than vice versa.

Layout for information seekers Wright (1986) argues strongly that task requirements must be viewed mainly in information processing terms. With such a view, she suggests, the material displayed needs to be compatible with the ways in which the operator is likely to process the information at a cognitive level. This means that presentation of the same type of material may have to be different in relation to the operator's needs, abilities and requirements.

Take, for example, a table of numbers within a spreadsheet and compare it with a table of numbers representing bus departure times. (Both of these, of course, may be presented either on paper or on a VDT screen.) Although both presentations provide numerical information in tabular form, they are likely to be used differently and may well require different forms of input. The spreadsheet user is likely to need the numerical information in order possibly to compare columns – profit and loss – to extract trends, etc. and will have the input data to hand in a particular format – finances, exam marks, etc. The timetable reader, on the other hand, will require that same sort of information – numbers – but for a different purpose. He or she will wish to know which bus to catch, at what time it arrives, whether there is a faster route, etc. A number of ergonomics studies are available which have considered the role of structure for different types of material to be presented.

It should be clear, then, that the ergonomics of the designed material presented to the user will need to vary in terms of what the task requires and in relation to the operator's processing and actions. In this case the advances provided by cognitive psychologists relating to perception, perceptual organization, thinking, and reasoning should all play a role in determining the extent to which displayed material can be designed to be compatible with the observer's own conceptions and abilities.

Layout for information readers   As well as the need to consider the form in which the user requires the information, a fundamental question also relates to the presentation for ease of reading itself. Studies of eye movements during reading and the extent to which the reader's cognitive structure imposes different reading patterns on the material are particularly germane in relation to text layout and arrangement.

Since a stable image is only formed when both the eyes and the object are stationary, the movement of the eyes over the material during reading is characterized by a succession of fast movements (saccades) and stationary periods (fixations). The importance of understanding and analyzing saccadic eye movements to the present discussion lies first in the fact that material presented that does not fit the saccadic movement is likely to be perceived less efficiently or, possibly, missed altogether. Secondly, saccadic patterns relate to the cognitive processing occurring within the perceiver (Rayner, 1977). Again, this indicates the need to consider the processes involved in the task and what the user wishes to obtain from the material.

The two important parameters of saccadic movements that relate to reading efficiency are the duration of each fixation and the number of fixations required. In this respect, the average length of a saccade appears to be about 2 degrees of visual angle (which conforms to about six 10-pitch or eight 12-pitch character spaces). For skilled readers the average fixation durations lie between 200 and 250 msec (Rayner, 1977), although there is a great deal of individual variability in this matter and this is thought to relate to reading skill.

Discussing the relationship of line saccades to the reading process, Bouma (1980) points to the importance of typographical design:

The horizontal extent of line saccades is controlled by visual information in the left visual field, concerning the far left-hand margin, which should therefore be in a straight vertical line . . . with a sufficiently wide margin . . . The vertical extent of line saccades is controlled by perceived inter-line distance. If this vertical component is inaccurate, the eye may mistakenly jump over two or perhaps even three lines.

Although information regarding the eye's saccadic movements indicates the reader's control movements and possible times taken to process a piece of text, it is not the full story. Information is also needed concerning the amount of information that the reader can process at any one fixation. This is known as the "span of perception" and is another aspect which determines reading speed and accuracy. Evidence from reading studies (McConkie and Rayner, 1975) suggests that the smaller the text area available to the subject, the longer it takes to read.

Furthermore, although material that appears central to the eye is most readily perceived and interpreted, readers also register information that falls outside the normal perceptual area. To what extent such material is used in comprehension rather than in eye control, however, is debatable. McConkie (1976), for example, has suggested that readers obtain different types of information from different regions within the perceptual span during a fixation in reading. Information falling on the fovea (the centre of the retina) is processed for its semantic content and information from the edge of the retina (the parafoveal area) is limited to rather gross featural information such as word shape and word length.

From an applied viewpoint, then, the importance of understanding the nature and parameters of saccadic eye movements during reading concerns the layout of textual and other material to fit in with these movements, and the division of words, phrases and sentences so that they are not frequently split in places that make comprehension difficult. Thus, the evidence that each saccade encompasses about six to eight character spaces should suggest that line lengths ought to be some multiple of this distance so that the eye does not need to make partial saccades. If the width is too small, however, only a few saccades may be possible on any one line, thus necessitating recursions to previous lines with the attendant problems of directing the eyes to the beginning of another line. On the other hand, if it is too large, too many saccades may be needed to scan the line.

More importantly, perhaps, it is necessary to ensure that when the eye is at the extreme right-hand end of one line it does not have too far to travel back to begin the next line (again, the optic control mechanism can lead the eye to the beginning of the wrong line). In this context, Bouma (1980) relates the length of a line of text (that is the distance between the left- and right-hand margins) to the angle over which the eye travels to reach the next line. This, he suggests, should be approximately 2. For long lines of text, therefore, the interline spacing should be reduced.

Linking the output to the input

Although considerable space has been given in this paper to the importance of displaying material in a way that suits the cognitive capacities and wishes of the operator, the other side of the coin – the way in which the operator presents his or her information to the machine – should not be forgotten. This, after all, represents the other half of the closed-loop system so dear to the hearts of ergonomists and it is as important to understand the user's abilities and capacities in this respect as it is to understand them in terms of the material displayed. However, before considering input devices in any detail, the cognitive link between input and output actions should be discussed. That is, the extent to which the operator's actions need to be compatible with those of the display and vice versa. This is an area of ergonomics study called *compatibility*.

The need to ensure compatibility arises for three reasons. First, an incompatible display–control relationship is likely to lead to reduced response speeds. Second, the learning time for the operation of equipment on which the controls are compatible with the display will be much shorter than if they were incompatible. Third, and perhaps most insidiously, when placed under stress an operator's performance on equipment with incompatible display–control relationships will deteriorate as he or she reverts to the relationship expected to occur.

Three main ways of arranging compatibility between control and display exist. The first is *spatial compatibility*, which occurs when the position of items in the display suggests the appropriate control response. Second is movement compatibility. In this case the movement of items in the display suggests the way in which the associated control should be operated, and vice versa. For example, most operators would expect the right-hand cursor control key to move the cursor to the right of a screen, and the left-hand key to move it leftwards. Relationships which are expected by the majority of the population are described as population stereotypes. Oborne (1982) and Loveless (1962) provide details of these types of compatibility relationships and suggest means of predicting their direction. Last is cognitive compatibility, in which the actions required of the operator by the program itself need to be compatible with the user's expectations of their effects.

The importance of ensuring cognitive compatibility in computer programs and system commands has been highlighted by workers at the Applied Psychology Unit in Cambridge (Morton et al., 1979; Barnard et. al., 1981; Hammond et. al. 1981; Barnard et al., 1982). In essence, they extract three forms of cognitive incompatibility: linguistic, memory, and perceptual.

Linguistic incompatibility can occur at both a syntactic and at a semantic level. It often arises at a syntactic level because the information following commands such as DELETE, MOVE, INSERT, are generally used in abbreviated forms, such as DELETE *x, y* or MOVE *x, y*. In "natural" language, that is the language used by the operator, the above abbreviated commands might well be interpreted as DELETE (information *x*), from (file *y*), or MOVE (information *x*), to (file *y*). If this is how the computer programmer or system designer intended the actions to take place, then there is no syntactic incompatibility. Often, however, commands of the form DELETE *x, y* imply the reverse of what is expected in natural language, that is DELETE *y* from file *x*.

Semantic linguistic incompatibility can occur in a similar way. In this case, however, the problem arises over meanings of commands – particularly when the commands are computer-centric. Examples might include the use of the terms PUT and GET or LOAD and DUMP. Both of these pairs of operations are often used to transfer information from the computer to some storage medium and vice versa. However, the direction of the transfer is only immediately obvious if the user has already accepted that the computer is at the center of the operation. Carroll (1982) also discusses some of these semantic incompatibility problems.

Memory incompatibility arises because the machine's requirements of the user's memory capabilities can be incompatible with the user's actual abilities. Again, linguistically incompatible terms can increase the memory load required because they require the user to remember, for each command, the relationship between the variables *x* and *y*.

Perceptual incompatibility relates primarily to the presentation of information as displayed on the computer screen and its relationship to the operations required of the user.

Presenting the information to the computer

Whereas the behavioral and ergonomic questions surrounding computer output – its design and presentation – relate essentially to the operator's cognitive capacities and requirements, inputting information from the operator to the computer concerns more the use of limbs. Thus, the considerations relate to the user's skill, and psychology's role in this respect is to understand and manipulate skilled behavior. However, the importance of cognition should be be forgotten because it is a simple and obvious fact that the execution of a skill depends on the cognitive structure available to the operator. For example typing, a skilled behavior that is very important to the efficient use of modern computer input devices, is seen to be as much a cognitive skill as it is a motor skill. In this case, considerable preprocessing of the material-to-be-typed occurs *before* the fingers hit the keys.

This part of the paper considers various types of input device that are currently available, and the extent to which ergonomists have had a significant part to play in their design for effective use.

In general, the primary ways in which information is passed (input) to the computer is via one of the operator's three effector systems: limb movement and touch (usually using the hands or fingers), speech, and even eye movement. A number of possible devices can be conceived, although unfortunately there have been very few comparative studies to investigate which is the best type of control for particular circumstances. Those studies that have been reported have generally been restricted in their application and have considered simply the relative efficiencies of different controls for the simple task of selecting an item from a screen. Furthermore, no study has been reported that has considered operator preference. The work which has been done, however, has consistently indicated keyboard controls to take longer and to be more prone to errors (Earl and Goff, 1965; Goodwin, 1975). For inputting discrete pieces of information, continuous positioning devices such as lightpens are the most efficient (Card et al., 1978).

Keyboards

Alphabetic keyboards   The normal QWERTY typewriter keyboard has been in existence since before the beginning of this century and was designed to conform to the mechanical constraints of contemporary typewriters: the apparent haphazard arrangement of letters was developed to slow typists down to prevent jamming of the keys. This presents a prime example of how a system can develop and become accepted within new technology for entirely the wrong reasons. Ergonomics needs constantly to expose inappropriate design and, possibly more importantly, inappropriate use of design.

Despite the apparent inappropriateness of the QWERTY arrangement it would appear to have some saving graces – particularly from the viewpoint of the physical loads placed on operators' hands. It does distribute evenly the workload assigned to each hand and thus may reduce fatigue. Noyes (1983a), for example, argues that common letter sequences typed on the QWERTY board involve either alternate hands being used, the whole hand being moved over the keyboard or non-adjacent fingers being moved sequentially.

A number of alternative keyboard arrangements have subsequently been proposed. All are based on the frequencies with which letters and letters pairs occur in the English language. The two which have captured most experimental time are the Dvorak and the alphabetic board.

The Dvorak board (patented by A. Dvorak in 1932) was produced as a result of a decade of physiological and language research. The essential feature of the key arrangement is that all vowels and the most used consonants are on the second (or "home") row, so that something like 70 percent of common words are typed on this row alone. Generally, the arrangement means that vowels are typed with the left hand and frequent (home row) consonants with the right hand, producing, it is argued, a more even distribution of finger movements and a bias towards the right hand. It also reduces the between-rows movement by 90 percent, and allows 35 percent of all words normally used to be typed on the middle row.

Controversy presently exists as to the relative merits of the QWERTY and the Dvorak boards. For example, a US government sponsored study in 1956 demonstrated little difference between the arrangements (Alden et al., 1976). Martin (1972), however, discusses (unreported) novice training experiments carried out in Great Britain which demonstrated a 10 percent saving in training time using the Dvorak board. Furthermore, Dunn (1971) argues that the Dvorak board is superior in terms of ease of learning, reduced likelihood of error and fatigue and increased speed of entry.

On the alphabetic board, keys are arranged as the name suggests: from A to Z. The argument behind the use of this arrangement is, quite simply, that an alphabetical ordering of the keys makes logical sense, particularly to inexperienced typists, who need to spend considerable time learning the QWERTY arrangement.

Despite the apparent logic of using an alphabetically arranged board, Norman and Fisher (1982) point out that the available studies do not support the view that inexperienced typists find the alphabetic board easier to use. Indeed both Hirsh (1970) and Michaels (1971) have shown that for semi-skilled typists, keying rates and error correction are better using the QWERTY board, and performance on the two boards is essentially the same for novices. Norman and Fisher suggest two reasons for these findings: first – an experimental one – it is difficult to find subjects who have not had some exposure to the QWERTY arrangement. Second, the alphabetic keyboard, although logically superior, still requires considerable visual search and mental processing (to remember, for example, that "m" appears after "k"). At the novice stage at least, therefore, all keyboard layouts are equivalent. Once the skill has been learned visual feedback gives way to more efficient feedback from the limbs themselves, so that the different board arrangements are likely to be equally efficient.

Numeric keyboards Fewer studies have been performed to determine the optimum arrangement of the numeric keys (i.e. 0–9) than the alphabetic keys – possibly because, with only ten keys, there are fewer sensible arrangements that can be accommodated. A number of these arrangements were investigated by Deininger (1960) in a study of pushbutton telephone sets. Four designs were shown to be roughly equally acceptable on criteria such as keying time, errors and "votes" for and against. For "engineering" reasons, however, Deininger suggested an arrangement of a 3 + 3 + 3 + 1 matrix starting with 1, 2, 3 on the top row and ending with 0 below the third row. Indeed, the "standard" telephone keypad has this arrangement.

Although this arrangement has become standard for telephone keypads, it is not currently used for numerical input on keyboards such as calculators. This is normally the reverse of the telephone arrangement, the keys on the 3 + 3 + 3 + 1 matrix having the order 7, 8, 9; 4, 5, 6; 1, 2, 3; and 0. Conrad and Hull (1968) compared the keying efficiency of these two types of arrangement. No significant differences were obtained in terms of the speed of data entry but they did find that significantly fewer errors were made using the telephone keypad (1, 2, 3; 4, 5, 6; etc.) than with the calculator pad arrangement (7, 8, 9; 4, 5, 6; etc) (6.4 percent versus 8.2 percent).

Chord keyboards   In the search for improved ways of keying data, particularly alphabetic data, the possibility of reducing the number of keys by requiring the operator to press more than one key at a time has often been suggested. Such key arrangements are called chord keyboards and they appear in many different forms. (Litterick, 1981, describes some of these boards, and Noyes, 1983b, describes the history and development of chord keying.) The efficiency of such boards, of course, will be determined by the combinations of keys used to produce particular letters – from the viewpoint both of the operator's ability to use various finger combinations and to learn and remember key sets (see Seibel, 1964).

Very few experiments have been performed to compare directly keying performance using a typewriter and a chord keyboard. Again, this is probably because of difficulties in obtaining matched groups of subjects and being able to train them for very long periods of time using the same instructor. Nevertheless, the comparative studies that are available have demonstrated a chord keyboard performance superiority (Bowen and Guiness, 1965) and reduced training time (Conrad and Longman, 1965).

Other types of input device

With the need to input varying forms of information, computer systems have caused a number of innovative designs to be created. Unfortunately, as will become apparent, the amount of behavioral and ergonomics input to the design of such devices has been minimal. Consequently, such devices are appearing more frequently on the market without having been considered in terms of user ability. As argued above, history is repeating itself. This time, however, users are unlikely to have to wait for nearly a century before the usable features of such devices are studied – as they did for evaluations of the QWERTY keyboard. This time, market forces will not allow it, since only the ergonomically designed devices – designed to fit the user and users' actions – will survive. The remainder of this section describes some of these devices and indicates areas of study that are sadly lacking.

Touch displays   These allow the user to input information to the machine simply by touching an appropriate part of the screen or some representation of the screen. Since the computer screen both presents information to and receives information from the operator, it combines the functions of keyboard and display. Both Hopkin (1971) and McEwing (1977) discuss the advantages of screen based displays, which can be summarized thus: they are easy and fast to use, training time is reduced (Usher, 1982), they minimize errors, they are flexible, and operator reaction is generally favorable. Against these advantages, however, Pfauth and Priest (1981) suggest a number of disadvantages: initial high cost for the system, increased programmer time, reduced flexibility for some types of input, possible screen glare, physical fatigue from reaching to the screen, and the finger and hand blocking the operator's line of sight to important areas of the screen.

Light pens   Like touch displays, light pens are fully interactive control devices. They can be used effectively to position the cursor on the screen or to select responses from a "menu" displayed to the operator. Unfortunately, little research appears to have been carried out to investigate either the design or the efficiency of this type of control, although Oborne (1985) discusses various features that should be important.

Bar code scanners   These are devices which both look and operate very much like light pens, but they are not used interactively with the computer screen; rather they are passed over alternate black and white bars, the composition of which contains the information to be input. They have a major advantage in that their operating postures are not constrained by the computer system itself so that the arm and hand do not need to be maintained under static load to enable the pen to touch the screen. However, Wilson and Grey (1983) point out that the fixed "pen" system of scanners, in which the material to be read is passed over the scanner, can create postural difficulties for the operator.

Levers and joysticks   The difference between a lever and a joystick is simply that joysticks operate in two dimensions whereas levers only operate in one. For this reason, joysticks are used more often for cursor positioning. Because they are used in situations in which precision adjustments are made, it is desirable that only the hand and fingers are used, since these muscles are more densely supplied with nerves than, for example, the arm. For this reason joysticks are generally smaller than levers. To aid precision they should have resistance in all directions with, perhaps, a return to center position if the hand is moved. Morgan et al. (1963) further suggest that the joystick should be designed to enable the operator to rest the wrist while making the movements, and that the pivot point should be positioned under the point at which the wrist is rested.

The roller ball and mouse   As the name suggests, "roller balls" are spherically shaped objects which the operator can rotate in any direction. Their distinctive characteristic is that they rotate within a socket; thus they are fixed pieces of equipment. The "mouse," on the other hand, operates in a similar fashion to the roller ball but it is not fixed; the operator is able to move it around, much like a pen is moved around paper to form characters. Card, English and Burr (1978) have demonstrated the superiority of these input devices over the conventional keyboard when used to move a cursor around the screen.

Summary

Through various examples, this paper has emphasized the need to consider all aspects of the operator's cognitive, physical and physiological behavior when interacting with computer systems. It has stressed the importance of understanding the many different uses to which computers can be put and adapting the hardware and software accordingly. Only when this occurs, when the user and the system are in harmony with each other, when a true symbiotic relationship can emerge, will users be able to apply the computer to their and its fullest potential. Since the users are the choosers, only when this occurs will current and potential computer systems become competitive and viable.

References

Alden, D.G., Daniels, R.W., and Kanarick, A.F. (1976) "Keyboard design and operation: A review of the major issues," *Human Factors*, 14, pp. 275–93.

Barnard, P.J., Hammond, N.V. and Morton, J. (1981) "Consistency and compatibility in human–computer dialogue," *International Journal of Man-Machine Studies*, 15, pp. 87–134.

Barnard, P.J., Hammond, N.V., Maclean, A., et al. (1982) "Learning and remembering interactive commands." IBM research report HF 055, Portsmouth, UK: IBM

Bouma, H. (1980) "Visual reading processes and the quality of text displays," in E. Grandjean and E. Vigliani (eds), *Ergonomic Aspects of Visual Display Terminals*, London: Taylor and Francis.

Bowen, H.M. and Guiness, G.V. (1965) "Preliminary experiments on keyboard design for semi-automatic mailsorting," *Journal of Applied Psychology*, 49, pp. 194–8.

Cakir, A., Hart, D.J. and Stewart, T.F.M. (1980) *Visual Display Terminals,* Chichester, UK: John Wiley.

Card, S.K., English, W.K. and Burr, B.J. (1978) "Evaluation of mouse, rate-controlled isometric joystick, step keys, and text keys for selection on a CRT," *Ergonomics*, 21, pp. 601–13

Carroll, J.M. (1982) "Learning, using and designing command paradigms," *Human Learning*, 1, pp. 31–62.

Coe, J.B., Cuttle, K., McClellon, W.C. et al. (1980) *Visual Display Units;* Report W/1/80, Wellington: New Zealand Department of Health.

Conrad, R. and Hull, A.J. (1968) "The preferred layout for data-entry keysets," *Ergonomics*, 11, pp. 165–73.

Conrad, R. and Longman, D.J.A. (1965) "Standard typewriter versus chord keyboard – an experimental comparison," *Ergonomics*, 8, pp. 77–88.

Deininger, R.L. (1960) "Human factors engineering studies of the design and use of pushbutton telephone sets." *The Bell System Technical Journal,* 39, pp. 995–1012.

Dunn, A.G. (1971) "Engineering the keyboard from the human factors viewpoint," *Computers and Automation*, February, pp. 32–3.

Earl, W.K. and Goff, J.D. (1965) "Comparison of two data entry methods," *Perceptual and Motor Skills*, 20, pp. 369–84.

Goodwin, N.C. (1975) "Cursor positioning on an electronic display using lightpen, lightgun or keyboard for three basic tasks," *Human Factors*, 17, pp. 289–95.

Gould, J. (1982) "Writing and speaking letters and messages," *International Journal of Man-Machine Studies*, 16, pp. 147–71.

Gotlieb, C.C. and Borodin, A. (1973) *Social Issues in Computing*, New York: Academic Press.

Grandjean, E. (1980) "Ergonomics of VDUs: Review of present knowledge," in E. Grandjean and E. Vigliani (eds), *Ergonomics Aspects of Visual Display Terminals*, London: Taylor and Francis.

Hammond, N.V., Long, J.B., Morton, J., et al. (1981) *Documenting Human–Computer Mismatch at the Individual and Organisational Levels*, IBM research report HF 040, Portsmouth: IBM.

Hirsh, R.S. (1970) "Effects of standard versus alphabetical keyboard formats on typing performance," *Journal of Applied Psychology*, 54, pp. 484–90.

Hopkins, V.D. (1971) "The evaluation of touch displays for air traffic control tasks," IEF Conference on Displays, publication no. 80.

Licklider, J.C. (1960) "Man–computer symbiosis," *Institute of Radio Engineers Transactions of Human Factors in Electronics.*

Litterick, I. (1981) "QWERTYUIOP – dinosaur in the computer age," *New Scientist*, 89, pp. 66–8.

Loveless, N.E. (1962) "Direction-of-motion stereotypes: A review," *Ergonomics*, 5, pp. 357–83.

Martin, A. (1972) "A new keyboard layout," *Applied Ergonomics*, 3, pp. 48–51.

McConkie, G.W. (1976) "The use of eye-movement data in determining the perceptual span in reading," in R.A. Monty and J.W. Senders (eds), *Eye Movements and Psychological Processes*, Hillsdale, NJ: Lawrence Erlbaum Associates.

McConkie, G.W. and Rayner, K. (1975) "The span of effective stimulus during a fixation in reading," *Perception and Psychophysics*, 17, pp. 578–86.

McEwing, R.W. (1977) "Touch displays in industrial computer systems," in *Displays for Man-Machine Systems*, London: IEE.

Michaels, S.E. (1971) "Qwerty versus alphabetic keyboards as a function of typing skill," *Human Factors*, 13, pp. 419–26.

Morgan, C.T., Cooks, J.S., Chapanis, A, et al. (1963) *Human Engineering Guide to Equipment Design*, New York: McGraw-Hill.

Morton, J., Barnard, P., Hammond, N., et al. (1979) "Interacting with the computer: A framework," in E. Boutmy and A. Danthine (eds), *Teleinformatics '79*, Amsterdam: North Holland.

Norman, D.A. and Fisher, D. (1982) "Why alphabetic keyboards are not easy to use: Keyboard layout doesn't much matter," *Human Factors*, 24, pp. 509–19.

Noyes, J. (1983a) "The QWERTY keyboard: A review," *International Journal of Man-Machine Studies*, 18, pp. 265–88.

Noyes, J. (1983b) "Chord keyboards," *Applied Ergonomics*, 14, pp. 55–9.

Oborne, D.J. (1982) *Ergonomics at Work*, Chichester, UK: John Wiley.

Oborne, D.J. (1985) *Computers at Work: A Behavioural Approach*, Chichester, UK: John Wiley.

Pfauth, M. and Priest, J. (1981) "Person–computer interface using touch screen devices," *Proceedings of the 25th Annual Meeting of the Human Factors Society*, Baltimore: HFS.

Rayner, K. (1977) "Visual attention in reading: Eye movements reflect cognitive processes," *Memory and Cognition*, 5, pp. 443–8.

Rayner, K. (1978) "Eye movements in reading and information processing," *Psychological Bulletin*, 85, pp. 618–60.

Seibel, R. (1964) "Data entry through chord, parallel entry devices," *Human Factors*, 6, pp. 189–92.

Shackel, B. (1985) "Ergonomics in information technology in Europe – a review," *Behaviour and Information Technology*, 4, pp. 263–89.

Usher, D.M. (1982) "A touch sensitive VDU compared with a computer-aided key pad for controlling power generating plant," Paper presented to IEE Conference on Man–Machine Systems.

Wilson, J. and Grey, S. (1983) "The ergonomics of laser scanner checkout systems," in K. Coombes (ed.), *Proceedings of the 1983 Ergonomics Society*, London: Taylor and Francis.

Wright, P. (1986) "Phenomena, function and design," in D.J. Oborne (ed.), *Contemporary Ergonomics 1986*, London: Taylor and Francis.

Wright, P. and Lickorish, A. (1983) "Proof-reading texts on screen and paper," *Behaviour and Information Technology*, 2, pp. 227–35.

Yamamoto, S. (1985) "A study of VDU operators' information processing based on saccadic eye movements and response time," *Ergonomics*, 28, pp. 855–68.

The VDT Debate

Kenneth R. Foster

The introduction of IT into the workplace has been marked by controversy over possible health hazards arising from the frequent use of VDTs. In particular, the use of VDTs has been linked to birth defects. Kenneth Foster provides a readable but sober account of the controversy and in so doing demonstrates the value of the scientific approach. The author is Associate Professor of Bioengineering at the University of Pennsylvania and this article first appeared in American Scientist, *vol. 74, March–April 1986.*

Within the past decade a great change has swept the workplace, with the nearly universal adoption of computers and word processors. An estimated 10 million Americans – travel agents, clerks, secretaries, students, and professors – now spend their days with keyboards and video display terminals (VDTs). Although the increase in efficiency has proved a great benefit, there have also been complaints of visual problems and fatigue associated with the use of VDTs.

In the early 1980s, concern spread about the possibility of a serious problem to users of VDTs: an increase in the risk of miscarriage or of having children with major birth defects. Despite repeated assurances by public officials that there was no reason for concern, the alarm grew, leaving effects that are still apparent today.

A history of this issue can be written on several levels: the events themselves, the different perceptions of their significance, secondary results of the controversy, and the more general problem of establishing hazard or its absence. For myself, I do not believe that the available evidence establishes any connection between the use of VDTs and reproductive problems, nor that any strong connection is likely to exist. More interesting is the evolution of the controversy, and the general problem of how to deal with suspected hazards whose possibility is raised by observations that are open to varying interpretations.

On July 23, 1980 the *Toronto Globe and Mail* carried an article under the headline "Work Conditions Probed at [*Toronto*] *Star* as Defects Found in 4 Employees' Babies."[1] Four women in the classified advertising department of the *Star* had given birth the previous autumn to children with birth defects, including a cleft palate, complex heart defects, an underdeveloped eye, and club feet. All four mothers had worked with VDTs during the early stages of their pregnancies.

Other news reports soon appeared, covering both the concerns of workers and the reassuring comments of authorities. An article in the *Toronto Star*, titled "VDT Operators Worry As Experts Pooh-pooh Fears," began: "Thousands of Canadians edged away from their television screens with a tinge of fear this week, but the experts say they see no reason for concern."[2] The article explained that the (Canadian) Radiation Protection Bureau had tested radiation emissions from VDTs, and the acting director of the bureau was quoted: "The machines are safe . . . There's absolutely nothing of any hazard emitted by VDTs."

On July 31, 1980 the *Toronto Star* reported the findings of the Toronto Department of Health.[3] The report concluded: "There is no scientific evidence whatever that radiation from VDTs is a health hazard, even to pregnant women, nor is there any evidence that four abnormal births by *Toronto Star* VDT operators were caused by VDT radiation . . . The energies of government should not be wasted over and over again on what is now quite clear." The reporter noted, however, that in Gander, Newfoundland, "VDTs . . . are being checked for radiation leakage after [a VDT] operator gave birth to a baby two months premature and with spinal problems."

Other suspicious groupings were soon reported: at the offices of the Solicitor General in Ottawa (7 adverse outcomes of 8 pregnancies) and of the Attorney General in Toronto (10 of 19), the Air Canada offices at Dorval Airport, Montreal (7 of 13), Sears, Roebuck in Dallas (8 of 12), the Defense Logistics Agency in Atlanta (10 of 15), Pacific Northwest Bell in Renton, Washington (3 of 5), and Surrey Memorial Hospital in Vancouver (5 of 6). The problems included birth defects, spontaneous abortions, respiratory problems in the newborns, Down's syndrome, spina bifida, and premature birth.[4]

The apparent danger to pregnancy quickly became an issue between management and employees. At the *Montreal Gazette*, pregnant employees refused to work on VDTs until the terminals could be tested to verify that they did not emit dangerous levels of radiation. The Federal Labour Minister of Canada endorsed the recommendation of a task force that pregnant workers should have the right to transfer without loss of seniority to jobs not requiring the use of VDTs. A union official at Surrey Memorial Hospital was quoted, "Enough is enough. We want those VDTs put out of service until they have been completely gone over."[5] In 1982 a public service arbitration board in Ontario ruled that the belief that radiation from a terminal could harm an unborn child was reasonable grounds for a pregnant government employee to refuse to work on a VDT.[6]

Several researchers followed up the early reports of reproductive disorders. At first, X-ray emissions were suspected as the agent of damage; however, a growing series of studies (which by 1983 had surveyed more than 2,000 VDTs in Canada alone) showed that levels of X-radiation were extremely low and in the overwhelming majority of cases unmeasurable.[7] Then other possible factors were considered. At Surrey Hospital, levels of ionizing and non-ionizing radiation associated with VDTs were measured in two departments: the accounting department, in which several abnormal pregnancies had been reported, and the medical records department, in which no grouping of problems was reported. Emissions of X-rays, microwaves, and ultraviolet and infrared radiation were very low or undetectable. The electric fields at very low frequencies were found to be more intense near the VDTs in the accounting department than in the medical records department. No toxic chemicals were detected in either area.[8]

A study conducted by the US Army Environmental Hygiene Agency at the Defense Logistics Agency failed to locate an obvious source of the problem there.[9] The study verified the initial reports of the cluster (three cases of congenital malformation and seven first-trimester miscarriages). It concluded that the grouping of birth defects was highly unlikely, but it was less sure about the grouping of first-trimester miscarriages, since the true background rate of such problems is not well established.

In a follow-up study at Sears, Roebuck by the Center for Disease Control, no characteristic could be found in the affected women that was significantly associated with adverse reproductive outcomes. A statistical analysis found no clear association between the extent of exposure to VDTs (hours per week or proximity to a terminal) and adverse outcomes of pregnancies.[10]

Clusters

No positive explanation has been found for the groupings of reproductive problems. While some reproductive hazard from VDTs might well be demonstrated in the future, another possibility is that the groupings, or clusters, as they are frequently called, were simply random occurrences.

The probability (P) of a cluster occurring in any single group of women is low – in the range 0.001 to 0.01 for the groups at the Defense Logistics Agency or at Sears, Roebuck.[11] However, in a sufficiently large number of groups, clusters are likely to be found. The "expected–unexpected cluster" is a phenomenon well known to epidemiologists (and also to gamblers). In their report, the Centers for Disease Control calculate that if 7 million VDT workers of both sexes were arbitrarily divided into 100,000 groups of 70 workers, 2,500 groups could be expected to contain an unlikely ($P < 0.05$) cluster of abnormal pregnancies over a three-year period. Of these, 50 groups would be expected to contain a highly unlikely ($P < 0.001$) cluster.

Thus, observed in retrospect, a cluster may have no epidemiological significance, however traumatic it may have been to the individuals involved. Roberts, writing for a task force on the possible health hazards of VDTs, notes: "The greatest problem facing us when interpreting a cluster of cases is that it has only come to our attention because it *is* an unusual cluster and not the result of a routine pregnancy outcome surveillance study."[12]

An epidemiologist would consider the reported clusters to be provocative, but inadequate to demonstrate any connection between reproductive problems and VDTs. Yet a number of people concluded that a connection existed. These differing perceptions bear closer examination.

In the news reports and other comment on the clusters of abnormal pregnancies, there emerged two distinct attitudes about what conclusions could be drawn from the observed events. People with different viewpoints frequently seemed not to be in communication but to be talking past each other.

Some participants quickly reified the observed connections among the events into "effects," a term that embodies assumptions of causality. Thus, the pamphlet *The Hazards of VDTs*, published by the Ontario Public Service Employees Union, contained a chapter entitled

"Radiation Injury among VDT Operators."[13] The pamphlet mentioned several clusters of reproductive problems as "cases of possible radiation damage." It concluded with an urgent call for research on long-term effects of low-level radiation from VDTs.

As to the repeated assurances by officials that no reason for concern existed, the pamphlet explained, "There is a fundamental conflict between physics and biology . . . The physical approach of the regulatory agencies simply applies the principles of physics to determine how, *in theory*, electromagnetic fields can produce biological effects. In this approach, *theory* is the touchstone: biological results not explained by the theory are viewed as oddities and placed in limbo." A similar view was expressed in a legal discussion of the controversy about possible hazards of low-level nonionizing radiation: "To say that there are no effects [of nonionizing radiation] when effects are in fact observed, simply because the effects cannot be explained, is like saying no apples fell until Newton discovered the law of gravity."[14]

If the clusters are regarded as an "effect," their lack of explanation is indeed troubling. The repeated assurances that levels of ionizing or nonionizing radiation from VDTs are unmeasurable or negligible could easily be interpreted as stonewalling.

In contrast, the government scientists who investigated the clusters were more critical in drawing and testing inferences from the data. Ruckelshaus, former administrator of the US Environmental Protection Agency, described this viewpoint: "The risks of effects from typical environmental exposures to toxic substances . . . are largely constructs or projections based on scientific findings. We would know nothing at all about chronic risks attributable to most toxic substances if scientists had not detected and evaluated them. Our response to such risks, therefore, must be based on a set of scientific findings."[15]

Thus, the authors of reports at the Centers for Disease Control and the Environmental Hygiene Agency critically weighed the hypothesis that increased frequency of miscarriage or birth defects is associated with the use of VDTs. They searched for other conditions that might increase risk. They separated questions of fact (whether the use of VDTs carries increased risk of reproductive problems) from questions of interpretation (whether radiation was responsible for the problems). Within the limits of a retrospective analysis of the events at Sears, Roebuck and the Defense Logistics Agency nothing emerged that seemed to connect the reproductive problems with the terminals.

A newspaper article about a study of one unidentified cluster illustrates the great difference between the two views. A consultant for the Department of Health and Welfare of Canada is quoted as saying: "So little is known about miscarriage anyway, and the numbers are too small to allow us to draw conclusions. . . . On looking through the details we can't see anything to connect anything to anything."[16] An employee who, since working with VDTs, had experienced a miscarriage and then borne a baby with respiratory distress was quoted, "They would have been better off testing the machines and not us."

How to detect increased risk

If the clusters themselves do not demonstrate the presence of a hazard, what would serve to do so? Roberts outlines a hypothetical study that could reliably show whether there is a connection between VDTs and reproductive problems. The preferred site of the study would be a large company that employs many women of reproductive age, some working with VDTs and some not; the company should not have previously been associated with clusters of cases. To ensure that any reproductive problems had an equal chance of being reported regardless of the group of women in which they occurred, a crucial step would be to recruit subjects into the study before the outcome of the pregnancy is known, preferably as soon as possible after pregnancy is diagnosed. To avoid other confounding variables, the "VDT" and "non-VDT" groups would have to be carefully matched in all respects except for use of the terminals.

To detect substantial increases in risk would require a large study. Prezant estimates that to detect with 80 percent probability a 40 percent increase in spontaneous abortions above a background rate of 14.4 percent would require monitoring a total of 672 pregnancies in the "VDT" and "non-VDT" groups.[18] Given normal fertility rates for women aged 18 to 29, this would entail keeping accurate records on approximately 13,000 women office workers for two years. A far larger study would be needed if older women were included (because of their lower fertility rates) or if major birth defects were also considered (because they are less frequent than spontaneous abortions).

Let us consider the possibility that a difference was found between the "VDT" and "non-VDT" groups. The challenge would lie in interpreting this result, particularly if the differences were small. Unavoidably, some doubt would remain that confounding variables or reporting bias had not been entirely eliminated from the study. The strength of the argument that the use of VDTs increases the risk of reproductive problems would build slowly, as the results were corroborated by other studies, a relation was established between extent of use and frequency of problems, and finally an underlying biological mechanism was demonstrated.

As discussion has continued, the assumption that the clusters were effects of "radiation" helped fuel the controversy. A news story in the *Toronto Globe and Mail* described the reluctance of the Ontario Ministry of Labour to continue its survey after having tested about 100 terminals for an unspecified radiation. According to a spokesman, "It would have taken two or three staff members about two years to test all the terminals in use in the province. There was no expectation that anything hazardous would be found, so testing the terminals is not an appropriate way to spend our time or the taxpayers' money." An editorial in the same issue asked, "Of what use is public support of a radiation protection service which, when its protection is sought, claims overwork and closes up shop?"[19] The Ministry continued its testing.

The concern about possible reproductive hazards from VDTs persists, six years after the first reports of the clusters. At a hotline telephone service for pregnant women in Philadelphia, 12 of 450 recent callers requested advice about the possible hazards from using VDTs during pregnancy;[20] questions about VDTs are among the 20 most frequently asked by the women calling the hotline. The National Association of Working Women (9 to 5) established a VDT hotline and received 6,000 calls during the first six months of its operations.[21] Legislation regulating the use of VDTs has been introduced in 22 states, in some cases with provisions for the transfer of pregnant workers, for radiation shielding, or for the monitoring of radiation.[22] Shields to reduce the levels of low-frequency electric fields from VDTs have recently come on the market.[23] Several government agencies (in the United States, the Food and Drug Administration) continue to monitor ionizing and nonionizing electromagnetic fields associated with VDTs.

The original reports of the clusters appear to consist of memoranda and private correspondence and are not readily available for critical assessment. However, a few studies on the supposed reproductive hazards of VDTs have appeared in the scientific literature. A letter in the British medical journal *The Lancet* reports a retrospective study of 1,475 Finnish women who gave birth to children with major birth defects; as a control, each woman was matched with another in the same district whose delivery immediately preceded her own.[24] The authors conclude that exposure to VDTs for at least four hours per day during early pregnancy was associated with no detectable increase in probability of having a child with a major birth defect. A retrospective Swedish study of 10,000 pregnancies found no evidence that VDT users run a higher risk of miscarriage or of delivering babies with major birth defects.[25]

Other reports of reproductive problems associated with VDTs have been described but not directly published in refereed scientific journals. In a survey of 6,000 respondents to its VDT hotline (873 completed the questionnaire), 9 to 5 found a rate of miscarriage approximately double that typically reported for the American population.[26] (Reporting bias may be a factor here, with women who had experienced problems more likely both to call the hotline and to complete the questionnaire.)

Two large epidemiological studies are now beginning. A two-year study by the US National Institute for Occupational Safety and Health will compare reproductive function in 2,000 women who use VDTs and 2,000 nonusers. It is designed to be able to detect with 90–95 percent probability, a 1.6-fold increase in the rate of spontaneous abortions, and a 3- to 3.5-fold increase in the rate of major birth defects.[27] A four-year study at Mount Sinai Hospital, in New York, will include 10,000 women, both users of VDTs and nonusers, to compare rates to reproductive problems.[28]

Concern about the possible ill effects of VDTs might arise from several factors. Some problems are frequently reported, such as visual fatigue, headache, or backache. A panel assembled by the US National Research Council judged radiation hazards to be highly unlikely, but focused in its report on the relatively mundane but important problems of glare, legibility of video displays, background lighting, and design of the workstation.[29]

One subtle factor could be the nature of the job itself. One of the ironies of the computer revolution is that many of the clerical jobs performed on computers provide little satisfaction for the worker, are repetitive, and are subject to excessively close supervision. A data entry clerk spending his days keying sequences of numbers into a computer, with rigid performance standards to meet and with every keystroke counted, may understandably experience emotional and perhaps physical problems as well. Such problems are evidently widespread, but difficult to study, and their connection with the terminals themselves might be indirect. One result may be a misplaced concern, for example about radiation.

Field strengths and frequencies

The issue of "radiation" is a complex matter that requires some elaboration. VDTs offer a smorgasbord of weak fields, at a time of great public awareness about the possibility of subtle hazards. Concern over possible hazards from low-level nonionizing electromagnetic energy has been a well-publicized issue surrounding the use of microwave ovens, microwave telephone communication facilities, radar installations, and power transmission lines. A scare in the late 1960s about X-radiation from color television sets helped set the stage for concern about VDTs.

Many VDTs have now been tested by several agencies. A report published by the Department of Health and Welfare of Canada summarizes the findings.[30] Although some VDTs can generate low-level X-rays internally, virtually all such radiation is absorbed within the set, and levels of emission are normally undetectable. (When severely overloaded, a few units tested by the US Bureau of Radiological Health emitted X-radiation at a level marginally above federal standards for television sets, but these were excluded from the market.) Levels of ultraviolet, visible, and infrared radiation are far lower than recommended limits, and microwave radiation has usually been undetectable. Electrostatic fields associated with VDTs vary widely, but in general are comparable to those already present in offices or homes. At the frequency of household current, 50–60 Hz, the maximum field strengths measured are of the order of 10 V/m, which is below or comparable to those associated with other common household appliances such as incandescent light bulbs (2 V/m at a distance of 30 cm), refrigerators (60 V/m), electric broilers (130 V/m), or electric blankets (250 V/m).[31]

Electric and magnetic fields with frequency components in the range of 10–100 kHz are generated by the flyback transformer and the circuits that move the electron beam across the screen. In small localized regions near the transformer the average (root-mean-square) electric field strengths can be as high as 300–500 V/m; 30 cm from the screen these average field strengths can be as high as 15 V/m rms but more typically they are less than 1 V/m rms.[32] These are far below the levels known to produce damage of the kind that is well established from electromagnetic fields, which generally involves excessive heating of tissues, or (for low-frequency currents) nerve excitation and shock.

The question of the "safety" of VDTs has been frequently raised. One difficulty is that "safety," if considered to be the absence of increased risk, can never be demonstrated. A hazard can be shown to exist; absence of hazard cannot. Human experience offers many observations (such as the cluster) that might be interpreted as pointing to a hazard, yet from which no convincing demonstration of hazard is possible. The possibility of hazard from weak electromagnetic fields that has been suggested in the lay press in the last several years illustrates the difficulties involved.

The primary research literature on biological effects of electromagnetic fields is vast and inconsistent. Medical literature over the centuries has presented many claims of therapeutic effects of electric or magnetic fields that could not be confirmed by later work. In recent years, thousands of studies have been completed and hundreds of effects of all sorts have been claimed, on the basis of evidence of widely varying credibility.

For electric fields at 50–60 Hz, for example, Carstensen has compiled a list of 127 effects that have been reported over a wide range of field intensities from 100 kV/m to 1 V/m, in a variety of organisms.[33] Of these roughly one-quarter have been independently confirmed, one-third could not be confirmed by other investigators, and the rest have not yet been followed far enough to be judged confirmed or negated. For magnetic fields at 50–60 Hz, Carstensen's list includes 51 reported effects, of which two have been subject to unsuccessful attempts at confirmation and five have been independently confirmed. Not surprisingly, the effects most clearly established are found at high field levels, and they have an easily recognized connection with the field – for example, damage to leaves of plants such as alfalfa, wheat, and corn by corona near their surfaces, which occurs at field strengths above about 20,000 V/m.[34] The ten or so effects reported at field strengths (measured in air) that are typical of VDTs tend to be subtle phenomena that are difficult to confirm.

There are several reasons for the difficulty in confirming these reports. Many of the studies involve screening experiments or other kinds of exploratory research, and the significance of any observed changes can be open to varying interpretations. Often the changes are just barely distinguishable from random variations in the data; in searching for new phenomena it is difficult to exclude subtle artifacts. An investigator might report an "effect" on the basis of some difference between the control and exposed subjects, whereas his readers might assume that the field has been shown directly to cause the change – which is a far more difficult result to establish.

Thus, there are many opportunities for speculation about the possible existence of some as yet undemonstrated hazard. The feeling is understandable that where there is all this smoke there must be a flame, somewhere. But to protect people against a hazard requires a more precise understanding about its nature and the conditions under which it is likely to occur. Whether such an understanding will develop about any specific hazard from weak electromagnetic fields is by no means certain; smoke and fog are hard to distinguish at a distance.

A recent study by Delgado and his associates [35] has been cited in the lay press as raising the possibility of hazard from the *magnetic* fields associated with VDTs. This group reported in 1982 that the exposure of eggs to weak pulsed magnetic fields, comparable in strength to those from VDTs and weaker than the earth's magnetic field, was associated with developmental anomalies in chick embryos. The extrapolation of these findings to humans is tenuous at present, however, in the absence of some positive explanation for the observations. Moreover, the presence or absence of anomalies seems to depend on small differences in the time-dependence of the pulse, much smaller than the differences between the pulses used in the experiment and the magnetic field pulses generated by VDTs.[36] Until more is known about the phenomenon, it is unwarranted to single out VDT operators as being at special risk. Several research groups are following up the study; one group has reported its unsuccessful attempt to confirm the original findings of Delgado and his co-workers.[37]

Lessons of the debate

This debate illustrates Weinberg's dictum that cognitive dissonance is all but unavoidable when the data are ambiguous and the social and political stakes are high.[38] But the costs of this dissonance are also high, in several respects. It is important to minimize anxiety while isolating and studying whatever real problems might exist. Several lessons can be drawn from the VDT debate.

First, anxiety can be minimized by more effective communication between scientists and laymen. I believe that the writers of the Canadian news reports tried to be objective, and their reports of the "clusters" included assurances by public officials that no radiation hazard existed. But the reports lacked critical evaluation of the inference from the clusters of reproductive problems that use of VDTs increases the risk of miscarriage or birth defects. A discussion of this inference would have been comprehensible to laymen, and perhaps more reassuring than flat assertions that the units are safe. A positive demonstration of safety is difficult in any event, and it is questionable to provide assurances about what cannot be proved.

Second, every attempt should be made to isolate and study suspected problems as directly as possible. It is preferable, at this point, to try to confirm and extend the results of Delgado and his associates rather than to undertake new exploratory research exposing animals to the weak fields produced by VDTs. If the phenomena reported by Delgado and his associates are significant, they will soon be widely studied and any pertinence to VDTs will soon be established. The other approach, unguided probing into the unknown, is likely merely to add to the scientific noise long associated with the bioeffects literature.

A third lesson concerns the need to avoid unconscious bias. The discussion about the clusters should have centered on what can be inferred from them, without assuming that a radiation hazard exists. Comments about biological effects of fields too easily confuse association (i.e., changed observed after exposure to fields) with causality (whether the fields directly caused the changes). The discussion about Delgado's observations should center not on how the magnetic fields could produce the changes, but on what can be reliably concluded from the data, what experiments are needed to rule out other possible interpretations, and how such interpretations can be reconciled with existing knowledge of other biological phenomena. A recommendation for caution about VDTs because the fields near the transformer are more intense than those in front of the screen should be made only if accompanied by some argument that the more intense fields do in fact approach the threshold for some specified hazard.

Debates about possible low-level hazards in the environment raise questions about what we know about the world and how we know it. Distinctions must be drawn that are not difficult but that might be unexpected to laymen who, I think, have too often been presented with scientific truths in neat packages. That reproductive problems occured in "clusters" to women users of VDTs is a fact; that they were causally connected with the terminals is an inference that has not been supported by subsequent work. Whether *any* association exists between the use of VDTs and reproductive problems is a question of fact – but one that is difficult, for the reasons discussed above, to answer reliably. Such discussion will not provide easy answers, but it can help to establish a civil and fair approach to what might otherwise be an intractable problem.

Notes

1 *Toronto Globe and Mail,* July 23, 1980.
2 *Toronto Star,* July 26, 1980.
3 *Toronto Star,* July 31, 1980.
4 L. Slesin and M. Zybko, *Video Display Terminals: Health and Safety* (New York, Microwave News, 1983), pp. 41–6.
5 *Vancouver Sun-Sentinel,* September 28, 1982.
6 Slesin and Zybko, *Terminals,* p. 53.
7 W. M. Zuk, M. A. Stuchly, P. Dvorak et al., *Investigations of Radiation Emissions from Video Display Terminals.* Public Affairs Directorate, Department of Health Welfare Canada, Report 83-EHD-91, 1983.
8 H. Sharma, "Preliminary report on adverse pregnancy outcome and other health effects at the Surrey Memorial Hospital." Unpublished.

9   US Army Environmental Hygiene Agency, *Investigations of Adverse Pregnancy Outcomes*. Defense Contract Administration Service Report 66-32-1359-81, 1981.

10 Family Planning Evaluation Division, *Cluster of Spontaneous Abortions*. Centers for Disease Control, Report EP1-80-113-2, 1981.

11 Ibid.

12 R. S. Roberts, *Adverse Pregnancy Outcomes Associated with VDUs: Interpreting the Evidence of Case Clusters* (Ontario Advisory Council on Occupational Health and Occupational Safety, 1982).

13 R. DeMatteo, *The Hazards of VDTs* (Ontario Public Service Employees Union, 1981).

14 K. A. Massey, "The Challenge of Nonionizing Radiation: A Proposal for Legislation," *Duke Law Journal,* 1979, pp. 105–89.

15 W. D. Ruckelshaus, "Risk, Science, and Democracy," *Issues in Science and Technology,* vol. 1, 1985, pp. 19–37.

16 *Ottawa Citizen,* October 21, 1982.

17 Roberts, *Adverse Pregnancy Outcomes.*

18 B. Prezant and G. S. Omenn, "Visual Display Terminals." Unpublished.

19 *Toronto Globe and Mail,* July 26, 1980.

20 B. Vogt, Personal communication, August 1985.

21 National Association of Working Women, "9 to 5 Campaign on VDT Risk: Analysis of VDT Operator Questionnaires of VDT Hotline Callers." Unpublished.

22 Office Systems Ergonomics Report, vol. 3 (5), 1984.

23 *New York Times,* September 3, 1985.

24 K. Kurppa, P. C. Holmberg, K. Rantala et al., "Birth Defects and Video Display Terminals," *The Lancet,* vol. 2, 1984, p. 1330.

25 B. Källén et al., "Dataskärmsarbete och Graviditet," *Läkartidningen,* vol. 82, 1985, pp. 1339–42.

26 National Association of Working Women, "9 to 5 Campaign."

27 National Institute of Occupational Safety and Health. Summary of NIOSH reproductive study of video display terminal operators. Unpublished.

28 *Wall Street Journal,* June 7, 1985.

29 *Video Displays, Work, and Vision* (National Academy Press, Washington, DC, 1983).

30 Zuk et al., *Investigations.*

31 D. A. Miller, "Electric and Magnetic Fields Produced by Commercial Power Systems," in *Biologic and Clinical Effects of Low-frequency Magnetic and Electric Fields,* eds J. G. Llaurado, A. Sances and J. H. Battocletti (Springfield, IL: Thomas, 1974), pp. 62–70.

32 M. A. Stuchly, "Health Aspects of Work with Video Display Units," *Science of the Total Environment,* forthcoming.

33 E. L. Carstensen, *Biological Effects of Transmission Line Fields* (Amsterdam: Elsevier, forthcoming).

34 G. W. McKee, D. P. Knievel, D. T. Poznaniak et al., "Effect of 60-Hz High Intensity Electric Fields on Living Plants," *IEEE Transactions on Power Apparatus and Systems,* PAS-97, pp. 1177–81.

35 J. M. R. Delgado, J. Leal, J. L. Monteagudo et al., "Embryological Changes Induced by Weak Extremely Low Frequency Electromagnetic Fields," *Journal of Anatomy,* vol. 134, 1982, pp. 533–51.

36 A. Ubeda, J. Leal, M. A. Trillo et al., "Pulse Shape of Magnetic Fields Influences Chick Embryogenesis," *Journal of Anatomy,* vol. 137, 1983, pp. 513–36.

37 S. Maffeo, M. W. Miller, and E. L. Carstensen, "Lack of Effect of Weak Low Frequency Electromagnetic Fields on Chick Embryogenesis," *Journal of Anatomy,* vol. 139, 1984, pp. 613–18.

38 A. M. Weinberg, "Science and Its Limits: The Regulator's Dilemma," *Issues in Science and Technology,* vol. 2, 1985, pp. 59–72.

6   IT in the Home

From IT in the Home to Home Informatics

Ian Miles

The term "Home Informatics" (HI) is used here by Miles to describe the consumer electronics gadgetry now available to households. In outlining the scope of HI and some general directions HI is taking, the author makes it clear that he believes that something very important is happening. Ian Miles is Senior Fellow at the Science Policy Research Unit, University of Sussex and this piece is adapted from a report prepared for the Six Countries Programme on Aspects of Government Policies towards Technological Innovation in Industry (TNO, Delft, Netherlands, 1987), later revised and published as Home Informatics: Information Technology and the Transformation of Everyday Life *(Pinter, London, 1988).*

In the formal economy, the cheapening of information processing means that there can be major innovations in the production process. IT can be used to consult stored knowledge, to record new data, to operate equipment on the basis of signals received and programs installed, to communicate across long distances, and to perform statistical and other analyses. It is often possible to do this in ways that are not notably time- and money-consuming, nor are they skill-intensive and laborious. While the motives of, and constraints upon, consumers are far from identical with those applying to organizations in the formal economy, similar sorts of innovation may be anticipated in the informal domestic economy.

Already in the home environment there are many technologies which perform informational functions. Figure 6.1 presents a picture of the broadening spectrum of consumer electronics, based entirely on products that are already widely diffused in one or more Western countries.

Within the contemporary household in Western societies, then, are devices that:

- *transmit* information into and out of the home (mail, newspapers, radio and TV, telephones have all supplemented word of mouth communications and personal transport);
- *monitor* and/or *control* the operations of domestic equipment (meters, dials and displays, and even fuses, which respond to abnormally high power loads);

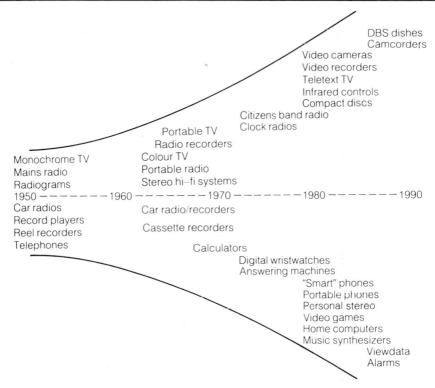

Figure 6.1 The spectrum of consumer electronic products. (Partly based on Mackintosh International, *The European Consumer Electronics Industry,* European Commission, 1984. Dates are approximate and vary from country to country.

- *store* information for subsequent reproduction and display (notepads and photographs have been supplemented by audio and video tapes).

IT-based innovation is already beginning to have an impact on these technologies. Often, what is involved is a transfer of technologies developed for industrial (or military) applications to consumer purposes. Among the most notable features of IT-based innovation are:

- First, *an improvement in the effectiveness, quality or power* of many of these technologies (e.g., better sound or video reproduction, higher levels of data storage, more versatile telephones).
- Second, *the addition of new functions* to equipment (e.g., being able to meter new things, being able to obtain more useful information from meters, being able to communicate in circumstances where this has been heretofore impossible).
- Third, *the development of new types of equipment* e.g., home computers, video tape recorders, interactive Compact Disk systems).

- Fourth, *the integration of many functions,* as the possibility of different items of equipment easily and cheaply intercommunicating allows for useful applications of integration to be implemented (e.g., TVs being able to carry alarm messages from home security devices or from malfunctioning equipment, power-consuming devices being controlled by electricity meters according to tariff rates).

There are several overlaps among these items, of course, but for convenience we shall discuss them in the order in which they have been presented above. The first area will be divided into three subsections: improved controls and displays, improved data storage and retrieval, and improved communication facilities.

Improvements in existing functions

Improved controls and displays

The improvement of controls and displays is already widely apparent: on more modern items of equipment, controls are often push-button or even touch switches, while information on the state of apparatus is supplied in the form of numerical data on an LED or liquid crystal display. There has been a shift from traditional mechanical and electromechanical dials and switches, to electronic and microelectronic ones, just as the controls within devices have also moved in this direction.

Often, the improvements in displays are accompanied by *improved quality in the information that is yielded.* For example, they may provide not only more readable, but also more precise data (e.g., seconds as well as hours and minutes). Frequently, additional low-cost informational functions are added (thus digital clocks, for example, are standard in many radios, microwave cookers, video recorders). And, corresponding to increasingly precise data outputs, so can more precise inputs be accommodated. One reason for incorporating clocks in many gadgets is to be able to use these to automatically control cooking times or the recording of TV programs; and these can be controlled with great precision.

Other features of controls and displays are also quite well established already. IT is often claimed to liberate users from traditional limitations of time and space: because information can be stored and transmitted readily, the user need no longer be at the right place at the right moment to make use of a facility. This is most clear in the development of "teleservices" (telebanking, teleshopping, etc.), but also already applies to the controls of domestic equipment in a modest way.

Remote control by hand-held infrared devices is common for TV and hi-fi systems, and is also becoming available for some other devices. For example, it is possible to operate some micro-computer keyboards at a distance from the VDT and other bulky components, so that, for example, the keyboard may be operated in one's lap from an armchair, rather than on a table or desktop. Telephone answering machines can be interrogated by their owners from distant locations.

Programmability has long been a gimmicky feature of household appliances like washing, knitting and sewing machines. In the main, this has really consisted of a number of pre-existing options being made available, so that they can be chosen by appropriately setting a dial or pressing buttons. Occasionally there has been external "software," in the form of a card – this is of course not electronic but mechanical software, rather like a music roll was software to drive a pianola. More recently, electronic and microelectronic systems have enabled devices to operate with more flexibility. More preprogrammed options are available on current washing machines, for example. Record and tape players need not just play the (ROM) software of the LP or tape, but can search for particular tracks and play them in a chosen order; and to the conventional tone and volume controls are added graphic equalizers that allow for more precise adjustment of the sound output to room features or personal tastes.

Each of these trends in controls and displays is accelerated considerably by the application of IT. The low cost of microelectronics, and the use of the technology within devices, means that improvements in these "human–machine interfaces" (HMIs) can form a relatively cheap way of improving products. Thus we can expect to see further innovation in the capability to operate domestic equipment at a distance, to have it controlled by inputs that do not require one's immediate physical presence, in its programmability to suit personal needs and tastes, and in the quality of the information that is provided for users.

Screens and finger-presses are not the only means of controlling and monitoring devices. In applications in the formal economy, *voice synthesis* is being used to provide some types of information, such as the prices of items being passed before a bar-code Electronic Point of Sale (EPOS) device. Similar innovations are apparent in some consumer goods. For example, warning systems in cars to inform drivers if seat belts are not fastened or oil is running low, and "speaking clocks" that announce the hour. Spoken output from equipment may be most appropriate where very simple data are provided or where urgent action is required, at least until speech synthesis can be made to sound more natural, and the information can be put into a form more closely resembling natural language.

Speech recognition on the part of equipment, beyond an extremely basic kind, seems further away; it requires high data-processing power and much research is under way around the appropriate software. However, microcomputers which can recognize a fairly large vocabulary are being developed, and over the coming decades the techniques for this sort of HMI will no doubt be vastly improved and cheapened. Speech-driven controls, that can accept verbal commands as a basis for operation, together with speech synthesis and systems that can process natural language (a goal of the Japanese Fifth Generation project) will ultimately allow for interaction between user and equipment to take place using natural language rather than single commands or restricted phrases; and with devices having the capacity to ask for clarification if there seem to be mistakes, misunderstandings, or ambiguous and insufficiently specified instructions.

A further development might be termed *"telecontrol."* This involves the ability to interact with remote devices, for example by telephone. Already, for example, some directory enquiry and mail order systems are able to process simple inputs from users, and to provide appropriate answers or set other procedures into operation. Domestic equipment may similarly be turned on or off, or interrogated as to its status, by telephone. An alternative form of within-home communication is termed "peritelevision," and involves equipping devices so that they can send messages as to their status to the domestic TV.

The issue of user-friendliness, which underlies efforts to develop menu-driven systems and speech recognition, reflects a problem that seems to be increasingly common. Simply put, it is that the "new freedom" of consumer choice may present an information overload, as in the fast food outlet where more time is spent choosing between the innumerable combinations of bread, filling, garnishes and drinks as is taken to prepare the meal. In practice, consumers may not always want high levels of feedback or a wide spectrum of choice.

It appears that part of the success of modern cameras and music centers is that they relieve users of choices which may be time-consuming and knowledge-demanding. It is far easier simply to point a camera in the right direction and press the button, to load a tape or CD into the music center and press a button than it is to be a photography or hi-fi enthusiast, and most of us have a range of enthusiasms that is more limited than our range of tastes. The two examples are worth pursuing, since they both point to rather different aspects of the problem, and indicate rather different solutions.

Thus, microprocessor-controlled cameras can actually make many of the operating decisions for the user; they ensure a higher proportion of successful shots than inexperienced photographers are liable to achieve (though use of these functions may rule out some special effects and more creative photography). A parallel innovation is under way in microwave cookers, into which some manufacturers are now placing sensors that weigh foodstuffs and monitor temperatures so as to achieve optimum results, relieving users of the need to make rule-of-thumb estimates. Music centers relieve consumers of the need to make decisions about the technical and aesthetic compatibility of different items of hi-fi equipment, and thus provide a packaged, integrated set of components. Although there may be inflexibility and costs in this approach (the system may well need to be repaired or replaced as a whole), it is likely to provide reproduction as well as any combination of items amounting to the same price.

The evolution of HI is liable to involve a large number of tradeoffs of this kind – tradeoffs between "information overload" and flexibility of operation. With the advent of devices that are more truly programmable, we may expect to see domestic equipment following the path taken by user-friendly microcomputer systems, presenting a variety of preset or default options, being capable of operating in default mode with no lengthy instructions, but having the capability of accepting – and storing for future reference – our own peculiar requirements. Eventually, we may anticipate appliances that can learn from our reactions to past operations, so as to "guess" our preferences.

Improved data storage and retrieval

One story (which is perhaps apocryphal) describes well a major limitation of the first wave of HI devices. It tells of an elderly lady encountered in one of the first displays of home computers in a high street store. After fingering a keyboard for a few moments, she was heard to mutter "what good are these computers if they can't tell me the price of eggs?"

The story underlines the point that the practical uses of high-powered information processing devices are very much limited by what information they have available to process. A recent study of home computer users illustrates this well: users who input large volumes of data themselves were usually motivated by a professional interest (e.g., those preparing texts via word processing) or a hobby (indexing one's stamp collection, for example). The tedium of typing in facts and figures makes current home computers a poor choice for many home tasks, and there have been few commercially available data bases which appeal to home users. Perhaps the most common reaction to this situation within the IT industry has been to advocate access to data via telecommunication as the answer: home computers will come into their own, it is suggested, when linked to viewdata systems which can provide near-instantaneous access to any of a large number of huge data bases.

The terminology used to describe data storage in computer systems can be applied to traditional consumer goods. Conventional audio records – and now compact disks (CDs) – are ROM (read-only memory) devices: the data they contain may be degraded, but they cannot be modified in any useful way. The same is effectively true of printed materials, although readers may jot in the margins or fill in crosswords! Audio and now video tapes are RAM (random access memory) in that data may be recorded and released repeatedly on the same medium – rather like a blackboard. Less familiar are WORM (write once read many times) media, which allow users to add data up to the limits of capacity of the medium, but not to rewrite it. A conventional notebook (without an effective eraser) is effectively a WORM system, as is photographic film.

As the examples suggest, many storage media are already in common use in the domestic environment. The most important developments that are under way concern advances in the storage and retrieval of large volumes of data encoded in digital form. CDs are the best-known example of such media at present, although digital tape recorders and digital VTRs are now in production. CDs use optical technology, in that the data are recorded in the form of dots which are read by laser light, enabling massive quantities of information to be stored on a small disk. First made familiar through audio CD systems for domestic use, CD is proving a powerful means of storing large data bases for computer use: thus many "electronic publishers" providing online information services for business users are now making their data available on CD. This data storage for microcomputer use is generally referred to as CD–ROM to distinguish it from the use of CD for audio storage. CD–WORM systems are currently considerably more expensive than CD–ROM, and have a correspondingly limited market.

Where the information is not such as to require rapid and frequent updating, optical ROM systems have proved a viable approach, especially as costs of CD–ROM systems have come within the reach of even small businesses – they are currently comparable with the costs of Winchester hard disk systems, but can store over 600 megabytes of data as compared to the 10–30 megabytes typical of hard disks. Furthermore, this is not just an application relevant to wealthy business environments. For example, it is already possible for libraries to acquire a CD version of a large encyclopedia (the Graunier encyclopedia, several volumes on a single disk), which is also promoted as being suitable for home education purposes. This system is not just a book read from a VDT; it also offers the possibility of vastly improved indexing functions, so a full-text search for the occurrence of particular words or phrases is possible. A CD–ROM system permits a microcomputer to access large volumes of data which are stored in a robust, transportable and secure form (it is predicted that disk life will be in excess of ten years in the typical office) – and while data retrieval from the system is somewhat slower than from conventional "hard disks," this is being improved.

An educational application of videodisk (rather than CD) technology has attracted attention in the UK. The "Domesday Project" consists of two videodisks used with a Philips interactive videodisk player and a BBC microcomputer. The system (on two disks) presents an hour of video film material, but it also contains tens of thousands of maps, tens of thousands of still photographs, and more than one hundred thousand teletext "pages" of information, together with material from the British census and the parliamentary record. Users can "zoom" in on local areas from national maps, take "walks" through a number of visual environments, call up census or survey data for processing, and search for material on a wide range of topics. Further videodisks under preparation are also oriented to education (and training), although some are being developed as new types of in-store shopping catalogue.

This system is relatively expensive (costing around £4,000, although the manufacture of each disk costs a mere £5). However, cost reductions are likely as the technology matures, and the key feature of interactivity is seen as central to the evolution of CD systems. Current audio CD is largely the passive replaying of data stored in a linear sequence (although it is possible to select tracks in particular orders, etc., as noted earlier). The concept of Interactive CD systems (CD-I) proposes access to the large volumes of data that may be stored on CD for a wide variety of purposes, not just those currently associated with CD-ROM systems as became available for microcomputers in the mid-1980s. Building on existing CD standards and the mass production of CD players for the consumer market (over 10 million have been shipped, well in excess of industry forecasts), the aim is to establish mass markets for the more advanced CD-I systems.

The CD can be used to store information of various kinds and at various levels of quality. For example, instead of one hour of stereo high-fidelity audio, some 700 hours of phonetic speech could be on tap (and in fact, even a CD of current capacity would be capable of storing 3,000 still pictures of higher quality than current TV pictures alongside an hour of stereo music). Like audio material, visual images (including text) can be stored at various levels of definition (and with possibilities for different numbers of colors being used). Simple animation is possible, though the scope for true "motion picture" video images is currently limited. Thus CD-I will make use of audio and video data like current home entertainment media, but will also be able to use computer data like CD-ROM systems. Potential applications include: new types of interactive book (e.g., speaking dictionaries, electronic encyclopedias and do-it-yourself manuals for home use), data bases, games and entertainment, media for music and graphics composition, and practical tools such as road map displays for motorists.

Improved communications

Three major developments may be cited here. First is the upgrading of the telecommunications infrastructure, as exemplified by the use of Direct Broadcast Satellites (DBS), the new cable TV networks, and the replacement of existing telephone systems by the Integrated Services Digital Network (ISDN) framework. Second is the emergence of new telecommunications services and improved telecommunications devices, such as cellular radio and portable telephones. Third is the development of in-house communications systems – which appear to be moving on from familiar remote control devices and baby alarms to "Small Area Networks" (SANs).

These developments all reflect the novel developments that have given rise to the concept of Information Technology, which is often defined as "the convergence of computers and telecommunications." Increasingly information-processing and transmission are taking advantage of the superior features of digitization. Thus the ISDN allows for the transmission of all types of data through the same network. Conventional telephone systems allow for a variety of telephone voice services (with fairly low quality sound reproduction), together with low-speed telex, facsimile, viewdata and other computer data communications. The latter may be routed through Packet Switch Stream Services, which take advantage of digitization to reduce costs and increase error-trapping, but a modem is necessary to link digital computer data to the analogue telephone system. The ISDN systems now under construction are intended to allow for much more rapid data transmission, and will be able to digitize voice communications. They will permit substantially better telecommunications services, such as photovideotex (near-photographic quality viewdata images).

However, even ISDN is far from the broadband system that is envisaged as the telecommunications network of the "information society." The channel capacity envisaged for the public networks (64 kilobits per second) is too low for the transmission of moving video images (although some slow-scan video images may be conveyed as in security applications and a primitive videotelephone that has recently been displayed under the name "teleport"). Optical fiber systems have the capacity to carry information at levels *millions* of times higher than that of the ISDN plans.

Already the more advanced cable TV systems that have been installed permit users to choose which of thousands of films on store in a video library they wish to have played into their home TV set, but many commentators are skeptical of the idea that such systems are sufficient as a base for market forces to rapidly establish a widespread broadband system. Thus they argue for ideas like "Eurogrid," an intergovernmental effort to set up such a system. The justifications for this vary, but the two most common are (1) that this will provide an incentive for the European IT industry to consolidate its innovative efforts and (2) that such a system is a necessary feature of the "information society," the infrastructure required for a wide variety of new IT-based goods and services to be developed and to find adequate markets.

Whatever the pace of change, it is clear that the telecommunications power available to private households will increase in coming decades. Access to telephony and computer-communications via the public telephone network, to broadcast TV via Direct Broadcast Satellites (DBS) and via cable TV (which, as noted, can also provide "narrowcast" services) is growing.

The capabilities of home reception/transmission equipment are also growing – devices are becoming smaller and more portable, memories are being installed, and the multi-telephone, multi-TV home is becoming as common now as the multi-radio home was after the advent of the transistor radio. This reflects the use of microelectronic components and the digitization of at least some information-processing activities in home equipment which is taking place in advance of the digitization of telephone, radio, and TV transmissions.

A number of new telecommunications services have been introduced to the mass market in the last decade. These include:

- Broadcast information services. Teletext transmission to television sets has widely diffused in a number of Western countries; this enables viewers to call up "pages" of information (e.g., news services, broadcasting schedules), and can also be used to provide, for example, subtitles for the hard-of-hearing and different language groups. A rather similar system for radio broadcasts, Radio Data Services, is currently in late stages of development: its main uses are likely to be the transmission of emergency messages and codings representing the class of program currently broadcast.

- Interactive telematics. The best-known system here is videotext (viewdata), which can be used like teletext to gain access to remote data bases (but with a wider selection), but can also be used for transactional services (teleshopping, telebooking, etc.), and for message services (electronic mail, chatlines, etc.).
- New telephone services. While message storing and similar services are mainly oriented to business users, new services for consumers include numerous stored messages (weather forecasts, information on AIDs, etc.) and "Talkabout" facilities (which enable callers to join in group discussions in a telephone equivalent of Citizens' Band radio).

In addition to telecommunications that relate the home to remote information sources, in-home communications are becoming more important. A number of communications media are already in use by domestic devices: infrared signals by the "autocommando", mains signalling by some baby alarms (these feature sound detectors that plug into an electricity mains socket in the baby's room, and set off signalling devices similarly located in the living room or elsewhere), and specialized wiring by most other alarm and security devices and by audio systems (the most recent Bang and Olufsen systems feature infrared controls and coaxial wiring to carry the high-fidelity audio). However, some security devices send radio signals, and radio is also used by portable telephones. There are thus numerous physical media available for in-home communications.

An important direction for the development of HI involves allowing household devices to intercommunicate. The existing electrical mains is exploited as an existing "infrastructure" in mains signalling. This only allows for the transmission of limited volumes of data, but, for instance, this is quite sufficient for signals concerning the state of apparatus, and for the transmission of messages instructing devices to turn on or off. A major problem that is confronted by mains signalling is that the mains network is not confined to a single home: various coding techniques are therefore required to prevent interference with neighbors' apparatus. Radio and infrared transmission require no rewiring and permit not only physical mobility on the part of users (within quite different limits!), but also allow for considerably higher levels of data transmission than does mains signalling. Although problems of interference arise again, standards have been developed for cordless phones and related devices that should provide a basis for overcoming these.

New capabilities

Our second feature of HI was the addition of *radically new functions* to domestic equipment. An example of this, already mentioned, is the addition of teletext capabilities to ordinary domestic TV sets. In this case the new function is (typically, but not always) incorporated within the established device. In other cases, a peripheral device (to borrow an item of computer terminology) is added. An example of the latter is the telephone answering machine, which enables callers to leave messages, but which is usually an additional device that sits alongside the conventional telephone.

There are several difficulties in providing a systematic account of the addition of functions to equipment. One problem is in defining which functions are being added to which devices – is a wristwatch with calculator, diary and address book functions really an augmented wristwatch, or a portable calculator with accessories? This may be more a matter of marketing strategy (or industry of origin) than of technical characteristics. Another problem is that it is often in practice difficult to draw a firm boundary between improvements in existing functions and the addition of radically new functions. Take, for example, the addition of an electronic clock/timer to a device that previously might have featured an electric or electro-mechanical one. Here there may not appear to be any real addition of functions. But in many such cases there is a tendency to capitalize on microprocessor control so as to increase the programmability of equipment which previously provided only a few fixed options.

In many cases, the substitution of microelectronic for electromechanical or even mechanical devices provides the basis for new functions. Consider another example, that of the CD player, which at first sight substitutes for the conventional record player, and merely improves upon it in terms of sound quality and size. But in addition, new levels of programmability are available: the player can be instructed to repeat, search for or skip certain tracks, for example – and such features are available in mass market systems, not merely as extras in top-of-the-range models. For another example, the digital wristwatch features an alarm, a timer, a calendar, and often other functions, as standard in the same way. (Again, this has promoted a surge of competitive innovation in conventional watches.)

It seems likely that the innovation process, adding new functions to both the CD player and the electronic wristwatch, has much further to run. Many of these functions will probably remain forever beyond the reach of the conventional technologies. Thus portable personal stereo CD players are already available (they can be carried on one's belt or in a pocket, and provide ample output to power headphones), and some CD players have output sockets which enable them to be linked directly to forthcoming generations of digital amplifiers and recorders; conventional record players will not be given these characteristics, we can say with some confidence. Likewise, it is already common to see digital watches which incorporate calculators, and memory to be used for minimal diaries or phone lists, and some wrist computers/terminals are now being marketed that include (retain?) watch functions but go so far beyond these as to be quite novel devices.

Four facets of the application of IT to household products contribute to the development of new functions. These are:

- the development of digital controls and displays in all types of device;
- the use of microprocessors in the central operating processes of audio and video equipment;
- the rapid cheapening of RAM memory costs, so that information can be stored by equipment;
- the addition of communications input/output interfaces to equipment.

It is almost inevitable that these features of HI will be used so as to lead to a proliferation of new functions. Indeed, this is such an elementary step that many innovations of this sort represent little more than unnecessary gimmicks. (How many LED clocks does one really need in a room?) Some of the new functions – perhaps particularly those displayed on portable devices like wristwatches – may be status symbols, whose main "informational function" is to demonstrate the owner's wealth, taste or infatuation with hi-tech. But a number of utilitarian functions are already being marketed or under development and are likely to emerge in the near future.

These utilitarian functions include:

Memories   Telephones, for example, have had answering machines added, so that they can receive and store messages when the owner is unavailable; and new phones can "dial" frequently required numbers in response to a few keypresses (and in products being developed, on the basis of a voice input).

Safety features   Examples of these are warning indicators and alarms that indicate that, for example, a refrigerator's power supplies have been interrupted, the device is overloaded, or that something appears to be amiss (blockages, burning, etc.); and simple triggers that turn off devices when they appear to be malfunctioning (e.g., when gas is not ignited). Automobiles are being equipped with such features to provide feedback to drivers – or even to disable the car – when seat belts are not fastened, speed limits are exceeded, or some threshold has been exceeded (e.g. low oil levels, or, as in a system on trial for alcohol abusers in the United States, high driver alcohol levels).

Maintenance features   These have perhaps been pioneered in the office environment by manufacturers of such as photocopying machines, who have installed displays that inform users where a paper jam has occurred or what they need to do (add ink, add toner, etc.) if copies are inadequate. Some automobiles are fitted with internal monitoring systems that allow garages to quickly establish the source of problems: with lowered microcomputer costs, these diagnostics could be performed automatically by the car itself. Such auto-diagnostic displays, perhaps indicating not only where the probable locus of a problem is, but also what steps should be taken to overcome it, could be installed on many durables.

Energy conservation features   Again innovation in automobiles prefigures developments that are emerging or foreseeable in many consumer goods. A considerable increase in the energy efficiency of motors has been achieved by regulating their fuel consumption and performance by microelectronic controls. Similar innovations may be applied to other energy-intensive goods, such as washing machines and dryers. In addition, energy conservation may be served by the provision of more information to users of the energy costs of particular operating choices ("what will the effect on the fuel bill be of choosing to keep this room one degree warmer?"), and the ability of microprocessor controls to be linked to sensors or communications systems so as to adjust their operations according to environmental changes (e.g., time of day, temperature rise), or to signals received from remote or distant sources (e.g., concerning changes in energy tariff rates or TV programming).

Communications   We mentioned telecontrol earlier, and shall enlarge upon this in more detail later, but we should note for completeness here that the addition of communications features can enhance the improved functions noted above. For example, prototype devices (some in use in advanced business installations) can transmit their emergency alarms by telephone, adjust their operations according to signals about electricity tariff rates transmitted together with their power supply, and be interrogated remotely about the reasons for their apparent malfunctioning.

Finally, we should point out that the development of household appliances, and especially the addition of new functions to equipment, is being driven along by more than just the application of IT to consumer goods. For example, one aspect of current product differentiation, reinforced by IT capabilities, but also reflecting social trends, is the development of smaller and more portable devices. In some cases, such as countertop dishwashers and mini-ovens, the main driving force seems to be the recognition of a market opportunity based on the increasing numbers of small, single-person households. Other instances, such as personal stereo systems, some cordless devices (those that involve data transmission – others are based on battery power) do benefit from the small scale (and low power consumption) of microelectronics. Whatever the driving force, it is apparent that many devices are becoming available in a wider variety of sizes, and being made more portable in other ways – to the extent of radios that can be used in the shower, cameras that can be taken swimming. One consequence of this tendency may be the dissemination of several varieties of the same item around households: it is not at all uncommon to fund multi-car, multi-TV, multi-music-center families, for example. If flexible manufacturing does permit wider product differentiation, such a trend may well be intensified.

New household products

A third class of development, again overlapping with the innovation trajectories discussed previously, involves *new household products* using IT. Several devices that we have already discussed are reasonably regarded as new products (microwave cookers, CD-I, viewdata services, home computers, etc.), and there is some difficulty in classifying what are new products as compared to what are simply improved products. By "new products" here we refer to those household goods and services which either permit households to undertake new activities, or which promote major change in the way in which household activities are carried out. Whether or not there are really any substantially new activities taking place in the household is very much a matter of definition. If we formulate activities in very specific ways (e.g., watching TV, using a washing machine), then we will be able to identify many new activities; but at a more general level, there are few, if any, additions to the familiar household functions such as childcare, entertainment, social and sexual intercourse, personal care, etc.

There are, however, also transfers of activities between the formal economy and the household. Traditionally, for example, many welfare state provisions were formerly left for families of small communities to supply to the best of their ability. In the past few decades, many transfers have gone the other way, these have often been associated with the introduction of new household technologies which permit functions formerly supplied by traditional services to be achieved in new ways. Over the post-war decades, cheap motor power (petrol engines and electric motors) and·electronics (valve and transistor-based systems) enabled households to evade the economies of scale in the production and delivery of services which previously underpinned the use of facilities like laundries, cinemas, and public transport utilities.

Before considering whether IT might further such trends, let us consider these examples a little further. The motor car and washing machine are used to provide services for consumers – transport and cleaning in these cases – which might otherwise be purchased as final services from the formal economy (e.g. by riding on a bus or sending washing to a laundry). The "self-service" mode of provision may not involve any radically new household goals, but it does require informal labor inputs to the core task. But some other household technologies call for very little (if any) labor input: watching TV, for example, requires less effort than going out to the cinema.

Two aspects of these new modes of service provision are significant: first, some new skills may be required to use the technologies (minimal in some cases, but in others – such as car driving – of a relatively high level). These skills may occasion new household goals and divisions of labor. Second, changes in the cost and effort associated with activities may change the final functions to which these are directed: motoring may itself become a pleasure activity, watching TV does not involve the socializing that theaters traditionally provided, for example.

There is a fuzzy boundary between a new product, as we have defined it above, and what is simply a considerably improved version of an existing product. Our approach has not been based on the technical methods employed (e.g., whether audio material is recorded in analogue or digital form), so much as on the change in activities that may be associated with the new product. For example, the microwave cooker involves a new way of carrying out the core function of cooking, and by altering the characteristics of the process, has led to some shift in activity. It seems that new patterns of family dining are emerging around the microwave cooker, since it becomes much easier to rapidly cook a convenience or pre-prepared meal; this means that men are more prepared to take up some cooking activities, and that individual members of families are eating at their own convenience rather than communally – though "mother" often remains encharged with doing the original meal planning and preparation.

The extent to which a qualitative change in activities may be associated with HI will depend upon the degree to which the new technology's design characteristics differ from that for which it is substituting. Key characteristics, for example, will include: costs, improvements in convenience (portability, skills required), and the variety of new functions provided. When a new device removes the need for relatively laborious or skilled physical or intellectual labor, the change in activities may be very marked. (This seems a likely consequence of home computers and computers-communications, for example.)

The development of HI, based on the low cost of information and data processing power, is liable to lead to the "informatization" of many current household activities. That is, the largely unrecognized work of planning stages of an activity, and testing out expectations against perceptions, which are involved in even the most mundane household activities, will often be augmented by IT. This is liable to promote substantial changes in a wide range of activities, with an even wider range of activities changing less markedly (e.g., with improvements in the quality of performance of the activities or the ability of relatively unskilled people to engage in them). On this last point, for example, it could be argued that many men's readiness to use convenience foods and microwave ovens reflects their perception that they will not need to acquire difficult and/or "feminine" skills to use them.

Improved controls and outputs, simplifying tasks or ensuring higher levels of quality control, will certainly contribute to this process. In addition, the provision of information from external data bases or from domestic mass data storage could be applied to various household activities. Examples of this might be: personal transport (e.g., trip planning), cooking (e.g., menu planning, recipes), the efficient use of energy (e.g., matching use of devices and the opening/closing of windows and doors to energy costs), shopping (consumer advice and product specifications), and some forms of entertainment (broadcasting schedules, hints and tips for games). Data might be accessed via new telephone services, broadcast teletext, narrowcast cable TV services, online computer-communications and viewdata, CD-I systems, and other technical modes of delivery. Likely developments here, then, are online and broadcast data services (building on current dial-a-menu and traffic/weather news) and the incorporation of "cookery books" and "home maintenance manuals" into household appliances and into new types of home information center.

The integration of equipment

The fourth, and last, general development in household technology identified was the *integration of equipment*. We have long been aware of tendencies to put different devices together, often in one box – ranging from the integrated music center to the simple combination of a clock and radio in the same housing. The use of microelectronics and digital controls makes it more feasible to consider relating together the operation of devices that are in the same box (so that the clock, for example, can be used to turn on the radio). But it also increases the utility of interrelating devices that are not in the same box, by getting them to communicate with each other through the home. Such a trajectory moves towards what is often known as "home automation:" in the United States and Japan the term "smart house" has some popularity, while in Western Europe the phrase "interactive home systems" conveys much the same image.

"Home automation" may carry connotations of office automation as it is taking place in the formal economy, and indeed there is a transfer of ideas and techniques from the "smart building," an office environment which is still in a relatively immature stage of development. But "automation" also conjures up the image of the automated factory; this is quite inappropriate, since the control of household equipment along the lines of factory robotics and assembly line technology will probably remain prohibitively expensive for general-purpose domestic use in the immediate future. (There may be applications in special instances, however: for example, for disabled people.) However, linkage of a wide range of household devices through a "homenet" or "Small Area Network," the domestic equivalent of the "Local Area Network" in business, could permit automation to the extent that devices are electronically controlled by changes in their own state or that of other devices or the environment, so that previous requirements for human decision-making and labor are substantially reduced.

Skepticism about HI reaches a peak where ideas of the "smart house" are discussed. And indeed, there does seem to be some contradiction between the decreased cost and increased portability of equipment and the idea of integrating it. Why have audio relayed from room to room (as traditional hi-fi enthusiasts would do) when a music center can be carried around or several systems can be installed around the house? However, HI allows for more than the relatively passive relaying of signals from a source room to a destination – it permits interactivity of devices. This means that it has considerably wider appeal than the hi-fi enthusiast example suggests.

In some instances, the rationale for integrating equipment may be *convenience* – being able to follow the same recording while one is moving around the house without depriving those who are remaining stationary, is certainly one example of this. But so too are in-home communications systems (e.g., being able to "telephone" someone who is in a distant part of the garden, being able to check that the baby is asleep). In some cases the rationale may be based more on *security* concerns – having the ability to monitor the state of the house from one's workplace, for example, or to see who is at the front door while staying in the sitting room. And in other cases it may be based on *automation*, going beyond simply being able to unlock the front door remotely to, for example, using "informed equipment," such as the "smart meters" which are capable of sending signals to other items of equipment to inform them that tariff rates have changed (so that, if they have been programmed to operate only in a low-cost energy mode, they should turn on or off).

There seem to be many circumstances under which the integration of equipment might be promoted. Whether this takes the form of specific items being related together, or that of a more comprehensive "smart house" system, will depend on these circumstances, together with issues such as the cost of equipment and of installing home communications systems.

The Myth of the Electronic Cottage

Tom Forester

In this article, I take Miles and others to task for over-estimating the capacity of IT in the home to bring about the changes in lifestyles envisaged in the "electronic cottage" scenario. It is reprinted from Futures, *vol. 20, 3, June 1988.*

An enduring theme in the literature on the impact of computers on society has been the prediction that we will see a big increase in home-based activities. Early visionaries of the "electronic cottage" forecast a rapid growth in working at home and the increased consumption of IT-based services, which together would amount to a revolutionary change in lifestyles. Now a new wave of theorists are making equally bullish statements about the impact of "home informatics" gadgetry.

This article reviews the evidence on participation across a range of home-based activities and discusses why home working, home banking, home shopping and home information services have not taken off as predicted. Drawing on case studies and personal experiences, I argue that (1) writers have consistently underestimated the *psychological* problems of working at home and (2) consumers have by and large not found new IT-based services to be cheaper, usable or useful – nor do they fulfill their *psychological* needs.

For these and other reasons, I conclude that any increase in home-based activity is likely to be gradual and that the vast majority of homes will *not* become the focus of new economic activity. The arrival of "home informatics" (HI) may lead to some increased consumption of IT-based services, but HI seems unlikely to (1) significantly boost economic activity in the home or (2) bring about the revolutionary change in lifestyles envisaged in the electronic cottage scenario.

Introduction

For 20 years or more, futurists have posited growth in cottage industry as part of a wider argument that computers and information technology (IT) play a decentralizing role in society. For example, James Martin and Adrian R.D. Norman, writing in the late 1960s: "we may see a return to cottage industry, with the spinning wheel replaced by the computer terminal . . . The time will come when the computer terminal is a natural adjunct to daily living . . . It is possible, indeed, that in the future some companies may have almost no offices."[1] A decade later, Alvin Toffler gave us the celebrated "electronic cottage.": ". . . we are about to revolutionize our homes . . . [the new mode of production makes possible] a return to cottage industry on a new, higher, electronic basis, and with it a new emphasis on the home as the center of society . . . powerful forces are converging to promote the electronic cottage . . . The fight for the electronic cottage is part of a larger super-struggle between the Second Wave past and the Third Wave future."[2] And more recently, Rowan A. Wakefield gave the argument a new twist with his notion of "family empowerment:" "Family empowerment means . . . using home computers to bring back into the home many functions that were there before the industrial revolution . . . 'Family empowerment' is a great social revolution in the making . . . Its coming is inevitable, a direct result of the marriage of the home computer with the family in our emerging information society."[3]

This is heady stuff, deliberately selected from writers who do not skimp on the hyperbole. But these are only colorful versions of a widely held view. For example, Jack Nilles, of the Center for Futures Research in California – and seen by many to be the "father" of the new homeworking movement – carried out studies in Los Angeles following the 1973 oil crisis on the economics of telecommuting. He concluded that for every 1 percent of the workforce who gave up urban commuting by car for telecommuting from home, the United States would save 5.4 million barrels of oil per year. If just one in seven of urban commuters dropped out, the United States would have no need to import oil and air pollution would decline.[4] In 1982, he wrote that telecommuters "now number in their thousands" and "By 1990, there should be as many as 10 million telecommuters" if certain conditions were met (three of the four conditions have been met). He concluded: "Telework and telecommuting are likely to increase at an accelerating pace over the next decade."[5]

The "electronic cottage" has fired the imagination of many writers and has become firmly implanted in the public consciousness as an allegedly widespread "social trend." The expected growth of homeworking in particular has been widely accepted as a "given" in discussions of the IT revolution – indeed, the *assumed* growth in all home-based activities has become an enduring theme in the literature. Most writers on the subject tend to point up the trend to homeworking and the consumption of home-based services (generalizing from a few well-known examples); review the available technology; state the vast potential for increased home activity and then conclude with a technologically determinist prediction for future growth which entirely glosses over the many problems encountered by actual participants. In summary, what the electronic cottage theorists have in common is a belief that we are witnessing (1) increased economic activity in the home, (2) increased consumption of IT-based services in the home, and (3) with it will come a fundamental change in lifestyles. It is these propositions that we will test against the evidence.

Working at home

The evidence

Working at home is quite common and is probably increasing, but it is by no means the norm. Establishing the true extent of homeworking is complicated by two problems. First, there are many different categories of homeworker, ranging from the factory outworker, the home-based salesman and self-employed person to telecommuting employees and executives who occasionally take work home. But broadly speaking there are two main types: those who do all their work at home and those who do just some of their work at home. The second problem arises from the confusion of statistics for self-employment and working at home, which are not necessarily the same.

Baer reports that 11 million Americans work at home – 7 percent of the total workforce work at home full-time and 6 percent part-time.[6] This roughly accords with another authority, Cross, who suggests that about 10 percent of the US workforce work at home for some or all of the time and that this figure will grow to 15 percent by the year 2000, which is of course just a decade away.[7] Electronic Services Unlimited, a New York consultancy, have been responsible for estimates ranging from "13 to 14 million" regularly working from home to "23.3 million" and "about 25 million."[8] In the UK, the Department of Employment in 1985 estimated that 7 percent of the workforce (or 1.7 million people) were homeworkers.[9]

When it comes to the figures for self-employment and/or home-based businesses, the picture gets even more confusing. The US Bureau of Labor Statistics put the number of self-employed in the US at about 8 million, but US Census and other sources estimate the total number of home-based businesses or individuals running businesses from home to be anything from 2 million to 24 million![10] As Atkinson is forced to conclude: "No one knows for sure how many people work at home, much less what the breakdown is. What *does* seem to be clear, though, is that the numbers are growing."[11]

But how true is this? First, the numbers have not grown as fast as many imagined. Ten percent perhaps rising to 15 percent by 2000 is hardly a social revolution and it's all a far cry from the heady days of the mid-1970s when Nilles was making his dramatic calculations. And while James Martin and Alvin Toffler hedged their predictions around with caveats, the clear implication of the "electronic cottage" literature was that working at home would be far more widespread than it is by now. Second, even Atkinson may have overestimated the *rate* of growth. Take actual telecommuting, for example: Cross says there are still only "about 100,000" telecommuters in the United States, while Baer and others point out that while many US corporations have experimented with telecommuting, the experiments have usually been on a small scale and have often been abandoned.[12] It is also very difficult to find new examples of telecommuting schemes: time and again the same few examples crop up in the literature – the Rank Xerox networkers and F International in the UK; Blue Cross/Blue Shield and Aetna Life in the United States – but none of these schemes appears to have expanded very much in recent years.

In fact, the historical trend in the self-employment statistics for the United States suggests that the electronic cottage theorists may have it all wrong. Dickson, for example, shows that no less than 34 percent of the US workforce were self-employed in 1870 (farming would have accounted for a large proportion). This declined steadily to 25 percent in 1910 and to 19.5 percent in 1950, finally bottoming-out at 6.7 percent in 1971. But in the 12 years to 1983, self-employment only climbed back to 7.6 percent.[13] We are thus left with the intriguing possibility that, if things go well for high-tech homeworking, we may get back to 1950s levels of self-employment sometime in the twenty-first century!!

Discussion

There is a vast literature on homeworking, much of it similar in content, as noted above. Some authors have contributed to the debate about the phenomenon by raising specific issues of financial exploitation, conditions of employment, and the lack of union representation,[14] possible problems with local planning laws,[15] or the management problems encountered by companies trying to run telecommuting programs.[16] Still others have written manifestos, which urge others to "break free" and partake of the joys of self-employment and/or home-working, usually in the way the author has.[17] But the majority are content to point up the trend, cite the well-known examples, state the vast potential and list the advantages and disadvantages.

Yet this listing of the pros and cons merely provides clues as to why working at home has apparently failed to grow in popularity. It does not provide an adequate explanation. Basic problems like the fact that the vast majority of people live in small houses or flats which are quite unsuitable for homeworking are conveniently overlooked. A second basic point usually ignored is that working at home is largely a middle-class issue since most of the occupations that can be done at home are middle class and that most computer owners are "well-off, well-educated and white."[18] Economies of scale and the dynamic of centralization in most corporate structures are rarely considered. The advantages and disadvantages of working at home are seldom explored in any real depth or in relation to empirical evidence – if they were, it might be possible to assess their relative importance and arrive at a more considered analysis. Most important of all, in my view, the literature (with a few honorable exceptions) glosses over and seriously underestimates the *psychological* problems of working at home. It is my contention that it is here that an explanation of the failure of homeworking to take off might be fruitfully sought.

Martin and Norman, for example, dismissed obstacles to the return to "cottage industry" in one short paragraph. Three factors, they declared, could counteract "the trend." First, management would be reluctant to provide employees with home terminals. Second, management might feel employees should be at their desks, 9 to 5, in the office. "The third is a feeling that people cannot work at home because the environment is not suitable. Perhaps some houses are unsuitable, *but the authors of this book had no difficulty in writing at home with a rate of productivity that would be regarded in industry as high"* (my emphasis – at the last count, James Martin had large homes in Bermuda and Vermont). Furthermore, "We believe that these views are not generally held by intelligent and enthusiastic members of the community."[19] So there.

Baer, in an otherwise realistic and non-deterministic account of IT is the home, declares in relation to self-employed professionals working at home: "The use of space at home need not change dramatically to support such professional work. If a separate office or study is not available, most people can place a computer and related equipment in their bedrooms. The bedroom can be used for work during nonsleeping hours."[20] Nobody who has ever worked full-time at home for any length of time could possibly take seriously a statement which overlooks so many practical and psychological problems. Again, in listing the barriers to more widespread homeworking, Baer chooses to focus on the institutional policies of government, the unions and "conservative" business organizations.[21] But there is little evidence that tax policies, zoning laws, and union opposition have created serious problems for homeworkers – certainly not enough to outweigh the alleged advantages.[22] Conservative management may well have restricted the growth of telecommuting schemes, but it should not have held back the growth of self-employed homeworking.

Cross is mainly concerned with the problems of managing successful telecommuting programs, a subject on which he consults through the Cross Information Company. Cross seems keen to sell the benefits of telecommuting, but nevertheless recognizes some of the problems and is quite realistic about its prospects. But his discussion of the "human factors" of telecommuting is, in my view, inadequate.[23] Likewise, Toffler mentions but does not discuss in any real depth the difficulties of transferring work to the electronic cottage (and, wishing to have it both ways, he actually concludes his hyped-up account by stating: "We cannot today know if, in fact, the electronic cottage will become the norm in the future."[24] Nilles lists a number of "undesirable side effects" of telecommuting and various "impediments" to its rapid spread, but these are not pursued in great detail.[25]

It is to Atkinson that we have to turn for an empirically grounded discussion of the difficulties posed by working at home,[26] although earlier skeptics such as Renfro earlier expressed similar feelings.[27] After talking to scores of homeworkers, Atkinson became convinced that the psychological problems associated with working at home were paramount:

It is very difficult – psychologically – to work at home. Almost without exception, "cottage industrialists" and "telecommuters" alike report a host of problems, including lack of motivation and discipline, inability to organize work and manage time effectively, loneliness, family tensions, fear of failure, burnout, stress and hypochondria. Essentially, these problems stem from an inability to be *self-managers*. In other words, the problems most often associated with working at home are triggered not so much by economic, legal, or technological factors as by the failure of these pioneers to manage themselves and their work.[28]

Concerned by the apparently high drop-out rate among homeworkers, Atkinson concluded that success or failure was determined by the individual's ability to cope with the stresses and strains imposed: "The primary factor determining success was a series of personal characteristics or traits."[29] Evidently, homeworking suits some people and not others.

In reaching this conclusion, Atkinson shows that homeworking is a much more complicated business than myriad articles have made out. Successful homeworkers, he says, need to possess the skills necessary to survive in their chosen career, they require an appropriate working environment and sufficient capital to get started, and they need the self-management skills necessary to organize their life efficiently. But most important of all, he says, they need the mental equipment to cope with the serious psychological problems that arise. Among the many problems: relations with the family or spouse; environmental problems such as noise; feelings of loneliness or isolation from colleagues; concern about social status, especially in the neighborhood; fear of failure; fear of poverty and the pressure to produce; workaholism; stress and burnout; hypochondria and computer anxiety.[30]

Under the first heading alone – relations with the family – Atkinson found that homeworking was rarely viewed favorably by the wives of homeworking husbands ("You ought to interview wives too! They're the ones who have to deal with the problems," called out the wife of one of his interviewees). The "problems," which can become a serious psychological drain on families, tend in my experience to include: explaining to the children that daddy is not available because he is "at work;" explaining the same to friends, neighbors and other callers; and keeping the children quiet or re-arranging the vacuuming so as not to disturb daddy. For the homeworker himself, there is the guilt and feelings engendered by hearing the children crying or arguing and not being able to intervene; hearing young children happily playing and not being able to join in; and the general problem of dividing "work" from "home" life. How do you explain to a 2-year-old that daddy in the kitchen making a cup of coffee is thinking about his next paragraph and is not to be interrupted? Similar illustrations could be provided under every heading in Atkinson's list.

Like Atkinson, I myself worked at home for seven years as a writer, full-time and wholly self-employed, based in Brighton, England. Prior to that, I commuted by train to work in London. To the problems of earning a living during a recession were added in this case the additional stresses arising from a heavy political involvement; a working spouse; the arrival of two young children, making a total of three; trouble with the neighbors; the death of close relatives; a lack of recognition, and so on. Like many of Atkinson's subjects, I went through a familiar cycle: an initial honeymoon period of 2–3 years, which was accompanied by feelings of elation and high productivity, was followed by a less satisfactory period which was accompanied by feelings of loneliness, isolation and a growing desire to escape the "same four walls." In 1986, I gave up full-time homeworking and took a three-days-a-week job on a computer paper near London to help resolve the problem. In 1987, the family emigrated to Queensland, Australia where my current position enables me to "get the best of both worlds" – the gregariousness of campus life for social contact and the peace and quiet (during school hours!) of a home office for serious work.

During the same period, I monitored the progress of five other homeworkers in the Brighton area – three of whom, like myself, had previously commuted to London by train. Of the five, two divorced, one became seriously depressed and one returned to working in London. For only one of the five did homeworking appear to be an unmitigated success – and even in that case there were serious question marks over aspects of the domestic situation which could lead to problems later.

I conclude that most of the existing literature on homeworking is written by people who haven't done it, it lacks an empirical basis for its assertions and in particular it seriously underestimates the psychological problems of working at home. As a result, it cannot account for the failure of homeworking to become more widespread. Theorists of the electronic cottage have failed to recognize that technological change is not always followed automatically by social change. Four statements therefore seem appropriate:

1 Not many people are or will be in a position to work at home in future because of space constraints and the nature of their occupations.
2 Of those who *could* work at home, not many will choose to do so, because homeworking suits only some people and not others. Even fewer people can cope with the psychological problems on a long-term basis.
3 We are thus most unlikely to see a major increase in homeworking (or the "mass return home after the industrial revolution" envisaged by the electronic cottage theorists).

4 We may, however, see a small but steady increase in the number of people doing some rather than all of their work at home, as flexible working patterns become more widespread and more people seek to get "the best of both worlds."

IT-based services

The evidence

If relatively few people will be *working* at home in the years to come, will more people be staying at home and using IT-based gadgetry to bank, shop and access videotex information services? The evidence to date is not encouraging for the electronic cottage theorists and those who, only a few years ago, were predicting a home banking revolution[31] or who were arguing that video games and personal computers would open up a vast market for home information services.[32] Baer estimates that "fewer than 1 percent" of US households use any videotex services,[33] while even videotex boosters admit that home information services are only likely to reach a "small, but affluent, audience."[34]

Home banking has been slow to take off in the United States and Europe. The two most successful US experiments are the Bank of America's service in San Francisco with a reported 15,000 subscribers and the Chemical Bank's Pronto service in New York which claims 21,000 users. But these totals are a far cry from the huge numbers envisaged when both services were launched back in 1982. Some US banks – like the Los Angeles First Interstate, San Francisco's Crocker National and Miami's Dadeland Bank – have dropped their planned home banking services altogether.[35] In the UK, the Nottingham Building Society's Homelink service, also launched in 1982, has apparently been a modest success, while the Bank of Scotland's Home Banking service (1985) and the Trustee Savings Bank's Speedlink (1987) have attracted some attention but no firm figures for the number of subscribers have been published. With a claimed 50,000 subscribers, the home banking service run by the Verbraucher Bank of Hamburg, West Germany, would appear to stand out as the most successful in the world. But for most banks, home banking is pretty low down their list of priorities (which include making high street banks more attractive places to visit) and customers aren't exactly clamoring for it, either.[36]

Home shopping or teleshopping has fared even worse. Back in the late 1970s, Warner-Amex showed that it was feasible with its famous Qube cable TV experiment in Columbus, Ohio. But since then a whole series of disasters have befallen the budding teleshopping/videotex industry in the United States. In 1983, Time Inc dropped its ambitious plans, but Knight–Ridder's Viewtron experiment in South Florida, Times–Mirror's Gateway service in Orange County, California and the Centel/Honeywell Keyfax service in Chicago went ahead. All three had folded by 1986 after making huge losses. Many saw Viewtron as the pioneer of electronic publishing in the United States and it was heavily promoted. Users could shop, bank, catch up with the news and access commercial data bases from home – for $600 down and $12 per month, plus telephone charges. But Knight-Ridder only managed to sign up a claimed 5,000 customers in the first year and Viewtron was shut down in March, 1986, after losing an astonishing $50 million. Two other videotex ventures – the IBM–Sears–CBS consortium's Trintex experiment and the AT&T-led Covidea venture – looked like going the same way.[37] In the UK, a home shopping service was started in Gateshead, County Durham as long ago as 1979. This was followed by the Club 403 experiment in Birmingham, started in 1983, and the Shop TV nationwide service (via British Telecom's Prestel) in 1985. But none has attracted much support. Although there has been a lot of speculation about planned home shopping services, nothing of major importance has materialized. The argument that home shopping would inevitably take off once cheap modems were available and/or the number of households with personal computers reached critical mass has proved to be erroneous.

It should be pointed out, however, that the period 1986–7 saw the sudden growth in popularity in the United States of home shopping via television and telephone. Home Shopping Network Inc. features actors and actresses who heavily promote special deals on consumer goods on cable TV shows. The goods may be obtained by placing an order over the telephone. But consumers soon appeared to tire of the gimmicks and strident sales pitches. By mid-1987, sales per viewer began to fall off.[38]

Likewise, videotex information services (other than the hybrids already discussed) have failed to capture the public's imagination, apart from one notable exception. In the UK, the two broadcast teletext services, the BBC's Ceefax and ITV's Oracle, have been operating since 1976, but only a minority of TV purchasers opt for this facility. Prestel, the viewdata service launched with great fanfare by British Telecom in 1979, has still only attracted about 60,000 subscribers – a fraction of the total originally predicted – and not all of these are residential. West Germany's similar Bildschirmtext has about 20,000 subscribers (in one of the most memorable predictions of the coming videotex bonanza, the Diebold group once forecast 2.8 million Bildschirmtext users by 1991!). Commercial data bases in the United States such as CompuServe, The Source and Dow Jones/News Retrieval and free, ad-supported local services like the Boston CitiNet have attracted users, but the only videotex service in the world to enjoy really widespread success in the domestic situation is the French Minitel system, which now boasts 2.2 million terminals – or about one in eight of all French telephone subscribers. Minitels are used for banking and shopping, but it is the personal message (or perhaps one should say "massage") services which have proved immensely popular. Some attribute this to the French penchant for conversation, gossip and forming liaisons with members of the opposite sex, including other people's wives. But even in the case of Minitel, there have been suggestions that recent rates of growth cannot be sustained.

Discussion

Boosters of videotex have consistently overestimated the market for home banking, shopping and information services. Far from attracting millions, participants may be counted in their thousands or even hundreds, with the exception of Minitel. Home banking has two basic drawbacks: it can't be used for cash transactions and most consumers don't do enough banking to justify the initial costs or recurring charges. Quite simply it's not very useful and it's unlikely that consumers or the banks themselves will push hard for it. Home shopping has failed because of practical problems such as complicated on-screen instructions, difficulties over payment systems, problems with arranging delivery times and a lack of choice of products. But perhaps most important of all, home shopping has failed because it does not fulfill the *psychological* needs of shoppers. Buyers like to shop around to compare prices and quality, and to handle potential purchases (especially high-value items). Many customers enjoy the social side of shopping, which offers a chance to bump into friends and to reacquaint themselves with other members of the community.[39] For housewives or househusbands stuck indoors all day, going out to the shops and/or the bank in the high street is a psychic safety valve, despite the hassles involved in modern-day shopping. Home shopping can be a useful service for disadvantaged groups such as the elderly, the housebound and the disabled, and maybe there is a market among hard-pressed two-career households, but it is a lonely business and most ordinary people positively welcome the opportunity to get *out* of the house and to go "down the shops".

The technological determinists who posited the "inevitable" growth of videotex information services once cheap personal computers and modems became available have been proved wrong over again. Videotex services are not easy to use, they are slow and they are inflexible. They are also costly and consumers have proved themselves unwilling to pay for mere information. Rather like the failure of cable TV enthusiasts in the early 1980s to accept that most people were quite happy with their existing TV channels,[40] the videotex boosters have badly overestimated the general public's ability to absorb more "infotainment." In the domestic environment, videotex remains a technologically glamorous solution looking for a problem.

Carey and Moss have looked at the diffusion of consumer electronics and new telecommunications services into the home,[41] reviewing the mixed fortunes of innovations such as CB radio, quadraphonic sound, cable TV, videophones and videotex. Pointing out that the marketing of many new services has been characterized by excessive hype and false expectations, Carey and Moss found that new services must meet three criteria in order to gain widespread acceptance: they must be cost-competitive or cheaper than existing ways of doing things; they must be usable ("compatible with user skills"); and they must be useful ("provide a specific service concept that the user values"). If new offerings are not cheaper, usable and useful, then they will inevitably fail. Thus consumer electronics and domestic telecommunications innovation would appear to be an area where there is a high degree of consumer sovereignty. In the final analysis, it is the consumers – not the manufacturers, not the banks, not the retailers, not the information providers, not governments, and not sociologists or futurologists, who will decide whether the new IT-based services meet their real needs.

Addendum: There is a point to be made which further undermines the notion that many people will be doing their banking and shopping from home in future. Retailers have, of course, been investing in IT for some years in an attempt to smooth the flow through the checkouts and to aid stock control. Banks have invested heavily in ATMs to facilitate 24-hour banking and many are completely revamping their interiors in order to make high street banking more relaxed and attractive. In the past year, a number of innovations have been introduced or announced which are aimed at making retail outlets more attractive and easier to use. In particular, the in-store marketing system – a stand-alone booth incorporating interactive videodisk technology – has made its appearance in thousands of US stores, shopping malls and airport concourses.[42] These devices are being used to sell everything from fabrics and cosmetics to cars, while others offer recipes, recommend wines or simply advise customers where items may be found in the store. And the electronic price tag on supermarket shelves is being developed into an information system which gives data on, for example, the nutritional content of grocery items. These gadgets have received a mixed reception, but they indicate a continuing effort by retailers and bankers to attract people *into* their outlets and *out* of their homes.

Home informatics

The argument

It is against this background of failure that we must evaluate the potential impact of "home informatics" (HI), to assess whether it offers any real prospect of increased economic activity in the home, increased consumption of IT-based services or a fundamental change in lifestyles. According to Miles, "The term 'Home Informatics' refers to the applications of Information Technology (IT) products that are emerging for use by members of private households."[43] These, he says, include home computers, consumer electronics, videotex services, and other IT products used in the home environment. With new products like compact disk (CD) storage systems, high definition TVs (HDTV), even smarter telephones, and home security systems on the way, the scene is set, he says, for a "revolution" in household equipment.[44] In a recent report, Miles reviews in detail the latest developments and makes a number of points about the importance of the HI market, the problem of technical standards, the necessity of developing a new telecommunications infrastructure and the need for governments to understand the links between consumer demand and industrial policy, as well as broadcasting policy and telecommunications policy.[45] He says there is a case for taking HI more seriously because of its impact on the economy and society at large.

The origins of this interest in the household as a possible locus of major social change can be traced back in its most recent form to Gershuny, who in 1978 argued that technology transfer into the home in the form of washing machines, dishwashers, freezers, food processors, microwave ovens, paint-strippers, hover-mowers, and VCRs could substitute for services purchased outside the home from launderettes, restaurants, decorators, gardeners, and cinemas. Any increase in such "self-servicing" would clearly have implications for the future of service sector employment.[46] The evidence for and against this thesis is mixed, but in any event Gershuny and Miles later brought IT more squarely into the picture by arguing that computing, telecommunications, and storage technologies would create a "new wave" of "social innovation" in the ways of receiving information, entertainment, education, and possibly medical services.[47] An important NEDO report, co-authored by Miles, devoted a section to exploring the links between the household economy, consumption, and economic growth.[48]

At the same time, Barras was developing his thesis that investment in IT goods in the home could provide the impetus for economic recovery from the downswing in the 1980s. Many writers such as Freeman have attempted to explain the possible links between perceived clusters of innovation and the alleged existence of long waves of economic development.[49] The general consensus of this literature seems to be that we may have to wait for IT innovations to fully diffuse into the economy before we can expect to experience an upswing which might offer some hope to the millions of unemployed.[50] Barras compares today's "service revolution" with the Industrial Revolution and the building of the new telecommunications network with the building of the railway network in the 1840s. The first phase of the Industrial

Revolution was accompanied by job losses and social dislocation, the second phase saw job gains and economic growth once the network was completed and the new goods and services could be moved around. In IT, Barras sees

> the potential to generate an enormous growth in new service activities, supported by an IT network capable of transmitting large volumes of information instantaneously over great distances . . . Under such circumstances, vast markets for new types of interactive services will be created. Some of these new services, such as home banking and home shopping, will consist of radically new ways of delivering established services to customers. Others . . . will involve new service products of a type which can now only be perceived in general terms . . .[51]

Barras, along with Gershuny, Miles and others who have looked at IT and the household economy, all seem to agree with Mackintosh[52] and Vitalari and Venkatesh[53] that developing a new telecommunications infrastructure of a broad-band fiber optic cable into every home is the *sine qua non* not only of home informatics, but of renewed economic growth and even the continued existence of a European IT industry.

Discussion

What we are primarily concerned with here is whether the burgeoning home informatics literature offers any compelling new evidence or convincing new arguments in support of the electronic cottage scenario, which envisages increased economic activity in the home, increased consumption of IT-based services in the home and a consequent revolutionary change in lifestyles. Miles, for example, writes: "A revolution in household equipment is looming which will be at least as wide-ranging as the white and brown goods revolution of the 1950s and 60s;"[54] "The home of the future is liable to be as different from the 1985 home as that was from the 1945 one;"[55] and "the cumulative impact of product innovation in home informatics is likely to be as revolutionary in terms of what equipment people have in their homes, and how they consequently organise their ways of life, as was the pattern of innovation over the postwar decades."[56]

These statements, of course, beg a number of questions such as the extent to which the gradual introduction of brown and white goods – and their subsequent steady upgrading – constituted a "revolution" in household equipment; whether the upgrading of household equipment necessarily leads to changes in lifestyles, and so on. But even if we accept the general thrust of the argument that there are some significant things going on and that the whole area of home informatics should be taken more seriously, there is little here[57] to suggest that the arrival of the electronic cottage will be hastened by any new generations of gadgetry. In respect of economic activity, working at home is not directly discussed in the HI literature and Miles himself concedes that there are no really new domestic activities in the offing.[58] In respect of IT-based services, the failure of home shopping and banking is recognized and briefly discussed by both Miles and Barras,[59] but neither in my view offers an adequate explanation of its failure. Likewise, Miles provides a useful discussion of the mixed fortunes of videotex in Europe,[60] but offers no compelling new evidence to suggest that it will fare any better in the future. As we argued above, it is consumers who decide which services to accept,[61] and the evidence so far is that these IT-based services have by and large been rejected by consumers.

In respect of lifestyles, the HI literature offers little support for the theory of the electronic cottage. A combination of home computers, consumer electronics goods, videotex services, and home security systems, even in a "smart" house, wired with heating and lighting sensors – and pseudo-useful devices which enable residents, for example, to listen to the same music as they move from room to room – hardly adds up to a revolution in ways of living comparable to the Industrial Revolution. Besides, a number of so-called "homes of the future" which incorporate all or most of these facilities have in fact been built in recent decades and they have stirred very little interest.[62] When Miles talks about fundamental and revolutionary changes in lifestyles, it becomes clear that what he actually has in mind are relatively modest changes in the process of housework (thanks to "smart" kitchen gadgetry, for instance, cooking can be accomplished faster, better, more conveniently, etc.); possible changes in the sexual division of labour (more role reversal); and relatively minor changes such as spreading family meal-times (thanks to microwaves).[63] While one wouldn't disagree with any of this, it hardly adds up to a major revolution in lifestyles of the kind envisaged by the electronic cottage theorists. Miles himself also concedes that no lasting changes will take place "without people's willingness to create changes in their ways of life"[64] – and it is my contention that there is precious little evidence that people are willing – or able – to make such changes.

One cannot deny that there are some interesting domestic applications of IT on the way. A cull of recent press cuttings revealed plans (nearly all, incidentally, of Japanese companies) to market videophones or TV telephones, home management systems for "smart" houses, 3-D camcorders, home fax machines, cheaper mobile phones, and even miniature home bakery systems, which enable people to bake single loaves at home, thus, in theory, eliminating many visits to the shops. But at the same time, plans are being announced for more "smart" office buildings and the Japanese are intending to upgrade their commercial centers to create the necessary infrastructure for the advanced information society.[65] As I pointed out above, just as there are IT developments which might serve to decentralize society and keep people IN their homes, so there are developments which might serve to further centralize facilities and keep people OUT of their homes.

I must therefore conclude that while "home informatics" may be of interest for various reasons, developments on this front are unlikely to lead to a substantial increase in economic activity in the home or an increase in the consumption of IT-based services in the home of a sufficient volume to amount to the revolutionary change in lifestyles depicted in the electronic cottage scenario. The process of technology transfer into the home is a slow and complex business. The mistake of some HI enthusiasts has been to assume that IT will transfer swiftly and smoothly into homes with inevitable social changes following on. Actually, things haven't changed very much – and nor are they likely to do so. Given the evidence and analysis presented on working at home, the consumption of IT-based services and the potential of "home informatics," I have to conclude that the electronic cottage is largely a myth.

Notes

1 James Martin and Adrian R. D. Norman, *The Computerized Society: An Appraisal of the Impact of Computers on Society in the Next Fifteen Years* (Prentice-Hall, Englewood Cliffs, NJ,) 1970, pp. 32, 155–6.

2 Alvin Toffler, *The Third Wave* (William Morrow, New York, 1980), pp. 204, 210, 214.

3 Rowan A. Wakefield, "Home Computers and Families: The Empowerment Revolution," *The Futurist*, vol. 20(5), September–October 1986, pp. 18–22.

4 J. M. Nilles, F. R. Carlson, P. Gray et al., *The Telecommunications-Transportation Tradeoff: Options for Tomorrow* (Wiley, New York, 1976).

5 Jack Nilles, "Teleworking From Home," in T. Forester (ed.), *The Information Technology Revolution* (Basil Blackwell, Oxford, 1985), p. 208. Reprinted from *Technology Review*, April 1982.

6 Walter S. Baer, "Information Technologies in the Home," in Bruce R. Guile (ed.), *Information Technologies and Social Transformation* (National Academy Press, Washington, DC, 1985), p. 128.

7 Thomas B. Cross, "Telecommuting – Future Options for Work," *Oxford Surveys in Information Technology*, vol. 3, 1986, p. 255.

8 Jonathan Friendly, "The Electronic Change: House Becomes Office," *The New York Times*, Thursday May 15, 1986, p. C1; ESU Telework study, reported in *The Australian*, September 8, 1987; William Atkinson, *Working at Home – Is It For You?* (Dow Jones-Irwin, Homewood, IL, 1985).

9 *Employment Gazette*, 92(1) (HMSO, London, 1985).

10 Atkinson, *Working at Home*, pp. 9–10.

11 Ibid., pp. 11–12.

12 Cross, p. 248; Baer, "Information Technologies," p. 132; and Atkinson, *Working at Home*.

13 Paul Dickson, *On Our Own: A Declaration of Independence for the Self-Employed* (Facts on File, New York, 1985).

14 For example, Arnold Cragg and Tim Dawson, *Qualitative Research Among Homeworkers*, Research Paper No. 21 (Department of Employment, London, May 1981); Ursula Huws, "Terminal Isolation," in Radical Science Collective (eds), *Making Waves: The Politics of Communications* (Free Association Books, London, 1985); *Telework: Impact on Living and Working Conditions* (European Foundation for the Improvement of Living and Working Conditions, Dublin, 1984); Gitte Vedel, *Just Pick Up a Telephone! Remote Office Work in Sweden* (Information Systems Research Group, Copenhagen School of Economics and Business Administration, 1984).

15 For example, John Herbers, "Rising Cottage Industry Stirring Concern in US," *The New York Times*, May 13, 1986, p. A18; "Telework May Violate Employment Laws," *Futures*, June 17, 1985, p. 313.

16 For example, Steve Shirley interviewed by Eliza G. C. Collins, "A Company Without Offices," *Harvard Business Review*, January–February, 1986, pp. 127–36; Miriam K. Mills, "Teleconferencing – Managing the Invisible Worker," *Sloan Management Review*, Summer 1984, pp. 63–7.

17 For example, Dickson, *On Our Own*; John Applegath, *Working Free: Practical Alternatives to the 9 to 5 Job* (Amacom, New York, 1982).

18 Holden in Baer, "Information Technologies," p. 137.

19 Martin and Norman, *The Computerized Society*, pp. 154–5.

20 Baer, "Information Technologies," p. 127.

21 Ibid., pp. 131–2.

22 See for example, Dickson, *On Our Own*; Atkinson, *Working at Home*.

23 Cross, "Telecommuting," pp. 255 and 261–3.

24 Toffler, *The Third Wave*, p. 217.

25 Nilles in Forester, *The Information Technology Revolution*, pp. 204–7.

26 Atkinson, *Working at Home*.

27 William L. Renfro, "Second Thoughts on Moving the Office Home," in Forester, *The Information Technology Revolution*, pp. 209–15, reprinted from *The Futurist*, June 1982.

28 Atkinson, *Working at Home*, p. 4. Emphasis in original.

29 Ibid., p. vii.

30 Ibid., pp. 34–5; 60–1; and 86–107.

31 Toffler, *The Third Wave*; Martin and Norman, *The Computerized Society* and Alan Cane, "The Banking Revolution – Home Sweet Bank," *Financial Times* (London), October 23, 1981.

32 Louise Kehoe, "The Home Workstation Is On The Line," *Financial Times* (London). September 27, 1983.

33 Baer, "Information Technologies," p. 134.

34 Ralph L. Lowenstein and Helen E. Aller, "The Inevitable March of Videotex," *Technology Review*, October, 1985, p. 27.

35 For discussion, see T. Forester, *High-Tech Society: The Story of the Information Technology Revolution* (Basil Blackwell, Oxford, 1987), pp. 237–40.

36 Forester, *High-Tech Society*, pp.129 and 239–40.

37 Ibid., pp. 128–30.

38 See reports in *Business Week*, December 15, 1986, March 30, 1987 and October 12, 1987.

39 Forester, p. 238 and *Financial Times* (London) February 28, 1985.

40 T. Forester, "The Cable That Snapped," *New Society*, January 24, 1985; see also "Cable TV's Journey From Promised Land to Wasteland," *Business Week*, September 14, 1987.

41 John Carey and Mitchell L. Moss, "The Diffusion of New Telecommunication Technologies," *Telecommunications Policy*, vol. 9(2), June, 1985.

42 Rifka Rosenwein, "Merchandisers Turn to Electronic Clerks," *The Wall Street Journal*, June 30, 1986; Paul Hurly, "Automated Retail," *High Technology*, September 1986; "Smart Shopping," *Fortune*, May 11, 1987.

43 Ian Miles, *Home Informatics: A Report to the Six Countries Programme on Aspects of Government Policies Towards Technical Innovation in Industry* (Six Countries Programme Secretariat, Delft, Netherlands, revised draft, July 1987)

44 Ian Miles, *The Convergent Economy*, Papers in Science, Technology and Public Policy No. 14 (Science Policy Research Unit, University of Sussex, 1987).

45 Miles, *Home Informatics*, pp. 148–50.

46 Jonathan Gershuny, *After Industrial Society? The Emerging Self-Service Economy* (Macmillan, London, 1978).

47 Jonathan Gershuny and Ian Miles, *The New Service Economy: The Transformation of Employment in Industrial Societies* (Frances Pinter, London, 1983).

48 John Bessant, Ken Guy, Ian Miles et al., *IT FUTURES: What Current Forecasting Literature Says About The Social Impact of Information Technology* (National Economic Development Office, London, 1985).

49 Christopher Freeman, John Clark, and Luc Soete, *Unemployment and Technical Innovation: A Study of Long Waves and Economic Development* (Frances Pinter, London, 1982).

50 For a popular summary, see Peter Hall, "The Geography of the Fifth Kondratieff," *New Society*, March 26, 1981.

51 Richard Barras, "Information Technology and the Service Revolution," *Policy Studies*, April 1985, pp. 14–23. It is only fair to point out that Barras acknowledges elsewhere the problems of home banking and shopping – see "New Technology and the New Services," *Futures*, vol. 18(6), December 1986, pp. 748–72.

52 Ian Mackintosh, *Sunrise Europe: The Dynamics of Information Technology* (Basil Blackwell, Oxford, 1986).

53 Nicholas P. Vitalari and Alladi Venkatesh, "In-Home Computing and Information Services: A Twenty-Year Analysis of the Technology and Its Impacts," *Telecommunications Policy*, vol. 11 (1), 1987, pp. 65–81.

54 Miles, *The Convergent Economy*, p. 13.

55 Ian Miles, *Social Implications of Information Technology*, Paper to Library Association Conference, Brighton, UK, August 1987; also p. 13 of Miles, *Home Informatics*.

56 Ian Miles, *Work in Information Society*, A Report to the Joseph Rowntree Memorial Trust (Science Policy Research Unit, University of Sussex, first draft, December, 1986), p. 218.

57 That is, in Miles, *Home Informatics* and Miles, *Work in Information Society*.

58 Miles, *Work in Information Society*, p. 237 and Miles, *Home Informatics*, p. 5.

59 Miles, *Work in Information Society*, p. 254; Barras, "New Technology and the New Services," pp. 755ff.
60 Miles, *Home Informatics*, pp. 70–9.
61 A point also made in, for example, J. Hartley, J. S. Metcalfe, J. Evans, et al., *Public Acceptance of New Technologies: New Communications Technology and the Consumer*, Report to the Economic and Social Research Council (PREST, University of Manchester, 1986), p. 1.
62 See, for example, T. Forester, "The House of the Future?" *New Society*, August 28, 1980.
63 Miles, *Home Informatics*, pp. 152–3.
64 Miles, *Work in Information Society*, p. 229.
65 On the latter point, see *Business Week*, November 2, 1987.

Postscript

General support for my argument comes from an unlikely source - Japan. In a rare English-language study of new communications technology in Japan (Prometheus, vol. 6, no. 2, December 1988), Tessa Morris-Suzuki reports on the 1984–7 Mitaka experiment, which involved giving 2,000 Japanese households fax machines, videotex terminals, videophones, etc. and their connection to INS, the Japanese version of ISDN. Surprisingly, she found that the subjects of the experiment were by no means enamored by the "electronic cottage" concept - using the home shopping facility, for example, on average only once a month, and even then merely as a substitute for mail-order. She also looks at the evidence for participation in home working, home medical care, and the use of videophones, concluding that "household use of new media in the immediate future is likely to be very limited." Tessa Morris-Suzuki is Lecturer at the University of New England, Armidale, New South Wales, Australia.

The Sexy Computer

Justine De Lacy

About the only domestic videotex system in the world that seems to be popular with the public is the now-famous Minitel service in France. In this amusing article, journalist Justine De Lacy explains that sexy messages have been a major cause of its success. I tell my students that this is an important example of how the diffusion of new technologies is influenced by cultural traits - though I'm still not sure whether the French really are over-sexed or whether they are just very lonely. Reprinted from The Atlantic, *July 1987.*

It has always been hard to tell what the French will fall in love with next. Their latest passion is sending anonymous messages on a squat nine-inch computer terminal to people they have never met. Designed in 1978 as the world's first electronic telephone directory, Minitel, which is distributed, free, to French telephone subscribers, today provides access to more than 4,500 consumer services 24 hours a day, revolutionizing business in a country in which home delivery is rare and few shops are open at night. But it is the French perception of Minitel as a passport to romance that has made France's first high-tech addiction.

Though officials are reluctant to give precise figures, roughly half the connection hours on Minitel's most popular network are to the more than 400 *messageries* – direct-dialogue services that, for many, are taking the place of confidante, confessor, psychiatrist, and lover. A user, protected by a pseudonym he or she chooses when signing on, sends a message to another "pseudo," listed on the screen, or waits to receive one.

Those looking for more than understanding consult *messageries roses*, sexual smorgasbords with something for every taste. (In France *le rose*, or "pink," refers to soft-core pornography.) Sextel, X-Tel, Désiropolis, Aphrodite, Aime-Moi Mimi, and Abélard et Héloïse advertise a selection of "Rambos, machos, Latin Lovers, Romeos, and Big Bad Wolves" for women, and "mermaids, man-eaters, Little Red Riding Hoods, and femmes fatales" for men. Pom, "the first encyclopedia of lovemaking," hears confessions and takes orders for lingerie. Canal Gay, Gai Pied, Voice of the Paranoid, Masked Ball, and many others cater to male and female homosexuals, voyeurs, and groups given to sexual *bizarrerie*.

As the conversations build from friendly to flirtatious to seriously seductive, some pseudos exchange phone numbers; a few eventually meet. But many choose to remain behind their protective shields. In an age when physical contact is often associated with contamination, Minitel's attraction is risk-free communication: the emotional equivalent of safe sex, conversation with a condom.

So many people have become addicted to these electronic singles bars and computer cafés, as they are called, that it is not uncommon for people to abandon human beings to run home to electronic rendezvous. The hunger for communication is even replacing the legendary French appetite for food – growing numbers of people are staying in their offices to "talk" on Minitels during lunchtime.

Adults are not the only ones who have become addicted to the Minitel. When a television call-in show asked children to answer questions by Minitel, instead of by telephone, five hundred responded, instead of the usual fifty. An amazed father wrote to *Minitel Magazine* to say that his four children didn't want to take any of the regular vacation paraphernalia to Brittany this year; the only "toy" they wanted was the Minitel.

Yet few people openly admit to seeking romance on their Minitels. In bourgeois circles using them for social reasons is still slightly taboo, in the same category as placing a personal ad. Then, too, there is the feeling that the French, internationally acknowledged experts in the art of love, shouldn't require the services of a machine – Real Frenchmen Don't Need Minitel. But the minute one guest at a dinner party confesses that he has tried looking for love on his, others soon relax and admit that they have too.

The love affair between the normally technology-shy French and their new high-tech toy is one of the most unusual success stories in France since the Second World War. Last year Telecom, the government telecommunications agency, had revenues of more than one billion francs ($167 million) from Minitel, making France the world leader in videotex, the system by which one computer communicates with another; in French it is called *télématique*.

These days Georges Nahon, the managing director of Intelmatique, Telecom's marketing arm, is eyeing the American market the way Tom eyes Jerry. A cartoon in *Intelmatique* magazine shows a tiny Minitel cooing "I love you" to an equally smitten American cowboy. In an office adorned with a gold-plated Minitel, the millionth manufactured, Nahon plies foreign journalists with tote bags that say I LOVE MINITEL and discusses "les chat lines" in fluent Franglais. (Minitel is "très user-friendly," "un bon business"; the BBC Minitel service, begun in March, "un package: message plus news.")

In recent months Nahon has spent much of his time studying "le break-up," the deregulation of the American telephone industry, and his nemesis, Judge Harold Greene, the author of the ruling that the French consider to be the main obstacle to the conquest of America by Minitel. Lately, however, Nahon has had more to worry about than Judge Greene. A controversy over the sexually explicit use of Minitel is threatening to tarnish its carefully polished image.

Many people who have logged on to the *messageries roses* out of curiosity have been shocked by the obscene language and semi-pornographic graphics. Starting last summer, however, they no longer had to turn on Minitel to see women in provocative poses. Racy ads for Minitel loomed at them from subway corridors, newspaper kiosks, and some of France's most illustrious historical monuments. In August a homosexual network promoting sex with children was brought to public attention. Then came the news that a woman in Nice had been tortured and raped by a man she had met on Minitel.

"MINITEL ROSE SCANDAL," "MINITEL SEX MACHINE," the headlines read. "A few are making fortunes preying on the sexual poverty of the many," *Le Monde* moralized. "We thought the *messageries roses* were just acne," François de Valence, the editor of *Minitel Magazine,* wrote. "They're turning out to be smallpox." Parisians joked that PTT no longer stood for Postes, Téléphone et Télégraph but had become "Prostitution Télématique et Téléphonique." By December the mayor of Paris, Jacques Chirac, had received so many letters from Parisians complaining that they couldn't go Christmas shopping without encountering technicolor genitalia that he ordered the most offensive posters taken down.

A special Commission Télématique was convened to decide whether existing laws on pornography apply to Minitel. But sessions for the most part resembled a town meeting discussing what to do about the flying saucer that landed on the village green. "A lot of time is spent laughing at the stories," one member admitted. The PTT was quick to duck responsibility. "The *messageries* are more mental than physical," Jean-Paul Maury, the head of Télématique services, says. "Two and a half million people use Minitel, and we don't have two and a half million people meeting in corners." Shifting blame to the private contractors who provide the software, he said, "Our role is to transport information, not to censor it. To blame us because somebody got raped is like blaming Gutenberg for pornography because he invented the printing press."

Ultimate responsibility belonged to the courts, everyone decided. But even the courts are confused. "A 1939 law forbids public incitation to debauchery," Monique Poignard, a judge assigned to the case, explains. "But are Minitel messages public or private? One-to-one messages and electronic mail are obviously private, but the personal ads and the forums where several people talk at once are public. We want the contractors to screen them. Some say it's technically impossible. Others tell us it can be done. We aren't sure whom to believe."

The truth no one really wants to admit is that the *messageries roses* are making too much money for anyone to want to do much of anything about them. Selling sex is, after all, as French as tarte aux pommes. In the country that made the brothel a respectable social institution (in a typically Cartesian Catch-22, prostitution is legal but soliciting is not), anything goes as long as the government gets its cut. "Let's face it," one official says, "people are not going to run up ten-thousand-franc bills sending messages to their banks."

A national sex network wasn't exactly what the technocrats had in mind. Strongly influenced by a 1978 report on the computerization of France, which warned that the technophobic French, unless they rapidly became computer-friendly, would be left home making Camembert and coq au vin while the Americans and the Japanese fought it out in the microchip major leagues, Telecom officials came up with a plan to force the French to the keyboard.

The telephone book, which was expensive to compile and print, and 10 percent of which was out of date by the time it was published, would be replaced by an easy-to-use computer terminal linking users to an electronic directory. As consumer services were added to its repertoire, the French would become hooked on high tech, and France would be a step closer to a longstanding dream: a French-language satellite data bank that would break the worldwide online monopoly of English. (Reportedly, President François Mitterrand has complained about having to talk to machines in English.)

This was an ambitious plan, considering that in 1977 only a third of French homes had telephones. As late as 1973 France had ranked only twenty-second among industrialized nations in the number of telephone lines *per capita*, behind Spain, Greece, and Iceland – a situation said to have cost France 2 percent of its GNP, or \$3.7 billion, in business that year.

But it was usually after the French got their telephones that their headaches began. As a form of communication, French telephones were only slightly less primitive than the tom-tom and often less effective. Half the calls in Paris regularly failed to go through. When they did, one had to expect that the dialogue might at any moment become a monologue. "Half of France is waiting for a telephone," a member of the National Assembly once remarked. "The other half is waiting for a dial tone."

Shocked by the state of French telecommunications when he returned to France in 1969, after working for a French firm in North America for 12 years, Jean-François Berry started France's first consumer lobby, the Association Française des Utilisateurs du Téléphone et des Télécommunications (AFUTT), and began bombarding the government with graphs that showed just how far France had to go.

The French failure to invest in telecommunications was not an oversight. From its introduction in France, in the early 1900s, the telephone had had two image problems: it was considered an instrument of women's liberation and of political subversion. "It acquired a risqué image because it was thought that women used it to carry on affairs behind their husbands' backs," Catherine Bertho, a historian at the Post Office Ministry, explains. "Belle Époque postcards showed the first call girls, holding telephones. The French adore hierarchy, and [the telephone] allowed one to bypass the hierarchy: social climbers had access without having first to leave their cards. It was also used to give orders to tradesmen, so anyone who jumped when a bell rang was acting like a servant."

Charles de Gaulle, never one to jump when a bell rang, despised the intrusiveness of the telephone and would not permit one near him. By allowing French telecommunications to languish, he also followed a longstanding French tradition: government control of information.

Not until 1974, the first time in 16 years that the Gaullists were out of power, did AFUTT's embarrassing graphs hit home. Ordering the then Post Office Minister Gérard Théry to "get the French connected," President Valéry Giscard d'Estaing allocated 100 billion francs (\$17 billion) over five years to make the telephone a national priority. As a result, telecommunications made a greater leap in one decade than any sector of the economy had since World War II. France has 24 million telephone subscribers today, as compared with 10 million in 1977, and anyone who wants a telephone can have one within several days, for an installation fee of 250 francs (\$42), a fourth of what it used to cost.

The one problem that remained was the telephone book, and Directory Inquiries was little better. It was often five or ten minutes before an operator answered, and when one did, it was usually to berate the caller for not having the party's address or middle initial. (I once tried to obtain the number of a hotel in rue des Beaux Arts called L'Hôtel. "We are in France, Madame," the operator announced. "And in France the hotels have names. Hotel Crillon. Hotel Ritz. You see – names. Call me back when you find the name.")

Enter Minitel! Not only does it find any number in France in seconds, but it does so when you give it an incorrect spelling or incomplete information. (As soon as I got mine, I typed in "L'Hôtel". Up came the number.) But superior service, officials knew, would not be enough to entice the French to use Minitel, let alone get them hooked. Aware that their thrifty compatriots would never pay for the machines, which cost 1,000 francs ($167) each to produce, Telecom decided to include them in the telephone subscription price – in effect giving them away. "It was an amazing thing to do," Alain Minc, a co-author of the 1978 report, says. "Like giving away television sets in 1955." Such unprecedented largesse got people's attention. Henri IV had promised the French a chicken in every pot. Now there was to be a Minitel in every *maison*. Next, Telecom officials decided on an enticing pay-as-you-go policy. Unlike videotex users in other countries, the French pay no access or subscription fees. They are charged for the time they use – from $4 to $10 an hour, depending on the service – on their telephone bills.

The electronic telephone directory was an immediate hit. But aside from that the French, overinformed and underloved, like many of us, remained largely indifferent. Then, in October of 1981, pirates in Strasbourg hijacked the internal message system of a small videotex network started by *Les Dernières Nouvelles d'Alsace*, one of the few newspapers that had seen Minitel as an opportunity rather than a threat. They began sending each other messages, and within days connection time on the network tripled.

Fascinated, Michel Landaret, the computer specialist who had set up the system, spent weeks at his terminal watching what he calls "the verbal tennis matches." (A jovial man, referred to as the "father of the *messagerie*" by the French press, Landaret recalls the day he spotted the first suggestive pseudo. It was "Peggy la Cochonne – Peggy the Pig," he says with a grin.)

Communication, not information, was Minitel's raison d'être, Landaret realized. He went to Paris to sell Telecom on the idea of a direct-dialogue service that would allow users to "talk" to each other. "They were scandalized," Landaret says. "They said it would be a waste of time for people to 'chat' on Minitel." Undeterred, Landaret returned to Strasbourg and created France's first *messagerie*, Gretel, whose logo is a heart with fluttering eyelashes.

It wasn't long before Gretel had revolutionized Strasbourg, a staid Alsatian town in France's gloomy northeastern corner which is known as the home of the European Parliament and for its citizens' lengthy silences. By the end of the first year the once taciturn Strasbourgeois had sent each other 18 million messages; Gretel was receiving 1,200 calls a day. The average "conversation" lasted an hour.

Those who had sneered began to see the *messageries* in a new light. First on the bandwagon was the press, which had seen Minitel as a rival and campaigned against it. Anxious to disarm the opposition, in November of 1984 Telecom accorded the press a virtual monopoly on 36.15, a network that includes the profitable *messageries* and is now known as *le kiosk*. As a result, far from being what *Le Monde* once called the "gravedigger of print," Minitel soon put many newspapers, including two of Paris's largest, into the black after years of financial chaos.

By June of 1985 the *messageries* were receiving so many calls that the network exploded, reducing its capacity substantially for more than a month. By 1986 *le kiosk* was generating 70 percent of the main traffic on Minitel and revenue had nearly quadrupled, from 286 million francs ($48 million) in 1985 to 822 million ($137 million). In the 12-month period ending in March 1987, traffic increased by 50 percent. Gretel had revenues of 1.5 million francs

($250,000) a month, two-thirds of it from the direct-dialogue service. (The other third came from news and consumer services.)

The French, it seemed, were hooked. As *messageries* sprang up all over France, the French succumbed to a desire to explain it all. True rationalists, the French don't just experience passion. They passionately analyze it, scrutinize it, assess it to excess. So many long-winded articles on the *messageries* soon appeared that one journalist challenged the intellectuals "to come off it and admit they are out for sex like everyone else." Why, they wanted to know, had videotex been such a success only in France? Were the French more lonely, isolated, frustrated, repressed, or up-tight than everybody else?

The answer, in many respects, seemed to be yes. The *messageries* are a response to a society that teaches people to be not only wary of strangers but also suspicious of friends, one in which a burden of rituals and rules regulates most activity. The first thing that children – and foreigners – learn is that there is one way to do things, the French way, *comme il faut*. Childhood in France is a never-ending litany of "Don't run, you'll trip," "Don't play, you'll get dirty," "Don't speak to someone unless you have been introduced." (It is not uncommon for people who have worked together for years to address each other as Monsieur and Madame. Not for nothing was "It is forbidden to forbid" the most enduring slogan of the mass demonstrations of May, 1968.)

Such a rigid system has produced a nation of inhibited, self-conscious people, despite their image of dash and flair, whose reputation for sexual expertise is largely a myth. Romain Gary wrote in *La Vie Devant Soi*, which won the Prix Goncourt in 1975, "What we call being alive in our country is having your papers in order." Sociologists considered it significant that France's first *messagerie* bloomed in the emotional desert of Strasbourg, and they flocked there to study it. In 1983 Gretel became nationally famous when the French got a glimpse of love à la Strasbourgeoise in *Minitel, Mon Amour*, a television documentary produced by Eddy Cherky, a sociologist at France's prestigious Centre Nationale de Recherche Scientifique. Viewers were as deeply fascinated by the adventures of Ulysse, Superman, Coeur d'Or, and La Fée aux Mille Yeux Miroirs (The Fairy with the Thousand Mirror Eyes) as they were by those of les Carringtons.

Ulysse is a university mathematics professor who, with his wife's approval, corresponds platonically but passionately with Maldita, a woman he had never seen until they appeared on television together. Not all Strasbourgeois were as relaxed as Ulysse's wife about their spouses' new friends. A woman incensed by the idea that her husband might be sending flirtatious messages to women while she was sitting in the same room logged on to a friend's Minitel with a lascivious pseudonym. She was soon besieged by racy propositions, including one from her husband. He awoke the next day to find his wife gone and the Minitel on the pillow.

A man who suspected his wife of having an affair cut the Minitel wires. She spliced them. With the finesse of a cordon bleu he cut them into inch-long pieces, and then threw the Minitel out the window. "So many have gone out the window that we have stopped counting!" Michel Landaret says. "Put a Minitel in a bad marriage and it's over." (There is now a 3,060-franc penalty for "voluntary destruction" of a Minitel.)

As spouses quickly realize, Minitel relationships are no less real because the partners are invisible. Many Minitelistes are telling their new electronic pen pals things they have never told anyone else. Some, as a result, experience greater intimacy than they have with their long-time spouses.

One woman told her friends that she was leaving her husband for a "wonderful man" she had met on Minitel. When they asked what he looked like, she admitted she had never met him. Another woman, who got her Minitel the day her husband left her, told Cherky that she had learned more about life in one night at the keyboard than she had in 25 years of marriage.

"People feel liberated because they are no longer being labeled and judged by the usual criteria," Jean-Pierre Talon, Landaret's assistant, explains. "Old, young, black, white, rich, poor, Arab, Jew, none of it has any significance on Minitel. Suddenly you are communicating in a different dimension, one in which the normal rules of social intercourse are missing. Le look doesn't count. It's totally democratic! It cuts across all barriers. You can be talking to an 80-year-old grandmother and have the feeling she is 22, or a woman and be certain it's a man. It's as if you are communicating directly with a person's soul.

"Before Minitel, everyone I met dressed like me, was educated like me, and thought like me. Minitel released me from this mental suburbia. One of the most interesting people I've met is a woman who drives a cart in a Heineken beer factory. When she talks about her job, it's like listening to a Grand Prix driver! One day we met for a drink. She had on a lot of makeup. She looked cheap. I realized that without Minitel, I never would have spoken to her, because of her physical appearance."

But Minitel's opacity also has less fortunate consequences. A woman was about to break up her marriage to move in with a Minitel suitor who had sent her many gifts. She was stricken when she learned that the suitor was a woman.

Some people are devastated by the defection of an electronic soulmate the way they would be by the desertion of a spouse, Landaret has discovered. "A man who had just moved to Strasbourg knew no one but the pseudos he had met on Minitel. When he was out of town, someone took his pseudo and was rude to the others. When he came back, no one would send him any messages, and he killed himself."

As the French are brought together by mutual interests and needs, networks are forming. They are something new in a country with little civic tradition, where people traditionally band together to fight against rather than for something. Strasbourg, like many French cities, now has Minitel support groups for single parents; the elderly; and people with cancer, multiple sclerosis, or AIDS; and dozens of hobby and sports "clubs."

Talon told me a story that exemplifies the new sense of cooperation and concern that Minitel has engendered. "One woman who was worried because her daughter had not come home typed her description on Minitel. Twenty-five people saw it and went looking for her. They found her in a nightclub at five a.m. and sent her home." A busy career woman got unexpected help when she encountered an 18-year-old longing to be given orders by a woman. "My apartment has never been so clean," she told a French women's magazine.

Another unexpected result is that Minitel, far from doing in the written word, has sparked a writing renaissance. Like Roxane in *Cyrano de Bergerac*, Minitelistes have no clue to each other's identity or the sincerity of each other's sentiments except what is put in writing. "There are no fingerprints, no witnesses, only masks at the 'Masked Ball,' which has become a carnival of words," *Le Monde* commented.

"The ability to write is now a major factor in seduction," Talon says. "Some people keep a dictionary beside the keyboard." Others, far from the baleful eyes of the Académie Française, which has kept the French language stagnant for years on the pretext of safeguarding its purity, are taking liberties with grammar and syntax to create a unique Minitel patois.

"Many people dream of writing, but where do they get a chance in their normal lives?" Talon says. "On Minitel people are discovering whole new personalities, defining themselves by new criteria. After a lifetime in a boring office many suddenly see themselves as artists!"

For some, who continue to write to each other on Minitel instead of talking on the telephone even after they have met, the medium is indeed the message. "We write things we could never say out loud," one woman told Talon. "It's easier to be honest." People are not just writing love letters. The minute Landaret put a word-processing program on Gretel, it was deluged with everything from classical Alexandrine verse to imitation e.e. cummings. "One man wrote a 650-page book!" he says. "He broke the system. I couldn't believe it." When an elderly man asked for a program for fishermen, Landaret suggested that he come in and write it. "He didn't think he could do it, but it was wonderful!" he recalls. "It was full of imaginative drawings. We still use it today." Others began trying their hands at programming. As a result, Gretel has more than 600 programs. (Most *messageries* offer a dozen or so.) "It's like an attic!" Landaret says. "We still don't know who wrote many of them."

Political *messageries* – even the French Communist Party is now on line – feature "graffiti" services and opinion polls that are giving the French a sense that their opinions matter. "After years of telling people what to think on television, they're asking what they think," Talon says. "It's flattering. Minitel has given a lot of people the sense that they are being listened to for the first time."

While Telecom officials have welcomed the enormous profits from the *messageries*, they are nervous about having so much revenue generated by what is essentially a fluke. If the *messageries* prove a fad, they are wondering, will the French someday abandon their Minitels the way they dump their dogs at the start of their summer vacations?

If they do, it will be not because of flagging passion but because of dwindling francs. Like all addictions, Minitel has its price. To many people in France, where the "play now, pay later" concept is far less common than it is in the United States, being given a Minitel is like being given a home video arcade and told they won't have to pay for two months. Many go into shock when they get the bills for their billets-doux. Several have stormed the Telecom office, swearing they couldn't have run up such high sums. The record, set by a single woman in Besançon, is 70,000 francs ($11,666) in a month. "She had to spend over five hundred hours on it, and there are only seven hundred and twenty hours in a month," Landaret says.

The only solution for some has been to go cold turkey, but it's not always that easy. One couple who returned their Minitel kept getting the same high bills; they discovered that their children had been plugging in a friend's Minitel. Others have chosen to stay with the paper telephone book. But the question is, how long can people hold out?

The sheer number of public services now available on Minitel is making it increasingly difficult to live without. The Ministère des Finances has started a tax-information service, the Ministère de la Santé answers questions about the baffling French social security system, and the Ministère de l'Éducation Nationale gives same-day baccalaureat examination results and tutorials. In what is perhaps the ultimate consecration, the Catholic Church recently opened a service. "God on Minitel," read the cover of *Minitel Magazine*.

People complain that railway information is now almost impossible to get by telephone, forcing them to make reservations by Minitel. Directory Inquiry plays a tape insolently informing callers that they would already have the number if they were using Minitel.

After waiting three years to see if Minitel would prove merely a passing fancy, *Le Monde* opened a service last September, with a 12-page special section billing Minitel as its *"plus beau bébé."* To prevent the baby from becoming an enfant terrible and to prove that there is life after sex on Minitel, it announced, its service would not include a *messagerie rose*. Its ads for "le Minitel intelligent" coyly boast that the service is for people interested in *"I. Q., pas cul." (Cul,* pronounced like the French letter *q*, means "derrière" – by extension, sex.)

So far *Le Monde* is winning its wager. The newspaper is receiving 10,000 calls a day and has almost caught up to its rival, *Libération*, which has one of the most popular *messageries*. Connection time doubles whenever there is breaking news, such as last December's train strike and student demonstrations. "It doesn't bother us to go slowly," Antoine Beaussant, the director of the paper's *télématique* service, says. "We're in for the long haul."

In an editorial suggesting that the sexual shenanigans were merely a phase that would soon be over, France's "good gray lady" commented drily, "If more French people know how to use a computer, so much the better. Passion has served its purpose."

7 IT in Schools

Computers in the Classroom

Alison B. Bass

The issue of computers in schools continues to cause controversy. In this readable article, journalist Alison Bass gives an account of Project Headlight, the attempt by MIT Professor Seymour Papert to improve public education through the use of computers in a run-down Boston school. The account is tempered by the inclusion of some critics of Papert's techniques – notably Professor Joe Weizenbaum. Reprinted from Technology Review, *April 1987.*

The rusting carcasses of two stripped cars border the street in front of the Hennigan Elementary School in Roxbury. The building's drab beige walls are pockmarked with graffiti and the grass is long and unkempt. All the doors fronting the street are locked, and the only open entrance is hidden around the side.

Inside, the environment is cheerier. Splotches of crayoned paper conceal the concrete walls, and a dark hallway opens up into two large, open rooms filled with noise, light, and children. The children are seated around three circular banks of computers, staring at the green VDT screens and chattering with one another. One little boy's screen shows a square inside a square, and the squares are different colors. The boy is proud of his accomplishment and eager to explain how he did it. But two desks down sits an even smaller child whose screen is blank. Her hands are silent and her eyes are on her lap.

Both students are part of "Project Headlight," a pilot program designed to incorporate computers into the regular curriculum at Hennigan School. Initiated in 1985 by Seymour Papert, professor of mathematics and education at MIT, Project Headlight is an ambitious attempt to improve the educational climate in one public school.

"We chose Hennigan because it is central to the problem of education in the United States," says Papert, a mathematician, computer scientist, and self-styled anthropologist. "It's an inner-city school with a range of problems: single parents who are just trying to survive, not much education at home. It is a culture on the margin of literate society."

Into this milieu Papert has introduced 252 personal computers donated by IBM and a programming language known as LOGO. Originally designed by Papert in the 1960s, LOGO has since spawned hundreds of other educational software programs and is close to becoming a cult. Every year a week-long LOGO conference is held at MIT – an event that one bemused observer calls "a chapel to LOGO." Two of LOGO's more promising spinoffs are included in the Hennigan experiment: LOGO writer, a package that combines programming with word processing, and LEGO/LOGO, software that allows children to use the computer to manipulate toys built with parts from LEGO building sets.

Based on plain English, LOGO allows children to draw all kinds of geometric shapes, symbols, and complex pictures with the computer. Their "pencil" is the Turtle, a fuzzy gray apparition that can be directed to move in any direction on the screen. The Turtle allows children to visualize and grasp mathematical concepts in a way that they can't with textbook problems.

When drawing a circle (or rather, a polygon that approximates a circle), for instance, children can command the Turtle to go forward (FD) 2 (a Turtle step is roughly the size of one pixel or dot on the screen), turn right (RT) 12 degrees, and then repeat that sequence 30 times. In creating that simple shape, children pick up some interesting facts. They learn that whenever a Turtle is turned around a total of 360 degrees (12 × 30), it'll be facing the same direction as when it started. They learn that 180 degrees is half a circle, or half of 360 degrees. And as they move on to other shapes, they learn that no matter what shape the Turtle draws, it must turn a total of 360 degrees if it creates a closed curve. According to Papert, these are powerful geometric concepts not always obvious to young children. With the Turtle they can see these concepts, make them happen, in front of their eyes.

"In directing the Turtle, children also have to make judgments about the size of numbers as well as spatial judgments," Papert says. "For instance, I've seen many small kids who don't know the difference between 10 and 10,000. But they pick up that difference very quickly with the Turtle; if they command it to go 10,000 steps, the computer will say, 'I don't like 10,000 as input.'"

Most important, Papert says, LOGO allows children to draw from their own experience in mastering a concept. He revealed that secret one day to a diminutive nine-year-old at Hennigan with braids almost as long as her pinafore. The girl, along with the rest of her fourth-grade class, had been assigned to draw a map of the solar system. But new to Hennigan and to LOGO, she was having difficulty designing a simple sun.

Papert, who had been watching the class work, gently drew the child to her feet. Holding her hand and talking quietly, he took a few steps forward and then turned to the right. He repeated that sequence with her until they had turned together in a complete circle. Intimidated at first by the big, gray-haired stranger, the little girl blushed fiercely through the first go-around. She stopped blushing when she understood.

"The reason why children don't learn math is not because it's hard, but because it's not related to their experience. They can't do anything with it that seems worth doing and so it feels deadly to them," Papert explains later in the "Turtlecove," a small room at Hennigan allotted to the MIT group. As usual, he is dressed casually in a white-ribbed turtleneck sweater and black wool pants. His eyes are large and luminous behind thick glasses, and his gray-pepper beard swallows up the lines on his face.

"In the real world, people always learn by experience," Papert says. "A lot of theorists and thinkers about education agree it would be a powerful way to learn in the classroom. But up till now nobody knew how to provide experiences that embody the kind of math knowledge that we think children need to have. So mathematics is taught mainly by rote and many children are turned off.

"Now we have a technology that children can use to make something they're interested in – whether it's pretty shapes with LOGO or cars with LEGO. The computer provides children with a way of appropriating mathematical knowledge – and using it in a very personal way."

Falling in love with gears

Papert first experienced the power of appropriating knowledge at the age of two or three while playing with an old truck near his home in Swaziland. His father, an entomologist studying the migration patterns of the tsetse fly, had brought his wife and young son with him into the jungle. The family lived in a succession of base camps on the east coast of Africa, following the lethal fly's trail.

"There was a lot of machinery in those camps, trucks being repaired," Papert recalls. "They used to let me drive this one truck – they put it in low gear so it could only go three miles an hour. If I ran it into anything, it wouldn't do any harm. And when the truck was stopped, I would climb underneath and watch the gears. I became fascinated by gears."

It wasn't until years later, Papert says, that he really understood how gears worked. But having fallen in love with them once, he did so again, playing with gears and building increasingly complicated gear systems. "Gears, serving as models, carried many otherwise abstract ideas into my head," he writes in *Mindstorms,* a book about computers and education. Papert's intimate knowledge of one particularly complex system – the differential gear – made algebraic equations easy for him.

The differential gear is a box of gears that connects the driveshaft to the two rear axles of a car. It allows the axles to turn at different speeds, making it possible for a car to turn corners smoothly. Without the differential, the outer wheel would have farther to travel when going around a bend but couldn't speed up. As a result, the car would skid, lurch, and tend to fly off the road.

"My first brush with equations in two variables immediately evoked the differential," Papert says. "By the time I had made a mental gear model of the relation between x and y, figuring out how many teeth each gear needed, the equation had become a comfortable friend."

Papert might well have pursued a career as a theoretical mathematician had it not been for another, very different childhood experience. After four years in the Swaziland base camp, where his family had been the only white people for miles around, the Paperts moved back to Johannesburg so their children could obtain a formal education. "The only children I saw or played with in the camp were black children," Papert says. "All of sudden I was in a world where black and white children were separated. It was a shock."

Segregation was a concept the young boy couldn't fully understand. So in fifth grade, he and a few friends came up with an idea: why not run a night school for the domestic servants in their Johannesburg neighborhood? "A lot of these people had come from the tribal areas and didn't know how to read or write," Papert says. "We thought it would be a great thing to teach them at night when no one else was using the school. It hadn't occurred to us that anyone would object."

But object they did and in ways that the precocious ten-year-old found baffling. "I remember clearly what I was told: that you can't have these people coming and sitting on the seats in school because they might have diseases. But I was old enough to respond to that. I said, 'These are the same people who are looking after your babies and cooking your food.' It didn't matter: the night classes were terminated and I almost got thrown out of school. That was the beginning of my interest in the nature of thought. I couldn't understand how people could think like that."

The boy continued to go to school in segregated South Africa, but the episode planted a seed that flowered years later in the mind of the man, when he met the child psychologist Jean Piaget. In Paris for a series of lectures, Piaget was discussing his theories on how thinking and logic evolve in human beings, and his ideas struck the 30-year-old mathematician with the force of revelation.

Papert explains:

Piaget was the first to take abstract questions about the nature of thought and translate them into scientific questions. Take the question: is our knowledge that space is three-dimensional something humans learn, or is it something intrinsic to the nature of thought? Kant believed that it was intrinsic to the human mind – we think a certain way and it is not something learned or changeable – whereas Hume argued that knowledge comes from experience. Piaget turned philosophical questions like this into empirical experiments. He said let's go look at children and see how it happens. If this thing is part of the nature of thought, it should be there from birth.

What Piaget learned is that neither Kant nor Hume was completely right: some know-how is innate – like the awareness of a baby on a table that the space beyond the edge of the table is different from the space on which she sits. But most human knowledge must be learned by trial and error, by experience. And some of that knowledge can be gleaned only after a certain point in childhood, when the brain is more fully developed.

"Piaget brought many things together for me," Papert says. "Before I met him, I had been intellectually torn between my interest in how people came to think and my interest in more abstract ideas. Piaget showed me a way in which my caring for math, for the philosophy of thinking, and for social reform all seemed to go together."

So when Piaget asked Papert to come to his new Center for Genetic Epistemology in Geneva, Papert's answer was a foregone conclusion. He spent the next five years in Geneva, helping Piaget study how children learn math.

Conquering math anxiety

In the 1950s, Piaget was not the only one who was turning abstract questions about the nature of thought into concrete scientific experiments. Primitive computers were on the scene, and the early pioneers of artificial intelligence were grappling with many of the same issues. While still based in Geneva, Papert began commuting to London to work with one of the most powerful computers then in existence. Built by the mathematician Alan Turing, the computer had a memory of about 2K – one-thirtieth the memory of a simple Apple IIc. Yet it filled a room as big as a barn. There Papert met John McCarthy and Marvin Minsky, now widely considered to be the founders of artificial intelligence (AI).

Minsky eventually persuaded Papert to come back with him to MIT, where they jointly ran the AI Lab through the late 1960s. But Papert was still working with Piaget when he conceived the idea of the computer as an element of cultural and educational change.

"On the one hand, Piaget is telling us that children are wonderful learners, that they rediscover this vast amount of knowledge as they grow," Papert explains. "But on the other hand, as I began to see in the schools, children, far from being wonderful learners, seem to be incapable of learning even the simplest things. How does one explain this paradox?"

He came to the conclusion that children learn best when they have materials from their own culture to build with. For instance, even children who drop out of school can readily count change or read comic books. But when knowledge is not well represented in the culture and, in fact, is feared by that culture – as is math and, to a certain extent, grammar – children falter. Computers, Papert theorized, could be the solution – if and when they became small and affordable enough to be used in the classroom.

By the 1980s, computers had indeed become manageable enough for the classroom, and the push to bring them into the schools began. IBM and Apple personal computers, often donated or discounted, found their way into elementary and secondary schools as well as universities. In the public schools, however, they were mainly used for drill and practice in the basic skills – something that could often be done just as effectively with paper and pencil. As one educational expert charged, computers were being cast in the same sad mold of rote teaching that has characterized much of US public education.

"Historically, American public shcools have embodied the idea of education as a passive experience for students," wrote Marc Tucker, executive director of the Carnegie Forum on Education and the Economy, in a national report on computers in education in 1985. "So it was natural that school personnel would view the machine as just one more device to deliver instruction, like a sort of automated drill sergeant delivering commands."

A year later, in a speech to a National Governors' Association task force, Tucker was a bit more optimistic. He reported that computers were being used in more "creative" ways in a few isolated places around the country. One of those places was the Hennigan School. Tucker had visited Project Headlight in its first year of operation and observed a group of nine-year-olds playing with LEGO/LOGO.

"But this was no ordinary LEGO set," Tucker told the governors. In addition to the building-block modules, gears, shafts, and wheels found in most LEGO sets, this set also contained electric motors that could be mounted onto the cars and other toys the children made. Also available were touch and light sensors that they could add to their creations. The sensors and motors could be connected to the computer,which, in turn, made it possible for the children to use data coming from the sensors to control the motion of the things they built.

One little boy, for instance, had built a car that was supposed to follow a track made by laying a piece of adhesive tape on the floor. The car stayed on the track with the aid of a light sensor placed under its "hood." When the car wandered from the adhesive tape, the sensor showed that the floor was dark, and the computer program the boy had written directed the wheels to turn until the sensor showed that the floor was light.

"In this workshop, boys and girls learned more math and science and technology at the fourth-grade level than I had ever thought possible," Tucker reported.

Consider the car that followed the adhesive tape. The instruction to the computer was in the form of: if the value returned by the sensor is equal to or less than x, then turn b degrees to the right. If, having maintained this direction for a specified interval, the value returned by the sensor does not increase above a specified value, turn so many degrees to the left, and so on . . .

Bear in mind that what is being given in this lab is a class in engineering, a first exposure to the pleasures of equipment design, in which the participants are exposed to the use of mathematics and science in a way that is clearly enthralling.

No longer sweating the mistakes

Kyle is a handsome nine-year-old from Roxbury who has trouble reading and writing. He has disrupted class so many times that he has been banished to a special-needs workshop. There he has been given the opportunity to play with LEGO/LOGO. Last week, he built a tractor and kept running it back and forth on the floor, making delighted vroom noises as the wheels spun along. This week, he is learning how to direct the computer to run his tractor for him. He likes the idea of being able to add a sensor that will keep his tractor from bumping into walls.

Jack Gray, a Harvard student who is working with Papert's group, tells Kyle he will help him write the tractor program. But Kyle will have to take notes so he doesn't forget how to do it. One of the teacher aides who has been sitting nearby interrupts: "I don't know if he can take notes." Gray looks momentarily discouraged. Then he says, "Okay, Kyle, I'll take the notes, you type them in."

Kyle types in TO and then turns to Gray and asks him, "How do you spell tractor?" "I don't know," Gray replies. "What do you think?" Kyle struggles for a few minutes with the TR sound. But after a few hints from Gray and a few more false starts, he finally spells it out loud and types in onto the screen: TO TRACTOR. Gray begins running through the instructions step by step:

TALK TO "C" (C is the power outlet where the motor is plugged into the computer)
ON FOR "40" (go forward for 4 seconds)
LISTEN TO "6" (the sensor is plugged into button number 6 on the computer interface)
WAIT UNTIL . . .

But Kyle has lost interest. He is no longer looking at the screen and is busy screwing and unscrewing the tiny wires that connect the tractor with its computer interface. A few minutes later, he throws a glance at me taking notes and asks suspiciously, "Is she a computer lady?" Gray replies, "Yeah, I think she is." But Kyle continues to squat moodily on his heels, his fingers busily working tiny strands of wire.

Later Steve Ocko, a filmmaker who helped develop LEGO/LOGO and has been working with the teachers at Hennigan, explains: "Kyle loves playing with LEGO. In class, he has a very short attention span, but we have to pull him off the LEGO toys. Kyle is also on the verge of getting thrown out of public shool and put in a special school. He knows this is his last chance. He probably thinks you are here to test him and that scares him."

In reality, no efforts are being made to test the Hennigan students on what they learn from LEGO/LOGO. The MIT researchers say that it is extremely difficult to measure in any systematic way what concepts the children are picking up. They view Project Headlight as an experiment to study how children learn with computers, not as a benchmark test from which to develop standards. As a result, they have little hard data to show experts in education and computer science.

"Tests tell how well kids learn by rote, which is why so much of their education consists of abstract facts and rules," says Mitch Resnick, an MIT graduate student in computer science who worked with Ocko in designing LEGO/LOGO. "But what's really important for kids to learn, the actual process of learning – that's a hard thing to test. And how do you test whether you've gotten kids excited and curious about learning?"

As Resnick is fond of saying, play is not a four-letter word at Project Headlight. The children are encouraged to learn by exploration, by discovery, and by making mistakes. And when they do, they are asked to figure out what went wrong, correct it, and move on. "The children learn they don't have to sweat the mistakes," Ocko says.

The same goes for the teachers. Papert is encouraging the Headlight teachers to experiment and to integrate the computer into their own curriculum – whether math, science, social studies, or English – and then study the results. He sees his role in all of this as advisor, not the all-knowing headmaster.

"The strategy is not to tell the teachers what to teach. There's already too much of that . . ." Papert pauses, and in a characteristic gesture drops the thought and starts afresh. "Yesterday, somebody from the US Department of Education came to MIT to talk to us about computers in education. He wanted to know how we can use computers to bypass the teachers. He had this idea: let's get the best teachers in the world and then embody in the computer their ways of teaching. Well, we're doing the opposite at Hennigan."

Papert freely acknowledges that Project Headlight is an attempt to bring back the open classroom of the 1960s. Only this time, he says, teachers have a more powerful and seductive medium to work with and a specific approach. "The free-school movement of the 1960s collapsed partly because it was tied to a political movement of the time, and partly because there were some subject matters that nobody knew how to teach in a noncoercive way. With the computer, we're in a much better position to have a second shot at free schools."

Some observers are not so sure. Joseph Weizenbaum, Professor of Computer Science at MIT, says that a more open, less rigid approach to education is a fine idea. "Seymour may, in fact, have found a better form of teaching. But what does that have to do with computers?" he asks. If anything, he says, an overemphasis on computers obscures the real issue, which is the need to fundamentally restructure the educational system and deal with the social problems that hinder children's natural urge to learn.

"Children may not be motivated in school because they're hungry or they've been abused at home or for any number of reasons," Weizenbaum says. "Simply introducing computers avoids the question of why children may not be motivated in school. It converts a social problem into a technological problem and then tries to solve it by technical means. In that sense, the computer serves to inhibit the asking of important questions about the way our society raises and teaches its young."

Will children think like computers?

Bonnie Brownstein is a former teacher who heads the Institute for Schools for the Future, a nonprofit educational think tank affiliated with the City University of New York. She worked with Papert in the early 1980s, training teachers in the New York schools to use computers. Their training workshop eventually gave rise to the Computer School, an alternative junior high school in Manhattan that has been highly successful in reducing absentee rates and raising reading and math scores. Brownstein believes that computers can be used effectively in education, particularly in math and writing. "With the computer, I've seen kids redo and redo what they write and experiment," she says. "Children never used to edit or critique what they wrote because they'd have to copy it over."

However, Brownstein agrees with Weizenbaum that any substantial improvements in the public schools will require a major restructuring of the system as it now exists. "Computers can't teach a powerful new way of thinking in a vacuum," Brownstein says. "We need more time and more money, and we need to look at the system as a whole. I mean, kids in the New York schools don't even have pencils to work with."

Still, Brownstein gives Papert high marks for seeking new avenues of change. "People like Papert are needed to keep stretching our thinking about what is possible," she says.

Other critics are not as sanguine. Weizenbaum and Hubert Dreyfus and his brother Stuart, both professors at the University of California at Berkeley, believe that Papert's approach is actually detrimental to the process of learning. They are particularly worried about his insistence that children learn how to think by programming. Papert has long believed that programming teaches children valuable cognitive skills. It isn't what they program that is so important, but rather the process of breaking problems down into sub-problems and solving them, he says. By programming computers to perform almost any kind of task, children learn how to think.

Weizenbaum argues that the kind of thinking learned through programming – logical step-by-step analysis – is only one, limited variation of human thought. And, in fact, it is not the way human beings solve most of their problems in everyday life, particularly complex problems. "Programming applies to a very narrow domain of problem-solving," Weizenbaum maintains. "But most human problems – whether to get married, whether to have children – are not solved that way."

The analytical approach to problem-solving is already emphasized "too much and too soon in our schools," he says. Both he and the Dreyfus brothers believe that computers will merely reinforce society's reliance on such thinking – with dangerous consequences. The Dreyfuses say that Papert's approach encourages children to discount their more important intuitive thought processes in favor of a more limited analytical approach (see "Why Computers May Never Think Like People" by Hubert and Stuart Dreyfus, pp. 125–43 above).

Even in Papert's group, a few researchers worry about the effect of computers on the mind. Edith Ackerman, a Swiss-born child psychologist who worked with Papert at Piaget's Center for Genetic Epistemology in Geneva, agrees that children exposed to computers "will be more likely to think of their own thinking like a computer." But the presence of computers is a fait accompli in this society, Ackerman points out, and Papert is doing his best to turn something that could be destructive into something positive and enormously creative.

"If somebody like Papert puts all his energy and years of life into having children control computers and not be controlled by them, that to me is very good," Ackerman says. "Computers are already here; we can no longer escape unless we go to a tropical forest."

Weizenbaum has other problems with Papert's vision. Computers may indeed help children learn by experience, but "I question the nature of the experience," he says. "We live in an increasingly abstract world where much of our experiences come to us via cathode-ray tube – television. Many kids have never had the experience of raising an animal or hammering a hut together. Learning by experience is important, but I would rather it be a different kind of experience."

Yet schools were created to teach abstract ideas not easily gleaned in the "real world." And it is those largely abstract ideas used in writing, science, and mathematics that children from impoverished families need most to learn. What Papert is trying to do, his supporters say, is teach the "basics" – but in more interesting and imaginative ways.

A cure for teacher burnout?

At the age of 42, Linda Moriarty has been teaching in the Boston public schools for 20 years. She is considered one of the best teachers at Hennigan, and the parents of her students – who come from a variety of ethnic backgrounds – have only good things to say about her.

But Moriarty is ready to quit. "I guess you could say I'm burnt out," says Moriarty, a slender woman with a thin, tired face."I'm going to stay in education, but not necessarily in the classroom. It's too emotionally draining."

Moriarty has been burnt out before. She was ready to leave four years ago, when the excitement of teaching in a "magnet school" had faded and Hennigan was becoming just one more inner-city school with too many problem students, too few dedicated teachers, and not enough money. But around that time a colleague, Joanne Rankin, persuaded Moriarty to take a few courses in LOGO with her. Moriarty became excited about using computers in elementary education, and a year or two later she and Rankin wrote the proposal that brought Project Headlight to Hennigan. (Papert offered his program to the Boston school system at large and a number of schools competed for it.)

"LOGO has a magic that nothing else has," Moriarty says. "Personally, I feel my instructional program is pretty exciting. But LOGO seems to add a dimension I wouldn't want to lose."

Like most of the other teachers in Project Headlight, Moriarty and Rankin use LOGO in their math, science, English, and social studies classes. This year, for instance, Rankin's fourth-grade class has used LOGO to study the parts of plants (they programmed the computer to build different kinds of plants). They also used LOGO to examine the complex relationships in *Charlotte's Web*. Their literature assignment was to create an animated scene from the classic children's story and discuss its ramifications. (The animation effect is created by programming the various figures in a scene to move, wait, and repeat those commands a number of times.)

In some of the scenes the children created, Charlotte (a spider) can be seen coming down from her web and saying, "I'll help you, Wilbur." Wilbur (a pig) is about to be caught and carved up for Christmas dinner, and Charlotte's offer of help brings the two animals closer together and ends up saving Wilbur's life. Rankin's students also chose to animate another climactic scene in the book – the time when sheep in the barnyard run over and inform Wilbur that the farmers are after him.

"Creating these scenes got the children more involved in the relationships between Wilbur and Charlotte and the other animals," Rankin says. "They thought more about what the book was about."

Rankin has found that her students love working with the computer – whatever the assignment. It excites them like little else in the classroom. "The kids really work at it," says Rankin. "Maybe it's because the computer is new and everything they're doing is new. Maybe it's because they know we don't have all the answers and they can teach us something."

For some children, just writing or drawing is a problem. "I have a number of children who find it almost painful to write. They bear down so hard and the letters are so thick. It may be they have poor manual dexterity. At the computer, that problem disappears. A lot of times the child who is a slow learner in class excels at the computer and there's a new respect for that child among the other kids."

Both Rankin and Moriarty have observed a different kind of rapport at the computer – between the teachers and students and among the children themselves. "Generally, when you put kids into groups, they talk about other things," Rankin says. "But with the computers, they tend to talk about their programs. And they share things with one another. They are always picking up one another's ideas."

"It's a more pleasant interaction between the teacher and the kids," Moriarty adds.

Perhaps that's because you're not in the position to criticize what the kids are doing. If you're teaching reading and a child is not learning to read, that's threatening for the teacher and she might turn it against the kids. But because you don't have to meet certain standards with LOGO, there's not as much pressure on the kids. They become more creative and relaxed about their creativity.

Moriarty hopes students are never tested on their LOGO skills "because that would defeat the purpose of having something the kids can control."

For Moriarty, Project Headlight is particularly compelling as a strategy for motivating teachers.

A lot of teachers just don't have the incentive to go out and learn new ways of doing things. After all, it's not a very rewarding field, given the money and the way you're treated as a teacher in this society. And it's very hard for teachers to change. If I've been teaching reading for years, I'm not going to sit there and let some young person tell me how to teach reading. But computers are not so threatening. We're all starting at the same point and the teachers are more willing to let the kids get head, let other teachers get ahead.

But why not concentrate on solving the education system's real problems instead, as Weizenbaum and Brownstein suggest? Why not bring in new and more talented teachers, reduce the student/teacher ratio, pay teachers more so you can expect more of them? Because, says Linda Moriarty, that isn't going to happen – at least not in her lifetime: "It's very unrealistic to expect that there is going to be enough money and enough people in education who are willing to spend all that extra time and energy."

Given that reality, Moriarty thinks it's important to put something in the schools that will appeal to the teachers who are already there. And she believes that computers – when used as Papert intends – could be that something.

Most of the teachers at Hennigan agree with Moriarty that Project Headlight has had a beneficial effect. Hennigan's overall reading scores are still below the national average (or, in a few grades, slightly above), but most of the school's math scores have climbed since the program began. In the third and fourth grades, math scores rose more than 10 percentage points between 1984 and 1985. While math scores dropped in the second grade during that time, they still remained above the national average. (The Boston school system changed its testing method in 1986, so no comparison can be made at Hennigan between 1985 and 1986.)

The teachers, however, have noticed other, less tangible signs of change.

"I've seen kids who have absolutely no confidence suddenly gain a lot of confidence," says May Macchi, a 20-year veteran of the Boston public schools.

I've seen kids who were true loners start cooperating with the other children when they realized that could help them solve problems on the computer. And it's definitely lowered the frustrations of the special-needs kids. They don't give up as easily and they're very proud of what they do. I think it's because they associate the mistakes with the machine. They no longer think it's them.

Macchi, however, is concerned that Project Headlight – in only its second year – is already fading out. "Last year, people were falling over us trying to help. Now we're lucky to see one person [from the MIT group] at least once a week." Macchi, a small, unflappable woman who is highly respected by her peers, says that funding from IBM seems to have dried up, and that Papert has not yet been able to locate alternative funding. At this point, neither she nor the other teachers are certain whether Project Headlight will last its designated three years.

But Macchi *is* sure of one thing: "Project Headlight has done some wonderful things for our kids. If it were up to me, it would never end."

The Promises of Educational Technology: A Reassessment

Donald P. Ely and Tjeerd Plomp

The authors of this authoritative paper say that the growing use of computers in schools should be seen in the context of the 50-year history of educational technology, which is largely one of failure. Ely and Plomp analyze in general terms why some projects have succeeded and why many more have not fulfilled their promise. They conclude that there is little evidence of a technological revolution in education. Donald Ely is Professor of Instructional Design at Syracuse University, New York, and Tjeerd Plomp is Professor of Education at Twente University of Technology, the Netherlands. This article first appeared in International Review of Education, *vol. 32, 1986, pp. 231–50.*

Over the past 50 years educational technology has evolved from its early emphasis on the protection and use of the media and instruments of communication to its current concern with the systematic approach to solving educational problems based on theories of learning and instruction. This time has been marked by the arrival of new technological developments, each one of which has been heralded as a major breakthrough with a potential for revolutionizing education. The historians of educational technology (Saettler, 1968; Cuban, 1985) have documented the movement from radio, motion pictures, and slides to television, programmed instruction, and computers. In each case the new technology has been touted as a replacement for textbooks, an extension of the classroom to the world, or a complement for some of the instructional functions. However, the present authors, in surveying the current scene, do not see evidence of significant, revolutionary use of the various communication technologies. Their isolated use in different areas of the world can be observed, but there are no major educational innovations or movements which promise to bring about the changes which are so desperately needed (Botkin et al., 1979; Faure et al., 1982).

What has happened to educational technology during the past 50 years? Is there any residue from the myriad efforts to introduce the concepts of media and technology into educational systems in many parts of the world? Are there lessons we can learn from these efforts which might enable us to consider more fully the merits of future technological developments?

The purpose of this article is to present an interpretation of educational technology, including its roots, its definition, its areas of application, and its development. This background survey is followed by a discussion of the educational problems which could be addressed by educational technology. There then follow a catalogue of applications of educational technology which have attempted to resolve some of the problems, and an analysis of the "successes" and "failures" of the programs described. The common threads that emerge from these analyses are picked out, and finally a listing is given of what has been learned in the process.

What is meant by educational technology?

When the term "educational technology" is used, it often carries the media connotation which focuses on equipment and materials, i.e., the delivery systems. In fact, in the United States, the Presidential Commission on Instructional Technology (Tickton, 1970) gave two definitions of the field and the first emphasized the hardware and software:

the media born of the communications revolution which can be used for instructional purposes alongside the teacher, textbook and blackboard . . . the pieces that make up instructional technology: television, films, overhead projectors, computers and the other items of "hardware" and "software". (p. 5)

But the report goes on to say that there is an emerging second definition which might be more important in the future:

A systematic way of designing, carrying out, and evaluating the total process of learning and teaching in terms of specific objectives, based on research in human learning and communication and employing a combination of human and nonhuman resources to bring about more effective instruction. (p. 5)

This process definition is much more amenable to emerging concepts in the field and is compatible with the first and second definitions of Lumsdaine (1964) and Romiszowski (1981). Davies (1978) proposes a third interpretation which combines the hardware and software aspects of the two definitions and builds a bridge between educational theory and practice yielding "a science and an art of teaching with a technology of its very own" (p. 15). Romiszowski (1981) speaks of a product versus a process approach of educational technology, and Davies (1978) of a hardware versus software approach. Historically, both approaches had their supporters. Those supporting the product definition came mainly from an audiovisual orientation and from media producers. The early advocates of the process approach could be found mainly in the circles of psychologists and training developers. It can be concluded from the early literature of the field that both groups operated rather independently from each other.

The definition of the field may be used in a variety of ways. For some, it is useful to help describe a profession; for others, it is a description of what practitioners do; and for still others, it helps to limit the scope of their activities so that individuals know who is "in" and who is "out" (Ely, 1983). Educational technology is an elusive field because it draws on such diverse roots and because it finds the bulk of its activities in many applied areas. Primary contributory fields include psychology, communications, management, and engineering (Stakenas and Kaufman, 1981). In its applications, educational technology can be viewed as *technology* when referring to the methodology of its problem-solving aspects; it can be viewed as *media* when aids to learning are required and instructional surrogates are appropriate; and it can mean *technique* when it is employed as a teaching/learning method as in a simulation/game or in computer-assisted learning. It may be a *change* paradigm in the classroom or school building at the microlevel or an entire school system at the macrolevel. Distinctions are often made in describing educational technology when it is used for training purposes and when it is used for the attainment of educational goals (Ely, 1985). Heinich (1984) insists that "the root of instructional technology is technology itself. Instructional technology as a field of study is better considered as a subset of technology in general than as a subset of Education (p. 67)." His meaning of technology is rooted in the problem-solving mode.

It may sound pretentious to say that educational technology is all of these but, in fact, it is. All the factors mentioned above are not simultaneously operational but most of the aspects of the field do come into play at one time or another in a systematic fashion if a solution is being sought following a technological approach.

Conceptual evolution of educational technology

In the 1960s it was realized that real improvement of education could not be attained by focusing on independent parts of the system. Instructional methods or modes of presentation could not be replaced by machines and/or methods in vogue without real changes in the configuration of the educational process. Curricular materials (including all types of media), teaching strategies and teaching philosophy are so interrelated and interconnected that one cannot change one without considering changes in the others (Fullan, 1985). Inspired by developments in other disciplines, like engineering and management science, a holistic approach gradually developed, i.e., a problem cannot be isolated from its context or environment, but has to be analyzed in that context or environment. It is not self-evident that every problem in education or training should be solved by using media or even by using new instructional strategies. Implicit in this holistic approach is the need to be alert to the many factors which determine a problem situation and to those which can play a role when searching for a solution. This new development has resulted in a broader meaning of educational technology to which the Association for Educational Communications and Technology (AECT) has given a comprehensive description/definition: "Educational technology is a complex, integrated process involving people, procedures, ideas, devices and organization, for analyzing problems and devising, implementing, evaluating and managing solutions to those problems, involved in all aspects of human learning" (AECT, 1977). Several other authors have associated themselves with the broader meaning of educational technology. Davies (1973) and Romiszowski (1981) characterize educational technology as a method for solving educational problems. This method is discussed by many authors, often for specific classes of problems (see Gerlach and Ely, 1971; Gagné and Briggs, 1974; Davies, 1978; Dick and Carey, 1978; Romiszowski, 1981; Plomp, 1982; Diamond, 1985). These authors all speak of a systematic or a systems approach consisting of the following general phases: (1) analysis and definition of the problem; (2) selection or design of a solution (from a set of alternatives); (3) development of the solution; (4) testing, evaluating and revising; (5) implementing and controlling. This process is not a linear but an iterative one in which creativity and a heuristic (instead of algorithmic) approach are important features. In such a technological approach one strives for acceptable and attainable solutions, and not always for the best one (from a scientific point of view). The limitations imposed by the problem context will ultimately be more influential on the choice of the best alternative than on scientific arguments. Although no guarantee can be given that the best solution will be achieved, the systems approach to educational problem-solving will result in an optimal chance of arriving at an acceptable solution.

The most important methodological aspects of an educational technology approach can be divided into three categories:

Educational technology as systems   Using concepts and approaches of systems theory and operations research in the analysis phase, the problem can be handled by defining the problem space as a system with boundaries, within which related subsystems can be defined. Complex problems can be unravelled to reveal well-ordered partial problems with enough known properties to make an acceptable solution possible.

Educational technology as methods and techniques   Many techniques, most of which are not specific to educational technology, can be used in the analysis, design, development, and evaluation phases. The specificity of these techniques lies in their order within the technological cycle. This cycle can be considered as the methodological basis for the design process. A typical characteristic of educational technology is that techniques for design decisions are considered to be a vital part of the process.

Educational technology project organization   A technological approach makes special demands on the organization of projects. This is partly due to the fact that the problem analysis will result in an overview of knowledge and skills needed for finding a solution. Many problems need expertise from a variety of disciplines. "Management of expertise" is the key phrase: the classification of a problem with the right expertise at the right time. Continuing attention to the implementation of the solution makes demands on the project organization. Planning has to be considered as one characteristic of a technological approach. The project organization is directed at achieving an optimal solution within the existing constraints such as budget, personnel and time.

Educational problems may occur at all levels. At the macrolevel there are the national problems concerning the educational needs of the society as a whole: policy, structure of the system, minimal facilities needed for giving everybody an opportunity for a basic education. At the mesolevel there are the problems of institutions (schools, colleges, universities, etc.) which are curricular and organizational in nature. At the microlevel there are the teaching and learning problems, the concerns of teachers and students. At each of these levels problems can be approached with recourse to educational technology. The expertise needed will differ from level to level and depend on the type of problem, e.g., choice of curricular materials or media, curriculum development, organization of higher education, etc. In solving these problems one has to draw not only upon many disciplines, such as psychology, pedagogy and sociology, but also upon theories of methodology, instruction and curriculum, media and communication, organization and systems, and sometimes the field of informatics or computer science. A combination of specialized knowledge from these disciplines, with educational technology as a problem-solving methodology, will fully cover the domain of education and training in terms of providing the capacity to tackle problems.

The educational technologist may often use educational technology in its older meanings:

technical products and the process of systematic design of instruction. This approach, and its history derived from the field of audiovisual media, creates in the minds of many people a technical image of educational technology. From the approach of the present authors it is clear that technology is not the same as technique. However, this technical image is not rapidly diminishing, one possible reason being that educational technology does not start from the primacy of the teacher. The role of the teacher will always be analyzed in relation to the educational setting as a whole. In this analysis there is a need to pay attention to alternative solutions in which new technological media, like computers and interactive video, are used and are reinforcing the technical image of educational technology. This technical image is convincing some people that educational technologists should in fact be educational technocrats. After the preceding dicussion we should be able to say that educational technology is nothing more or less than a methodology for solving educational problems. A large number of its practitioners have adopted this methodology, but there remain many more who are still wedded to the older concepts of the field.

Educational problems which could be addressed by educational technology

One basic premise in regard to the use of educational technology is that it ought to be used in response to appropriate problems. In the past, some of the less successful uses of educational technology occurred when it was offered as a solution to a problem which had not been clearly defined. In the early days media (and to some extent computers today) were viewed as solutions looking for a problem rather than the other way round. The mystique which surrounds the new technologies causes enthusiasts to try to apply them in almost any setting without, however, raising the "right" questions. It is far better to define and describe the problems facing a country, an organization or an individual and *then* consider alternative solutions which may involve technology. Unless this view is held by technology's leaders and implementers, most technological innovations are doomed to failure. There is much to recommend Schumacher's concept of appropriate technology (1973): "One can also call it self-help technology, or democratic or people's technology – a technology to which everybody can gain admittance . . . Although we are in possession of all requisite knowledge, it still requires a systematic, creative effort to bring this technology into active existence and make it generally visible and available (p. 154)."

What are some of the most critical problems in the educational sector? The problems differ depending upon the level of development attained. In the developing nations of the world, increasing numbers of children are seeking education. More and more of these students are seeking higher levels of education and training but are being thwarted by other realities. There is a shortage of qualified teachers in most countries of the world and many teachers are not fully trained. In many parts of the world, classrooms tend to be dull places where students are putting in time without developing an appetite for learning. These problems, coupled with insufficient funds for education, inevitably lead to poor student performance. The inadequacy of funding also limits the resources available to the teacher and the learner: there are insufficient numbers of textbooks, blackboards are poor, and no media other than the teacher are present. Such a bleak picture often discourages educators and government officials from trying to overcome the problems which exist. In the more developed nations, the problems relate to the quality of education, the societal concerns which can be dealt with in the schools, the organizational implications for multicultural education, and the cost-effectiveness of the investment made in education. Educational technology, it can be said, offers potential solutions to some of the most pressing problems in all areas of the world.

Proposals to alleviate the problems

Over the past 50 years many projects have been established by international agencies and various bilateral agreements have been made between nations in an attempt to use the mass media to resolve some of the educational problems facing developing countries. The emphasis seems to be on providing instruction on a large scale, usually through radio or television, to students who could not attend local schools. Schramm (1977) reports on most of these programs and concludes: "Students learn from *any* medium, in school or out, whether they intend to or not, whether it is intended or not that they should learn . . . providing that the content of the medium leads them to pay attention to it (p. 267)." While it appeared that the media were being deployed to solve some of the critical educational problems facing a country, they were in many instances being seen as contemporary delivery systems which would help to modernize a developing nation. In the more highly developed countries, media and technology have been used as a showpiece by local schools eager to impress upon parents and community leaders that the school was on the cutting edge of the technological revolution sweeping through other sectors of society. The presence of hardware seemed to convince people inside and outside the schools that modern devices were being used. However, there is little data available on how these devices were used and what the results were. Hardware (and random software) did not appear to bring about the changes that were originally envisaged.

Assumptions about the use of instructional technology

In advancing the technologies of radio, television, film, and other more traditional audiovisual media, advocates made certain assumptions. Some of these assumptions are logical and reasonable; others need to be questioned and clarified. By definition, a medium is a vehicle through which something is accomplished or conveyed. Thus, a teacher is a medium. When an instructional medium is used, it acts as a means of performing one or more instructional functions of a teacher. Perceptions that teachers are being "replaced" by a medium seemed to override the value of the surrogate. A related assumption was that logical or reasonable justification for the use of media and technology would bring about easy acceptance by teachers, principals, and parents. It was thought that each of these groups would value educational technology.

The assumptions that economies of scale would eventually reduce costs pervaded almost every project in which media and technology were used. After the initial installation, development of materials, and training of teachers (the argument went) costs could be amortized over time for an actual net saving of educational expenses.

A final assumption was that educational problems, especially in teaching and learning, could be solved in ways similar to other sectors of society where technology had intervened to help find solutions to problems, create better lifestyles, and deliver services in an efficient and effective manner. If problems of transportation, food production and family planning could be solved by new technologies, the argument in support of educational technology seemed to be a logical one. There appeared to be a role for technology in instructional improvement, but that role was never clearly stated.

What has happened?

Some projects have succeeded and continue today. One of the most notable is the Open University in the UK, but there are others in China, Japan, the Federal Republic of Germany, the Netherlands, Thailand, and Pakistan, to mention but a few. Some aspects of other projects succeeded and vestiges of them remain. TV College in Chicago is still operating after more than 30 years but in a more limited way and for a different clientele. Other projects succeeded until the money ran out; that is, they accomplished what they set out to do and, as long as there was financial support from a donor agency, the programs continued. The Satellite Instructional Television Experiment (SITE) in India was implemented for a specified period of time, but no continued support was forthcoming and no attempt was made to revive it, despite the fact that the data indicate that SITE achieved most of its objectives. Lastly, many other projects simply failed.

Today there appears to be less hostility toward media and technology than in earlier times, especially in the more developed areas of the world. There is an acceptance of the tools and products of our time as legitimate resources for the classroom. However, media and technology still seem to be used more as adjunct materials than as an integral part of the teaching/learning process. They remain as audiovisual *aids* rather than as fundamental substantive resources for learning. They are used more for instruction than for learning and they help the teacher more than the learner. This may be because teachers are more apt to use media and technology when they can maintain control of classroom events, and do not have to make major changes in the routine of the classroom. It may also reflect the generally acknowledged poor quality of instructional materials and inadequate supplies of equipment and materials.

Where are the successes?

Some problems are so obvious that the solutions do not seem to be particularly inventive. In Australia, for example, radio has been used for more than 50 years to reach students in the outback. (Supplementary materials sometimes have to be dropped by aeroplane.) An insufficient number of trained teachers, especially in mathematics, led to the use of educational radio in Mexico, El Salvador, and Nicaragua. These radio lessons provide comprehensive instructional units especially in remote areas of these countries. In an attempt to prepare youngsters for primary school, *Sesame Street* was produced and shown in the United States and has been translated into several languages in other countries; it is not uncommon to see "Big Bird" in many countries of the world. Microteaching, which began as a procedure for improving the training of teachers at Stanford University, has become a standard activity for teacher education around the world, permitting a teacher trainee to teach a small group of students as the lesson is being videotaped for later analysis. Audiotutorial instruction, which began as an attempt to individualize instruction for university-level botany classes, has gradually spread to other colleges and universities throughout North America. As a result, the number of lecture classes has been reduced and students spend more time in a laboratory carrel where the instructor's lecture is available on tape and the materials for experiments are nearby. With this form of instruction, students proceed at their own pace and their performance is usually better than that of students who attend traditionally organized classes and laboratories.

Educational technology, in its process sense, has been discovered by business, industry, the military, and health professions. When life or death matters are paramount, training programs designed by educational technologists become very important. It should be noted that the emphasis is on *training*, not on education, which is broader and more general in its goals. Training programs use the concepts and principles of educational technology to ensure the optimum performance of employees. Many of the same principles are used in education, but they are not usually as pervasive.

One very successful application of educational technology is the use of low-cost learning systems in Indonesia, Liberia, the Philippines, and Thailand. These programs are designed for maximum student involvement, peer tutoring, and the use of simple print and audio media all organized in a systematic way in order to ensure that learning takes place (Nichols, 1982).

What about the unfulfilled promises?

An understanding of what makes programs "successful" or "unsuccessful" can be acquired by examining the common elements which would appear to be inherent in successful projects, and those elements which would appear to be lacking in less successful programs. What follows is a brief list of some of the reasons why some projects did not fulfill their expectations.

Goals were confused People participating in the project did not know why educational technology was being used. They tended to think of it as a *means* rather than as a systematic approach to instructional development. The hidden objective was to prove the value of a specific medium or technique. Sometimes goals were set not by the users themselves but by organizations which were "on the outside." Ambiguity of goals leads to diffuse activities by personnel who lack the guidance of having specific goals in mind.

Emphasis on the medium Greater importance seemed to be attached to the equipment used than to the design of the program or accompanying materials. In these cases, a new medium was being tried out for its own sake, the problems to be solved taking second place to the actual use of the equipment. Instructional television in American Samoa (Schramm, 1977) was installed to provide more and better education but the emphasis was on television rather than on learning. With each new medium the advocates seemed to follow the same pattern, i.e., prove its value in comparison with traditional approaches.

Research and development in both major streams of the field have enlarged our knowledge and understanding of the possibilities of media and the instrumentation of teaching and learning processes, as well as the use of systematic design and development of instruction, curricula, and courseware.

Ultimately, the influence of both developments on educational practice appears to be very limited. Most of the research conducted on the effectiveness of different modes of presentation has not yielded unequivocal results: a "no significant difference" was almost always reported.

However, when significant results *were* reported, there was insufficient consistency to be able to draw meaningful conclusions (see e.g., Dubin and Taveggia, 1968; Schramm, 1977; Chadwick, 1979). The early product and process approach of educational technology usually referred to physical aspects of the educational process: new aids, new media of presentation, new learning programs, etc. The technology, i.e., the products and/or the process, was the focus of attention, but the very structure and organization of the educational processes were never part of the discussion.

Resistance to change   There are people who for various reasons simply do not want change and who are wont to scuttle the work of agents of change and innovators. The application of technology to the teaching/learning process posed a special threat for such people because, when its use was optimized, it replaced in many cases the traditional information-giving function ascribed to the teacher. Moreover, in schools where factors affecting change (commitment to change, availability of resources, etc.) are not taken into consideration, resistance to technology seems to escalate.

Lack of support systems   Basic ideas may be sound and initial resources may be provided, but without a management support system, including logistics on a day-to-day basis, project objectives become difficult to achieve. Sometimes social support systems are also lacking, and individuals trying to adopt an innovation may feel alone and without help. More sophisticated equipment often requires continual looking after, usually by technical and management personnel. If a computer or videotape recorder does not operate, provision for replacement and repair needs to be made. Support services should make it easier to use the hardware – sometimes the lack of such services is an impediment to its use. The new user also needs peers who are themselves trying out a new procedure and who can therefore help one another to carry through a program. Without this type of encouragement, volunteers for innovation are not very forthcoming.

Lack of skills   Some people who are designated to use new technologies do not receive adequate training or, at worst, do not receive any training whatsoever. Opportunities to practise using the new technology must be found in the individual's own time and there is therefore little incentive to become skilled. Under such circumstances it is reasonable to expect a lack of enthusiasm and an unwillingness to risk failure.

Expense   In some cases project implementers are not aware of the expenses that will accrue during the course of operation of the project. If people have not been trained or if all the equipment has not arrived by the time the funds run out, the project is likely to fail. If new money is allocated and documented results are not available some time during the first year of operation, it is likely that financial support for the project will be cut. Sometimes alternative uses for the money become more attractive than the experiment, for example purchasing new textbooks seems to be a far better use of scarce resources than purchasing a microcomputer or videodisk unit.

Lack of quality software   After costly and visible equipment is installed, many project participants realize that they must create the "software" to use with the hardware. If software is imported, it may be culturally inappropriate. If it is produced locally, people have to be trained in the process of instructional design. Rarely is there any type of educational technology project that has sufficient amounts of quality software, probably the most important element of the total delivery system. In addition, the general inflexibility of most software requires high fidelity between its designated pattern of use and its actual implementation. Without the opportunity for local adaptation, users have little "ownership" in the use of software that they cannot adapt for their own purposes.

Lack of system focus   Some projects are concerned with only one (or a limited number of) aspects of the problem rather than the totality. They tend to focus on one important objective and neglect the rest. All too often, cause and effect mentality, especially in different cultures, brings about incorrect perceptions of people, procedures, and processes. Attention is given to only a few aspects of a program and not to the entire operation. Where vision is limited, it is unlikely that systems which require substantial changes can be implemented. When a user does not perceive a new procedure as one contributory element of a larger structure, it is likely to fail or to have its effectiveness reduced.

What are the threads which run through successful programs?

When successful problem-oriented, technology-based programs are analyzed, there appears to be a series of strands which run through most of them. Some of the most frequently found themes are given below:

- Successful programs using technology meet such *critical* educational needs as a shortage of teachers, insufficient space for classrooms, or escalating costs.
- Such programs are oriented toward the *individual learner* rather than toward the teacher. When instruction is designed on the basis of what the learner must be able to do, new software based on the principles of instructional design often emerges. If these principles have been followed, the problem rests with the materials rather than the teacher if the student does not learn.
- Successful programs are cost-effective. The best examples come from the use of radio in developing countries. With increasing sophistication in accounting for the outputs of educational programs, measures of effectiveness are emerging along with measures of efficiency.
- Delivery systems are relatively simple and available. Less exotic media such as audio cassettes and programmed learning courses are having remarkable success in a large number of developing countries. In many cases where simple media are used, the emphasis is not on the medium, but on the systematic approach to instruction.
- Closely related to the use of simple delivery systems in the emphasis on the *design* of the system. New, research-based (Gagné and Briggs, 1974) procedures are being recognized as important elements in the process of teaching and learning.
- Projects and programs which succeed are more often involved in training than in education. Since the purposes of training are more often directed toward measurable skill competencies, it is logical that such efforts would yield specific positive results. The

wider range and amorphous quality of education makes it difficult to assess whether goals have been attained, for these goals are usually of a more general nature.

What have we learned?

The results of our analysis have produced a number of general guidelines which, if followed, would be likely to bring about the successful implementation of educational programs. These guidelines should continue to be tested and altered as necessary. They may be followed using either the product or process approach to educational technology, but they would work best at the problem-solving level where all aspects which impinge upon the teaching/learning process are factored into a comprehensive design.

1 Begin with a problem to be solved, not with a medium or instrument to be used. Selection of the hardware and software should grow out of specific needs which have already been identified. In its best sense, educational technology uses a systematic approach to problem-solving in teaching/learning contexts. It serves users most effectively when it addresses the total problem rather than one part of it. Open universities begin by exploring the need to provide tertiary education to large numbers of secondary school graduates and adults who do not have access to a college or university setting.

2 Analyze the context in which the teaching and learning will take place. Consider all of the elements which will influence the process. (Some would suggest carrying out a needs assessment as part of the analysis of the contextual environment.) With these data in hand, develop a comprehensive plan for the design, installation, and maintenance of any new practice. Such a plan would involve potential users in the process and would provide for training along the way. Organizing for the management of a project is as important as the substance of the effort.

3 Let the design of the materials reflect the philosophy of the program and the strategies which will be used in implementation. These elements (materials, beliefs, and strategies) work together – attention to one without concern for the others will eventually lead to a mismatch of materials and learners.

4 Focus on the individual learner – build in active participation – provide feedback. This shift from teacher to learner is a major change in the teaching/learning process. It begins with a series of statements about student outcomes, i.e., what students should be able to do at certain points in the process. What the teacher does is to arrange the right conditions for learning to take place; these conditions include facilities, materials, time, grouping, and opportunities for practice.

5 Select simple, available media. These should be integrated into the design and not be considered as optional or ancillary. Research shows that media can teach content at least as effectively as traditional instruction. Moreover, well-designed media can help learners to gain more than from traditional instruction.

6 Determine the role of the teacher. If media are to carry some of the content, the teacher's role must change. The teacher will be less of an information-giver and more of a learning facilitator. Fewer professional teachers may be required if roles are modified and teacher aides or assistants are used alongside professional teachers. In no way should the teacher be denigrated; he/she is still the primary resource person but now serves as more of a

manager than as a fountain of knowledge. The more a teacher participates in the planning of instructional delivery, the greater the fidelity to an agreed-upon implementation design.

7 Set up support systems to assist the teachers and students. Support systems might include logistic help, counselling, resource people, and technical assistance. They are as important as all other elements of the system. Without support, the instructional delivery will not "work" at an optimum level. Again, as with the teacher, roles must be defined and criteria for using the support systems should be developed.

These guidelines have been derived from actual practice and stem from current thinking about educational technology as a problem-solving process for teaching and learning.

What is past is prologue . . . or is it?

Some historians believe that events are cyclical over time; some psychologists believe that the best indicator of future behavior is past behavior; some philosophers say that we learn from our mistakes. All of these viewpoints seem to describe the activities of educational technology over the past 50 years.

What might be viewed as a failure to install many of the instruments and artifacts of educational technology might in fact be a sign of maturity, a sign that advocates have learned what the proper role of educational technology really is. In a world where the products of a technological age are visible in many sectors of society, it is reasonable to think that these fruits of our labors are potentially useful in the educational sector as well. We have learned that we must buy products that have been originally designed for other purposes and adapt them to educational settings. We thought that mere acquisition was sufficient to begin using these new technological delights, but soon learned that there were no quick and easy roads to success. We have learned that hardware was insufficient to achieve educational goals. We have learned that the goals of education were quite different from those of other sectors of society.

To say that we have failed or learned very little is to miss the point. We have learned about education, teaching, and learning. We have learned that there is no easy road to educational success. We have learned that media that entertain do not necessarily teach. We have learned that there are better ways to design software. We have learned that we must deal with the whole rather than the parts. We have learned that education is not an institution that can be revolutionized easily – but that evolution can be accelerated. We have learned that educational technology is a problem-solving process, not a product.

The current innovation is information technology or, more specifically, the computer. What will happen in the future? Will the mistakes of the past be repeated? Will the next 50-year analysis be similar to this one? The potential for failure is still there. We have a visible piece of hardware with software that has been developed largely for business, industry, the military, or government purposes. Worldwide problems in education still exist, and the urgent calls for a "quick fix" are creating pressure to embrace new technologies. The basic structures of education are the same, and most teaching continues to be offered in classrooms with groups of learners being taught by an individual teacher. This age-old practice is probably the single most effective deterrent to improvements in learning. Until educators realize that new times demand new configurations for teaching and learning, we will continue to find pockets of innovation which may or may not make much difference to the advancement of learning. Teachers have a role to play in this new configuration; so does technology. The past 50 years have taught us how to bring about changes that will improve learning and make it more exciting. Critical problems of numbers and space, especially in developing nations, can be addressed by new and systematic configurations of learning environments where teachers, technology, and techniques make their optimum contribution to the process of teaching and learning. To do less is to deny the advances of the past 50 years. To do more is to launch education on a path towards the twenty-first century.

References

Association for Educational Communications and Technology (1977), *The Definition of Educational Technology*, Washington, DC: AECT.

Botkin, J. W., Elmandjra, M., and Mailitza, M. (1979), *No Limits to Learning: Bridging the Human Gap: The Club of Rome Report*, Oxford: Pergamon Press.

Chadwick, C. B. (1979), "Why educational technology is failing (and what should be done to create success)," *Educational Technology*, January, pp. 7–19.

Cuban, L. (1985), *Teachers and Machines: The Classroom Use of Technology*, New York: Teachers College Press.

Davies, I. K. (1978), "Educational technology: archetypes, paradigms and models," In Hartley, J. and Davies, I. K. (eds), *Contributing to Educational Technology*, vol. 2, London: Kogan Page.

Diamond, R. (1985), "Instructional design: systems approach," In Husén, T. and Postlethwaite, T. N. (eds), *The International Encyclopedia of Education*, Oxford: Pergamon Press, pp. 2258–563.

Dick, W. and Carey, L. (1978), *The Systematic Design of Instruction*, Glenview, IL: Scott, Foresman and Co.

Dubin, R. and Taveggia, T. C. (1968), *The Teaching Learning Paradox*, Eugene, OR: University of Oregon Press.

Ely, D. P. (1983), "The definition of educational technology: an emerging stability," *Educational Considerations*, X (2), Spring, pp. 2–4.

Ely, D. P. (1985), "Education and training: two paths or one?" *Programmed Learning & Educational Technology*, 22 (1), pp. 75–7.

Faure, E. et al. (1982), *Learning to Be: The World of Education Today and Tomorrow*, Paris: UNESCO.

Fullan, M. (1985), "Curriculum Implementation." In Husén, T. and Postlethwaite, T. N. (eds), *The International Encyclopedia of Education*, Oxford: Pergamon Press, 1985, pp. 1208–15.

Gagné, R. and Briggs, L. (1974), *Principles of Instructional Design*, New York: Holt, Rinehart and Winston.

Gerlach, V. S. and Ely, D. P. (1971), *Teaching and Media: A Systematic Approach*, Englewood Cliffs, NJ: Prentice Hall.

Heinich, R. (1984), "The proper study of instructional technology," *Educational Communications and Technology Journal*, 32, pp. 67–87.

Lumsdaine, A. A. (1964), "Educational technology, programmed learning, and instructional science." In Hilgard, E. R. (ed.), *Theories of Learning and Instruction*, Chicago: University of Chicago Press, pp. 371–401.

Nichols, D. G. (1982), "Low-cost learning systems: the general concept and some specific examples," *NSPI Journal*, September, pp. 4–8.

Plomp, T. (1982), *Enige verkenningen*, Enschede: T. H. Twente (in Dutch).

Romiszowski, A. J. (1981), *Designing Instructional Systems*, London: Kogan Page.

Saettler, P. (1968), *A History of Instructional Technology,* New York: McGraw-Hill.

Schramm, W. (1977), *Big Media, Little Media,* Beverly Hills, CA: Sage Publications.

Schumacher, E. F. (1973) *Small is Beautiful,* London: Blond & Briggs.

Stakenas, R. G. and Kaufman, R. (1981), *Technology in Education: Its Human Potential,* Bloomington (1970): Phi Delta Kappa.

Tickton, S. G. (1970), *To Improve Learning: An Evaluation of Instructional Technology,* New York: Bowker.

Selected Further Reading

Artificial intelligence

Igor Aleksander and Piers Burnett, *Thinking Machines: The Search for Artificial Intelligence* (Oxford University Press, Oxford, 1987).

Eugene Charniak and Drew McDermott, *Introduction to Artificial Intelligence* (Addison-Wesley, Reading, MA, 1985).

Dwight B. Davis, "Artificial Intelligence Enters the Mainstream," *High Technology*, July 1986.

Karamjit S. Gill (ed.), *Artificial Intelligence for Society* (Wiley, New York, 1986).

Paul Harmon and David King, *Expert Systems: Artificial Intelligence in Business* (Wiley, New York, 1985).

John Haugeland, *Artificial Intelligence: The Very Idea* (MIT Press, Cambridge, MA, 1985).

Peter Jackson, *Introduction to Expert Systems* (Addison-Wesley, Reading, MA, 1986).

Jeffrey Rothfeder, *Minds Over Matter* (Prentice-Hall, Englewood Cliffs, NJ, 1985).

William B. Schwartz, Ramesh S. Patil, and Peter Szolovits, "Artificial Intelligence in Medicine: Where Do We Stand?" *The New England Journal of Medicine*, vol. 316 (11), March 12, 1987.

J. Marshall Unger, *The Fifth Generation Fallacy: Why Japan is Betting Its Future on Artificial Intelligence* (Oxford University Press, New York, 1987).

Terry Winograd and Fernando Flores, *Understanding Computers and Cognition* (Ablex, Norwood, NJ, and Addison-Wesley, Reading, MA, 1988.)

Masoud Yazdani (ed.), *Artificial Intelligence: Principles and Applications* (Chapman and Hall, London, 1986).

The user interface

Hugh Aldersley-Williams, "Design With People in Mind," *High Technology*, July 1987.

John P. Crecine, "The Next Generation of Personal Computers," *Science*, vol. 231 (4741), February 28, 1986.

James N. Danziger and Kenneth L. Kraemer, *People and Computers: The Impacts of Computing on End Users in Organisations* (Columbia University Press, New York, 1986).

William H. Dutton, Everett M. Rogers, and Suk-Ho-Jun, "Diffusion and Social Impacts of Personal Computers," *Communications Research*, vol. 14 (2), April 1987.

Sara Kiesler, Jane Siegel, and Timothy W. McGuire, "Social Psychological Aspects of Computer-Mediated Communication," *American Psychologist*, vol. 39 (10), October 1984.

Raymond S. Nickerson, *Using Computers: The Human Factors of Information Systems* (MIT Press, Cambridge, MA, 1986).

Dan Shafer, *Silicon Visions: The Future of Microcomputer Technology* (Prentice-Hall, New York, 1986).
Sherry Turkle, *The Second Self: Computers and the Human Spirit* (Simon & Schuster, New York, 1984).

IT in the home

Larry Armstrong et al., "The Electronic Battle Goes Home," *Business Week*, February 29, 1988.
William Atkinson, *Working From Home: Is It For You?* (Dow Jones-Irwin, Homewood, IL, 1985).
Jerome Aumente, *New Electronic Pathways: Videotex, Teletext and Online Databases* (Sage, Newbury Park, CA, 1987).
Walter S. Baer, "Information Technologies in the Home," in Bruce R. Guile (ed.), *Information Technologies and Social Transformation* (National Academy Press, Washington, DC, 1985).
Herb Brody, "Companies Struggle to Automate Homes," *High Technology Business*, March 1988.
Thomas B. Cross, "Telecommuting – Future Options for Work," *Oxford Surveys in Information Technology*, vol. 3, 1986, pp. 247–69.
Gladys D. Ganley and Oswald H. Ganley, *Global Political Fallout: The First Decade of the VCR 1976–1985* (Ablex, Norwood, NJ, 1987).
Ralph L. Lowenstein and Helen E. Aller, "The Inevitable March of Videotex," *Technology Review*, vol. 88 (7), October 1985.
Joshua Meyrowitz, *No Sense of Place: The Impact of Electronic Media on Social Behaviour* (Oxford University Press, New York, 1985).
Ralph Lee Smith, *Smart House: The Coming Revolution in Housing* (GP Publishing, Columbia, MD, 1987).
Nicholas P. Vitalari and Alladi Venkatesh, "In-Home Computing and Information Services: A Twenty-Year Analysis of the Technology and Its Impacts," *Telecommunications Policy*, vol. 11 (1), March 1987.
Roger Williams and Stephen Mills (eds.), *Public Acceptance of New Technologies: An International Overview* (Croom Helm, Beckenham, UK, 1986).

IT in schools

"Computers and Research," special issue of *Science*, vol. 228 (4698), April 26, 1985. A variety of articles on uses in tertiary education.
New Information Technologies: A Challenge for Education, Centre for Educational Research and Innovation, OECD (HMSO, London, 1986).
Steven Frankel, "Finally, the Revolution in Teaching," *The Washington Post*, Sunday November 23, 1986, p. D3.
Peter Gywnne, "Computers are Sprouting in the Groves of Academe," *Technology Review*, October, 1984.
Margie Ploch, "Computers in Schools: Can They Make the Grade?" *High Technology*, September 1986.
Nick Rushby and Anne Howe (eds), *Educational, Training and Information Technologies: Economics and Other Realities* (Kogan Page, London, 1986).
Harold G. Shane, *Teaching and Learning in a Microelectronic Age* (Phi Delta Kappa, Bloomington, IN, 1987).

Part Three: Computers and Organizations

8 The Productivity Puzzle

The Puny Payoff from Office Computers

William Bowen

As I noted in my Introduction to this volume, there is a new wave of skepticism about the benefits of computerization. After the expenditure of billions of dollars on hardware and software in factories, offices, and banks, people are asking where the productivity payoff is. One of the first to seriously question the value of IT in offices was technology writer William Bowen, whose piece appeared in Fortune, *May 26, 1986. Bowen argues forcefully that getting results usually involves redesigning the work process before computerization.*

Have the millions of computers purchased by US businesses brought any overall improvement in productivity? Surprisingly, the best information available says no.

This collides with many people's beliefs regarding computers. Without computers, present-day credit card operations, check processing, and airline reservation systems would be unthinkable. But the figures indicate that, on a national scale, business's investment of hundreds of billions of dollars in computers and computer-aided communications has failed to bring about a discernible improvement in productivity. "The puzzling thing," observes economist Martin Neil Baily, a senior fellow at the Brookings Institution think-tank in Washington, DC, "is that the computer revolution has not yet paid off in productivity growth as did the earlier generations of innovation."

So far productivity has grown more slowly in the computer age than it did before computers came into wide use. Growth in white-collar productivity has been especially weak, and white-collar employees account for something like three-fourths of total business payroll costs in the United States. White-collar work is also where most computers are. Only about 10 percent of computers are used in manufacturing processes.

Managers and consultants who have studied the problem offer several explanations for why computers have not improved white-collar productivity. Getting large productivity benefits from computer systems usually requires a learning process. Often management has to change work flow to realize the benefits of automation. Sometimes computers have been set to doing the wrong tasks, or simply have sat idle. Most of the productivity payoff from computers now in place may still lie ahead. The experiences of companies that have already managed to achieve substantial white-collar productivity gains provide an instructive, hopeful lesson for other companies, both in the United States and abroad.

The only way to calculate white-collar productivity in the United States is to break down statistics on the productivity of the entire workforce. The federal government puts out no figures for white-collar productivity, but it does collect information that makes it possible to sort white collars from blue collars with a heroic amount of work. Credit for taking on this task goes to Stephen S. Roach, a senior economist at the investment banking house of Morgan Stanley.

By Roach's reckoning, white-collar productivity – output per worker hour – stands just about where it was in the late 1960s. Improvements in blue-collar productivity account for all the productivity gain realized since then. The lack of growth in white-collar productivity may largely explain last year's dramatic deceleration in business spending for computers and telecommunications equipment. The dramatic slowdown, Roach says, reflects "a growing dissatisfaction with high tech's productivity payback."

To some extent the failure of computers to improve white-collar productivity is accounted for by what might be called the down-escalator factor. In some instances computers may have been pushing white-collar productivity up while other influences have been pulling it down. Thanks to the upward impetus computers have provided, productivity has stayed more or less at the same level on a down escalator.

One indication of this is that the phrase "cost avoidance" often comes up when managers or consultants explain what computers have done for productivity. With variations, these people seem to have much the same theme in mind: circumstances have forced business to devote additional staff to nonproductive work, and if computers had not been improving efficiency somewhere, companies would have needed more white-collar workers to produce the same output. "If you didn't have computers," a Du Pont executive observes, "you might have had a big increase in staff."

What nonproductive work? Government-imposed paperwork and the complexity of the tax code catch some of the blame. Monstrous awards in liability cases have entailed more work by lawyers to cope with litigation and more monitoring by companies to try to avoid it. The expansion of employee rights in matters such as firing or retirement has made additional work for legal staffs and personnel departments.

Down-escalator effects on productivity may also derive from what Harvard economist Harvey Leibenstein calls X-inefficiency – inefficiency that results from an organization's failure to make the best use of resources. In some cases, X-inefficiency comes from failures of managers or their employees to work as hard or smart as they can. Workers, Leibenstein argues, have some degree of "effort discretion." How effectively they do their jobs partly depends on such intangible influences as morale and quality of supervision.

Since X-inefficiency exists in most organizations most of the time, it would have a down-escalator influence on productivity only if it were increasing. Has it been? Some managers and consultants think so. Donald A. Sachar, vice chairman of Environetics International, a leading office design firm, argues that employee effort has waned to a degree that "without information technology, we would be in a disaster." While that may overstate the case, discretion clearly increases as professionals and people in clerical and staff jobs come to make up more of the work force.

Underuse represents a possible contributing reason for the failure of computers to improve productivity. Many personal computers, especially machines bought during the personal computer boom of 1983 and 1984, sit idle much of the time. Consultants refer to them as dusty.

Some computers are used in ways that partly wipe out their efficiencies. Electronic mail, for example, produces lots of electronic junk mail. Some managers like electronic mail because it eliminates "telephone tag" between those on the system. Within an organization, you can send messages to people who are not at their desks and receive messages when you are not at your own. You can also store your distribution list and then send a message to everybody on the list just by tapping a few keys. But the very ease of communication leads to abuses. People send trivial messages. Sometimes messages of value to only a few people on a distribution list go to everyone on the list.

The principal application of personal computers in businesses is word processing, and the ease of revision can bring out perfectionism. Doing an additional draft or two beyond what would have been done in the typewriter era may achieve gains in quality – more effective letters, more readable reports – but the number of drafts sometimes reaches double digits.

Excessive redrafting and electronic junk mail can be expected to recede as time goes by, restrained by overt or subtle forms of disapproval. Far more important than such transient abuse is that computers are often used for applications with low payoffs. David L. Shay, a top productivity consultant at the Peat Marwick & Mitchell accounting firm in New York, says, "Automating office tasks rarely leads to substantive savings." The large payoffs come not from increasing the efficiency with which people perform their old jobs, but from changing the way work is done.

In upbeat stories that some managers tell about computers and productivity, two themes recur. One, work is done differently from the way it was done in precomputer days. Two, getting there took time.

Ideally, you should change the way work is done *before* you put in new equipment. Nancy Bancroft, manager of office systems consulting at Digital Equipment Corp., advises prospective customers to scrutinize their procedures before they decide what to buy, "If people are doing the wrong things when you automate," she says, "you get them to do the wrong things faster." Advises Paul Strassmann, former vice president of the information products group at Xerox and now a consultant: "Automate only after you simplify."

Northern Telecom, the big Canadian manufacturer of telecommunications equipment, has so-called business methods staffs that scrutinize procedures before automation gear is ordered. Sometimes they carry Strassmann's counsel a step further: they simplify *instead* of automating. Says William D. Bradshaw, a business methods manager at a Northern Telecom facility in North Carolina: "We try to limit the use of technology by improving the methods."

As an example, Bradshaw and his former boss William H. Murdaugh point to a job they did in an operation that ships hardware to buyers of telephone switching equipment. Workers packed the hardware in boxes, which they sealed and dispatched to the shipping department. There every box was opened so quality-control inspectors could inspect the contents. Then the hardware was repacked for shipping. Doesn't sound quite right, does it?

Understandably, the process was slow. Managers yearned for help from automation of some sort. In came Murdaugh and Bradshaw, who quickly saw that the inspectors were doing their work at the wrong state of the operation. The absurdity of it had not been noticed because no one had bothered to look across departmental boundaries to see the whole process. Now the inspectors do their inspecting at the packing end, before the boxes are sealed. Automation proved unnecessary. A Northern Telecom employee describes business methods work as "doing what should have been done years ago."

In most cases managers do not scrutinize before they automate. They automate, then begin a sometimes painful learning process. One thing everybody who has been through it agrees on is that you do not get the benefits just by plugging in the equipment, even if it is the right equipment. The learning process often takes years.

Consider Allied Stores, a big retailer headquartered in New York, whose domain includes department stores such as Jordan Marsh and Stern's and specialty stores such as Brooks Brothers and Bonwit Teller. Like all large retailers, class and mass, Allied has to have an operation to call people who have not paid their bills. In 1982 the collection departments of certain Allied divisions computerized. The job used to involve a lot of paper handling, but now relevant information regarding a call automatically appears on a terminal in front of the caller.

For the first three months the productivity gain was zilch, but as the callers got the feel of the new system, productivity picked up. By the end of the first year the staffs in collections had decreased by about 25 percent. As time went by, productivity improved further, and a change in work structure helped. On most calls all the needed information came up on the screen, but sometimes the caller had to get up and find the customer's paper file. Peter Duggan, director of credit operations, observed that some divisions were getting better productivity by providing callers with clerical support to retrieve necessary papers, and so he provided such support in most divisions of the company. Now people who are good at calling stay with that, and other employees fetch information from the files. By the end of 1985, staffing was down 50 percent from the end of 1982, with no falloff in the number of calls being placed. In other words, productivity was about double the level of precomputer days. "We had a longer learning curve than we expected," says Duggan, "but also greater benefits."

Another company that has achieved good productivity gains partly by changing procedures is PPG Industries, a manufacturer of glass, paint, and chemicals. The accounts payable department, for example, used to pay dozens, even hundreds, of invoices to some PPG suppliers every month. Now it consolidates and pays one invoice a month to each supplier. In credit accounts receivable, the standard procedure for checking customer credit has undergone much simplification. Says Thomas A. Headlee, director of management information systems: "We recognize that automating what you're doing isn't enough. There are some savings in the game in that regard, but the larger savings come from automating what you're doing and then doing it better."

Few companies in any field have done much better at improving productivity than Federal Kemper Life Assurance Co., part of Kemper Group, a big insurance company headquartered near Chicago. From 1972 to 1985 productivity increased fivefold, as measured by policies issued per employee per year. Federal Kemper installed a new computer system in 1974, but for a while things were done much the same as before. Work moved from one station to another in a sort of assembly line. Employees at terminals had faster access to information than before, but clerks still moved stacks of paper from one workstation to the next. Productivity gains were imperceptible. Employees jokingly referred to the computer system as an electric pencil.

After a year or so Gerald F. McCann, vice president for operations, proposed a radical transformation of the work process, and management adopted his idea. Federal Kemper abandoned the assembly-line work flow and regrouped employees into self-contained three-person teams, each handling all the functions involved in the issuance of policies. John B. Scott, who succeeded McCann as vice president for operations, remarks that his predecessor's revolution "created a bunch of small companies." It worked. McCann subsequently moved up to executive vice president.

As the Federal Kemper story indicates, the achievement of large productivity gains from applying computers to white-collar work depends on managers' taking an active role. William J. Stapleton, vice president and head of data processing at Allied Stores, draws the same lesson from his experience. "To get vivid results," he says, "you need a leader, a manager who pulls the process along instead of waiting to be pushed."

Finn Caspersen, chairman and chief executive of Beneficial Corp., a big financial services company, is a notable example of an executive who pulled the process along. Less than two years ago Beneficial began putting in an extensive management information system manufactured by Data General. Among other things, the system provides electronic mail and access to data from deep within the organization. In a rare departure from the usual pattern, use of the system spread through the company from the top down. Caspersen got the first terminal, and he used it. Today the system connects 1,200 managers, professionals, and other white-collar employees in the United States, Canada, and the UK. All written communication between managers travels in the system. Paper is out.

Caspersen says the system is "magnificent." He thinks it has already paid for itself in enhanced managerial effectiveness. "I can communicate with or yank figures from any manager anywhere," he says. "We can make a decision now in a quarter to half the time it took before." Eventually, he predicts, the system will change the management structure, perhaps enabling the company to operate with fewer layers of management. "The span of control is so much better," he says, meaning that he can effectively deal with a larger number of people than before.

Raymond E. Cairns, Jr, head of the information systems department at Du Pont, also uses the expression "span of control" with regard to electronic mail. The improved ability to communicate, he says, enables him to have more people report directly to him, and that may make it possible to reduce the number of levels. At PPG, Raymond LeBoeuf, vice president for purchasing, foresees "a flattening of management" after top managers begin using electronic mail. "You're going to have fewer top managers and more people reporting to each of them," he says. Vistas of important reductions in overhead costs open up here. It is often remarked that US companies have more layers of management than Japanese companies. The intrepid management expert Peter Drucker ventures that most US companies have 20 percent to 30 percent more managers than they need.

Some of the disappointment with productivity payoff comes from expecting results too soon. Learning lags have occurred before in the annals of technology. For a while after typewriters came along, businesses used the machine to prepare drafts of a document, then had the final version copied by hand for sending out. When it comes to using computers, many managers are still at the stage of redoing letters in longhand.

Information Technology as a Competitive Burden

Timothy N. Warner

Following on nicely from Bowen, Warner's paper ridicules the notion that IT is an infallible competitive weapon – in this instance, in manufacturing. Citing a number of high-tech horror stories, Warner warns of the dangers of the high-tech "fix" in factories and, like Bowen, suggests that IT solutions to production problems should only be considered after *conventional techniques of system reorganization have been exhausted. Tim Warner is Assistant Professor in the Faculty of Administrative Studies, York University, Toronto. This piece first appeared in* Sloan Management Review, *vol. 29 (1), Fall 1987.*

A major electronics manufacturer establishes an automated warehouse for incoming components. Robots glide up and down the high-rise bays, selecting bins of components under computer control; the bins are passed to a conveyor system; they move around on a path determined by bar code scanners that identify each bin and route it to a stock picker. The stock picker removes items for dispatch to the factory floor as instructed by a computer workstation. An automated guided vehicle rolls off to the factory along a track painted on the floor.

At a cost of many millions of dollars, the system epitomizes the technology of the "factory of the future." But it is now idle. The firm now delivers the bulk of its supplies directly to the factory floor, bypassing the automated warehouse.

Perhaps the managers of this firm thought that information technology was a competitive weapon; perhaps they thought that advanced manufacturing technologies incorporating microelectronics were the key to manufacturing cost reduction. At least, finally, they recognized an organizational design alternative to the use of information technology. Had they not done so, information technology would have continued to be for them as for many others, a competitive burden.

The purpose of this paper is to review the role of information technology in manufacturing enterprises and to point to alternative strategies for achieving the results that information technology promises. It will also argue that the proper role of information technology in a production system cannot be correctly assessed until the system has been restructured for maximum efficiency using conventional means.

Information technology in manufacturing

When we consider the use of information technology in manufacturing, we find three main components. The first is the use on the shop floor of devices containing some level of intelligence – robots, numerically controlled machines, flexible manufacturing systems, automated guided vehicles, and the like – and falling under the rubric of *flexible automation,* or *advanced manufacturing technologies*. The second is the use of computer-aided design techniques, and the third is the use of computerized manufacturing information and control systems. Together these components are capable of becoming computer-integrated manufacturing systems (CIM). Businesses most affected by them tend to be from the aerospace, automotive, electrical equipment, electronics, machinery, and metal-fabricating industries. Many observers see these technologies as truly strategic in impact. For example, rapidly shifting consumer tastes and increased global competition necessitate short product design cycles and responsive manufacturing facilities; economies of scope replace economies of scale. Indeed, some observers see in these information-technology-based approaches the solution to the problem of North American competitiveness.[1]

Information technology and organizational design

Information systems, whether they incorporate "information technology" or not, serve a coordinating function in the firm, allowing it to cope with complexity and uncertainty. Jay Galbraith's work provides a framework for understanding how this occurs.[2] He starts with the issue of how to organize for a task that grows in complexity and uncertainty, and considers the problems of coordination. As soon as the task becomes so large that several persons are engaged in it, they face a management problem. This can be resolved in a variety of ways. For example, a hierarchy of authority is more or less essential, as are agreed-upon rules, programs, and procedures. If the task to be performed is known and standardized, little more needs to be done. But uncertainty in the task creates problems because, to resolve the issues created by uncertainty, more and more information passes up the channels of authority, ultimately overloading them. Galbraith suggests a number of generic strategies for dealing with this problem, which he divides into two broad categories.

Reduce the need for information processing

- Give organizational units more discretionary authority so that the need for upper-management intervention is diminished. Doing this is associated with redesign of tasks into larger, firewalled modules that are carried out by craft or skilled workers.
- Manage the environment to reduce the amount of uncertainty.
- Create slack resources, often in the form of inventory or order backlogs.

Increase information-processing capacity

- Increase vertical-channel capacity in the hierarchy.

- Increase information-processing capacity of selected nodes in the hierarchy.
- Increase the amount of lateral coordination, not involving higher levels of management.

These strategies are not so much mutually exclusive as they are complementary. The important thing to realize is that sometimes one can meet an apparent information-processing problem not by throwing computer power at it, but by removing the conditions that caused the need for information processing in the first place. The example with which I opened this paper demonstrates this possibility well. The control of raw materials inventory and of its movement within the factory are such complicated jobs that advanced computer systems, and computerized devices, are needed to cope with them in an efficient manner – that is, in an analysis comparing manual and automated systems, the automated system would appear more efficient. A better alternative (ignored if one focuses on the use of information technology) might be to remove the conditions that cause inventory to be held.

The Japanese have taught us to regard inventory as "waste." Galbraith's analysis shows us that, if inventory is waste, then information-processing capacity that serves the same function as inventory is also waste.

Information-processing capacity is used to cope with uncertainty and complexity, but much of the uncertainty and complexity faced by a firm is created by the firm itself, because, for example, the product is too complex, contains components from too many suppliers, and is produced by systems of high variability. Let us examine four cases where dealing directly with these conditions replaces attempting to compute one's way around them.

Design for manufacturability

Complex products are reflected in complex productions systems. It is instructive to analyze examples where sophisticated companies have taken a hard look at their production systems, intending to raise the level of manufacturing efficiency, perhaps to become the industry's low-cost producer. Generally there are three elements in their strategies: product design, automation, and manufacturing control systems. While it is hard to disentangle the relative benefits of each, a strong case can be made that much of the gain in efficiency comes from a process of change that may well have been precipitated by the adoption of automation but is otherwise unrelated to it.

Consider the example of Northern Telecom, a major multinational corporation in the telecommunications industry that was faced with the challenge of low-cost telephones produced in Pacific Rim countries. The company's response was to redesign the telephone and reduce its labor content through automation. The redesign is especially interesting because it succeeded in reducing the parts count from 325 to 156.[3] The original labor content was twenty-three minutes per handset. A crude computation shows that if labor content were proportional to parts count, then manual assembly of the revised product would take eleven minutes. Actual labor content, after automation, was nine minutes. It is clear where the major leverage was achieved.

A similar analysis could be conducted with another well-documented automation success – the IBM Proprinter.[4] Redesign for manufacturability reduced the parts count by 60 percent (the printer has 60 parts, compared to 150 in a competitor's product), and the product was simplified for robotic assembly. A similar emphasis on product design at Ford Motor

Company reduced the number of pieces in a car-body side panel from 15 to two. What these examples tell us is that product redesign has tremendous leverage to reduce complexity and its concomitant variability. The important thing is to manage what we might call the internal environment; automation is secondary.

Group technology

A second example, from the secondary manufacturing sector, is the job shop – a production system in which jumbled flow dominates. Scheduling problems in job shops are severe. The result is that the typical machined part spends 95 percent of its total time on the factory floor waiting, and only 5 percent on a machine, being cut. A machine tool might spend only a small fraction of its time cutting metal, the bulk of its day being taken up waiting for work or being set up. The consequent waste of resources has motivated considerable research into job shop scheduling, and the development of shop floor data acquisition systems to aid in managing the flow of work through the shop. With few exceptions the North American solution has been to throw computer power at the problem.[5]

Information processing is not the only, or necessarily the best, solution. People who didn't have the luxury of computers established the concept of "group technology," which in essence is the classification of parts produced by the job shop in terms of similar fabrication sequence, shape, and size.[6] Suppose we can, via such a classification scheme, allocate 80 percent of the shop's volume to families of like parts. Then we can process each family through a manufacturing cell whose machines are placed in the correct sequence and are tailored for the family. The job shop starts to look like a flow shop; scheduling problems are reduced; the prospect for dramatic reductions in work-in-process inventory is enhanced. (As it happens, information technology can play a key role in the application of group technology concepts, and is perhaps essential to that process, but at least when this is the case we know that the technology is being applied reasonably.) In Galbraith's terms, we have redesigned the task into selfcontained modules, as opposed to finding the information-processing capacity to schedule the more complex task.

Manufacturing cells

Jelinek and Goldhar have pointed out that the new technologies of flexible automation – particularly the use of numerically controlled machine tools, robots, and flexible manufacturing systems – give rise to new production system possibilities based on short production runs and rapid switching (at near-zero cost) from one product to another.[7] These provide economies of scope, contrasted with economies of scale. The essential component here is the programmable device, say the numerical control (NC) machine or industrial robot, that can switch immediately from performing one kind of task to another under program control. Once switching costs are zero, then small lot sizes become feasible, indeed optimal. Combining the concepts of rapid changeover through programmability, and group technology, one arrives at the flexible manufacturing cell – the first step toward CIM.[8] It may consist of an integrated multifunctional NC machining center, or a circle of NC tools with automatic tool-changing and raw material loading and unloading, perhaps with automated guided vehicles moving the pieces from one machine to the next. Its purpose is to produce, in small lot sizes, the components in a particular family.

It is incorrect to think that only programmable multifunctional machines are capable of instant zero-cost switching. The Japanese have shown us that conventional technology can be used in the same way.[9] The trick is to reduce set-up times to very small amounts through ingenious engineering and the application of what is, in retrospect, common sense. The "multifunctional" machine can be created from an assemblage of low-cost conventional machines in a manufacturing cell. Hence a concept – economies of scope – that appeared to depend on the advent of high technology on the factory floor is applicable in a much more modest manufacturing environment.[10]

In its simplest form a manufacturing cell is a line (or U-configuration, or circle) of simple machine tools, say, for the production of a family of parts. In order to produce a part, a worker starts with the raw material piece and walks it down the line, performing each operation sequentially, until he or she reaches the end. Note, lot size equals one, and set-ups must be one-touch, not involving other workers. To speed up the line one simply adds another worker; each takes roughly half the work of the cell. One can keep adding workers until the physical ability of the cell to accommodate them is exhausted.

The conventional manufacturing cell achieves flexibility with slack machine resources (which can be cheap, because the machines are simple) and multifunction workers. (Galbraith suggests that a function of "craft" workers is to reduce the costs of coordination.) The cell is a low-fixed-cost increment to a firm's manufacturing capacity, a feature not shared by the information-technology-intensive flexible manufacturing cell, which achieves flexibility through machine-based intelligence.

There is a further consideration – the flexibility of the fully automated "flexible manufacturing cell" is deceptive, because of the extent to which inflexible materials-handling equipment is integral to its operation. This factor limits the number of different items that can in fact be processed by the cell, rather undermining the notion of flexibility.[11]

Just-in-time systems

Another complementary approach to uncertainty and complexity arises out of the problem of management control in repetitive discrete manufacturing (of cars, airplanes, computers, or lawnmowers, for example). In this situation, an information-technology approach (material requirements planning) contrasts strongly with a non-information-technology approach (continuous flow manufacturing).

The manufacture of such goods is information intensive. It is said, for example, that the engineering documentation for a Boeing 747 weighs more than the plane itself. The manufacturing process involves many separate suppliers, spread across the globe, whose activities must be coordinated. The production system for these goods is an industry, not a single enterprise. The sheer volume of transactions required to manage such a production system makes it a natural target for information technology.

Material requirements planning (MRP) is an approach to the management of fabrication and assembly of products of this type. The key concept is that the demand for low-level components derives from the production of an end product whose production level is planned. Traditionally a component of, say, a lawnmower (a particular blade, perhaps) is manufactured in an economic lot size, stored in a warehouse, and used as needed until a reorder point is reached, at which point another batch is fabricated. The inventory of blades constitutes *slack* in the sense that it exists because nobody bothered to figure out exactly when the blades would be needed based on the production schedule for end-items, or perhaps because the number of end-items required could not be accurately forecasted or determined.

Clearly, if we know the precise production schedule of all the lawnmowers into which this particular blade goes, then we can establish, by back scheduling, when to produce or order the blades, so that inventory never builds up much in excess of requirements. MRP, then, substitutes information processing for slack in the way that Galbraith envisions. But MRP systems are notoriously difficult to implement and consume substantial resources in the form of computing power and indirect manufacturing labor.[12] Further, although they deal with the slack created by the earlier inability to back schedule production, they trap and institutionalize other slack that is generally more significant. In order to back schedule you have to estimate lead times for production. As mentioned earlier, *95* percent of the manufacturing lead time in a job shop is wasted, and building this exorbitant lead time into a computer system merely institutionalizes waste. In addition, the buffering function of inventory – allowing for variations in lead time or quantity delivered – is generally handled by artificially inflating the lead time or the quantity produced, which again casts inefficient organizational processes in stone. A final point is that the occurrence of stockouts on the shop floor can be ascribed to "the computer" rather than to some individual who could take corrective action. The system does not contain the levers that would motivate the workforce to more efficient behavior; standing apart from the system on the shop floor, the MRP system introduces a fatal bifurcation of responsibility for overall performance.

Contrast this with what has been called just-in-time (JIT) or stockless production, or continuous flow manufacturing.[13] Suppose for a moment that production of all components could be accomplished instantly. Then back scheduling from the number of different lawnmowers required to the number of blades required in a given period is simplified. But even this is unnecessary. If there is almost no work-in-process inventory (WIP), then replacement of the components required for a particular lawnmower must occur soon after its production. All we need is a signaling system that lets the blade production worker know when to produce. This is accomplished through the well-known *kanban* system. No computers are necessary to accomplish job-order release and dispatching, since these happen because of the pull system in place.

But there is a radical change in the organization of production. Set-up times must be very low; lot sizes are correspondingly small – otherwise a machine would be occupied running large lots at the time it is required to produce a component "on demand." The flow of work might be reorganized so that travel times between successive workstations are minimized, and so that visual signaling methods (*kanban* squares, colored golf balls, etc.) can be used. There can be absolutely no defective parts passed along the system, because there is little WIP to absorb the discrepancies between planned and actual production.

Because there is so little WIP, it can all be located on the factory floor. No elaborate materials-handling or inventory control systems are required. The benefits are legion, well documented, and persuasive to the increasing number of US manufacturers adopting these techniques.

In Galbraith's terms, the firm adopting JIT seems to be doing the impossible – lowering the information-processing requirement *and* removing slack from the system. This is not a complete picture, because the JIT firm plans slack resources in the form of machinery running more slowly, people working less than complete shifts, heavy maintenance, and idle equipment. In addition, the JIT firm eventually manages the uncertainty in its external environment by negotiating supply and delivery schedules to which all parties firmly adhere.[14]

We see here the competitive use of information systems, to be sure, but the use is not necessarily based on high technology. We also see whole industries being transformed by the impact of JIT methods, and corporations such as Hewlett-Packard and IBM relying on the cost and quality benefits of JIT to achieve a competitive edge.[15] One authority at IBM, which has reportedly invested $22 billion in manufacturing in the last five years, comments, "Of all the aspects of IBM's investment in manufacturing . . . the least expensive – Continuous Flow Manufacturing – is the most significant."[16]

I do not intend to give the impression that JIT systems are universally applicable in place of MRP systems. A balanced view might be that each has its place, or that some blend of the two is appropriate.[17] Certain conditions (long lead times for production, uncertain reject rates, fluctuating demand, high set up costs) favor MRP systems.[18] The tragedy is that an information-technology approach treats these conditions as immutable, whereas in many cases they are not. Rather than reducing waste, an information-technology approach adds to it by burdening an already inefficient system with the cost of computation.

Conclusions

Just as piles of work-in-process inventory can signal inefficient production, so also can the elaborate information system, or the machine tool with more axes than it needs, or the automatic storage and retrieval system. The paradox here is that some of the finest examples of manufacturing efficiency incorporate the most advanced computer control systems and factory automation. For example, comparing North American to Japanese manufacturers, we find in North America a lower rate of adoption of NC machines and robots, the building blocks of flexible automation. The reason is that for the well-organized production system the benefits of automation are clear. The Japanese, having paid more attention to basics than the North Americans, are in a better position to evaluate new technologies *and* have production systems into which devices such as robots and NC machines more readily fit.

The analysis presented above suggests that the twin strategies of product design and production system design around conventional technologies can achieve the lion's share of the benefits associated with moving from an unexamined, poorly organized production system to a world-class manufacturing facility. The issue is one of timing – a firm should forgo information-technology-based approaches to solving production problems until it has exhausted conventional approaches, and then move forward into flexible automation. At that point it can examine the benefits of flexible automation relative to the best alternative practice.

Information technology is seen as a new competitive weapon; "strategic systems" take their place alongside decision support systems and traditional data processing;[19] and the "chief information officer" commands a seat at the table where strategic decisions are made.[20] Indeed, in the five years or so since early work on information technology as a competitive weapon appeared, the topic has achieved the status of cliché. Cliché or not, many firms look to information technology as a key weapon in their strategic arsenal.

When one considers what kinds of competitive advantage firms hope to achieve using information technology, one finds a depressingly high proportion of firms hoping to reduce competition through raising switching costs, reducing the amount of information available to the customer, and so forth – that is, using information technology to secure a local monopoly.[21] Depressing, because innovations in the service sector, or in the distribution, marketing, or purchasing functions of manufacturing enterprises, do little to counter the concern that North American enterprises are becoming "hollow corporations."[22] Meanwhile, a naive faith in technological silver bullets diverts manufacturers from the hard work of rebuilding North America's industrial base, and tempts them into alarming, high-risk forays toward the factory of the future. A recent report describes the experience of Deere and Company:

The giant farm equipment manufacturer broke fresh ground a decade ago with factory automation that was then regarded as the model for all others to emulate. FMS technology worth $1.5 billion was designed to provide a choice of 5,000 process changes on ten basic tractor models.

As Deere had to weather a depressed farm equipment market and then a strike, it became apparent that the company had invested too much in its state-of-the-art FMS without regard to the process being automated. . . .

Billion-dollar losses were followed by rationalization of the production process, and today automated manufacturing at Deere is a much more organized, simplified affair. John Lardner, a company vice-president, said: "The FMS was a retrofit to a production design problem that shouldn't have existed in the first place."[23]

Manufacturing competitiveness is the only enduring base for a viable modern economy. Information technology will play a key role in transforming manufacturing. But not now, not for most firms. For them it is the hard road of conventional process improvement and production system organization that will lead to manufacturing competitiveness.

The author wishes to thank I. A. Litvak for his comments on this paper.

Notes

1 R. I. Benjamin, J. F. Rockart, M. S. Scott Morton, et al., "Information Technology: A Strategic Opportunity," *Sloan Management Review*, Spring 1984, pp. 3–10; Cyert, R. M., "The Plight of Manufacturing: What Can Be Done?" *Issues in Science and Technology*, vol. 1, 1985, pp. 87–100.

2 J. R. Galbraith, *Organization Design* (Reading, MA, Addison-Wesley, 1977).

3 R. McClean, "Quality and Productivity at Northern Telecom," in *Proceedings of the Fourth Annual Operations Management Association Meeting*, 1985, pp. 1–9.

4 "Less is More in Automation," *IBM Engineering/Scientific Innovation*, Fall 1986, pp. 4–5.

5 W. K. Holstein and W. L. Berry, "Work Flow Structure: An Analysis for Planning and Control," *Management Science*, vol. 16, February, 1970, pp. B324–B336.

6 N. L. Hyer, and U Wemmerlöv, "Group Technology and Productivity," *Harvard Business Review*, July–August, 1984, pp. 140–9.

7   M. Jelinek and J. D. Goldhar, "The Strategic Implications of the Factory of the Future," *Sloan Management Review*, Summer 1984, pp. 29–37.

8   P. Huang and B. Houck, "Cellular Manufacturing: An Overview and Bibliography," *Production and Inventory Management*, Fourth Quarter, 1985, pp. 83–92.

9   S. Shingo, *A Revolution in Manufacturing: The SMED System* (Stamford, CT, Productivity Press, 1985).

10 U. Wemmerlöv and N. L. Hyer, "Research Issues in Cellular Manufacturing," *International Journal of Production Research*, vol. 25, March, 1987, pp. 413–31.

11 R. Jaikumar, "Postindustrial Manufacturing," *Harvard Business Review*, November–December, 1986, pp. 69–76.

12 J. C. Anderson, R. G. Schroeder, S. E. Tupy et al., "Material Requirements Planning Systems: The State of the Art," *Production and Inventory Management*, Fourth Quarter, 1982, pp. 51–66.

13 R. W. Hall, *Zero Inventories* (Homewood, IL: Dow Jones–Irwin, 1983); R. Schonberger, "Applications of Single-Card and Dual-Card Kanban," *Interfaces*, August, 1983, pp. 56–67; "Integrated Manufacturing: Nothing Succeeds Like Successful Implementation," *Production Engineering*, May, 1987, pp. IM4–IM32.

14 S. Chapman and M Schimke, "Towards a Theoretical Understanding of Just-in-time Manufacturing," *Operations Management Review*, Summer 1986, pp. 32–6.

15 R. C. Walleigh, "What's Your Excuse for Not Using JIT?" *Harvard Business Review*, March–April, 1986, pp. 38–54.

16 "What Did IBM Buy for $22 Billion?" *Computerworld*, June 15, 1987, pp. 69–83.

17 Schonberger, "Applications of Kanban."

18 L. J. Krajewski, B. E. King, L. P. Ritzman et al., "Kanban, MRP, and Shaping the Manufacturing Environment," *Management Science, 33*, January 1987, pp. 39–57.

19 M. E. Porter and V. E. Millar, "How Information Gives You Competitive Advantage," *Harvard Business Review*, July–August, 1985, pp. 149–60.

20 "Management's Newest Star: Meet the Chief Information Officer," *Business Week*, October 13, 1986, pp. 160–72.

21 G. L. Parsons, "Information Technology: A New Competitive Weapon," *Sloan Management Review*, Fall 1983, pp. 3–14; B. Ives and G. P. Learmonth, "The Information System as a Competitive Weapon," *Communications of the ACM*, December, 1984, pp. 1193–201; J. Y. Bakos and M. E. Treacy, "Information Technology and Corporate Strategy: A Research Perspective," *MIS Quarterly*, June, 1986, pp. 107–19.

22 "The Hollow Corporation," *Business Week*, March 3, 1986, pp. 56–78.

23 T. Davis, "Manufacturers Revise Their Strategy on Factory Automation," *Globe and Mail* (Toronto) July 4, 1987, p. B7.

Technological Revolution and Productivity Decline: The Case of US Banks

Richard H. Franke

What Bowen and Warner have done for offices and factories, Franke does for banks (albeit in a different style!). In this impressive paper, the author shows that computerization of US banks was associated initially with a decline in the productivity of capital and a fall in profits. Although there are now definite signs of an improvement, it will still be some time (like early in the twenty-first century) before we reap the economic benefits of IT, says Franke. The author is Professor of Management at the Sellinger School of Business and Management, Loyola College, Baltimore, MD, and this piece is adapted from an article which appeared in Technological Forecasting and Social Change, *vol. 31, 1987, pp. 143–54.*

Introduction

Major technological change may not yield productivity improvement in the short term. For example, during the British Industrial Revolution following the introduction of Watt's coal-fired steam engine in 1775, there were not early increases of output and efficiency. Instead, time appears to have been needed for technology diffusion and for human and organizational adjustment. It was not until the 1820s, about a half century later, that there began substantial increases of output, productivity, and income (von Tunzelmann, 1981; Harley, 1982; Crafts, 1983, 1985; Lindert and Williamson, 1983, 1985; Schwartz, 1985). Economic benefits from the Industrial Revolution may have been delayed through the crowding-out of industrial investment by British government debt for military expenditures (Williamson, 1984, 1985). On the other hand, introduction of new technology might also be fostered through application to military needs, with national debt used to leverage economic power (Raster and Thompson, 1983, but see Melman, 1983, 1986). Under similar conditions, a second technological transformation now has progressed in the United States, its place of origin, since the introduction of reliable computers in the 1950s (Rosen, 1983).

Although impacts on society are not yet clear (Danziger, 1985), it does appear that work and life have begun to change in what promises to be "the biggest technological revolution men have known, far more intimately affecting men's daily lives . . . than either the agricultural transformation in Neolithic times or the early industrial revolution" (Snow, 1966, p. 652).

The purpose of this paper is to appraise the impact of the computer upon economic performance. This is attempted by analysis of apparent effects in the initial large industry to adopt computers. The first major sector of the US economy to employ the technology widely was the financial industry, beginning in the 1950s. Introduction of standard procedures for magnetic ink character recognition in 1958 made possible the financial industry's "breakthrough of electronic data processing" and a rise of computer use by commercial banks to 97 percent by 1980 (Brand and Duke, 1982, pp. 22–3; Ernst, 1985). Applications include check handling, administration and bookkeeping, ongoing credit analysis, electronic funds transfer, and automated teller machines. Computers facilitated expansion of services and the growth of branch banking, but they also accounted for much of the industry's growing capital input. By 1980, half of banks' fixed capital expenditure other than for structures was for computers and accessories (Brand and Duke, 1982), and other capital expenditure was computer-related.

Expected positive effects from the introduction of computer technology were increased growth of labor and/or capital productivity, achieved either by accelerated output growth or by decreases in the growth of labor or capital inputs. However, expectations do not seem to have been realized (Baily, 1986). As noted by Strassmann (1985), there are hidden costs of fitting computers into office work processes, which can delay performance benefits. Financial industry productivity stagnated during the 1970s (Grossman and Sadler, 1962), as clerical employment continued its long-term expansion (Roessner, 1985). While integrating people and organizations in a new order of work can be costly, it is especially the huge capital outlay for computing equipment that appears to have affected the industry negatively. In America's financial industry, a key sector of a capitalistic economy, performance per unit of capital seems particularly important and is the focus of study here.

Analytical method

Data for the financial industry (banking and insurance) over the 36 years from 1948 to 1983, obtained from the American Productivity Center (1984), were based on US Department of Commerce and other statistics. Industry output and inputs were formulated as indices recalculated to equal 100 for the initial year (1948). Output was the real product (inflation-adjusted value added) of the industry, based upon deposit turnover, new insurance written, and sales of stocks and bonds (Kendrick and Grossman, 1980). Capital was viewed as a real cost, regardless of rates of utilization. Capital input estimates were of real capital stock, proportionate to real gross stocks of tangible capital in structures, land, equipment, and inventories. Assuming adequate maintenance, deterioration with age in output-producing capacity was not considered substantial prior to retirement. Real investments remaining in stock from prior years' outlays (not retired) were summed to obtain total real gross capital stock (Kendrick, 1976; Kendrick and Grossman, 1980). Labor input was the number of person-hours worked, without weighting by occupational category (Kendrick and Grossman, 1980).

Combining these elements, total factor input was a weighted sum of the two inputs (Kendrick, 1961; Kendrick and Grossman, 1980), capital intensity was computed as the ratio of capital to labor input, total factor productivity was the ratio of output to total factor input, and the partial productivities of labor and of capital were computed as the ratios of total output to labor and to capital. Data tracing technological changes in computers and changes in background economic conditions were compared. Technology developed from vacuum tubes to transistors, integrated circuits, and metal oxide semiconductors, representing the first through fourth generations of computers (Ralston and Reilly, 1983). In the current fourth generation, microcomputers based on 16-bit microprocessors have accelerated the pace of computer application (Calhoun, 1981; Ilan and Shapira, 1986).

Analysis relates the productivity of capital in the US financial industry, first, to the level of capital intensity – largely from investment in computers and accessories – and, then, to the changing technology of computing equipment and to changing economic conditions. Stepwise multiple regression is employed in time series analyses over 36 years. Technological and economic background variables are entered following capital intensity – subject to significance constraint ($p < 0.10$, two-tailed), to monitoring serial correlation, and to monitoring multicollinearity for results consistent with first-order observations (cf. Franke, 1980, pp. 1010–13).

A second analysis replicates the US financial industry study at a lower level of aggregation to test generalizability and applicability of results (cf. Franke and Kaul, 1978, n. 11), using data obtained from a large Northeastern bank for 1960–84. The dependent variable in this analysis is capital profitability, or real return on equity, with before-tax net income and equity capital expressed in 1972 dollars (cumulation of real equity valued at times of acquisition). Again, multiple regression evaluates effects of technological and economic factors in addition to capital intensity.

Results: performance of the financial industry

As shown in figure 8.1, industry output rose fourfold over 1948–83. Output growth was 4.7 percent/year from 1948 to 1958, but declined to 3.6 percent/year coincident with the expansion of computer use from 1958 to 1983. Capital input rose 14-fold overall, growing 2.7 percent/year up to 1958 but 9.8 percent/year thereafter – with investment increasingly concentrated in computers, in ancillary equipment and structures, and in facilities such as branch banks made feasible by computers. Labor hours rose almost threefold overall. After 1958, with decreased output growth and increased capital investment, a decline in the growth rate of labor input might have been expected. Instead the growth of labor rose slightly, from 2.8 percent/year before 1958 to 3.1 percent/year over the next quarter century.

Financial industry capital intensity, labor productivity, and capital productivity are presented in figure 8.2. Capital stock per labor hour declined slightly in the late 1940s and early 1950s, but rose fivefold from 1958 to 1983. Labor productivity rose more slowly after 1958 than before, peaking in 1975 at a level 41 percent above the 1948 figure, and declining slightly over the subsequent 8 years. Perhaps most important as an index of business performance in a capitalistic economy, capital productivity rose over a quarter by 1957, but with

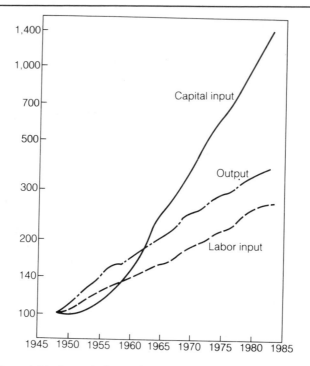

Figure 8.1 Financial industry indices of output, capital output, and labor input in real terms (semilogarithmic, 1948 = 100).

more rapid computer introduction after 1958 began a steady decline. By 1983, capital productivity had decreased to a level only 28 percent of that in 1948 and 22 percent of the peak value achieved in 1957, just prior to the accelerated introduction of computers.

From the plots in figure 8.2, it is apparent that the industry's increasing ratio of capital to labor inputs explains much of the dramatic decline in capital productivity which began in 1958. Indeed, since capital productivity is the ratio of output to capital, any increase in capital investment which did not bring forth a compensating labor productivity increase would lead to declining capital productivity.

Regression on capital intensity does explain much of the variance in capital productivity, yielding a negative slope coefficient. The coefficient of determination is 88 percent, but there is severe serial correlation (a low Durbin–Watson coefficient), suggesting that additional explanatory variables remain to be specified. The equation is presented below:

capital productivity = 134.43 (t = 35.18[a]) − 0.27 capital intensity (t = − 16.04[a]),
variance explanation = 88.33%,
Durbin–Watson coefficient = 0.11 (significant serial correlation).

[a] p appears < 0.00005, neglecting serial correlation.

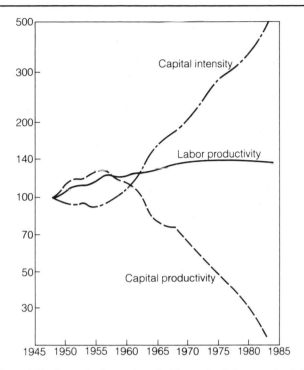

Figure 8.2 Financial industry indices of capital intensity, labor productivity, and capital productivity (semilogarithmic, 1948 = 100).

Differences between actual levels of capital productivity in the financial industry and those predicted by this regression equation were calculated for 1948–83. The residual moved fairly smoothly from year to year, as indicated by a low index of serial correlation. However, it appeared that the difference between actual and expected capital productivity was related to the computer technology available at the time, with the residual pattern changing direction at times of technological change.

Stepwise regression on the technical and economic variables yields a more comprehensive equation for the dependent variable of capital productivity:

	Intercepts	Slope coefficients
capital productivity =	150.67 (t = 73.53[b])	capital −0.53[b] intensity (t = −22.69[b])
	—	+2.80 pre-MICR yrs (t = 18.06[b])
	+23.61 (t = 14.95[b]) when MICR	−1.80 MICR yrs (t = −5.38[b])
	−39.96 (t = −16.16[b])	

[b] $p < 0.00005.$

when Comp. Gen. 3
$- 37.22$ ($t = -10.69^b$) $+ 2.80$ Comp. Gen. 4 yrs ($t = 5.84^b$)
when Comp. Gen. 4
$+ 9.79$ ($t = -5.01^b$) $+ 9.76$ microcomp. yrs ($t = 13.41^b$)
when microcomputers
— $+ 0.20$ GNP growth ($t = 1.94^c$),
variance explanation = 99.86% (99.80% corrected),
Durbin–Watson coefficient = 2.10 (little serial correlation).

Intercepts indicate residual value at the time of technological change, while slope coefficients show yearly rate of change in capital productivity while the new technology is adopted. It appears that, holding constant the negative impact of increasing capital intensity, productivity tended upward until reversed by accelerated computer use following introduction of magnetic ink character recognition (MICR) in 1958. Incremental decline halted with the introduction of third generation computers, and there were positive influences from the fourth computer generation and from microcomputer technology. Finally, productivity was slightly higher with stronger national economic growth. The equation explains all but 0.2 percent of the variance in capital productivity over the 36-year period, with little serial correlation to indicate misspecification and inhibit significance testing.

Results: performance of a large Northeastern bank

Replication tests industry-level results in an individual bank. The initial equation for real before-tax return on equity is presented below:

capital profitability = 29.64 ($t = 4.59^a$) $- 0.34$ capital intensity ($t = 2.67^d$),
variance explanation = 23.62%,
Durbin–Watson coefficient = 0.46 (significant serial correlation).

As for capital productivity in the industry as a whole, the bank's capital profitability is associated negatively with increasing capital intensity (real equity per employee). However, there is relatively low variance explanation, which together with significant serial correlation indicates that additional explanatory variables remain to be specified.

Analysis appraising additional effects of technological and economic changes yields the following equation:

	Intercepts	Slope coefficients
capital		capital
profitability =	21.99 ($t = 6.25^b$)	$- 0.13$ intensity ($t = -1.86^c$)
	—	$- 1.26$ ATM yrs ($t = -8.26^b$)
	—	$+ 1.62$ reg. proc. yrs ($t = 4.93^b$),

variance explanation = 84.81% (82.64% corrected),
Durbin–Watson coefficient = 1.78 (no significant serial correlation).

[c] $p < 0.10$.
[d] p appears < 0.05, neglecting serial correlation.

Multiple regression indicates that installation of automatic teller machines (ATMs) beginning in 1972 was associated with decreased real return on equity, the technological variable adding to negative effects of increasing capital intensity. Beginning in 1978, the banks' establishment of integrated regional data processing centers, eliminating numerous peripheral systems, appears to have led to some performance recovery. However, by 1984 the profitability of capital had regained only about half the level extant prior to the more intensive introduction of computer technology. Over 80 percent of the variance in the bank's before-tax real return on equity is explained, in an equation which is free of serial correlation.

Extension to other industry

By 1982 in US industry, a third of all investment in producer's durable equipment was for computer equipment. Yet there is no conclusive evidence as to the profitability of this investment (Strassman, 1985, p. 152; Baily, 1986). Computer adoption has coincided with productivity decline in the machine tool industry (Melman, 1983), and since the mid-1960s in manufacturing industry as a whole (Franke, 1983). In addition, analysis at the firm level for 138 wholesalers by Cron and Sobol (1983) showed higher returns on assets in organizations without computers. Some medium and heavy users of the computer obtained high ROAs, but more experienced higher operating expense and lower capital profitability. In industry other than finance, the computer revolution also coincided with diminished economic performance, and it seems possible that costs of adapting to new conditions of work may be responsible for declines which cannot be explained otherwise (Denison, 1984).

Conclusion

Thus far in the second major transformation of industrial economies, as in the early decades of the first technological revolution (Deane, 1965), there appears to have been more technical progress than economic success. Analysis in this paper indicates that the adoption of computer technology initially led to decreased capital productivity and profitability. The transformation of the US financial industry, an early adopter of computers, has resulted in movement from low to moderately high capital intensity during recent decades, bringing this traditionally labor-intensive industry's capital/labor ratio up to about 60 percent that of the business economy as a whole. With the rapid increase in capital intensity, the financial industry experienced sharp decline in the productivity of capital. Although this decrease could have been exaggerated by statistical understatement of qualitative improvement (Baily, 1986), profitability also declined. Real return on equity of the large bank analyzed here dropped below 10 percent before taxes, to half the level of 1960. By the mid-1980s bank failures were numerous (*Fortune*, 1986). It appears that the primary economic effect of the large-scale adoption of computers has been to raise capital intensity without proportionately increasing output or the productivity of labor, and thus initially to reduce the productivity and profitability of capital.

Leontief and Duchin (1986, p. 25) observed that:

the great industrial revolution inaugurated by the introduction of mechanical power continued to transform western economies and society over a period of some 200 years. The computer revolution became visible only a few years ago, and by the year 2000 it will be no more advanced than the mechanization of European economies had advanced by, let us say, the year 1820.

According to this assessment, it will be early in the twenty-first century when the accumulated experience in producing and using the equipment of the second technological revolution leads to more effective utilization of human and capital resources and to major increases in output.

Just as Britain assumed world leadership while its entrepreneurs were introducing the tools of the first technological revolution, the United States's clear ascendancy to leadership coincided with its introduction of the tools for the second revolution. As has been observed (Melman, 1983; Rasfer and Thompson, 1983; Williamson, 1985), heavy military expenditures in Britain and the United States may have delayed effective application of new technology. But that can be only part of the explanation for economic malaise in the early stages of technological revolution. Fundamental changes in the distribution and organization of work, due to the new technology, result initially in diseconomies. Only with time can enterprises adjust to become productive (Haustein and Neuwirth, 1982).

In the first large US industry to adopt computers, signs of improvement already can be discerned. Early in the next century, the machinery of the second technological revolution may become generally useful, removing humans one step further away from uninspiring and routine work and providing a basis for dramatic economic expansion.

The author is grateful for assistance with company and industry analysis by Pamela S. Glasgow, Gregory L. Stephenson, Patricia J. White, Linda S. Robinson, Karen A. Miller, and Tomai A. Webb; for suggestions by Walter R. Holman and by referees; for guidance in economic history from Ed Duggan; and for editing by Elke K. Franke.

References

American Productivity Center (1984), *Multiple Input Productivity Indexes*, American Productivity Center, Houston, vol. 5(1).

Baily, Martin Neil (1986), "What has happened to productivity growth?" *Science*, vol. 234, pp. 443–51.

Brand, Horst and Duke, John (1982) "Productivity in commercial banking: computers spur the advance," *Monthly Labor Review*; vol. 105(12). pp. 19–27.

Calhoun, Craig J. (1981), "The microcomputer revolution? Technical possibilities and social choices," *Sociological Methods and Research*, vol. 9. pp. 397–437.

Crafts, N. F. R. (1983), "British economic growth, 1700–1831: a review of the evidence," *Economic History Review*; vol 36, pp. 177–99.

Crafts, N. F. R. (1985), "English workers' real wages during the Industrial Revolution: some remaining problems," *Journal of Economic History*, vol. 45, pp. 139–44.

Cron, William L. and Sobol, Marion G. (1983), "The relationship between computerization and performance: a strategy for maximizing the economic benefits of computerization," *Information and Management*, vol. 6, pp. 171–81.

Danziger, James N. (1985), "Social science and the social impacts of computer technology," *Social Science Quarterly*, vol. 66, pp. 3–21.

Deane, Phyllis (1965), *The First Industrial Revolution*, Cambridge: Cambridge University Press.

Denison, Edward L. (1984), "Accounting for slower economic growth: an update," in John W. Kendrick (ed.), *International Comparisons of Productivity and Causes of the Slowdown*, Cambridge, MA: Ballinger.

Ernst, Martin L. (1985), "Electronics in commerce," in Tom Forester (ed.), *The Information Technology Revolution*, Cambridge, MA: MIT Press.

Fortune (1986), "The FDIC wants more muscle," vol. 113(8), p. 10.

Franke, Richard H. (1980), "Worker productivity at Hawthorne," *American Sociological Review*, vol. 45, pp. 1006–27.

Franke, Richard H. (1983), "The impact of cybernetics technology upon management, labor, and productivity in the United States," paper presented at the Tsukuba Conference on the Problems of Bureaucracy in the Advanced Industrial Societies, Tsukuba, Japan.

Franke, Richard H. and Kaul, James D. (1978), "The Hawthorne Experiments: first statistical interpretation," *American Sociological Review*, vol. 43, pp. 623–43.

Grossman, Elliott S. and Sadler, George E. (1982), *Comparative Productivity Dynamics*, American Productivity Center, Houston.

Harley, C. Knick (1982), "British industrialization before 1841: evidence of slower growth during the Industrial Revolution," *Journal of Economic History*, vol. 42, pp. 267–89.

Haustein, Heinz-Dieter and Neuwirth, Erich (1982), "Long waves in world industrial production, energy, consumption, innovation, inventions, and patents and their identification by spectral analysis," *Technological Forecasting and Social Change*, vol. 22, pp. 53–89.

Ilan, Yael and Shapira, Zur (1986), "The introduction and use of microcomputers by professionals in an industrial corporation," *Technological Forecasting and Social Change*, vol. 29. pp. 183–94.

Kendrick, John W. (1961), *Productivity Trends in the United States*, National Bureau of Economic Research, Washington, DC.

Kendrick, John W. (1976), *The National Wealth of the United States by Major Sector and Industry*, Report No. 698, The Conference Board, New York.

Kendrick, John W. and Grossman, Elliot S. (1980), *Productivity in the United States: Trends and Cycles*, Baltimore, MD: Johns Hopkins University Press.

Leontief, Wassily W. and Duchin, Faye (1986), *The Future Impact of Automation on Workers*, New York: Oxford University Press.

Lindert, Peter H. and Williamson, Jeffrey G, (1983), "English workers' living standards during the Industrial Revolution: a new look," *Economic History Review*, vol. 36, pp. 1 25.

Lindert, Peter H. and Williamson, Jeffrey G. (1985), "English workers' real wages: reply to Crafts," *Journal of Economic History*, vol. 45, pp. 145–53.

Melman, Seymour (1983), *Profits without Production*, New York: Knopf.

Melman, Seymour (1986), "Swords into plowshares: converting from military to civilian production," *Technology Review*, vol. 89, pp. 62–71.

Ralston, Anthony and Reilly, Edwin D., Jr (eds) (1983), *Encyclopedia of Computer Science and Engineering*, 2nd edn, New York: Van Nostrand.

Rasler, Karen A. and Thompson, William R. (1983), "Global wars, public debts, and the long cycle," *World Politics*, vol. 35, pp. 489–516.

Roessner, J. David (1985), "Forecasting the impact of office automation on clerical employment, 1985–2000," *Technological Forecasting and Social Change*, vol. 28, pp. 203–16.

Rosen, S. (1983), "Contemporary and future," in Anthony Ralston and Edwin D. Reilly, Jr (eds), *Encyclopedia of Computer Science and Engineering*, 2nd edn, New York: Van Nostrand.

Schwarz, L.D. (1985), "The standard of living in the long run: London, 1700–1860," *Economic History Review*, vol. 38, pp. 24–41.

Snow, C.P. (1966), "Government, science, and public policy," *Science*, vol. 151, pp. 650–3.

Strassmann, Paul A. (1985), *Information Payoff: The Transformation of Work in the Electronic Age*, New York: Free Press.

von Tunzelmann, G.N. (1981), "Technical progress during the Industrial Revolution," in Roderick

Flaud and Donald McCloskey (eds), *The Economic History of Britain Since 1700*, vol. 1: *1700–1860*, Cambridge: Cambridge University Press.

Williamson, Jeffrey G. (1984), "Why was British growth so slow during the Industrial Revolution?" *Journal of Economic History*, vol. 44, pp. 687–712.

Williamson, Jeffrey G. (1985), "The historical content of the classical labor surplus model," *Population and Development Review*, vol. 11, pp. 171–91.

9 People and Computers in Factories

The Automated Factory: Vision and Reality

Harley Shaiken

In this clear statement of the argument that computers "de-skill" workers and degrade the quality of working life, Harley Shaiken contends that managers don't like skilled workers because they are semi-autonomous: therefore managers intent on control seek to remove skill from workers and to transfer it to machines. This article, reporting on work carried out for the US Office of Technology Assessment, is reprinted from Technology Review, *January 1985. It also reflects the argument in Shaiken's book,* Work Transformed: Automation and Labor in the Computer Age *(Holt, Rinehart and Winston, New York, 1985).*

As usual, at last year's International Machine Tool Show, held in the cavernous exhibition halls of McCormack Center on the edge of Lake Michigan, manufacturers displayed acres of computer-controlled machining centers, lathes, grinders, robots, and other automated equipment. These machines shape raw blocks of metal into the precision parts essential for any advanced industrial economy – from the parts that make up the wings of Boeing 747s to those used to build machines that package breakfast cereals.

The latest trend at the show, as throughout industry, is to use computers to link individual pieces of automated production equipment into automatic manufacturing cells, or even entire factories. Walking down the aisles in Chicago, you can envision vast plants operating under the control of a handful of skilled technicians. All that is needed to increase productivity spectacularly is to move these machines from the show to the factory floor. And no doubt workers will benefit from more satisfying high-technology jobs.

However, visions of automation that seem fine at machine-tool shows ignore the actual experience of supervisors and workers on the factory floor. To begin with, although computer-based technologies can indeed help make jobs more satisfying, that is often not what actually happens. In their attempt to create the automatically controlled factory, managers and engineers often wind up making jobs as tedious as those on the assembly line.

A skilled machinist I talked with who had been assigned to operate a computerized machine tool said he felt like a "rat in a cage." The machine had not eliminated his job – but was used in a way that degraded it by requiring little creative input. "You don't have time to light a cigarette," said a worker on a robotic welding system. "I'd take my old job hand welding any day."

Manufacturing systems never seem to break down at machine tool shows, but I have visited automated factories that were down a third or more of the time. The cause is not hard to discover. Reducing human input often means instituting complex technologies that are prone to trouble. To put it another way, the drive to eliminate uncertainties arising from human influence only winds up creating mechanical and electronic uncertainties. Thus, despite the vision of total automation, workers must in the end play critical roles in operating, as well as unjamming and repairing, computer-based production systems.

Too often public debate centers simply on figuring out how to automate as rapidly as possible, rather than on finding ways to develop and install the best technology – one that both improves life on the job and provides efficient production.

Along with my MIT colleagues Steven Herzenberg and Sarah Kuhn, I recently had the opportunity to explore the way automation affects worklife. As part of a project by the congressional Office of Technology Assessment to study computer-based automation in factories, we visited an automobile plant, a commercial aircraft plant, an agricultural equipment plant, and seven small metalworking shops. These firms differ in many respects, but all are leading and experienced users of automation.

We agreed not to divulge company names and in exchange were allowed a free hand to observe factories and obtain private interviews with everyone from top management to hourly workers. When I presented our findings to engineers who had actually designed many of the kinds of equipment we studied, some were surprised to learn about traps that they had not imagined would occur on the road to automation.

The individual machinists

Before the arrival of computer-based automation, the machinist's skill provided the missing link between a blueprint and a finished part. Using intricate fixtures and making careful measurements, machinists would orient parts to be machined in just the right way, and would then turn the necessary cranks and run the cutting tools.

In numerical control (NC), a computer punches holes in a paper or plastic tape, and when the tape is fed into a machine tool, these holes control the way it cuts metal. Most of the shops we studied used computer numerical control (CNC), a newer form of the technology in which a computer at the machine directly controls its operation. Both NC and CNC (the terms are often used interchangeably) can be far superior technically to manual control. The computer is able to guide the cutting tool through complex arcs and angles that no machinist could duplicate. Furthermore, intricate fixtures to hold parts at special angles are often unnecessary. Since all operations are preprogrammed, NC enables a machine to proceed from cut to cut far more rapidly than is possible with manual control, thereby reducing the time required to make a part. However, the machinist must still set up the workpiece to be cut, make adjustments to correct for tool wear, and stop the machine if anything goes wrong.

The technology of CNC leaves a wide latitude as to who programs the computer. At one extreme, a full-time parts programmer sits in front of a video screen and determines how a part will be made. At the other extreme, a machinist does the same thing at a minicomputer at the machine.

There are sometimes compelling technical reasons for programming to be done off the shop floor. Devising long, complex programs may require intricate calculations taking several days. In other cases, it may be more efficient for machinists to write programs – particularly for making simpler parts. Operators at the machines are also especially well situated for debugging flawed programs. For example, in one shop we visited, a program called for making a heavy cut across a block of aluminum – an operation that generates considerable heat – and then boring two holes a precise distance apart. When the steps were carried out in this order, the distance between the holes decreased as the aluminum cooled. The machinist was able to correct the problem by editing the program to drill the holes first.

Managers in the small shops we visited organized production on CNC machines in different ways. In one shop, prototype machinists, who make the initial prototypes of parts, did the programming. Another shop rotated some machinists through the programming department. However, in the vast majority of cases, the responsibility for writing instructions for the machines had been removed from the shop floor and given to programmers working in offices, even when this was far from optimal technically.

Understanding why requires taking a look at owners' motivations in introducing CNC. They told us they introduced CNC partly to improve the machines' speed and flexibility, but also to tighten control over shop operations. By concentrating planning in the relatively small, white-collar programming department, they believed they could specify more uniform procedures for carrying out jobs. Also, since programmers are not responsible for actually running the machines, they have little incentive to use programming to slow the pace of production, the owners felt. As the officers of the Numerical Control Society, an organization of managers and engineers concerned with computers in manufacturing, wrote in 1981, CNC has put important decisions "in the hands of managerial and professional personnel rather than machine operators."

Shop owners were also concerned by what they saw as a shortage of skilled machinists and by the leverage of those who were available. "Five, six years ago, we were very dependent on skilled labor, to the point where I spent half my life on my hands and knees begging somebody to stay and do something," said one shop owner. "Machinists tend to be prima donnas. This is one of the motivations for bringing in NC equipment. It reduced our dependence on skilled labor." Another shop owner was so impressed by the power of CNC that he was considering firing most of his ten employees and starting over with a more amenable group. "Sometimes too much knowledge is dangerous," he said.

In practice, visions of firing the entire shop floor workforce and hiring pliable new people off the street are probably not workable. Nor can CNC eliminate the need for machining skill somewhere in the production process. However, managers did report that this technology gave them more control in determining which jobs require that skill. They could employ machinists with considerably less expertise than that needed to run conventional tools – in effect moving that skill to the programming department.

However, using the lowest level of skill necessary to run CNC machines is not necessarily the way to make production most efficient from a technical standpoint – especially in machining small quantities of intricate parts. Not only can machinists contribute to programming; they must also often intervene in operations even after the program has been debugged, many owners admitted. An operator may find that the rough casting to be machined is larger than the programmer expected and thus requires more cutting. An alloy may turn out to be harder than expected, in which case the part must be fed more slowly into the cutting tool. "In a small business, when you invest a lot of money in a piece of NC equipment you don't want to save two dollars an hour by putting an unskilled operator on it," said one head of manufacturing engineering. "The higher the operator's skill, the more we get out of the machine."

The paradox is that, though skill and experience are required for operators of some CNC equipment, that very skill and experience may make operators dislike the equipment. Skilled machinists were particularly frustrated by CNC if they did no programming. "I'm a worker, not a sitter," said one. "I like to be kept busy. My day goes by faster, my mind is more active. You get a little weak-minded on NC." Another complained that CNC "was supposed to be made idiot-proof," and that he would rather quit than run such a machine full time. "The hardest thing to do is to keep yourself on your toes checking the measurements," said a machinist at the aircraft-manufacturing plant. "Just because the tape says the part is good doesn't mean that it necessarily is. But you get to relying on that tape because of the boredom. You know, you'd just as soon put another part in and sit down again."

Not surprisingly, managers do not find it easy to fill such jobs. "You'll find somebody who can do the job," admitted one shop floor supervisor. "but once he's learned it, he'll get quickly bored and want to do something else."

It is true that machinists who formerly loaded hundreds of identical parts on conventional machines generally preferred CNC machines. The new technology tends to make work cleaner and physically lighter – not so much because of computer control as because of mechanical improvements. For example, workpieces are often shielded while being cut, preventing the dispersion of small metal particles and the cooling fluids that are sprayed on the cutting tools.

Skilled machinists, who had formerly planned production on conventional machines, told us that they would be more interested in using CNC machines if they had responsibility for writing programs. "Get a good operator and give him a chance to do set up and learn how to program the machine," said a machinist in a small shop. "That way he can look at the readout and understand what the machine is doing, not just stand there." The chance to program would not eliminate boredom during long running times or repeated production of a single type of part, but it would make jobs more creative and could increase productivity. Some machinists said that they already do some programming unofficially and felt that managers should give them formal recognition for it.

Spy in the sky

CNC enhances managerial control in the workplace but does not make it complete. This technology affects only what happens when a part is actually being machined – and not, for example, how parts move from one production step to another through the shop. And machinists have a certain measure of control even while a part is being cut. They usually have a dial to override programmed feed rates (the rates at which workpieces are fed into cutting tools) to compensate for special factors such as unexpectedly hard alloys. Thus, operators can slow down or speed up the work pace.

To secure more control over this aspect of the machinist's job, and to better estimate the efficiency of the operation, the managers at the aircraft company implemented a computerized monitoring system on 66 NC machines. The system categorizes each machine as running, running at less than 80 percent of programmed feed rate, temporarily halted, or down. A panel in a control room above the shop floor displays the status of each machine with colored lights. A supervisor can check these lights and gain further information by glancing out at the floor below. Daily reports tell supervisors not only about production levels, but also about how each worker spends his or her time. Upper management receives weekly and monthly reports. Obviously, such a system has the potential to weave an electronic net of control through the shop.

Shop floor workers generally tolerate the monitoring system, in part because of an agreement between the company and the union that the system will not be used for disciplinary purposes. Nevertheless, some operators told us that individual supervisors do use the system to exercise subtle discipline, constantly telling operators that their feed rates are too low. "It's like having a big television camera looking over my shoulder," said one machinist. The workers sardonically refer to the system as the "spy in the sky."

Management set up the system to ensure that the machines are operated at over 80 percent of the programmed feed rate. However, the system has no way of evaluating whether that feed was established correctly in the first place: the programmer could have set it faster – or slower – than was practical. And of course, if the rate is too slow, machinists have little incentive to raise it: since the programmers are so sure they are right, why not just let the machine poke along?

The information that the system produces may also be extremely misleading. One machinist told us that he had to work long and furiously to set up a particularly intricate part to be cut. As a result, his machine sat idle most of the day. While he felt that he had never worked harder, his supervisor reprimanded him because the system reported that his machine was idle.

The domino effect

A common managerial vision is to combine CNC machine tools, automated carts, robots, and other computer-controlled equipment into an entire production unit – a flexible manufacturing system (FMS) – that can run with as little human intervention as possible. An aspect of this vision was expressed bluntly in a survey report published in the September 1981 issue of *Iron Age*, a respected trade journal: "Workers and their unions have too much say in manufacturers' destiny, many metalworking executives feel, and large, sophisticated FMSs can help wrest some of that control away from labor and put it back in the hands of management, where it belongs."

One FMS we visited – in effect, a computer-controlled machine shop – produces transmission cases and clutch housings for a line of heavy-duty tractors. At one end of the system, workers load a large iron casting on to a chain-driven cart. Guided by computers, the cart carries this workpiece to one of 12 computer-controlled machine tools. Here it is unloaded, machined, reloaded, and shuttled off to another station. A complex formula ensures that the various operations are scheduled efficiently. Finally, workers unload precision-machined cases and housings – untouched, at least in theory, by human hands.

Three supervisors and 11 production workers are assigned to the day shift, fewer to the other two shifts. One operator is responsible for every three machines, changing tools when the computer indicates it is time, inspecting parts to be sure they are correctly cut, cleaning the area, and solving any problems.

The system is intended to minimize operator intervention – particularly in setting the pace of production. "You don't have people you're relying on," said the project manager. "Once the computerized system gets the part, it doesn't wait for a guy who is drinking a cup of coffee." Another manager noted that "quality is no longer dependent on the skill of an individual operator."

However, there is something of a dichotomy between what the managers of an FMS intend and what actually happens. Though the project manager spoke of not having to rely on people, he also admitted that operators must minister to this complex system with considerable "tender loving care." A tool may wear in such a way that it fails to cut accurately, or the boring head, which turns and maneuvers the cutting tool, may be slightly out of alignment. In both cases the operator has to make sensitive adjustments. Or a cart may jam and have to be unstuck.

Problems inevitably occur in such complex electronic systems, and when they do, they can spread in a domino effect. The planners of the FMS were able to limit this effect to some extent by designing the system with some redundancy. If one machining center goes down, the program and the part can be shuttled to another. However, it is hard to foresee all eventualities. Even the designers of the FMS expected that it might be down as much as 33 percent of the time. Managers' estimates of actual downtime, after the initial debugging period, range from an unbelievably low 4 percent up to 20 percent. Some workers told us that downtime was far higher than that.

Our own research team's experience at the plant, admittedly limited, suggested that downtime is a serious problem. While we were there, an air conditioner malfunctioned, causing a machine control to overheat and the machine to go down. This stopped the entire system. While it was down, the carts drifted slightly, and the computer lost track of their exact locations. Setting up everything again took three-quarters of an hour. On the following night the system was down for several more hours. Although managers scheduled work for the weekend to catch up, problems with the software caused that shift to be canceled.

High downtime does not necessarily imply that automated systems are unproductive. They work so fast when they are up that they do typically increase total output. However, high downtime does indicate that an automated system is falling short of its potential – a serious consideration, given the cost of the technology.

Upper management's response to the problem of downtime has not been to alter the technology or the organization of work, but to pressure supervisors to keep these complex mechanical and electronics systems working. The supervisors in turn pass that pressure down the chain of command. "They think you shouldn't make mistakes, so they come down hard," said an operator at the FMS. "After you make a mistake, you're so scared it gets so you can't do your work."

Robogate

The robotized welding system that we visited in the bodyshop of the automaker shed further light on some of these problems. Before robots were introduced, workers wielded heavy hand-held welding guns. The long black cables that connected these guns to overhead racks looked like vines and gave the body shop its nickname: the jungle. The welders working in this spark-showered jungle had some of the most unpleasant jobs in the plant. Thus, one might expect that using robots – programmable mechanical arms – to do the welding would improve the work environment even though it eliminated jobs. However, many of the 100-odd workers who remained on the new welding system disliked it because it had intensified the pace and eroded the quality of their worklife.

Under the new system, workers assemble the floor, sides, and some roof members of each car and secure them by hammering small metal tabs into slots, much as model tin cars are built. Then a gate, or large metal frame, cradles the body and holds it while robots weld it. This set up is referred to as a "Robogate" system. Mini-Robogates cradle and weld together subassemblies such as floors and sides before they are fed into the main line. Over 60 robots and other welding machines are employed in the entire operation.

Before the company installed the Robogates, workers welded some subassemblies at largely independent workstations. After they had completed the wheel-wells or other body parts, they could either place them on the main assembly line to be put together into car bodies, or store them in piles known as banks. This gave the workers some control over the pace of their work: to break the monotony of the day, they could push ahead quickly, bank a lot of parts, and then have some free time later on. Supervisors did not object to banking because it assured a continuous supply to the main assembly line even if unexpected problems occurred, such as a breakdown of the welding machines.

In contrast, the Robogate system ties subassembly workers directly to the line. They now operate welding machines working side by side with robots. There is no bank: when the subassembly is complete, they place it directly on the conveyor to the main line. The Japanese "just-in-time" concept, in which supplies arrive just before they are needed, is the theory behind this new approach. The company's director of manufacturing engineering argues that with fewer parts waiting to be worked on, defects are spotted quickly, and productivity increases.

However, managers have not considered the effects of these changes on workers. Almost every subassembly worker we spoke with complained about the hectic and sometimes erratic pace. "The work is lighter but faster," said one who was doing tabbing. "They want us to work like machines, too. But we're not machines, we're people." The new system also produces stress because of the lack of autonomy. The harried manager, stewing over decisions, is often considered the prototypical candidate for a heart attack. However, several studies, notably one by Robert Karasek at Columbia University, show that stress on the job stems not only from a hectic work pace but also from a lack of authority to make decisions.

Promoters of automation often claim that it broadens the scope of maintenance jobs. At both the tractor plant's FMS and the automaker's Robogate, maintenance jobs did indeed become more challenging. Workers told us that maintaining computerized control systems requires expertise in electronics and broader diagnostic skills than are needed for conventional equipment. However, automation puts those responsible for maintenance, particularly supervisors, under extraordinary stress, because a failure of one critical component could paralyze the system and even the entire plant.

The main Robogate line processes car bodies at the rate of more than one per minute, and any number of things can go wrong. The photocells installed to count car bodies may tell the computer to fit too many bodies into too little space. Then the carriers that transport the bodies along the line become jammed, and the robots sometimes keep on welding anyway. The scene that ensues resembles a crash on the freeway more than the effortless grace of automatic production.

The Robogate was initially built with storage areas capable of holding a two-hour supply of bodies at a number of critical points. But because the storage systems proved less reliable than the main system, managers told us they plan to eliminate them. Then, if the main robogate line goes down, the factory will be able to run for a short time. However, as soon as the storage capacity in the main line is exhausted, the entire bodyshop, with its millions of dollars worth of equipment and hundreds of workers, will stand idle.

The interconnected nature of the system puts tremendous pressure on repair crews. Welding-repair supervisors had an annual turnover rate of 150 percent in the first several years of operation. "This has been the hardest three years of my life," said a general foreman who has lasted longer than most. "There isn't any relaxation. I've walked out of here and sat in my car, unable to move, getting myself together."

Engineers next

Computer technology can be used as a powerful tool to restructure the jobs of engineers as well as production workers. We discovered this in our visits to the manufacturer of commercial aircraft, a subsidiary of a larger aerospace firm. Only about one-third of the division's 40,000 employees actually "touch" the aircraft during production. Management plans to revamp most of the remaining two-thirds of the jobs through automation.

Engineering is now organized so that knowledgeable people in various departments and levels make decisions, communicating in meetings and by exchanging drawings. For example, the design engineer sends a blueprint of a part to the tooling engineer, who is responsible for figuring out how to make the devices to hold intricate aircraft components during production. The tooling engineer then generally modifies the design engineer's drawing and sends it back for checking. "All the engineers add their thoughts," said one manager. "Everybody is innovative. You end up with a product touched by a lot of people."

Introducing computer-aided design (CAD) systems, in which engineers work on computer terminals and video screens rather than on paper, need not mean changing this organizational structure. However, the aircraft company we visited is using computers to give elite engineering teams greater control.

Such teams will soon establish the basic design of an airplane and feed it into the computer system, along with fundamental decisions about tooling and manufacturing. This information will be launched throughout the rest of the company via the CAD network. Tooling and manufacturing departments will still be necessary, but only to work closely with the elite team in fleshing out the details of decisions that have already been made. One manager sees this system as "putting the smarts up front."

The design teams at the source of this stream of information will have broader responsibility, but, for a given volume of work, as many as a third of the engineers and technicians downstream are likely to find their jobs eliminated. Up to 80 percent of the manufacturing engineers, who plan how parts proceed from step to step during production, could be eliminated, according to company officials. And the downstream jobs that remain will be more constrained. "Many of the people who are left will be elements in a very controlled process," said the co-director of the computer-integration project. "The ingenuity of the craft will be removed. The advantage will be in having more consistent outcomes with fewer hiccups."

However, removing the hiccups without sacrificing creativity may be difficult if not impossible. "If you carry a process like this too far, you tend to suppress new ideas," said a former vice president of engineering. "We don't want to standardize one landing gear to the extent that we don't give anybody the opportunity of building a better one."

Another problem is that engineers working on computer terminals may find themselves mistaking computer simulations for reality. A story has been going around among engineers about a young designer at a British aircraft company, who created an igniter for a jet engine on the computer screen. Although it was a fine igniter, somewhere along the way a decimal point was moved one place. The computer therefore instructed a machine tool to cut out a part that was ten times too big. When the machine operator brought the part up to the designer, the designer didn't see anything wrong.

Like many hourly workers in automated factories engineers working downstream will have less autonomy yet faster-paced work. "Some computer-aided design systems we have looked at increase the decision-making rate by 1,800 or 1,900 percent," says Mike Cooley, a former senior design engineer at Lucas Aerospace and now with the Greater London Enterprise Board. As the engineers try to handle data at that pace, making low-level judgments yet being overseen by superiors upstream, says Cooley, "the stress is enormous."

Technological control or humane work?

The managerial obsession with technology as a way to establish tighter control over production became an overriding theme in our study of automation. Managers often find it hard to exert close control over a skilled worker such as a machinist, who is making many intricate cuts to produce a complex part. The task is so difficult that a manager must simply rely on the machinist to work at a reasonable pace and to produce a good part. Skilled workers also have substantial bargaining power: if they walk off the job, untrained hands cannot fill in. Thus, managers intent on control seek to remove skill from workers and transfer it to complex machinery. The resulting jobs are tedious, high-paced, and stressful.

Moreover, there are hidden costs to this path. Observers of industrial management widely agree that workers are more productive and do a better job if they are motivated and able to use their skill, experience, and creativity. These abilities are especially important in the case of computer-based technologies, which – in reality if not in theory – depend intimately upon workers for smooth functioning.

Under certain circumstances, managers can increase output while making work more routine and stressful. However, concern for improving production should not outweigh consideration for what workers do on the job. Degrading the work people do ultimately demeans their lives – a cost that is seldom figured into calculations as to which system is more efficient. Computer-based automation holds extraordinary promise for improving life on the job. The emphasis should be on realizing that promise.

Robots Can't Run Factories

Larry Hirschhorn

The contrary view on factory automation is put by Hirschhorn, in a piece specially prepared for this volume. Unlike Shaiken, Hirschhorn argues that the troublesome nature of IT actually increases the dependence of managers on their skilled workers, and not the opposite. The common notion that computers de-skill workers and degrade work is wrong, he says. The author is a senior researcher at the Wharton Center for Applied Research, University of Pennsylvania, and this article is largely based on the author's notable book Beyond Mechanization: Work and Technology in the Post-Industrial Age *(MIT Press, Cambridge, MA, 1984).*

Failure and vigilance in automated factories

Can robots run factories? In the past, critics of job design practice argued that industrial jobs were boring and dehumanizing. They urged managers and engineers to upgrade skills and give workers greater responsibility on the shop floor. But computers, robots and microprocessors pose an even more dramatic question: responsibility over what and for what? What role can workers possibly play in the production process when cybernetic controls manage the flow of materials and objects from beginning to end? How can work be humanized if there are no work roles left, if workers simply watch dials and turn screws? Why worry about the humanization of work? Worry about the superfluity of the worker instead.

This argument is misplaced. Robots can't run factories. The cybernetic image of the perfect machine is utopian. The new technologies introduce new modes of machine failure, new flaws in the control systems themselves, and new challenges to the design of jobs. In such settings, workers must *control the controls*. Nuclear reactor accidents provide insight here. Reactors are typical of most continuous process technologies. They use electrical, hydraulic, and pneumatic control systems, accidents pose significant dangers, and workers observe the production process indirectly, using dials, printouts, and displays. Consider the following two accidents.

1 In the Ginna nuclear reactor in Rochester, New York, a tube holding "dirty" irradiated

water burst, spilling its contents into the clean water used to power the generator. Sensing a pressure drop in the dirty water system, the automatic controls pumped water into it. But because the tube was broken, the subsequent rise in water pressure pushed irradiated steam through an open valve into the clean water and the air outside the containment. The Nuclear Regulatory Commission suggested that a new type of accident, based on the punctured tube, had emerged. Such an accident, if not stopped, would have led to an uncovered and dangerously overheated core. Paradoxically, operators could easily have used a valve to equalize pressure between the clean and dirty water systems, but the automatics, programmed to close the "non-essentials" in an emergency, shut the air valve controlling this "pressurizer" valve.

2   The broad features of the Three Mile Island accident, triggered by a stuck valve, were never anticipated. Prior contingency analysis assumed that an accidental loss of coolant from the core would be sudden. Instead, the loss was gradual, creating a degraded core rather than a meltdown. Entirely new contingencies appeared. In particular, operators faced the unexpected problem of managing a hydrogen bubble that threatened to block the circulation of the coolant water. In the first few days of the accident, some scientists feared that the bubble might explode. The fear proved groundless. This anxiety indicated the confusion of scientists and engineers.

In both cases, a particular local failure, such as a punctured tube, or stuck valve, set off a train of events which created an entirely new system of relationships within the reactor system. The very interconnectedness of the machine system, the basis for its efficiency, is also the source of unanticipated accidents. In such accidents, the control systems themselves may create accidents. Thus, at the Ginna reactor, an automatic control shut off a valve needed to control the consequences of the punctured tube. In sum, engineers cannot anticipate all the modes of machine failure. As one engineer writes, in such systems "only an improbable combination of events is consistent with known facts." The control systems are "incomplete". Workers must consequently control the controls if the machinery is to operate smoothly and safely.

But can workers successfully manage cybernetic systems? To do so, they must not only be vigilant, but curious and committed. "Human Factors" engineers have argued that we need to design better "machine–man interfaces," better displays, alarms and knobs. Certainly, the control room displays in most nuclear reactors are primitive and confusing. At Three Mile Island, critical displays were on the back sides of panels, too many warning lights came on during an accident ("It looked like a Christmas tree," as one supervisor said), and the relative location of different controls and alarms did not match the underlying flow of steam and water.

But design improvements will not prove sufficient. The levels of worker vigilance, attention and curiosity are determined primarily by *subjective* factors, such as the nature of supervision, incentives for worker learning, and feelings of anxiety as workers face dangerous situations. Consider the following five examples.

1   A worker inspecting air cooling pipes at the Indian Point Reactor in New York jiggled a float that measured possible water leakage into the containment. An indicator light on the control panel lit up. After he completed his inspection, water in fact began leaking through a corroded fitting in a fan cooler. Over the next two weeks, whenever water leakage was sufficient to trigger the indicator light, workers assumed that the earlier jiggle accounted for the warning. (They were also relying on two automatic sump pumps

in the containment to push out water, not realizing that both pumps were broken.)

2 Workers at Three Mile Island continued to believe that they faced a typical problem of "excessive pressure" in the containment, despite other indications that water and steam were leaking rapidly from the core. They were beguiled in part by poor displays. Yet investigative evidence suggests that they were also inflexible in their thinking. Once they hit upon a particular theory or model of the accident, they could not change their minds, despite the appearance of contradictory evidence.

3 Safety inspectors in nuclear power plants, called quality assurance engineers, review operators' work procedures and the certifying documents that record these procedures, to ensure that work is done safely. At most nuclear power plants, such engineers work within a distinct quality assurance (QA) department and are not part of the operating team. This has three consequences. First, QA engineers often lack concrete knowledge of plant problems. Consequently, operating personnel resent the quality assurance engineer's meddling. Second, operating personnel abdicate their responsibility for working in a safe manner. Safety practices become identified with the meddlesome and ill-informed quality assurance engineer. These practices become *his* business. Moreover, since safety is entrusted to the low status QA engineer, the operator comes to believe that things cannot be so dangerous at all! Third, the QA engineer, sensing his dilemma, tries not to make waves. The resulting surface peace between the QA division and the operating (line) division, leads senior managers to believe that the plant is operating safely! This affirms their assumption that they can delegate the problem of safety to subordinates and not worry about it.

4 In the 1982 Washington, DC National Airport crash, the co-pilot did not aggressively challenge the pilot to reconsider his decision to take off despite his serious misgivings – there was ice on the wings. Instead, he posed his grave doubts as tentative questions ("That doesn't seem right does it?") allowing the pilot to continue his own self-deception that conditions warranted take-off. The social relationship between pilot and co pilot led to a tragedy.

5 High steel construction workers have a norm of not talking about felt anxieties and dangers, despite their deep-seated fear of "going into the hole." They psychologically ostracize workers who are overtly fearful and anxious. These norms can lead a worker to ignore a danger sign which can threaten the whole crew.

These examples highlight at least five obstacles to creating and sustaining worker vigilance and attention. First, the social relationship between a subordinate and superior may inhibit the former from taking authority, from assuming leadership when an accident threatens. Second, the dangerous character of the work itself may paradoxically lead workers to suppress their vigilance. Third, managers may not invest adequate time, money, and effort in assuring safety and quality. Fourth, the anxiety surrounding difficult and dangerous control work may lead workers to project their anxieties on to other groups, to create scapegoats, who, like the messengers of bad news, appear as the source rather than as the monitors of potential threats. Fifth and finally, workers may lack conceptual flexibility when they face novel threats. This may happen because anxiety makes them think rigidly, or because they have not learned how to be diagnosticians, how to solve novel problems.

These obstacles suggest that engineers cannot "design" curiosity and vigilance into their display systems. Instead, managers must find ways to create a *climate* of work in which curiosity, vigilance and commitment emerge as natural concomitants of the total system of working relationships. Managers face a social and cultural problem rather than a technical one. But how can they create such a climate?

The new sociotechnical factories

Over the past 15 years, between 500 and 1,000 plants have been established which deploy novel principles of job design:

- Workers are organized into teams.
- They are paid salaries based on how many skill clusters they master.
- A worker rotates into different parts of the plant by temporarily joining other teams.
- Team members frequently evaluate one another's skills.
- The first-line supervisor develops a facilitating rather than commanding style.
- An elaborate system of committees and task forces is used to solve recurrent problems, accomplish specific projects and "govern" the plant.

Thus, for example, at "Big Chem," a world-class chemical plant, a team member works as a maintenance worker, operator and lab technician, the controls produce economic as well as technical data so that operators can estimate the monetary consequences of different control decisions, and teams send delegates to a "norm review board" which writes and updates the plant's good practices handbook. Researchers in the UK first developed this "sociotechnical" design when studying coal mining work in the early 1950s.

Proponents and critics are deeply divided on the meaning and import of this new design. On the one side, proponents argue that it promises to improve "the quality of worklife" for plant employees and so humanize work. On the other, critics argue that it is one more familiar human relations program, whose function is to co-opt workers, excuse poor management, and bust unions.

Both arguments miss the point. Irrespective of its historical roots, this design is the most effective method we have for sustaining worker vigilance and curiosity. It does so by *integrating doing with learning*. Three processes are central here.

First, the pay system creates incentives for a worker to master several skills and to deepen his or her competence in at least one. The worker becomes progressively more knowledgeable about many different parts of the plant's operations.

Second, workers can advance only if each team in the plant is functioning well and is therefore willing to accept and effectively train rotations from other teams. Thus, for example, at a soft goods plant called "Fall Mills," one team developed an elite conception of itself, it wanted to be the first "fully autonomous team" in the plant, and therefore did not accept rotations from other teams. Similarly, at Big Chem, one team temporarily withdrew from the norm review board (which regulated such processes as rotation, training, and career ladders) because too few of its members had become assistant team coordinators in other parts of the plant. In such a system, a worker cannot mind his own business and ignore the conditions of work and group life in other parts of the plant. His advancement depends on those conditions. His commitment and interest in plant life are high.

Third, the team system gives individual workers a chance to take authority and become leaders. Since supervisors play a background role, members rotate through different leadership roles such as job scheduler, vacation scheduler, safety specialist, and recorder. Indeed, in some plants workers advance only if their performance in these social roles is positively evaluated. In addition, workers must frequently solve difficult team problems such as disciplining a perpetual latecomer, enforcing a "drinking at lunch prohibition," or failing a technically incompetent but personable teammate. Such conundrums, when resolved successfully, enable workers to experience their own *personal authority* in a complex group process. They learn (as many managers never do) to confront and hold one another accountable for effective performance.

In effect, with this design, a worker increases his understanding of plant operations, his commitment to overall plant functioning and his experience of his own personal authority. Consequently, he maintains his curiosity, attention, and capacity for leadership at a high level.

Do these plants work?

No researcher has rigorously studied how workers in sociotechnical plants respond to problems and accidents when compared to workers in traditional settings. Yet, three pieces of evidence indirectly suggest that workers in sociotechnical plants are more responsive. First, case studies suggest that such plants produce a higher quality of product than conventional ones. Second, several studies suggest that workers in such plants respond efficiently and quickly to the introduction of new product lines. An observer of Farm Inc., a grain dryer plant, writes,

During an unforeseen slump in the market for grain dryers, management decided to produce fans in order to avoid a layoff. The manufacturing of this new product started rapidly with great effectiveness. . . . this enhanced systems response capability is especially beneficial to Farm Inc. Their business, primarily in agricultural products, is cyclical, often with expected fluctuations. The capacity to continue productively through changing demands is, therefore, especially desirable.

Indeed, many observers suggest that these new designs will be most valuable when the plant managers must produce small runs, on short notice for a changing mix of customers. Under these conditions, the plant must continually solve the problems of quality and delivery time, as opposed to the traditional problems of cost and capacity. Third, managers frequently use these designs when introducing new technologies at new manufacturing sites. The technologies must be broken in through a frequently painful process, and the plant crew must be trained, responsive, and willing to learn. In short, the indirect evidence suggests that workers in these plants are attentive, curious, and committed.

But experience also suggests that managers and workers frequently face social, psychological and political problems in implementing this new work design. Consider the following.

Workers and managers at Big Chem, a new factory designed according to sociotechnical principles, faced a critical juncture in the first winter of the plant's operation. The plant was highly automated, the technology was new, and workers played a critical role in controlling the production process. Yet the workers could not fully master the machinery. The plant was based on a solid plastics technology, the first of its kind in North America, and 60 percent of plant personnel were unfamiliar with the equipment. When the feed would back up, there was little time to search for causes. Instead the team on shift would shut the process down and take the plastic out of the machine. But as one worker noted, "you have to take it out by hand, and it's messy junk. There we were in the middle of the winter, up to our knees in the junk because we didn't know how to manage the technology."

Top management, afraid of year-end losses, installed temporary assistant coordinators to help the management-appointed team coordinator supervise the work teams. One manager argued that the assistant coordinators were "helping hands," and that the teams needed "more structure, more training and more boundaries between them and the rest of the organization." The plant, he said, "was not moving toward a traditional supervision system." "I have talked to all the workers, they all want more authority."

But an active worker and union steward disagreed. She argued that plant management had panicked. "They were watching the bottom line fall away from them." They appointed the assistants "to cover their ass and get the head office off their backs. But it was a unilateral decision. Why were they being so paternalistic and authoritarian? I guess we had a misconception. We thought we were on our way to autonomous work groups." Yet the worker admits that the new assistant coordinator stabilized the teams. Before management installed them, "when an informal leader [of a team] would emerge, he was cut off at the head. People got too comfortable with committees. The assistant coordinator had a unifying effect. You had two people now . . . Before that, the coordinator was chasing his shadow. The teams settled down."

This example highlights some of the critical problems that both workers and managers face in implementing the new sociotechnical design. If managers are to create a climate that fosters committed and vigilant workers, they must give the worker teams the authority and power to make shopfloor and personnel decisions. Yet, plant supervisors are frequently more skilled than operators. In a pinch, managers may push them to take over the teams, to protect profits and production. Workers, however, may resent this assistance, feeling that though they have invested much in the development of their team systems, they are about to lose them to management. None the less, workers may face their own intra-team conflicts and limits. While they may resent the plant managers' authority, they may also undermine the authority and leadership of their own members. They may "cut the head off" of a natural team leader.

Thus workers and managers *have to strike an optimum balance in the distribution of authority between the teams and plant management.* Too little authority for the teams may ultimately reduce their commitments to plant production and individual learning. But too much may demoralize them if they cannot cope with the technical novelty of the plant and the social novelty of their own team processes.

Research suggests that the new factories fail most frequently when managers and workers are unable to strike this balance. Six failure modes seem typical. First, managers take too little or too much authority in response to technical novelty. Second, there is too little technical novelty and challenge so that workers grow disinterested in mastering new skills. The plant and the workers "plateau." Third, in response to technical and social anxiety, workers create overly closed teams so that inter-team cooperation deteriorates and plant performance suffers. Fourth, workers create dysfunctional team processes so that a few informal leaders dominate the team.

Finally, two contextual processes seem important as well. If corporate managers are only partly sympathetic to the new design they will give the plant manager little leeway to make mistakes and lose money in the plant's early years of operation. The plant manager may in turn take over the teams at the first sign of trouble, and so quickly undermine the spirit of the design. Second, management careers frequently reward short stays in particular plants. Under these conditions, the informal norms of authority developed by one plant manager may be overturned by the next. In response workers become cynical and abdicate their right to take authority for their technical and social competence.

These failure modes suggest that managers and workers must become interpersonally and politically sophisticated if they are to successfully implement the new designs. The plant manager must frequently develop a political strategy to protect his or her plant from head-quarters pressure and must be aware of how and under what conditions he must take and relinquish authority from and to the teams. Similarly, workers must develop interpersonal skills to manage their own team processes and must develop political skills to manage inter-team and plant-wide relationships.

The complexity of these processes transcends the informal social systems which organized traditional plants. In those plants social relationships were organized by a simpler antagonistic "we–they" set of relationships between workers and managers. Workers were "brothers" and managers were the enemies. Managers were loyal to the company and believed that workers were lazy. These divisions don't disappear. Rather, they are submerged in a more multi-dimensional set of relationships in which workers must manage more of their own conflicts, and plant managers see the workers as allies in the "game" against a complex technology.

We arrive at an ironic conclusion. Robots can't run factories. The new cybernetic systems pose new modes of failure while stressing old systems of organizing work. Workers must become vigilant, committed, and curious but managers cannot "command" them to do so. Recent experiences have taught us much about work designs which foster such behavior. But to implement such designs, both managers and workers must develop forms of behavior which transcend their inherited patterns of taking authority, sharing power and managing the politics of intra-group and inter-group life. The emergence of a new technology places new demands on management's social and cultural skills. The new worker must be matched by a new manager. If robots can't run factories, neither can the traditional manager. But how, where and through what processes, will this economy develop the new manager, and the new system of corporate relationships, so that we can appropriate our new technologies? We had best find out. Post-industrial development may hang in the balance.

Human Factors in Computer-integrated Manufacturing

John Bessant and Alec Chisholm

Following on from Hirschhorn's discussion of "sociotechnical" systems and team-working, Bessant and Chisholm make a powerful case for developing more human-centered systems. A comprehensive survey of research into manufacturing automation leads to a discussion of the pros and cons of this approach. Their conclusion is similar to that of Warner (above), Hoerr et al. and Smith (below). Professor Bessant is Head of the Centre for Business Research, Brighton Polytechnic, UK, and Chisholm is Research Professor of Engineering at the University of Salford, UK. This paper was prepared for the 18th CIRP Manufacturing Systems Seminar at Stuttgart, West Germany, June 1986.

Summary

Whereas some commentators have appeared to stress the use of advanced technology as the most potent factor in improving manufacturing productivity, this paper first seeks to redress the balance by suggesting that human beings will remain crucially important in computer-integrated manufacturing (CIM) systems, however "intelligent" these systems become. By using people at all levels in a non-Tayloristic way, the potential improvements in productivity through the better utilization of people can be considerable.

On the assumption that the trend to CIM is generally incremental rather than revolutionary, and that lessons about the future can therefore be learned from recent developments, some results of recent research into human factors in manufacturing are reviewed. After the very broad scope of this is outlined, the concept of choice is introduced. The scope of the choices available appears to permit many different relationships to be established in practice between people and technology, all with the objective of improving manufacturing performance.

Strategic preparations for CIM may be made best through, first, organizational integration, followed then by integration of the technology. But in all aspects of organizational integration, human factors are fundamental and crucially important and continuing research in this field is important and necessary.

Introduction

Merchant has drawn attention to some data on the relative contributions to productivity growth in manufacturing of labor, capital, and technology[1]. In three separate studies, technology was found to be the major contributing factor whilst the quality of labor accounted for only 10–20 percent. Merchant uses these data to suggest that future increases in the cost-effectiveness of manufacturing should be sought from technological developments, specifically the move to computer-integrated manufacturing (CIM). Although this might be construed as supporting the trend towards the truly "automatic" factory, we believe that there will still be an important human element in the management and operation of future manufacturing systems, no matter how intelligent the overall control systems may become.

Moreover, the actual transition to any computer-integrated manufacturing systems of the future will have to be managed by people and the many variants of the manufacturing systems required to suit the wide variety of products and particular circumstances of different industrial sectors will also continue to involve people in many different roles. People will remain crucially important in manufacturing systems, but in exactly what roles and with what skills remains very uncertain.

Many commentators have observed that traditional ways of designing work systems in manufacturing have produced inefficient systems because they take insufficient account of human needs and capabilities, indeed that the human element is in many ways a neglected resource. Different, and less traditional "Tayloristic" ways of treating the human beings in manufacturing, based on research and empirical trial and observation, may make substantial improvements in performance possible to an extent hitherto unenvisaged (just as, to take an example from "technology" itself, refining a product design ready for "automatic assembly" may be so successful as to make the automation unnecessary).

A notable statement expressing the human-centered approach was made by Konosuke Matsushita of the giant Matsushita Corporation. He said "we are going to win and the industrial West is going to lose." Of particular relevance was his comment that "we are beyond the Taylor model. . . . the survival of firms . . . depends on the day-to-day mobilization of every ounce of intelligence. For us the core of management is precisely this art of mobilizing and pulling together the intellectual resources of all employees in the service of the firm. . . . The intelligence of a handful of technocrats . . . is no longer enough to take up [the new technological and economic challenges] with a real chance of success."[2]

The introduction of new technology into manufacturing with its possible adverse effects on the people employed, together with a heightened social interest in improving the quality of working life, are among the influences which have led to extensive interest in the broad field of what have been termed "human factors" in manufacturing.

Human factors in manufacturing

There has been extensive research in the field of human factors for nearly 100 years; examples include the work of Taylor, the Gilbreths, the "human relations" school of Mayo, Roethlisberger, and Dickson and Kurt Lewin, and more recently the sociotechnical systems

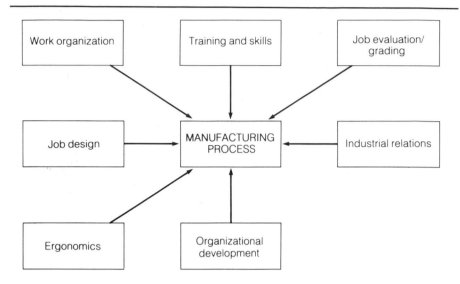

Figure 9.1   Some areas of interest in the field of human factors in manufacturing.

group including Trist, Rice and others from the Tavistock Institute. In each case – from the "scientific management" approaches developed in engineering plants in the early 1900s through to the realization in the UK coal industry of the 1950s that introducing new technology involved a "people" system working with the technology – there has been an appreciation of the breadth of influence which human factors have on the successful operation (or otherwise) of the manufacturing process. Such work has illuminated and assisted in the development of strategies aimed at getting the best out of the manufacturing system.

Current interest in the field of human factors involved in the manufacturing process covers a broad spectrum of issues; figure 9.1 summarizes these.

Although this picture might suggest an incoherent and fragmentary approach, these different streams are united in so far as they are all concerned with ways of trying to establish an optimum relationship between people and technology in the manufacturing systems of the future. This belief is not founded on a collection of "motherhood statements" about how nice it would be if people were considered more in the manufacturing process. Rather, the evidence is already widespread and growing that without adequate consideration of human factors across this broad field, the increasingly sophisticated manufacturing systems now being developed will not operate effectively.

In a sense this is axiomatic: clearly without suitable training and a ready supply of trained manpower on the labor market progress in using new technologies will be inhibited.[3] Equally, failure to take account of ergonomic characteristics in man–machine interaction is likely to result in ineffectual or slow response to emergency situations.[4] Problems which have occurred in the nuclear industry, and in particular the Three Mile Island plant, are good examples. Or again, there is growing evidence that better systems can be designed if there is an element of employee participation in their design and implementation. A number of sets of guidelines for obtaining employee participation have appeared in recent years, including those of the Work Research Unit,[5] or Mumford's ETHICS method.[6]

Finally, there is the whole question of workforce acceptance, both on an individual level and in the context of industrial relations as a whole; the recent crisis in the UK newspaper printing industry illustrates the effects that can emerge when – for whatever reasons – there is a failure to accept and implement change.

Perhaps the most eloquent testimony to the importance of human factors comes from those situations in which they were not considered. For example, Clegg and Kemp[7] describe the implementation of a flexible manufacturing system (FMS) in the computer industry. In particular they mention the absence of consultation between the various groups involved in the project: "one result of this dearth of discussion and consultation was that . . . a year after the first pieces of the FMS were introduced, demarcation disputes between engineers, machine operators and programmers over who does routine edits of programme tapes remains unresolved."

In another case, reported by Henderson and Horsley,[8] the commissioning and subsequent early stage operation of large scale methanol and ammonia plants within ICI Agricultural Division was plagued with problems. These included long delays, failures to achieve the design efficiencies (despite being built to a proven licensed design) and continuous labor relations problems. All these were eventually dealt with by taking an alternative approach to the whole commissioning project. A crucial element of this was to build in the role of a "people technologist" who produced a "people plan" as part of the project plan. Subsequently, all major plants within the division have been commissioned using the same approach.

Human factors and advanced manufacturing technology

Such general considerations about the importance of human factors in the manufacturing process can be given specific emphasis in the case of advanced manufacturing technology (AMT), a major step along the road to computer-integrated manufacturing. Throughout the industrialized countries, emphasis is being given to the rapid adoption of AMT as a means of restoring competitive advantage. The choice for many firms is stark: "automate or liquidate!" Yet successful implementation of AMT depends crucially on the human dimension.

A number of commentators have pointed out the importance of human factors in the case of various examples of AMT. Dempsey[9] suggests that successful implementation of FMS requires "a new way of thinking" about production organization and management. In his work with Ingersoll Engineers and in a study by Bessant and Haywood[10] the experience of users of FMS was that most of the benefits – 60 percent or more – came, not from the technology, but from the way in which they had been forced to change their patterns of organization and management.

Equally, commentators such as Voss[11] on computer-aided production management systems, Fleck[12] on robots and Arnold and Senker[13] on computer-aided design identify significant time lag between adoption of these technologies and actually getting the best out of them. Indeed, as Greenhalgh[14] comments, successful utilization may never be reached and the organization may be forced to reject what may have been a costly new technology. In each case the reasons are essentially on the human factors side, concerned with the organization's ability to learn to use the technology and to adapt to coping with it.

Whilst it could be argued that these are simply manifestations of the well-known "learning curve" effect, we suggest that this learning is in fact a complex function of acquiring technological skills and also of learning to organize to get the most out of the new technology; it is in this latter area that concern about human factors achieves central importance.[15]

In their comprehensive review of the diffusion of innovations, Rogers and Shoemaker[16] identify five characteristics of innovations which exert a strong influence on the likelihood of successful adoption and implementation. In particular they found – for a variety of different innovations and adopting populations – that successful implementation is very much a function of compatibility – that is, of how good a fit is achieved between the technological innovation and the context into which it is introduced. In the sense of our discussion it is clear that achieving a good fit – and hence exploiting the benefits offered by AMT – will depend on adaptation of both the technology and the organization. Human factors are a critical consideration in this adaptive process. While most managers and engineering designers of manufacturing systems now recognize the potential importance of human factors and of organization structure, they are often handicapped by lack of relevant knowledge about the human element and inhibited by inability to influence organizational structures.

The concept of choice

We do not have the space to discuss the whole range of factors indicated in figure 9.1, but will instead consider some issues to highlight the importance of human factors in making AMT systems work. In particular, we aim to emphasize the choice which is available in the integration of people and technology.

At the level of direct operators, a great deal of work has been done in the case of computer-guided numerically controlled machine tools (CNC) to try to identify the best patterns of work organization and job design for such systems.[17, 18, 19] Such work concerns itself with questions of what skills are required, who should perform tasks like programming and maintenance, whether the option of eliminating the skilled machinist is justified or whether instead of machine minders some form of job design involving greater autonomy for the individual operator should be used, and so on. Although it might be expected that the technology implied one particular "best" way of doing this, research suggests strongly that there is, in fact, considerable choice. Rempp,[20] for example, identifies no less than five arrangements of programming and operating skills, each of which has technological, economic and social advantages for particular circumstances.

As Sorge et al.[21] put it, "all our results serve to stress the extreme malleability of CNC technology . . . [this] shows in the fact that its technical specification in detail, and its organizational and labor conditions are closely adjusted to company and departmental strategies, existing production engineering and organization strategies and manpower policies."

This conclusion is also drawn by other workers such as Jones,[22] Bessant and Dickson,[23] and Scott,[24] and also appears to have applicability in cases of other, related technologies such as FMS. Work by Wall et al.,[25] a team of psychologists working alongside engineers in the design and implementation of new technology in the computer industry, has shown that two very different roles can be identified for operators. The first – the "operator monitor" – is essentially one of limited skill and autonomy; this follows the apparent logic of designing towards the eventual goal of excluding the operator altogether in some future configuration. However, the other – the "operator midwife" – is a broadly skilled role, requiring a variety of different interventions and activities by the operator to support an automated system. Table 9.1 summarizes the key dimensions of these two roles: the significance of this is that it demonstrates clearly that the latter role is more effective in keeping expensive AMT systems efficiently utilized.

This breakdown into two alternative options – both of which are applicable and appropriate under different operating conditions and within different factory contexts – is echoed in work by Kohler and Schultz-Wild.[26] They looked at flexible manufacturing systems in West Germany and commented that "theoretical reasoning and empirical evidence demonstrate that job structures and manpower policies are not determined by manufacturing technology in

Table 9.1 Different operator roles in AMT facilities

Operator monitor	Operator midwife
Emphasizes division of labor and centralized control through specialists	Emphasizes local responsibility and expertise, devolved control with support from experts
Applicable where technology needs managing and controlling by many different specialists (who support several machines)	Applicable when technology needs a single dedicated expert to solve problems at source
Operator role is to mind machine and call for help when required	Operator role is to set machine and tools, prove out tapes, edit programs write simple programs and carry out routine maintenance work
Needs additional back-up from: • machine setters • tool setters • more programmers (to write and prove out programs) • more engineers (for maintenance, need electrical, mechanical and electronic skills)	Needs less support: • no setters needed • no setters needed • fewer programmers needed • fewer engineers needed (no routine maintenance work)
Involves low direct labor costs but high indirect costs	Involves high direct labor costs and also training costs Lower indirect costs
May involve coordination and operator motivation problems	Offers better operator motivation

Source: Wall (1986)

general or by the technical characteristics of FMS. Different work organizations, recruitment, and training policies are compatible with FMS which are technically similar." Indeed, in the many studies of direct operators employed in machining, the general pattern is the same; changes in the task and skill content of jobs bring out the importance of the choices which are available about how to use people within the manufacturing process.

One set of choices follows the trend towards manufacturing integration through technology. This choice reduces the scope of the operator task to one of machine loading and unloading, and of general minding and monitoring duties; however, it also requires complex automated machinery at high cost. This follows the conventional logic originally developed by Taylor and Ford in applying the principles of scientific management which emphasizes the division of labor within the manufacturing process. Over time, tasks are reduced to the level where they can be automated and the human element replaced altogether; such approaches may be highly suitable in monotonous and simple assembly tasks such as those involved in mass production on assembly lines, but may be less appropriate in flexible and integrated production systems. Those plants which have tended to emphasize a pattern of work organization involving low division of labor and high individual skill input have traditionally been those involved in small batch and custom or jobbing work.

The arguments in favor of the high division of labor route include the fact that training costs are kept low because only low level skills are required at operator level; concentration of resources like programming in a separate department can bring economies of scale if other computer applications are also present within the factory; a further advantage is the relative ease with which work organization can be implemented around a new technology because it does not require any radical change in the way things are done.

Another motive has been identified by a number of commentators, notably Braverman, who suggest that management introduce technology in order to reduce the level of human intervention and thus to increase managerial control over the manufacturing process.[27]

The apparent dominance of this traditional model of "technological determinism" has been challenged by a number of recent commentators – e.g. Wilkinson[28] and Jones[29] – drawing upon experience with many of the newer innovations involving AMT. This indicates that the awareness of the existence of choices is growing, coupled with better understanding of the costs and benefits of different alternatives. For example, as Kohler and Schultz-Wild point out, the benefits of the "traditional" model need to be offset by disadvantages such as the risk of extended downtime. Lack of training investment results in overdependence on external resources (such as machinery suppliers) for maintenance back-up. Further, flexibility in the case of an FMS can be severely curtailed if the operating workforce is not trained beyond a particular envelope of skills and working practices.

It is, therefore, tempting to assume that the non-traditional human-centered approach solves these difficulties and offers a better way of working. However, research evidence does not necessarily support this view. Kohler and Schultz-Wild again report that the second model – one involving features like high skill input from operators, high training investment, job rotation within the team and so on – can also be problem-generating as well as problem-solving. Amongst the problem issues raised in one example of a gear manufacturer were the following:

- High training costs, both in infrastructure provision and in actual training.

- Lack of suitable software and hardware for shop floor programming to support what they call homogeneous job structures for operators.
- Problems of integrating such homogeneous work structures into a factory with more conventional arrangements – in some cases leading to demarcation disputes.
- Problems posed by pay differentials since operators under the new system are paid more.

Overall, they conclude that "the alternative approach will entail relatively high costs during the process of introduction and will produce significant problems of implementation in general. However, there seems to be a high problem-solving capability in the long-run" – in other words, the long-term development of a flexible and responsive workforce may offset these initial costs.

The general picture is thus one in which there is no single "best" way of organizing or structuring the jobs of operators involved in AMT facilities. Rather the motives for introducing the technology and the way in which it is implemented are both determined by the local situation and are the product of negotiation amongst the various parties involved. As Wilkinson[30] observes, this is essentially a political process, involving many actors with different goals and levels of power and influence over the final outcome. Boddy and Buchanan[31] make a similar point in reviewing their analysis of a wide range of IT applications in manufacturing; they conclude that, although it is likely to be the exercise of what Child[32] calls "strategic choice" by management which determines the final outcome, there is a danger that "the advantages of new technology may be lost if it is applied with traditional management values and assumptions. The effective use of new information and computing technologies may be dependent on new forms of work organization."

Conclusion

To summarize, empirical evidence suggests the possibility of alternative ways of using technology, moving away from the further division of labor to expand the range of tasks performed and the level of skills required to perform them, essentially integrating several elements into a new and more responsible job. The two should be seen as poles on a continuum along which management can exert choice about the way to operate AMT systems. How those choices get made is, as Wilkinson suggests, a negotiated and political process in which the relative power of different interest groups is a key factor. It can thus be argued that there is no technologically determined single "best" way of using new technology but rather a range of choice across this continuum. The emphasis is thus placed on finding the most appropriate option for given circumstances. This shifts attention away from the technology as the shaping factor, and replaces it with the idea of a "design space" in which the room to maneuver in arriving at job design, work organization design, and other characteristics of new manufacturing systems is bounded by local conditions and requirements.[33]

The trend towards integration in computer-integrated manufacturing (CIM) reinforces the crucial importance of human factors. In essence, the pattern has been one of convergence for some time. Stand-alone machine tools have evolved through machining centers to direct numerical control (DNC) manufacturing cells and thence to flexible manufacturing systems which integrate processing, handling, and the overall monitoring and scheduling of the entire cell. Similarly, in the field of design, the designer, draughtsman, production planner, and industrial designer have all converged on the computer-aided design (CAD) workstation. Stock control, progress chasing, production planning and scheduling, purchasing, and other related functions have converged in systems such as materials requirements planning. The direct linking of design and production through CAD/CAM (computer-aided manufacturing) systems is fast growing in many applications.

A consequence of this technological trend toward the integration of the entire manufacturing system is the growing need for organizational integration, in which traditional departmental boundaries and management hierarchies are changed or broken down, and where skill areas are changed.[34]

Trying to implement CIM within the context of an inappropriate organization is likely to lead to mismatches at a number of levels which may account for many of the difficulties currently experienced in practice.

The appropriate strategy for moving toward CIM is therefore first to solve the organizational problems and then to build up technological integration, that is, to "first simplify, then integrate."[35] Schonberger[36] considers that the key pillars in the success of Japanese manufacturing industry – such as just-in-time scheduling or total quality control – are primarily the product of organizational rather than technological change.

Radical organizational change of the kind envisaged has wide-ranging and fundamental implications for people: in their ability to produce change and to adapt to change; in the need for different skills and the way they are utilized; for new manufacturing philosophies; for different company strategies; and for society as a whole. In some areas, the pace of change is extremely rapid, though very non-uniform across manufacturing industry as a whole. This non-uniformity is not necessarily solely the result of slow diffusion caused by uncompetitive incompetence and ignorance, but may reflect valid assessments of economic advantage in different manufacturing sectors, and with different products and scales of operation.

Continuing research is clearly needed which is aimed at trying to understand better the parts to be played by human beings in integrated manufacturing plants in the future. It is also needed to provide independent assessments of the experience gained so far and of future likely trends for the guidance of those who are responsible for initiating and executing the changes involved.

Notes

1   M. E. Merchant, "Flexible Manufacturing Systems: Robotics and Computerized Automation," *Annals of the American Academy of Political and Social Science*, vol. 470, 1984, pp. 123–35.
2   Private communication to A. W. J. Chisholm.
3   M. Beesley and P. Senker, "Towards the Automatic Factory?," in *Proceedings of "Technology Management '85"*, IERE, Eastbourne, October 3–4, 1985.
4   C. Perrow, "The Organizational Context of Human Factors Engineering," *Administrative Science Quarterly*, vol. 28, 1983, pp. 521–41.
5   A. Mackenzie, "People in Manufacturing," in *Proceedings of Human-2* (IFS Publications, Kempston, Bedfordshire, UK, 1984).
6   E. Mumford, *Designing Human Systems – the ETHICS Method* (Manchester Business School, Manchester, UK, 1983).

7   C. Clegg and N. Kemp, "Information Technology Personnel, Where Are You?," *Institute of Personnel Management Magazine*, April 1986.

8   D. Henderson and B. Horsley, "Commissioning of Large-scale Methanol Plants in ICI Agricultural Division," in *Proceedings of "Production '78"* (Institution of Chemical Engineers, Rugby, UK).

9   P. Dempsey, "New Corporate Perspectives in FMS," in *Proceedings of 2nd International Conference on FMS* (IFS Publications, Kempston, Bedfordshire, UK, 1983).

10 J. Bessant and W. Haywood, *"The Introduction of Flexible Manufacturing Systems as an Example of Computer-integrated Manufacturing,"* Occasional Paper No. 1 (Innovation Research Group, Department of Business Management, Brighton Polytechnic, UK, 1985).

11 C. Voss, "Implementation – a New Field of Innovation Research," paper presented to ESRC Workshop on Innovation, Windsor, UK, May 28–9, 1985.

12 J. Fleck, "The Employment Effects of Robots", in *Proceedings of Human-1* (IFS Publications, Kempston, Bedfordshire, UK, 1984).

13 P. Senker and E. Arnold, *Designing the Future: the Skills Implications of Interactive CAD* (EITB, Watford, UK, 1983).

14 K. Greenhalgh, "Counterimplementation: Management and Implementation of High Technology Systems," paper presented at conference on Economic, Social, Financial and Technical Effects of Automation, Salford University, UK, November 1984.

15 J. Bessant, "The Integration Barrier," *Robotica*, vol. 3, 1985, pp. 97–103.

16 E. Rogers and F. Shoemaker, *Communication of Innovations* (Free Press/Macmillan, London, 1971).

17 A. Sorge et al., *Microelectronics and Manpower in Manufacturing* (Gower Press, Aldershot, UK, 1982).

18 W. Cavestro, "Automation, Evolution of Skills in Small and Medium Size Firms: the Case of Numerical Control," in T. Martin (ed.), *Design of Work in Automated Manufacturing Systems* Pergamon, Oxford, 1984).

19 J. Bessant, "Microelectronics and Manufacturing Innovation," in G. Winch (ed.), *Information Technology in Manufacturing Processes* (Rossendale, London, 1985).

20 H. Rempp, *Wirtschaftliche und Soziale Auswirkungen des CNC-Werkzeugmaschineneinsatzes* (RKW, Eschborn, 1982).

21 Sorge et al., *Microelectronics and Manpower*.

22 B. Jones, "Destruction or Redistribution of Engineering Skills?" in S. Wood (ed.), *The Degradation of Work? Skill, Deskilling and the Labour Process* (Hutchinson, London, 1982).

23 J. Bessant and K. Dickson, *Issues in the Adoption of Microelectronics* (Frances Pinter, London, 1982).

24 P. Scott, "Automated Machining Systems and the Role of Engineering Craft Skills," in *Proceedings of Human-2* (IFS Publications, Kempston, Bedfordshire, UK, 1985).

25 T. Wall, Results presented at MSC Workshop on "New Technology and Skills", Aston University, Birmingham, UK, 24–25 March, 1986.

26 C. Kohler and R. Schultz-Wild, "Flexible Manufacturing Systems: Manpower Problems and Policies," paper presented at the World Congress on Human Aspects of Manufacturing, Ann Arbor, Michigan, 1983.

27 H. Braverman, *Labour and Monopoly Capital* (Monthly Review Press, London, 1974).

28 B. Wilkinson, *The Shopfloor Politics of New Technology* (Heinemann, London, 1983).

29 Jones, "Destruction or Redistribution?".

30 Wilkinson, *Shopfloor Politics*.

31 D. Boddy and D. Buchanan, *Organizations in the Computer Age* (Gower Press, Aldershot, UK, 1984).

32 J. Child, *Organizations* (Harper and Row, London, 1977).

33 J. Bessant and K. Dickson, "Determinism or Design?" in *Proceedings of "Design '82"* (Institution of Chemical Engineers, Rugby, UK, 1982).

34 Bessant and Haywood, *The Introduction of FMS*.

35 J. Mortimer, *Integrated Manufacture* (Ingersoll Engineers/IFS Publications, Kempston, Bedfordshire, UK, 1985).

36 R. Schonberger, *Japanese Manufacturing Techniques* (Macmillan/Free Press, London, 1982).

10 People and Computers in Commerce

A Spreadsheet Way of Knowledge

Steven Levy

This classic account of the origins and development of computer spreadsheets suggests that they represent a whole new world view – or "reality by numbers." Although they may be superficially attractive, the author warns that their use can be obsessive. They are also prone to errors and manipulation. Levy is author of Hackers: Heroes of the Computer Revolution *(Doubleday, New York, 1985) and this piece first appeared in* Harper's *November 1984.*

As Dan Bricklin remembers it, the idea first came to him in the spring of 1978 while he was sitting in a classroom at the Harvard Business School. It was the kind of idea – so obvious, so *right* – that made him immediately wonder why no one else had thought of it. And yet it was no accident that this breakthrough should have been his.

Bricklin had graduated from MIT, where – and this is crucial to the idea he would have that afternoon in 1978 – he had worked intimately with computers. Before deciding to go to graduate school he had worked for two major computer companies – first for Wang, then for the Digital Equipment Corporation, for whom he helped design a word-processing program. Like most Harvard MBA candidates, he wanted to be a businessman; but more often than not, his thoughts strayed to the technological.

The question Bricklin was pondering that day in 1978 concerned how he might use what he knew about computers to help him in his finance course. This was the assignment: he and several other students had been asked to project the complicated financial implications – the shift in numbers and dollars, and the shifts resulting from *these* shifts – of one company's acquisition of another.

Bricklin and his classmates would need ledger sheets, often called spreadsheets. Only by painstakingly filling in the pale green grids of the spreadsheets would they get an accurate picture of the merger and its consequences. A row on the ledger might represent an expense or a category of revenue; a column might represent a specific period of time – a day, a month, a year. Run your finger across, say, a row of figures representing mortgage payments for a certain property, and the number in each "cell" of the horizontal row would be the figure paid in the time period represented by that particular vertical column. Somewhere on the sheet the columns and rows would be tallied, and that information would be entered on even larger sheets.

The problem with ledger sheets was that if one monthly expense went up or down, every-thing – *everything* – had to be recalculated. It was a tedious task, and few people who earned their MBAs at Harvard expected to work with spreadsheets very much. Making spreadsheets, however necessary, was a dull chore best left to accountants, junior analysts, or secretaries. As for sophisticated "modeling" tasks – which, among other things, enable executives to project costs for their companies – these tasks could be done only on big mainframe computers by the data-processing people who worked for the companies Harvard MBAs managed.

Bricklin knew all this, but he also knew that spreadsheets were needed for the exercise; he wanted an easier way to do them. It occurred to him: why not create the spreadsheets on a *microcomputer*? Why not design a program that would produce on a computer screen a green, glowing ledger, so that the calculations, as well as the final tabulations, would be visible to the person "crunching" the numbers? Why not make an *electronic* spreadsheet, a word processor for figures?

Bricklin's teachers at Harvard thought he was wasting his time: why would a manager want to do a spreadsheet on one of those "toy" computers? What were secretaries and accountants and the people down in DP for? But Bricklin could not be dissuaded. With a computer programmer friend from MIT named Bob Frankston, he set to work developing the first electronic spreadsheet program. It would be contained on a floppy disk and run on the then brand-new Apple personal computer. Bricklin and Frankston released VisiCalc (the name was derived from *Visi*ble *Calc*ulation) in late 1979.

Today, VisiCalc and its newer rivals – most notably, a more powerful spreadsheet program designed by the Lotus Development Corporation called 1-2-3 – are making fundamental changes in the way American businesses work. For the first time, businessmen have at their fingertips sophisticated and flexible means to chart all the variables – from interest rates to warehouse space – that make (and break) businesses. The biggest firms, the most diversified corporations, can be neatly translated into spreadsheet "models" – each box of the grid a window on to once-overlooked facts or relationships. These models can be used not only to keep track of transactions but also to analyze the nature of a business itself. They allow businessmen to calculate the effects of sudden changes in the corporate environment (a decrease in the prime rate) and to experiment with scenarios (anything from the expansion of a product line to a merger) – all with an ease inconceivable five years ago.

More than a million computer spreadsheet programs worth more than $250 million will be purchased in the United States this year. There are corporate executives, wholesalers, retailers, and small-business owners who talk about their business lives in two time periods: before and after the electronic spreadsheet. They cite prodigious gains in productivity. They speak of having a better handle on their businesses, of knowing more and planning better, of approaching their work more imaginatively. A virtual cult of the spreadsheet has formed, complete with gurus and initiates, detailed lore, arcane rituals – and an unshakable belief that the way the world works can be embodied in rows and columns of numbers and formulas.

It is not far-fetched to imagine that the introduction of the electronic spreadsheet will have an effect like that brought about by the development during the Renaissance of double-entry bookkeeping. Like the new spreadsheet, the double-entry ledger, with its separation of debits and credits, gave merchants a more accurate picture of their businesses and let them see – there, on the page – how they might grow by pruning here, investing there. The electronic spreadsheet is to double-entry what an oil painting is to a sketch. And just as double-entry changed not only individual businesses but *business*, so has the electronic spreadsheet.

Already, the spreadsheet has redefined the nature of some jobs; to be an accountant in the age of spreadsheet programs is – well, almost *sexy*. And the spreadsheet has begun to be a forceful agent of decentralization, breaking down hierarchies in large companies and diminishing the power of data processing.

There has been much talk in recent years about an "entrepreneurial renaissance" and a new breed of risk-taker who creates businesses where none previously existed. Entrepreneurs and their venture-capitalist backers are emerging as new culture heroes, settlers of another American frontier. Less well known is that most of these new entrepreneurs depend on their electronic spreadsheets as much as movie cowboys depended on their horses.

Mitch Kapor, age 34, a former teacher of transcendental meditation, is chairman of the board of the Lotus Development Corporation. In 1983, less than a year after selling its first 1-2-3 package, Lotus went public, a move that brought Kapor's personal net worth to more than $75 million. "Compare the expansion of business today to the conquering of the continent in the nineteenth century," Kapor told me recently as he pulled himself away from his IBM-PC. We were talking in his modest office in the old iron-casting factory in Cambridge, Massachusetts, that is now Lotus's headquarters. "The spreadsheet in that comparison is like the transcontinental railroad. It accelerated the movement, made it possible, and changed the course of the nation."

Kapor's comparison is an apt one. The computer spreadsheet, like the transcontinental railroad, is more than a means to an end. The spreadsheet embodies, *embraces*, that end, and ultimately serves to reinforce it. As Marshall McLuhan observed, "We shape our tools and thereafter our tools shape us." The spreadsheet is a tool, and it is also a world view – reality by the numbers. If the perceptions of those who play a large part in shaping our world are shaped by spreadsheets, it is important that all of us understand what this tool can and cannot do.

One measure of the spreadsheet's impact is clear, however, and it is a source of satisfaction to Dan Bricklin: every student in the Harvard Business School is now required to be proficient in using electronic spreadsheets.

Ezra Gottheil, 34, is the senior product-design planner at Lotus. He shows up for work in casual clothes, and his small office is cluttered with piles of manuals and software. When I visited Gottheil he gave me a quick introduction to electronic spreadsheeting. Computer programs are said to use different "metaphors" to organize their tasks; a program might use the metaphor of a Rolodex, or a file cabinet. When you "boot" almost any spreadsheet program into your personal computer, you see little more than some letters running across the top of the display screen and some numbers running down the side. This serves to indicate the grid of a ledger sheet, the metaphor used by Lotus and other best-selling spreadsheets like VisiCalc, Multiplan, and SuperCalc. The "cursor," a tiny block of light on the screen that acts like a kind of electronic pencil, can be moved (by a touch of the computer keyboard) to any cell on the spreadsheet in order to "input" numbers or formulas. By placing in the cells either figures or formulas that adjust figures according to different variables, it is possible to duplicate the relationships between various aspects of a business and create a "model." The basic model for a restaurant, for example, would include expenses such as salaries, food and liquor costs, and mortgage or rent payments; revenues might be broken down into "bar" and "food," perhaps even further by specific dishes. Every week, the figures would be updated, the formulas reworked if necessary (perhaps the price of olive oil had risen) and the recalculated model provides an accurate snapshot of the business.

Gottheil turned to the keyboard of the IBM-PC on a table beside his desk and booted a spreadsheet. The screen lit up with the familiar grid, and Gottheil's hands arched over the keys as gracefully as the hands of a pianist. He pressed the keys that make the blinking cursor hopscotch across the cells, and as he changed an item in one cell, there was a ripple-like movement in the other cells: the spreadsheet program was recalculating. His eyebrows rose as he saw the result. Then he punched in another variable, and another ripple of figures washed across the screen. He was offering the computer different hypothetical developments, and it was feeding back to him their probable consequences. "It's a good tool," Gottheil noted matter-of-factly.

In these, the early days of electronic spreadsheeting, it is most frequently seen as a tool for saving time. Don Jackson is a certified public accountant in Cincinnati. He has between 40 and 50 clients, mostly small businesses. Before he bought an Apple three years ago, he painstakingly did his calculations on light green crosshatched ledger sheets. A client would come in to work out a billing procedure, and after Jackson had put the relevant numbers on a sheet – in light pencil, so erasures could be easily made – various questions would come up. For example, if the billing procedure was based on a 15 percent interest rate, what would happen if the rate went up to 18 percent? To find out, the whole sheet would have to be redone. Each figure would have to be punched into a hand calculator and then checked by one of Jackson's employees. "I would work for twenty hours," Jackson said. "With a spreadsheet, it takes me fifteen minutes."

Jackson's story is a common one. In the first days of electronic spreadsheets – that is, two or three years ago – those who used them got things done so quickly that, despite the evidence of finished reports, bosses and co-workers often had trouble believing the tasks had been completed. Gottheil told me of an accountant who got "a rush task, sat down with his micro and his spreadsheet, finished it in an hour or two, and left it on his desk for two days. Then he Fed Ex-ed it to the client and got all sorts of accolades for working overtime."

But saving time is hardly the only benefit of spreadsheets. They encourage businesses to keep track of things that were previously unquantified or altogether overlooked. Executives no longer have to be satisfied with quarterly updates, for it is now an easy matter to compile monthly, weekly, even daily updates. People use spreadsheets to make daily inventory checks, to find out who has paid their bills, to chart the performance of truck drivers over a period of weeks or months. How-to manuals for spreadsheets often use as an example a performance chart for salespeople – the model breaks down how many items they sell week by week and instantly calculates commissions and even bonuses due. If word comes down that a belt-tightening is in order, a few keystrokes will create a sheet that clearly identifies the worst performers.

Bob Frankston, the programmer who designed VisiCalc with Dan Bricklin, noted that instant hard figures, so recently a luxury, are quickly becoming a necessity. The spreadsheet tool is shaping us. "There's an increasing demand for quantitative rather than qualitative justification for decisions," he said. "In the past, before spreadsheets, people would have taken a guess. Now they feel obligated to run the numbers."

Yet what really has the spreadsheet users charmed is not the hard and fast figures but the "what-if" factor: the ability to create scenarios, explore hypothetical developments, try out different options. The spreadsheet, as one executive put it, allows the user to create and then experiment with "a phantom business within the computer."

"Before the spreadsheet, you barely had enough time to do the totals," said Archie Barrett, a Capitol Hill staff member who uses an IBM PC-XT to work up spreadsheets for the House Armed Services Committee. "Now you put in a number and see whether you're above or below the total. You can play what-if games. What if we don't order as many tanks? What if we order more?"

The what-if factor has changed the way Allen Sneider, a partner in the Boston office of Laventhol & Horwath, a national accounting firm, approaches his job. Sneider bought an Apple in 1978, but he was not able to make it useful in his business until he saw an early copy of VisiCalc and became one of the first professionals to use the program. He explained:

Before, you would suggest a change to a client, get a staff member to calculate it, send it to the typist, to the proofreader, and recalculate it to make sure there weren't any errors. Now you have a machine right there with the client. Want to see what happens with a different return on investment? Sheltering? Interest rates changing by half of a percent? It's done in a minute. Before you'd be tempted to say, "Let's leave it the way it was." The whole mental attitude toward preparing projections has changed.

The what-if factor has not only changed the nature of jobs such as accounting; it has altered once rigid organizational structures. Junior analysts, without benefit of secretaries or support from data processing departments, can work up 50-page reports, complete with graphs and charts, advocating a complicated course of action for a client. And senior executives who take the time to learn how to use spreadsheets are no longer forced to rely on their subordinates for information.

Theodore Stein is an assistant vice president in data processing at the Connecticut Mutual Life Insurance Company in Hartford. After seeing what VisiCalc and the more powerful Lotus 1-2-3 could do, Stein became a passionate disciple of the spreadsheet. Until recently, Connecticut Mutual, like many large corporations, centralized its computer services in one division – data processing. People out in the field, or even at corporate headquarters, were generally not satisfied with the information they got from DP. Stein said

DP always has more requests than it can handle. There are two kinds of backlog – the obvious one, of things requested, and a hidden one. People say, "I won't ask for the information because I won't get it anyway." When those two guys designed VisiCalc, they opened up a whole new way. We realized that in three or four years, you might as well take your big minicomputer out on a boat and make an anchor out of it. With spreadsheets, a microcomputer gives you more power at a tenth of the cost. Now people can do the calculations themselves, and they don't have to deal with the bureaucracy.

Since it is easy to learn how to use spreadsheets – no programming experience is required – all it takes to get into the game is a $3,000 personal computer and a $500 copy of 1-2-3, or even a copy of VisiCalc or the Micro-Soft Company's Multiplan, both of which cost less than $200. Stein learned this early in Connecticut Mutual's spreadsheeting days. The company's chief financial officer wanted certain information, and his top "experts" had difficulty providing it. So one weekend he brought an Apple computer and a copy of VisiCalc home with him. Monday morning, he called his people in and showed them how he had gotten the information he had been clamoring for. "With one swipe of a diskette, he cut them off at the knees," Stein said. "He out-teched them. His experts! He'd cut the chain. The following week, they all came down to learn VisiCalc – fast."

All of this powerful scenario-testing machinery right there on the desktop induces some people to experiment with elaborate models. They talk of "playing" with the numbers, "massaging" the model. Computer "hackers" lose themselves in the intricacies of programming; spreadsheet hackers lose themselves in the world of what-if. Some, like Theodore Stein of Connecticut Mutual, admit that their habit goes beyond the point of diminishing returns: "I can't begin to tell you how many hours I spend at this," he said. "This is my pet, in a way. Scratching its ears and brushing its code . . . it's almost an obsession."

The experiments Stein and those like him carry out are far-flung attempts to formulate the ultimate model, the spreadsheet that behaves just like an actual business. Allerton J. Cushman of Morgan Stanley has been a connoisseur of these models since discovering that computer spreadsheets could make forecasts of the property-casualty insurance industry. Cushman wrote a pamphlet about his projections entitled "Confessions of an Apple Byter," which offered the observation that with VisiCalc, "getting your arms around the future seems a trifle easier." Cushman's office, high above midtown Manhattan, is dominated by IBM-compatible computers and printers, and when I visited him there he explained his fascination with modeling this way: "People like to build elegant models, whether of balsa wood or numbers."

Spreadsheet models have become a form of expression, and the very act of creating them seems to yield a pleasure unrelated to their utility. Unusual models are duplicated and passed around; these "templates" are sometimes used by other modelers – and sometimes only admired for their elegance.

Stein, Cushman, and other so-called gurus lose themselves in the more esthetic possibilities of spreadsheeting: the perfect model is an end in itself. "Power users" learn from gurus, but have other ends in mind – they can use sophisticated models to gain significant professional advantages. When a guru is not available, there are courses to take, self-help books to study, and magazine articles to examine, like the one in the July 1984 issue of *Personal Computing* entitled "Power Spreadsheeting," which warns of "arrested spreadsheet development" and urges users to "think like a spreadsheet."

Mastery is important, not for art's sake but to *win*. A brilliant model is not only beautiful, it yields insights impossible to attain by any other method. Dick York, a private real estate investor in Sausalito, changed his entire business to revolve around his Lotus 1-2-3. "I've used it to reduce everything in my operation to cash flow," he said. "The spreadsheets give me constant updates, and I'm able to pinpoint property that isn't bringing in money – I dump those properties immediately. This is information I'd always tried to get manually, but couldn't." York told me about the time he negotiated a commercial lease that included both a monthly rental and a percentage of the profit of his operation. In the course of making the spreadsheet model, he discovered there was a point at which going along with a raise in his rent would actually *decrease* the amount he'd pay the landlord. (The landlord did not have his own spreadsheet to divine this fact.)

Allen Sneider of Lowenthol & Horwath once worked a spreadsheet masterpiece. A client representing a finance company wanted to know whether it would be a good idea to pay $12 million for a factory that made artificial turf. Sneider and the client made a model that was sensitive to all sorts of variables. It would let you know the consequences of any change you might want to make in the business. Add a new production line, decrease production, increase inventory, widen the collateral base, change the mortgage rate, increase hourly wages . . . it was all there, calculated according to highly refined formulas. What happened? Sneider's client did not buy the factory (the factory employees bought it). Instead, he started his own business – buying and selling spreadsheet templates.

Because spreadsheets can do so many important things, those who use them have a tendency to lose sight of the crucial fact that the imaginary businesses they create on their computers are just that – imaginary. You can't really duplicate a business inside a computer, just aspects of a business. And since numbers are the strength of spreadsheets, the aspects that get emphasized are the ones easily embodied by numbers. Intangible factors aren't so easily quantified. Jim McNitt, in *The Art of Computer Management,* tells the story of a restaurant owner named Maxwell who was trying to decide whether to undertake a costly renovation. He ran 15 different scenarios on his computer, including one in which he took the money set aside for renovation and invested it elsewhere. What Maxwell found was startling: not only would renovation be foolhardy, but "even the 'best case' numbers showed I'd get nearly as good a rate of return on my investment in a money market fund as staying in the restaurant business." Get out of the restaurant business! the spreadsheet said. What the spreadsheet left out, of course, was the unquantifiable emotional factor – Maxwell loved what he did. He kept the restaurant (though he scuttled the renovation).

Maxwell was his own boss, and could follow his instincts. But a corporate executive who ignored such a clear-cut bottom-line conclusion might be risking his professional life. He is more likely to follow the numbers turned out by spreadsheets.

And so it is that spreadsheets help in the drive for paper profits, and are a prime tool of takeover architects. An executive in an acquisitions-hungry company might spend his time spreadsheeting in order to find a company ripe for takeover. If his spreadsheet projections were to produce a likely candidate – if the numbers looked good – he would naturally recommend making a takeover bid. Even a hostile takeover seems cut-and-dried, perfectly logical, in the world of spreadsheets. The spreadsheet user has no way of quantifying a corporate tradition or the misery of stockholders or whether the headaches of a drawn-out takeover bid will ultimately harm the corporate climates of the firms involved.

The flexibility of spreadsheets can encourage other heartless moves from headquarters. It is no great drain on a spreadsheeting executive's time to experiment with all sorts of odd, even insidious scenarios. He might ask: "What if we dropped our pension plan?" Then he might run the idea through a spreadsheet and find a huge gain in capital – and there would be the unthinkable, in hard figures.

Spreadsheets have no way of dealing with hunches, either, no formulas for telling their users when lightning will strike – when a product will be not merely a product but a trend-setting blockbuster. There were no formulas in Lotus's spreadsheet projections that did justice to the fantastic consumer acceptance of 1-2-3. "Our own projections were violated on a daily basis," said Ezra Gottheil. "It was beyond our wildest assumptions."

People tend to forget that even the most elegantly crafted spreadsheet is a house of cards, ready to collapse at the first erroneous assumption. The spreadsheet that looks good but turns out to be tragically wrong is becoming a familiar phenomenon. Sometimes the erring model-makers themselves pay the price. In August 1984, the *Wall Street Journal* reported that a Texas-based oil and gas company had fired several executives after the firm lost millions of dollars in an acquisition deal because of "errors traced to a faulty financial analysis spreadsheet model."

An often-repeated truism about computers is "Garbage In, Garbage Out." Any computer program, no matter how costly, sophisticated, or popular, will yield worthless results if the data fed into it is faulty. With spreadsheets, the danger is not so much that incorrect figures can be fed into them as that "garbage" can be embedded in the models themselves. The accuracy of a spreadsheet model is dependent on the accuracy of the *formulas* that govern the relationships between various figures. These formulas are based on assumptions made by the modelmaker. An assumption might be an educated guess about a complicated cause-and-effect relationship. It might also be a wild guess, or a dishonestly optimistic view.

For instance, a 5 percent increase in the cost of raw materials used to make widgets might lead to a 10 percent increase in the retail price, according to an established cost-price ratio. Anyone projecting a budget for a widget company could confidently integrate that formula into his model. But to determine the effect of a 10 percent price increase on the number of widgets actually sold, he would have to take into account all sorts of market factors, as well as how people tend to behave in certain situations. Perhaps the spreadsheeter has access to a study that definitively shows that a 5 percent increase in widget prices results in a 6 percent decrease in sales. But maybe no study exists. Or maybe the spreadsheeter knows that the widget company plans to use the projection to seek new financing and therefore doesn't want to reveal the company's vulnerability to fluctuations in the price of raw materials. So he might make the ludicrously optimistic assumption that a 5 percent price increase would result in only a 1 percent decrease in sales.

A notorious example of this kind of fiddling occurred when David Stockman, director of the Office of Management and Budget, was drawing up the budget for Ronald Reagan's first presidential term. According to William Greider's book *The Education of David Stockman and Other Americans*, a mainframe computer had been programmed with an elaborate model of the nation's economic behavior. When Stockman used the model to project the effects of Reagan's plan to reduce income taxes and increase defense spending, the computer calculated that the plan would lead to unprecedented federal deficits. Did Stockman warn his President that they were on a disastrous course? No. "He changed the economic assumptions fed into the computer model," writes Greider. "[He] assumed a swift decline in prices and interest rates. . . . The new model was based on a dramatic surge in the nation's productivity." So Stockman was able to fortify the Administration with figures – generated by a computer! – showing that the deficit would not be a problem.

Stockman's sleight of hand was fairly easy to discern. In 1981, electronic spreadsheets were just coming into their own, and the kind of sophisticated modeling Stockman did was still done chiefly on mainframe computers. The output he was working with wasn't in the now-familiar spreadsheet format; instead, the formulas appeared in one place and the results in another. You could see what you were getting. That cannot be said of electronic spreadsheets, which don't display the formulas that govern their calculations.

As Mitch Kapor explained, with electronic spreadsheets, "You can just randomly make formulas, all of which depend on each other. And when you look at the final results, you have no way of knowing what the rules are, unless somebody tells you."

Increasingly, however, businessmen are not telling but letting their spreadsheets do the talking. Because a spreadsheet looks so authoritative – *and it was done by a computer, wasn't it?* – the hypothetical models get accepted as gospel. The spreadsheet presentation is becoming both more commonplace and more sophisticated: not only the numbers but the formats of the sheets themselves are designed to make eloquent points.

This use of spreadsheets has less to do with productivity or insightful analysis than with the art of persuasion. "People doing negotiations now sit down with spreadsheets," Bob Frankston said. "When you're trying to sell a car, the standard technique is to ask for the other person's objections, and then argue them away. If two people are in front of a spreadsheet, and one says, 'Well, the numbers say this,' the other can't say, 'Yes, but there's something I can't quite point to.' "

As spreadsheets are used more for persuasion and negotiation, people are becoming rather sly about their design. Lotus 1-2-3 can turn figures and formulas into graphs – graphs that spreadsheeters can use to skew and oversimplify reality. "With graphs, things take on greater weight," Allen Sneider said. Sneider expects spreadsheets to become more persuasive – and the distortion of reality greater – when color printers become more common. "If I wanted to, I could skew the picture by choosing a particular color in a bar graph. Some people think red is very negative. They might think green indicates profitability."

All of this has made some people who work with spreadsheets regularly skeptical of what they see. "I know of one venture capital firm that *assumes* people manipulate spreadsheets," Kapor said. "So they have this other model to put against the first one, to factor the stuff out."

Obviously, not all of the millions of people who use spreadsheets (VisiCalc alone has sold over 700,000 copies) are accountants, financial analysts, or middle managers. VisiCalc's co-designer Bob Frankston attributes some of his program's popularity to these other users: "It turns out there are a number of people who are either running their own businesses or doing financial management. The 'own business' might be something like renting an apartment. If you've got to project costs for a year, it makes sense to do it with a spreadsheet."

More than 10 million people filed Schedule C "self-employment" reports with the IRS last year: we are becoming a nation of businesspeople. Moreover, we are becoming a *society* of businesspeople. We speak in jargon derived from the business world ("What's the bottom line on this?"). We read columns on "personal money management" that urge us to speculate in markets once reserved for the very few. We have accepted the venture capitalist as a role model. The buzz word these days in computer software firms looking to expand their markets is "personal productivity," as if the home itself – maybe *life* itself – were best viewed as a business.

Spreadsheets are at the heart of this movement. Using electronic spreadsheets, everyone can run his or her own business. Thousands of Americans are attending classes to learn about the spreadsheet way of knowledge. Some will lose themselves in the rows of columns, the grids becoming their windows on the world. They will spend their evenings in front of their computers, the dark dimly lit by the glow of green phosphorescent numbers, fiddling with scenarios, trying to make the profit line perfect.

There is no doubt that the electronic spreadsheet saves time and provides insight; there is no doubt that even greater benefits will one day be derived from these grids. Yet all these benefits will be meaningless if the spreadsheet metaphor is taken too much to heart. After all, it is only a metaphor. Fortunately, few would argue that all relations between people can be quantified and manipulated by formulas. Of human behavior, no faultless assumptions – and so no perfect model – can be made.

Human Issues in New Office Technology

Richard J. Long

Pursuing our theme that human and organizational factors heavily influence the effectiveness of new technologies, Rick Long identifies the key human resource issues involved in office computerization. In a cogent analysis of the literature, the author describes three possible roles for human resource specialists, concluding that a "proactive" approach is the most desirable. Professor Richard Long is Head of the Department of Industrial Relations and Organizational Behaviour at the College of Commerce, University of Saskatchewan, and this specially written paper draws on material from his book New Office Information Technology: Human and Managerial Implications *(Croom Helm, London, 1987).*

Organizations have been implementing new office information technology at a dramatic pace in recent years.[1] Some of the consequences that are sought include higher productivity, cost reduction, better decision-making, improved customer service, and an enhanced ability to respond to environmental change.

However, in many cases, actual results have fallen well short of expectations. For instance, a major study of 2,000 US firms that had implemented new office systems[2] revealed that at least 40 percent of these systems failed to achieve the intended results. Interestingly, less than 10 percent of the failures were attributed to technical failure. The majority of the reasons given were human and organizational. As Levinson puts it: "While the 1960s were the era of hardware failures, and the 1970s of software deficiencies, the issues for system failure in the 1980s have become organizational and managerial."[3]

In order to achieve successful implementation and ongoing effectiveness of new information systems, a large number of human resource (HR) issues need to be effectively dealt with. These include training and support, recruiting and selection, job design and structuring, health and safety, ergonomics, compensation policies, performance evaluation, and industrial relations. Yet, empirical studies[4] suggest that these issues rarely receive the attention they deserve during the implementation process, and that human resource specialists are seldom involved at an early enough stage in the process to do other than react to human and organizational problems as they emerge.

Although technical specialists are frequently blamed for these omissions, observation suggests that human resource specialists themselves are frequently at fault by not aggressively seeking to be involved in planning and implementation. However, line management may also contribute to this problem by abdicating responsibility to technical specialists, in the belief that new office systems are technical, not behavioral systems. For example, a study of 125 Canadian firms by Templer[5] found that not only did most line managers see little role for the HR department in setting technology policy, neither did the HR managers themselves. Clegg and Kemp[6] found similar results in their UK study.

Lack of timely involvement by HR specialists may have far-reaching consequences. New office technology can be implemented in such a way as to enhance or expand human abilities, increase user discretion and autonomy, and generally improve the quality of work life experienced by organization members. Or, it can be used to do the exact opposite. Fortunately, there is a considerable body of evidence to suggest that not only is the former approach more socially desirable, it also results in the most productive use of the technology in most instances.[7]

This paper will first identify and describe some of the key human resource issues that need to be dealt with when implementing new office technology. It then describes three possible roles that HR specialists in organizations can assume regarding the technology – reactive, supportive, and proactive. It suggests that a proactive approach is necessary to bring about the most desirable of the scenarios described above, and urges both line managers and human resource specialists to do all they can to promote adoption of this role.

Key human resource issues

While there is a wide variety of specific human issues associated with new office technology, perhaps the most fundamental has to do with the place of human beings in the overall conception of the technology, and the orientation taken by the organization in this regard. Does the organization see the new technology as an opportunity to tighten control, reduce skill levels needed for job performance, and eliminate labor? Or does it see it as an opportunity to allow greater worker autonomy, broader jobs, and increased employee participation in decision-making? The evidence is clear that either is possible.[8]

Those organizations seeking the first set of results tend to adopt what is known as the "technology driven" approach to implementation of new office technology, while those seeking the second set of results tend to adopt the "user driven/participative" approach. The approach that is taken and the underlying philosophy about the technology that is adopted can have dramatic effects on the types of human issues which emerge, and the way they are handled.

Let us take the practice of computer monitoring of performance as a case in point. Numerous studies have concluded that it can lead to the reduction of worker autonomy and increased stress, particularly when used for performance evaluation.[9] (For example, ad takers for the *New York Times* are reported to work under a system that times not only their average time per ad taken, but also their bathroom breaks![10]) In addition to its possible impact on the performance evaluation process, this type of usage may lead to reduced employee job satisfaction, higher employee turnover, increased absenteeism, and performance problems, all of which must be dealt with in some manner.

On the other hand, empirical findings by Rothwell provide an interesting counterpoint to these findings. In her UK sample, she found that "while the potential use of information technology for monitoring worker effort and errors is resented by trade unions . . . workers appear to be less resentful of errors unambiguously attributable to them than being blamed for omissions that were largely the responsibility of others."[11] Similarly, a study by Westin and his associates found that many US video display operators reacted positively to computer monitoring, citing increased objectivity in performance evaluation and the ability to more easily monitor their own output.[12] In West Germany, Sydow found that only 15 percent of VDT operators "strongly agreed" that introduction of the VDT had resulted in greater intensity of supervision, while 32 percent strongly disagreed.[13]

Overall, it appears that computer monitoring can be either beneficial or detrimental to employee discretion and satisfaction, depending on how it is used. On the one hand, it has the potential to be a valuable source of feedback to employees, one of the five core dimensions of psychologically healthy work.[14] On the other hand, when implemented in an autocratic, mechanistic, and simplistic fashion it can lead to a reduction in worker autonomy and discretion, as well as dysfunctional employee attitudes and behavior. Which of these outcomes occurs will have a major impact on the nature of the human issues to be dealt with.

The specific human resource issues surrounding new office technology can be grouped into two categories: (i) those associated with the implementation itself, and (ii) those associated with the *consequences* of implementation. The first category centers around creating conditions such that those who will be operating the new system will be willing and able to do so. Part of this may involve selecting people with the right skills and abilities. To do so, changes to recruitment and selection procedures may be necessary. Compensation policies and performance appraisal procedures may need to be changed. Old job categories may be eliminated and new ones created. Effort needs to be directed at ensuring that the jobs that result from the new system possess as much motivating potential[15] as possible. Possible health and safety issues need to be anticipated and dealt with, and efforts made to ensure that ergonomic standards and principles have been considered and utilized.[16] In unionized organizations, many of these issues are subject to negotiation, and may take some time to change.

To take just one issue, providing the necessary training and education is a much more complicated and difficult task than it may appear to be at first glance. This is because several types and levels of training and education are usually necessary in order to realize the full benefits of the new system. First, there is the relatively straightforward matter of what buttons to push, and Curley terms this "Type A" learning.[17] But beyond that, users need to understand the relationship between the technology and the organization, which will better enable them to utilize the full potential of the technology. Curley suggests that "Type B" learning, which can only occur with ongoing usage, is crucial but frequently neglected.

Users should also be provided with an understanding of the ergonomics of the technology, so as to be able to adjust it to their best advantage and minimize potential health problems such as eyestrain or muscle aches, which can otherwise arise.[18] Although frequently neglected, managers and supervisors also need to be educated about what the equipment is and is not capable of, as well as the human and policy issues surrounding use of the technology.

Finally, a major issue relates to the implementation process itself. It is axiomatic that the process by which any significant organizational change is implemented has a major impact on the success of that change. One of the most important contributions that HR professionals could make would be to encourage use of an implementation process that is based on sound behavioral principles. Key among these would be user participation in the change process and measures to reduce the insecurity and uncertainty that change inevitably brings. The well-known sociotechnical approach can also be employed in the application of new information technology.[19]

Although these are difficult and complex issues, the human resource issues that *result* from implementation of the new technology typically require as much or more attention and planning. For example, if the new system requires fewer people to operate, or people who are different from those now employed, what is to be done with the "surplus" people? Possible options for retraining and transfer need to be explored, and this requires considerable long-range planning. "Bridging" positions may be necessary in assisting surplus "clerical workers" to become needed "knowledge workers," dealing with higher-level tasks.

To take another example, assume that introduction of technology results in considerable time savings for office workers. How is this time to be used? What new tasks will they assume? From whom? In order for lower-level office workers to take on new tasks formerly carried out by their superiors, they may need additional training. But will superiors be willing to give up these tasks? How can they be encouraged to delegate more, and how will they use *their* time savings?

Indeed, what about managers? There is considerable evidence that the roles of supervisors and managers could change dramatically as a result of new office technology. For example, it has been suggested that there will be a need for fewer supervisors, and that those who remain will see their roles change from routine surveillance to focus more on training, helping to implement new systems and procedures, boundary roles, and promoting innovation.[20] What kind of training and support will be necessary to help them adapt to or even create their new roles? How will performance standards have to change as qualitative aspects of performance become more important than quantitative results? How will the major organizational processes – such as communication and decision-making – have to be changed to support these new roles?

Possible roles for the HR department

As mentioned earlier, there are three main roles that a human resource department could assume regarding the implementation of new office information technology – reactive, supportive, and proactive – and each will now be discussed in turn.

In the *reactive role*, human resource specialists become involved only after implementation, when problems such as ineffective performance and employee dissatisfaction emerge. At that time they may have to deal with problems such as unexpected turnover, a mismatch between available and needed human resources, employee complaints and grievances, high stress among both workers and supervisors, unsatisfactory performance levels, and possible difficulties with the union. Organizational policies which prove to be inappropriate are identified and dealt with in a piecemeal, ad hoc manner.

This approach may not only lead to unsatisfactory results, but may also damage the credibility of the HR department. This problem was accurately foreseen some years ago by Williams, who contended that "late entry [by HR specialists] too often involves playing catch-up with problems that are too far advanced to be handled well. In this instance, the personnel department runs the risk of being seen as ineffective."[21] Yet, observation suggests that this role remains the norm.

In the *supportive role*, HR specialists become involved in anticipating some of the problems that may occur, and developing policies to either prevent or deal with them. For example, they may assist in designing effective training and support programs. They may engage in human resource planning to develop policies and procedures for dealing with a potential shortage or surplus of employees. Changes in job classifications, job descriptions, and reporting relationships may be required. All of this is aimed at maximizing the success of the new technical system, which is taken as a given by the HR department.

Although not as complex as the proactive role, this role is still a challenging one. A major challenge is simply to be able to anticipate and identify what the human resource issues will be at each stage of system development. However, a number of useful vehicles have been developed to assist this process, one of them by the Personnel Policy branch of the Treasury Board of Canada (the agency charged with promoting effective management in the Canadian federal civil service). It consists of a detailed checklist geared to the various stages of the Systems Development Life Cycle, a popular methodology for designing information systems.[22] Although still not the norm, a number of the more sophisticated HR departments are taking on this role.

In the *proactive role*, human resource specialists become involved right at the first stages of planning, and assist in designing new systems not only to avoid potential problems, but to create a *more* productive and satisfying work environment than previously existed. This is accomplished by identifying what the "ideal" work structure should be, from both a social and technical point of view, identifying problems currently hindering this, and then using the technology to move in this direction.

Walton and Vittori term this an "opportunity orientation, . . . which explores the possibility that system design and implementation activities may be used to move toward preconceived organizational ideals and preferences."[23] They suggest that firms can move toward this orientation by developing an "organizational impact statement" as part of the implementation process. This involves, first, careful examination of the proposed information system. The objective in so doing is to identify changes that would occur in such areas as degree of job specialization, locus of control, skill requirements, amount of individual discretion, and performance measures. These are termed "first order consequences."

After that, an attempt is made to predict the human dynamics that will flow from the first order consequences. Examples of these "second order consequences" include job security or insecurity, status gains or losses, increased or reduced sense of autonomy, and career optimism or pessimism. Finally, management must assess whether these consequences are consistent with their organizational ideals, or whether these consequences would move them in the wrong direction. As a formal requirement of the go-ahead decision, the organizational impact statement becomes part of the broader calculation of the costs and benefits of the new system. On this basis the decision could be made to proceed, or to send the plan back to the developers for modification. In extreme cases, a decision to abandon the new system altogether might be made.

Since the proactive role recognizes that use of the "technology driven" approach to the implementation of new office technology is undesirable, a key part of this role involves actively lobbying for use of the "user driven/participative" approach. This can be done by both pointing out the unintended negative consequences that frequently arise from the technology driven approach, and by helping to provide the behavioral knowledge that is essential for the user/driven participative approach to work.

Overall, there is little evidence to suggest that the proactive role has been adopted in other than a very few isolated instances. However, as knowledge about the most effective utilization of the new technology continues to spread, this role is likely to be increasingly adopted by HR departments in the more progressive organizations.

Conclusions

To bring about effective implementation of new office information technology, the involvement of human resource specialists must be seen as not only legitimate but essential. As a first step, they – along with technical specialists and line managers – need to recognize that new office systems are not technical systems, but behavioral systems which depend for success on the effective integration of both their social and technical components.

Once the HR department recognizes that it can and should play a crucial role in the planning and implementation process, how can it convince others of this? Based on his research, Templer concludes that the HR specialists "must *earn the right to participate* in introducing new technology by demonstrating convincingly their technological credibility, their support for organizational goals, and the essential and indispensable nature of this knowledge of the human side of technology."[24]

This can be facilitated by demonstrating acceptance and effective utilization of the new technology within the HR function, which may in itself be an area where major improvement is required. For example, research by Hall and Torrington[25] found that while HR specialists have experienced a dramatic increase in access to computing technology in recent years, it is rarely used for other than routine record-keeping functions.

This is unfortunate, since there are a large number of different possibilities. For example, computerized personnel records can facilitate personnel research of a variety of types. Unusual patterns of absenteeism could be identified, along with possible causes. The health and safety officer could systematically investigate accident records. Wage and salary research could be conducted more easily. Human resource planning could be facilitated. The technology could even be used to facilitate introduction of various innovative personnel policies, such as a "cafeteria style" benefits plan or flexible working hours.

Beyond this, however, HR specialists must make a conscious effort to educate themselves by learning from the experiences of other organizations that have implemented new information technology. Admittedly, a well-documented body of knowledge dealing with human issues in the implementation of new information technology has only begun to emerge, and much remains to be learned. None the less, recent years have seen the appearance of some works which attempt to synthesize the evidence to date and draw out the managerial implications.[26]

Once some expertise has been acquired, the case must be sold to top management that there is something to be gained, in terms of organizational objectives, from intensive HR involvement right from the earliest stages of planning. What would be most effective would be a credible estimate of the potential costs of failure to adequately consider the human side of implementation, including opportunity costs if possible. At the least, a well-documented assessment of the possible negative consequences that can flow from reliance on a reactive approach, and the potential benefits of a proactive approach, can be prepared. In so doing, it is important to place these consequences within the context of organizational objectives whenever possible.

In sum, those organizations that recognize the key role of human issues in successful implementation and utilization of new office information technology, and actively encourage the involvement of human resource specialists right from the outset, can expect to be rewarded with more effective use of that technology.

Notes

1 J. W. Verity and G. Lewis, "Computers: The New Look," *Business Week*, November 30, 1987, pp. 112–23.

2 T. K. Bikson and B. Gutek, *Implementation of Office Automation* (Rand Corporation, Santa Monica, CA, 1984).

3 E. Levinson, "Implementation Path Analysis: A Method for Studying Implementation of Information Technology," *Office: Technology and People*, vol. 2, 1985, pp. 287–304.

4 See C. Clegg and N. Kemp, "Information Technology: Personnel, Where are You?" *Personnel Review*, vol. 15(1), 1986, pp. 8–15; R. J. Long, *New Office Information Technology: Human and Managerial Implications* (Croom Helm, London, 1987); S. G. Rothwell, "Company Employment Policies and New Technology," paper presented at EGOS Conference on the Organizational Consequences of New Technology, University of Antwerp, 1983; A. Templer, "Managers Downplay the Role of the HR Function in Introducing New Technology," *Personnel Administrator*, July 1985, pp. 88–96.

5 Templer, "Managers Downplay the Role of the HR Function."

6 Clegg and Kemp, "Information Technology."

7 See Long, *New Office Information Technology*, for a review of the evidence on this issue.

8 ibid.

9 See for example A. F. Westin, H. A. Schweder, M. A. Baker, et al., *The Changing Workplace: A Guide to Managing the People, Organizational and Regulatory Aspects of Office Technology* (Knowledge Industry Publications, White Plains, NY, 1985); Labour Canada, *In the Chips: Opportunities, People, Partnerships*, Report of the Labour Canada Task force on Micro-Electronics and Employment (Labour Canada, Ottawa, 1982).

10 Westin et al., *The Changing Workplace*.

11 S. G. Rothwell, "Supervisors and New Technology," *Employment Gazette*, January, 1984, p. 23.

12 Westin et al., *The Changing Workplace*.

13 J. Sydow, "Sociotechnical Change and Perceived Work Situations: Some Conceptual Propositions and an Empirical Investigation in Different Office Settings," *Office: Technology and People*, vol. 2, 1984, pp. 121–32.

14 See R. J. Hackman and G. Oldham, *Work Redesign* (Addison-Wesley, Reading, MA, 1980).

15 Motivating potential is determined by the extent to which each of the five core dimensions of desirable jobs (skill variety, task identity, task significance, autonomy, and feedback) is present in a given job. See Hackman and Oldham, *Work Redesign*.

16 Ergonomics is a term used to describe the systematic consideration of physical, psychological, and social characteristics of human beings in the design of tools and equipment, the workplace, and the job itself. Effective application of ergonomics can enhance both employee wellbeing and performance. Ergonomic guidelines as applied to new office technology can be found in Long, *New Office Information Technology*, pp. 270–80.

17   K. F. Curley, *Word Processing: First Step to the Office of the Future?* (Praeger Publishers, New York, 1983).

18   For an excellent discussion of the possible health effects of new office technology see S. L. Sauter, L. J. Chapman, and S. J. Knutson, *Improving VDT Work: Causes and Control of Health Concerns in VDT Use* (The Report Store, Lawrence, KA, 1985).

19   See E. Mumford, "Participative Systems Design: Practice and Theory," *Journal of Occupational Behaviour*, vol. 4, 1983, pp. 47–57; or C. Pava, *Managing New Office Technology: An Organizational Strategy* (The Free Press, New York, 1983).

20   Long, *New Office Information Technology*.

21   L. K. Williams, "Office Automation – Some Problems and Opportunities," AFIPS Office Automation Conference, Houston, Texas, 1981, p. 261.

22   See Treasury Board of Canada, *Changing Technologies: Human Resource Management Considerations* (Ottawa 1984). Also reproduced in Long, *New Office Information Technology*, pp. 296–305.

23   R. E. Walton and W. Vittori, "New Information Technology: Organizational Problem or Opportunity?" *Office: Technology and People*, vol. 1, 1983, pp. 249–73.

24   Templer, "Managers Downplay the Role of the HR Function," p. 94.

25   L. Hall and D. Torrington, "Why Not Use the Computer? The Use and Lack of Use of Computers in Personnel," *Personnel Review*, vol. 15, 1986, pp. 3–7.

26   See Long, *New Office Information Technology* for a comprehensive discussion of these issues and a detailed guide to implementation. Other useful sources include R. A. Hirschheim, *Office Automation: A Social and Organizational Perspective* (Wiley, Chichester, UK, 1985); and A. F. Westin, H. A. Schweder, M. A. Baker, et al., *The Changing Workplace: A Guide to Managing the People, Organizational and Regulatory Aspects of Office Technology* (Knowledge Industry Publications, White Plains, NY, 1985).

Desktop Computerization and the Organization of Work

Rob Kling and Suzanne Iacono

Like the previous author, Kling and Iacono emphasize the role of choice in office computerization, arguing that specific interventions lead to either increased flexibility in worklife and streamlined work groups, or regimented work organization and muddled work procedures. The authors don't agree with the "optimists" or the "pessimists," whose views on the quality of office worklife are seen as deterministic. Kling and Iacono say they don't expect to see any single form of "office of the future" emerging. Professor Kling and Suzanne Iacono are in the Department of Information and Computer Science, University of California, Irvine, and this paper is based on their new book, Computerization at Work.

Causal arguments about computerization and worklife

Most work is carried out with specialized equipment or techniques. As a consequence, sociologists of work have often tried to account for the roles of technology in organizing work, and the effects of changing technologies in changing work organization. Despite the rich literatures about technology and work, there are few key theoretical ideas to help deepen our understanding about the link between technology and work organization. This paper examines changes in technology as a *complex social and technical intervention* into a work process and argues that the "intervention" concept can sharpen our research and theorizing. We will examine a particular form of computerization – desktop computing – as an intervention into white-collar work organizations.

Many sociological analyses of changing technologies – especially office technologies – rest on some form of social or economic determinism. C. Wright Mills, for example, characterizes the social influence of mechanized office equipment in mid-century in these terms:

As machines spread, they began to prompt newer divisions of labor . . . The newer machines, especially the more complex and costly ones, require central control of offices previously scattered throughout the enterprise. This centralization, which prompts more new divisions of labor . . . is facilitated . . . through the urge to cut costs, and . . . through the increased volume of office work . . . Machines and centralization go together in company after company: and together they increase output and lower unit costs. They also open the full range of organization to factory techniques.[1]

Harry Braverman[2] stimulated a new line of research about technology and the labor process by amplifying Mills' argument and suggesting that new technologies are exploited by managers so as to help them tighten control over workers: de-skilling and job fragmentation were expected outcomes of this process.[3] In contrast with these grim visions of the roles of technology in enhancing bureaucratic regimens and tightening work organization, a small group of authors portray relatively utopian work worlds as the likely outcomes of technological change. In the case of computerization, they suggest that most jobs will be more flexible and intellectually challenging.[4]

"Determinism" has become a stigmatizing label, and few analysts would characterize themselves as enthusiastic determinists. A hallmark of deterministic analyses is the focus on *either* flexible *or* regimented work organizations as the primary outcome of technological change. Deterministic analyses can be enticing because they are simple and make strong unambiguous claims about the way that technological innovations have altered worklife and are most likely to continue changing worklife. However, they also vastly oversimplify and mislead when they ignore the contingencies that can lead to opposite outcomes.

Our own research does not show that computerization, one form of technological change, leads to the same outcomes in all situations. Instead, outcomes depend upon several contingencies, which include: the strategies for implementing technological change, the social organization of technical support and work for a particular work group, the occupational power of the worker and her work group, and the degree of integration of the technology into the worklife of the user and her work group. We examine some of these dimensions throughout the rest of the paper by examining the role of an important class of office technologies – desktop computing – in worklife. We base our analyses on three kinds of evidence:

1 Evidence from research studies done by others and cited below.
2 Our own observation as participants in university departments, research institutes, and administrative offices which have adopted a variety of desktop computing environments.
3 The preliminary findings of our own case studies of work groups in several private firms which have adopted rich desktop computing environments.

We use this evidence informally and usually implicitly. The main points of this paper are to identify the ways that desktop computerization works rather than to carefully test explicit hypotheses against a specific set of data.

Desktop computing

Many analysts and public commentators expect computer-based "desktop" office automation to be the most significant technological innovation in white-collar workplaces in the 1980s and 1990s.[5] We view desktop computing as an information service in which people get access to specific information or information-manipulating capabilities in their immediate work area.[6] Desktop computing can be delivered by a variety of equipment from stand-alone microcomputers through multi-user computer systems. Many organizations are adopting microcomputers and the office support packages which computer vendors are adding to larger multi-user computers. These adoptions facilitate a move toward more extensively automated office environments. About 7 million personal computers (PCs) and 300,000 multi-user systems were installed in the United States by early 1985; and these numbers are still growing at about 15 percent annually. By 1985, there were terminals or microcomputers for at least 10 million people, or 20 percent of the United States' white-collar workforce. Desktop computing is spreading rapidly, even with periodic slumps in equipment sales relative to the relatively strong average growth rates.

The earliest forms of desktop computing were located in two very different kinds of work places: scientific laboratories and clerical data entry offices. In the laboratories, many programmers, scientists, and engineers utilized terminals at their desks linked to general-purpose time-shared computers. Their jobs were relatively flexible and their modes of computer use were highly discretionary. In contrast, the other major class of desktop computing users had highly repetitive, and routinized jobs, e.g. airline reservationists took phone calls from customers and helped them make reservations by using highly structured transaction processing systems. Today, desktop computing has spread well beyond R&D labs and regimented clerical work groups. Some analysts argue that providing sophisticated computer terminals for most office workers will transform office work and jobs on a vast scale.[7]

Accounts of computerization and worklife

Deterministic analyses

Analysts who project significant social changes disagree about the character and quality of these transformations and their implications for people working in extensively automated environments. Regardless of the theoretical differences, however, most analysts discuss these changes in a similar context: "the office of the future." Many analysts portray each office of the future as effectively similar. There is little variation in the major elements which comprise each extensively automated office: types of computing equipment, occupational mix of workers, and types of work for which computing is used. They characterize work as information processing or knowledge work. Computing use is usually portrayed as a simple smooth-functioning process. A worker keyboards data or text, the computer computes, and the printer produces adequately correct output. Or, managers routinely access the proper data – online or through printed reports. Problems of access, training, or unreliable machinery are exceptional. Most workers are relatively similar in their jobs and status. As a result they are viewed as sharing similar fates with computerization.

Many professional articles and books about desktop computing are permeated with powerful images of favorable working conditions for computer users.[8] Sparse computerization will have minor impacts on worklife.[9] Extensive computerization may profoundly change worklife by enabling managers to change the division of labor and temporal patterns of workers. Work groups extensively automated with multifunctional desktop computing are especially interesting because they are a major model for future work groups and they are likely to be the sites of the most substantial transformations in work that can be attributed to computerization.[10] Few work groups are so extensively automated that the majority of workers routinely use desktop computing services. Most work groups have terminals or micro-computers for a small fraction of their workforce. Today, the most extensively automated work groups are clerical work groups or small professional work groups which specialize in activities like financial analysis or engineering design. However, it is likely that a wider variety of work groups will become increasingly computerized in the next 20 years.

Some analysts view the poor working conditions for back office clericals as the most likely fate of all office workers.[11] In contrast, some technological enthusiasts consider the flexibility of many professional jobs as the likely direction of social change.[12] In this more optimistic scenario, the differences between job levels and their related restrictions, opportunities and status will diminish. Finally, both lines of analysis usually imply that most workers will work with computer systems and that most significant work will be done on them. We simplify the primary debate about the direction of "the office of the future" by characterizing the two extreme alternatives as *flexible work groups* versus *regimented work groups*. These alternatives are opposite conceptions typically implied by "optimistic" and "pessimistic" analyses of extensive computerization[13] These one-sided analyses make it seem that computerization will make one of these alternatives far more dominant in the future.

Optimistic analyses portray extensively automated offices as flexible and implicitly professional workplaces. They idealize the capabilities of computer-based technologies in transforming worklife. They argue that most white-collar workers could readily have immediate access to multifunctional workstations at their desks. The workers will intensively use the equipment to enhance a variety of work activities. They can communicate better and faster via electronic mail. Information will be at their fingertips through online data bases. They can speed through other tasks such as analyzing data and preparing correspondence using sophisticated equipment.[14] In general the optimistic analyses view desktop computing systems as potentially very accessible, reliable, and easy to use. Information handling tasks can be simplified through automation with appropriate equipment. Office workers perform more varied and interesting jobs through a reduction in routinized work. The nature of white-collar work will be transformed to be substantially more interesting and creative.[15]

Pessimistic analyses portray extensively automated workplaces as primarily regimented workplaces. They infer that computerization will degrade work by examining workers at the lowest levels of the office hierarchy where jobs are the most routinized and the division of labor is the most rigid. They view the implementation of desktop computing as another method for management to gain more control over the work processes and extract more work from the workers. Data entry clerks, such as telephone travel reservationists, insurance claims clerks, and word processing specialists are examples of office workers who use single function systems, work in relatively regimented work groups, and maintain positions at the lowest levels of the work group hierarchy. Pessimistic analyses characterize offices of the future as workplaces where there will be major differences between a few good jobs and many bad jobs. They hold that computerization readily degrades work, and that computerized clerical jobs will be highly feminized, poorly paid, and relatively unsatisfying.[16] Zuboff characterizes computer users as performing "computer-mediated" work; she criticizes computerization as buffering workers from each other, from their clients, and from the "real" concrete subject of their work.[17]

These lines of analysis which portray one outcome as dominant usually rest on economic and technological determinism: the character of work in extensively computerized settings is determined by the nature of the technology and the structure of economic interests. The arguments are simple and appealing, albeit conflicting, depending upon the "optimism" or "pessimism" that underlies one's analysis. To resolve these disputes and gain some deeper insights into the possible changes in work organization we can expect with extensive desktop computerization, it helps to examine studies of earlier modes of computerization.

Empirical studies of computerization and work

Scholars have studied work groups which employ large-scale computerized information systems such as accounting;[18] police property and suspect enquiry systems;[19] claims processing in insurance; and inventory control systems in manufacturing firms.[21] There are two difficulties in drawing upon this body of research in a literal way to understand extensive desktop computing.

First, clerical workers are more frequently studied[22] than managerial and professional workers.[23] However, many extensively automated work groups are primarily managerial and professional work groups in which clerical workers provide critical support. As a consequence, we should not anticipate the same changes in worklife reported in other studies of other modes of computerization to be necessarily repeated with desktop computing (e.g., de-skilling of clerical workers or slight job enlargement for professional workers).

Second, few studies link work outcomes to careful descriptions of the technology and social organization of work. The presence of computer technologies is often viewed as the main independent variable.[24]

Despite these two limitations, we can learn about computerization and worklife from earlier studies. For example, Turner reports that social workers who used a fast online information system to determine a client's eligibility showed more mental strain symptoms, increased absenteeism, and decreased job satisfaction than those who used an older teletype system.[25] The improved system enabled users to interact with more clients each day due to a decrease in the length of each interview. As a result, productivity increased. However, the strain of additional problems and emotional interchanges due to increased client contact led to increased stress and decreased job satisfaction.

Turner reports a second case study in which the use of an electronic mail system improved the quality of worklife for a group of bank loan officers who marketed international loans but did not increase their overall performance.[26] They worked in New York City, managed loans in the Orient, and often stayed late at work to phone Tokyo and Hong Kong. The electronic mail system enabled them to send and receive messages during normal working hours, and to reduce their number of phone calls. With the new system, they could leave the office at normal hours. But it did not improve their effectiveness. Even though the group became more satisfied with their working conditions, they were unable to increase the number of loans granted.

Turner's studies are interesting because they examine a transition from a primitive computer-based system to one which approaches desktop computing in one dimension: speed of interaction. Recently, Tora Bikson and Barbara Gutek found that people who did share workstations or terminals reported more substantial integration of computer systems into their work, greater satisfaction with systems, and greater productivity.[27] These studies suggest that improving one dimension such as speed of interaction or access alone can improve productivity or quality of working life. These improvements can go hand in hand, but are not necessarily simultaneous.

Carter argues that the structure of the work organization (e.g., its size and control structures) might help predict when good outcomes will occur.[28] This line of reasoning presumes that the practices that accompany the introduction of computer equipment or changes in equipment are quite different in work groups with different structural arrangements. For example, clerks in work groups that are already regimented may be told explicitly how to use computer-based systems and have their productivity closely monitored while clerks in more flexible groups may have substantial control about the ways in which they integrate computer equipment into their own work and be less accountable for producing measurable work products. Ideas like these are usually implicit in contingency analyses like Carter's. In this paper we make them explicit by viewing desktop computerization as a complex strategic intervention.[29]

Danziger and Kraemer provide additional support for the thesis that computerization should be viewed as an intervention which varies across work groups. They report that when computing users have greater discretion in their jobs, "the characteristics of the user have the greatest effect on computer impacts."[30] They also observe that when computing users have relatively little discretion in their jobs, that "the nature of the computer package has the greatest effect on computer impacts." Danziger and Kraemer analyzed their data about 2,500 managers, professionals, and clerks by occupational differences. But it is plausible to interpret their findings in terms of work groups since they gathered most of their data from computer users who worked in groups that were relatively homogeneous by occupation. (For example, the clerks worked in offices which processed traffic tickets and the majority of their professional respondents worked in specialized professional groups such as urban planning and police detective details.)

Hirschheim advances beyond simple determinisms and argues that computerization may have different outcomes depending upon the social processes that accompany a system's design and implementation: more control by end users will lead to better outcomes.[31] Technological determinism has not been a viable model for predicting changes in worklife. The overall body of empirical research does not find that better jobs are necessary byproducts of better systems or that technological change necessarily de-skills and fragments jobs.[32] Work groups differ in many ways besides the sheer content of the tasks done: size, occupational mix, compliance or commitment-oriented control patterns, turnover rates, relative resources, etc. Work groups also vary in the quality of working conditions. It would be remarkable if technological changes alone were powerful enough to make these other differences minor and to force groups into developing toward a common future.

Many alterations in worklife will depend upon both existing work conditions (e.g., the organization of work, resources, and the actual technologies in use) and upon the social interventions that accompany changes in computing equipment. For example, interpersonal communication patterns will change where electronic mail – a technical intervention – is routinely used and especially where its use is commonplace. Professional jobs will change in content most frequently when professional workers do not have secretarial support to which they can delegate certain routine tasks (e.g., data entry, printing letters) – a social intervention.

How desktop computerization has consequences

Technological and economic determinism dominate most analyses of computerization. In the previous section, we briefly examined optimistic and pessimistic perspectives. Our alternative to a deterministic analysis of the outcomes of extensive desktop computerization is to characterize the process of implementation as a *complex intervention*. It is a *strategic intervention* in so far as some participants have a vision and strategy for linking work and computerization. Organizations and their sub-units vary in the kinds of strategies that they employ to facilitate specific goals. Some organizations which are particularly cost-conscious may require extensive cost justifications for any desktop computing equipment. In these organizations, some managers, professionals and even clerical workers have to fight to get the equipment they want. Other organizations may be more concerned about their image in the market place and insist that everyone use desktop computing. And still other organizations may vary the use of equipment across the hierarchy of job levels with clerks on terminals, secretaries and analysts on "fully loaded" PCs, and managers on small portable PCs. The combinations of strategies within and across organizations are endless.

The intervention is *sociotechnical* since social dimensions are coupled with the technical choices that are usually part of any substantial computerization effort. When new equipment is brought in, decisions are made about who will use it, under what conditions and with what expectations. The meaning of desktop computing for secretaries who have managerial expectations of high use and who use equipment in public areas differs significantly from the meaning of desktop computing for managers who use equipment in private offices and with expectations of low use. Workers who use terminals can be monitored much more closely than workers who use stand-alone PCs. In some work groups, "fully loaded" PCs are seen as status symbols just like expensive cars with sunroofs and leather upholstery. When new expensive equipment comes into the office, older equipment may be passed down to lower status workers while the best equipment is used at the highest levels. These are examples of the kinds of social choices which surround equipment use. Similar kinds of social choices are made about other dimensions of desktop computing technologies such as software use, access to organizational data, the distribution of electronic mail accounts, and how much support an organization will offer any or all of their desktop computer users.

Organizations have many choices about which technologies to use, how to organize them, and how people can work with them.[33] In this view, some mixes of computing technologies and work organization can be extremely beneficial for most participants. Other mixes of computing equipment and work organization can lead to poor working conditions. Some outcomes may be anticipated and intended – such as a reduction in labor or a reduction in the amount of time spent with a customer using a computerized system. Other outcomes may be unanticipated – such as increased stress or time pressures or workload – and as a result may become a hidden dimension of the job and difficult for workers to change.[34]

Some analysts recognize these contingencies, but rivet their attention on the opportunities for improving work conditions with computerization.[35] They emphasize methods for achieving positive outcomes such as more flexible work, integrating discrete tasks into more complex jobs, or allowing more self-supervision. They acknowledge that computerization may degrade working conditions and still not improve productivity, but they pay little attention to these problems. Moreover, they do not inquire about whether there are any social or organizational conditions under which powerful actors are likely to stress the improvement of working conditions over other goals which may have negative consequences.

We share the optimists' preferences that groups should computerize in ways that enhance working conditions. However, it is important to understand that the most common changes need not be benign. Rather than presuming positive outcomes for widespread desktop computerization we need to understand which alternatives seem most likely and under which conditions. We will examine four dimensions in more detail: *the social organization of work, equipment, infrastructure,* and *control patterns.*

Desktop computerization as a complex intervention

Some potential transformations of white-collar work which analysts attribute to the use of desktop computers are actually shaped by strategies that accompany their implementation. If a sales organization adopts extensive automation including electronic mail and simultaneously reduces the amount of office space and face-to-face meetings, then the salesmen will know each other better by their electronic signatures than their looks. In this case, reductions in face-to-face contact are not a necessary consequence of desktop computers, but are part of the social and technical strategies of desktop computerization.

Powerful organizational actors typically make these kinds of decisions, although some smaller scale computerization projects can arise from grass-roots efforts. The social impact of computerization may be less of a concern to upper-level managers than other goals such as cost reduction, space savings or faster communications times. One school of analysis, socio-technical design, focuses upon the importance of users' participation in computing implementations.[36] These analysts highlight the social dimensions which accompany technical decisions and believe that user participation early in the design of systems will lessen the negative social impacts of system use. Typically, the social-technical design approach is used normatively; in this paper we use it analytically.

We view desktop computerization as a complex social and technical intervention since a user of desktop computing interacts with the social dimensions of the computing environment and work arrangements, as well as with the equipment. This approach is derived from our *web model* of computerization which views computerization as dependent on mixes of equipment and social practices which develop with a history in a particular social setting.[37] When an organization or work group implements desktop computing for most or all of its workers, there are likely to be changes in the character of jobs, policies, practices, and the use of resources. Sometimes the desktop computing environment develops slowly over time and the resulting environment appears as the product of an incremental evolution. In other situations, there may be a large-scale conscious intervention at a particular time. (For example, an organization with 1,500 employees may purchase 400 microcomputers with common software during a short time period.) Further, some practices, like training staff, may be planned and routinized while in other cases staff training is an afterthought and informal. The term "intervention" covers all these cases and highlights the social and technical choices made, even if by oversight.[38]

We have identified four major arenas in which organizations make key social choices about computerization: *the social organization of work, equipment, infrastructure,* and *control patterns* (table 10.1). We will briefly examine these arenas and how organizations structure computing and work along these dimensions.

Table 10.1 Elements of a desktop computerization intervention

Social organization of work
    Changes in the division of labor
    Rewards/demands for learning new systems
    Access to machines and data

Equipment
    Shared vs independent systems
    Standardization
    Extensiveness

Infrastructure
    Training
    Adjunct resources (e.g., space)

Control patterns
    Implementation strategy and operations
    Daily working conditions
    Division of labor

Social organization of work

The ways in which work is organized or reorganized is a critical part of any computerization effort.[39]

Changes in the division of labor Changes in work roles are sometimes an explicit element in an intervention. For example, a Dean of Social Sciences at a medium-sized public university purchased microcomputers for about 40 of his faculty in the mid-1980s. He used funds including the money he saved by not replacing two secretaries who had left for personal reasons. He required these professors to reduce the amount of work they delegated to the remaining secretaries. As a consequence, the faculty with microcomputers had their jobs more clericized. Changes in the division of labor, therefore, are sometimes *explicit elements* of an intervention – actions by design. At other times, they are outcomes of a computerization strategy.

Rewards/demands for learning new systems The rewards and demands for learning to use new computer-based systems vary among workers. A manager may find the use of a spreadsheet on a microcomputer helps her better organize her budgets. Her spreadsheet use may be entirely discretionary with little time pressure or demand. On the other hand, a secretary who must help her manager enter data on a spreadsheet in a given time frame may perceive this activity as another burden in an already demanding time schedule. Another secretary may find such an activity an opportunity for learning a new software package and improving job opportunities within the organization.

    The first computer users in many organizations are self-selected and are often willing to bear the additional personal costs of learning. Later users often have less discretion in computer use, and also usually have less interest in spending many hours mastering a word processing package, a data base or a spreadsheet.[40] We have observed a variety of reward systems in practice – from requiring clerks to learn new systems on their own time to giving staff raises as they learn new systems.

Access to machines and data   Machines and data are different kinds of resources, but they are both subject to organization-wide control. In most organizations, access to data – budgets, sales records, etc. – is relatively tightly controlled. In contrast, organizations vary widely in the extent to which they control access to computer services. In some organizations micro-computers or terminals are hard to obtain while other organizations support widely diffused desktop computing services.[41]

Only a few organizations allow some employees to work at home freely and use computer systems as a medium of communication.[42] Few organizations give their employees desktop computing equipment for permanent use outside their immediate workplaces. It is more common for work groups to have transportable microcomputers for employees to take home for work in the evenings or on weekends or when they travel. In most cases, work at home extends the normal work week. While some computer firms have invested considerable funds in marketing very portable "lap top computers," they have not become commonplace.

Equipment: the kinds of hardware and software to be acquired

The kinds of hardware and software acquired play a special role in computerization strategies. Different kinds of equipment *enable* or *facilitate* certain organizational behaviors, but they do not shape them. For example, shared systems can allow people to communicate by electronic mail. However, the presence of electronic mail – in itself – does not mean that people will use it routinely.

Shared versus independent systems   Some organizations acquire minicomputers or mainframe computers and link to them. Other organizations acquire independent microcomputers. There are mixed strategies in which microcomputers serve as terminals for shared systems. Whether a system is independent or shared is an important distinction since environments built around each strategy facilitate different forms of work organization.

Organizations that provide microcomputers to their staff can start computerization efforts at relatively low initial costs and in a relatively graduated manner.[43] In addition, using micro-computers opens up a wide range of software choices. However, sharing files between isolated machines requires that diskettes or tapes be physically swapped, and electronic mail is impossible. Shared machines and local area nets simplify file sharing, enable electronic mail, and facilitate centralized file archiving. Many work groups have adopted mixed strategies in which microcomputers are used as isolated systems in parallel with larger shared systems. In addition, systems which are shared within a particular department are sometimes incompatible with systems shared within other departments. A department that has chosen to go its own direction may find that it is isolated from the rest of the organization. Users may be unable to benefit from the skills, expertise, and training available to others in the organization.

The use of isolated microcomputers tends to allow individuals more control over their work, except for elements of work life which are imposed from other work relationships. Generally workloads are set by higher-level managers, especially for lower-level staff. In addition, as we have suggested earlier, the time needed to learn to use new equipment skillfully or deal with equipment failures can effectively increase workloads and job pressures.

Workers can lose control over some important aspects of their worklife in a shared computing environment which could be more self-controlled in an isolated computing environment. We have observed the newsroom of one newspaper where reporters and editors use a shared computer system to write and edit stories. Editors have been given the capability to electronically browse reporters' files and copy their stories. Some editors will now take stories electronically before reporters are finished with them. In the world of typewriters and paper copy, reporters had to physically hand stories to their editors. This gave reporters more influence in the face-to-face negotiations about the readiness of a story. A newsroom automated with isolated stand-alone microcomputers would make file sharing more difficult than with most shared computer systems. Editors would receive stories on diskettes, and reporters could retain more influence over the timing and conditions for passing their stories on to editors.

Standardization Many organizations standardize computing arrangements in order to simplify coordination and training and to gain economies of scale in purchase, maintenance, and other operations. Each time an organization standardizes another aspect of its computing environment, it increases regimentation and global efficiency and decreases opportunities for individuals or work-units to control their own destinies and maintain some flexibility in their work arrangements. There is no optimal set of tradeoffs that uniformly benefits all participants.

Organizations typically restrict major hardware purchases to one or two major brands.[44] Software is also commonly standardized to single packages that perform a specific function (e.g., data base) on shared computer systems while microcomputer environments are usually less controlled and less easily controlled by central administrators.[45]

In our field studies we have found that software is usually standardized within work groups, except for academics who use microcomputers, since they have substantially more autonomy over their tools than do many other workers. Coordinating work takes work, and groups which agree upon standard equipment can simplify the mechanical efforts required to coordinate electronic documents and data files. But it is not uncommon to find people trying to coordinate work and feeling frustrated by the complications of moving data across incompatible kinds of equipment. As a consequence, one should not assume that computerization guarantees streamlined work. Moreover, for reasons too complex to develop here, it is unlikely that there will be universal equipment standards that will fit the preferences of all workers in organizations where groups have diverse tasks and occupational cultures.

Extensiveness Extensiveness denotes the extent to which members of a work group have their own terminals or microcomputers. The extensiveness of a desktop computing environment appears important since certain practices appear as a byproduct of having many co-workers routinely utilize computing. Service like electronic mail is more feasible and useful. It is also more likely that computerized text handling and data management will become routinized rather than completely discretionary as a group adopts terminals and microcomputers for a larger fraction of its members.

Infrastructure

Computing infrastructure denotes all the resources and practices required to help people adequately use computer systems to carry out their work.[46]

Training: practices for training staff in new technologies and developments   Computer use requires skill and the "consequences of computerization" can hinge on skill levels as much as on other elements of the intervention. People who do not have the skills to use computing equipment in the way their managers, co-workers or clients expect can feel much more pressure and perform less well, ceteris paribus.

Training people to use computing systems can be as expensive as the purchase price of the cheaper equipment. For a variety of reasons, many organizations often underinvest in skills training. Vendors and the mass media have convinced many naive computer users that computer use is as simple as "pushing a button." This image of "easy to use" systems has lead many managers to have unrealistic expectations about what their workers can do in a specific time period with little or no training. Some software packages are relatively easy to use for elementary activities. In our own observations, we have found that supervisors of clerical work groups that process relatively routine documents and transactions take greater pains to systematically train their staff than managers of professional work groups or groups that mix clerical staff and professionals.

Practices for training people to use new software vary from organization to organization. At one extreme, some organizations institutionalize relatively high levels of training for workers who use particular packages. These organizations will routinely send workers to computer courses[47] or provide specialized "one-on-one" sessions for their staff. Other organizations offer no systematic training – all training is on-the-job. The use of local courses can vary from work group to work group within an organization. Training classes usually take clerical workers out of an office and some managers are reluctant to lose clerical support for the four to 80 hours that the courses require. However, managers who require that their staff learn software packages on top of other work or "on their own time" also impose substantial job pressures upon them.

Adjunct resources: the use of related resources like space or support staff   Computer systems often require additional resources besides hardware and software: reliable electrical power, paper for printers, space for equipment, manuals, data archives, and support staff. In most accounts of computerization, these adjunct resources are taken for granted or assumed to be available on demand. They only become an issue when computer users find these resources unavailable. Most organizations do not invest heavily in a large support staff. Several support staff may be responsible for several hundred microcomputers throughout an organization. As a result, they may become so backlogged in their work that they can no longer do their jobs effectively. Users in this situation may find that when they have problems they have to resolve them themselves or work around them.

Control over desktop computerization

Implementation strategy and operations Most intervention strategies are one of two kinds: "top down" or "grass roots." Most analyses of desktop computerization focus on the former where top-level management define specific strategies and then follow through with large-scale implementations. "Top down" interventions are most common in work groups where managers desire control over data entry. Examples of top down interventions with terminals attached to multi-user systems include the work group of reporters at a large local newspaper previously discussed, data entry for an inventory control system and a work group of buyers in the purchasing department of a large manufacturing organization. More recently, top down interventions have included the implementation of PCs in accounting work groups of savings and loan companies or the financial analysis sections of large conglomerates. Top down interventions receive the most attention from analysts and public commentators because they are most visible. But they can also symbolize unwelcome managerial impositions on the staff who use them.

The most common desktop computerization strategy in organizations today are "grass roots." That is, in any given organization, most departments have had to struggle to get access to computing services by requesting terminals or PCs. Or they have had to give extensive cost justifications to purchase their own equipment. As a result, these work groups are usually not as extensively automated as those which were part of top down implementations and they typically suffer from a lack of computing resources. However, users in these work groups have more local control over their computing environment. Top management often pays little attention to these small pockets of desktop computerization because they are not considered a high priority compared with the development and operation of big information systems. However, when key actors in an organization do an inventory of these small pockets of local computing, they are often amazed at the amount of money that has been spent on distributed computing resources. Often, it is more money than has been spent on the mainframe. As these pockets grow in size and number, centralized staff often attempt to gain back control over the distributed computing environments.

Regardless of the specific intervention strategies of desktop computerization, the central organization will maintain at least a minimum of control through budget allocations and lists of approved hardware and software.

Daily working conditions People working under conditions of top down implementations will suffer most from increased control over their work behaviors if only for management to justify the cost of the equipment. Workers will be expected to be disciplined in their transactions with systems. Management will establish many standard policies and practices which they will enforce. At the same time, workers will not suffer the frustrations of a lack of training or a lack of support staff to take care of their equipment should it break down.

Grass roots implementations usually occur in work groups with a mixture of activities and a high division of labor. Workers want access to machine capabilities or organizational data to aid them in their work. In these workplaces, management cares little about a worker's particular interaction with the machine since machine inputs or outputs are not the final products of their work. Control issues will not be a dominant factor in these workers' interactions with the desktop computing equipment. Their problem will stem more from the lack of services provided by the central organization. Staff usually receive little or no formal training. Individuals are expected to learn on their own or from other workers in the department. When equipment breaks down, staff often manage repairs themselves. These workers will suffer most from increased managerial expectations, increased workloads and increased time pressure. This is particularly true if a worker had to convince her manager that she should get the equipment by indicating that she could do more work.

Division of labor   Top down implementations in the past have occurred most often in work groups with flat hierarchies – one manager or supervisor with an army of clerks, sales people, or buyers under her, for example. More recently, these implementations have also occurred in professional work groups with a greater division of labor – but where there is still one dominant activity, like financial analysis. Top down strategies tend to focus in the first stage of the implementation at the lowest levels of the work group hierarchy and then over time move up to include the professionals and managers.

Grass roots strategies are the reverse. Staff at higher levels of the work group hierarchy are the first users and then the implementation moves down over time. Usually, an influential manager or worker in a work group has fought for access to desktop computing services or equipment. This person and her immediate staff will probably be the first users in the work group. Over time, others in the work group may come to believe in the capabilities and benefits of desktop computing use. As more of the work group principals come to be users, they require that their secretarial staff also be users.

Interventions into the organization of work

The decisions made in the four broad arenas identified in table 10.1 structure the opportunities and constraints of desktop computer use within a work group. The detailed arrangements and expectations that accompany the introduction, alteration, or expansion of worklife around computing are as important as the information processing capabilities of a computer system in shaping worklife. In particular, the complexity of desktop computerization makes it difficult for managers to exert total control over the interventions, except in the extreme cases of larger scale top down implementations. As a consequence, there is often room for workers and managers to negotiate some aspects of their computing and work arrangements that are situationally specific.

Work groups that share microcomputers with other work groups or even among themselves are likely to integrate computing into their work organization differently than groups that provide each user with a dedicated microcomputer or terminal.[48] People are more likely to integrate various computing tasks into their daily work routines when they have computer systems close at hand. The discretion that people have in using desktop computing is also critical. Computer systems can become critical structures in regimented work groups. In more flexible work groups, like university departments, faculty (and some students and staff) may have substantial discretion in computer use. They can select whether to use computing and for which tasks. Work groups where staff are well trained in using desktop computing services are likely to be less hectic and operate more smoothly than those where staff are casually trained.[49]

Practices such as discretion over computer use and staff training are part of the interventions "chosen" by organizations. They shape the meaning and character of desktop computerization beyond that which is given by a particular application, such as text processing or electronic mail.

The social elements that accompany computerization are *as central* as the information processing capabilities in predicting changes in worklife. In public discourse, the technological capabilities of desktop computing are placed in the foreground – the ability to rapidly reformat text, merge stored text into new documents, rapidly reanalyze small data sets, and communicate asynchronously over modest distances and across time zones via electronic mail. Yet these versatile, rapid, and flexible information processing capabilities don't *necessarily* translate directly into more flexible, productive, and versatile work for all participants.[50, 51]

Flexible or regimented work groups

Work groups usually routinize some activities – by specializing in certain kinds of work, by having a stable division of labor, by enacting procedures and schedules that are constructed for their members or are responsive to outside interests. No work group is arbitrarily flexible; but some work groups have more routines than others. Regimentation is usually associated with a rigid division of labor and tight management control over many workplace behaviors.

Whether worklife in extensively computerized work groups becomes more flexible or more regimented depends upon (1) the occupational mix of white-collar staff in the work group; (2) the type of desktop computing implementation; and (3) the type of computing equipment in use. In the following paragraphs we discuss some of the links among the flexibility of work groups and these three dimensions. We suggest some of the ways in which there are subtle, but important interactions between these dimensions. For simplicity, we are discussing different occupational mixes separately.

Clerical work groups

Work groups that are predominantly clerical are usually support groups, although they also include customer enquiry (and record updating) in the entertainment, service, and finance industries. These groups are usually lower status than purely professional groups. In predominantly clerical work groups where the systems are shared and the implementations are top down, one finds the most regimented uses of computing and also the most regimented worklives for group members.

In those clerical work groups (with shared systems and top down implementations), regimentation can mean fine-grained monitoring, management concern that the equipment be used continually, and workers feeling that they are "tied to the machine." Supervisors often maintain strict control over work hours and breaks. The division of labor may be rigid and non-negotiable. Work procedures may be set and clerical workers may be unable to delegate extra work to others. Unlike work groups with mixed staff, work that could enlarge clerical jobs may not be delegated to them from higher status workers since the mix of skills and status is relatively homogeneous. Most clerical work groups are not exempt from charging for overtime, and their managers are usually reluctant to increase costs by allowing them to push extra work into paid overtime hours. Consequently, additional work may result in increased time pressure and stress on the job. As a result, clerical workers may be viewed as resistant to changes that may cause their workloads to increase (e.g., new systems may mean hours of learning and teaching each other).

Clerical work groups which use stand-alone systems are often somewhat less regimented than those that use shared systems. We have found stand-alone systems in use by decentralized department secretaries. They have little problem with regimentation or monitoring but many problems from a lack of training and support. They are often confused about specific procedures and don't know where to turn for help. Grass roots implementations may further reduce regimentation but grass roots implementations are rare in predominantly clerical work groups.

Professional work groups

We have found the most flexibility in the use of desktop computing in predominantly professional work groups which have implemented stand-alone systems in a grass roots style. The flexibility in computer use is also associated with greater flexibility in work, generally. Higher status workers are rarely more tightly monitored, particularly if they have computerized on their own. They often influence the kinds of equipment and software they will use, when they will obtain it and where it will be located. These work groups have control over much of the desktop computing implementations in their worklives. They are more likely to allow members to carry portable computing equipment home or on business trips so that they may have more flexibility in the location and time of their work. In addition, some professionals are able to train secretaries to edit their documents and enter data into spreadsheets and files so that they can delegate some of the more routine aspects of their desktop computer work.

Since these professionals have some autonomy in their worklives, they are able to take the time to learn about new equipment, search for better software or systems that will benefit the groups. Not all professionals are interested in actively exploring their computing worlds, but those who have the interest will have some discretion to do so. Increased workloads from increasing desktop computerization tasks may be delegated to support staff if they are available or pushed into overtime hours. The division of labor may be less rigid and more negotiable so that computing responsibilities may be shared by many in the group. At the same time, those who take major responsibility may find that it takes them more hours a week to get their work done. Those who end up working more may push for equipment that they can take home so that they can work at home nights and weekends.

However, if the implementations are top down with multi-user shared systems, then we have seen more regimentation but rarely as much as for clerical work groups. Where top management has invested substantial resources into the work group, they are often concerned with returns on investment reflected in productivity gains or improved products or services.

Mixed white-collar staff   Similar to work groups with other occupational compositions, top down implementations and shared systems will foster the most regimentation and grass roots implementations in combination with stand-alone systems would create the most flexible working arrangements. The division of labor in these groups is the most fluid. They also support the greatest transfer of work tasks among workers with different occupations. Secretaries and other clerical staff may take on routine tasks that were previously done by managers, professionals or technicians. And managers and professionals may take on some clerical activities, such as keyboarding memos, in order to gain more control over the product and the timing of activities. Tasks newly controlled by the professionals themselves may be pushed up closer to the actual deadlines so that they can gather more information or write more drafts where formerly the work was put into a support staff queue some time prior to the deadline.

Conclusions

We have examined technological change as an intervention into an ongoing work process through the case of desktop computerization. Extensive desktop computing may become a commonplace innovation in white-collar offices. Many work groups in the United States already have some form of computer equipment for a fraction of their workers. And an increasing number of organizations are providing desktop computing for the majority of workers in selected work groups.

Most professional and many scholarly articles about desktop computing are permeated with powerful images of favorable working conditions for computer users. There is also a critical literature which argues that managers are likely to use any technology, including desktop computing, to exploit workers and not to improve their working lives. These accounts, both optimistic and pessimistic, usually assume a form of technological or economic determinism. The deterministic imagery of flexible and regimented work groups is built on simple causality. We have shown that deterministic analyses are poor predictors of the changes in work organization that accompany computerization. At this time there are few empirical studies of desktop computerization in sufficient depth and detail to allow strong generalizations across the wide mixture of work, occupational mixes, computing interventions, and prior forms of work group organization.

This paper develops a conceptual scheme which we hope will influence future research so that meaningful generalizations are easier. We view desktop computerization as a complex social and technical intervention. Organizations don't computerize with a single logic. The working lives of people who use desktop computing are shaped by the opportunity structures created by specific *computerization strategies*, such as grass roots or top down. Desktop computerization is not simply desktop computers in use. Particular social choices lead to increasing flexibility in worklife and streamlined work groups or regimented work organizations and muddled work procedures. These choices hinge on strategies of developing equipment, organizing work and providing infrastructure. We do not argue that all strategies – benign or oppressive – are equally likely. It is naive to blindly generalize from the top down computerization strategies which have shaped the computerization of larger clerical work groups to all computerization strategies and all workers. Some structural conditions, such as occupational power, labor market conditions, professional and organizational ideologies will influence the computerization strategies specific work groups adopt in practice. Moreover, the social complexity of computerization as an intervention makes it difficult for managers to completely control all the relevant practices about the division of labor, patterns of computer use, and infrastructure – even if they would wish to. As a consequence, computerization is often much more open-ended than simple deterministic models would predict.

In this paper we have identified some of the key social dimensions along which actors are likely to develop computerization strategies. This approach is derived from our *web model* of computerization which views computerization as dependent on mixes of equipment and social practices which develop with a history in a particular social setting.[52] This view of desktop computerization as a social and technical intervention demands that researchers report the specific implementation practices in various work groups, the organization of work before the intervention, the social organization of computing (which includes the desktop computing technologies and services and the infrastructure for their use), the relative power and influence of workers and their work groups in the organization, and the degree of integration of computerized work into worklife. Unfortunately, it is difficult to find many research reports which are so carefully fine grained – about computerization or other technological changes in work. We hope that these analyses help enrich future social studies of computerization, as well as other technologies.

Notes

1 C. Wright Mills, *White Collar: The American Middle Class* (New York, Oxford University Press, 1951), pp. 195–6.
2 Harry Braverman, *Labor and Monopoly Capital* (Monthly Review Press, New York, 1974).
3 See, for example, Andrew Zimbalist (ed.), *Case Studies in the Labor Process* (Monthly Review Press, New York, 1979).
4 Vincent Giuliano, "The Mechanization of Office Work," *Scientific American*, vol. 247, 1982, pp. 148–64; H. Poppel, "Who Needs the Office of the Future?" *Harvard Business Review*, vol. 60(6), 1982, pp. 146–55; Paul A. Strassman, *Information Payoff: The Transformation of Work in the Electronic Age* (Free Press, New York, 1985).
5 Organizations also purchase other office technologies, such as high speed photocopiers and new telephone systems. These technologies alter relatively few procedures. They are easier to manage and are less sweeping than computerization in their implications for worklife. White-collar work has changed steadily during the twentieth century. See Rob Kling and Clark Turner "The Structure of the Information Labor Force: Good Jobs and Bad Jobs," in Rob Kling, Mark Poster and Spencer Olin (eds), *California's Informational Utopia: Orange County's Postwar Social Transformation* (University of California Press, Berkeley, CA, forthcoming), for a detailed study of the relative growth of clerical workers and stability of professional workers in the information labor force between 1900 and 1980. See Susanne Iacono and Rob Kling, "Office Technologies and Changes in Clerical Work: A Historical Perspective," in Robert Kraut (ed.), *Technology and the Transformation of White-Collar Work* (Lawrence Erlbaum, New Jersey, 1986), for an assessment of changes in clerical work in response to changing office technologies between 1880 and 1980.
6 Desktop computing is broader than "desktop publishing" or the use of microcomputers because many activities other than "desktop publishing" are usually emphasized and multifunctional systems are shared.
7 For example, Giuliano, "The Mechanization of Office Work."
8 ibid.; Strassman, *Information Payoff*. There is a small professional literature which argues that desktop computerization is difficult to manage: *Business Week*, July 12, 1982, pp. 56–60; Peter Keen and Lawrence A. Woodman, "What to Do with All Those Micros," *Harvard Business Review*, vol. 85(6), 1985, pp. 129–38. These analysts indicate that managers are often too optimistic about the

productivity gains and ease of managing desktop computing. However, they don't suggest that a technologically well-managed competitive environment can be troublesome for workers.

9   Rob Kling, "The Impact of Computing on Job Characteristics of Managers, Data Analysts and Clerks" (Working Paper, Public Policy Research Organization, University of California, Irvine, 1978); E. Wilde, "Personal Computers in the Corporate Environment: The Users' Perspective," unpublished Master's thesis (MIT, Cambridge, MA, 1983).

10 Extensive automation may become a common thing in the near future. The exceptional work groups which are extensively automated today represent the "leading edge" of early adopters.

11 Robert Howard, *Brave New Workplace* (Viking Press, New York, 1985); Abbe Mowshowitz, "The Social Dimensions of Office Automation," in *Advances in Computers, 25* (Academic Press, New York, 1986).

12 Giuliano, "The Mechanization of Office Work;" Strassman, *Information Payoff.*

13 R. A. Hirschheim, *Office Automation: A Social and Organizational Perspective* (Wiley, Chichester, UK, 1986), of which see chapter 6 for a more detailed exposition of optimistic and pessimistic analyses of office automation in general.

14 Giuliano, "The Mechanization of Office Work;" Poppel, "Who Needs the Office of the Future?"; Ron Uhlig, David Farber and James Bair, *The Office of the Future: Communication and Computers* (North-Holland, New York, 1979).

15 Strassman, *Information Payoff.*

16 Evelyn N. Glenn and Roslyn L. Feldberg, "Proletarianizing Clerical Work: Technology and Organizational Control in the Office," in Zimbalist, *Case Studies in the Labour Process*; Judith Gregory and Karen Nussbaum, "Race Against Time: Automation of the Office," *Office: Technology and People*, vol. 1, 1982, pp. 197–236; Howard, *Brave New Workplace*; Mowshowitz, "Social Dimensions of Office Automation."

Mowshowitz summarizes his sharp vision in these concise terms: "Our principal point is that the lessons of the factory are the guiding principles of office automation. In large offices, clerical work has already been transformed into factory-like production systems. The latest technology – office automation – is simply being used to consolidate and further a well-established trend. For most clerical workers, this spells an intensification of factory discipline. For many professionals and managers, it signals a gradual loss of autonomy, task fragmentation and closer supervision – courtesy of computerized monitoring. Communication and interaction will increasingly be mediated by computer. Work will become more abstract . . . and opportunities for direct social interaction will diminish."

Not all deterministic analysts ignore alternative possibilities. Howard, for example, devotes the last chapter of his book which examines how regimentation is a byproduct of computerization to examining alternative possibilities *if* workers have greater voice in shaping computerization. However, the weight of Howard's analysis is unrelentingly pessimistic. Carter's forthright report about her surprise at finding many clerical workers who were enthusiastic about using computer-based systems is instructive. She was originally inspired by pessimistic analyses and began field studies expecting to find almost universal discontent with computerization. Had she begun expecting widespread enthusiasm for new technologies, she might also have been surprised by finding some level of discontent as well as enthusiasm: Valerie J. Carter, "Office Technology and Relations of Control in Clerical Work Organisations," in Barbara D. Wright (ed.), *Women, Work, and Technology: Transformations* (University of Michigan Press, Ann Arbor, 1987).

17 Shoshana Zuboff, "New Worlds of Computer-mediated Work," *Harvard Business Review*, vol. 60(5), 1982, pp. 142–52.

18 Kling, "The Impact of Computing;" James N. Danziger and Kenneth K. Kraemer, *People and Computers: The Impacts of Computing on End-user Organizations* (Columbia Press, New York, 1986).

19 ibid.

20 Barbara Baran and S. Teegarden, "Women's Labor in the Office of the Future," unpublished MS (University of California, Berkeley, Department of City and Regional Planning, Berkeley, CA, 1984). Jon A. Turner, "Computer Mediated Work: The Interplay between Technology and Structured

Jobs-claims representatives in the Social Security Administration," *Communications of the ACM*, vol. 27(12), 1984.

21 Rob Kling and Suzanne Iacono, "The Control of Information Systems after Implementation," *Communications of the ACM*, vol. 27, 1984, pp. 1218–26.

22 For example, Baran and Teegarden, "Women's Labour;" Niels Bjorn-Anderson, "The Changing Roles of Secretaries and Clerks," in H. J. Otway and M. Peltu (eds), *New Office Technology: Human and Organizational Aspects* (Ablex, Norwood, NJ, 1983), pp. 120–37; Carter, "Office Technology and Relations of Control;" Turner, "Computer-mediated Work."

23 cf. Barbara Gutek, Tora Bikson and Don Mankin, "Individual and Organizational Consequences of Computer-based Office Technology," *Applied Social Psychology Annual*, vol. 5, 1984, pp. 231–54; Kling, "The Impact of Computing;" Danziger and Kraemer, *People and Computers*.

24 See, for example, Zuboff, "New Worlds of Computer-mediated Work;" Tora Bikson, Cathy Stasz and Don Mankin, "Computer-mediated Work: Individual and Organizational Impact in one Corporate Headquarters," Report No. R-3308-OTA (Rand Corporation, Santa Monica, CA, 1985). The primary exceptions are recent studies by Turner, "Computer-mediated Work;" Kling and Iacono, "The Control of Information Systems;" Rob Rittenhouse, "The Social Dynamics of Computer-based Text Processing," unpublished PhD dissertation (University of California, Irvine, 1986); Baran and Teegarden, *Women's Labor*; Tora Bikson, "Understanding the Implementation of Office Technology," in Kraut (ed.), *Technology and . . . Transformation*; Carter, "Office Technology and Relations of Control."

25 Turner, "Computer-mediated work."

26 Jon A. Turner, "The Organization of Work with Integrated Office Systems: A Case Study in Commercial Banking," unpublished MS (New York University, 1985).

27 Tora Bikson, "Understanding the Implementation of Office Technology."

28 Carter, "Office Technology and Relations of Control."

29 Suzanne Iacono and Rob Kling, "Desktop Computerization and Work in Future Offices," in R. Gordon and L. Kimball (eds), *High Technology: Industrial, Regional and Social Transformation* (Ablex, Norwood, NJ, forthcoming); Rob Kling, "Value Conflicts in the Development of Computing Applications: Cases in Developed and Developing Countries," *Telecommunications Policy*, March 1983, pp. 12–34.

30 Danziger and Kraemer, *People and Computers*.

31 Hirschheim, *Office Automation*. Our approach differs from Hirschheim's "pluralism" which sees the different outcomes linked to the kinds of participation users have in systems designs. We see participation in design and implementation as only one pair of contingencies among many.

32 Paul Attewell and James Rule, "Computing and Organizations: What We Know and What We Don't Know," *Communications of the ACM*, vol. 27, 1984, pp. 1184–92; Arthur Francis, *New Technology at Work* (Clarendon Press, Oxford, 1986).

33 Iacono and Kling, "Office Technologies and Changes in Clerical Work;" Kling, "Value Conflicts;" Enid Mumford, *Designing Secretaries* (University of Manchester Business School Press, Manchester, UK, 1982); Calvin Pava, *Managing New Office Technology: An Organizational Strategy* (Free Press, New York, 1983); Walton and Vittori, "New Information Technology."

34 Baran and Teegarden argue in *Women's Labor* that computerization in insurance will transform work in a somewhat complex pattern: data entry work will be reduced; some professional work will be automated and passed along to clerical workers whose jobs will appear upgraded; and the remaining professional work will become substantially more specialized.

35 Margarethe H. Olson and Jon Turner, "Rethinking Office Automation," in *Proceedings of the International Conference on Informational Systems* (Indianapolis, IN, 1985); Phillip Store and D. Dunphy, "Office Productivity and Quality of Work Life," unpublished MS (Harvard University, Cambridge, MA, and University of New South Wales, 1985); Phillip Stone and R. Luchetti, "Your Office Where You Are," *Harvard Business Review*, vol. 85(6), 1985, pp. 129–38.

36 Robert Johansen and E. Baker, "User Needs Workshop: A New Approach to Anticipating User

Needs for Advanced Office Systems," *Office: Technology and People*, vol. 2, 1984, pp. 103–19; Mumford, *Designing Secretaries*; Pava, *Managing New Office Technology*.

37   Rob Kling and Walt Scacchi, "The Web of Computing: Computer Technology and Social Organization," *Advances in Computers*, vol. 21, 1982, pp. 1–90; Rob Kling, "Defining the Boundaries of Computing across Complex Organizations," in Richard Boland and Rudy Hirschheim (eds), *Critical Issues in Information Systems Research* (Wiley, Chichester, UK, 1987).

38   Organizational actors do not all share the same values and job demands. Choices in computing equipment, infrastructural support, and work organization will not satisfy all people simultaneously. Some choices may lead to conflict and even failure while others may enhance productivity and improve working conditions.

39   This is the main dimension of an intervention that links to the differences between flexible and regimented work groups.

40   Packages like word processing and spreadsheets take more time to learn skillfully than vendors and the media usually suggest. Commonplace applications like spreadsheets and word processors can take 10–20 hours of class time and an equivalent amount of practice to develop a broad set of skills. The learning time can be much longer for people who teach themselves.

41   This section does not take account of costs, and systems costs can be relatively high for extensive desktop computing environments. In practice, many organizations vary between loose and tight control over the purchase of terminals, microcomputers, and software. Part of the temporal variations in particular organizations can be accounted for by the amount of slack money available and the scale of the adjunct costs for new infrastructure – such as communication ports and shared disk space.

42   Cf. Margarethe Olson, "Remote Office Work: Changing Patterns in Space and Time," *Communications of the ACM*, vol. 26, 1983, pp. 182ff.

43   We have observed one organization which has provided about 300 microcomputers for about 500 professionals and clerks. The information systems staff distributed about 60 microcomputers with a word processing package to secretaries during the first phase of their project. They labeled these machines as "word processors" and only revealed their broader capabilities after some managers began asking for microcomputers.

44   Much depends upon an organization's size and the extent to which acquisitions are centralized. Larger organizations are more likely to purchase equipment from a wider variety of vendors, especially if subunits choose their own hardware. UC–Irvine may be an extreme case. The campus has over 14,000 students and 700 faculty. Its schools operate over 50 minicomputers and mainframes manufactured by DEC, Harris, CDC, IBM, Hewlett Packard, Ridge, Integrated Solutions, Sequent, and Honeywell in addition to hundreds of microcomputers which are assembled by about ten different vendors. On the other hand, many large organizations are basically "IBM shops," "IBM and Wang shops" or similarly committed to one or two primary computer vendors.

45   At a major insurance company in Southern California which has deployed about 200 IBM PCs, Multimate is the standard word processor and Lotus 1-2-3 is the standard spreadsheet. In contrast, at UC–Irvine, microcomputer software is standardized at the departmental level. Multimate, Microsoft Word, Word Perfect, Volkswriter, PC-Write and Note Bene are all used in different departments.

46   Kling and Scacchi, "The Web of Computing."

47   Some of these may be courses which are taught on the premises. Other courses may be organized through a local software training center.

48   We have observed microcomputers on carts that can be wheeled from desk to desk. We have also observed microcomputers shared by workers in a public room and accessible only through sign up sheets in two hour time blocks. Even though the machines were IBM brand "personal computers," they were actually organizational computers.

49   There can be many variations within a broad structure in any particular organization. For example, we have observed different divisions in one insurance company which provide substantially different

levels of training for microcomputer users – from negligible training, except "on the job," to fairly intensive classes and coaching.

50 See the previous discussion about Turner's study ("Computer-mediated Work") of the ways in which an improved computer system leads to higher stress and mental strain for workers.

51 For example, in mid-1985, the office automation vendors faced a relative slump in sales because many managers had become disillusioned with the gap between the promise and performance of microcomputers and advanced computer systems.

52 Kling and Scacchi, "The Web of Computing;" Kling, "Defining the Boundaries of Computing."

11 The Management of Change

Management Discovers the Human Side of Automation

John Hoerr, Michael A. Pollock, and David E. Whiteside

The poor productivity payoff from computers has led many managers to re-examine the "people" side of the equation, say the authors of this notable article. Getting people and technology working together in harmony is the key to high productivity, they say. This can best be achieved through the adoption of innovative work practices such as "teamwork." Reprinted from Business Week, *September 29, 1986.*

Like thousands of companies in the early 1980s, Shenandoah Life Insurance Co. marched eagerly into the world of high technology. It installed a $2 million system to computerize processing and claims operations at its Roanoke (VA) headquarters. But the results were disappointing. It still took 27 working days – and handling by 32 clerks in three departments – to process a typical application for a policy conversion.

Shenandoah's problem stemmed from its bureaucratic maze, not from defects in the technology. Only by radically reorganizing its work system could it reap the benefits of automation. The company grouped the clerks in "semiautonomous" teams of five to seven members. Each team now performs all the functions that once were spread over three departments. Team members learned new skills, bringing them greater job satisfaction – and better pay. As a result, the typical case-handling time dropped to two days, and service complaints were practically eliminated. By 1986, Shenandoah was processing 50 percent more applications and queries with 10 percent fewer employees than it did in 1980.

The productivity gains at Shenandoah Life are part of a powerful synergism taking root in the United States – the pairing of people with automation. American managers are finally learning what the Japanese discovered years ago. The solution to fading competitive ability, sluggish productivity growth, and poor quality cannot be found in the mythical black box of a miraculous technology. To realize the full potential of automation, leading-edge companies are integrating workers and technology in "sociotechnical" systems that revolutionize the way work is organized and managed.

This is an immensely important trend, one that is producing a new model of job design and work relations that will shape the workplace well into the twenty-first century. Nevertheless, the changeover isn't occurring fast enough. The great wave of automation that has swept through offices and factories since 1980 is losing momentum, largely because not enough companies are adopting the innovative work practices that get the most out of automation. Many managers are reluctant to "run the kind of social revolution at work that is needed to make technology pay for itself," says productivity expert George H. Kuper, who heads the Manufacturing Studies Board, a research arm of the National Academy of Sciences.

People problems

With or without work reforms, computer-based technology is having an enormous impact on workers. In one way or another, it has changed the jobs of 40 million to 50 million people, almost half of the US work force. It has made some jobs more challenging and "de-skilled" others. It has caused severe dislocations at specific work sites by eliminating jobs, raising a fundamental question of whether government and business are investing enough money and expertise in retraining displaced workers (see below). For the entire nonfarm economy, however, technological change helped produce a 10.4 million increase in jobs between 1979 and 1986.

But contrary to the engineers' vision of factories run by robots, the high-tech workplace depends more than ever on people. "There will be fewer of them, but the ones who are there will be critical," says Gerald I. Susman, an expert on work and technology at Pennsylvania State University. Mistakes by poorly trained, poorly motivated workers can cause enormous damage, as demonstrated by the nuclear accidents at Three Mile Island and Chernobyl. Says Lyman D. Ketchum, a pioneering consultant on teamwork: "We're moving increasingly into dangerous, unforgiving technologies that can't be operated safely with uncommitted people."

Most important, it is becoming evident that advanced computer technology calls for a radical change in traditional work practices. The old "scientific management" method of dividing work into discrete tasks that require little skill or training becomes obsolete in a computerized workplace where many functions – including materials handling, assembly, inventory control, and testing – are integrated by computer. "The integration no longer makes it possible to define jobs individually or measure individual performance," says Richard E. Walton of Harvard University. "It requires a collection of people to manage a segment of technology and perform as a team."

Global competition

For these reasons, more companies are installing work systems that emphasize broader-based jobs, teamwork, participative managers, and multiskilled workers. The innovations include a range of other labor policies aimed at developing "committed" workers, including enhanced job security, continuous training programs, and compensation schemes that reward group performance (see figure 11.1). Industries such as autos, steel, and communications have been moving slowly in this direction with the cooperation of their unions since the beginning of the "quality-of-worklife" (QWL) movement in the 1970s.

But the new innovations go far beyond QWL reforms that involve workers in problem-solving groups or otherwise aim at making jobs more satisfying. Now the movement is being fueled by global competition and the need for a high rate of product innovation. The average life cycle of an electronics product, for example, is only three to five years. Experts say that while the United States may not be able to compete with countries that turn out standardized products and parts at low wages, it can create new market niches for customized products. But manufacturers must be able to switch quickly from one product line to another, and flexible work systems – when combined with computer-based technology – give them that ability.

The new "paradigm," as organizational behavior specialists call it, will gradually replace the old system characterized by authoritarian management and an extreme division of labor epitomized by the assembly line. The new approach often entails sociotechnical planning – that is, integrating the psychological and social needs of workers with technological requirements in designing a new plant or redesigning an old one. Harvard's Walton contrasts the old "control" paradigm with the new model of "commitment."

The payoff can be significant. Many plants that were designed with sociotechnical methods and use the most radical innovation, semiautonomous teams, are 30 percent to 50 percent more productive than their conventional counterparts. In most plants, these teams manage themselves without first-line supervisors, determine their own work pace within parameters set by management, schedule their own vacations, and have a voice in hiring and firing team members and deciding when they qualify for raises. This is a relatively new creature on the US industrial scene, and both managers and workers give it high praise.

Ten years ago, fewer than two dozen manufacturing plants in the United States organized work on a team basis. Today teamwork is used in several hundred offices and factories, especially new, highly automated plants with small workforces of 25 to 500 people. One example is a diesel engine plant jointly owned by Cummins Engine Co. and J. I. Case Co. in Whittakers, NC. Teamwork, says plant manager John C. Read, brings out "an entrepreneurial cowboy spirit" in American workers. "When this spirit gets wrapped into team efforts to figure out why a machine went down – and if management gets out of the way – it's a tremendously powerful tool."

Many workers like teamwork for its greater variety of tasks, compared with repetitive jobs on a conventional assembly line. That's true of Randy Gilbert, a ten year veteran at General Motors Corp. who now is an elected team coordinator in Buick City, GM's showcase plant that combines high technology and Japanese management methods. "Once in a while I get bored and switch jobs with someone just to relieve the tedium," he says. That wasn't possible before.

Not fast enough?

But technology experts say teamwork and other innovative practices are not spreading fast enough. Although the sociotechnical revolution is here to stay, plants that use teamwork still constitute only a small minority of US workplaces.

If teamwork produces such good results, why haven't more companies tried it? For one thing, it requires a drastic change in management style and methods. The old idea that a manager's main function is to control workers is replaced with the concept that a manager should encourage employees to use initiative. This goes against the grain of everything

In Americus, GA, robots are writing the script for a tragedy. Michigan–based Ex-Cell-O Corp. employs 400 hourly workers in this hamlet of 17,000 people to make plastic car parts, including brightly colored urethane shells for masking auto bumpers. But now robots are taking over the spray-painting of the shells. The resulting gains in quality and productivity will help secure the jobs of most Ex-Cell-O employees. But that isn't any consolation to as many as 100 workers who will be replaced by the robots.

Only a handful of the painters qualify for the highly skilled and technical job of servicing the robots. Others may be able to transfer to lower-skilled slots at Ex-Cell-O, but that would displace workers with less seniority. The remainder may have to job-hunt elsewhere. "These people may have heard that there will be new jobs for them in plants that manufacture robots," says a company executive. "But that won't be in Americus."

The Ex-Cell-O example illustrates an important public policy issue raised by automation: Who is responsible for retraining workers who are thrown into the labor market by new technology? Traditionally, most companies have left this role to government. But public concern may force them to reassess this position – or face greater pressure from Washington to act.

Painful predicament

More and more workers across the nation are finding themselves in the painters' predicament. From insurance companies to machine shops, new technology is altering work radically. Many of the technologically unemployed will drop into relatively unskilled service industry jobs. But occupational experts say the demand is rising for workers in new, more technically oriented jobs being created by automation. If displaced workers are to get these jobs, however, they will have to be retrained.

"The new jobs require much greater literacy and skill," says Roger D. Semerad, Assistant Labor Secretary for employment and training, who worries that displaced workers may not be equipped to fill the new high-tech slots. "There could hardly be any more significant issue with respect to employment policy than this one," adds Harvard Business School professor D. Quinn Mills, a member of the National Commission on Employment Policy, an independent group that reports to the President.

Dislocation is not the only serious problem caused by technology. Some workers complain about being de-skilled; others say their employers use the computer as a control device. For example, reservations clerk Toni M. Watson works at a computer terminal in the San Diego office of a regional airline. Her performance, including how many minutes she devotes to each incoming call, is continuously monitored by computer. Three years ago she suffered a nervous breakdown, largely because of job pressures, and entered eight months of therapy. Management, she says, is acting as if "I am supposed to have a digital clock in my head. I'm not a machine."

Government policy, of course, can't solve these kinds of problems. But retraining dislocated workers is another matter. Currently, as many as 2 million jobs are thought to be vanishing each year in the United States. Most economists believe that foreign competition is more to blame for this than automation, and in any case the economy is generating more jobs overall than are being lost.

Last-minute lobbying

Nevertheless, the National Commission on Employment Policy estimates that through the rest of this decade 400,000 workers a year may need extensive retraining to find new jobs. This includes people who must acquire higher technical skills, as well as those who will need remedial training in basic English and mathematics, whether they are active employees or just entering the work force. The federal government's primary jobs program, the Job Training Partnership Act of 1982, serves less than 200,000 dislocated workers, and its budget is being halved to $100 million a year.

Labor experts and union leaders contend that the government should spend far more on retraining. But the Reagan Administration's opposition to big domestic spending has made the White House unlikely to support such an idea. With unemployment edging downward to 6.8 percent in August 1986 and federal deficits headed in the opposite direction, even Congress would look askance at new spending programs.

Some legislation to limit dislocation by restricting plant shutdowns is gaining momentum, however. In mid-1985, for instance, support was strong for plant-closing legislation because of a widespread perception in Washington that plant shutdowns were on the rise. A bill requiring employers to notify workers well in advance of shutdowns was voted down in the House only after an intense, last-ditch lobbying effort by business. Warns Randolph M. Hale, a vice president of the National Association of Manufacturers: "If employers expect to have the flexibility to close plants when they want, they are going to have to do a better job at retraining and placing workers where there are jobs."

Hale and other business lobbyists are urging companies not to wait for Washington to act. They point out that retraining workers with obsolete skills and keeping them at work fosters corporate loyalty. By giving workers the knowledge to perform several jobs, companies also would benefit from a more flexible and adaptable work force. A few companies go even further and retrain workers for jobs outside the company if none is available inside. Ford Motor Co., for example, runs a joint training program with the United Auto Workers and has retrained some 1,700 displaced Ford workers for other jobs since 1982.

A more visible effort by companies to beef up training and improve the quality of worklife would reduce the political heat being generated by the issue. In the long run, that could help industry considerably. For if employers ignore the problem and dislocations increase substantially, the federal government will step in sooner or later – with results that business may not like.

managers have been taught since the early years of the century, says Lyman Ketchum, who helped design one of the first sociotechnical plants in the United States, a Gaines Foods Inc. plant that opened in Topeka, Kan., in 1971. To accept the commitment model of work, he says, managers have to go through a "personal paradigm shift, which is a deep psychological process."

John B. Myers, vice president for human resources at Shenandoah Life, adds that most managers are comfortable with old-style bureaucracies in which orders are passed from top to bottom. "Bureaucratic organizations become habit-forming, just like cigarettes," he says. "That's why they don't change."

The slowness to change may have implications for productivity growth. The rise in output per man-hour in the United States has lagged behind that of Japan and European nations for more than a decade. Bureau of Labor Statistics economists estimate that productivity will increase at an average annual rate of 1.7 percent through the mid-1990s, about double the rate of the past ten years, largely because of new technology.

This projection, however, is based on a continuing high rate of technological innovation that may not happen. The 1980s started with glowing predictions of pushbutton factories linked to

What management assumes about workers

Old way Worker wants nothing
from the job except pay, avoids
responsibility, and must be
controlled and coerced

New way worker desires
challenging job and will seek
responsibility and autonomy if
management permits

How the job is designed

Old way Work is fragmented
and deskilled. Worker is confined
to narrow job. Doing and
thinking are separated

New way Work is multiskilled
and performed by teamwork
where possible. Worker can upgrade whole system. Doing and
thinking are combined

Management's organization and style

Old way Top–down military
command with worker at bottom
of many supervisory layers;
worker is expected to obey orders
and has no power

New way Relatively flat structure
with few layers; worker makes
suggestions and has power to
implement changes

Job training and security

Old way Worker is regarded as
a replaceable part and is given
little initial training or retraining
for new jobs. Layoffs are routine
when business declines

New way Worker is considered
a valuable resource and is
constantly retrained in new skills.
Layoffs are avoided if possible in
a downturn

How wages are determined

Old way Pay is geared to the
job, not the person, and is determined
by evaluation and job classification
systems

New way Pay is linked to skills
acquired. Group incentive and
profit–sharing plans are used
to enhance commitment

Labor relations

Old way Labor and management
interests are considered incompatible.
Conflict arises on the shop floor
and in bargaining

New way Mutual interests are
emphasized. Management shares
information about the business.
Labor shares responsibility for
making it succeed

Figure 11.1   The changing approach to organizing work. (Source: Richard E. Walton,
Harvard University; *Business Week*.)

executive suites in vast computer networks. And the "paperless" electronic office was said to
be just around the corner.

But the unmanned factory has not arrived. Computer-integrated manufacturing (CIM), in
which shop floor machines are operated by a central computer, is a reality in only a few plants.
And offices are still struggling with primitive computer networks.

Pulling back

Investment in new technology is not increasing nearly as fast as was predicted in the early 1980s. In early September, Dataquest Inc., a San Jose (CA) market research firm, lowered its projection of industrial automation sales in 1990 by 13 percent, to $34 billion. Robot sales are also slowing down. "I'm very discouraged," says Richard M. Cyert, president of Carnegie-Mellon University. "For the future of manufacturing in this country, we have to find a way to move automation ahead at a faster pace."

Many companies are pulling back from overambitious automation projects. In its blueprint to convert seven plants to produce a new midsize car, GM had intended to install more than 1,000 robots and replace conventional car assembly lines with the automatic guided vehicle (AGV), a moving "island" of car parts. Now, however, only three plants will be converted. In addition to financial and marketing reasons, GM has had problems integrating technology with its management systems, observers say.

The complexities involved in making CIM work are stymieing automation efforts at many companies. Few have managed to tie the major management functions of engineering, production, and marketing into a single, computerized information system. This kind of linking is necessary for companies to gain one of the larger benefits of computer technology – eliminating layers of middle managers and technicians who now do this work. In addition, computerizing new techniques such as just-in-time inventory control may have as much impact in cutting production costs as eliminating direct labor and managers, says Penn State's Susman. "But reducing inventory tightens the couplings between parts of an organization," he adds, "and this requires workers who know what they're doing."

GM is going ahead with other projects, including a highly automated front-axle plant in Saginaw, Mich. When this plant reaches full production in late 1987, it will be run entirely by robots part of each working day. This plant illustrates the new US emphasis on human skills. It will be operated by 38 hourly employees, all members of the United Auto Workers, who survived a stringent selection process. They are now being schooled in electronic, mechanical, and problem-solving skills and will have more than a year of training before the plant begins making axles.

This amount of training is new in the United States, although the Japanese have routinely engaged in such comprehensive programs for years. It is one of the ways Japan invests in human resources so that automation will "make people more productive," says Thomas J. Gallogly, a metalworking expert in the Commerce Department's International Trade Administration. The Japanese also enlist workers in "quality circles" to solve production and quality problems. Lifetime job security is emphasized in Japan as well, although for limited numbers of workers in the larger companies.

Wider scope

When American managers began touring Japanese plants in the mid-1970s, the Japanese stressed the importance of these human factors, recalls Kuper of the Manufacturing Studies Board, who led some of those tours. "Our managers kept looking for the technological solution to the growing Japanese success," he says. "The Japanese were trying to be honest with us, but we were too stupid to listen."

Now, US employers are belatedly turning to the human side of technology, partly by borrowing the Japanese techniques but also by using other methods. For example, Japanese companies do not emphasize a fundamental redesign of jobs to make them more appealing to workers. Furthermore, when the Japanese use production teams, they usually keep them under the control of first-line foremen.

Indeed, the semiautonomous team idea originated in experiments at British coal mines in the late 1940s. Behavioral scientists at London's Tavistock Institute of Human Relations, led by Eric Trist – now professor emeritus at the Wharton School – concluded that industry needed a new paradigm of work organization. By stressing autonomous work groups, jobs of wider scope, and worker involvement in decision-making, Trist and his colleagues said, companies could adjust much more easily to fast-changing market and political conditions.

Trist and others developed the "sociotechnical systems" (STS) concept of work design. STS calls for involving workers whenever possible in planning a new or redesigned plant, as auto workers have been involved in GM's Saturn project. Usually, the technical design came first, and work flow and the placement of workstations followed. In designing an auto plant, for example, engineers would specify a conventional assembly line that allows only one social system: Workers must stay at fixed stations along the line, performing the same task every 30 seconds or so.

"Traditionally, jobs were designed with no capacity for people to initiate anything," says Harvey F. Kolodny, a professor at the University of Toronto. "If things went wrong, you'd get an inflexible response. We should design jobs so that workers can be more than a pair of hands behaving in a mechanical way."

To give workers a greater variety of duties, a sociotechnical auto plant design would call for teams to assemble entire subunits of a car from parts moved through the plant on AGVs. Team members would be free to move around, rotate jobs, pace themselves within a much longer work cycle of perhaps five minutes or more, and have more control over product quality. Studies show that group assembly not only makes workers feel better but also produces higher quality.

The STS concept moved from Britain to Norway and Sweden, where Volvo used it in designing its plant at Kalmar, Sweden, which opened in 1974. Kalmar's work force is divided into about 20 production teams; each assembles a major unit of a car in an average of 20 minutes to 40 minutes. Production costs at Kalmar are 25 percent lower than at Volvo's conventional plants, and the company is building a new plant at Uddevalla based on the Kalmar experience.

Teamwork also began to appear in the United States in the 1960s. But for years it was confined to a handful of pioneering companies, including Procter & Gamble, Cummins Engine, Gaines Foods, Sherwin-Williams, the Packard Electric Div. of GM, Hewlett-Packard, TRW, and Best Food, a unit of CPC International.

In the past few years, scores of companies that traditionally set the patterns in industrial relations have adopted the concept. Among them are General Electric, Ford, most GM divisions, and Westinghouse, as well as Xerox, Honeywell, Digital Equipment, and other high-tech companies. Shell Canada Ltd runs four chemical and refinery plants with sociotechnical principles. Even the financial services industry is picking up the concept. In addition to

Shenandoah Life, Lincoln National Life and American Transtech have reorganized their paper-processing operations into teams, and one giant insurance company, Aetna, is on the verge of doing so.

For the most part, the teamwork movement has been a quiet revolution. Many of the leading companies have not trumpeted their findings, partly because they believed their innovations provided a competitive edge. Now some of the pioneers are opening up a bit, and their evidence of superior performance in teamwork is impressive.

Procter & Gamble Co., which established its first team-based plants in the 1960s and now has 18 such sites, has always refused to comment publicly on the matter. However, it confirms remarks made in late 1984 by Senior Vice President David Swanson in a closed meeting at Harvard. Swanson said P&G's teamwork plants were "30 percent to 40 percent more productive than their traditional counterparts and significantly more able to adapt quickly to the changing needs of the business."

Person to person

Cummins Engine has three teamwork plants, including the North Carolina site, and has used elements of the team approach at its older plants in Columbus, IN. Cummins also has been reticent about the new-style plants. But in a recent interview with *Business Week*, Vice President Ted L. Marsten said that Cummins is convinced that "this is the most cost-effective way to run plants. In traditional plants, work was broken down to the lowest common denominator, and there was not a lot of flexibility. We created teams to get the work to flow in the most productive way. The people felt a lot better about the work they did, and we got a much higher-quality product."

In Oregon, Tektronix Inc. converted a few years ago from assembly-line-manufacturing in its metals group to teams. Each "cell" of six to 12 workers turns out a product that can be manufactured in relatively few steps. One particular cell now turns out as many defect-free products in three days as an entire assembly line did in 14 days with twice as many people. Xerox Corp. began using teams in some of its operations a few years ago and has found them to be "at least 30 percent more productive" than conventionally organized operations, says Dominick R. Argona, manager of employee involvement.

The Gaines Foods plant in Topeka, which received heavy publicity in the early 1970s for its new style of management, has proved that teamwork there was not a passing fad. Fifteen years after it started production, the plant still uses teamwork – both in the office and on the shop floor. Plant manager Herman R. Simon says Topeka produces the same pet foods as a sister plant in Kankakee, IL, at 7 percent lower labor costs. Once a unit of General Foods Corp., Gaines is now a wholly owned subsidiary of Anderson, Clayton & Co.

Shenandoah Life's decision to embrace teamwork is a classic illustration of why technology can't solve all problems. Even after installing an automated system, the company found that processing clerks were still, in effect, "passing papers from person to person electronically," says Myers. "It made no sense to have a new technology and yet operate the old system."

Since experimenting with one clerical team in 1983, Shenandoah has formed nine teams of employees who before worked in separate departments. Former first-line supervisors belong to a team that "advises" the processing groups. Shenandoah has never laid off employees, but the team system has enabled it to reduce the workforce by 14 percent, down to 229, over a year and a half.

"Turf issues"

The team approach also can help shape the kinds of goods and services a company produces. Shenandoah's disability income team – which includes an actuary, an underwriter, and a marketing specialist – took only six months to develop and market a policy amendment designed to attract new business. If all the skills needed to design a new product are contained in one team, Myers says, product development doesn't get hung up on the "turf issues" that arise when several departments are involved in planning a new product.

Because of the difficulty in changing the culture and management style in existing plants, most teamwork plants are "greenfield" sites, and most are nonunion. Indeed, the sociotechnical trend can present a problem for unions. Where employees have been allowed a strong voice in decision-making and largely manage themselves in teams, organizers have had a tough time presenting a case for unionization.

A number of unions, however, have worked jointly with management to convert existing plants to the team concept. These include the Auto Workers, Electronic Workers, Clothing & Textile Workers, and Steelworkers. One successful example involves the Aluminum Workers and a Rohm & Haas Co. plexiglass plant in Knoxville, Tenn. Within four years after the plant began changing to team organization, productivity – measured as square feet of plexiglass produced per worker-hour – had risen some 60 percent.

But resistance to the concept remains fairly strong in these and other unions because it requires changes in many traditional union–management relations. Instead of multiple job classifications, for example, a teamwork plant usually has only one or two. Production and maintenance work, traditionally separated under the scientific management organization of work, tend to merge into one fluid work system.

High anxiety

For all its productiveness, teamwork is very difficult to implement and keep working successfully. Changes in plant and corporate management, from participative to old-style managers, have doomed many a promising teamwork experiment. Personality conflicts in teams also cause problems. Indeed, says Cummins' John Read, tension levels in sociotechnical plants tend to be higher than in conventional workplaces. "It's wrong to think of teamwork plants as merely happy places," he says. "But the tensions tend to be constructive, and they produce high performance."

High performance is what US industry needs if it is to make the most of computer-based automation, say technology experts. While the United States is still behind Japan in matching workers and new manufacturing techniques, it is trying to catch up. "We need work environments that produce continuous innovation in a highly competitive global economy," says Eric Trist. The new model of work relations is not yet the dominant one, he adds, but "I'd be sad if we weren't getting close to that point by the end of the century."

Office Automation: Making it Pay Off

Catherine L. Harris et al.

In a more upbeat article, the authors recount a number of office automation success stories. These show how computers can improve the effectiveness of organizations. Harris and her co-authors say that information is a weapon which, if used intelligently, can significantly boost productivity and thus competitive advantage. This article first appeared in Business Week, *October 12, 1987.*

It's one of the great business debates of the 1980s: Has office automation really made companies more productive? Clearly, financial analysts can now churn out spreadsheets in minutes, not hours. Marketing people can generate reports in hours, not days. And secretaries can type more letters, without typos. But look what it has cost: Almost 40 percent of US capital spending now goes to information processing systems, and more than half a trillion dollars has now been spent on the technology. Has this helped or hurt the corporate bottom line?

Until recently the debate had been a standoff. Hardware makers and management consultants who help install the technology toss out estimates like 20 percent and 40 percent to convey how much more productive these systems can make customers. Government figures tend to show the opposite: that even as corporate spending on computers and related equipment has bounded upward, white-collar productivity has been stagnant since 1973. But then measuring productivity is tricky indeed, since managers can hardly be judged by how many decisions they make per hour.

Now, however, after a decade of trial and error, leaders in the use of office automation finally are learning to focus their efforts on clearly measurable goals. In the process they are proving that automation does pay off. Haphazard application of office technology still produces poor results. But what pacesetters are finding is that if the right technology is used where it can do the most good – and if the organization's work structure is adjusted to take advantage of the benefits – huge gains will result.

Broader results

The benefits may be as simple as lowering head counts or doing much more work with the same number of people. More than that, though, the technology is turning out to be pivotal in accomplishing wider business goals: boosting revenues and profits by improving quality, for instance, or developing new products. The term that's being used to describe these broader results is effectiveness. There are still no figures to quantify what that concept means for the economy as a whole. Maybe there never will be. But individual companies know how they have fared. Those that haven't discovered the secrets of successful office automation are still frustrated and inefficient. Those that have are seeing the results on the bottom line.

For the past 18 months, for example, American President Cos. has had the marketing people at its American President Lines Ltd use microcomputer networks to help determine APL's market share in hauling everything from Taiwanese lawn furniture to frozen shrimp from Bangladesh. Such reports let the big Oakland (CA) transporter's sales force spot the best customers in the most lucrative markets so resources can be allocated more effectively. The reports used to take a week or more. Now they take about half an hour.

The result: using about half as much labor, the marketing department now turns out 28 times as many one-page market reports. Although many other factors obviously affect performance, it may not be coincidental that APL's ocean-cargo volume was up 28 percent last year – while the market grew only 17 percent. And even as one major rival, US Lines Inc., left the business, APL was among the few companies in shipping to turn a profit: its parent reported making $18 million on $1.5 billion in revenues.

Goal-tending

APL has learned what most companies have yet to grasp: to get productivity out of office systems, they must be aimed at a clear goal. And that goal can't be as generic as better planning. It must be something as specific as getting sales representatives to spend 10 percent more of their time with customers. "Winners use their systems in a highly focused way, targeting them at a person or a group and a business 'deliverable,' such as closing more sales," says N. Dean Meyer, a Ridgefield (CT) technology management consultant and co-author of *The Information Edge*. The result, he says, can be up to a 1,000 percent return on investment.

One thousand percent? In his book, Meyer cites the efforts of an unidentified company to get a new product to market. The company put together a team with members in Connecticut, Florida, and Texas. They estimated that it would take 12 months to finish the job. Later, though, they decided to save time by using electronic mail to send documents back and forth, and they ended up finishing in only ten months. "Even ignoring the competitive advantage of getting the product out early, the company got two months of additional profits, in this case $110,000, vs $10,000 for the cost of the electronic mail," Meyer notes. "Return on investment: 1,000 percent."

Most companies have less happy stories to tell. In some cases, office technology works its way up from the bottom, with no companywide or departmental goals in mind. Workers ask for personal computers so that they can work faster or more easily, and the productivity gains go no further than that. "The individual rarely creates a product – a group does," notes Leon Jackson, who recently founded Management Focus Inc., a Hudson (Mass.) consulting firm. "If he gets an analysis done in 30 minutes instead of eight hours but it still takes five days for someone else to make a decision, what difference does it really make?"

In other cases, office systems are sent in from on high, on the assumption that they will spur productivity and efficiency but with no plan to make that happen. "The least effective organizations use the personal computer as a better typewriter," says Paul Saffo, an analyst at the Institute for the Future in Menlo Park, CA. What often happens in such cases is that a lack of understanding of how employees really work dooms the automation to failure.

Many companies simply assume there will be a benefit from automation and sit back and wait for it to happen. "It never does," says Peter G. W. Keen, executive director of the International Center for Information Technologies in Washington. "If you don't know where you're going, how do you get there?"

That's a lesson learned by executives at GTEL, the retail subsidiary of General Telephone Co. of California. Management thought that personal computers and spreadsheets "would somehow impact the bottom line, so they put one on everybody's desk," recalls Denise E. Schubert, the end user support manager who helped familiarize employees with the machines. The company "assumed that [Lotus Development Corp.'s] 1-2-3 [spreadsheet] would be able to generate more revenue." But though personal productivity did go up, "spreadsheets actually have been more of an expense."

How so? Lotus can cut number-crunching time from 40 minutes to ten. If employees are efficient, they might then use that extra 30 minutes for something else. But they might not. If managers don't see that the time saved is used productively, either by reducing the workforce or assigning new tasks, the efficiencies won't show up in profits.

Hard lesson

That doesn't mean GTEL has wasted time and money on office automation, says Amy Wohl, a veteran office automation consultant in Bala-Cynwyd, PA. "Everyone has to make mistakes and find out what works in their company," she says. "They're training people to use the technology and they're getting experience in how to organize and implement technology – that's the really hard lesson to learn. Whenever you change the way you do your job, it's likely you'll be less productive, not more, at first."

That's particularly true with office automation, given the number of new tools that exist. They include – in addition to personal computers and spreadsheets – decision support systems, business graphics, electronic calendars, internal and external data bases, desktop publishing systems, electronic mail, voice messaging, and teleconferencing, just to name a few. "It takes time for people to become proficient," notes William H. Howard, vice president for information services at Bechtel Group Inc. "Some people forget that."

The problem is not only learning how to use the equipment. It is also dealing with the resulting flood of information. "A computer is like pencil and paper, just faster," says John D. Moynahan, Jr, executive vice president for Metropolitan Life Insurance Co.'s group insurance operations. "You can end up with stacks of reports with 14 pages of numbers in columns and rows." Moynahan put up with that for a while, but then he told the

Five steps to success

◄ Plan ahead

Real office productivity comes from changing work processes and eliminating steps throughout the organization, not just speeding up work. That may mean rethinking the entire management system and structure to tap automation's full potential. This is a job for top executives, not information systems managers

Be selective ►

Don't automate across the board. Identify one or two, well–defined tasks that are critical to the company's mission, and make sure the objective is measurable. Don't give everyone computers at first. Target the 20 percent who can assure the success of your initial experiments. The other 80 percent will follow

◄ Be patient

Climbing the learning curve takes time. Technology will change your organization's culture, as well as its methods, and it could take two years or more for employees to adjust. Don't let data processing managers try to protect their own turf. Reward them for actively anticipating the needs of employees

Measure the benefits ►

Doing things faster is a change but not necessarily a benefit. Monitor whether the technology alters behavior, assess whether that is good, and calculate the value of that change. Figure out where the time went. The highest payoff may come not from cutting staff but from using that extra time to do a better job such as closing more sales

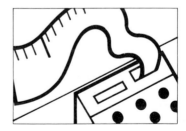

◄ Communicate

Tell your employees why you want to automate, and get their help in designing and implementing the system. Appoint a complaint czar and encourage employees to identify what's not going smoothly. Fix it quickly. If the new equipment includes personal computers, expect to spend about the same amount on training and support that you spend on the computers

Figure 11.2   Five steps to success.

If only Willy Loman had used a laptop

For eight months, William Rorison diligently called on the pension-fund manager of a small Chicago company, trying to sell him an annuity program that lets clients tailor their investments in six various funds. It was all in vain until mid-August, when Rorison, an account representative for Metropolitan Life Insurance Co., showed up with a sample plan on a laptop computer. The salesman and the client started blue-skying: What would happen to the client's total return if, say, he switched money from this investment to that. Rather than schedule a follow-up appointment, Rorison produced answers on the spot.

Within three weeks he made the sale, for $633,000, and picked up a $28,500 commission. Rorison eventually would have succeeded anyway, he says with salesman-like confidence, "but the computer analysis pushed it over the top." Now he's closing half his deals on the first call, up from almost none before. And his commissions are up about 20 percent.

Sales boost

Few cases so clearly demonstrate the benefits of automating a sales force. US companies are rapidly discovering that for an investment of a few thousand dollars, they can raise the productivity of a sales rep almost overnight. And there's more to it than demonstrating new products. By automating everything from order entries to checks on the status of orders and the scheduling of sales calls, companies are eliminating the time-honored, and time-wasting, methods of managing by telephone and memo.

You needn't look far for the reasons. According to a recent Conference Board study, most sales reps devote up to 40 percent of their time to paperwork and spend $200 or more per sales call. Management may not always control what's done with the time freed by automation, but "the feeling is that the more you can reduce overhead burden, the more you increase selling time and sales," says Louis A. Wallis, a senior research associate at the Conference Board. His survey of 45 companies showed that 45 percent recouped their computer investments – from $4,000 to $7,000 per salesperson – in under two years. But because portable computer technology has not been available until recently, fewer than 10 percent of US salespeople currently carry the machines.

Just as automation affects work patterns in the office, it often radically changes selling. Last year, Hewlett-Packard Co. equipped 135 sales representatives with laptop computers to help with such time consuming chores as retrieving account histories and tracking the status of orders from the corporate mainframe. After a six-month pilot effort, HP found that the machines cut time spent in meetings by 46 percent and travel time between customers and the office by 13 percent. "We changed the way people communicate with their boss and peers," says Richard S. Burgess, an HP marketing manager. As a result, time spent with customers shot up 27 percent and sales rose by 10 percent. Even if sales go up only half that much as HP rolls out the program to 1,700 reps this year, it will still generate $30 million in pretax profits – or five times the project's cost.

Cincinnati Milacron Inc.'s representatives had a different problem: information overload. With a line of some 65,000 grinding wheels and hundreds of cutting fluids to sell to metal shops, its distributors' sales forces of 1,500 people couldn't master enough detail to recommend the right product easily. The question was: "How do we open up to all of these people the full art of selling?" says Alan L. Shaffer, group vice president for industrial products.

The answer: give them product information via portable computers. Then have the software identify the appropriate product by leading a representative through a series of questions about the customer's needs. The system has been such a hit that Milacron has added more than 50 distributors, a 40 percent increase, and it has helped the company roughly double its market share, to more than 10 percent – without adding any new employees.

Close call

Information at the point of sale can also be a competitive weapon. In one recent case, a large hospital was considering switching from Merck & Co.'s Mefoxin, an antibiotic, to a competitor's product that was half the price. Armed with a laptop tied to a data base, the Merck salesperson searched clinical and lab studies from the Food & Drug Administration to find that the competing drug had not shown efficacy in treating gynaecological infections. That convinced the client to stick with Mefoxin – and saved Merck a major account.

Many companies are finding that automating the field force helps other parts of the organization as well. Every segment, from marketing and production to shipping and accounting, needs information gathered in the trenches. Westinghouse Electric Corp.'s advanced industrial systems division, for example, has reduced accounts receivable in the past 18 months by almost half. That's because its 500 service technicians now file their job reports electronically, cutting ten days off the manual billing process.

In time, computer-armed field representatives may even influence product development. When HP salespeople receive leads from the marketing department, they now use electronic forms to report whether they win or lose the business and why. For most sales reps, generating that information used to be a low priority. Now the form pops up in the rep's electronic mailbox after each lead is sent – a constant reminder to fill it out – and the company can use the results to position and price products and to design future features. "There isn't a marketing executive around who wouldn't give his left hand to get that kind of information," says Richard C. Alberding, executive vice president for marketing. With more productive salespeople, such drastic measures won't be necessary.

report-senders: "Give me knowledge, not data." Now the reports tend to be short narratives, with numerical details appended. And "if a report is going out routinely, we check every few months to see if people really need it," says Moynahan. "It's a matter of learning how to use a tool."

At American President Lines, turning data into knowledge had a big payoff for Michael E. Cromar. When Cromar was corporate controller and wanted to keep track of expenses, he got 1,500-page reports from the corporate mainframe. The reports listed every line item in each of more than 500 cost centers. But they offered no way to focus on variances from the budget. When Cromar got his own microcomputer system, however, he could break out who was spending what on, say, travel and entertainment. And when he started sending out periodic one-page T&E summaries listing in descending order which cost centers were the biggest spenders, expenditures quickly fell: Nobody wanted to be No. 1. "Simply putting out the information seems to generate the desired behavior – without inordinate management time doing it," says Cromar, who has since been promoted to director of information resources.

Feeling their way

Many companies are just starting to deal with information overload. Dataquest, a San Jose (CA) market researcher, recently studied 400 companies to assess the payback in office automation. It discovered that more than half of them had not started automating their offices until 1984 or later. Many of these companies are still feeling their way.

Once they've mastered the early learning curve, which can easily take a couple of years, the first thing companies generally do is look to reduce head counts. In the US government, for example, where budgets have been shrinking in recent years, eliminating staff was a key goal cited by agencies in a 1987 study by New York market researcher Quantum Consultants Inc.

Some of those agencies have already seen gains. The US Forest Service, one of the few organizations that has done before-and-after studies of its automation efforts, signed a $125 million contract with Data General Corp. in 1983 to automate and electronically link its 900 offices. Environmental-impact statements now take 39 percent less time, while timber sales contracts take 27 percent less time to draw up. The service has sliced 30 percent off the hours needed to do its work and cut staff by 25 percent, to 37,000. "In 1985 alone we had savings of $125 million," says Charles R. Hargraves, associate deputy chief for administration. He "conservatively" expects a 250 percent return on investment between 1983 and 1990.

Michael Spatz, president of the nation's 38th-largest shopping center management company, has done even better by holding his head count down and doing much more work. Spatz & Co., in Northbrook (IL), started off with four properties in 1981, with three bookkeepers sharing one computer. Today it oversees 65 properties, with only one more bookkeeper, thanks to a mainframe with 15 terminals bought in 1984. Spatz estimates that without automation, he'd need 20 bookkeepers, plus 24 property managers – 16 more than he has now. At that rate, his annual payroll would be $886,000, not $412,000. That, he concludes, would make "the difference between being bankrupt or profitable."

The tough part

The greatest benefit of office automation lies not just in doing existing work faster, however. It comes from shaking down the organization to eliminate whole chunks of redundant work. Ford Motor Co., a leader in using office automation as well as factory technology, has cut white-collar staff for 32 consecutive quarters, in large part by automating existing jobs. And it did so even as it put out more car lines than at the start of the decade, says S. I. Gilman, Ford's executive director for information systems. Now "the future opportunities are in changing the process, not eliminating fat," he says. "And that's tough."

Tough but doable, as Ford is proving. Look at its system for paying suppliers. Once upon a time the process started when an invoice arrived. A Ford clerk would call the plant to confirm that the parts in question had indeed arrived in the stated quantity. The clerk then would call purchasing to confirm that the stated prices were correct. If everything was in order, the clerk would authorize payment. If not, he began a long checking process.

Ford had 500 people in the US paying bills this way when management decided in early 1986 to computerize in hopes of eliminating 100 jobs. "Big improvement, 20 percent right?" recalls Gilman. "Then someone said wait a minute, why pay bills this cumbersome way at all?" Now the document attached to the incoming parts is taken at the receiving dock and fed into a computer terminal there. A central computer multiplies the parts price in its memory with the quantity received and authorizes a check-writing machine to make payment. Suppliers don't even send Ford an invoice any more. Under the new system, instead of eliminating 100 jobs, Ford will do away with 375 by 1990. And it will take that long only because the company will do it by attrition and transfers.

Ford's achievement may sound simple, but it wasn't. The company had to bring together people from manufacturing, finance, purchasing, and data processing to change basic work patterns. For example, purchasing agents who used to negotiate prices with suppliers now are also responsible for ensuring that the prices in the computer's memory are up to date. "The hardest job is crossing organizational lines," says Gilman.

A faster mess

Ford's experience makes another thing clear: High-level management attention is essential to get the full benefit of office technology. Just having data processing people install hardware won't do the trick: Automating a mess will only produce a faster mess. Says Cyrus F. Gibson, a technology consultant at the Index Group in Cambridge (MA), and co-author of a new book called *The Information Imperative*: "Real office productivity comes from changing the work itself, and that has nothing to do with technology."

He won't get any argument from Anthony C. Mondello, International Business Machines Corp. vice president for office-product development and sales. Mondello advocates that office automation "be installed at the top of the organization first," so that management will learn a few tricks of the trade. When IBM put in its own office-communications network, Mondello was the first to get it. "I would send out requests, and it became obvious that if you were not on the system, you'd miss important discussions," he notes.

Mondello learned firsthand many of the lessons he now tries to communicate to clients. "I found myself changing how I did my job," he recalls. New-product design proposals were sent around so people could add comments and ship them back quicker. That cut development time by 15 percent to 20 percent. The result: "The company looks at itself and says, 'Now that we can communicate in an hour, not a day, we can do things differently.' So now you adapt to all the things tools make possible. It's hard to quantify things that weren't even possible before. You have to look at productivity in a much broader way."

When top managers realize this, productivity starts to zoom. And the changes can be measured in orders of magnitude, not just percentage points. In late 1984, American Express Co. executives decided they had to improve the company's credit-authorization services. Bad decisions in authorizing credit when merchants called in for approval were leading to losses said to be in the hundreds of millions of dollars. The company decided to develop a so-called expert system that would pull together the experience of American Express' best authorizers and make their skills available to all the others via computer.

Today the system, dubbed the Authorizer's Assistant, gathers pertinent information on cardholders from 14 data bases and squeezes it down to two screens so human authorizers can easily scan it and make a final decision. The computer itself can handle those authorizations where the data do not raise any red flags – about 25 percent to 30 percent. The rest of the time, when cases are referred to humans for a decision, the system shaves off 20 percent of the handling time because it packages the cardholder information so tightly.

The result: a 45–60 percent annual internal rate of return on the cost of the new system, according to Robert H. Slast, American Express' vice president for technology strategy. Even more important, the system has reduced by 50 percent the number of approved transactions that end up as bad debts. How much money does that save? Slast won't tell. But he does say

Table 11.1   Where office systems save money

Market researcher Dataquest studied 400 companies to see where office systems cut costs. The results:

Area of saving	Percent of respondents that cut costs by 10% or more	
	Smaller companies*	Larger companies**
Communications	36.5%	39.3%
Photocopying	33.5	33.3
Clerical workers	34.5	29.9
Storage	27.0	26.4
Paper	31.5	25.4
Printing	27.5	25.4
Professionals	6.0	5.5
Middle-level managers	6.5	5.0
Top-level managers	1.5	1.0

*200 companies with 100–999 employees
**200 companies with 1,000 or more employees
DATA: DATAQUEST INC.

that the losses avoided through improved screening are five times as great as the productivity savings.

"Drudgery into fun"

Both figures are substantially more than the $2 million cost of developing the pilot system, which was installed in late 1986 in American Express' Fort Lauderdale (FA) facility to serve 100 authorizers. By October, 1988, 2,900 more will have the system. "The managerial climate is extremely important," says Slast. "Having senior management that's willing to place these kinds of bets on technology goes right to the heart of effectiveness in productivity."

That's true for companies of every size. At Midwest Metal Products, a small manufacturer in Michigan City, IN, William H. Wendt, the 45-year-old founder and president, says the computer has "turned the drudgery into fun" and saved about $100,000 a year in salaries. Wendt, who is also the company's No. 1 estimator and computer operator, managed a family-owned metal-fabricating shop in Chicago before starting his own business from scratch. He sold his old Mercedes-Benz to buy a personal computer system, on which he developed programs that let his office staff of six make price estimates on their own.

In his old business, a careful estimate could have taken 15 to 20 minutes. "Now it takes 15 to 20 seconds," he says. "All I have to do is plug in the quantity, the material, and the diameter, and bingo, I have the price and weight. Without the system, I'd probably need a staff of ten or 12 instead of six."

Wendt's system has brought him a competitive advantage. But for many businesses, technology offers something more basic: survival. Increasingly, companies will find it harder to compete effectively without a technological infrastructure. The nation's six largest airlines, for example, all have their own electronic reservation systems – a trend started by American Airlines Inc. and United Airlines Inc. And Federal Express Corp.'s success has been widely attributed to its ability to use technology to dispatch and track packages. Imitators are now legion.

Catch-22

Ironically, though, for some industries, technology will be a catch-22: something they can't afford to live without but can't live with, either. Commercial banking is a good example. To be competitive, every money-center bank has had to develop its own electronic communications networks for transferring funds and instructions internationally. In all, commercial banks spent $9 billion last year on hardware, software, data communications, and operations for international funds-transfer systems that move a total of $300 billion a day through New York, according to Thomas D. Steiner, a McKinsey & Co. technology management consultant to financial institutions.

According to Steiner, each management group was right to invest in systems. Otherwise they couldn't have competed. "In the paper world, moving funds internationally costs $10 to $12," he says. "Electronically it costs $2 or less." But, Steiner says, because each bank has created virtually unlimited capacity, the net result will be intensified competition and price wars in transferring funds. Ultimately, that will mean a shakeout. "This new electronic world leads to tougher competitive environments, and fewer institutions will be needed. You don't need 25 electronic funds-transfer systems doing the same thing – all you need is maybe half a dozen," he says. "That will produce more efficiency and productivity in the long run, but it's a long and painful and costly process that will kill the profitability of many businesses."

The same thing could happen to many other industries. "What motivates companies to raise productivity is to get a jump on the competition for awhile," points out Martin N. Baily, an expert in productivity issues at the Brookings Institution in Washington. "But if all companies are equally progressive, then the benefit goes to the consumer."

That may come as dismaying news to businesses that are trying to assess the wisdom of investing huge sums in office automation systems. But for many companies, making that investment may be the only way to stay in the game at all.

Information Technology in Banks: Taylorization or Human-centered Systems?

Steve Smith

In this paper the author argues that regimented work systems on Tayloristic lines in UK banks have not only degraded the quality of worklife: they have actually failed to boost productivity. The solution lies in the development of more "human-centered" systems, which retain human skills, intuition, and discretion, says Smith. The author is Lecturer in the School of Sociology, Kingston Polytechnic, UK, and this piece first appeared in Science and Public Policy, *vol. 14 (3), June 1987.*

There are many prescriptions as to how work ought to be organized and how managers ought to manage the introduction of new technology. Yet the thoroughly rational management strategy for technical change has proved to be an elusive chimera.

The paper focuses on a few key approaches to organizational and new technology in the context of "retail" or high street banking. I look at some of the achievements as well as some of the problems that have been generated as a result of one particular management strategy for technical change: Taylorism.

I begin by presenting simplified outlines of four key theoretical approaches to the design of work and technology. Each of these has tended to be conceived in terms of the "shop floor" whether in the factory or in the office. Yet, I will argue, relatively little attention has been given to the implications which organizational theories of technical change carry for managers *per se*.

In the second part I describe the main features of technical and organizational change in the bank's branch networks, the chosen rationale for change, and the difficulties which have arisen as a direct result of it.

Finally I return to consider the concept of the "human centered" office system and ask whether or not this unorthodox approach to work and new technology might not only meet the interests of shop floor workers for whom it has been conceived but also curtail the burgeoning management functions of large corporations.

Labor process

The rising tide of information technology (IT) has been accompanied by a multitude of invocations that managers must embrace the new technology, and must think theoretically about how they organize technical change and direct work. "Unprofessional" management by hunch, rule of thumb or custom and practice is definitely out of favor.

Nowhere is this more so than in the UK, whose relatively weak economic performance is frequently explained in terms of a lack of professionalism and "conceptual" thinking among managers, and a lacklustre record on the adoption of new technologies. Managers, it is said, are going to have to change.

But managers are aware of the practical limits of organizational theory and have learnt to mistrust fanciful claims made for new technology. This is true even in industries that are very heavily professionalized, like banking, which also has a long record of computerization.

In any case the choice of a management strategy is no mere technical decision: it is subject to all kinds of conflicting demands and interests, not least among managers. Banking research which begins and ends with technology itself therefore contains very misleading impressions of the employment impact of technical change.

A recently completed two-year research project on new technologies in banking,[1] the service industry with arguably the greatest investment in IT, suggests that there is nothing less than a crisis among managers: "New School" managers have been prepared to embrace an explicit and distinct theory of work organization and technical change. Yet this overtly theoretical strategy for technical change has generated major snags which we will explain later.

On the other hand, "Old School" managers remain reluctant to give up the complex "knowledge" that they have gained through life-long apprenticeship in the intricacies of banking practice and task organization. Implicit in the Old School view is also a theory of sorts. Old Schoolers hold to a neo-craft conception of bank work and organization that is easily as distinctive as the New School approach now being pursued.[2]

Before going into detail about banking, let us summarize some of the key academic theories of work organization and technical change in order to spell out just what is at stake. In particular, and at the risk of over-simplification, the labour process debate may be described thus.

Taylor's doctrines

The doctrines of F. W. Taylor probably remain the main, if understated, orthodoxy among managements in the UK.

Taylorism claims to offer the most efficient approach to technical design, the most rational way of organizing work and the most complete form of managerial control over workers. It bases this claim on what Taylor saw as a scientific view of human nature. Known also as "Scientific Management," Taylorism thus presented itself as the most rational way of matching an organization's means to profitable ends.

In practice, it is based on an instrumental, egoistic conception of human nature, and therefore would design labor around a system of money incentives. Work, it is supposed, is done not for its own sake, but for anticipated extrinsic benefits. It could therefore be broken down into a series of very small, cheap and simple operations. Many machines are designed on these assumptions.

Management work is similarly specialized while the function of coordination and control in a Taylorian organization is progressively concentrated at the apex. In an extreme division of labor, each layer of management controls the layer below and is controlled by the level above.

On the other side of the debate stands an unstable alliance between the followers and revisionists of the late Harry Braverman and the followers of a Human Relations School.

Braverman's rejection

For Braverman, Taylorism, or Scientific Management is to be seen as the "managerial ideology of advanced capitalism," having little to do with science or rationality. Braverman thus rejects its scientific status outright.

However, he agrees that a Tayloristic approach to technology *does* represent the most effective form of (class) control over labor at the workplace. Thus he equates, or has been interpreted as equating, the economic triumph of capitalism with the triumph of control brought by Taylorism: the detailed breakdown of the labor-process into minute divisions, the separation of conception from execution, the progressive destruction of craft skills, the elimination of worker-autonomy over the pace, order, and timing of tasks.

For Braverman these elements of Taylorism had nothing to do with human nature, and were no more than an attempt to secure the interests of capital against those of labor in the battle for control on the shop floor.[3]

Human Relations School

The Human Relations School also opposes itself to Scientific Management. But unlike Braverman's "class approach," Human Relations bases its critique on an alternative view of human nature to that held by Taylor.

According to Human Relations, people and machines ought to be organized in a way that would satisfy a complex of supposed moral as well as instrumental "motivations." (The "moral" side, originally a part of Taylor's writing has long since been forgotten by his own practitioners.)

This school contends that there is a wider range of human natures.[4] Displacing Scientific Management's egoistical view of human nature, Human Relations emphasizes the need for moral satisfaction in work especially through allowing and encouraging sociability among groups of workers.

Rather than divide workers up by setting them to do a range of highly differentiated and repetitive assembly line jobs, the Human Relations School would set up small groups of workers who would have some discretion to arrange how tasks are organized. The work group is left to decide the work rota, and where possible to determine the pace of work at any one moment.

Payment would be based on group performance, not individual output, while the group should develop its own collective work discipline, thus managing itself to a degree. Machine layout would facilitate this.

Human Relations appears to share Braverman's abhorrence of Taylorism and work degradation but disagrees that it is effective. Instead it contends that a Human Relations approach to work organization would be the most efficient form of work organization under a capitalistic or, indeed, any other economic system. For the Human Relations School, humane work is entirely compatible with private ownership and control of the means of production – so much so that ownership is hardly raised as an issue.

But for Braverman capitalism represents the negation of worker integrity: his thesis on the relationship between technology and work organization is thus revolutionary by implication. According to Braverman, only under socialism could work be organized in a way that was truly rewarding and non-alienating.

Human-centered systems

There is yet one more group who would seek to "humanize" labor, by developing human-centered manufacturing and office systems. Here the desire is particularly to over-turn the Taylorist orthodoxy in the design of work and new technology. Instead of taking skills, control and discretion *away* from the operator and absorbing them into the machine and organization, so rendering work meaningless, the human-centered approach seeks to retain the centrality of human skills and intuitive knowledge.

If experimental projects at UMIST (Manchester) and Sheffield Polytechnic in the UK and also in Sweden were to be generalized, operators would have the discretion to disagree with machine intelligence on the basis of their own long developed grasp of the processes in question. They would also see through their work from the beginning to the end of a discrete process. They would literally know what they were doing.

One implication of the human-centered approach (although this does not seem to be spelt out) would be that the human-centered organization could get by with far fewer managers. Instead of being mere cogs in a complex machine, with all the coordination functions that Taylorism gives birth to, the human-centered approach promises that operators will be "left to get on with it" so to speak.

Operators' commitment would originate from a pride in skill and competence and would depend on halting and reversing an alleged long historical process of de-skilling. Skill is seen as functional here.

There is the further implication that the human-centered school would be highly mistrustful of what they would see as the sham autonomy of semi-autonomous group working.

Human Relations is thus viewed as a *post hoc* attempt to reconcile human needs with inhuman work – a mere share out and rotation of otherwise boring, meaningless and specialized tasks.

These theories and counter positions generate a wealth of further issues. How, for example, might a human-centered system come about, and could, say, bank branches ever look like human-centered organizations, so defined? Could the anti-managerial strategy of the Human-centred School be launched without curtailing the rights of owners of capital?

Rosenbrock thinks so, but others do not.[5] Are some organizations so segmented, de-skilled, and specialized that they are too far gone to be rescued from Taylorism, and could not possibly be reformed on a new craft basis? Or is de-skilled work truly as de-skilled as it first appears? Can all large organizations be fairly categorized as Tayloristic in any case? The prescriptions may seem reasonable, but what about the organizational power and interests of those involved?

These are not just academic niceties; they are fundamental to the development of living organizations.

One way to begin to come to terms with these questions is to specify more clearly the technical and organizational stage of development reached in particular industries and companies. The next section presents an exemplar from UK branch banking.

To summarize the argument so far, the debate on the organization of work has occurred between four poles. First, there are two managerial approaches to work organization: one, Taylorism, advocates an extreme division of labor coupled with a graduated incentives system to gain worker effort; a second, Human Relations, approach seeks to accommodate workers' claimed need for moral solidarity or sense of belonging at work by setting up semi-autonomous work groups with job rotation. The latter approach seeks to gain working commitment.

On the other hand there are two counter-orthodox positions. The first, following Braverman, foresees liberated, worker-determination of the labor process only on the demise of the capitalistic economic system. Some supporters of the second, human-centered approach are, however, primarily anti-*managerial* rather than anti-*capitalistic*.

Thus in contrast to Braverman some adherents of the human-centered approach (especially Rosenbrock) would contemplate possible reforms of work under both capitalist and state socialist systems, and they would see no necessary incompatibility between the private ownership of the means of production and human-centered employment. Thus, here the issue of the control of work is far more crucial than the issue of social ownership.

The point, as Rosenbrock claims to show from his human-centered flexible manufacturing system at UMIST, is that a human-centered labor process may be several times more efficient, not because ownership has changed but because a more favorable form of control has been devised.

Technical change

At first sight banking seems an unlikely focus for contention between these theories of work organization and technical change, but in the past two decades, all four leading UK clearing banks have experimented with recognizably Tayloristic forms of work organization in their branch networks.

This strategy implies a certain view of recruitment, training, technology and efficiency and has been characterized as a competitive response to "non-bank" financial institutions such as building societies, retailers, finance houses, and money shops, as well as to the Post Office, Girobank and so on. Taylorization was seen as a means of gaining fitness in competition.

Yet Taylorism has not proved entirely successful and a second view of work organization is now emerging. In some ways the (latest) new approach represents the reassertion of a more conservative view of bank work. I will now look at some of these changes in corporate thinking.

Banking apprenticeship

The established ideal in banking was that every branch manager was theoretically capable of performing most if not every branch operation, on the basis of his (sic) training and practical experience. In theory promotion was open to anyone who could demonstrate the necessary aptitude and dedication.

The apprenticeship was long and comprehensive. It began with employment as a "junior" at 15 or 16 years of age and might (and for some did) end in a General Managership at corporate headquarters (HQ). Some recruits joined believing they carried the proverbial "Chief General Manager's baton in their knapsacks."

The dominant principle for promotion was that one would be nominated for career steps to jobs one *could not yet do* (the opposite of Taylorian specialization, which regards this as wasteful). The newly promoted would learn the job side-by-side with somebody who had already mastered it, and who would eventually be moved on in turn to a task which he/she was not yet competent to perform. Over time this knowledge would be entrusted to the next generation of employees.

The ethos of the banking apprenticeship was paternal-autocratic: employees were held in trust and promised a career in return for deference to the bank's code of ethics. Non-conformity was devalued. However, if an employee managed to reach senior management – it might take 40 years – then he was finally granted autonomy to make radical strategic technical and organizational decisions on the basis of his wide experience and knowledge as a "general practitioner" in banking. At the local level, one individual branch manager might be a loan manager, a personnel manager, a production or operational manager all rolled into one.

Clearly this picture is somewhat over-drawn but it is a reasonable indication of how "Old School" bankers were promoted; authority and confidence to manage came with age, experience, "generalist" skills, and a particular outlook. The prerequisite "passport to success" was, and to an extent still is, the examination leading to recognition by the Institute of Bankers.

In banking perhaps even more so than in many service sector industries, even at the clerical level people have been trained to do a comparatively wide range of tasks, and for very good reasons. Because the "banking day" involves considerable qualitative and quantitative variations in inputs and outputs, staff flexibility is crucial if a branch is to operate efficiently. At the very least an Enquiry Clerk should be able to cashier and to input on a terminal, and may move around the branch doing different operations at different times of the day. This is how the "traditional" branch meets its peak loads.

There is a certain camaraderie and collective pressure amongst clerks to work well, and not to create difficulties for others to deal with later; in a crisis employees will help each other out. There is reciprocity. The person who is mainly responsible for staff deployment and training is the branch "Accountant," a role which requires very detailed knowledge of bank work to be effective. The term "apprenticeship" was earlier used quite deliberately in order to suggest parallels between banking and crafts normally associated with manufacturing industry.

Design values

As new technology was introduced into banking, what design values were incorporated in it? What of the employees who did not pass out as managers? How has the recruitment of women been pursued?

Partly on the basis of the design values of the technology suppliers, corporate managements in banking have overseen profound changes in bank work and organization. The most extreme and widely quoted statement of these values was made by Franco de Benedetti, Managing Director of Olivetti, at a *Financial Times* conference in March 1979. It appears to fulfill Braverman's worst nightmare:

The Taylorism of the first factories . . . enabled the labor force to be controlled and was the necessary prerequisite to the subsequent mechanization and automation of the productive processes. In this way Taylorized industries were able to win competition over the putting out system . . . information technology is basically a technology of coordination and control of the labor force, the white-collar workers, which Taylorian organization does not cover . . .

However EDP [Electronic Data Processing] seems to be one of the most important tools with which company management institutes policies directly concerning the work process conditioned by complex economic and social factors. In this sense EDP is in fact an organizational technology, and like the organization of labor, has a dual function as a productive force and a control tool for capital.

Similarly Docherty observed that within the branch "increased automation converted tellers who were in effect mini-bankers into automatons."[6]

In announcing its proposals for work reorganization a large clearing bank effectively announced that managers would be Taylorized too: "For some time, we have been moving away from the concept of a generalist banker and have now decided that we must provide a greater degree of specialization to serve our personal and corporate customers."[7] The primary application of new technology in banking so far has been the automation of the branch accounting system. Branch ledgers have been replaced by mainframe files, the italic hand by operators at keyboards: encoders, back office terminals, single entry machines. This has contributed to moderate and steady increases in the efficiency of bank workers.

Indeed, business growth could not have been handled without new technology. However, the social organization of the branch accounting system has also changed in important ways and recent management strategy towards technical change has generated some new problems.

There has been progressive task specialization, and several tiers of entry have replaced common entrance at 15 or 16. The career structure has become horizontally and vertically segmented, and men and women tend to do different jobs often physically segregated within a branch. What were once stages in a long career have tended to become more or less permanently staffed by one segment of the labor force.

Several banks have taken this clearly Tayloristic approach to an extreme and piloted "hub and satellite" banking, where specialist tasks are geographically defined. At the hub branch a full range of services are provided and this is where a management "team" of specialist lenders, administratives and training managers may be found.

The sorting of vouchers (like checks and credits) may be undertaken in this building, or in a separate data processing office. Voucher handling is usually done by women, sometimes working part-time or in shifts. This layout has been strongly advocated by US suppliers as the best counter to rising costs.

Standing Order clerks and many "appointed" grades are also grouped centrally in this local network, as is typing/word processing. The hub and DP office are linked to satellite or service branches, which offer a narrower range of services to the personal customer, and which therefore house only a fraction of the range of bank jobs. Some satellite branches have no managers. The lines between the branches represent van-runs for vouchers and other collections and deliveries, relief staff cover, and journeys by the management team who oversee the network.

Branch network reorganization

This form of branch network reorganization (BNR) has been highly successful on the lending-side – so long as the network is not too geographically dispersed. It does not suit rural areas. Specialist lending managers are almost unanimously pleased with BNR because it enables them to concentrate on marketing the banks' services. This is seen by them as rewarding work.

However, BNR in this form has brought a series of new problems. Above all the management administrative and coordination input is considerably increased with specialization. The banks who have piloted BNR find that there are few if any clerical staff savings – clerical staffing seems to rise, and "appointed" or intermediate staffing also seems to increase slightly.

These changes in some branches can be more than proportionate to the increase in business which banks have been enjoying. In other words, recent moves towards Taylorization at least in retail branches have not markedly increased labor productivity. It certainly does not "revolutionize" clerical work performance.

Furthermore, we have found that Taylorian specialization tends to reduce staff flexibility. (There are also major architectural constraints.) The banking day involves large qualitative and quantitative variations in inputs and outputs, yet these are inconsistent with Taylorism which depends on continuous inputs and outputs for its success – think of the assembly-line. A Tayloristic new technology strategy is bound to create some important new difficulties.

For example, branch reorganization involves first centralizing paper vouchers to process them. This has created new messengers' jobs and considerable van mileages: one quantifiable symptom of the new control difficulties of BNR.

Taylorization also highlights important differences between groups of employees that further affect work organization. Differences are discernible between "Old School" and "New School" bank managers, and between women clerks and "fast track" career program men. It also breaks the link between the professional examinations of the Institute of Bankers and banking careers.

Young "specialist" graduate managers, and older general practitioner (GP) managers are conscious of profound differences of outlook which separate them. The graduates have intimated that they may feel uncomfortable in a branch environment, while one Old School manager complained that "you can't just inject people with 30 years' experience."

Old Schoolers are inclined to argue that they can understand balance sheets in a rapid, intuitive way, and better understand the branch staff *milieux*. This only comes with experience.

However, New Schoolers suspect that such GP "intuition" represents benign prejudice rather than strict business sense. The new managers seem more inclined to treat branches as industrial systems rather than as a particular or special way of working life. GPs regard this as a regrettable offence against a revered way of working life.

There are also differences between women clerks who predominantly work as cashiers, standing order clerks, personnel bankers and "mech" (machine) room operators, and men on "the accelerated career program." Men appear to be put through these grades more quickly, particularly through the mech rooms, probably as a gesture towards the old notion of a banking apprenticeship. Men have thus been found managing machine rooms otherwise staffed by women as part of their "man-management training."

Staff morale in data processing sections is quite variable; however, I have frequently heard the complaint that staff who joined to be bank employees find themselves "dedicated" to repetitive "factory work:" "This isn't banking, it's factory work." The declining morale of staff and the undermining of certain incentives to work hard – collective pressure to finish and go home, the satisfaction of seeing a task through to completion, the promise of a career in return for conscientious work – may have contributed to some "proletarianization" of staff in these areas.[8]

Taylorism has also had an impact on the Institute of Bankers' (IOB) examinations which have tended to become somewhat devalued in the eyes of the employers. This is because the IOB's rule as a "passport to success" contradicts the growing horizontal and vertical segmentation of the labor force.

Day release for IOB courses has been restricted. Yet the IOB continues to attract record numbers of students (60,000 +) including women, who may study through correspondence or night classes, and who clearly have not given up hope of some career progression and the pay rise on completion of Part One.

This places the IOB in a difficult position. A compromise is being sought which would channel students either to an upgraded form of banking qualification or to a new diploma in financial sector services work possibly in and beyond banking as such. This development could have further effects on the gender and career structure of banking employment and might conceivably underscore the separation of women's and men's work in banking.

These differences and difficulties arise from the gradual insinuation of Taylorism into banking as branch accounting has been progressively automated.

Banking revolution

Banking employment has changed with the impact of new information technology (IT) and in certain areas, especially the updating of customer accounts ("inputting") and in voucher handling, considerable efficiency gains have been made compared with manual systems. For many General Practitioner bankers, banking has indeed gone through a "revolution." It is not that the rules of the accounting system have changed. It is more that the organization of tasks, training, and the career structure have disrupted the Old Schooler's ideal of "what banking is all about."

For many GP managers the advent of specialization, segmentation, and the introduction of career ceilings is perceived with a sense of sadness and loss. But it would be premature to announce the complete demise of the established assumptions about work organization in banking.

Technical and organizational changes have, for example, brought surprises for the New Schoolers too. One major clearing bank was surprised to find that the most operationally efficient branch was the "traditional" 15 person branch and that BNR "hasn't produced any staff savings really."[9] Yet three of the Big Four have invested heavily in BNR for some time.

It is now realized that the interaction of inputs and outputs at branch level is extremely complex, and not capable of at-a-stroke technology fixes. According to one clearing bank, even the most important process innovations envisaged in the next five to ten years "may not produce as much as one whole staff or equivalent time saving per branch!" Far from wiping out clerical staff, one further "revolutionary" innovation will save a mere five hours per branch per week.

Some technology suppliers have been perilously ill-informed as to the nature of branch operations. The case of the Automated Teller Machine (ATM) illustrates this well. Again it is clear that Tayloristic assumptions about work can be wide of the mark.

To the US suppliers who coined the term, the terminal was strictly an automated teller and sold as such. Obtaining cash by customer self-service at one machine was thought equivalent to between one-third and one human cashier, a calculation initially accepted by the UK clearing banks.

The problem was that this equivalence did not turn out to be hard and fast, and, as in the rest of the service sector, productivity is very difficult to measure. Any staff savings (or more accurately, any non-recruitment of otherwise necessary new staff) was more a question of "political" judgment in the organization.

Despite the progress of Taylorism, UK bankers were initially adamant that they still employed cashiers not tellers. They therefore drew attention to the (several) operations a cashier did and the career they could expect to lead. The ethos of the job dictated that cashiering represented much more than plain "teller" duties.

Unlike the Taylorized form (telling), cashiering was invested with responsibility, trust, duty, and career rewards. It was not just a job. It could not be automated as such, because it had not yet been degraded sufficiently.

Furthermore, because the customers used ATMs in a quite unanticipated way, the employment effects cannot really be judged. The most frequent cash withdrawal at an ATM turned out to be surprisingly small and the customers come back again and again.

This pattern simply has no equivalence with customer behavior at the cashier position. (Paper transactions continue to rise in both volume and value despite ATM usage.) Here IT has made a difference, but not necessarily the one that was anticipated. Useful, but not "revolutionary."

Expected failure

However, the suppliers did not rest their efficiency arguments there. They have tried for years to persuade British clearing banks that the ATM should not just dispense cash and balances or order check books. It should be a much more sophisticated "self-service banking terminal."

Sited in the wall, the lobby or a remote site, customers might transfer funds across their accounts, initiate payments, set up standing orders, all without the intervention of bank staff or, in supplier terminology, without a "warm body."

The clearing banks are not at all sure. Certainly experiments with such terminals are under way, including "home banking" terminals. However, their rather cautious use of pilot projects should show that they remain to be convinced.

Bankers interviewed in my research reported that even the simple, limited function ATM is not necessarily a proven innovation. Because ATMs have been put in many sites where usage is low, it may actually be costing more to dispense cash through such ATMs than via a human cashier.

In short, many innovations have failed to meet expectations; banks have become increasingly cautious in buying new technology; and the organization of work in branches is far from fully understood by Organization and Methods Departments. There is enough evidence to cast doubt on the Tayloristic strategy, and certainly to question the assumptions of Taylor (and Braverman) that Scientific Management is the optimal form of branch systems design. It is difficult to see how the employers can effect any substantial net staff savings in the next five to ten years on this strategy, and even beyond.

It is much more likely that new technology will be used to partially automate parts of various people's jobs, while preserving or renewing existing "first generation" techniques of doing the same functions. Check truncation, which involves "stopping" checks and sending information about their value electronically (so avoiding paper-based clearings), will fall into this category.

So too will electronic funds transfer at the point of sale (EFT/POS). This involves persuading customers not to use their check books in shops but to pay by electronic means directly from their bank accounts into the retailers' account – itself a dubious privilege.

Again, far from eliminating the clearings, the most the banks can hope for from the "EFT/POS Revolution" is that a proportion of customers will move from checks at the point of sale to EFT/POS. But as only a minority of checks are written in stores anyway, the potential employment impact of EFT/POS must be considered small.

Fundamental reconsideration

We, therefore, conclude that, because experience shows that it is hard to eliminate whole tasks, and even harder to make whole individuals redundant in banking, a fundamental reconsideration of what new technologies are supposed to do is necessary.

Until recently, employers have concentrated on gaining clerical productivity increases through Taylorization, which occurs in a pronounced form in hub/satellite/DP center reorganization. The idea seems to have been that if you tidy up bank work so that particular people do only particular operations then there should be efficiency gains.

In a few instances managers and staff have accepted the factory atmosphere and Taylorization has worked moderately well, though not brilliantly. However, the results have been mostly disappointing.

Paradoxically, the search for organizational simplicity has caused serious complications – including increased overtime, loss of flexibility, increased difficulties in finding sickness and holiday cover, in organizing temporary work, part-time staff, and shift working, certain difficulties in "motivating" staff and so on. Finding bank staff and managers who can meet the new requirements of Taylorism is a gamble.

The alternative is to think about bank work in traditional terms. Instead of aiming at getting individual staff to do particular operations on a fixed one-to-one basis, why not view the inherent organizational untidiness of traditional bank branch clerical work organization as a positive virtue. By all means automate-out those fractions of jobs that can be automated; but view these as time-gains to be shared among several individual clerks and to be used in a whole range of possible ways.

The first step in this direction might be to realize that Taylorism, to paraphrase Rosenbrock, "rejects skills which exist and creates a demand for skills that do not exist." Work tends to become more routinized, morale tends to decline. And the integration problems associated with an excessively complex division of labor inevitably absorb increasing levels of overt managerial work.

Recent attempts to bring Human Relations to the rescue of Taylorism by fostering staff commitment will always to some extent be compromised if the reality of work shifts further toward non-career "factory-like" employment. In such circumstances, asking for employee commitment and "motivation" is like asking something for nothing extra in return. Is such a radical recomposition of the workforce – including its managers – necessarily appropriate?

The tentative outlines of an alternative quasi-human-centered view can already be seen.

First, the major banks have drawn back from the true Taylorization of branch operations and the suppliers are finally moving with them. Local branch network DP centers are being shut down and their "dedicated-machine" staffs reintegrated into the branches. These centers "did not prove cost effective" and they will not be missed. New branch processors allow for this return to more traditional flexible working.

Experimental branch layouts are a physical recognition that cashier and "mech" operations are best shared by several employees. These arrangements have recovered much of the camaraderie and spirit of mutual helpfulness (and coercion) among clerks.

For clerks at least, the notion of knowing each other's jobs and seeing work through at least a reasonable number of steps is becoming re-established. I have seen just how well this can work in a branch that was very short staffed through sickness and leave, yet which was coping well with the most intensive peak loads of the week.

Second, and partly by default, some managerial control is being devolved on to non-managerial staff. Some branches without managers are left in the charge of grade four clerks – often women. It is quite clear that this does involve true management responsibilities and, like the principle of the integrity of clerical skills just described, represents a partial recovery of the (control) skills of the clerk.

The problem is that these skills are not actually recognized or rewarded as management skills – especially as clerk-managers spend much time cashiering and machining alongside more junior clerks (wherein lies the secret of their success). Spurious organization complexity has been cleared away.

Thirdly, and again partly by accident, some of the under-rated interpersonal skills of cashiers have been recently enhanced by creating a new kind of job, the "personal banker," who sits in the enlarged lobby of some banks answering general enquiries about financial services. Like clerks-in-charge, personal bankers also do cashiering and mech room work. They are effectively upgraded enquiry clerks, but have been invited to develop marketing skills in selling personal financial services.

Such skills can truly only be gained with practice; they certainly cannot be "injected" *ad hoc*; they are not fully encompassed in the appropriate training "packages," and the personal bankers interviewed appeared to be adding their own techniques to what is wrongly supposed to be a de-skilled and mechanical job. Unfortunately, there is no logical career progression beyond this job at present, and some of the customer contact involved in being a personal banker has been bought at the expense of other cashiers.

Fourthly, despite the development of automated load assessment, or "credit scoring" and even some initial research on replacing managers under the national Alvey programme on Fifth Generation computing, there are also new developments in IT that move in a different direction. GP managers often lament their loss of customer knowledge during the period of rapid business growth and the automation of branch accounting which merely recognizes isolated accounts and cannot integrate information from all possible accounts of a customer.

However, recent proposed developments would establish a transparent "information" system operating separately to the opaque "data" generated by the automated accounting system. Personnel would be able to ask the system sensible questions on the nature and spread of customer accounts in order, say, to get to know about their account holders and make marketing strategies. "It's back to the old days!" said one supplier.

There are no technical reasons why, for example, personal bankers should not be given access to any such system and be allowed to develop "banking" skills further, thus demonstrating old style "commitment." What is more critical here is whether the entrenched gender stereotyping of work in banking and the long standing de-skilling strategy of Taylorization can be overturned.

The outcome will be settled by what may be called "political" struggles in the organizational hierarchies, between the recent orthodoxy of Scientific Management and a new, yet paradoxically more conservative view of bank work. The future involves choices, and these cannot be isolated from the different stakes of different interests.

Summary

Although automation in banking has enabled far more accounts to be handled than ever before, the Tayloristic assumptions of technical change have resulted in certain sub-optimal outcomes. Technologists have under-estimated the value and importance of skill, knowledge, flexibility and career.

Technical change strategies have disrupted bank work and ways of working life, with mixed costs and benefits. Taylorization has also undermined autocratic-paternalism and this may be welcomed. But Taylorism has also tended to alienate bank workers from the material they are working on, as well as from each other.

An approximately human-centered alternative strategy can be contemplated. Organizational developments including network data processing center closures, job reintegration, clerks-in-charge, personal bankers and transparent information systems could arguably be prefigurative developments of human-centered bank work.

The outcome will depend on an ideological struggle over what bank work ought to look like. Different schools of management, different kinds of technologists, educators, training managers, the IOB, men, women, and trade unions are already implicated in this contest of ideas and practices.

I tentatively suggest that in banking at least, contrary to scientific management, efficiency actually improves and control is made easier if the "labor process" is as coherent as possible. There should be a presumption in favor of skills, pride in the job, staff flexibility, apprentice-based careers (which recognize the skills of "women's jobs" as skills) and intuitive knowledge.

Staff must be permitted to float up to their own levels of ability, rather than be rigidly pre-categorized according to formal, educational qualifications and recruitment tiers. Managers might fundamentally reconsider the claimed control benefits of Taylorism and contemplate placing more trust in skilled workers. All this points towards a much more imaginative approach to systems design and technology agreements than we have seen to date.

Notes

1   The paper is based on research entitled "New Technology, Employment and Skills", funded by the Open University and conducted by David Wield and myself.
2   For discussion of managerial "schools," see B. Wilkinson and S.L. Smith, "Management Strategies for Technical Change," *Science and Public Policy*, vol. 10(2), April, 1983. S.L. Smith and B. Wilkinson, "From Old School Hunches to Departmental Lunches," *The Sociological Review*, vol. 32(1), February 1984. A.W. Gouldner, *Patterns of Industrial Bureaucracy* (Free Press of Glencoe, New York, 1954). A.W. Gouldner, *Wildcat Strike* (Antioch Press, Yellow Springs, Ohio, 1954), or T. Spybey, "Tradition and Professional Frames of Meaning for Managers," *Sociology*, vol. 18(4), November 1984.
3   H. Braverman, *Labor and Monopoly Capital* (Monthly Review Press, New York, 1974). B. Wilkinson, *The Shop-floor Politics of New Technology* (Heinemann, London, 1983).
4   E. Mayo, *The Human Problems of an Industrial Civilisation* (Macmillan): F. Hertzberg, *Work and the Nature of Man* (World Publishing Company).
5   H. Rosenbrock, "The Redirection of Technology," *FAC Symposiums*, Bari, May 21–23, 1979 and H. Rosenbrock, "Technical Redundancy: Designing Automated Systems – Need Skill be Lost?" *Science and Public Policy*, December 1983.
6   P. Docherty, "Automation of the Service Industries," *IFAC Round Table*, 1978.
7   "Barclays Bank to Restructure Branch Network," Barclays Bank Press Release, June 27, 1983.
8   R. Crompton, *White-collar Proletariat: De-skilling and Gender in Clerical Work* (Macmillan, London, 1984). D. Bunyan and R. Youdale, *Report of a Case Study on the Impact of New Technology on Women and Trade Union Organisations in Banking* (Bristol Resource Centre, Bristol, UK, 1981).
9   This research interview finding fits with A. Rajan, *New Technology and Employment in the UK Financial Services Sector: Past Impact and Future Prospects*, (IMS, Sussex University, 1984) but conflicts with the view of others that "substantial" job-loss will occur in banking. For example, E.R. Shaw and N.S. Coulbeck, *UK Retail Banking Prospects in the Competitive 1980s* UK (Staniland Hall Associates, Loughborough, UK); L.S. Palmer, *Technical Change and Employment in Banking*, University of Sussex, mimeo August 1980; or N. Hewlett, "New Technology and Banking Employment in the EEC," *Futures*, vol. 17(1), February 1985.

Selected Further Reading

Factories

Computerized Manufacturing Automation: Employment, Education, and the Workplace, Office of Technology Assessment (OTA) report to US Congress, Washington, DC, 1984.

"The Hollow Corporation," a *Business Week* special report, March 3, 1986.

Marjory Blumenthal and Jim Dray, "The Automated Factory: Vision and Reality," *Technology Review,* vol. 88(1), January 1985.

Joseph Deken, *Silico Sapiens: The Fundamentals and Future of Robots* (Bantam, New York, 1986).

Arnoud De Meyer, "The Integration of Information Systems in Manufacturing," *Omega,* vol. 15(3), 1987.

Bela Gold, "On the Potential, Requirements and Limitations of Information Technology in Manufacturing," *Prometheus,* vol. 4(2), December 1986.

Thomas G. Gunn, *Manufacturing for Competitive Advantage: Becoming a World Class Manufacturer* (Ballinger, Cambridge, MA, 1987).

Ramchandran Jaikumar, "Postindustrial Manufacturing," *Harvard Business Review,* November–December 1986.

John K. Krouse, "Engineering without Paper," *High Technology,* March 1986.

Jack R. Meredith, "The Strategic Advantages of the Factory of the Future," *California Management Review,* vol. 29(3), Spring 1987.

Jack R. Meredith and Marianne M. Hill, "Justifying New Manufacturing Systems: A Managerial Approach," *Sloan Management Review,* Summer 1987.

Karen Pennar, Otis Port, Resa King, and William J. Hampton, "The Productivity Paradox: Why the Payoff from Automation Is Still So Elusive," *Business Week,* June 6, 1988.

Charles F. Sabel, Gary Herrigel, Richard Kazis, and Richard Deeg, "How to Keep Mature Industries Innovative," *Technology Review,* April 1987.

Richard J. Schonberger, *World Class Manufacturing* (Free Press, New York, 1986).

Jeffrey Zygmont, "Guided Vehicles Set Manufacturing in Motion," *High Technology,* December 1986.

Commerce

Automation of America's Offices, Office of Technology Assessment (OTA) report to the US Congress, Washington, DC, 1985.

"Computers Make the Sale," *Newsweek,* September 23, 1985.

Effects of Information Technology on Financial Services, Office of Technology Assessment (OTA) report to the US Congress, Washington, DC, 1984.

Robert D. Buzzell (ed.), *Marketing in an Electronic Age* (Harvard Business School Press, Boston, MA, 1985).

J. Daniel Couger, "E Pluribus Computum," *Harvard Business Review*, September–October 1986.

Fe Josefina F. Dy, *Visual Display Units: Job Content and Stress in the Office* (ILO, Geneva, 1985).

Gerald Faulhaber, Eli Noam, and Roberta Tasley, *Services in Transition: The Impact of Information Technology on the Service Sector* (Ballinger, Cambridge, MA, 1986).

Barbara Garson, *The Electronic Sweatshop: How Computers are Transforming the Office of the Past into the Factory of the Future* (Simon and Schuster, New York, 1988).

R. A. Hirschheim, *Office Automation: A Social and Organisational Perspective* (John Wiley, New York, 1985).

Peter G. W. Keen and Lynda A. Woodman, "What to Do with All Those Micros," *Harvard Business Review*, September–October 1984.

Robert McIvor, "Smart Cards," *Scientific American*, vol. 253(5), November 1985.

Michael E. Porter and Victor E. Millar, "How Information Gives You Competitive Advantage," *Harvard Business Review*, July–August 1985.

David E. Sanger, "Wall Street's Tomorrow Machine," *The New York Times*, October 19, 1986, p. F1.

Anthony Saunders and Lawrence J. White (eds), *Technology and the Regulation of Financial Markets: Securities, Futures and Banking* (Lexington Books, Lexington, MA, 1986).

Paul A. Strassman, *Information Payoff: The Transformation of Work in the Electronic Age* (Free Press, New York, 1985).

The future of work

Technology and Structural Unemployment: Re-employing Displaced Adults, Office of Technology Assessment (OTA) report to the US Congress, Washington, DC, 1986.

"Technology in the Workplace," special 100-page report in *The Wall Street Journal*, September 16, 1985, p. C1.

David Birch, *Job Generation in America* (Free Press, New York, 1986).

Efren Cordova, "From Full-time Wage Employment to Atypical Employment: A Major Shift in the Evolution of Labour Relations?" *International Labour Review*, vol. 125(6), November–December 1986.

Colin Gill, *Work, Unemployment and the New Technology* (Polity Press, Cambridge, UK and New York, 1985).

Eli Ginzberg, Thierry J. Noyelle, and Thomas M. Stanback, Jr, *Technology and Employment: Concepts and Clarifications* (Westview, Boulder, CO, 1986).

William B. Johnston and Arnold E. Packer, *Workforce 2000: Work and Workers for the 21st Century* (Hudson Institute, Indianapolis, IN, 1987).

Raphael Kaplinsky, *Microelectronics and Employment Revisited: A Review* (International Labour Office, Geneva, 1987).

Wassily Leontief and Faye Duchin, *The Future Impact of Automation on Workers* (Oxford University Press, New York, 1986).

Janet L. Norwood, "The Future of Employment: Demographic and Economic Factors," *Vital Speeches of the Day*, vol. 53(4) December 1, 1986.

Russell W. Rumberger and Henry M. Levin, "Forecasting the Impact of New Technologies on the Future Job Market," *Technological Forecasting and Social Change*, vol. 27(4), July 1985.

Thomas M. Stanback, Jr, *Computerization and the Transformation of Employment: Governments, Hospitals and Universities* (Westview, Boulder, CO, 1987).

Shoshana Zuboff, *In the Age of the Smart Machine* (Basic Books, New York, 1988).

Managing change

John Bessant and Bill Haywood, "Flexibility in Manufacturing Systems," *Omega*, vol. 14(6), 1986.

David Boddy and David Buchanan, *Managing New Technology* (Basil Blackwell, Oxford, 1986).

Jon Clark, Ian McLoughlin, Howard Rose, and Robin King, *The Process of Technological Change: New Technology and Social Choice in the Workplace* (Cambridge University Press, Cambridge, and New York, 1987).

Chris DeBresson, *Understanding Technological Change* (Black Rose Books, Montreal, 1987).

N. F. Dufty, L. K. Savery, and G. N. Soutar, "Banking Industry Employees and Technological Change," *Prometheus*, vol. 5(2), December 1987.

Steve Early and Rand Wilson, "Do Unions Have a Future in High Technology?" *Technology Review*, October 1986.

Donald Gerwin, "Organizational Implications of CAM," *Omega*, vol. 13(5), 1985.

Philip R. Harris, *Management in Transition* (Jossey-Bass, San Francisco, 1985).

Larry Hirschhorn, *The Workplace Within: Psychodynamics of Organizational Life* (MIT Press, Cambridge, MA, 1988).

Harry C. Katz and Charles F. Sabel, "The Future of Automaking: What Role for the Unions?" *Technology Review*, October 1985.

Clark Kerr and Paul D. Staudohar (eds), *Industrial Relations in a New Age* (Jossey-Bass, San Francisco, 1986).

Dorothy Leonard-Barton and William A. Kraus, "Implementing New Technology," *Harvard Business Review*, November–December 1985.

Henry C. Lucas, Jr, "Utilizing Information Technology: Guidelines for Managers," *Sloan Management Review*, Fall 1986.

Fred L. Luconi, Thomas W. Malone and Michael S. Scott Morton, "Expert Systems: The Next Challenge for Managers," *Sloan Management Review*, Summer 1986.

Ian McLaughlin and Jon Clark, *Technological Change at Work* (Open University Press, Milton Keynes, UK, 1988).

Ian McLoughlin, Howard Rose, and Jon Clark, "Managing the Introduction of New Technology," *Omega*, vol. 13(4), 1985.

Rex Maus and Randall Allsup, *Robotics: A Manager's Guide* (Wiley, New York, 1986).

John S. Rydz, *Managing Innovation: From the Executive Suite to the Shop Floor* (Ballinger, Cambridge, MA, 1986).

Richard E. Walton, "From Control to Commitment in the Workplace," *Harvard Business Review*, March–April 1985.

Part Four: Computers and the Future

12 Ethical Issues

Monitoring on the Job

Gary T. Marx and Sanford Sherizen

In this fascinating account of modern employee surveillance techniques, the authors show how computers have put a new weapon in the hands of managers. Monitoring technology can be used to improve workplace security, but it can also threaten traditional privacy rights. Steps must be taken to improve matters – for instance, by establishing a code of computer ethics, say the authors. Gary Marx is Professor of Sociology in the Department of Urban Studies and Planning at MIT, while Sanford Sherizen is a computer-security consultant. Both have contributed to recent US Office of Technology Assessment reports on employee monitoring. Reprinted from Technology Review, *November–December 1986.*

A large manufacturing company hid microphones in the bathrooms of one of its plants in an effort to ferret out drug sales at work. The microphones were accidentally discovered, and the local union complained, claiming violation of a basic privacy right. Management defended the action as part of a program to eliminate drug use at work.

A bank conducted a random check of an employee's microcomputer and found a file of personal letters and a program for preparing income tax forms. The employee was warned to use the company's computer only for company business. The employee felt that her privacy had been invaded: it was as if the company had looked in her desk or purse and told her what could and could not be there.

Two workers left a factory as their shift ended, engaged in a heated discussion. A fist fight ensued, and a video camera designed to protect the company's parking lot recorded the fight. The employees were later fired. They protested that their activity outside factory gates was a private matter. A judge agreed and ordered that they be rehired.

The monitoring of workers is hardly a new phenomenon. Indeed, it has always been the responsibility of supervisors to watch workers. From the very beginning, factory systems were designed to facilitate managerial control. With the rise of mass production and the spread of the "Scientific Management" ideas of Frederick Taylor, jobs were divided into their smallest components. Time and motion studies were done to establish work standards and quotas. However, even then monitoring was essentially personal. It relied on individual supervisors, and workers were likely to know when they were being watched.

In many ways, contemporary monitoring is a continuation of Taylorism. But new developments in electronic technology are taking that ethos to new heights (or lows, depending upon
your point of view). The monitoring of employees is increasingly being done by machines.
Much more is being monitored, and the monitoring has expanded from the production line to
the office.

People may not know they are being watched. Furthermore, monitoring is no longer
restricted to a bounded work setting such as a factory or an office. It can be done anytime, day
or night, and from a location far removed from the actual work setting. Thus, an employee
using a company computer at home can be observed, and a simple electronic transmitter can
monitor the movement of people and vehicles far from the central office. Traditional social
and legal protections are not as clearly applicable.

US managers are under increasing pressure to monitor and improve productivity. Many
companies also share a growing concern about product security and employee theft.
Manufacturing processes and electronic systems for transmitting data and transferring funds
are far more complex than they used to be, increasing the potential for costly abuses and errors.
Rising concern over drug use at work, AIDS, and escalating health insurance costs also exerts
pressure on managers to conduct more intensive screening and monitoring.

As a result, the concept of privacy itself is changing. In the name of improving company
security and enhancing worker productivity, intrusions that would have been questioned or
rejected in the past are now being accepted. The boundaries between acceptable and unacceptable intrusions are less clearly drawn. Where is the line between on- and off-duty behavior?
When does the factory or office stop and the home begin? In the future, we may even have to
confront questions about the right to control brainwaves and other biometric indicators
thought to be relevant to work.

US companies today are at a crossroads. They can use new electronic technologies to
increase their control over worker behavior and reinforce traditional patterns of nonparticipa-
tory management. But such efforts will erode individual rights to privacy and may cause
psychological stress and reduce productivity. Fortunately, companies can use the new
monitoring technologies in a restricted fashion, recognizing that just because an intrusive form
of monitoring can be done does not mean it *should* be done. With employee participation in
setting standards and fair guidelines, some monitoring can even enhance privacy, security, and
productivity.

The value of privacy

Privacy is not a simple concept with only one meaning. It embodies a variety of meanings and
expectations. For instance, most Americans expect that an individual's behavior will not be
observed, monitored, or recorded without that person's consent. They expect not to have to
divulge personal information that is not directly relevant to the issue at hand. And they expect
that the information they do divulge will be treated confidentially and not used in unexpected
ways. Laws and administrative rules often tend to support these views.

But why is privacy so important in the first place? Privacy is an essential component of
individual autonomy and dignity. Our sense of liberty is partly defined by the ability to control
our own lives – whether this be the kind of work we undertake, whom we choose to associate

with, where we live, the kind of religious and political beliefs we hold, or the information we wish to divulge about ourselves.

Control over personal information is particularly important for our sense of self. When an individual's room, pocketbook, or body can be searched at will, when conversations and even thoughts are available for instant inspection by outsiders, openness and honesty lose their value. Distrust becomes institutionalized and an important and even sacred element of the social bond is damaged.

In practice, of course, privacy is not easy to protect. The privacy rights of different individuals or groups sometimes conflict. For instance, an employee's right to keep personal certain information about his or her health conflicts with an employer's interest in knowing about health conditions that may affect performance and medical insurance costs. An employee's right to know about hazardous conditions at work may conflict with an employer's right to protect proprietary information.

The issue is also complicated by the fact that privacy rights depend heavily on context. Intrusive behavior considered acceptable on the job is not always acceptable off-duty. Police wiretapping of suspected drug dealers with a warrant is one thing; employers wiretapping employee telephone calls is quite another. A supervisor watching employees on an assembly line is not likely to be questioned. But the use of a hidden camera and bug to gather equivalent data is. There are few, if any, forms of intrusive behavior that all people would agree are always illegitimate.

The maximum-security workplace?

In a less technological age, our expectations about privacy were defined partly by what the unaided senses – sight, sound, smell, taste, and touch – were capable of detecting. The traditional physical boundaries of the workplace offered other limits to the gathering of information. Today's monitoring technologies easily transcend traditional barriers to data collection. Since monitoring is increasingly done automatically by machines, supervisors are no longer limited to what they can immediately observe. Nor are workers always able to know when they are being monitored. Phone systems designed as intercoms or paging devices permit managers to listen to conversations in other offices without being detected. Even in the few cases when union contracts or state laws require that notice of monitoring be given, workers will not necessarily know when the monitoring is being done.

Compare, for example, a video camera or video recorder with the traditional supervisor who occasionally walks by. Workers usually know when the supervisor is present. They also know that the monitoring is episodic – the supervisor can't be everywhere all the time. In contrast, camera and recorder are omnipresent and tireless; the worker can never be sure whether they are in operation or if their results will be reviewed. Moreover, in the past, the economics of monitoring tended to work against intensive mass surveillance. But technological breakthroughs have greatly reduced the cost of monitoring. Some companies are even using satellite technology to pinpoint the location of their trucks on a television screen.

Furthermore, monitoring devices with built-in microprocessors can now be made very small. This means that they can be placed in hidden locations and activated from distant places. By installing a tiny pinhole lens and video on the plane, for instance, it is possible for people on the ground to see and hear all activity on an aircraft up to 200 miles away. The market for such security products is expected to grow from $774 million in 1985 to $2.1 billion by 1992.

Workers increasingly participate in their own monitoring – even though such participation may be unwilling or unconscious. Technical devices automatically record data that workers generate: they capture information from the workers' voices or movements such as keystrokes or assembly-line actions, and they measure workers' effectiveness by monitoring security and quality-control systems. In data processing jobs, for instance, the devices monitor the number of errors and corrections made, the speed of work, and time away from the desk. One Bank of America vice president, commenting upon the 200 criteria he uses to assess productivity among workers in his credit card division, notes: "I measure everything that moves."

The workers most likely to be monitored are those who use computers for telecommunications, word processing, programming, and service contacts. Companies such as AT&T, United Airlines, Equitable Life Insurance, and American Express use sophisticated devices to regularly monitor their employees.

Take, for instance, the development of a technique called station message detail recording (SMDR). Telephone systems often have built-in SMDR features that record on what telephone each call is made, what user identification code and extension is used, where the call goes, what time it is made, and how long it lasts. SMDR systems generate detailed reports that management can use for planning budgets, allocating and controlling costs, and monitoring activities. Among the functions that can be monitored are toll calls made after official business hours and telephone use during lunch hours. Employees who use the telephone to make personal calls can readily be identified, as can employees who leak information to the press or to competitors. Calls from one extension to another within the company can also be monitored. New developments in software also make it possible to capture the content of a conversation, although this is much less frequently done.

The monitoring of telephone communication is likely to become pervasive. In 1985, 20,000 SMDR and related systems were sold in the United States, and that number is likely to grow. As one airline-company executive put it, "Communications performance monitoring is going to be one of the major computer service fields in the next five to ten years."

Thanks to other advances in software, employers can monitor employees working on microcomputers from the time they log on to the time they log off. One software product now on the market allows management to document the activities of anybody using the company computer system – without the user's knowledge. With the program, marketed by Clyde Digital Systems of Provo, Utah, and called "CNTRL," managers can observe on their own screen all input entered by the employee and all output from the computer to the user's terminal as it occurs. It can also be captured in a log, "creating a certifiable record to be used for disciplinary or legal proceedings," as the company's literature promises.

Software companies have even developed programs that allow employers to tell workers how their productivity compares with that of their co-workers. One program can be used to display messages on the video display terminal such as: "You are not working as fast as the person next to you."

A report by 9 to 5, the national organization of working women, describes a program called "The Messenger" that can be called up by the VDT operator. Calming images of mountains and streams are displayed along with subliminal messages such as "My world is calm." More ominous are subliminal programs that the worker may have no knowledge or control over. One such program entitled "Subliminal Suggestions and Self-Hypnosis" permits management to send any kind of message – such as "relax," "concentrate," or "work faster" – unbeknown to the worker. The messages pass so quickly in front of the watchers' eyes they cannot be consciously detected.

Your retinal pattern or your life

Information security is a growing priority for many companies, particularly those involved in complex electronic fund transfers or confidential communications. The ability to gain remote access to computer systems had long posed a security problem, largely because both hackers and those with much less technical knowledge have found ways to bypass traditional precautions such as passwords and special cards.

To prevent unauthorized use, security firms are now developing biometric identification products for the commercial marketplace. These are based on the sensing of individual characteristics such as fingerprints, handwriting, voice, typing rhythms, hand geometry, and the distinct patterns of people's retinas. *Personal Identification News* magazine estimates that private companies spent more than $35 million in 1985 to develop biometric products.

These products can indeed improve the ability of federal agencies and private companies to limit access to top-security data. But they are also being used as a substitute for other managerial controls and supervision. A leading hotel, for example, used retinal-pattern identification to prevent workers from punching in one another's timecards. And a growing number of organizations ranging from Avis, Con Edison, and Equitable Life Insurance to the Universities of Tennessee and Georgia use hand geometry to identify employees.

The new technologies, of course, may bring greater equity. After all, "pre-technological" monitoring by a human supervisor sometimes meant high-handed or discriminatory treatment. Technological monitors have no favorites; all workers are treated alike. Because so many parameters of job performance can now be monitored, the total result might be a fairer system. Furthermore, monitoring can extend up as well as down the organizational hierarchy. Video cameras, card key systems required to enter a room, and computer access codes make demands on all who encounter them.

However, intrusive monitoring may conflict with workers' traditional expectations of what is fair on the job. There is, of course, no formal protection for the privilege of whispering at work or of being free from observation. But most of us feel entitled to a sense of privacy in our communications at work. The new technologies are threatening that privacy and – for some workers – making it obsolete.

The use of biologically based technologies could jeopardize people's privacy off as well as on the job. Workers have already been fired from their jobs when drug tests have revealed evidence of marijuana use, even though the drug was used at a weekend party and job performance was not in question.

When deception becomes the rule

The increased use of monitoring in the workplace could well backfire. People are wonderfully ingenious at finding ways to disrupt, distort, and deceive monitors. For example, typists may hold one key down to increase the number of key strokes recorded. They can always delete the file containing the errors later. Telephone reservation agents may learn to avoid calls that add to their average case time – by either disconnecting the call or simply withholding information. And workers required to provide urine samples may add chemicals that distort the test results or even turn in someone else's urine.

Monitoring may also create more adversarial relationships in the workplace. Workers may feel violated and powerless in the face of the new monitoring technologies. The result could be low morale, reduced productivity, and destructive countermeasures. Monitoring may even increase the violations or abuses it is intended to stop. Workers may feel challenged to beat the system or react out of anger and estrangement. When people feel they are not trusted, they often adopt an attitude similar to that of some police regarding corruption: "If you've got the name, play the game." In other words, as long as everyone thinks that you will take graft, you might as well do it.

One truck driver for the Safeway Co. with 40 years of experience recalled that he used to love his job because "you were on your own – no one was looking over your shoulder. You felt like a human being." But now a small computer on the dashboard of his truck (with the apt name of Tripmaster) keeps track of speed, shifting, excessive idling and when and how long he stops for lunch or a coffee break. As a result, the driver says he will retire early. He complains, "They push you around, spy on you. There's no trust, no respect anymore."

No comprehensive information exists on how technological monitoring affects productivity, but anecdotal evidence shows that overly zealous monitoring can be counterproductive. One large Mid-western electronics company, for instance, found that productivity declined and absenteeism, stress, and turnover increased after a highly touted monitoring system was installed. The company eliminated the system within the year. The employees may have reacted like the directory-assistance operator who couldn't understand why her company had started monitoring her: "I worked all those years before monitoring. Why don't they trust me now? I will continue to be a good worker, but I won't do any more than necessary now."

Increased monitoring can breed other problems as well. The emphasis on quantity at the expense of quality may result in an inferior product. With monitoring, employers can automatically speed up the work process so it is no longer in the employees' control. Also, to the extent that electronic supervisors displace people, the potential for growth and learning on the job may be diminished. Less contact with a supervisor may mean a more impersonal, less satisfying work environment.

New types of monitoring may also disrupt understandings between labor and management. The technologies may eliminate activities that workers have traditionally taken for granted as "perks" of the job. For instance, many employees (and enlightened employers) equate the custom of keeping personal letters in an office computer with the tradition of taking home paper and pencils. Yet under the new form of monitoring, such previously "tolerated" behavior may no longer be accepted.

Surveillance also has a tendency to expand. Under the Reagan administration, government agencies have already begun monitoring their employees extensively, and further monitoring is planned. Polygraph testing, once restricted to top-secret matters of national security, is now applied to leaks to the press. In an effort to stem such leaks, some government agencies also monitor employee phone use. One new computer program even compares a list of calls with reporters' phone numbers. Concern about employee drug abuse has led President Reagan to urge drug testing of many government employees as well as employees of government contractors.

There is another reason for making sure technological monitoring in the workplace does not get out of hand: monitoring could become much more extensive in society at large. Practices developed at work can easily spill over into other areas. The new biometric forms of identification are one example. The more widespread this practice becomes in the workplace, the easier it will be to create a mandatory national ID system.

A permanent class of undesirables?

Another danger is that monitoring – in the form of pre-employment screening – may help create a class of permanently unemployed and underemployed people. Because traditional records systems were inefficient, many people, particularly those who had been imprisoned, were given a second chance. In the old days, moving to a frontier town meant the opportunity to start over. But this traditional freedom may be severely constricted as credit institutions and other organizations gather comprehensive data bases on US citizens and sell them to other companies. The past becomes haunting: there is no second chance.

An increasing number of data base companies gather and sell information to prospective employers on everything from an individual's political activism to the filing of worker-compensation claims. These companies are relatively unregulated in their use of the data bases. One factory worker was fired from a new job after his employer checked with a private computer network that tracked such claims. The employee had filed two claims for minor injuries (such as a broken finger) with previous employers and had collected modest compensation.

Many companies also use written tests to screen out job applicants. The Knight-Ridder newspaper chain, which owns the *Miami Herald* and the *Philadephia Inquirer*, routinely requires applicants for reporting positions to take a battery of written tests designed to reveal their personality traits and philosophical views.

Other forms of monitoring – such as genetic screening – could eventually be used to discriminate against individuals not because of their past but because of statistical expectations about their future. People who carry antibodies to the AIDS virus but have not developed the disease are already being discharged from the US military and isolated or fired from other jobs. Scientific advances are making it increasingly possible to identify the genetic traits that predispose people to widespread diseases such as diabetes and heart disease.

Eventually, the workforce may become divided between people thought to be good risks and others. Not only would this create an enormous waste of human resources as people are locked out of jobs for which they are otherwise qualified, but some of these people could turn to crime to support themselves. The demands on the welfare system would certainly expand.

Omnipresent monitoring will almost certainly chill political and social expression. Security and control may be enhanced but at the cost of a less creative and dynamic society. If American democracy is to be destroyed, it is unlikely to happen by sudden catastrophic events. Rather, it will occur by slow, incremental changes defined in benign terms. As Justice Louis Brandeis said, "The greatest dangers to liberty lurk in insidious encroachment by men of zeal, well-meaning but without understanding."

Using technology to enhance privacy

Monitoring need not always mean invading some aspect of privacy. In some cases, technological monitoring is actually less intrusive than direct human monitoring. Electronic monitoring of hand luggage at airports eliminates the need for direct searches of passengers' purses and persons. The use of electronic markers on library books and consumer goods also makes costly and demanding physical searches unnecessary.

New technologies can also be used to reduce the need for monitoring and protect privacy. Monitoring in some ways is an admission of the potential for a system to fail. One watches because things *can* go wrong. However, work situations can be structured so that violations, abuses, and errors are less possible. Under these conditions, technological developments can enhance privacy.

For instance, data encrypted on fiberoptic telecommunications lines are clearly more secure from unauthorized use than information left in a desk drawer or file cabinet. Telephones can be designed to allow users to dial only local calls, eliminating the need to monitor for long-distance abuse.

Access keys or codes for using computers and copying machines reduce the need for visual surveillance. Before such systems were developed, supervisors had to watch who was using copying machines and in some cases resort to informers to locate abusers. Where once telephone company staff had to listen to conversations to verify the quality of connections, technical developments now make it possible to do this without listening in on voice communications.

In the future, "smart cards" containing personal data carried by everyone may eliminate the need for central data bases, returning us to an earlier period when personal data were much more in the possession and control of the individual. In one inexpensive "smart card" system, laser technology is used to encode and read a wallet-sized card that contains up to 800 pages of information. The information on such cards is constitutionally protected from unauthorized use – which is not the case for records held by a third party such as a bank. However, back-up copies would have to be made, creating the potential for abuse. Furthermore, if carrying such cards became mandatory, they might well seem more Orwellian than central data bases.

Even technologies that have the potential to invade privacy may have positive benefits for employees. Some workers welcome close monitoring when it is tied to a system of merit pay. The permanent records from monitoring can also protect the innocent from false accusations and document violations by the guilty. Video cameras designed to prevent theft from loading areas may increase safety in adjacent parking lots. And drug screens may prevent accidents and protect the health of employees.

Establishing a code of ethics

Given the new technologies' wide range of advantages and disadvantages, how best can we manage their use? Companies should begin by analyzing why they want to institute monitoring. For instance, will the monitoring be a direct part of the work process, or will it be added on – a procedure apart from the work process such as a drug screen?

Most monitoring technologies can be applied in a number of ways. A video monitor can be hidden or visible, operated randomly or only when a light is on. Drug testing can be based on an inexpensive and relatively unreliable test or the opposite. Drug tests, polygraphs, and other forms of inspection can be general or specific, scheduled or random.

Given the variety of instruments, uses, and contexts, sweeping generalizations about monitoring technologies are inappropriate. In general, however, privacy is best protected when monitoring is minimally intrusive, is directly relevant to job performance, and is visible – i.e., a supervisor is walking by or a video camera has a flashing red light that indicates it is on. Highly intrusive forms of checking that are not directly related to work output should be restricted to situations where there are some grounds for suspicion.

A code of ethics does exist among certain manufacturers and vendors of monitoring technology. For example, AT&T, which provides telephone companies' equipment for checking phone lines, requires subscribers to agree that they will use it solely for quality control and training. AT&T also requires that employees be notified in writing that they will be subject to such monitoring.

Some firms ask employees to help establish behavioral norms at work and thus cut down on the need for monitoring. For example, some companies have instituted programs whereby, if losses from employee theft are less than the previous year, employees split the money saved. Following a widespread practice in Europe, a few US companies have agreed to use work monitoring only for group, rather than individual, output.

As the new monitoring technologies become pervasive and affordable, however, misuses are bound to increase unless clear guidelines are developed. Our work in analyzing and developing information-security and privacy programs for companies and government agencies has made it clear that legislation and company policies must:

- Apply to monitoring the same protection that applies to pre-employment background checks – that is, permit only information directly relevant to the job to be collected. The burden of proof for the need to monitor should lie with the employer.
- Require employers to provide employees with advance notice of monitoring as well as appropriate mechanisms for appeal.
- Require people to verify machine-produced information before using it to evaluate employees.
- Provide workers with access to information on themselves.
- Provide mechanisms for monetary redress for employees whose rights are violated or who are victims of erroneous information generated by a monitoring system.
- Apply a "statute of limitations" on data from monitoring. The older the data, the less their potential relevance and the greater the difficulty employees have in challenging the information.

Little is known about the extent of employee monitoring in the United States and the policies that govern its use. Research by companies and government agencies could provide policy-makers with a greater awareness of monitoring as a social phenomenon.

In sum, technology is neither the enemy nor the solution. More and more US companies are turning to monitoring devices to increase their control over employee behavior and improve internal security. But thus far, society has paid insufficient attention to protecting individuals' rights. The US government and the private sector must work together to make sure that in our haste to protect our property, we do not destroy our basic freedoms.

Who Owns Creativity?

Anne W. Branscomb

New information and communication technologies have made copying intellectual property much easier. The privatization of information producers and the global marketplace have further eroded existing legal protections of intellectual property, posing economic and ethical dilemmas for scientists, policy-makers, and the public. Realistic legal solutions, says the author, depend upon a new consensus about what kind of behavior is socially acceptable and what is not. Anne W. Branscomb is an attorney associated with Harvard University and the Fletcher School of Law and Diplomacy. This piece first appeared in Technology Review, *May–June 1988.*

In the coming months, a Boston, MA, federal district court may settle a $10 million lawsuit by deciding who owns the "look and feel" of a popular computer program. The result will only intensify the controversy over the impact of new information technologies on intellectual property rights.

In January, 1987, the Lotus Development Corp. filed suit against two small software houses for violating its copyright on the enormously successful Lotus 1-2-3 computerized spreadsheet. The defendants had developed and marketed "work-alike" spreadsheet programs that incorporate the program functions and screen design of 1-2-3 without duplicating the programming code traditionally protected by copyright. Nevertheless, Lotus argued that the work-alike programs are unauthorized copies. The name of one clone is – revealingly – "Twin," and an advertisement for the other boasts that it is "a feature-for-feature work-alike for 1-2-3 . . . designed to work like Lotus . . . keystroke for keystroke." According to Lotus, the essence of a program is not its code but its distinctive "look and feel," which the copyright should protect.

The defendants disagreed. From their perspective, the work-alikes are not imitations but innovations, providing all that Lotus offers and more and at a lower price. Indeed, what the defendants have done is not so different from what Lotus did some five years ago when it built upon the first computerized spreadsheet, VisiCalc, to create a technically superior product.

Ironically, three months after Lotus filed its suit, the company itself became the defendant in another copyright-infringement case, this time brought by the parent company of the firm that created VisiCalc. The claim was that Lotus had borrowed the look and feel of the original spreadsheet.

The desire of individuals – and corporations – to profit from their own intellectual creativity has often clashed with the public's wish for relatively free access to ideas and innovations. Over the centuries, many different legal mechanisms have been invented to strike a balance between the two. However, what suited the age of print and mechanical inventions is proving inadequate to that of the computer program, expert system, and distributed data base. The attempt to force these new technologies into outmoded categories can create absurd and contradictory situations that threaten to undermine public confidence in the principle of intellectual property rights itself.

Software is a good example. Copyright is designed to protect literary expression. But what makes a computer program a literary work? Is it the code written to make the program function? Or is it, as Lotus argues, the look of the screen and feel of its commands?

To make matters even more confusing, software manufacturers simultaneously employ other legal protections to safeguard their intellectual property rights, because they are doubtful that any one will prove effective. The principle of trade secrets underlines the "shrink-wrap license" to which every software user supposedly agrees upon opening the package of a new program (see below).

Some computer programs are also eligible for patents, most notably software embedded in computer hardware. And while operating systems that are not built into hardware have traditionally been excluded from patent protection, the US Patent Office has recently been considerably more lenient toward such applications.

As the forms of protection increase, the gap between legal precedent and everyday behavior grows wider. The new technologies make copying intellectual property easier and legal protections much more difficult to enforce. Some degree of unauthorized copying has become accepted social practice – despite the legal prohibitions against it: journal articles are photocopied at universities, recorded music is taped on to blank cassettes, and computer software is commonly reproduced.

Although disputes about technology and intellectual property are usually cast in narrow legal terms, they are intimately related to public attitudes. Realistic legal rules depend upon a social consensus about what kind of behavior is acceptable and what is not.

"To promote Science and useful Arts"

The idea of intellectual property rights has been around since the late Middle Ages, but the roots of US intellectual property law go back to the Constitution: "The Congress shall have Power . . . To promote the Progress of Science and useful Arts, by securing for limited Times to Authors and Inventors the exclusive Right to their respective Writing and Discoveries."

As this language suggests, the fundamental goal of intellectual property rights is not to benefit the creators of works but to further the public good. Authors and inventors are given a limited right to their work as an incentive to create and disseminate ideas and information. Thus, intellectual property law makes protection conditional on public disclosure.

For example, copyright law covers original "works of authorship" as long as they are "fixed" in a "tangible medium" such as a book. Copyright protects the literary expression of an idea, rather than the idea itself, from unauthorized copying for the life of the creator plus 50 years (or, for corporations, for a total of 75 to 100 years). Other authors can make "fair use" of a copyrighted work – for example, quoting a passage in an article of review – without asking the original author's permission. More extensive use requires permission and often the payment of a royalty.

Patent law protects inventions or discoveries that are registered with the US Patent Office. Unlike copyright, a patent protects not only the expression but the actual useful features of a product or process for 17 years. A design receives protection for 14 years. Patent rights grant a monopoly, good against those who independently discover the same design or product. But rights can be licensed to other users.

However, a patent is much harder to get than copyright. To be eligible for patent protection, a work must have distinguishing features that are innovative, useful, and not obvious. And the application process often takes two years or more.

Not all forms of intellectual property protection require public disclosure. The oldest and probably most common form of protection is secrecy. Trade secrets are protected by contracts designed to ensure confidentiality on the part of licensed users. To be enforceable in court, the information considered a trade secret must be used commercially and relevant to a firm's competitive advantage. Also, the firm must have evidence that it has actively attempted to keep the information secret.

The intellectual property system breaks down

These traditional mechanisms for balancing public and private claims worked relatively well during the industrial era. As long as the publication of books and journals depended on a relatively small number of commercial printers, it was easy to identify copyright violations. As long as most industrial innovations had a relatively long life, the patent process successfully protected their economic value. And as long as most violations took place either within a single nation or between nations with relatively compatible legal systems, effective sanctions could be easily enforced.

Recently, however, three interrelated factors have eroded the effectiveness of traditional protection mechanisms: the development of new information and communications technologies, the globalization of the marketplace, and the privatization of information providers.

The traditional categories of intellectual property law depend on a set of clearly defined "products" or "processes" – literary works, inventions, designs, etc. But with the new technologies, boundaries between media are blurred and intellectual assets become increasingly abstract and intangible. The same work or even parts of a work can be stored and presented in a bewildering variety of forms – not only paper, but magnetic tape, floppy disk, or laser disk. The work can be made available to large numbers of people via broadcasting, computer networks, or telephone lines. Data bases can be packaged and re-packaged. Pieces of music or video images can be electronically re-mixed, re-formatted, or otherwise altered. And easy-to-use technologies like video graphics and desktop publishing allow more individuals and small businesses to enter the information marketplace than ever before, making enforcement of intellectual property rights nearly impossible.

The globalization of the world economy, caused partly by the new technologies, has also contributed to the breakdown of the old system. International conflicts over intellectual property have always been a problem, as developing countries, anxious for economic growth, have been unwilling to extend protection to foreign works. This was true of nineteenth-century America, and it is true of much of the Third World today.

But the increasing integration of the world economy has multiplied both the incentives for international violations of intellectual property rights and the economic harm of such violations. Today, the products of newly industrialized countries such as Korea or Taiwan are sold all over the world. "Borrowing" intellectual property allows these countries to successfully compete in markets for many advanced products without bearing the cost of research and development.

Finally, the growing trend toward using market mechanisms to gather and disseminate information has disrupted the traditional public infrastructure for sharing intellectual assets. For example, before the break-up of the regulated Bell Telephone system, Bell Labs was the equivalent of a national basic-research laboratory, supported by corporate cross-subsidies. Today, institutions like Bell Labs face growing pressures to pay their own way. The federal government has mandated that agencies such as the National Technical Information Service and the National Library of Medicine become self-supporting through user fees. And even universities are turning to patent rights and copyright royalties to recoup their investment in faculty research and development.

The high costs of copying

Thus, at the very moment when information is becoming a valuable commodity, protecting the economic value of intellectual assets is proving more difficult. While the loss of income is difficult to ascertain, estimates range anywhere from $20 billion to $60 billion each year.

Most serious is the deliberate commercial pirating of both low- and high-tech products in foreign countries. For example, videotaped copies of Hollywood films are often illegally released in foreign markets before the US release. The Motion Picture Association of America estimates the loss at about $6 billion annually. And illegal publishing of books and technical manuals abroad costs the US publishing industry about $1 billion every year. In Korea alone, nearly 1 million US titles have been pirated.

Other violations of intellectual property rights – for personal rather than commercial use – are more difficult to track. The rule of thumb in the software industry is that at least one unauthorized copy exists for every authorized sale of a software program. According to the Software Publishing Association, software manufacturers lost approximately $1 billion in sales to piracy (both for profit and for personal use) in 1986. Lotus claims that over half of its potential sales of 1-2-3 are lost – at a cost of about $160 million every year. And Wordstar estimates that in 1984 it lost $177 million in potential sales, compared with $67 million in revenues from actual sales of the program.

Such reports need to be taken with a grain of salt, as they assume that every user of an unauthorized copy would buy the program in question were the copies to disappear – an unlikely proposition. Still, the numbers suggest the scope of the problem.

Violations of intellectual property also have public costs. Widespread copying is one factor in high software prices, as firms try to recoup their investment in a program as quickly as possible. If unauthorized copying could be eliminated, it is likely that the costs of software could be greatly reduced – a net gain for society as a whole.

Owners of intellectual property have tried a variety of methods to combat unauthorized copying. In some cases, technology itself seems to offer a solution. To stop satellite-dish owners from capturing broadcast signals without subscribing to local cable services, programmers scramble their signals. Today, the most popular programs cannot be received by satellite unless viewers pay a monthly fee to gain access to the special code of each cable channel.

However, technical protections can spawn their own technical countermeasures or result in a consumer backlash. For example, the practice of "copy protection," once widespread in the software industry, has given birth to special programs whose sole purpose is to override copy-protection code. And consumer dissatisfaction with the inconvenience of using copy-protected software has led most software companies, Lotus included, to give up on copy protecting their programs altogether.

On the international front, the federal government has encouraged trading partners to enact intellectual property laws or expand coverage of laws that already exist. Under recent provisions in trade and foreign aid laws, countries whose copyright and patent practices do not conform to US standards can be penalized, even to the point of restricting their imports to the US market. The federal government is also promoting a multilateral agreement on intellectual property as part of the Geneva Agreement on Tariffs and Trade.

So far, such efforts have had only limited effect. The sanctions available to federal trade officials are miniscule compared with the enormous profits foreign companies can make by using US processes and designs in the international market. Even money damages and confiscation of goods are simply absorbed by pirate firms as a cost of doing business.

Copyrighting the user interface?

In the absence of effective protection, owners of intellectual property have tried to fit their products into any and all of the available legal categories. The results are legally contradictory and confusing to the general public. They also undermine traditional rationales for intellectual property protection.

For years, the legal status of computer programs was unclear. Although the US Copyright Office began tentatively registering software under its "rule of doubt" provision in 1964, many analysts suspected that computer code written to be read by a machine rather than a human couldn't qualify for copyright. And the Patent Office considered most programs a collection of algorithms – which, like other mathematical equations, are excluded from patent protection.

So the computer software industry relied primarily on trade secrecy. This has worked reasonably well for larger computer installations with custom-made software. However, the mass distribution of easily available software made possible by the personal computer created a new legal situation.

Any personal computer user has seen the long and complicated agreement, usually set in type so small that it is barely legible, on the cover or inserted underneath the outer protection of most software diskettes. This is the "shrink-wrap license" to which the purchaser is assumed to agree upon opening the package. Most such licenses stipulate that the buyer cannot "use, copy, modify, merge, translate, or transfer" the software "except as expressly provided in this agreement."

The "shrink-wrap license" treats software as a trade secret. This poses an immediate practical problem. To consider a computer program used by millions of people as a trade secret offends common sense – the fact that so much copying takes place indicates how few users take the agreement seriously. What's more, at least one court has held such licenses legally invalid.

In 1980, Congress amended the 1976 Copyright Act to explicitly include software, partly because there seemed no other adequate mechanism for protecting what was clearly a valuable asset. Since then, the courts have steadily extended copyright protection for software. At first, it applied only to the source code, written in a programming language such as FORTRAN or COBOL. Later court cases established that a program's object code, the sequence of 0s and 1s read directly by the computer, was covered as well. In 1986, the flow diagrams that encapsulate the logic and sequence of the program were also included under copyright.

That same year, in *Jaslow* v. *Whelan*, the Third Circuit Court of Appeals affirmed a lower court ruling that copyright protection extends to certain "non-literal" features of the program. The court decided that the screen design and the commands of the program represented the time and effort the computer software programmer had expended in understanding the needs of the application in question – an inventory system for dental laboratories. The conclusion was that such laborious intellectual analysis should be protected. This has set the stage for the "look and feel" cases currently under consideration.

At the same time that copyright protection is being expanded, software firms are again turning to patent protection. Court cases have redefined the status of computer programs under patent law, considering operating systems just like other industrial processes and therefore eligible for patents. In 1986, the artificial intelligence firm Teknowledge received patents on two new software products.

The dangers of ad hoc protection

There are a number of dangers inherent in this ad hoc approach. First, it is contradictory to claim that a computer program is a trade secret and yet deserves copyright protection, which assumes broad public dissemination. And saying that the same software can come under both copyright and patent law similarly defies people's sense of what belongs in what category.

Second, ad hoc measures run the risk of shifting the emphasis toward too much protection, even to the point of threatening innovation itself. Protecting the "look and feel" of a computer program could become a serious obstacle to standardizing software applications and could prove extremely costly as well.

For example, should the federal district court in Boston decide that the look and feel of Lotus 1-2-3 can be copyrighted, then every maker of computerized spreadsheets will have to create distinctively different screen designs. This could mean that the techniques and skills acquired by using Lotus spreadsheets wouldn't be transferable to other spreadsheet programs. Individuals and firms would face increased training costs, and even the most innovative software would encounter substantial barriers to entering the spreadsheet market.

Third, as communications technology becomes more complex, the ad hoc approach will become even more cumbersome. For instance, a single "read-only" compact disk (CD ROM) can store a 20-volume encyclopedia. What uses of the CD ROM are permissible within the limits of current law? Can users print the entire 20 volumes, or is this a violation of copyright? If so, how much of the encyclopedia can they reprint? Can portions of the encyclopedia be transferred to another computer, or does this constitute making a copy? Can portions be displayed in the classroom, or might this legally qualify as a performance or retransmission? May the contents be simultaneously networked to many locations, such as different classrooms at a university?

Some lawyers argue that since different mechanisms protect different rights, the proliferation of mechanisms covering the same intellectual asset is both effective and reasonable. So, for example, design of the laser videodisk may be patented; the process by which it is manufactured may be a trade secret; the content of a specific disk can be copyrighted; the commercial name under which the product is marketed will be a trademark; the talent whose performance is captured on the disk will be subject to performance rights; and the work, if retransmitted by a cable system, may be subject to royalties.

The problem is that such an elaborate system is costly and, when it comes to competing in the world economy, a distinct disadvantage. The price of a product must reflect not only the high costs of research and development but also the legal fees necessary to document legal protections and enforce them.

Toward a new rationale of protection

As long as the United States depends on the private sector to create and disseminate information, we need a simpler, less costly system for protecting intellectual property. Such a system should recognize that effective protection of intellectual property is not just a legal matter. It is also a function of public attitudes and opinions. No law, no matter how carefully worded, can prohibit widespread practices that the public considers acceptable.

While ethical standards for using new information technologies are still in an early stage of development, it seems clear that the public favors flexibility – as long as the original owner of the copied product enjoys no commercial advantage. The rationale seems to be that if you can loan your friends books, why not let them copy your software programs and musical tapes?

A public opinion poll conducted by the congressional Office of Technology Assessment found that 70 percent of those questioned thought copying a record, tape, software, or TV program in one's personal possession is permissible. About half agreed that such copies should be publicly available, for example in a library. However, some 80 percent opposed circumventing commercial offerings such as pay TV or cable television. And nearly all deplored the reselling of data bases for personal gain.

Both Congress and the courts have begun to take these attitudes into account. Under the Cable Communications Act of 1984, satellite-dish owners do not have to pay to capture the broadcast signals of copyrighted programs, as long as those programs are not available to them on cable television.

And in the now-famous "Betamax" case (*Sony Corp.* v. *Universal City Studios*), the Supreme Court recognized that it would be fruitless to try to turn the tide against the massive purchase of video cassette recorders able to record television programs for later use. Although collecting copied programs for a personal video library might violate the Copyright Act, the Court made a distinction between commercial exploitation and copying for "private use."

Owners of intellectual property are beginning to realize that they must cultivate public awareness and sympathy to protect capital investment. Numerous trade organizations are selecting this route and allocating more dollars to public education than litigation. For example, the Association of Data Processing Service Organizations has initiated a "Thou Shalt Not Dupe" campaign to discourage corporations from copying programs. The association has sent out hundreds of thousands of brochures urging companies to adopt a sample policy statement against copying. Similarly, the recently formed American Copyright Council is launching an advertisement campaign on the legalities of copyright infringement. And in addition to prosecuting flagrant cases of cable piracy, the cable television industry is spending millions of dollars advertising the impropriety of tapping into cable lines.

However, initiatives like these do not address systematic commercial pirating or complicated conflicts between innovation and imitation such as the look-and-feel lawsuits. Here, we need to articulate a new rationale for legal protection.

The starting point should be an understanding that information technology makes the form a product takes easy to separate from the intellectual assets that go into it. This suggests that copyright law, with its focus on the expression of an idea rather than on the idea itself, is inappropriate for protecting what is really valuable in the new kinds of intellectual property.

More suitable would be a system that emphasized the actual use of intellectual assets. For example, the entertainment industry has developed its own legally binding arrangements to determine who benefits from the use of entertainment programs. Standard contracts govern the division of earnings among all those necessary to produce works for continued use on radio, television, and videotapes. Perhaps the software industry could develop similar mechanisms.

Another possibility is a modified form of patent rights with registration procedures, monopoly time limits, and rules for licensing all shaped to the unique realities of the computer industry.

Of course, such efforts may eventually demonstrate that simple and effective protection of new kinds of intellectual property is largely impossible. If so, policy-makers will have to re-evaluate recent trends toward the privatization of information. When the private creators of intellectual assets cannot be adequately protected for their efforts, then new kinds of public support may be necessary.

Whatever the specific mechanisms for addressing the problems of intellectual property protection, those who are creating the new information and communications technologies – and who best understand their capabilities and limits – need to play a more active role in policy debates. Too often, the lawyers and legislators who write and litigate intellectual property laws have only a superficial understanding of the technology in question.

One possibility would be to create teams of technical experts to serve as negotiators or mediators in complex technological controversies. Or professional associations could develop codes of ethics for what constitutes acceptable – and unacceptable – borrowing of others' intellectual work.

Only when we hear from technologists will we begin to meet the real challenge of intellectual property rights: encouraging creativity while preventing exploitation inimical to investment and the rational allocation of R&D funds.

Computer Criminals are Human, Too

Keith Hearnden

Practically everyone agrees that computer crime constitutes a major new threat to society, but nobody really knows the true extent of the problem. The author has brought together data from the UK and elsewhere which shed some light on how computer crime is committed, and by whom. Key findings: most crimes are opportunistic and nearly all computer criminals are first-time offenders motivated by greed, pressing financial worries, and other personal problems. Keith Hearnden is with the Centre for Extension Studies, Loughborough University, UK and this paper first appeared in Long Range Planning, *vol. 19(5), October 1986.*

For too long, the "experts" have overlooked the human dimension of computer crime. Much research, many learned publications and a wealth of sophisticated computer hardware and software are evidence of the direction the computer industry has taken in its attempt to contain computer crime. I would not deny that this "mechanistic" approach has provided many valuable aids to improved security, but I do feel sometimes that its proponents have lost sight of a fundamental truth – that it is *people* who commit computer crimes, and that attempting to deal with the problem in human terms often offers a cost-effective and more securely based solution.

One of the difficulties with this line of reasoning, however, is the absence of any great volume of data about computer-linked crime and the people who commit it, so that to some extent we are forced into making assumptions about important things like motivations, attitudes to crime, profiles of computer criminals and so on. However, it is perhaps also true that we have not made the best use of the information that is available, nor extracted from it those items that could be significant in our attempt to understand more about the people involved in computer-linked crime.

In this article I have looked again at those cases recorded in UK studies such as the Audit Inspectorate Report of 1981; the Audit Commission Report of 1985; the BIS *Computer Related Fraud Casebook* (where this gives details of cases not covered by the 1981 Audit Inspectorate Survey); the 1984 EEC Report, *The Vulnerability of the Information Conscious Society*; a survey, *Computer Related Crime in Australia*, by the Computer Abuse Research Bureau in Victoria; some statistics produced by the American CPA about banking and insurance crime;

and some crimes newly reported in press and journal articles.[1] I hope that what these reveal will give a clearer insight into how computer crime is committed and what kinds of people become involved in it; and that from this greater understanding we can deduce some lines of action designed to counter the problem and reduce our exposure to risk.

What kind of crime?

Let us first define what types of activity are included in this analysis (see table 12.1). One omission from this survey is data on the theft of computer equipment. Whilst some information exists (in the EEC and Australian reports) it seems to me that this is a physical security problem, capable of being tackled by conventional crime prevention methods; which is why the subject is not dealt with here. I would just mention in passing, though, that theft of computers and associated equipment appears to be escalating, and there is some evidence to suggest that ready markets exist for high-technology second-hand products.

Our concern here, then, is primarily with fraud, embezzlement, misuse of computer resources and deliberately inflicted physical damage. In a computer context, fraud can be carried out in one of three ways. The first of these is by manipulating information fed into the system and falsifying data relating to accounts, stock records, funds transfer, etc.: this is commonly called "input" fraud. This is the type most commonly reported, and probably is genuinely the most widespread. Whether its ascendancy also in some way reflects the difficulty of ever discovering more sophisticated crimes that involve the alteration of computer programs, our second method, is an open question. Certainly, as we shall see, there is little evidence of fraud having been committed in this way.

The third technique involves the manipulation or misappropriation of computer output: theft of cheques, destruction of delivery notes, etc. This is also rarely in evidence and reflects the relatively limited opportunity up to now for fraud in this area. With the recent explosion in the use of micros at work, however, theft of output probably represents the area of most potential danger, due to the transportability of floppy disks and the poor performance of passwords and other control systems on such machines. "As microcomputer users convert their confidential information to disk files, that information which represents a competitive edge will become a target for industrial espionage."[2]

Misuse of resources covers a range of activities that in many ways are less serious than fraud, but which, nevertheless, represent an abuse of computer facilities. Unchecked and in excess they can seriously disrupt computer production schedules, by using resources required for legitimate work. A typical example is using an employer's computer to undertake private work – where effective controls are difficult to impose and will become an even greater problem as more employees have access to remote terminals and micros.

Sabotage, arson, and acts of vandalism directed against computers figure only in the EEC and Australian surveys, which makes widespread comparison impossible here. Nevertheless, even the limited information available provides some valuable insights into what are invariably high-cost incidents. Sometimes such acts appear to be politically motivated, whilst on other occasions they stem from employee frustration or aggression.

Table 12.1 What kind of crime?

Source of data	Types of crime included
1981 Audit Report	UK fraud (including misuse of computer
1985 Audit Report	resources)
BIS Fraud Survey	
EEC Report	EEC fraud; sabotage; deliberate attacks
CARB Report	Fraud; sabotage; vandalism; misuse of resources
USA CPA Survey	Banking and insurance fraud
press and journal reports	Fraud; extortion; industrial espionage

How much crime is there?

One aspect of computer-linked crime about which there seems to be general agreement is that "input" crimes dominate. This was not always the case. When business computing was in its infancy, it was conducted almost entirely by computer "experts," who operated on the fringes of mainstream company activity, secure both physically in their isolated computer suites and emotionally in the knowledge that they alone possessed the key that could unlock this new technological treasure-chest – and turn it into something at least partially useful to the businesses that employed them! What crimes there were that came to light back in the early 1960s always involved computer staff and were usually accomplished by amending the programs (software) in fraudulent ways.

Gradually, as computing technology has changed, so has the pattern of computer crime. The main thrust of recent years has been to progress from a batch production system, controlled by full-time computer operators, to widespread time-sharing systems that are capable of supporting simultaneously many separate terminals, usually remote from the actual computer.

Accompanying this fundamental change has been an improvement in the presentation of computer information and a facilitation of the way in which data can be entered into and processed by the computer. This is the so-called "user-friendly interface." The result is that computing has moved out of the era of black box mystique and is now just another business tool, available to a wide spectrum of staff from senior managers to first-line supervisors and clerical personnel. This has meant that the opportunity to misappropriate some of the wealth processed by the computer system is now available to many more people than used to be the case; for there is nothing like the daily use of a computer system for revealing any loopholes or imperfections that exist in its security.

Since manipulation of input data is perhaps the easiest avenue open to would-be computer criminals, this is where most evidence exists of attempts at fraudulent conversion. Table 12.2 shows the statistics culled from the various reports studied.

From these figures, it appears that well over half of all known computer-linked crimes are perpetrated by falsifying in some way or another the information fed into the computer. Thus, typically, supernumeraries will be entered on the company payroll; fictitious invoices from non-existent suppliers will be passed for payment; genuine debts due to an organization will be

Table 12.2   How much computer crime?

Source of data	Input	Output	Program	Misuse of resources	Sabotage/ vandalism
1981 Audit Report	42	2	1	22	n/a
1985 Audit Report	58	2	—	17	n/a
BIS Fraud Survey	46	1	5	2	n/a
EEC Report	25	8	4	2	21
CARB Report[3]	39	13	19	29	9
USA CPA (Banks)	('Most' out of total of 120 crimes)				
1985 press reports	5	4	2	2	—
Totals	215	30	31	74	30
Percent	57	8	8	19	8

written off the sales ledger balances; stock records will be falsified, in order to cover thefts; or, in a banking context, a cashier will manipulate say a spouse's checks so as to bypass the account debiting procedure.

From such examples, it can be appreciated that much of the computer crime that has been reported contains very little that is original or very sophisticated – perhaps that is why it was discovered in the first place! Most of it exploits weaknesses in the system controls, whilst it also reflects badly on the quality of management that often fails to implement such basic principles as the separation of duties between those responsible for handling goods or cash and those whose task it is to record all such transactions. In essence, much of what is now considered "computer crime" has existed since well before computers assumed their dominant role. Rather is it the case that, as the use of computers has mushroomed, so the means of committing fraud have adjusted to the new technology.

Less frequent, but of equal occurrence amongst themselves, are three other types of crime. These are those which involve the theft of computer output (checks, master programs), sabotage or vandalism, and those which involve the unauthorized adjustment of computer software. These all individually represent less than one in ten of recorded crimes but, as we shall see later, they have led to substantial financial losses where they have occurred.

You will notice an anomaly between the proportion of software-oriented crimes in Australia (17.5 percent) and that in our other surveys (3.5 percent). It is difficult to postulate reasons, unless it is that the Computer Abuse Research Bureau (CARB) there has more successfully teased out information than we have so far in Europe. Certainly, they are unequivocal in their concern:

The categories that should perhaps cause us most concern are the ones that we do not know so much about; the processing oriented techniques and the output oriented techniques. These techniques probably represented the majority of the 'under-water iceberg'; the part we cannot see, because they are being executed either without detection or, if they have been detected, management has been too reticent to reveal the abuse.[4]

Table 12.3 Who commits computer crimes?

Source of data	Managers/ supvrs	Clerks/ cashiers	Computer staff	Customers/ outsiders	Others/ unknown
1981 Audit Report	20	17	21	1	8
1985 Audit Report	29	27	8	6	7
BIS Fraud Survey	21	11	12	6	4
EEC Report	n/a	n/a	n/a	n/a	n/a
CARB Report	18[5]	18[5]	49	18	20
USA CPA Survey	26	68	13	0	13
1985 press reports	1	0	6	6	0
Totals	115	141	109	37	52
Percent	25	31	24	8	12

Table 12.4 Crimes by type and occupation

Type of crime	Managers/ supvrs	Clerks/ cashiers	Computer staff	Customers/ outsiders	Others/ unknown
Input	64	51	9	11	16
Output	0	1	5	2	1
Program (software)	0	0	8	0	0
Resources	4	3	28	3	5
Totals	68	55	50	16	22

Who commits the crimes?

Using the same source data, one conclusion is immediately clear: almost all the crimes involving computers are carried out by employees (see table 12.3). From this broad analysis it is possible to refine the information, so as to link occupation with types of computer crime. By doing this, we can more accurately define the risks facing us and thereby concentrate on devising appropriate strategies to deal with them (see table 12.4). (This further analysis is not possible from the data supplied in any of the foreign reports, and is therefore restricted to the UK information.)

Presented in this way, we can immediately see that clerical, supervisory, and managerial computer crime is almost exclusively undertaken by manipulating input data. This pattern of computer input crime (76 percent committed by end-users) is striking evidence of where the greatest risks now lie. As the authors of the 1985 Audit Commission Computer Fraud Survey have observed:

The risk is not just that a greater number of staff in organizations are more computerate; rather it is that while the generation of new entrants are familiar with computing, middle and senior management are invariably not so familiar. One generation is ready to grasp the potential, whereas another may well fail to grasp the implications . . . The risk is enhanced as computer facilities are provided on the office desk, rather than in a central processing area. As the number of users increases, so there is increased need for greater control, security and auditability.

Computer staff, on the other hand, are much more prone to misuse the computer resource, have a not unexpected monopoly on program fraud, and are the major cause of output-oriented crime. The latter two techniques can be (and already have been) employed to defraud organizations of large sums of money, but abuse of resources in itself does not usually incur significant losses. Even including this last in our statistics, computer staff still account for only a quarter of all reported crimes.

Motivations: the image and reality

There is a commonly held image of the computer criminal, widely promoted by the media, which depicts him as something of a "whiz kid." The respected American computer crime expert Donn Parker has described such people as, "Usually bright, eager, highly motivated, courageous, adventuresome and qualified people, willing to accept a technical challenge. They have exactly the characteristics that make them highly desirable employees in data processing." Match this personality profile with the assessment by F. W. Dennis in an article in *Security World* that "The common denominator in nearly all cases of computer fraud has been that the individual is very much like the mountain climber – he or she must beat the system because it is there," and you have all the ingredients for a successful Hollywood film.

However, when you are able to analyze how the (relatively few) reported computer crimes were committed, the substance for such an assessment is not really there. Not many of the crimes reported in the BIS *Computer Related Fraud Casebook*, for example, demonstrate high technical ingenuity on the part of the perpetrator. Most exhibit an opportunistic exploitation of an inherent weakness in the computer system being used.

On the question of the motivations behind computer-linked crimes, a US attorney, Jay BloomBecker, has produced a perceptive analogy which likens the criminal's attitude to the computer as either a "playpen" or a "cookie jar" (*Computerworld*, May, 1981). Some people, he says, view the computer as a playpen, where crime can result from an attempt to gain satisfaction from working with the computer that gets out of hand. He illustrates this by reference to attempts to gain use of computer time without paying for it: through, for instance, gaining unauthorized access to a time-sharing service; by illegally using a program, knowing that it was copyrighted and by running personal programs on your employer's computer. It is a theory that acknowledges the inherent satisfaction gained by many, adults and children alike, merely from manipulating a computer.

Others, perhaps the more dangerous category, view the computer world they live in as a cookie jar. In this case, personal problems like a gambling debt, drug-taking or investment losses may motivate an employee to view the funds available in the computer system as a solution to the problem. The criminal may try to take what he needs from the computer system; just like dipping into a "cookie jar." In such circumstances, the motivation is much more pressing than the observation of a loophole in the system security. In support of this view, an American study of white-collar crime has concluded that "situational pressures, such as a debt or loss" are a major factor in criminality.[6]

One of the crimes reported in the BIS Casebook refers to a classic illustration of this. In 1981, a 23-year-old, rather naive bank clerk, earning only £200 a month, became infatuated with a 32-year-old, wordly wise woman. In order to meet what he perceived to be her expectations of him, he lavished money on expensive gifts, travel and general "good-living." He stole £23,000 from four bank accounts, covering the theft by transferring cash through a computer from seventeen other accounts. He then lost £10,000 in casinos, trying to repay the money. When he was finally caught, the woman deserted him!

Attitudes to crime

Jack Bologna has spent longer than most examining the motivational aspects of computer crime and has published a collection of his own articles under the title *Computer Crime Wave of the Future*. In this, he reports the results of a fascinating questionnaire about attitudes to crime, which he put to two disparate groups in the United States – 100 accountants from public practice, industry and government and 90 data processing professionals of middle to higher rank, who were delegates to a Honeywell conference on computer security. The group were asked to express their agreement or disagreement with a series of statements seeking to rationalize why employees steal or embezzle from their employers. The statements were an attempt to synthesize the positions of the various schools of thought (from moral philosophers, through sociologists to economists and politicians) on crime motivations and causes.

There were both interesting similarities and differences in the responses he obtained. For both groups, the top four items were the same. They agreed that employees steal because:

1 "They feel they can get away with it and not be caught."
2 "They think stealing a little from a big company won't hurt it."
3 "Each theft has its own preceding conditions and each thief has his own motives, so there is no general rule."
4 "Most employee thieves are caught by accident, rather than by audit or design. Therefore, fear of being caught is not a deterrent to theft."

The fact that 70 percent of the accountants and 78 percent of the DP professionals believed that most thieves were caught by accident is a startling admission of the vulnerability of the accounting controls, audit trails, and programming documentation for which their professions are responsible.

However, the differences in the responses from the two groups provided equally interesting revelations. For the DP professionals gave significantly greater accord to the propositions that:

1 "They feel that 'beating the company' is a challenge and not a matter of economic gain alone." (DP = 70 percent v. Acc. = 57 percent.)
2 "They feel frustrated or dissatisfied about some aspect of their personal life that is not job-related." (DP = 68 percent v. Acc. = 48 percent.)
3 "They feel frustrated or dissatisfied about some aspect of their job." (DP = 75 percent v. Acc. = 63 percent.)

In their identification of personal and job-related "frustration" as a contributory cause of criminality, it may be that the DP professionals were accurately reflecting the lack of autonomy, minimal job variety, and poor management communications often endemic in data processing work.

How much does it cost?

To ask this question is akin to the enquiry about the proverbial piece of string! The scale of losses ranges from that involving the simple misuse of a computer resource, with virtually no quantifiable costs, to a handful of sophisticated frauds perpetrated against banks and other financial institutions, where the costs have been measured in millions of pounds.

What I have undertaken here is a consolidation of the published information about computer crime costs right across the spectrum, followed by a detailed analysis of input crimes on their own. As we have already seen, input crimes are probably the major problem facing us and therefore represent the greatest potential return, if we tackle them successfully. No adjustment has been made for the effects of inflation on the values of crimes which, in a few cases, go back to the 1960s. Furthermore, these values seldom reflect the full costs of an incident, since the less easily quantifiable costs of disruption and subsequent recovery are missing from most calculations. To this extent, true costs are understated in the figures that follow.

The overall costs, analyzed by type of crime in pounds sterling are shown in table 12.5. One or two aspects of these figures call for comment. The two UK Audit Commission Surveys revealed a lower average cost per incident than any of the other reports; something they recognized, but for which they offered no explanation. The EEC Survey and the 1985 press reports include three major banking frauds achieved by program manipulation; together these account for about £20 million of the total £21 million in that category. The latest press reports

Table 12.5   The cost of computer crime

Source of data	Input (£)	Output (£)	Program	Resource	Sabotage
1981 Audit Report	858,170	3600	26,000	17,379	n/a
1985 Audit Report	901,001	230,185	0	2301	n/a
BIS Fraud Survey	3,774,089	56	23,050	2000	n/a
EEC Report[7]	6,112,800	n/a	11,880,000	n/a	1,674,000
CARB Report[8]	1,580,925	106,845	152,038	34,323	461,550
1985 press reports	14,993,500	68,500	9,030,000	0	n/a
Totals	28,220,485	409,186	21,111,088	56,003	2,135,550
Percentage of total value	54	0.8	41	0.1	4
Number of cases with value assessed	193	13	21	27	8
Average value	146,220	31,476	1,005,290	2074	266,944

also include nearly £15 million bank losses resulting from two cases of false input information, again greatly inflating the figures.

Obviously, cases of this magnitude tend to distort the "run-of-the-mill" crimes and inflate the "average" values given. However, we must also recognize that the computer systems of financial institutions do routinely process vast sums of money, and to that extent can expect to be the subject of regular fraudulent attacks. Banks themselves have been conspicuously reluctant to admit to losses through fraud – a fact strongly criticized by the authors of the Australian CARB report, whose data include no banking information at all. In some measure, then, the five high-value cases included here only help to balance earlier (suspected) omissions.

Most of us, however, do not work in banks, and are therefore more likely to encounter the kind of input fraud covered so well by the two Audit Commission surveys and in the BIS Casebook. Between them, these three surveys examine 137 such cases,[9] enough to provide us with a number of useful insights.

First, let us look at how crimes relate to jobs (see table 12.6). Whilst the number of cases involving computer staff is too small to provide a reliable result, there is an immediate comparison possible between the senior staff grades of manager and supervisor on the one hand and the more junior clerical and cash-handling roles on the other. Those in positions involving trust, responsibility and (presumably) greater technical know-how manage on average to extract five times greater value than their humbler counterparts. When you also take into account that there are fewer of them, the potential for causing harm where technical expertise co-exists with authority and opportunity can be readily appreciated. This message is

Table 12.6 Crimes by value and occupation

Status	Source of data	No. of crimes	Total value (£)	Average value (£)
Managers/supvrs	1981	19	720,254	37,908
	1985	23	788,956	34,302
	BIS	20	678,081	33,904
		62	2,187,291	35,279
Clerks/cashiers	1981	14	77,619	5544
	1985	24	100,920	4205
	BIS	11	175,526	15,957
		49	354,065	7226
Computer staff	1981	2	5295	2647
	1985	1	452	452
	BIS	4	201,405	50,351
		7	207,152	29,593
Outsiders/unknown	1981	5	54,802	10,960
Customers/others	1985	8	10,673	1334
	BIS	9	2,719,077	302,120
		22	2,784,552	126,571

Table 12.7   Length and value of crimes

Job roles	Average value (£)	Average duration (months)	Value per month (£)
Managers/supvrs	35,279	19	1857
Clerks/cashiers	7226	11	657

reinforced by examination of the length of time such crimes go on before detection, and the rate at which value (normally money) is extracted (see table 12.7).

Finally, the 1985 Audit Commission Survey has some additional information about the people who committed the crimes it reported. The information is interesting for the light it sheds on this particular manifestation of white-collar crime. For every grade of staff, I have calculated the average time both in service to the one employer and also in the particular job occupied at the time the crime was committed. I have then compared them with the average duration of the frauds (see figure 12.1). Remember, these are averages, which makes it a sobering thought indeed that staff with such long records of service can and do feature in the annals of computer crime.

All the information we have indicates that nearly all computer criminals are first-time offenders, motivated by greed, pressing financial problems or other personal difficulties. There seems to be no strong relation between the extent of the financial loss and length of service, for some trusted employees have been prepared to commit fraud for a relatively small reward. Like all fraud, it is the opportunity, rather than the actual sum involved, that determines behavior.

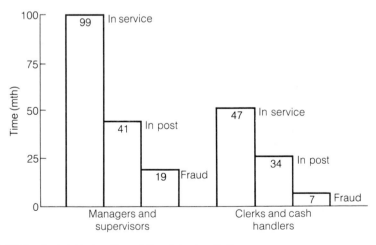

Figure 12.1   Average duration of fraudulent activity.

What can be done?

If we start from an acknowledgment that very few cases of computer fraud exhibit the ingenious application of technical skills (but that, on the contrary, most take advantage of inherent weaknesses in the basic system controls and procedures) then there is a range of counter-measures available for us to consider. The security manager should have a role to play in any such scheme, though it would be idle to pretend his is the only one.

The Audit Commission Survey makes the following observations:

If basic controls were introduced and enforced by management the risk of further frauds would be minimized. The ability to enforce such controls (particularly where there are increasingly complex terminal-based systems) will call for additional skills. A combination of accounting and computing knowledge will be essential for those responsible for verifying the adequacy of such controls – the auditor will need to be "computerate" if he is to function effectively in the future.

The risks of fraud and abuse will be all the greater if internal controls and internal audit are inadequate. Poor supervision and ineffective audit will almost certainly encourage the opportunity for large-scale and long-running losses. Where the organization sustains such an environment and still encourages the widespread introduction of computing, the risks will be considerable.

I am a great believer in a four-pronged approach to computer security. For many reasons, I think it is completely impractical to rely on any single person or job role to carry out the security function effectively. I would not, therefore, rely on computer staff alone to develop system security; nor do I see it as just the auditors' responsibility to ensure effective controls. Both approaches would be rapidly undermined without the involvement of the managers using the computer and without the insights brought by them to the actual operation of the systems. Even an approach that combined these three elements would be missing the professional skills of the security expert in analyzing risks and probing for any weaknesses in the agreed security strategy

To conclude, then, here are a few thoughts in the form of an aide-memoire about the contributions that could and should be made by those most closely involved.

Managers

- Define responsibilities of those involved:
    in systems design;
    in system use and
    in auditing.
- Develop for all users a "Code of Practice."
- Ensure adequate training is given at all levels.
- Become personally computer literate.
- Allow realistic time and budget schedules for developing security in computer systems.
- Counsel staff.

Auditors

- Liaise with computer staff in the development of systems.

- Ensure provision of adequate audit trails.
- Liaise with computer users.
- Become personally computer literate.

Computer Staff

- Be aware of the need for security.
- Ensure programmers and analysts possess general business skills, as well as technical expertise.
- Allow sufficient time to develop secure systems during program development.

Security Managers

- Become computer literate.
- Analyze the risks.
- Ask "awkward" questions:
    of computer staff;
    of auditors and
    of users.
- Apply security experience to the computer situation.
- Liaise with managers, auditors, and computer staff.

Notes

1 The full details of the reports referred to in this article are: *Computer Fraud Survey*, by the Local Government Audit Inspectorate (1981), now obtainable as *Computer Fraud Survey*, The Audit Commission for Local Authorities in England and Wales (HMSO, London, 1985). *Computer Related Fraud Casebook*, BIS Applied Systems Ltd (Manchester, UK, 1983). *The Vulnerability of the Information Conscious Society*, Commission of the European Communities, Information Technologies and Telecommunications Task Force (Brussels, 1984). *Computer Related Crime in Australia*, Computer Abuse Research Bureau, Chisholm Institute of Technology (Victoria, 1984). *Banking and Insurance EDP Fraud*, Certified Public Accountants, EDP Fraud Review Task Force (USA, 1984).
2 Kevin Fitzgerald in CIT – CARB Report.
3 The CARB Report lists a total of 123 crimes. Those not included here are eight cases of theft of equipment and six cases where the technique used was not known.
4 *Computer Related Crime in Australia*.
5 Available data only identify 36 cases in these two categories, without subdividing them between clerks and managers, etc. This division is therefore arbitrary.
6 Albrecht and Romney in *Prosecutor's Brief*, 1979.
7 European Currency Units (ecus) converted at 1 ecu = 54p (UK).
8 Australian dollars converted at $1 = 51p (UK).
9 In total, 144 cases, of which seven have no assessed value and have therefore been omitted here.

13 Political Issues

The New Capitalism

William E. Halal

What will be the overall political impact of information technology? Deregulation and privatization suggest a strengthening of free enterprise competition, yet capitalist corporations are also developing self-management ventures and forming cooperative links between each other and with governments. Meanwhile, the socialist states are allowing more free enterprise. All this suggests to the author that a "New Capitalism" is emerging, which represents a synthesis of liberal and conservative ideals. William E. Halal is Professor of Management at the George Washington University, Washington, DC. This article, adapted from his book, The New Capitalism: Democratic Free Enterprise in Post-Industrial Society *(Wiley, New York, 1986), first appeared in* Futures, *June 1985.*

One of the most disturbing features of our time is a perennial antagonism of left *versus* right wing political persuasions that hinders corporations, nations and the entire world economy. Major business firms have been impaled for decades on the horns of a dilemma in which liberals escalated demands for corporate social responsibility – while conservatives grew concerned that the economic survival of major industries was being threatened. The same conflict is reflected at the national level between the old liberal policies of big government that led to a "welfare state" – which has been attacked recently by neoconservatives promoting "supply-side economics" to free up the private sector. Even the major disorders that beset the globe – the world *problematique* composed of the multiple crises of resource depletion, environmental decay, international conflict, etc. – go unaddressed largely because of an enduring hostility between the capitalist and socialist superpowers.

All this conflict grew out of the paradigm developed for an industrial past – the "Old Capitalism" – in which the philosophies of liberalism and conservatism were diametrically opposed to each other. Lately, however, the realities of a new era have forced these views to begin changing so that a broader synthesis may become the most striking feature of the future.

I have been studying these issues for years, and the results of this work show that a "New Capitalism" is emerging. The New Capitalism is a "post-industrial paradigm" in business and economics appearing now in the form of 40 or so long-term trends that have been accelerating dramatically since the imminent transition to an Information Age reached crisis levels during the early 1980s.[1] Furthermore, a "technological imperative" seems to flow from the revolutionary power of information technology now spreading like wildfire to produce two central themes running through all these trends: both the liberal idea of democratic cooperation and the conservative ideal of free enterprise competition are rapidly becoming the major structural features of economic systems.

This creative union of the left and right is occurring – not out of dedication to political principles, economic altruism, or moral virtue – but because a powerful combination of democracy and free enterprise is becoming the most practical, indispensable course of action to handle the complexity of a knowledge-based society.

The corporation: democratically governed confederations of entrepreneurs

A prophetic event occurred in 1983 when *Time* magazine chose the personal computer as "Man of the Year" to signal a major step towards the Information Age. Suddenly, computers were no longer esoteric devices used by scientists, corporations, and bright kids, but common tools entering ordinary offices and homes by the million to irrevocably transform organizational structures from the machine-like, ossified bureaucracies of the industrial past into fluid new forms that are compatible with the flow of knowledge. The microcomputer, smart robots, telecommunications, and other technical breakthroughs are converting entire organizations into "integrated information systems" that should soon eliminate most of the routine jobs of blue-collar workers, office staff, and even middle-managers who formerly occupied the lower half of the organizational pyramid. *Business Week* noted: "Rigid hierarchical structures have begun to crumble at the best managed companies . . . considering the impetus behind the electronics revolution, these early changes may represent only the first tremors of an earthquake."[2] With these old internal routines fading in importance, the emphasis is shifting to external "boundary-spanning" functions like strategic planning and creating ventures to handle the quantum leap in complexity presented by a new era and to survive the intense competition caused by deregulation and growing foreign competition. Corporations like IBM, TRW, GE, HP, 3M, Kollmorgan, TI, and AT&T are being transformed into flexible, decentralized systems of numerous small, self-managed enterprises. IBM, for instance, took the lead from Apple by using a self-contained "Independent Business Unit" to develop its Personal Computer. The result is that progressive organizations are evolving from the traditional "hierarchy of decision-makers" into "organic networks" that are specifically suited for fostering entrepreneurial change – what Norman McCrae called a "confederation of entrepreneurs." Executives at GE Company described the emerging view:

Our philosophy is to encourage talented managers to act as entrepreneurs expert in their businesses, markets, and communities with direction and support from the corporate headquarters. . . . We're trying to reshape GE in the minds of its employees as a band of small businesses . . . to take the strength of a large company and act with the agility of a small company.[3]

This form of organization also fits in well with the values of a new breed of younger workers motivated by autonomy and achievement who are encouraging other arrangements that enhance employee freedom.[4] It is estimated that half of West German workers and 30 percent of the US workforce now use some variation of flexitime. Interest is also rising in having employees start new ventures within large organizations – "intrapreneurship" – which *The Economist* called "a major social invention." Even in Japan the tradition of lifetime loyalty to one employer is breaking down as talented professionals switch jobs.

The most exotic impetus is coming from the growing use of computers and teleconferencing systems that are converting white-collar and professional employees into "teleworkers" able to operate virtually anywhere rather than being confined to an office. About 5 million Americans work out of their home now because productivity gains can reach 50 percent. It is estimated that at least 10 percent of the labour force should be telecommuting by 1990, and some believe almost half could do so now. Authorities in the field offer some startling visions: "Over the next 10–20 years, most people in all levels of business will work at home at least two or three days a week. . . . The way we work in this society is going to be transformed . . . The 9–5 era is over."[5] As the growth of information technology urges the development of such fluid structures, institutions should become organic networks of semi-autonomous units that pass resources, employees and information freely across the organizational hierarchy and its permeable external boundaries. The resulting conditions – numerous small competing enterprises, freedom of entry and exit into contracts, and, above all, the widespread availability of accurate market information – constitute the requirements that economists have always defined for "perfect markets." Large institutions are thereby becoming part of the open marketplace, bringing the advantages we have always attributed to the free enterprise system directly into the internal operation of organizations themselves – flexibility for adaptive change, easier management of complexity, freedom for innovation, and other means for coping with a turbulent world.

But this flowering of enterprise represents only half the transformation now taking place. Organic networks may foster the entrepreneurial responsiveness needed for a more complex era; however, there is an equally great need to unify this mass of diversity into a coherent whole and to integrate it into society at large. This other half of the solution is also under way as progressive corporations slowly absorb various business stakeholders into a democratic form of governance that serves "multiple goals" while enhancing profit. Much of this has been taking place for decades in Europe, Japan and other nations, and now it is being extended to the US stronghold of the Old Capitalism as well. A good example is the way Chairman Lee Iacocca saved Chrysler from bankruptcy by rallying investors, labor, government, customers and other critical interests into a unified community that worked together far more effectively.

The resistance is enormous, of course, because deviations from the traditional form of profit-centered capitalism provoke strong ideological reactions, especially now that a neoconservative revolt has temporarily eclipsed these trends. But, ultimately, the move to a broader form of business may be inevitable because it seems to represent a historic shift in the critical factors of production. In Agricultural Society, those who owned land were accorded the power to govern because land was the most critical economic resource. In Industrial Society, holders of capital governed the social order for the same reason. The Old Capitalism was formed when the major task was to build manufacturing plants for producing goods, and since capital was the main requirement for constructing this physical infrastructure, profit became the dominant goal of business.

Although money and self-interest will obviously remain vital, now the move to a post-industrial era is bringing higher-order concerns to the forefront. Cultural values are shifting to emphasize social, intellectual, and political resources because these are becoming the primary factors that determine economic success and because society demands improving the quality of life. Peter Drucker summed it up: "The new demand is . . . that business and businessmen make concern for society central to the conduct of business itself. It is a demand that the quality of life become the business of business."[6] To resolve this conflict between traditional profit goals and the newer social goals, *avant-garde* US companies like 3M, Aetna, HP, Dayton–Hudson, IBM, and Kollmorgan are now shaping strategies that reconcile both sets of needs. They have developed social reporting methods to evaluate the impact of their operations on society. The insights gained from this knowledge reveal a different reality, showing the intrinsically political character of any institution created by the intersecting interests of employees, customers, and other constituencies that comprise this "extended corporate community." Enlightened executives are carving out roles as "economic states-men" to form a "social contract" that welds these stakeholders into a political coalition – what some have called "corporatism." Derek Bok, President of Harvard University, described this new institutional role: "Management arguably exists not simply to serve shareholders but to exercise leadership in reconciling the needs of stockholders, customers, employees, and suppliers, along with members of the public and their representatives in government."[7] It is important to stress that there is a critical difference between the older notion of "social *responsibility*" *versus* the "social *contract*." Social responsibility became an empty piety because it was a one-sided relationship that only concerned the obligations of the firm. Now that the conservative revolt and an economic crisis have challenged this view, the solution is emerging in the form of a *two-way contract* between the corporation and its constituent groups. Rather than some vague set of social obligations, the social contract is a pragmatic, "business-like" form of bargaining that unifies profit and social goals to create more successful corporate performance.

Good examples are provided by the "giveback" bargaining in industries like automobile manufacture and air travel. Driven by the need to compete with tough new competition, management is being forced to demand concessions from labor in wages, fringe benefits, and work rules – in return for providing profit-sharing, job security and participation in major decisions. As a result of these unyielding economic forces that seem likely to increase with further competition, no-nonsense executives who abhor any whiff of democratic values are almost unwittingly moving towards the democratization of capitalism simply because it is more productive. Employee directors are now seated on the boards of Chrysler, Eastern Airlines, Pan Am, and about a dozen other major corporations – which would have been unthinkable just a few years ago. One manager noted the advantage: "Our way of operating is just so far superior in organizational and human terms to the way most companies work, others will have a hard time competing. In a free society, this is the most potent force for change."[8] This transformation should realize the original vision which Adam Smith and others saw only dimly at the start of the Industrial Revolution. Before this century ends, I suspect that modern business is likely to become alive with myriad small, innovative, constantly changing enterprises offering an endless variety of sophisticated goods and services, and governed by democratically elected representatives of their various constituencies. This transition will require many years of disruptive change, and some traditional forms of business will always remain. But over the long term the relentless growth of information technology should cause modern corporations generally to bloom into full flower as vastly more productive and liberating institutions.

The national economy: markets combining both cooperation and competition

This synthesis of democratic cooperation and free enterprise competition may also restructure entire macroeconomic systems for a new era because neither the right nor the left alone seems able to solve the economic crisis that grips advanced nations.

Despite all the furore over the Thatcher and Reagan "revolutions," the right wing has not succeeded in reducing big government or revitalizing big business. Central government spending in the UK and the United States has continued to climb because of solid opposition to decreasing essential public services and regulatory protection. Stagflation has been reduced and there is renewed interest in enterprise, but the British economy still suffers from recession, and the growth in the US economy has been purchased at the cost of unprecedented budget deficits that threaten the future. US Senator Charles Mathias voiced a common fear: "We are living in an economic fantasy world."[9]

The biggest accomplishment of the neoconservative revolt was soundly to discredit the old liberal policies of the welfare state that carry the stigma of big spending and meddlesome intervention into the efficiency of the market. Big government is so out of favor that the socialist revolt in France is collapsing. President Mitterrand himself acknowledged, "We were dreaming a bit, it is true, in 1981."[10]

If this impasse is viewed from a dispassionate, long-range perspective, however, a broader solution is apparent that involves both the liberal and conservative positions. Liberals are defining a new role for government that uses collaborative labor–management–government alliances to improve the operation of the marketplace, and this more responsible form of business should also allow conservatives to wean the economy from its dependence on government assistance and regulations. Such a union of the left and the right would comprise a "decentralization strategy" that passes economic control from the public sector to a self-regulating private sector, permitting greater entrepreneurial freedom, a more benign economic system that serves the public good, and robust, equitable growth.

This possibility may be emerging now in a centrist movement that unites the neoconservative and neoliberal positions. Extreme groups will always remain at the fringe, of course, but there are signs of growing interest in "progressive moderates" – Gary Hart in the United States, the Social Democrats in the UK, the Greens in West Germany, the "radical center" in Denmark, etc. – which could easily swell into a populist wave of reform.

The key to this approach is the creation of democratic bodies to guide economic policy decisions that are unavoidably political matters. Just as the New Capitalism is urging major corporations to develop a new role as a political coalition of stakeholder interests, so should cities, states, entire industries, and nations be managed as a coalition of corporations, labor unions, local governments, and other political actors. Europe and Japan have been developing a similar form of policy-making for years, and now there is growing acceptance in the United States. Polls show that the American public, business leaders, Democrats, and some Republicans favor tripartite policy bodies. Congressman Timothy Wirth observed: "the clearest message we heard from hundreds of Americans was that the politics of confrontation among business, government, and labor must give way to the politics of cooperation."[11] Collaborative policy-making would allow liberals more effectively to foster economic progress and social welfare – not through the national planning implied in "industrial policy" – but by extending democratic principles to create productive working relations that serve various interest groups. Creative politicians in the United States today are providing statesmanlike leadership to form business–government partnerships that convert the difficult problems plaguing modern economies into opportunities for progress. Wang Laboratories worked with the community in Lowell, MA, to turn this decaying mill town into a model of high-tech prosperity. A coalition of banks, hospitals and universities brought new life to Indianapolis as a cultural center. Firms like Control Data have opened facilities in some of the nation's worst ghettos, alleviating poverty while also earning handsome profits. Research consortia are forming among competitors in electronics, aerospace and other high-tech industries. Life insurance executive Stanley Karson noted: "something exciting has been happening at the local level [that is evolving into a new social] fabric: the emergence of community coalitions of business, government, community groups and non-profit institutions to address common needs."[12]

An especially powerful outcome would be to redefine the way the economy works, the "rules of the game," by developing a more sophisticated infrastructure for a new era. "Market supplements" are being used to control social impacts while maintaining business freedom, as in the internalization of pollution costs through fees in lieu of the old "command and control" regulations. Government bureaucracy is being eliminated as functions of the public sector are "privatized" to be conducted more effectively by contractors. Joint government–business– university R & D programs are being developed to spur technological advances and train displaced workers. Modern nations long ago moved beyond the conservative ideal of an untrammelled, *laissez-faire* economy dominated by a brutal struggle for survival, and they also rejected the liberal vision of centralized national planning. The New Capitalism solves this conflict by drawing on the strong points of both philosophies – voluntary collaboration to create a more "perfect" form of market competition that fosters both productivity and social welfare – in short, by redefining capitalism as a system that combines cooperation and competition. Sinichiro Asao, US counsel from Japan, attributed his country's success to a similar strategy: "Competition and cooperation are both essential to healthy economic development . . . deliberation by the government with all interested parties: business, banking, labor, consumers, academic experts, etc. . . . to foster a climate in which the mechanisms of a free and competitive market operate most vigorously."[13]

A final change would be to redefine the roles of big business *vis-à-vis* big government. If the large quasi-public corporations that comprise the primary actors in modern economies were to adopt this broader and more benign role, they would be converted into institutions that are politically legitimate and vastly more productive. The mission of big business would thereby be expanded into a more democratic posture that formally serves the interests of society at large, while retaining the flexible, voluntary nature of a private institution in a system of free enterprise. These "soft corporations" of the future could eliminate much of the present maze of regulations because they would be fairly self-regulating, and they would reduce the need for government programs by alleviating unemployment, poverty, and other social ills that have fed the growth of the welfare state.

These are only a few of the more prominent concepts being considered, but they illustrate the evolution of a far more creative system of political economy that goes beyond the old dichotomy between interfering big government versus *laissez-faire* big business – a unique new combination of Western ideals that I call "Democratic Free Enterprise." This powerful union of cooperation and competition should provide the necessary conditions for strong, equitable growth: reduced regulation, lower taxes, entrepreneurial freedom, accurate market information, rapid technological innovation, collaborative working relations, an educated workforce, and other advantages.

If such a system could be implemented, it would form a modern version of the physical infrastructure created by government to foster growth during the industrial past – the federal banking system, unemployment insurance, the national highway system, and other features that comprised the basis of the Old Capitalism. Now we are simply adding a new infrastructure for a post-industrial era, a New Capitalism. As US business professor George Steiner noted, "We are now, in this nation, redefining capitalism."[14]

The world system: hybrids of capitalism and socialism

A similar metamorphosis is under way around the globe that offers the promise of resolving the obdurate antagonism between the superpowers that lies at the heart of the global crisis. In 1983, President Reagan delivered what has become a famous condemnation of the Soviet Union: "The Soviets have not slowed the pace of their enormous military buildup . . . they are the focus of evil in the modern world." But his counterpart, President Yuri Andropov, had precisely the same harsh view of the United States: "[the USA is] the root of evil perpetuated in the world, the evil which threatens the very existence of mankind."[15]

This mutual hostility is largely the result of ideological differences between the two major systems of political economy – capitalism and socialism – that have polarized the earth into warring camps. Most of us are unable to see this conflict for what it is because there is such fierce self-righteousness pervading both capitalist and socialist nations, which is exactly why it continues. But lately people are beginning to realize this is a senseless struggle that can only lead to disaster and that a new conceptual framework is needed to free us from this morbid state of mind. Richard Barnet warned, "Neither 'communism' nor 'capitalism' remains a credible philosophical system for organizing society in the contemporary world."[16]

If this sensitive issue is examined free of prejudice, however, a far richer perspective emerges of the two ideologies as part of a larger world system. The United States and the Soviet Union share strong similarities because they are both great industrial powers that govern vast empires covering half the globe using sophisticated technologies and authoritarian institutions. Their forms of political economy may be very different, but each system is an extreme version of the same basic "industrial" paradigm, so they complement one another to form a remarkable symmetry. Capitalism permits an efficient form of entrepreneurial freedom that has produced a high standard of living, but at the cost of harsh competition, great inequities and a precarious existence. Socialism uses centralized state control to provide personal security, many welfare benefits and more uniform social equity, but it is inefficient and dictatorial. The two systems are polar opposites that have their unique advantages and drawbacks.

As the worldwide economic crisis escalates rapidly, however, both systems are being forced to search for new solutions through a variety of economic–political experiments. The result has been a proliferation of "hybrid economies" that represent various combinations of capitalism and socialism as countries around the world struggle to find their way through the transition to an Information Age.

Many capitalist nations are deviating from the traditional *laissez-faire* model, such as Japan's form of "people's capitalism," the many variations on "economic democracy" practised in Europe, and countries like France, Italy, Spain, Greece, Egypt, and Hong Kong that are incorporating elements of socialism. Greece, for instance, is developing a unique system that uses democratically governed enterprises and free markets.

What is more astonishing is the way many socialist nations are adopting some desirable aspects of free enterprise, such as China, Vietnam, and the communist bloc in Eastern Europe, including Hungary, East Germany, Bulgaria, and Yugoslavia. These experiments in "market socialism" seem to be moving towards small business ownership, incentive systems for workers, prices set by market forces, and entrepreneurial freedom for managers of state enterprises. Chinese Premier Zhao Ziyang told his people, "if we do not remove the obstacles to the effective management of socialism . . . we cannot advance . . . we must encourage competition," while a US businessman dealing with the Chinese noted: "The difference now is like night and day. They are really talking concrete deals, they have a business-like approach."[17]

Even the Soviet Union is moving in this direction because there is a growing realization that the old planned economy has reached its limits so elements of free enterprise must be incorporated into the system. Soviet plant managers are being allowed to do more local planning and retain profits. Workers are being offered a voice in decisions and financial incentives to gain the support of a more sophisticated younger population that wants interesting jobs, autonomy and control over their work, just as in the West. Shortly before his death, President Andropov described young Russians in terms that are reminiscent of the way older Americans speak of the postwar baby boom: "The young generation is not foreign to ours; it is just different." Here's how Soviet officials describe their thinking: "[We plan to] restructure the economic mechanism. It cannot continue to operate the way it did 10 or 15 years ago. . . . But we cannot simply copy the methods of capitalism; we are trying to develop means natural to our own system."[18] If these trends continue, the consequences are so enormous that they cannot be fully comprehended, but one conclusion stands out: both sets of nations seem to be moving along a common path towards free enterprise and democracy. The outcome could be the creation of an international standard of political economy that synthesizes the capitalist and socialist ideologies into a more powerful "generic model" that combines the best features of both systems while overcoming their disadvantages, producing the "convergence" that many anticipated long ago.[19]

For instance, both capitalist and socialist nations are adopting free market principles to revive their stagnating economies. As noted, the West is deregulating industries and breaking up big corporate bureaucracies into networks of small ventures to realize the productivity of free enterprise that has often been simply a distant ideal in capitalism – while Red China and the Soviet bloc are doing the same to overcome the bureaucratic inefficiencies that have plagued socialism, albeit without relinquishing some form of state control. Thus, both ideologies are moving towards a common ground that takes advantage of the attractive features of market mechanisms to avoid the drawbacks of oligopolistic capitalism on the one hand and centralized state planning on the other.

The same convergence is also moving both systems towards democratic forms of economic governance. Europe, Japan, and more recently the United States are all incorporating some form of participation into their economic systems which represents a move toward the social welfare goals advocated by socialism, although they are doing so by using democratic principles rather than through the centralized control of the state – and likewise some socialist nations are broadening and decentralizing their old form of state control to move towards democratic plant governance, as in Hungary, Yugoslavia, and the USSR. The crisis in Poland indicates the fierce strength behind these demands for worker participation that are likely to persist until reforms are made. Franz Loeser, a former official in the East German Communist Party, believes such changes are inevitable.[20]

The communist countries are losing the economic race with the West. People in the communist countries feel it and the party membership know it. . . . What we are likely to witness is the painful dying out of an outmoded model of socialism and a fierce struggle for new, diversified and more democratic forms . . . neither the western capitalist world nor the communist countries have a clear vision of how to resolve their antagonisms peacefully . . . The best hope . . . is for both socialism and capitalism to become more democratic.

Thus both systems seem to be converging toward a common form of political economy that would be roughly similar to the model described in the last section – Democratic Free Enterprise – although it may be viewed differently in terms of each ideology. In capitalist states, the traditional goals of "profit making" are being "broadened" and "modernized" to encompass Western ideals of "democratic human values" and "entrepreneurial freedom" to increase "business productivity." For communist nations, socialist principles are being extended so that workers, local communities, and other members of the "proletariat" share directly in controlling the "means of production" to serve the "common welfare" using "decentralized planning."

However, it would be misleading to believe that such a single "ideal" system may become universal because the opposite tendency towards *divergence* can also be seen in the above examples. The world is growing far too complex for a monolithic approach, so it seems more likely that hybrid variations will "fill in the gap" that now separates capitalism and socialism, turning the barren no man's land lying between these two extremes into a rich field of fertile alternatives. Thus a full spectrum of diverse models of political economy may spring up over the next few decades to suit the unique cultural backgrounds of various nations. The "generic standard" at the center of this economic spectrum may be most popular in Europe, Japan, Greece, Yugoslavia, and other "moderate" nations. Brazil, South Korea, Taiwan, and other countries with a preference for dictatorial *laissez-faire* economies will tend toward the "capitalist" end, while the Soviet Union, Red China, Cuba, and other nations favoring collectivist values will lean toward the "socialist" end.

But notwithstanding these variations, I suggest that the Democratic Free Enterprise model seems likely to be a central focus of the emerging world economic system simply because it should prove to be most effective in solving the economic–political problems of the Information Age. After all, there has to be something between the jungle of *laissez-faire* capitalism and the dictatorship of state-controlled socialism. So when this standard of political economy does emerge, it will not only be the New Capitalism, it should also be the "New Socialism."

The twin imperatives of democracy and free enterprise

It should be clear that such momentous changes are not inevitable, they will take decades to evolve, they are likely to occur in a more unpredictable manner than we can foresee, and they are certain to meet enormous resistance. However, the most salient event of our time is that a revolution in information technology is spreading to cover the globe. And as we have seen, this new form of power seems to exert two imperatives that are moving on inexorably to urge both entrepreneurial freedom as well as democratic governance – simply out of sheer self-interest as growing competition and a turbulent era demand these changes to survive. The Information Age seems to be inevitably driving the development of free enterprise to manage an exploding level of diversity, while also fostering democratic systems to integrate these differences into a coherent whole.

On one hand, the new economic order is evolving into an extremely complex mix of highly diverse societies that are modernizing rapidly to create a huge increase in consumption, thereby placing difficult new demands on resource allocation, ecological controls, and other such limits as the planet's population grows to roughly 10 billion people living at an industrial level of development. Such massive levels of complexity can only be handled with economic systems that permit innovation, flexibility and local control, moving the world relentlessly toward the "free enterprise" feature that forms one component of Democratic Free Enterprise.

The other major imperative is the equally important need to foster the growth of collaborative institutions that integrate communities, global corporations and the entire world into some form of unified order. A rich diversity may be inevitable, but collaboration is also essential to create productive synergy out of these disparate elements. One of the most powerful new ideas today is that earnest cooperation far outperforms adversarial relationships because the dynamics of a knowledge-based society favor "positive-sum" relations over "zero-sum" relations. This unyielding imperative drives the second principle of "democracy" that forms the model of Democratic Free Enterprise.

So the transformation to a new world order should be characterized by both "divergence and convergence," or what some call "differentiation and integration." Where the force of growing complexity requires entrepreneurial freedom to accommodate diversity, there is an equivalent need for democratic collaboration to hold these explosive differences together so as to avoid destructive conflict and instead produce economic gains.

These twin imperatives are now fueling an international race of economic experimentation among corporations and entire nations to discover the principles of success for a very difficult world that lies ahead – as if the planet had become a great social laboratory working to unlock the secrets of the post-industrial future. Vast uncertainties abound in this frontier that nobody really understands very well, but my guess is that those who successfully perfect this unique blend of both democracy and free enterprise should lead the transition to an Information Age.

Notes

1 These trends cannot be adequately substantiated here because this brief article simply provides a broad conceptual overview. Some references are noted, but only to cite the source of quotes and other specific points. For fuller information see the author's book, *The New Capitalism* (Wiley, New York, 1986).

2 "A new era for management," *Business Week*, April 25, 1983.

3 N. McCrae, "Intrapreneur now," *The Economist*, April 17, 1982. The GE executives are quoted by Laura Landro, "Electric switch," *The Wall Street Journal*, July 12, 1982.

4 See Jerome Rosow and Robert Zager, "Punch out the time clocks," *Harvard Business Review*, March–April, 1983; and Gifford Pinchot, *Intrapreneuring* (Harper and Row, New York, 1984).

5 "It's rush hour for telecommuting," *Business Week*, January 23, 1984.

6 P. Drucker, *Preparing Tomorrow's Business Leaders Today* (Prentice-Hall, Englewood Cliffs, NJ, 1969), p. 77.

7 D. Bok, *President's Report*, Harvard University, 1977–78.

8 Charles F. Kiefer and Peter M. Senge, "Metanoic organizations in the transition to a sustainable society," *Technological Forecasting and Social Change*, October 1982, p. 122.

9 Charles Mathias, "We're ignoring the outside world," *The Washington Post*, January 22, 1984.

10 George Will, "Where socialists seem bent on suicide," *The Washington Post*, October 2, 1984.

11 T. Wirth, "A democratic policy agenda for the future," *The Wall Street Journal*, October 19, 1982.

12 S. Karson, "An appeal to the Presidential candidates," *Response*, January 1984.

13 S. Asao, "Myths and realities of Japan's industrial policies," *The Wall Street Journal*, October 24, 1983.

14 George Steiner and John Miner, *Management Policy and Strategy* (Macmillan, New York, 1977), p. 46.

15 Reagan's comments were reported in "Hardening the line," *Time*, March 21, 1983; and Andropov's in Dusko Doder, "Soviets offer to cut warheads," *The Washington Post*, May 4, 1984.

16 R. Barnet, "We need new rules," *The Washington Post*, January 20, 1980.

17 See "Capitalism in China," *Business Week*, January 14, 1985.

18 Dusko Doder, "Soviet study urges economic changes," *The Washington Post*, August 3, 1983.

19 For an excellent summary of the "convergence theory," see Clark Kerr, *The Future of Industrial Societies* (Harvard University Press, Cambridge, MA, 1983).

20 F. Loeser, "Communism won't change until the party machine goes," *The Washington Post*, August 19, 1984.

Teledemocracy Reconsidered

F. Christopher Arterton

Will the new communications technologies transform citizen participation in politics? The term "teledemocracy" has been used to describe the possible creation of direct democracy through the use of high-tech gadgetry. But after closely examining some 13 teledemocracy projects, the author concludes that a major transformation of our political system is unlikely – although new technologies can be used to improve participation in some respects. F. Christopher Arterton is Dean of the Graduate School of Political Management in New York City and this is an excerpt from his book Teledemocracy: Can Technology Protect Democracy? *(Sage, Newbury Park, CA, 1987).*

What could the developments of cable television, satellites, computer networks, and videotex mean for our political life? Does it matter politically whether the television industry is dominated by three national networks or fragmented into a host of channels on the basis of specialized programming tastes? Can we envision possibilities for improving our political institutions by using emerging technologies to promote citizen participation in public policy-making? Can the communications revolution deliver on the unfulfilled promise of television by creating a vibrant citizenship in America? Can push-button democracy become a practical reality?

The proponents

A few prominent forecasters and thinkers have begun to argue that we stand on the threshold of a major transformation of our political system. Not only will the emerging technologies of communication make possible new forms of association and political discourse, they will also unleash strong forces for political change. John Naisbitt (1982) and Alvin Toffler (1980), to cite two popular "futurists," take the view that a "communications revolution" will transform our politics. Electronics will enable a vast polity to function like a New England town meeting in which citizens can hear and contribute to the community discussion of issues. Electronic voting will both make possible and stimulate the holding of referenda or plebiscites. Citizens will be able to decide matters for themselves rather than surrendering decision-making power to representatives.

Toffler and Naisbitt write of this trend as inexorable. They are joined by Ted Becker (1981, p. 8) who predicts that "public opinion will become the law of the land." Becker and Scarce (1984), Barber (1982, 1984a, 1984b), Hollander (1985), Martin (1978), Tydeman et al. (1982, p. 265), Williams (1982), and Wolff (1976) are more cautious in their predictions of the inevitability of this transformation, but they are no less persuaded of the desirability of such a change.

The advocates of "teledemocracy" – as this evolution is being called – have, nevertheless, given little attention to the process by which such a transformation will come about. The evidence cited by Toffler and Naisbitt is largely anecdotal and nonsystematic. They gathered reports of many instances in which technology had underwritten participation, often accepting uncritically the claims of the project initiators. By reciting numerous examples, they appear to argue that accelerating experimentation will perfect ways of using the technology and will generate broad demand in society for replacing or modifying existing institutions so as to increase the power exercised directly by citizens.

Frederick Williams (1982, p. 199) appears to view these two processes of change as one:

The political order of nations is being rapidly transformed from the written document and spoken word to an electronic communications network enveloping everyone. The new political order is the communications structure. . . . The new communication technologies offer the opportunity for citizen information and participation undreamed of by our Founding Fathers . . . we may have to adjust our democracy away from the constraints of the eighteenth century and toward the advantages of the twenty-first.

For some, like Williams (1982) and Hollander (1985), the engines of this political revolution are the technologies themselves. Recognizing that modern telecommunications can permit large numbers of citizens to register their preferences, some contend that direct legislation "by the people" is inevitable. For others, the argument is that a communications revolution will generate a new social class that will restructure political institutions to its liking. In unison they argue that our current political institutions – parties, representative legislatures, bureaucratic agencies – will prove increasingly incapable of dealing with the demands of a large and ever more complex society. Valaskakis and Arnopoulis (1982) are a little more specific; they believe the communications revolution will generate a class of information producers and transmitters. As this group increasingly occupies a dominant position in society, its members will develop an interest in and the power to reshape political institutions and processes. They will naturally seek to ensure that information exchange becomes the basis for the new polity, though the precise institutional form cannot be predicted now.

Becker and Scarce (1984) argue that through teledemocracy experiments in direct democracy, "the representative system itself can be substantially improved by augmenting it through imaginative and bold uses of telecommunications." But they also conclude that "The participatory democracy movement . . . has advanced as present forms of government have weakened under the stress of size, increasing demands upon them, citizen dissatisfaction, and growing awareness that the people on the street are often as capable of making decisions as their 'representative' (p. 29)."

The most elaborate proposal for experimenting with institutional transformation has been advanced by Benjamin Barber in *Strong Democracy* (1984a). If new mechanisms – such as a lottery system of elections or a civic videotex service provided as a free channel by every cable company – were gradually put into place, citizens would learn the civic values of public responsibility and involvement. The result would be a stronger form of participatory democracy, though one in which many of the present representative institutions still functioned. Barber believes that the idea of true self-government would take root, producing "a campaign to win the substance of citizenship promised but never conferred by the victory of the vote." He offers ten proposals that, if adopted wholesale, would provide sufficient checks to safeguard democracy, whereas if adopted piecemeal they might be used to undermine democracy.

Thus even within the small community of those advocating the use of technology to strengthen democracy, one finds differences of emphasis and elaboration. They all agree, however, that the decline of participant behavior is a sign that our political institutions are not functioning adequately to meet today's needs. They tie the observed drop in voting to cynical and alienated attitudes produced by "an ever more meaningless and weak form of democracy" (Barber, 1984b). And they propose that the remedy lies in making citizen participation more abundant and more effective, aided by communications technologies.

Most of their speculation has revolved around the possibility of conducting votes or plebiscites electronically so that decisions could be made by all the people. Barber calls for both a national initiative and referendum process and experimentation with electronic balloting. Hollander (1985) believes that local experimentation with "video votes" will increase and gradually create a climate of legitimacy surrounding electronic plebiscites. Then, the stage will be set for national legislation that will create the legal authority for what he calls "video democracy." Wolff (1976) calls for a system of national voting through an unspecified electronic system linked to television. Becker's experiments with "teledemocracy" involve voting via telephone lines by a randomly selected sample of citizens who have been given detailed information and sufficient time to consider their choices.

But voting is only one form of citizen participation. With the exception of Barber, whose ideas go well beyond voting, less attention has been directed toward other ways in which technology might be used to promote participatory politics. The potentials are also significant for using modern hardware to forge closer bonds among individuals and groups (Laudon, 1984). The emerging telecommunication systems could be harnessed to make possible the exchange of large volumes of written and visual information (Blomquist, 1984) and to permit citizens to advocate their viewpoints to others either individually or in groups. By so doing, the role of citizen participation in the processes of agenda formation and policy determination might be expanded.

Using new telecommunication technology for electronic plebiscites, though no mean feat, would be functionally equivalent to placing a polling booth in every person's home or workplace. Some hope this might reverse the downward trend in voter turnout. The state of Oregon, for example, has had considerable success in increasing turnout by allowing citizens to vote in local bond issues by mailed ballots. Even so, such uses do not come close to tapping the participatory potential of more rapid and convenient information exchange. Recall that interest group membership, campaign work, writing to elected officials, and engaging in political discussion are fuller, and often more effective, forms of participation in politics than mere voting. Therefore, why should electronic referenda be the ultimate goal for the political application of telecommunication technologies? Voting is a limited notion of participation, whether by means of a paper ballot, a voting machine, a computer punch card, or an electronic box. The new technologies certainly have important applications here, but they can also be used more ambitiously. They can be used to facilitate the means by which citizens communicate with each other and with their chosen leaders. Communication, dialogue and information exchange are, after all, the cornerstone of an informed body politic.

The critics

As in most topics relating to political processes, the advocacy of teledemocracy has not gone unchallenged. Critics such as Elstain (1982), Gitlin (1981), Malbin (1982), Pool (1973b), and Laudon (1977, 1984) argue that direct democracy would be unworkable even with instantaneous, universal communications. For example, Laudon argues that putting citizens into greater contact with leaders also provides those leaders with greater direct access to citizens. He fears that public accountability will be lessened by the great inequalities of power in such a relationship. Without an intermediating stratum of secondary leadership to provide alternative opinions and information, the result could be less democracy, in the sense of less power, initiative, volition, and alternative choices for citizens.

Jean Elstain (1982, p. 108) expands this argument by strongly rejecting the contention that voting can be equated with real democracy. She notes that authoritarian politics can be carried out "under the guise of, or with the convenience of, majority opinion. That opinion can be registered by easily manipulated, ritualistic plebiscites." Beyond aggregated opinions that cannot constitute a civic culture, she points to our need for a deliberative process, involving discussion with other citizens, developing a shared sense of moral responsibility for society, and enhancing individual action and identity through mutual involvement. She reserves a special ire for systems, such as Warner-Amex's Qube, through which citizens participate as autonomous individuals, systems that privatize what should be a social discourse.

Ithiel Pool (1973b) adds to our understanding by pointing out that teledemocracy will complicate the policy-making process considerably since public consultation will inevitably be time-consuming and costly and will raise the prospect for stymie. In the process, policy matters will become more visible and public concerns heightened. He then puts his finger on a critical dilemma for teledemocracy:

> The more intense and real the involvement that electronic feedback creates for the citizen in public affairs, the more crucial it is to limit the scope of its operation and what is affected. If citizens are brought, by effective personal participation, to the point of caring very deeply about political outcomes, then there had better not be too many important political decisions, for every time one is made there are losers as well as winners (1973b, p. 244).

There are other arguments that can be raised against direct democracy, technologically induced or not. One results from the fact that citizens vary dramatically in the intensity with which they desire certain public outcomes. A majoritarian solution does not handle very adequately circumstances in which a majority is lukewarm in its support for one alternative and a minority ardently desires another. Another frequently voiced complaint is that many citizens do not care deeply about political matters and will refuse to become involved. Others argue that, even when they are interested, average citizens cannot possibly master all the details that go into policy decisions. Congressmen, for example, are full-time policy-makers yet even they have to specialize in a limited range of issues. Finally, there is the fear that the public will be irresponsible and fickle in its support of different policies; majorities will form and rapidly dissipate, policy will shift with ephemeral public opinion.

Proponents and opponents often talk past each other on different levels. The former, accepting without question the normative proposition that individuals and groups should decide for themselves, concentrate their attention on the fact that hardware may overcome the problems created by large numbers of citizens. In their view, the sole justification for representative institutions is that they constitute an expedient compromise necessary to make democracy feasible in large-scale societies. This rationale will be removed by the communications capabilities of emerging technologies.

Meanwhile, the critics of direct "teledemocracy," considering this problem on a theoretical and institutional level rather than as a normative assertion, argue that representative machinery is necessary to ameliorate divisive conflicts over political interest, to contain political ambition, to balance inequalities of participation and knowledge, and to safeguard minority rights.

The proponents and critics of direct, electronically induced democracy agree that declining rates of political participation – principally voting – and high levels of cynicism and civic distrust constitute severe threats to the health of the American political system. The question for both is whether modern communications can eliminate this cancer. While the answer of those advocating a transformation of our political institutions toward direct democracy is clear, their critics are less unified. After rehearsing the impact of changes brought by television, some of them feel that technological change cannot offer much of an improvement. Other critics of direct democracy wish to harness these new media to improve and strengthen existing representative institutions.

Here we encounter a different version of teledemocracy that has not received a great deal of attention. Even the most staunch defender of the status quo will admit that our political institutions do exhibit some problems that might be mitigated by technology. Low rates of citizen involvement is one such problem. A related concern results from the vast inequalities in participation across different social classes. Less well-off citizens simply are not as involved in political matters as are the more wealthy and better educated. Presumably, the outcomes of politics more closely reflect the preferences and wishes of those who are involved. Perhaps communications technologies can be used to redress this bias.

Consider another problem in the functioning of our political institutions that technology might help. Political figures often confront difficulties in surmounting the institutions that ostensibly they direct. Bureaucracies can become powerful filters of information, isolating elected leadership from the citizens they represent. Legislators frequently find themselves surrounded by staff, lobbyists, and interest groups who purportedly speak for the public. In these circumstances, communications media may be useful in putting representatives in direct contact with their constituents. Enhancing their capacity to respond to citizens will, however, potentially expand their capacity to influence the public; as Pool (1973) notes, electronic manipulation is the other side of the electronic democracy coin.

Neither side of the debate over teledemocracy, however, has much systematic evidence to support its assumptions about the potential of telecommunications media for strengthening political participation. This present study was first conceived because the arguments over teledemocracy raised some very important issues for American democracy, and yet both sides of the debate lacked factual information. Rather than speculating broadly about the benefits or detriments of using technology to strengthen democracy, I set out to investigate systematically a number of teledemocracy projects, instances in which communications media have actually been used to encourage citizen involvement. I wanted to find out how the media have been used and what the consequences have been.

The participation projects

For this article, I will analyze thirteen different projects in which elites set out to encourage political activity by citizens. Analytically, these projects constitute a degree of tinkering or experimenting with various institutional arrangements for containing political participation. As such, they take a different approach than that employed by most academic writings on participation, that gives attention to explanations of the ways individuals behave. By examining the institutional context within which participation occurs, we may gain insights beyond the numerical instance of participation, moving on to investigate the quality and effectiveness of citizen involvement.

Many of the projects studied were demonstration or pilot projects deliberately conceived to research the possibilities offered by new technology. About half of them, however, were serious attempts to establish new mechanisms that would involve the public more extensively in public policy formation.

Alaska's legislative teleconferencing network State legislative committees can take testimony from citizens scattered all over our largest state. The system is supplemented by a computer network containing information about pending legislation and amendments and the timing of floor and committee action. Electronic mail messages may be sent via the computer network to legislators in Juneau.

Alternatives for Washington From 1974 to 1976, then Governor Daniel Evans of Washington organized a planning project to consider future directions across a range of state policy issues. A group of citizens, nominated by political leaders and interest groups, was assembled to discuss future directions in detail. Their work was subsequently submitted to broad public choice in the form of mailed back newspaper ballots. The project also solicited citizen participation in the form of numerous community meetings, questionnaires, and telephone polls.

Berks Community Television (BCTV) Located in Reading, Pennsylvania, BCTV provides city and county officials with regular opportunities to discuss via a cable channel their policies and actions with citizens who telephone questions and complaints to the studio. In addition to "electronic office hours," Reading public officials frequently hold official hearings to discuss and solicit citizen input in their planning processes.

Choices for '76 Designed in 1973 to facilitate planning in the New York metropolitan region, Choices for '76 consisted of five films aired on 18 stations in the New York area. Citizens returned ballots printed in local newspapers covering five different regional issues.

Computer conferences on The Source and EIES   Computer conferences are just beginning to emerge as a communications vehicle open to a growing number of owners of personal and minicomputers. The Electronic Information Exchange System (EIES) and The Source Tele-computing Corporation (STC) provide to the public the most extensively used computer conferencing systems open to their subscribers. I examined both the political content of open conferences and the pattern of participation within discussions of public policy issues.

Des Moines Health Vote '82   Sponsored by the Public Agenda Forum in December 1982, Health Vote '82 involved a substantial proportion of the Des Moines, Iowa, community in a sophisticated campaign combining public relations skills with a detailed presentation of the significant trade-offs in health care service delivery. Citizens returned ballots printed in the Des Moines Register.

Domestic policy association: national issues forum   The Domestic Policy Association (DPA), a joint project of the Kettering Foundation and the Public Agenda Foundation, stages each fall a nationwide series of community meetings or issue forums to discuss and debate three selected policy matters each year. After the local meetings have concluded, the DPA holds a large, national meeting in which representatives from around the country can discuss these same matters with "decision makers" linked through a satellite distributed videoconference to an increasingly large number of sites around the country.

Hawaii Televote   Actually the Televote project is a series of discrete efforts undertaken by Professor Ted Becker at the University of Hawaii. First, a random sample of citizens are telephoned and asked if they are willing to participate in the vote. The project staff sends those who agree ballots and information describing all aspects of the selected policy question. They are given a certain interval to read about the topic and to consider and discuss it with others. Finally, the participants either call in to cast their votes or are called back by the project's initiators.

Honolulu electronic town meetings   The electronic town meetings in Hawaii combine television shows on the pro's and con's of a particular issue with two forms of voting. Citizens who wish to express an opinion are able to participate by mailing back the ballots from the newspapers or by calling in to register their opinions during and after the broadcast.

Markey's "electure"   From December 1983 to February 1984, subscribers to The Source Telecomputing Network could participate in an "electure" lead by Congressman Edward Markey (D-Mass). By entering his position papers into a computer conference, Markey initiated a series of discussions on different aspects of American nuclear arms policy. Those who joined the conference could react to his thoughts and those of other contributors.

MINERVA electronic town meeting   Designed by a sociologist (Amitai Etzioni) and an engineer, MINERVA was an attempt to broaden participation in the regular meetings of a community group without diminishing the quality of participation. Panelists discussed the various aspects of an issue over a cable access channel serving the apartment complex, and residents could walk to a convenient room in order to videotape their response to the presentation or the comments of others. At the end of this electronically mediated discussion, viewers were asked to fill out a questionnaire in which they stated their response to the show, their opinions as to how the matter should be handled, and their satisfaction with the experiment.

North Carolina's OPEN/net　North Carolina's OPEN/net is a continuing project of the state's Agency for Public Telecommunications. Weekly three-hour shows are produced on matters under consideration by various legislative and executive agencies and are distributed by satellites to over 50 cable systems around the state. During the first half, viewers watch an unedited, videotaped meeting or hearing in which state government officials deal with a pending policy matter. Then, citizens from around the state have an opportunity to telephone comments, complaints or questions to studio guests who are usually the key decision makers in the areas under consideration.

Upper Arlington town meeting over Qube　Installed by Warner–Amex in Columbus, Ohio, as part of its franchise agreements, the Qube interactive system gave the paying subscriber a box of push buttons with which to signal a response to questions posed during a cablecast. A central computer quickly processed the results, allowing viewers and others interested to learn the outcome of such a poll instantaneously. One of the most dramatic uses of Qube involved a four-hour planning meeting held in the Columbus suburb of Upper Arlington. A presentation by the Planning Board on traffic and zoning problems evoked considerable discussion and a high level of "voting" over Qube by the town's residents.

Lessons from the teledemocracy projects

The 13 teledemocracy experiments examined were divided conceptually. First, some projects placed government officials on the receiving end of citizen participation, while others did not. Where public figures were involved, the organizers appeared to be interested in setting up the conditions in which citizens might directly influence public policy. When public officials were not involved, the project initiators were most likely to emphasize the value of civic education. The second dichotomy involved the nature of the participant act: some experiments encouraged dialogues and others staged plebiscites. This distinction reflects differences in the project organizers' belief about the nature of politics. Some feel that its essence involves disputes among competing groups that must be harmonized; others believe that a common will exists among the citizenry and must be made manifest by citizen participation in plebiscites.

Behind this schema lies the formative principle that the goals and values of teledemocracy organizers are more important in understanding the differences among projects than are the technologies employed. I could have described these projects according to the media (broadcast television versus cable versus computer networks). But a technology-based schema would not have been nearly as insightful.

In any case, an effort to evaluate projects – grouped under four rubrics and employing six different technologies – along 11 different dimensions of participation is not likely to yield a single, simple conclusion. Can telecommunication technologies be used to improve the quantity and quality of citizen participation in politics? Yes. Can these uses also mitigate the inequalities now found in the rates of participation of different social groups? Yes. Do these projects collectively point toward one technology that best facilitates participation? No. Does this research suggest that technological change will produce an inevitable transition of our political institutions toward direct democracy? No. Can teledemocracy contribute to the functioning of America's political institutions? It depends upon what you mean by "teledemocracy."

The most straightforward manner of summarizing our conclusions from these investigations is to group them according to whether they are consequences of the technology or derived from the social planning of the project initiators.

Before doing so, however, I should restate succinctly the major limitations of the research. First, I have not examined all applications of technology to political communication. I have observed only instances designed to elicit citizen participation. The internal use of video-conferencing by interest groups, or the rapidly increasing sharing of data across levels of our federal system, to cite two examples, fall outside our purview. Second, the projects selected for study are all instances in which the organizers took an "outcome neutral" posture; they sought to encourage involvement as a value in its own right. The electronic ministers, the Chamber of Commerce, or the expanding apparatus at the Republican National Committee were excluded from this analysis. Third, rather than predicting the use of communication technologies that may become available in the future, I have tried to remain empirical, studying actual situations in which technology has been used. While some of the projects studied are on the forefront of technological developments, many of them are really jury-rigged efforts to use existing technologies, rather than experiments in "hi-tech" politics.

In truth, I cannot maintain a tidy separation between developments induced by hardware and those produced by the initiator's objectives. Abstractly, we confront a range of causes from those that are more dependent on the physical capabilities of technology to those that are primarily a result of the values brought to the exercise by participants and organizers. There is no pure case of technological imperative; when we speak of a communications medium, we refer to more than hardware. For example, beyond the transmission of sound, the telephone as a medium refers to private messages exchanged between individuals, near universal service, and monopoly utilities regulated as to rates and service, protected from liability for the messages they transmit, and unable to determine or limit access. In short, a huge number of value choices are already implicit in the regulatory policies under which a medium is established. Those who would use a given media such as the telephone to encourage partic-ipation must accept these inherent value choices as their starting point. But one should not pretend that those uses are purely a product of the technology of telephony. The most one can do in this situation is to discuss here those factors that *primarily* depend upon the capacities of the technology and the characteristics of the communications media.

Each medium has a distinctly different capacity to reach people. Some succeed in engaging a large, diffuse audience; others reach a much smaller group with definable characteristics; still others can be used to contact almost everybody, but they do so one at a time. Many of the new media are "semipublic" in that they are available to the broad public but, practically, because of choices made by receivers, they reach only limited segments of their potential audience. Others are "semiprivate" in that the sender can designate recipients, but the emerging tech-nology can include vastly more people in these conduits than can a point-to-point medium.

Political actors use these different media for accomplishing different tasks, according to these characteristics.

Plebiscites demand broad-gauged mass media. For these purposes, the communications media as they currently exist in the United States are less than ideal. Events such as the attempted assassination of Ronald Reagan amply demonstrate that the mechanisms do exist to communicate to all our citizens relatively rapidly. But an analogy drawn from times of crisis does not conform to the requirements of a functioning political system. As currently structured, the media available in the United States simply cannot be used to conduct the extensive and more-or-less continuous efforts that would be necessary to allow citizens to express their views of policy questions on a daily basis.

Among the projects examined, competition for the attention of potential voters has been the most persistent problem encountered by project organizers, especially by those who have sought to conduct plebiscites. The plethora of media is the single most difficult institutional barrier they face. The organizers of projects such as the Honolulu Electronic Town Meetings, Alternatives for Washington, Choices for '76, or the Des Moines Health Vote, have commandeered broadcast television because that medium has the most extensive reach to the citizenry. Their experience, however, documents that despite the capabilities of the medium, repetition and the use of multiple channels are necessary to involve anything approaching all the people. The most successful of these plebiscitarian projects, the Des Moines Health Vote, relied upon frequent public service advertisements, newspaper articles, radio talk shows, and even billboards and bus placards in addition to top public affairs broadcast programming. Yet even Health Vote had sharp limitations that circumscribe the degree to which it met the requirements of an effective, ongoing political system. It was a one-time effort staged over a lengthy time interval (to allow more opportunity to reach citizens and stimulate their thinking). It was concentrated upon a single policy area in a definable media market. And it proved to be expensive and taxing. The project amply demonstrated the capacity of technology to involve citizens in policy discussions, but it also documented how costly and extensive are the exertions needed to achieve even a 25 percent rate of involvement.

Can these projects serve as a model for a fully developed, effective political system? Evidently not. Consider the fact that, at present, broadcast channels require "roadblocking" and considerable repetition, which necessitates either substantial financial expenditures or a level of cooperation from private broadcasters that seems unlikely.

Moreover, the direction of change in the communications industry appears to be in a direction that will complicate the management of effective plebiscites. That is, competition for the communications industry is expanding the number of available channels. A larger number of conduits will aggravate the problems of getting the public's attention.

Perhaps the communications revolution will, as Barber (1984) suggests, allow society to establish a completely separate conduit reserved for political information exchange and voting. The problem then will become whether citizens are interested enough in public affairs to pay attention to this conduit, given all the other streams of information and entertainment available. These projects emphatically illustrate that public life is in a severe, and often losing, competition with other aspects of individual and social activity.

The evolution of the communications industry appears, on the other hand, to be improving the prospects for "pluralist" forms of teledemocracy. For example, in North Carolina and

Reading, public officials reach out to solicit constituent opinions using semipublic cable channels. While the technology may look much like a plebiscite (television programming out, telephone calls in), the difference is really one of expectation. Since everyone knows that the cable medium reaches a small audience, the organizers cannot pretend that they are receiving back the "voice of the people."

The more innovative experiments involve the political uses of semiprivate media. The legislature of Alaska, for example, holds committee hearings over a voice-only tele-conferencing network and citizens who wish to testify must go to one of 71 sites located throughout the vast state where those state-owned facilities are located. Computer conferences have been arranged allowing a congressman to discuss arms control policy with a limited group of citizens. Another congressman held videoconferences with constituents back home in California.

In addition, the evolving mix of communications media appears to be more conducive to the development of stronger interest groups; they will be able to use these narrower, private links to mobilize their membership. For example, several national interest groups now hold strategy sessions with affiliate state-level organizations to map out a lobbying strategy by a video-conference. As a result, any effective mechanism for embracing citizen participation will have to build into its design a positive role for interest groups and pluralist politics.

At present, however, there is still a long way to go before we reach the point at which the available media will be ideal for pluralist dialogues. Many of the efforts studied here employed cable television and a call-in format – mechanisms that are not totally satisfactory. The televised call-in has the potential of reaching large numbers of citizens, yet the number who can voice their opinions via the feedback loop is quite small.

If the currently available conduits are inadequate, what of the future? Audio- and video-conferencing hold better prospects for the few-to-few pattern of communication that is needed for a detailed, interactive exchange of views. In the process, they also give citizens much greater agenda-setting powers than does network television. But they impose additional burdens upon citizen participants over the convenience of cable television: they require that those who would become involved travel to a meeting site. The Alaska example demonstrates that in order to surmount (or reduce) these burdens, systems employing video- or audio-conferencing need to be backstopped by a staff specifically responsible for reaching out to potential participants.

Videotex and computer conferencing may become a suitable middle ground. Videotex can certainly convey outward a substantial amount of information about policy matters and can collect inward opinions from a substantial number of participants. The "voice" given partic-ipants may range from a simple yes/no choice to the opportunity for an individual citizen to poll the opinions of everyone else. That citizens have greater control over the timing and extent of information provided them is another benefit of these systems. Computer con-ferencing, moreover, facilitates horizontal exchange of information permitting citizens to organize politically or negotiate a set of common interests.

Videotex and computer conferencing systems, however, will also exhibit limitations as vehicles of political discourse. As a medium of dialogue, each of these vehicles may be conveniently used by modest numbers of communicators; the emerging technologies do not promise that everyone can have his or her individual say in a national dialogue. Another major problem, shared with cable television, is that videotex and computer conferencing carry material pertaining to a wide variety of human activity. As a result, in a single medium, politics comes into direct competition with these other facets of life for the attention of citizens. Many citizens may choose to spend their time in front of the computer screen engaging in commercial activity or being entertained rather than discussing or influencing politics.

At present, moreover, access to these systems is so severely limited by cost that they cannot be considered practical, and this condition will probably last for a substantial period of time (Blomquist, 1984). Yet they do promise a reduction in the inconveniences associated with the present state of audio- and videoconferencing, and, at the same time, they will permit a more extensive amount of feedback than systems employing the telephone. While they may greatly ease the mechanical problems of conducting plebiscites, they provide no solution to the political problems that this research has documented in plebiscites. Instead, they offer the prospect of facilitating genuine government-to-citizen dialogue patterned on the pluralist model of politics generated by self-interest and self-initiative rather than the populist-plebiscitarian perspective.

The principal observed impact of the use of technology for democratic politics is to reduce the costs and burdens of participation for citizens. These costs may be financial or they may be associated with time, travel, and information necessary to participate politically. Technology does not, however, reduce these costs and burdens across the board. In financial terms, communications technology can be very expensive.

Another important point, however, can be gleaned from the relationship between technology and the costs of participation. Across the range of project designs, technology served to distribute the burdens between those who would elicit participation and citizens who might become involved. Generally speaking, the lower the burdens placed on citizens, the greater the demands (both financial and in an obligatory sense) upon project organizers. For example, where the news media are used to "spoon feed" citizens the information they need to consider a policy matter, the initiators must assume consequentially higher duties of inclusiveness, fairness, and balance in presenting that information. Similarly, through electronic voting systems, a much larger number of citizens can be induced to participate in a plebiscite than will attend a discussion; but the organizers of plebiscites must be held to higher standards of openness in view of their more substantial control over the agenda of policy considered.

I am speaking conceptually of costs and burdens, and accordingly cannot come to any simple additive notion of whether the costs to society as a whole are reduced or simply redistributed by technology. Clearly, if institutions that have functioned quite smoothly through direct human contact now begin employing technology to conduct communications, they may incur additional costs of operation. There is no evidence that technology can open up the political process while saving money.

But since citizen participation has been rather low in these traditional mechanisms and inequitably distributed across social classes, the advantages of using the emerging communications technology to allocate costs and burdens away from citizens appear rather clear. The principal questions involve the nature of participation that can be encouraged and the institutional patterns that are most successful for generating citizen involvement.

Conclusion

These investigations of 13 different experiments provide greater support for a conception of teledemocracy in which technology is used to underwrite representative processes and a pluralist conception of political interest. Ultimately, of course, the choice remains a normative judgment. But where does this leave us? The use of communications technology to promote this notion of teledemocracy offers us only a slight improvement over the widely recognized difficulties that characterize our present political institutions. On the whole, however, settling for modest improvements may be more satisfactory than yearning for a miraculous technological fix for these problems. On the basis of evidence presented here, such a dramatic cure appears to be largely unfounded. Instead, we may take some comfort from the finding that technology can ease some of the major problems in American democracy. Teledemocracy offers us improvements in democracy, not a major transformation nor a final fulfillment.

References

Barber, B.J. (1982), "The second American Revolution," *Channels*, vol. 2(1).

Barber, B.J. (1984a), *Strong Democracy: Participatory Politics for a New Age;* Berkeley, CA: University of California Press.

Barber, B.J. (1984b), "Voting is not enough," *Atlantic Monthly, June*, pp. 45–52.

Becker, T.L. (1981), "Teledemocracy: Bringing power back to the people," *Futurist*, vol. 15(6), pp. 6–9.

Becker, T.L. and Scarce, R. (1983), "Teledemocracy: Past, present, future," Honolulu: University of Hawaii, mimeo.

Blomquist, D. (1984) "The more things change . . . Videotex and American politics," paper presented at the annual meetings of the American Political Science Association, Washington, DC, August, 30–September, 2.

Elstain, J.B. (1982), "Democracy and the Qube tube," *The Nation*, August 7–14, pp. 180–10.

Gitlin, T. (1981), "New video technology: Pluralism or banality," *Democracy*, October, pp. 60–76.

Hollander, R. (1985), *Video Democracy: The Vote-from-home Revolution*, Mt Airy, MD: Lomond.

Laudon, K.C. (1977), *Communications Technology and Democratic Participation*, New York: Praeger Special Studies.

Laudon, K.C. (1984), "New possibilities for participation in the democratic process," in K.W. Grewlich and F.H. Pederson (eds), *Power and Participation in an Information Society*, Luxembourg: Commission of European Communities.

Malbin, M. (1982), "Teledemocracy and its discontents," *Public Opinion*, June–July, pp. 57–8.

Martin, J. (1978), *The Wired Society*, Englewood Cliffs, NJ: Prentice-Hall.

Naisbitt, J. (1982), *Megatrends: Ten New Directions Transforming our Lives*, New York: Warner Brothers.

Pool, I. de Sola (1973b), "Citizen feedback in political philosophy," in I. de Sola Pool (ed), *Talking back: Citizen Feedback and Cable Technology, Cambridge*, MA: MIT Press.

Toffler, A. (1980), *The Third Wave*, New York: Bantam.

Tydeman, J., Lipinski, H., Alder, R., et al. (1982), *Teletex and Videotex in the United States: Market Potential, Technology and Public Policy Issues*, New York: McGraw-Hill.

Valaskakis, K., and Arnopoulis, P. (1982), *Telecommunitary Democracy: Utopian Vision or Probable Future*, Montreal: McGill and Montreal Universities, Gamma Research Service.

Williams, F. (1982), *The Communications Revolution*, New York: New American Library.

Wolff, R.P. (1976), *In Defense of Anarchy*, New York: Harper Colophon.

The Dangers of Information Control

John Shattuck and Muriel Morisey Spence

We're told that information is power and that we now live in an "Information Society", so it's not surprising that governments have taken an interest. In this disturbing article, the authors argue that an unprecedented web of new government rules is limiting the free exchange of information and ideas in the United States. This is justified by national security and the desire to save money. John Shattuck is Lecturer at the Harvard Law School and Muriel Morisey Spence is Director of Policy Analysis in the Office of Government, Community, and Public Affairs at Harvard University. Reprinted from Technology Review, *April 1988.*

For the past decade, the federal government has established a network of policies that restrict the availability, shape the content, and limit the communication of information. This net includes an expanded classification system, limits on the exchange of unclassified information, the use of export controls to restrict technical data, and restraints on contacts between US and foreign citizens. The architects of the new policy have also curtailed the role of government in both collecting and publishing many categories of scientific and statistical information.

The cumulative impact has been to restrain academic freedom, hamper technological progress, and undermine democratic decision-making. Consider the following examples:

- In 1983 the White House issued a directive requiring more than 120,000 government employees with access to classified materials to sign a lifetime agreement: they would submit for prior clearance any material they wished to publish.
- In 1985, the Department of Defense (DoD) required the Society of Photo-Optical Instrumentation Engineers (SPIE) to restrict attendance at a conference where unclassified papers would be presented to US and Canadian citizens and permanent US residents. Scientists allowed to attend had to sign an "Export Controlled DoD Technical Data Agreement," promising that they would obtain an export license before sharing information from the conference with foreign citizens.
- The Federal Communications Commission (FCC) decided in 1986 to publish its proposed actions in the Federal Register only in summary form, making public comment more difficult.

- The FBI has asked some librarians to report library users who might be "hostile intelligence people."
- In 1984, the Department of Housing and Urban Development (HUD) drafted a research contract with a Harvard scholar that would have required him to submit results of HUD–sponsored research for review six months before publication. The scholar would also have had to submit results on related work not funded by HUD. The contract would have given the agency the right to demand that the scholar make "corrections" in data, methodology, and analyses. After months of negotiation, Harvard decided to refuse the contract.

The trend toward greater control of information is predictable is some respects: information is an important national resource that the government understandably seeks to manage. Nevertheless, the government's efforts in these areas should be fundamentally different from its management of other public resources: it should be guided by a heavy presumption, based on the Constitution and our national history, that open communication and the free flow of information have great social utility. This presumption should be overcome only in particular cases where the government can show a substantial public necessity, such as a concrete risk to national security.

Advocates of extensive government control of information have relied on two justifications. The first is the need to protect national security – a concept that under the Reagan administration has become nearly limitless. The idea that broad categories of information must be kept from hostile ears and eyes has shaped a growing array of government decisions. This philosophy has supplanted the long and widely held view expressed by Vannevar Bush, President Truman's science advisor, that "a sounder foundation for our national security rests in a broad dissemination of scientific knowledge upon which further advances can more readily be made than in a policy of restrictions which would impede our further advances in the hope that our potential enemies will not catch up with us."

The second asserted justification for restrictive information controls is that the federal government must curtail its deficit spending and excessive regulation. The policies that result, however – including the FCC decision not to publish the complete text of its proposed rules – limit access to much information about government decision-making.

The negative effects of these policies could be substantial. As a 1982 report by the National Academy of Science (NAS) concluded, the continued health of US science requires open exchanges among researchers worldwide. The Soviet Union's experience illustrates the danger of a restrictive information policy. The American Physical Society cites official controls on scientific communication as the cause of the well-known Soviet lags in solid-state electronics and biology.

Restraints on the flow of scientific information can also hurt the US economy. An April 1987 NAS report indicates that controls on the export of manufactured goods and information cost the US economy 188,000 jobs and $9 billion a year. Exporters report sales losses to Japan and other nations because of these controls. And limits on the participation of foreign citizens in the US economy deprive the nation of needed foreign expertise. For example, 40 percent of all doctoral engineers entering the workforce every year are foreign citizens.

A further victim of controls, ironically, is likely to be US security itself, as the long-term technological progress on which it depends is impeded. Finally, if these trends persist, they will erode a long national tradition of free speech and public access to information.

The US tradition of openness

The pattern of government information controls is one of historical shifts between openness and secrecy. The US tradition of open communication stems from the Constitution, which guarantees freedom of speech, thought, religion, and the press. It also obliges the federal government to publish regularly information on its spending and taxing activities and their effects on the citizenry.

The late nineteenth century saw the beginnings of a long period of growth in the amount of economic and social data collected and circulated by government. During the first half of the twentieth century Congress repeatedly resisted efforts by the executive branch to impose official secrecy on the expanding number of federal agencies.

World War II ushered in an era of increased consciousness of national security and more restrictive information policies. President Roosevelt instituted procedures for classifying information in 1940, relying on a 1938 statute restricting public access to military installations, equipment, and "information relative thereto." World War II also prompted the founding of a large intelligence bureaucracy. After the war Congress gave agencies such as the Atomic Energy Commission and the Central Intelligence Agency authority to bar communication of some information to protect national security.

A countertrend toward more open government began with enactment of the Freedom of Information Act (FOIA) in 1966. Congress strengthened the FOIA in 1974, and two years later passed the Government in the Sunshine Act requiring federal agencies to open more of their meetings to the public. During the 1970s the Ford and Carter administrations both issued executive orders designed to curb the excessive secrecy of intelligence agencies over the previous decade.

Presidents Nixon and Carter also narrowed the classification system. In a far-reaching 1978 executive order, President Carter stipulated that even if information fell into one of seven restricted categories, it was not to be classified unless its unauthorized disclosure reasonably could be expected to cause "identifiable damage" to the national security. The order also called for documents to be automatically declassified after six years and prevented them from being reclassified. Significantly, information could not be restricted for the first time after an agency received a request for it under the Freedom of Information Act.

Meanwhile, demand for government information mushroomed with the expanding federal role in areas such as civil rights, environmental and consumer protection, public health and safety, and employment relations. This demand was spurred by a technological revolution that enabled both public and private sectors to store and disseminate growing amounts of information. But in the early 1980s, as demand for government-collected information continued to climb, the principles of public access again began to erode – this time to an unprecedented degree.

Expanding the classification system

The Reagan administration has used a panoramic definition of national security to justify an extensive network of restrictions on many categories of government information. Richard V.

Allen, former national security advisor to President Reagan, asserted in 1983 that national security "must include virtually every facet of international activity, including (but not limited to) foreign affairs, defense, intelligence, research and development policy, outer space, international economic and trade policy, and reaching deeply into the domains of the Departments of Commerce and Agriculture."

Supplementing this concept is the theory of an "information mosaic" – the idea that hostile elements can use sophisticated search techniques to assemble bits of seemingly harmless information into insights that threaten national security. An often-cited example of how this could be done is the blueprint for manufacturing an H-bomb published by *Progressive* magazine in 1979. The authors of the article amassed their information from unclassified data scattered through scientific journals.

Proponents of the mosaic theory have used it to fashion a broad expansion of the classification system. President Reagan issued a 1982 executive order giving federal officials authority to classify more information than ever before. Instead of having to demonstrate "identifiable damage" to national security, today officials need only point out that "disclosure reasonably could be expected to cause damage to the national security." The order created a new presumption in favor of classification when officials are in doubt about whether secrecy is necessary. It also eliminated the requirement that information be declassified within a prescribed length of time, and gave officials new authority to classify documents already in the public domain.

The Reagan system appears to allow classification to occur at any stage of a project and to be maintained indefinitely. The net effect could be to inhibit researchers from making long-term intellectual investments in fields that are likely to be classified at a later date, such as cryptography and laser science.

Language from a research contract with the Department of Energy reflects this new policy: "If the grantee believes any information developed or acquired may be classifiable, the grantee shall . . . protect such information as if it were classified." This provision places the burden on researchers to determine what data to withold, and does not specify how long they must comply. Such policies have prompted fears, in the words of one scholar, that "academic research not born classified may die classified." There is recent evidence that fears of retroactive classification are justified. In 1987 a federal appeals court upheld the National Security Agency's right to remove 33 documents from a library at the Virginia Military Institute.

New use for export controls

The current administration has used the export control laws to extend its sweeping view of national security. These laws – particularly the 1979 Export Administration Act – were enacted primarily to regulate the flow of goods and machinery. Yet they are increasingly being used to restrict the flow of intangible items such as unclassified technical information, both domestically and abroad. The asserted justification is that technical data are different from other information protected by the First Amendment because they can be used to create dangerous items such as weapons. And since technical information has immediate economic use, it resembles commodities more than ideas, according to this philosophy.

Such an outlook is new because there have traditionally been only two ways to restrict information. One is the classification system, for information controlled by government. The other is the doctrine of prior restraint, used for information not controlled by government in extraordinary circumstances involving a clear and present danger to national security. The government's burden of proof in such situations is very heavy, as illustrated by its unsuccessful effort to enjoin the *New York Times* from publishing the Pentagon Papers.

The Department of Defense has cited the export control laws in pressuring scientific societies to limit foreign access to DoD-sponsored research results – as evidenced by the restrictions on the 1985 meeting of the Photo-Optical Society. When the presidents of 12 leading scientific organizations – including the American Association for the Advancement of Science and the American Chemical Society – protested these restrictions, the administration attempted to clarify the situation. The White House issued National Security Decision Directive (NSDD) 189, which exempts unclassified basic research from control – "except as provided in applicable US statutes." But this did not assuage fears. One such statute, of course, is the Export Administration Act. DoD also issued a rule early in 1986 requiring scientists to submit all DoD-funded research for prior review "for consideration of national security at conferences and meetings."

Events at a June 1986 Linear Accelerator Conference, a biennial international gathering of nuclear physicists, revealed that not much had changed. The authors of 13 DoD-sponsored papers submitted them for clearance six weeks before the conference, as required. On the morning of the conference the Defense Department informed the authors for the first time that they could not present their papers – on the grounds that doing so would violate the export control laws. Conference organizers appealed the decision, and after a hastily called meeting DoD officials cleared ten of the papers – approving one only five minutes before it was delivered. One of the papers not approved had already been published.

To avoid such problems, some societies have informally barred foreign researchers from conferences. These include the Society of Manufacturing Engineers, the American Ceramics Society, and the Society for the Advancement of Material and Process Engineering. Nevertheless, restricted meetings are still more the exception than the rule. According to a 1986 survey by the American Association for the Advancement of Science, two thirds of scientific societies with policies on foreign participation prohibit restricted meetings.

The Reagan administration's interpretation of the export control laws has also forced scientists to be wary in their contacts with foreign citizens in classrooms, libraries, and research laboratories. The FBI's notice to librarians that they must report on "hostile intelligence people" is one such example. Another occurred in 1984, when DoD initially told UCLA's Extension Division that it could enroll only US citizens in a course entitled "Metal Matrix Composites" because it involved unclassified technical data appearing on an export control list. In 1981 the State Department attempted to require universities to report campus contacts between US citizens and Chinese exchange students. Strong objections from universities led the department to abandon the policy.

The administration has also tried to restrict foreign nationals' use of US scientific instruments. Supercomputers are a prominent example. The National Science Foundation (NSF) is the major funder of supercomputers at five universities, which will act as consortia for unclassified basic research. The Defense Department wants the universities to limit foreign scholars' access to these machines. Scientists have reacted with dismay, fearing that such restraints on unclassified work will undermine the quality of their research. Universities object to the prospect of policing researchers on campus.

The NSF has proposed guidelines designed to balance these concerns. Under the proposal, students from all countries could use supercomputers for regular course work. Soviet-bloc scientists could also use the machines for research in fields with no direct links to defense or intelligence functions. Officials from the departments of Defense and State as well as the White House have been reviewing the NSF proposals for more than two years without resolution.

The National Security Agency has designated some scientific fields as inherently sensitive and therefore subject to scrutiny under the export laws. A prominent example is cryptography, which has been so designated since 1981. Many cryptologists now submit their work to NSA for review before it is published to forestall even more stringent controls. The field of nuclear energy is also becoming increasingly secret. In 1981, at the request of the Reagan administration, Congress authorized the secretary of energy to regulate "the unauthorized dissemination of unclassified nuclear information."

By far the broadest category of information targeted for control is that maintained in electronic data bases throughout academia, industry, and government. A National Security Council directive issued in October 1986 by John Poindexter, former national security advisor, laid out the policy. The directive sought to restrict unclassified information affecting not only national security but also "other government interests," including "government or government-derived economic, human, financial, industrial, agricultural, technological, and law enforcement information."

Poindexter's directive prompted fears that US intelligence agencies would monitor virtually all computerized data bases and information exchanges in the United States. The White House withdrew the notice in March 1987 under pressure from Congress, but the underlying policy – as set out in NSDD 145 – is still in place. This calls for "a comprehensive and coordinated approach" to restricting foreign access to all telecommunications and automated information systems. The justification is again the mosaic theory – that "information, even if unclassified in isolation, often can reveal sensitive information when taken in the aggregate."

In December 1987, partially in response to the data base controversy, Congress passed the Computer Security Act. This legislation transfers responsibility for developing a government-wide computer security system from the National Security Agency to the National Bureau of Standards. But the act is silent on whether new categories of restricted information can be introduced as part of the security program.

Prepublication reviews as censorship

The Federal government's funding of many information-producing activities puts it in a unique position to influence the content of research or restrict its publication. Recent developments show that such restraints can undermine the objectivity of research, and sometimes constitute official censorship.

A 1980 Supreme Court decision set the stage for allowing the government to examine a wide range of documents before they are published. In *Snepp* v. *United States* the Court accepted the government's argument that a former CIA agent's book violated his agreement to give the CIA a chance to determine whether the material "would compromise classified information or sources." This ruling led to a CIA review of all proposed publications by current and former employees, not only those necessary to "protect intelligence sources and methods from unauthorized disclosure."

Three years after the Snepp decision, the White House issued NSDD 84 requiring 120,000 federal employees and contractors to agree to lifetime reviews of anything they wished to publish. This directive also allowed the government to give employees polygraph tests while investigating unauthorized disclosures of classified information. The new policy further required agencies to set up regulations governing "contacts between media representatives and agency personnel, so as to reduce the opportunity for negligent or deliberate disclosures."

Testifying before Congress on NSDD 84, Thomas Ehrlich, then provost of the University of Pennsylvania, noted that prepublication review would discourage academics from serving in government, depriving the country of their expertise and insight. Ehrlich noted that the policy would also thwart criticism of government, since those "in the best position to provide that criticism" – academics who have served in Washington – would be enjoined from discussing their experience.

Under pressure from Congress, the administration suspended the prepublication review provision in September 1984. However, it left in place a similar 1981 requirement that government employees with high-level security clearances sign a lifetime agreement – Form 4193 – to submit all writings, including fiction, for prepublication review.

A 1986 General Accounting Office report concluded that suspension of the supposedly broader requirement has had little effect. The GAO found that the government had examined 21,718 books, articles, speeches, and other materials as part of the review process in 1984. In 1985, after the policy supposedly changed, the number grew to 22,820. By the end of 1985, at least 240,766 individuals had signed Form 4193. From 1984 through 1985, current or former government employees made only 15 unauthorized disclosures in their books, articles, and speeches.

Restrictions on publication can also be a source of conflict between the CIA and its civilian researchers, many of whom are academic scholars. Until recently, most CIA contracts required consultants and researchers to submit all their writings for prepublication review. Many universities chose to forgo such contracts rather than agree to the restrictions.

In 1986 the CIA narrowed prepublication review to "the specific subject area in which a scholar had access to classified information." But the new rule continues to pose problems for scholars because they are likely to concentrate their research in their fields of specialization. Any later writing they do in those fields will apparently still be subject to CIA review.

Tension between funding agencies' interest in obtaining a certain research product and scholars' desire to avoid constraints are not uncommon, but this tension has risen to new levels. The conflict between Harvard and the Department of Housing and Urban Development, which wanted to review a scholar's research results for six months before publication, is one example. Harvard also objected to a NASA policy requiring grantees to obtain the agency's permission before copyrighting, publishing, or otherwise releasing computer software produced under contract. Harvard obtained an exception to this rule for one contract, but the underlying policy remains in place.

CIA contracts are a source of tension for scholars because the agency has traditionally required that the scholars not reveal that it funds their research. In 1986 the CIA recognized that a blanket rule would create "misunderstandings and suspicion," so contractors now can name their sponsor unless "public association of the CIA with a specific topic or subject would prove damaging to the United States." But this exception seems to apply to a broad range of circumstances, including where "acknowledged CIA interest in its affairs" would "create difficulty with a foreign government," or where "CIA interest in a specific subject . . . could affect the situation itself." Such secrecy undermines the credibility of academic work.

Reducing paperwork – and influencing policy

A pivotal point in the evolution of government information policy occurred in 1980 when Congress enacted the Paperwork Reduction Act (PRA). The current administration has used the act to cut back to a troubling degree the amount of information agencies collect and publish.

The Paperwork Reduction Act was a response to growing public concern about the burden of complying with federal requests for information, including tax and health-care forms and a wide variety of other required reports. The Commission on Federal Paperwork estimated in 1974 that these requirements cost citizens and government a total of $100 billion a year. Yet as the Senate Committee on Governmental Affairs noted when approving the PRA, the government must collect information to fulfill important national goals, including promoting research, protecting civil rights, ensuring safe working conditions, and – above all – informing the public about the workings of government itself.

To streamline the process of collecting data, the PRA established an Office of Information and Regulatory Affairs (OIRA) within the Office of Management and Budget (OMB). The OIRA director is charged with determining whether the information a federal agency collects is "necessary for the proper performance of its functions," including "whether the information will have practical utility."

Concerned about potential abuse of these provisions, Congress explicitly stated that they do not authorize interference with "the substantive policies and programs of departments, agencies and offices." Such interference, however, has become increasingly common.

An early example was a 1981 OMB directive requiring departments to cut the costs of producing both written and audiovisual materials. In response, the Department of Education created the Publications and Audiovisual Advisory Council (PAVAC), which rejected numerous requests from grantees to publish research results and information for the public. Yet as one research director pointed out, many contracts require grantees to publish the results of their work.

After examining the pattern of refusals, the House Committee on Government Operations concluded that the PAVAC review process was based on vague and content-related criteria – including whether the publication was "essential" or "timely" – that amounted to censorship. Moreover, the committee found that the review process had had no "cost-effective" results.

Since 1981 the administration has taken further steps to transform OIRA – and thus OMB – into a policy-making agency. The administration greatly expanded OIRA's authority with a January 1985 executive order requiring agencies to submit their regulatory plans to OIRA before making them public. OMB then reviews them for "consistency with the administration's policies and priorities." The agency has used this authority to interfere with efforts by the Department of Health and Human Services to require aspirin manufacturers to include warnings about the dangers of Reye syndrome on their labels. OMB has also hampered efforts by the Environmental Protection Agency to ban some uses of asbestos.

OMB has used the criteria of "necessity" and "public utility" in the Paperwork Reduction Act to decide which projects other agencies can fund. A prominent example has been research sponsored by the Centers for Disease Control (CDC) – which OMB must approve, under the PRA provision that it review plans by federal agencies to collect information from ten or more people.

A congressional committee asked researchers at the Harvard School of Public Health and New York's Mount Sinai School of Medicine to examine this process. After reviewing 51 projects CDC had submitted between 1984 and 1986, the study authors concluded that OMB was more likely to reject projects focusing on environmental or occupational health than those concerned with infectious diseases or other conventional illnesses. Research on reproductive topics, such as birth defects and venereal disease, was also more likely to be rejected. The authors noted that the proposed research had withstood the scrutiny of the peer-review process, and that OMB lacked the expertise to evaluate its practical utility. The authors concluded that the agency showed a "demonstrable bias" in thwarting efforts "to answer public demands for information on serious public health questions."

The administration has also tried to shift the burden of collecting and publishing information to the private sector. According to a 1985 OMB directive – Circular A-130 – agencies must see that information is disseminated with "maximum feasible reliance on the private sector" and the use of charges to recover costs. This policy led in 1986 to efforts to scale down the National Technical Information Service (NTIS) – a clearing-house for a wide range of scientific and technical data. The Commerce Department originally proposed discontinuing the NTIS entirely, selling it to the private sector, or contracting with a private entity for some or all of its functions.

This proposal prompted extensive criticism by legislators, libraries, universities, and industries that rely on the service, as well as by officials in the Public Health Service and the departments of Energy, Agriculture, and Defense. The Commerce Department's own staff concluded that "extensive privatization presents substantial costs and risks for the government, for NTIS customers and for the information industry as a whole." Critics worry that information without commercial appeal might go unpublished, and that private companies might be unwilling to maintain information over a long period of time. Changing the structure of NTIS could also hamper the influx of foreign technical information, which occurs through government-to-government agreements involving the NTIS.

The administration has responded by announcing – in a brief paragraph in the proposed 1988 budget – its decision to offer the private sector "the opportunity to operate NTIS on contract, with the government retaining overall policy direction." This has convinced neither the House nor the Senate. Both have voted in separate legislation to prohibit further privatization of NTIS without express congressional authorization. This prohibition has not yet received final approval.

Congressional dismay over OMB's attempts to manage information has also sparked efforts to cut OIRA's funding. This prompted OIRA director Wendy Gramm to set up a policy of disclosing OMB exchanges with other agencies regarding draft and final regulations. When

Congress reauthorized the Paperwork Reduction Act in October 1986, it made this disclosure policy law and included a separate budget line for OIRA to allow close congressional oversight.

Undermining the Freedom of Information Act

The Freedom of Information Act (FOIA) has become an increasingly important tool for gaining public access to government information, but recent actions by the administration have made it harder to use.

In amending the act in 1986, Congress stipulated that fees for searching and reproducing documents could be waived or reduced when "disclosure of the information is in the public interest." The legislators recognized that exorbitant fees can be a substantial impediment to academic researchers and non-profit groups that apply for information. The legislation's sponsors further specified that "a request from a public interest group, non-profit organization, labor union, library or . . . individual may not be presumed to be for commercial use" unless the information is being sought solely for a profit-making purpose.

Despite these indicators of congressional intent, the fee guidelines issued by OMB in March 1987 could significantly raise the cost of requesting information under the act. The new guidelines allow "educational institution(s)" to obtain documents for the cost of reproduction alone, excluding the first 100 pages. However, OMB defines educational institutions as entities that "operate a program or programs of scholarly research." This excludes public libraries, vocational schools, and a wide variety of other educational groups that may not be associated with research. The new OMB guidelines also expressly reject the presumption that a request "on the letterhead of a non-profit organization [is] for a noncommercial request."

The nonprofit National Security Archive has challenged these restrictions in federal district court. The case was argued in late January; a decision is still pending.

Reversing the trend

A decade of restrictive information policies has significantly affected important aspects of national life. The United States has lost some of its ability to innovate in a world increasingly driven by technology. Excessive secrecy – partly the result of an expanded classification system – has led to compartmentalized federal decision-making, manifested in its extreme form in the Iran-Contra affair. The public has been deprived of information it has paid for with tax dollars, and important values of free speech, academic inquiry, and democratic participation have been undermined.

The recent race to develop a high-temperature superconductor, in contrast, provides dramatic evidence of the advantages of open communication especially in science. The two scientists who first succeeded in creating a relatively high-temperature superconductor were German and Swiss nationals working for IBM, an American company, in Zurich. Their research, funded by the US Defense Department, set off a race around the world to develop practical ways of putting the discoveries to use. If federal policies had prevented these scientists from sharing their results, their work might still be unknown.

In mid-March 1987 thousands of physicists from around the world gathered in New York at a meeting of the American Physical Society to discuss the latest developments in this field. Such a meeting would not have been possible if DoD had prevented foreign nationals from attending.

Only one segment of the industrialized world has been left out in the cold during this extraordinarily fertile period of discovery and exchange. The Warsaw Pact nations have played no part in the superconductor frenzy. No one has sought to exclude them, but they are weighted down with bureaucratic restraints on travel, contacts with foreigners, and the use of telephones and copying machines.

Reversing the trend toward more government control of information should be a top priority of the president. Within the first 100 days, the new administration should issue an executive order on information policy liberalizing the classification and export control systems, and curtailing OMB's authority over the collection and dissemination of information. The president should also work with Congress to amend the export control laws, the Paperwork Reduction Act, and the Freedom of Information Act.

The new executive order should establish a presumption that information generated both inside and outside the government will be freely available – except where it can demonstrate a substantial public need, such as a clearly defined threat to national security. The government should not restrict any information based on its speculative relationship with other data: the mosaic theory leaves no chance for practical limits on information controls.

In a democracy, the management of information and ideas must be guided by a heavy presumption that open communication is essential to society's well-being. Experience shows that the free flow of ideas is vital to the fabric of national life, powering the engines of innovation, guaranteeing national security, and protecting personal freedom.

14 Economic and Social Issues

High Tech and Economic Development: Hope or Hype?

Edward J. Malecki

*Nations all over the world are feverishly pursuing the Holy Grail of high tech. But is it worth it? The author takes a critical look at the efforts of US states to attract and/or generate high tech industries. He says that success depends upon a number of factors – especially **patience** – but high tech should not be seen as a magic "cure-all" for regional economic problems. Edward Malecki is Professor of Geography at the University of Florida, Gainesville, and this article first appeared in* Technology Review, *October 1987.*

The allure of replicating California's Silicon Valley, Massachusetts's Route 128, and other high-tech centers has spawned a dizzying array of government policies intended to attract growing industries and nurture new firms. Hundreds, if not thousands, of communities and all 50 states are tying at least part of their economic future to high technology. By the end of 1985, a total of 35 state programs to recruit advanced technology industry were in place, compared with only four in 1979.

Many of these programs, proposals, and platforms are doomed to failure. Public programs can foster economic growth, but only if they consider the unique local conditions that bring about success.

The world's most ambitious high-technology development endeavor is Japan's Technopolis Concept, a plan to build 19 high-tech cities and link them to Tokyo by bullet trains. Japan's Ministry of Trade and Industry (MITI) selects the locations for these science cities. It looks for good transportation facilities; an integrated complex of industrial, academic, and residential areas; a pleasant living environment; and access to a "mother city." Tsukuba Science City, conceived in the 1960s and now home to two universities, 50 national research institutes, and over 11,000 researchers and staff, is in part a prototype technopolis.

In the United States, without strong central government support or guidance, the prospect of reproducing the Silicon Valley or Route 128 technopolises seems unlikely. Communities with existing high-tech concentrations have a huge advantage over areas seeking their first piece of the action. It is clear that success breeds success by providing a critical mass of workers, researchers, investors, and supporting businesses and services.

The high-tech route to economic development is susceptible to social control. The funda-mental dilemma for states and communities is that policy can't influence all variables – and most are alterable only in the long run and after substantial investment. Pools of professional and technical employees and employers, bastions of top-rank university research, and sources of seed and venture capital are critical for high-tech industry. None is created quickly.

Moreover, high-technology industry is misunderstood and probably overrated as a generator of jobs. The number of jobs it produces *directly* is relatively low. The Department of Labor defines high-tech industries as those employing a high proportion of engineers and scientists. Under that definition, high-tech employment is unlikely to exceed 10 percent of the US workforce. Only a few of the service industries coming to dominate the US economy are high-tech; computer software and information processing are at the top of that short list.

At the same time, high tech is the most probable source of innovations, successful entrepre-neurs, new firms, and new industries. Through this indirect and more long term route, high tech *is* an important employment generator. For example, high tech has spawned industries such as electronics, computers, and biotechnology that employ thousands of people. However, many of the jobs are semi-skilled.

Since branch plants have less need for skilled workers and large research components, they are more prone to move or close. Thus, farsighted industrial recruitment encourages firms to establish mainly R&D facilities rather than manufacturing plants. R&D labs employ better-paid, professional workers and require larger capital investments. This makes them less likely to close during economic downturns or to move on short notice to lower-wage sites.

Industrial recruitment the old way

The most popular – and often least beneficial – high-tech development programs simply modify or extend existing strategies to strengthen local or state economies. As with traditional programs, the goal is to woo any and all investment and jobs.

Targeting high-tech industries is the most common modification. Industrial-recruitment advertising in specialized publications emphasizes an area's high-tech traditions, skilled labor, and universities in addition to the usual lures of low taxes, low wage levels, limited unioniza-tion, and other elements of a "good business climate."

A refurbished recruiting style accompanies the high-tech focus. Slick brochures that convey quality of life with photographs replace dry statistics that measure economic advantages. These appeals answer to the preference of professional and technical employees, expressed in survey after survey, for locations with a mix of amenities. For example, a poll by Fantus Corp. and *Industrial Research and Development* magazine found that climate, recreational oppor-tunities, primary and secondary schools, and availability and cost of housing are most important for attracting and holding research engineers.

Pennsylvania's Department of Commerce touts the state's open spaces with a photo of a fisherman in a swift-running stream: "Your business would be a better place to work if it were in a better place to live." Maine boasts of its small-town atmosphere, and Colorado calls itself "the ultimate fringe benefit." Oregon has been notably successful in winning firms who want the Pacific Coast quality of life without California's high costs. In addition to branches of Intel and National Semiconductor, Oregon has won over several Japanese firms, including Fujitsu,

Kyocera, NEC, and the Epson subsidiary of Seiko. These Japanese companies desired Pacific Coasts sites but also wished to avoid a California tax on multinational firms.

Many state policies are dominated by the industrial-recruitment traditions from which they have evolved. Colorado's Silicon Mountain corridor from Boulder to Colorado Springs, advertising its low costs, now has several Silicon Valley firms. The reason, says Bob Nordeman, who has directed the Colorado Springs Marketing Task Force, is that "the cost of doing business here is half – across the board – of what it is in Silicon Valley."

Designating "high-tech highways" or "silicon strips" is a cut-rate and popular way to add high tech to conventional industrial recruiting. By itself, it is of little use. Whether named by journalists (like Silicon Valley) or by local boosters (like Oregon's Sunset Corridor), these areas are intended to elicit images of the next Route 128. The names have proliferated along with the interest in high tech. Examples include Silicon Bayou around Lafayette, Louisiana; Florida's Silicon Swamp; Silicon Gulch between Austin and San Antonio, Texas; Bionic Valley in Salt Lake City, Utah; and the Tennessee Technology Corridor.

A catchy name will not attract high-tech industry. Many technology regions are only vaguely delineated; others are clearly optimistic about their resemblance to Silicon Valley or Route 128. For example, Oklahoma's High-Tech Triangle encompasses large areas of empty prairie.

To succeed, future technology centers must meet at least some of the criteria underlying those that are already established. Several elements characterize the leaders: a large urban region, abundant air transportation, and strong universities that provide ideas and technical workers. Perhaps equally important but even harder to replicate is a large and continual flow of government research funding, such as the Boston and San Francisco Bay areas have received since World War II. In both regions, the funding has augmented local advantages, and high-tech concentrations existed before this industrial genre had a name.

Fulfilling any of the requirements for success is impossible without one key factor that industrial recruiters and promoters often ignore: patience. The long-term character of high-tech development is especially striking in Scotland's Silicon Glen, the region from Glasgow to Edinburgh. In the 1940s, US firms set up manufacturing plants in what is now labeled Silicon Glen to gain access to European markets and to take advantage of Scotland's sizable subsidies for industrial investment. Only in the 1970s did the more lucrative high-tech R&D enterprises become common. The US counterpart to Silicon Glen is North Carolina's Research Triangle, which started in 1959 when the state-supported Research Triangle Park opened. The area did not begin to compete with other regions for major R&D facilities until the late 1970s.

Building the base

Having accepted the need to adopt a long-term approach, states and communities can do much to attract out-of-state and foreign high-tech firms. One strategy is to improve the local infrastructure – utilities, roads, schools, and other public facilities. This strategy has the additional benefit of helping an area encourage and hold existing enterprises.

Boosting funding levels at state-supported universities enhances the high-tech image and attractiveness of a state. Unfortunately, university research is highly concentrated. Fifty universities account for over 60 percent of the total research funds. The state universities in

Arkansas, Tennessee, and West Virginia don't even rank among the top 100 in the country.

Since creating and maintaining top-notch universities is neither easy nor cheap, some state programs focus on selected high-tech fields, typically those in which there is already some local strength. With a mixture of state support and commitments from local firms, Arizona and North Carolina have established large microelectronics research centers. New York, New Jersey, and Ohio also sponsor advanced technology centers devoted mainly to one field of technology. In Ohio, for example, the University of Cincinnati concentrates on manufacturing technology, Ohio State University on welding research, and Case Western Reserve and the University of Akron on polymers. In Massachusetts, state funds are spread among institutions with strong programs in selected high-tech fields, such as marine science, polymer science, and biotechnology.

Texas took a focused approach as part of the deal that brought the Microelectronics and Computer Technology Corporation (MCC), a semiconductor industry consortium, to Austin. In addition to agreeing to build MCC a $20 million facility, the state set up an endowment for science and engineering departments at the University of Texas at Austin of interest to the microelectronics center.

While universities appear on nearly all checklists of high-tech companies looking for a place to settle, their actual effect on a decision is less clear. Faculty research and a pool of graduates alone are not enough to spawn local firms. The successful regions have several top universities *plus* abundant venture capital and urban services. And research – especially the best research – can be procured from a distance as industry–university agreements for biotechnology research have shown. Geography has not affected Du Pont support of Harvard Medical School and Caltech, Hoechst AG's agreement with Massachusetts General Hospital, or Exxon's arrangement with MIT.

On the other hand, long-term investment in higher education can pay off, as Texas demonstrated during the 1970s, when it rose into the top ranks of university research. This investment may be one reason why Texas now ranks among the leading states in the founding of new computer and software firms. Again, patience is crucial: the state's endowment of its universities dates from the 1920s. Less frequently noted is that oil revenue is almost the sole source of university funding. That revenue is fragile, booming with oil prices in the 1970s, and plummeting recently along with the oil market. To attract high-tech industry, university funding requires both a long-term commitment and a balanced source of support.

A second infrastructure improvement, access to other areas, is one of the most underappreciated means of drawing in high-tech industry. Professional workers depend on face-to-face communication with people inside and outside their firm. Increasingly, this requires good air service. Raleigh-Durham, North Carolina, and Colorado Springs, Colorado, have strengthened their appeal by acquiring additional air carriers or becoming major airline hubs. To a large extent, the success of Silicon Swamp and Central Florida Research Park, with 14 tenants, is attributable to Orlando's plentiful air connections. Gainesville's University of Florida Research and Technology Park, a two-hour drive north, has limited air service and half as many tenants.

A third infrastructure attraction amenable to public policy is the quality of life. Many cities, such as Baltimore, Maryland; Columbus, Ohio; and Pittsburg, Pennsylvania, are attempting to brighten their images with downtown development, funding for local schools, and bond issues for parks and other civic improvements. Building up university research potential also contributes to the sense of an "intellectual atmosphere" that attracts high-tech enterprises. For many people, art and similar activities are standard components of cultural richness, and they, too, depend heavily on public support and enthusiasm. The Research Triangle; Ithaca, New York; Athens, Georgia; and State College, Pennsylvania, compare culturally to much larger cities because of facilities available on campuses. These examples show that other places, if they can attain some of the attributes of metropolitan areas, can get at least a small slice of the high-tech pie.

The kicker is that a desirable quality of life has a price: higher taxes. And successful high-tech areas must continually maintain and upgrade their services to keep their quality of life competitive with that of other regions.

Building new firms

Encouraging and nurturing new companies bears more fruit than trying to lure firms from elsewhere. As a result, some state-level financial incentives are based on the fact that high tech evolves and grows in large part because of continual entrepreneurship. The hope is that rapidly growing local high-tech firms might replace declining industries.

To nurture enterprises that might be unable to secure private finances, at least 20 states have created public venture capital funds. Such policies attempt to imitate the model of private venture capitalists who provide money for risky start-ups in return for part ownership. The investors – whether private or public – hope to reap a high profit by picking the winning young firms in dynamic industries. This speculative investment may be lost entirely if the firms fail, which is what distinguishes venture capital from arrangements such as small business loans that expect a full and predictable payback. Extending the principle, some states and communities offer seed financing – small investments to get the riskiest projects going and encourage larger private venture capital involvement.

Connecticut, Indiana, Massachusetts, Michigan, New York, Ohio, and Pennsylvania are the major players. Most stretch the public investment with matching funds from private sources. Pennsylvania offers one dollar of state money to match three dollars in private money. The New York State Science and Technology Foundation's Corporation for Innovation Development has invested $3.2 million in young firms, leveraging an additional $15.1 million from the private sector and other public sources.

Even local communities are getting into the seed-and-venture act. North Greenbush, New York, near Rensselaer Polytechnic Institute (RPI), has raised over $1 million in grants from the Department of Housing and Urban Development. It invests up to $100,000 in small companies, some of which have been start-ups at RPI's high-tech park that were unable to find private capital.

One problem with public venture capital funds is that they have difficulty matching the personal relationships that are the heart of the private venture capital industry. Contacts between individuals inform investors about opportunities much more than do applications "off the street." With the proliferation of venture funds, expert managers are hard to find. Moreover, the networks are decidedly local. According to William Barnum, of the Los Angeles venture capital firm of Brentwood Associates, "There's definitely a bias toward companies that are close to home. I wouldn't say that we'd never do a deal more than 50 miles away, but you won't get a guy to fly to Biloxi, Mississippi, from Los Angeles every week."

The private venture capital industry is also highly concentrated geographically. California received 44 percent of the $2.6 billion in venture capital invested by private firms in 1985. Another 13 percent went to Massachusetts.

It is too soon to tell whether public venture capital or seed money can substitute for a lack of private funds. Most state funds are too new to have any track record, especially since return on investment is slow. Only Connecticut and Massachusetts began such programs before 1980, and most have started investing since 1985. New York has received only $420,000 in dividends and repayments on its $3.2 million invested through March 1987.

Moreover, although some funds have been established to counter the geographical concentration of private money, a number of the biggest are in states like New York and Connecticut that have the best access to such resources. Venture capital is still scarce in North Carolina's Research Triangle; consequently, very few new companies have taken root despite the area's attraction for the headquarters and R&D operations of large firms.

The science park route

Another popular way to encourage young companies is to cater to the preference of R&D firms for a campus-like setting. Called science parks, research parks, and technology parks, these specialized industrial developments reflects the clean office image of high-tech activities.

Business Facilities magazine recently listed 104 university-affiliated research parks in 37 states. Florida led the parade with nine parks, followed by Pennsylvania with seven, and Illinois and New York with six each. Occupancy rates tend to be highest in places where high tech has caught on for other reasons. Some of the more successful parks, each with over 50 tenants, are the Princeton Forrestal Center, Philadelphia's University Science Center, and New Haven Science Park. Each is near a major urban region and is affiliated with a world-class research university.

Metropolitan areas with their amenities and infrastructure remain the prime sites for new firms. It is not surprising, then, that so few science parks in the United States have thrived, or that the most successful tend to be in large urban centers. Those in out-of-the-way towns like Fayetteville, Arkansas, and Pullman, Washington have few, if any, tenants.

A more promising tactic is to create incubator facilities that "nurture" firms and allow them to "grow up" and find permanent local homes. Many incubators – called innovation centers when they serve exclusively high-tech companies – feature shared tenant services that can significantly reduce the need for start-up capital. David Allen of Pennsylvania State University has examined 12 incubator facilities in Pennsylvania and found that at least half provide in-house assistance on government regulations, government procurement processes, business, strategy preparation, and plans to relocate. Tenants in New Haven Science Park share a common word-processing service, receptionist, copy center, and personal computer rental.

Rather than charging rent for incubator space, a landlord (often a major university) may take some equity in its tenant companies. The Utah Innovation Center takes the highest cut – 30 percent of equity. At the low end of the scale, tenants in Rensselaer Polytech's incubator in Troy, New York, pay low rent while giving up 2 percent of their equity.

Incubators are a welcome policy shift away from wooing distant firms and toward supporting local entrepreneurs. Moreover, they are prominent in the comprehensive approach that a few states have undertaken. Pennsylvania's Ben Franklin Partnership combines incubators and venture capital with existing strong bases of university research and industry R&D.

Because the Ben Franklin Partnership addresses several elements of high-tech economic development at once, it has attracted significant private-sector support. The first $28 million in state funds for joint industry–university R&D projects in 1984 and 1985 was matched by $84 million from industry and foundation sources. The visibility and potential of the Franklin Partnership's four advanced technology centers has also made venture capital more available. At least two new seed-capital funds began in 1986 – one in Pittsburgh, the other in State College.

The limits and potential of public policy

In trying to foster economic growth through high technology, states and communities must focus on what they can control. While public policy can't create entrepreneurs, public venture capital pools *can* encourage local entrepreneurs to remain in the area rather than seek better investment opportunities elsewhere. Public policies can also bring entrepreneurs together through incubator facilities and integrate universities into civic and economic life. But since entrepreneurship is very much a local phenomenon, states must capitalize on and build up existing local strengths.

In addition, public policy must recognize its limited power to speed up the high-tech development process. Silicon Valley and Route 128 started at least 20 years before they were recognizable as high-tech regions. Others, such as Silicon Glen, have only recently begun to develop entrepreneurial activity. But the 25-year evolution of North Carolina's deliberate efforts to promote the Research Triangle shows that high-tech policies can bear fruit if they are focused on a small region with potential for economic development.

Moreover, while the employment gains from high technology may not be large or necessarily permanent, a well-designed state or local development policy can do much to strengthen a high-tech base. And such strategies have already contributed beneficial policy spin-offs. They have prompted a longer-term perspective about economic development and more patience to wait for small firms to grow and science parks to fill. They have demonstrated the connections between universities and the economy, and they have shown the significant advantages to be gained from investments in human capital, especially through education.

Thus, communities can profit even if industrial recruiting fails to create new high-tech regions. Everyone wins when towns de-emphasize the traditional lures of low taxes, low wages, and limited unionization and instead improve their airport facilities, schools, research infrastructure, local entrepreneurship, quality of life, and training for technical workers.

Even if undertaken only partially and half-heartedly, high-tech incentives can produce benefits. It remains to be seen whether farsighted policies will win out over those aimed at short-term gains.

Growing the Next Silicon Valley

Roger Miller and Marcel Côté

A more detailed strategy for developing a self-sustaining high-tech cluster is spelt out by these authors, who studied ten localities in Europe and North America. They argue that a sound approach must be based on existing strengths and must be accompanied by the long-term commitment of public and private leaders. Roger Miller is Director of the Technology and Management Program at the University of Quebec, Montreal and Marcel Côté is at the Center for International Affairs, Harvard University. This article, which appeared in Harvard Business Review, *July–August 1985, evolved into a book,* Growing the Next Silicon Valley: A Guide for Successful Regional Economic Planning *(Lexington Books, Lexington, MA, 1987).*

In recent years, both government officials and business executives have become increasingly involved in pursuing high-technology companies. Government leaders usually regard the effort as an essential part of an economic development strategy. Community business executives are frequently called on to lend their credibility, expertise, and contacts to help sell the area to interested entrepreneurs.

But experience shows that these recruitment activities are often unsuccessful and sometimes even misguided. Few regions have been able to grow their own version of Silicon Valley despite numerous and progressively more expensive efforts. This article offers insights for private and public leaders on how to grow a high-technology cluster.

It is important to recognize at the outset that high technology is not a universal panacea for economic development. Indeed, high-tech industries represent only one-third of high-growth industries. Moreover, even in a state like Massachusetts, renowned for its high-tech industries, they account for only 12 percent of total employment. Nevertheless, sound and sensible reasons exist for government and business to promote high technology. For the region, it means an industrial base that will last far into the future as today's innovations become tomorrow's common technologies. For corporations, it creates an economically vibrant community that can strengthen participants' performance, stimulate innovations, and point toward opportunities.

Why should executives care?

Business executives have traditionally been involved in promoting local economic development for a number of reasons. Some participate because it is part of their corporate civic duty. Many executives believe that they have particular expertise in the promotion of community economic development. In many instances, a corporation's self-interest meshes with development of the local economy. Companies that service the local economy, like banks, real estate developers, and utilities, generally stand to benefit from a strong regional economy.

But why should a manufacturing company that may not depend on the local market care about having high-tech businesses in the region? Close proximity to high-tech operations can help a company for two important strategic reasons:

1 Physical proximity facilitates the absorption of new technologies. Technology diffusion is still a geographical phenomenon. Recruitment, consulting services, and informal contacts among engineers, scientists, and executives enhance the transfer of technology. Local suppliers and subcontractors with state-of-the-art technologies allow companies to keep abreast of competitors. High-tech businesses in a region build awareness of new developments and thus help with cost reduction, productivity improvement, and product enhancement. Finally, with their own Silicon Valley nearby, executives can directly tap information networks otherwise accessible only at high cost.

2 Physical proximity exposes a corporation to a large number of leading-edge enterprises that can play a critical role in its diversification strategy. Candidates for acquisitions abound among fast-growing but capital-hungry high-tech businesses. Vigorous technological entrepreneurship offers numerous models to executives for internal venturing. Proximity also simplifies joint venturing with emerging high-tech companies, allowing a corporation to explore strategic opportunities in areas beyond its own activities. In joint ventures, physical proximity not only improves control but also allows more interaction – and thus more technology transfers.

Some business executives are concerned that the development of high-tech start-ups in their region may hurt their corporations by making it more difficult to keep technical personnel. Indeed, if a region is rich in technological entrepreneurship, employees may leave to start their own businesses and take with them costly technologies, processes, and products. Most corporations know this risk very well and have learned to manage it. Overall, this cost is insignificant in comparison with the benefits of agglomerating with other high-tech companies.

What makes a good environment?

A region's business conditions and institutional arrangements influence the emergence of a cluster of high-technology businesses. Our research indicates that the growth and multiplication of local companies creates a self-sustaining process that ultimately produces a healthy cluster. Some institutional factors enhance this development, and others slow it down. Any sound economic development strategy will try to favor the factors that stimulate the process.

Three conditions that support the start-up and growth of high-tech enterprises are: the presence of incubators – companies and laboratories where entrepreneurs can learn their trade and polish their skills before going off on their own; the wide availability of contracts that help start-ups survive their critical early years; and the emergence of success models, which not only stimulate entrepreneurship but also reduce risks for investors, suppliers, and bankers who are called on to assist new endeavors.

In addition to these business conditions, three institutional factors have strongly influenced the dynamism of the clustering process in a region: the availability of state-of-the-art technical knowledge, the presence of local venture capitalists, and strong community support for high technology.

Technological inputs

The presence of research-oriented universities in the San Francisco and Boston areas illustrates the importance of technical inputs on the formation of high-tech clusters. While a university is necessary, however, it is not sufficient in itself to activate the clustering process. Many fine research-oriented universities have not spawned high-tech clusters.

Four points define the technical inputs necessary to activate and accelerate cluster formation:

1 High-tech companies thrive on state-of-the-art knowledge, which they harvest and apply to market opportunities. Therefore, pertinent technological know-how is important. A run-of-the-mill research program is not likely to yield significant discoveries and useful new applications. Not all universities and research centers can be at the vanguard of science. Only a limited number attract the highest qualified scientists and graduate students who can explore these avenues.

2 An important difference exists between generic and applied research. Most commercially successful applied research is conducted in private companies or under contract in research centers and universities. Generic research takes place mostly in universities, research centers, and the advanced laboratories of large corporations. At some point in its development, a generic technology becomes fertile with marketable applications and spawns numerous new enterprises. Technological entrepreneurs are adept at harvesting technologies ripe for the marketplace while advanced laboratories are slower to profit from the same opportunities.

3 Most scientists are not entrepreneurs. Research shows that few scientists contribute directly to high-tech ventures; few MIT and Stanford professors or researchers have actually founded high-technology companies. On the other hand, many entrepreneurs have established their businesses near these institutions to profit in various ways from their creativity and technological output. This distinction is fundamental. Research institutions tend to be passive suppliers, and entrepreneurs, active developers of high technology.

4 The most useful applied research and development activities are market oriented. Applied research that takes place in nonprofit organizations like universities and government laboratories is usually not market driven and therefore seldom gets translated into products or ideas that lead to the formation of new enterprises.

The process of transferring technology from research institutions and universities to high-technology companies is complex and multifaceted. One important channel for developing applications for state-of-the-art technology has been government contracts for research and procurement. For instance, in the electronics and aerospace industries, direct government support for research and development, early contracts for process development, and the establishment of initial production capacities were powerful levers for technology transfers.

Another source of new products is contract research conducted at universities and research centers that have a commitment to state-of-the-art technology. The first minicomputers were largely developed under contract research at MIT, Harvard, and the University of Pennsylvania. Digital Equipment Corporation was built on the success of its PDP minicomputer, which was a spin-off of MIT's TX-O minicomputer project.

Finally, despite these legitimate roles for the government and universities, most government laboratories and universities are poor incubators of entrepreneurs and high-tech products. Usually, neither their researchers nor their laboratories have any significant contact with the marketplace. A potential entrepreneur working in such an institution is not exposed to the market, its needs, its organization, or its people. Product ideas generated in government laboratories and universities seldom meet marketplace standards, either technologically or in terms of cost.

The ideal research environment to support a high-tech cluster has the following characteristics:

- The region has several research institutions, like research-oriented universities and laboratories, which are recognized as leaders in their field and boast a sufficient reputation to attract "the best and the brightest."
- A tradition of contract research exists in these institutions.
- A few large corporations have set up advanced laboratories in the region, where they conduct their basic and generic research.
- A tradition of close relationships between these research institutions and local high-tech companies has taken root through consulting contracts, hiring of graduate students, and occasional joint venturing.

Venture capitalists

As a rule, local venture capitalists play a significant role in assisting technological entrepreneurs. But money, like technology, is not enough. More crucial is the business advice that venture capitalists can provide start-up enterprises.

The distinction between venture capital and venture capitalists is fundamental to understanding the process of the emergence of high-tech businesses. Technological entrepreneurs often lack many of the skills necessary to launch a company successfully. An experienced venture capitalist's advice can be critical to a new company's success in its first years.

The emergence of large, nationally active venture capital firms has blurred the fact that most start-up investments come from local sources. Because start-ups require significant interactions between entrepreneurs and investors, venture capitalists tend to concentrate first-round financing in their own areas. Both the Boston and San Francisco areas have always had a sufficient supply of active, local venture capitalists.

But not all venture capitalists are good first-stage investors. In fact, only a minority of venture capital firms succeed in this high-risk, time-consuming segment of the business. Good first-stage venture capitalists play three roles. First, they identify and sort out high-potential entrepreneurs. For that purpose, they maintain extensive informal networks that reach out to local high-tech companies, research centers, and universities. Second, they assist the entrepreneurial team in preparing a business plan and often raise the initial capital. Third, they give strategic advice on building and managing a rapidly growing organization. The venture capitalists' experience, contacts, and credibility are vital assets for high-tech companies in their early years.

Most small business investment corporations and government-supported venture capital organizations are not good first-stage venture capitalists. They can provide the funds but not the business acumen. In contrast, first-stage venture capitalists are themselves entrepreneurs who are able to identify opportunities and other entrepreneurs. They can also easily raise the funds needed for their investments. Usually these venture capitalists are not attracted to taxpayer-subsidized organizations. Rather, their activities are better suited to small partnerships where intuitive judgment is vital.

Not all regions have a local supply of venture capitalists. We have found, however, that government efforts to supply risk capital in substitute forms – like generous grants or government-supported venture capital pools – have actually retarded the emergence of local professional venture capitalists. No schools exist to train successful investors. Opportunities and experimentation are necessary.

High tech as a way of life

Another institutional factor is social support for high-tech industries and, in particular, high-tech entrepreneurs in the region. Fundamentally, the people in the region must recognize the virtues of technology and its contribution to economic growth. A Silicon Valley-like cluster requires a base of community support and encouragement for individuals taking economic risks.

First, this support sustains both private and public leadership in building and maintaining the institutions that contribute to the development of a high-tech base. Thus local political authorities will consistently back public expenditures to promote high technology. Senior managers will also be committed to high-tech research and teaching, which they will indicate by their recruiting practices, by how they award contracts, by their support for research institutions, and by their cooperation with government authorities to foster high-tech projects.

Second, community support increases the social rewards of high-technology successes. The most important barrier to the emergence of high-tech businesses in a region is often the resistance to technical entrepreneurs. The higher the rewards, the more would-be entrepreneurs will be tempted to abandon the security of salaried employment for the high risk of a new venture. Encouragement in the form of social recognition by the local intellectual, financial, and business communities can do much to promote an entrepreneurial climate.

The evidence of a social contract is strong around most high-tech clusters. The banking and industrial communities were important partners in founding MIT at the end of the nineteenth century. Today, high-tech business leaders still communicate their expected scientific manpower needs to the Boston and Cambridge universities. The purchase of land around Stanford University for eventual high-tech business sites dates back to the early 1930s. A consensus among university leaders, bankers, and managers of technology-based companies led to the formation of Stanford Research Institute and the development of contract research between Stanford and numerous corporations. A similar consensus exists in North Carolina, where the Research Triangle Industrial Park has consistently received strong support during its 20 years of existence.

In a similar fashion, the success in Lyons, France of Institut Mérieux, which developed human and animal vaccines after World War II, grew out of a strong commitment by the local business community and public leaders. During the same period in Paris, the publicly funded Institut Pasteur stagnated even though many technical discoveries had been made there.

Pitfalls of simplistic strategies

Simplistic strategies abound in efforts toward economic development. Most often, well-intentioned tactics, useful in a specific context and at a particular time, are dressed up as grandiose strategies. They seldom work. Both public officials and business executives who are called on to offer their advice as members of blue-ribbon committees should be ready to criticize these inadequate strategies:

Buying your way Attracting branch plants into a region with generous grants is the most common mistake. In the short run, this policy can yield impressive results, but at a high cost.

The areas that attract branch plants are provided with visible symbols of high technology, but they usually end up with symbols only. Branch plants are self-contained operations with minimal links to local suppliers or markets, which is one reason they can be located almost anywhere. Moreover, they house a limited number of managerial functions. For the most part, their management follows instructions and rarely gets involved in developing new products. Branch plants are also poor incubators, and they seldom award contracts that could form the basis for new companies nearby.

Thus branch plants contribute little to the process of the emergence of a new Silicon Valley. Even worse, the long-term impact of a branch-plant strategy can be expensive. For example, in the 1960s, by offering incentives, the Belgian government attracted numerous branch plants of international corporations. Later, these companies began to disinvest, closing plants as competition from Common Market businesses required aggressive strategic actions that local managers were not allowed to take. More recently, New Haven, Connecticut offered United Technologies tax breaks to locate a branch plant there, with the understanding that the company would make further investments. Instead, the original plant eventually left New Haven over the objections of city officials who insisted that the company had made a commitment to the community.

Under the right circumstances, however, branch plants can sometimes provide the basis for the emergence of a high-tech cluster. Two examples are in central Scotland and in North Carolina's Research Triangle Industrial Park. This is more likely to occur when branch plants are given product mandates or worldwide market responsibility. This gives them some degree of autonomy despite interdependence with the head office, research laboratories, and other factories. Over the years, such plants can become incubators, offer initial contracts, and grant subcontracts.

Looking in ivory towers The most forceful proponents of an industrial strategy are often universities and research organizations located in the region. The policies they advocate usually involve additional funding for their institutions, the establishment of innovation centers, and the development of programs to foster the commercialization of inventions. Their sources give these proposals much credibility. Yet this approach seldom produces satisfying results because the organizations involved are too far removed from marketplace realities.

Agglomerations of research laboratories vaguely connected to market activities can form nice neighborhoods with all the symbols of high technology. They do not, however, host many would-be entrepreneurs and do not act as initial customers. Once established, these agglomerations ossify into respectable research islands artificially maintained at public expense. Sophia-Antipolis ("city of wisdom"), near Nice, France, was designated a high-technology park. Heavily subsidized by the French government, it attracted Air France, several public research institutes, and a few research laboratories of multinationals. But it never took off. Start-ups are minimal. And few local companies are expanding. In contrast, Toulouse, France is a more vibrant high-tech area, spurred by a long history of aerospace production.

Toronto's Sheridan Park is another research park that did not trigger a self-sustaining process. It has attracted mainly government-funded research centers. Similarly, the Japanese have established a research park in Tsukuba, outside Tokyo, that has led to an agglomeration of research installations. The distance that separates it from industrial companies, however, has significantly reduced the expected level of exchange and the Tsukuba park has not given birth to self-sustaining growth.

Government programs to manage the transfer of technology also fall into this category. They assume that innovation results from a chain that starts with research, proceeds to the development of new products, and leads to their market introduction. This approach attributes a central role to technological push at the expense of market pull; it often leads to technologies in search of markets.

The experience of innovation centers established to manage the new company creation process is instructive. These centers were set up in the mid-1970s in selected universities both in Canada and the United States to commercialize new ideas and to develop start-ups. Most centers either have been closed after a few years of operation or have been reoriented as schools. None has achieved self-financing. None has worked as an innovation center.

Another popular policy is the establishment of greenhouses in industrial parks. A greenhouse is an industrial establishment where fledgling high-tech businesses rent space at subsidized rates. Any would-be entrepreneur would readily say that a good contract is worth many months of free rent. But greenhouses are popular because they are highly visible and are successful at concentrating entrepreneurs in one area. In the absence of a greenhouse, however, these start-ups would simply rent commercial space. Thus on the whole, greenhouses have little, if any, impact on the generation of new enterprises.

Picking the winners   Picking-the-winners strategies involve channeling public funds into high-potential endeavors and industries that public officials select. Such strategies have been hotly debated. On the one hand, people see them as effective ways of rationing limited government funds earmarked for high technology through logical economic analyses. On the other hand, some opponents argue that government officials are poor marksmen, spend public funds on the wrong targets, and suffer no loss for misinformed decisions.

Our experience suggests that picking the winners should be left to market forces and to venture capitalists. The weeding out of good investment opportunities is a skill that only successful venture capitalists have. Risks in start-ups are much higher than those in more common investments. As far as we can tell, committees staffed by well-intentioned civil servants are not better than the marketplace in evaluating high-risk investments

In fact, public officials are often tempted to make their choices for the wrong reasons. They can be attracted to glamorous technologies that promise a high profile. They often believe simplistically that early government funding and support are all that is necessary to push a technology into the marketplace. The competitiveness of the marketplace, however, is shaped by many factors, including technological virtuosity. Recently, Canadian officials promoted good airplane designs and nuclear reactors with little success. But in the 1970s, they missed two of Montreal's pioneering companies in word processing, Micom and AES.

Designing a strategy that works

A development strategy is a vision of what the future could be and a dedication by a coalition of leaders to achieve it. We believe that a long-term development strategy can be designed and implemented successfully in a region if it is based on a good understanding of the dynamics involved.

No global, all-purpose solution exists. Each region must design a strategy that fits its resources and competencies. At the same time, any successful strategy will have to display certain characteristics.

The success of the strategy   This rests on a long-term commitment by a sustained coalition of regional public officials and corporate leaders. It took more than 20 years for the Boston and San Francisco areas to develop large clusters. Building a sustained regional coalition requires going beyond conventional wisdom about the necessity of cooperation among business, government, and labor. Positive institutional factors have to be created and maintained over several decades through concrete actions. This length of time is needed to build a few generations of high-tech companies that will become incubators and initial contractors. Only strong leadership can ensure such long-term commitments in a region.

The focus of the strategy   This should be on multiplying homegrown enterprises. Developing and strengthening favorable conditions is not the end of the game. The strategy should focus on multiplying local companies. Many of these businesses will remain small. A few will grow fast and serve national and international markets. The emergence of successful new endeavors results from much trial and error and some failures. Consequently, a development strategy should favor experimentation by as many ventures as possible.

The role of corporate leaders   Business leaders should promote policies in their own companies that lead to contracting out and venturing. Establishing an effective strategy depends on private initiatives, not on public funding. Corporate leaders should implement high-technology procurement programs and maintain them over the years. The successful implementation of such programs requires dedication by executives. The temptation is always strong to do things in-house. One challenge of a high-tech procurement program is to maintain reasonable levels of risk-taking in the process. Thus new companies and innovative enterprises are favored as suppliers.

Venturing is the process by which a corporation nurtures and develops new activities. A company can do this in-house or through joint ventures with other businesses. Tektronix, Inc., a Beaverton, Oregon electronic instrument manufacturer, has a formal corporate program to help its employees who want to branch out on their own. Through this plan, Tektronix keeps partial ownership and maintains close contacts with the ventures.

The role of the government   This role is supportive and aims mainly at creating a hospitable environment and encouraging state-of-the-art research in the area. The government's role is secondary. It should focus on encouraging advanced research in the region's institutions and on supporting local companies in their pursuit of contracts. Government can also adopt contracting-out policies. For example, Montreal is home for three of the ten largest engineering corporations in the world as a result of Hydro-Québec's commitment to contracting out most of its engineering work.

Gathering information

A good strategy is based on a sound diagnosis. An appropriate diagnosis requires solid information. Unfortunately, official industrial statistics offer little useful information. Companies that want to diversify and venture into emerging technical fields will find SIC codes totally inadequate. The traditional statistics government agencies gather often fail to reflect the technological developments under way in a region – like fail-safe computers and gallium arsenide wafers. Influencing and encouraging the multiplication of linkages among emerging businesses, existing corporations, and venture capitalists requires new kinds of information. New codes and categories for data collection must be devised to deal with the dynamic qualities of certain technologies and industries.

Information necessary for stimulating venture activities is often informal and personal. For that reason, executives in companies where venturing has become a path for corporate development find that formal information networks are often useless. Before they can track and identify companies to joint venture with, they often must build personal, informal, and highly specialized networks. Public officials involved in economic development discover that they need to attend technical meetings and venture capital conferences to become a legitimate party in the informal network. In turn, they may direct entrepreneurs to influential buyers or first-round venture capitalists.

Designing a balanced strategy also depends on an assessment of a region's potential, especially the presence of incubators and the availability of initial contracts. A census of the technology-based enterprises in the region will indicate how best to proceed with a strategy. Two broad starting points exist:

1 A region may already contain an agglomeration of emerging and mature technology-based companies. Among these, growing high-tech enterprises are the most efficient incubators. In the Boston region, such businesses provide 3 percent to 5 percent of total employment

and about a third of all high-tech jobs. Many public and private leaders are not aware of the presence of hundreds of small high-tech companies in their area. For example, Minneapolis –St Paul, Minnesota; San Diego, California; Portland, Oregon, and London, England, to name but a few, each contain several hundred enterprises that offer a ready base for action. Many regions, however, have few such starting points. Thus out of necessity, mature technology-based businesses are often at the core of the strategy. These former stars still incorporate technologies in their products and processes that require extensive research activities.

2 Alternatively, a region may contain only a recent agglomeration of research laboratories and branch plants. For such an area, attracting plants and laboratories with a worldwide responsibility or a product development mandate could help compensate for the lack of an industrial agglomeration as a starting point. Nevertheless, communities must pursue new enterprises vigorously to create a critical mass – an expensive undertaking. A few plants and laboratories will not trigger a self-sustaining process.

Going into action

Depending on the starting point and a region's assets, public and private leaders must design and implement an appropriate action program. A partial list of policies, both private and public, to enhance the development of a high-tech cluster follows:

Ensure the development of incubators   The maintenance and development of active incubator institutions is a fundamental element of the strategy. In a region where the clustering process has started, private and public leaders should choose tactics that will help ensure that growing high-tech enterprises can thrive.

In an area where no clustering process has begun, strategies should aim at creating incubators. Mature technology-based companies can provide starting points. Research, spin-offs, and new ventures should be encouraged. Many corporations can benefit from venture programs that stimulate internal entrepreneurship or lead to outside joint ventures with employees or partners. Signing initial contracts, offering marketing assistance, and supplying venture capital can help promote ventures and spin-offs.

Branch plants can also become incubators if management has strategic responsibilities. But parent companies can be hard to influence. The time to establish the conditions that will lead to branch plants' becoming incubators is when they are first attracted into a region. Central Scotland's success in building a high-tech cluster from branch plants proves that it can be done.

Develop linkages through initial contracts   Entrepreneurs seldom forget their first contract. An open local market rich in subcontracting opportunities will stimulate technical entrepreneurs. As initial customers, mature technology-based companies can play a critical role in a region's triggering strategy. Private and public leaders should strongly encourage local procurement from start-ups or emerging enterprises. A positive attitude by the senior managers of mature companies can overcome staff resistance to buying from new ventures or from outside suppliers.

Several corporations have local procurement programs that can serve as models. IBM has a worldwide program to help local suppliers bid on work anywhere in the IBM system. Control Data Corporation has been a pioneer in the Minneapolis area in this direction.

An analysis of 50 start-ups in the Montreal region revealed that, for most of them, their first contract was the critical element during their launching. Most of these initial contracts come from mature technology-based corporations rather than from government. These contracts allowed final product development and streamlining of operations. Contracting out product development, sponsoring procurement projects, and subcontracting research are all sound ways to channel critical sales revenues to start-ups and emerging enterprises.

A balanced strategy should include initial customer programs addressed to mature high-tech businesses in the region. Private sector initiatives, coordinated by a regional development council or by a chamber of commerce, can produce such programs. The program coordinator should monitor the actual performance of participating companies and reward outstanding achievements with public recognition.

Fund R&D to maintain technological vitality   Sustaining technical vigor in a region requires private support for R&D and for universities and extensive public funding of research activities. But money is not always the limiting factor. First, because good researchers tend to gather in centers of excellence, private and public leaders in a region should ensure that their basic research institutions achieve a superior reputation and retain it.

Second, how the research money is spent is as important as how much is spent. Market-driven and applied R&D is fundamental to start-ups. Therefore, the development strategy should also ensure that sufficient R&D funds are channeled into profit-seeking companies, preferably small businesses with growth potential. When universities and nonprofit organizations bid on projects, they should be encouraged to team up with private companies. Moreover, government laboratories should be required to subcontract a certain percentage of their applied R&D work to private enterprises. Finally, defense and aerospace contractors should be encouraged to subcontract applied R&D to small businesses. The turbulence that results from applying these few rules can turn research institutions into incubators.

Encourage contractual links between universities and businesses   Universities are not good incubators because they are too removed from the marketplace. Moreover, universities should not try to usurp the role of incubators just because they have easier access to funds.

The principal contribution that universities and technical institutes can make to a region's development is simply to educate, transmit knowledge, and commit students to excellence. As far as economic development is concerned, basic research should be a second priority. Particularly in technical institutes, professors should be encouraged to develop consulting and research links with the business community.

Develop professional venture capitalists   Venture capitalists are skillful at discovering innovation opportunities and the entrepreneurs who propose to exploit them. Professional venture capitalists can be trained through experimentation – they flourish in high-tech clusters. A development strategy should therefore ensure that the local available risk capital ends up in "smart" hands. This does not always happen.

On the whole, government-sponsored venture capital firms and nonprofit venture capital funds have a dismal record in first-round financing. Corporate venture capital centers share this dubious record for financing start-ups.

An effective development strategy should therefore attempt to spawn a regional network of financial entrepreneurs oriented toward high-technology ventures. A limited number can do the job. For instance, the Boston region has only about ten early-stage venture capital firms, although officially, countless firms are involved in the overall venture capital industry. Most regions can get along with many fewer. Successful entrepreneurs themselves often become early-stage venture capitalists.

Second-round financing is more national in scope. Good first-round venture capitalists will attract national and international capital for second-stage financing. Thus a development strategy should not be concerned with second-round venture capital. Policies aimed at stimulating first-round venture capital can be tax-oriented. But the real lever is the joint decision by public leaders and financial institutions' managers to channel funds into venture partnerships that will experiment with start-ups and emerging businesses. The Massachusetts Capital Resource Company is a good example.

Growing the future

The benefits high-tech development gives a region are well known. High technology provides good jobs and the promise of a sound industrial base for many years to come. Manufacturing companies in mature technologies also benefit, as we have already discussed.

A deep understanding of the process can also influence the plant location searches of multiplant corporations. Indeed, technical vitality should be considered along with labor, land, and transportation costs when making decisions about locating any plant that involves state-of-the-art technology. Regions such as the San Jose area and New England are constantly losing plants through the branching-out process, and new plants always replace them. The departing plants are in more mature technologies, the new plants in more vital technologies. High-tech areas are better suited to handle the flux inherent in manufacturing operations where the technology changes rapidly. Workers are used to job shifts, the talent pool is much more mobile, executives are used to changes, and suppliers and vendors deal routinely with major plant reorganizations.

In the long run, a region that can develop businesses in the new technologies ensures its economic future. A regional economy can be compared to a forest. The large, mature trees stand out by their importance. But the source of future growth lies among the seedlings and young saplings. In the same way, the economic growth of a region depends on new or growing companies that have the potential to become large. A significant proportion of such enterprises are high-tech businesses. A development strategy should focus on stimulating their growth and regular renewal by continuously creating new ventures, to be in time the large corporations of tomorrow.

Computers and Gender

Elisabeth Gerver

Why does computing appear to be a male preserve? The author provides an impressive survey of the evidence on gender imbalance in computing and looks at the reasons behind it – in particular, the ways in which girls are "turned off" computer studies at school. Gerver then describes some projects created for women to learn about computing in New Zealand, Britain and the United States. Taken from chapter 2 of Elisabeth Gerver's book Humanizing Technology *(Plenum Press, London and New York, 1985).*

> *Microcomputers offer a golden, and perhaps unprecedented, opportunity to women.*
> Rose Deakin, *Women and Computing*

In the initial enthusiastic introduction of computers into various forms of community education in many parts of the developed world, grandiose claims were sometimes made for the beneficial effects that computerization could have on entire communities. It was against such a background of enthusiasm that I started to work in 1981 in the Scottish Community Education Microelectronics Project (SCEMP). Two impressions of that time are particularly vivid. The first is that there was already an extraordinarily high level of interest in using computers for individualized learning and for community information. The second is that, among the large number of people who expressed interest in the project, there were very few women. As a collaborative venture, the project drew heavily on the help of volunteers to create computer programs to demonstrate some of the possibilities of using individualized learning in community education. Nearly all of the volunteer programmers were men and boys. The project also required the help of voluntary organizations to coordinate and manage computer exhibitions which would give ordinary people a chance to experience the machines for themselves. Nearly all of the individuals who offered to help with these exhibitions were men. At that time, there were no women among the senior staff and computer programmers employed by the government-funded project to introduce computers into schools in Scotland, a project with which SCEMP was closely associated, and most of the visitors to both projects appeared to be men.

When the public exhibitions of computer programs began, their most notable feature at first was the large number of young people who wanted to use the equipment, and who often had to be tactfully or even bluntly steered away so that the adults, for whom the exhibitions were primarily intended, could also sample the programs. Almost all the young people were young and adolescent boys, and most of the adults for whom they made way were young men. Yet, the exhibitions were intended as an educational experience for adults, and in Britain, as in most of the developed world, most of the students in adult education are women.

At first glance, then, the phenomenon was puzzling. The programs used in the exhibitions were intended to have a reasonably wide appeal; they included programs on managing personal finance, assessing one's current state of health, choosing well-balanced meals, answering quiz questions about road safety, and a number of programs illustrating the kinds of educational games which children often played at school. Several exhibitions even included a program designed to help women make well-informed decisions about whether to breast or to bottle feed their babies! On the face of it, then, there was no explicit appeal primarily to male users.

Yet the users were predominantly male. At about the same time, I attended a conference for providers of computer literacy courses in support of the BBC Computer Literacy Project, which was expected to, and did, rouse a great deal of public interest in computers. Again, despite the fact that there are many female tutors in adult education, nearly all of those present were men.

The next evidence of the strangely single-gendered world of computers was visual. The overwhelming impression created by all the computer magazines and advertisements for microcomputers in Britain in the early 1980s was that this was a world only for men and their sons. "Son, where's my Epson?" demanded a happy father in an advertisement, as his school-age child sheepishly hid the computer behind his back. Early figures for sales of the extra-ordinarily popular BBC Computer indicated that over 90 percent of the purchasers were male (BBC, 1983).

Printed material for the computer hobbyist or for the serious computer educationalist seemed to assume that its reader would be a man. In magazines in 1983, there were about ten males to every one female, and she was usually there in a decorative capacity (Gerver, 1984). Even in the Open University, which usually avoids explicitly sexist material, the original leaflet for a course for teachers to learn about computers depicted far more men than women (Gerver, 1984). These visual impressions are confirmed by Bernstein (1984), who has found that there are three types of advertisements for computers: "men as decision-makers; women as attention-getters; and family-oriented ads which do not include the whole family." Those women who are included in advertisements portraying family life are shown only as being in charge of young children. Where the children are older, women tend to disappear, and girls, where they are depicted at all, are merely shown as watching the boys admiringly.

Advertisers are now beginning – more so in the United States than in Britain – to include women more often as users of computers. Deakin (1984) cites one advertisement on television in the UK in which a mother and father were shown as creeping down to use the home computer when they thought the children were not around. The commercial need for new markets for computers means that the representation of women in advertisements for computers is likely to increase, as women form 50 percent of the potential market. But until the mid-1980s, the message of most computer advertising was that computers were for men and boys.

The phenomenon seemed to me not merely striking, because unexpected, but also very dangerous, because it appeared to be so little noticed in the world of community education. Attention had already been drawn to the under-representation of women in the field of computing as a whole (Simons, 1981), but the largely male tutors of computer courses and the male observers at computer exhibitions seemed not even to notice that the great majority of the participants were men. Since then, increasing attention has been paid to the single gender of computers in publications (Deakin, 1984; Gerver and Lewis, 1984; among many others), at international conferences on the new information technologies, in action groups, and in many projects which have been started to try to redress the sexual balance in this field. Before considering the various ways in which adult educators and feminist groups have been trying to address the problem, however, I should like first to sketch the dimensions of the situation which has caused so much concern.

Gender bias in learning about computers

The land of computing is a frontier country, and, as in the development of most frontier territories, there are many more men than women. Indeed, it appears that at all levels of learning about computers – in school, in higher education, in further education, in training, in adult education classes, and in independent learning – women tend to be strikingly under-represented. The extent of their under-representation varies from sector to sector and to some extent from country to country, but the fact of it is so ubiquitous that the evidence tends to become monotonous. The statistical evidence that follows gives an indication of the scope of the problem, but it does not attempt to cover the phenomenon at all comprehensively.

Anyone observing the use of computers in schools in the UK and the United States will find many male teachers and students – and few females – among the enthusiasts. Even in the recently developing use of computers in primary school, there is already evidence in the UK that "girls are failing to seize the opportunity. There seems to be a preponderance of boys even in the more imaginative and exciting courses . . . designed for primary schools and intended to stimulate children before there is any firmly recognizable division of activities according to gender" (Deakin, 1984). In the United States, the pattern appears to be that seen in California, where at elementary school both sexes participate nearly equally in using computers, but by the time of junior high school, girls form only 37 percent of the users (Beyers, 1983).

In courses in computing in American secondary schools, males outnumber females by nearly 2:1 in a pattern that remains remarkably similar over a number of states (PEER, 1983). In the UK, the sexual bias in computing in schools may be seen in the finding that computer studies are assumed by many schools to be boys' subjects, along with nearly all the other sciences (Rogers, 1983). At the most senior level of work in computer studies in schools in England and Wales – that of A level examinations in computer science – the ratio of boys to girls is 4:1 (EOC, 1984).

In the more informal uses of computers in schools, the same pattern is evident. In the UK, "there are a few schools where an imaginative teacher has managed to stimulate girls into using computers, but in general there is a distressingly low take-up" (Deakin, 1984). The situation described by Deakin in one school is emblematic:

At one north London comprehensive school, the current fifth-year computer studies group has no girls at all. The current fourth year shows an improvement with six girls, but alongside them are seventeen boys. . . . A computer was available in the library, and here again boys tended to dominate. In the opinion of the deputy head, this was because "girls were not assertive or confident enough to resist the boys' 'helpful' suggestions about programming and gradually the girls would be eased out. . . . " Girls would not join the lunchtime computer club.

At the university level of study, in 1970–80 in the United States, only 30.3 percent of all first degrees in computer and information sciences were earned by women (National Science Foundation, undated). In the same year, only 20.9 percent of all masters degrees in the same subject were awarded to women, while at the doctoral level, the figure falls to 11.2 percent. In the UK in 1979, women formed only 27 percent of all the applicants for computer science undergraduate courses at the university level (Simons, 1981).

The pattern is not restricted to the level of undergraduate work. In the UK where the shortage in computing skills led the government to fund a 500 percent increase in places for postgraduate studies in information technology in 1983–4, only 10 percent of those qualifying in 1984 were women (Women's National Commission, 1984). The low percentage is unexpected and striking, especially as some of the new courses are "conversion" courses for graduates with degrees in the arts or social sciences and, therefore, could have offered women an opportunity to change direction and to enhance their chances of employment.

In computer courses within adult education, the pattern at first seems encouragingly less sexist: in the UK in 1982–3 the proportion of males to females in enrollment in adult education classes in computing appeared to be about only 2:1 (Banks, 1983; Gerver, 1984). In 1983–4, there was an encouraging increase in the number of women in computer classes in at least one local authority area, where the proportion of women rose to 43 percent (Banks, 1984). These figures, however, need to be treated with some caution. They should be seen in the light of the fact that, whereas there are roughly equal numbers of boys and girls in the school population, far more women than men traditionally take part in adult education classes, so that the population, from which such an apparently encouraging proportion of women is drawn, does not consist equally of men and women.

Among the providers of education in computers, there appears to be an even more pronounced male bias. Within schools in the UK, most work with computers is carried out by teachers of mathematics and physics, by far the great majority of whom are male. In 1983–4 in the UK, no woman was among the "new blood" university appointments in information technology.

Within the field of training unemployed people for new careers, the same pattern seems to persist. In Scotland in 1983, for instance, there was a striking difference in the numbers of unemployed men and women who completed training in higher level computer skills: 83 percent of those completing courses in computing at higher levels were male (Gerver, 1984). At the new Information Technology Centers, which have been established in the UK to provide skills in computing for school-leavers, there are far more young men than young women: in 1984, less than one-third of the trainees at these centers were women (Women's National Commission, 1984). The manager of one such center reported that he "is rather concerned about the lack of female applicants. . . . Girl[s] . . . are just not interested enough to apply" (Deakin, 1984).

Among those who are addicted to working with computers – the "compulsive programmers" or "computer junkies" – there appear to be no women. Research being currently conducted into the social pathology of computer addiction, has so far failed to uncover any examples of women who fall into this category (Shotton, 1984). In the United States, the compulsive programmers described by Weizenbaum (1976) are all "bright young *men* of disheveled appearance."

At the level of leisure pursuits, there is ample evidence that fascination with computers is largely a male phenomenon. Almost all the users of computer-based games are boys and young men, and the games appeal primarily to traditionally male preferences. In a review of computer games on the market for sale at Christmas in the UK, Hetherington (1984) noted that "all of the games have heroes, not heroines, and are in other ways oriented toward boys. This unfortunately reflects the current market, which apart from a few patronizing 'games for girls' is almost entirely aimed at boys." The predominantly male appeal of most leisure computer magazines is overwhelmingly evident. The articles, written mainly by men, assume that the reader is male; the advertisements sometimes verge on being offensive to women; the illustrations are primarily of men using computers, with women occupying a lesser, mainly picturesque, role.

Studies on the use of computers at home also show a pronounced sexual imbalance. Beyers (1983) reports that interviews with typical computer-owning families in the United States "indicated that sons used the machine most. They spent an average of two to three hours a day playing and programming games. The father used the computer regularly for business, while the mother did not use it at all."

In the informal learning that takes place in computer camps, where learning about computers is chosen purely as a form of pleasure, there are fewer girls than boys in the UK (Deakin, 1984) and in the United States (Beyers, 1983). In American computer camps, in 1983, "boys outnumbered girls by three to one. The proportion of girls in beginning and intermediate classes was 27 percent. This dropped to 14 percent in advanced programming classes and to 5 percent in higher level courses teaching assembly language" (Beyers, 1983).

In the setting of the public library, whose users tend to be female, it has been shown by Yeates (1982) that far more men than women will use computer-based systems to provide information. At central lending libraries in the UK, the ratio of users of Prestel (a computer-based information system) was seven men to every three women, while at reference libraries the gender imbalance was even more pronounced, with nearly four men to every one woman.

Such an apparently ubiquitous gender imbalance in the use of computers cries out for systematic research which would allow informed speculation about the reasons as a firm basis for trying to redress the imbalance. The field of computing is relatively new, and the studies which directly address the very complex problem of the reasons for the imbalance are scattered. Nevertheless, sufficient evidence has already been accumulated to provide indicators of some of the major factors at work.

Factors in the gender imbalance of computer use

In trying to assess the major sources of the difficulties here, one might be tempted to look at the world of employment as the overriding factor, and at the ability of girls and women to use computers effectively as a second major factor. As I shall suggest, however, both of these approaches lead to blind alleys, and one has to seek elsewhere for possible explanations.

At first sight it appears as if the situation in employment is one of the chief factors: women are significantly underrepresented in employment at most levels of working with computers. At the lowest levels – that of merely entering data into computers – there are far more women than men. In 1980 in the United States, women formed 78 percent of those employed as keypunchers or computer operators (Wider Opportunities for Women, 1983), while, in the UK of the same year, a survey showed that between 75 and 100 percent of all workers at the lowest level of computing were women (Simons, 1981).

At the more advanced levels of working with computers, in the United States in 1980, only 29 percent of computer programmers and 22 percent of systems analysts were women (Wider Opportunities for Women, 1983). In the UK, the gender imbalance was even more dramatic: females comprised only between 5 and 15 percent of all computer programmers, and less than 5 percent of systems analysts (Simons, 1981). In Germany in 1979, female systems analysts, programmers, and sales staff comprised only 18 percent of the total employed in these areas of computing (Simons, 1981).

But there is evidence that companies involved in the computer industry, far from discriminating against women, are trying actively to encourage their participation. Moreover, there are certain characteristics of working with computers which make such work particularly attractive to women who place a high value on their domestic roles. In the UK, the Women's National Commission (1984) has found that:

The new technology industries are the least resistant to the employment of women at all levels, provided qualified women come forward. Some companies have made special efforts to make their recruitment literature attractive to women. Companies like "F International" which employ women computing experts as "home workers", together with women managers of this now large-scale operation, show that skills in computing can offer women a special kind of compatibility between home and work responsibilities; isolation is also alleviated by the high-powered nature of much of the work and the need for periods of working contact with the client firm. Many women working for such companies have been able to make geographical moves following their husband's career without jeopardising their own; levels of work commitment can be varied over time, and there are opportunities to take wider responsibilities for managing others.

In the United States, evidence adduced in the mid-1970s suggested that the computer industry represented a relatively favorable employment environment for women (Simons, 1981), and the position appears, if anything, to have improved since that time. In varying degrees, throughout the developed world, women still suffer from multifarious patterns of stereotyping and of direct and indirect discrimination, and their progress up the hierarchy of the world of computing is often as tenuous as it is in many other fields. But, as Simons (1981) suggests, "compared with other, older industries, it is arguable that women have done well in data processing;" indeed, as Chivers (1984) reports, "some of the large high technology companies in computing and electronics . . . have actively supported the very able women technologists entering their ranks."

It appears, then, as if the reasons for the under-representation of women at all levels of computing do not stem primarily from discriminatory practices within the computer industry itself. Perhaps, then, women simply have less ability to use computers? There often appear to be connections between using computers and using mathematical ideas, and women and girls seem to perform less well at mathematics than men and boys. Perhaps, then, the problem lies in the lesser mathematical ability of females?

So far, nearly all the evidence available seems to suggest that women have abilities to work with computers which are at least equal to those of men. As Deakin (1984) points out, "computing is a discipline that requires some (but not necessarily great) mathematical ability, logic, . . . and a grasp of the principles of language systems and communication methods."

But even the assumption that girls and women are "bad" at mathematics needs further investigation. More females than males do say that they are afraid of mathematics and of technology, but there is evidence to suggest that such anxiety is a learned rather than an innate response. At primary school level, it appears that girls and boys perform almost equally in mathematics. It is only after elementary school that there appears to be a decline in the aptitude and achievement of girls. Thus, girls' attitudes toward mathematics tend to take a turn for the worse during the years of their early adolescence, at a time when they tend not to want to compete with boys. It has been shown that, in the United States, where mathematically gifted boys often take advanced courses, mathematically gifted girls are reluctant to do so because of their fear of social rejection (Stanley, 1973).

From the UK, there is a growing body of evidence to suggest that, when girls are taught mathematics in single-sex settings, their academic results are at least equal to those of boys taught in mixed-sex groupings, where boys have consistently been shown to be superior to girls in their results in mathematics. In a cautious review of the evidence in the UK so far, Smith (1984) concluded that "secondary school girls are likely to do better at maths when segregated from boys." This finding was confirmed in an experiment in England at Stamford High School, where a single-sex setting for the teaching of mathematics appeared to have a pronounced beneficial effect on the final marks of the girls during the two years in which it operated. It appears then, that, at least in mathematics, the performance of girls is at least as good as that of boys. The factors affecting the apparent decline in secondary school appear to be social rather than innate.

But the significant dropout of girls from computer courses discussed above seems to imply that they may have less ability at working with computers than boys. In the United States, as Rossen (1982) shows, girls have been doing slightly less well than boys on computer programming tests. However, when they have good exposure to computers, the girls perform as well as, or better than, boys (Rossen, 1982). Here again as in the question of mathematical performance, social factors rather than innate abilities appear to be the main cause of the apparent lesser performance by girls. There is now a mass of anecdotal evidence to suggest that girls will be discouraged from computing by the attitudes of their male peers. In one US high school, for instance, adolescent boys harassed the girls in order to discourage them from registering for the after-school computer courses. The boys admitted that they were doing this deliberately to limit enrollment, so that they could have more computer time for themselves (Rossen, 1982). In the UK, the Equal Opportunities Commission has graphically depicted one example of a ubiquitous problem with mixed-sex teaching of computer courses in secondary school:

Because the number of boys in the course far outweighed the number of girls, the girls felt as though they were interlopers, and that they had fewer rights than the boys when the computers were being used.

There was not enough time in class for adequate programming on the computers. The boys compensated for this by using the computer room at other times, but they did this in a way that forced the girls out or discouraged them from entering at all. This caused many girls to drop out of the course as they felt they had little or no chance of completing their project work. The sheer size and power of the average boy, determined to take more than his fair share of computer time, gradually forced the more timid girls to give up altogether. (EOC, 1983)

It appears, then, that the factors involved in the under-representation of women in computing can be traced neither to the beginning of their formal learning at school nor to their employment at the end of their formal education. Instead, the first of our clues may lie in the interaction that takes place between girls and computers at school.

Girls and computers

Even where girls do choose to take part in computer studies and in other ways of using computers at school, they have a particularly pronounced dropout rate. In one local education authority in England, for instance, twice as many girls as boys failed to take the final, qualifying examination in Computer Studies (EOC, 1983). As we have already seen, the ways in which boys effectively exclude girls from using the few machines available in many schools clearly contribute to such a wastage rate; competition between boys and girls for what is still a relatively scarce resource is likely to benefit those who are more aggressive and competitive. But other factors seem to interact with such sexist exclusion to create a situation in which girls choose to exclude themselves from the specific opportunities that are available to them.

A number of features about the way in which computer studies are presented in school seem to alienate girls. Indeed, it appears that some of the same characteristics are at least partially responsible for the extent to which many women also feel alienated from the new information technologies, including computers.

In the first place, work with computers in schools often focuses primarily on the machine itself, the theories behind its functioning and the electronics that implement those theories. The Deputy Director of the Microelectronics Education Programme in England and Wales, for instance, believes that Computer Studies should emphasize "the concepts which underlie electronic systems, electronics, and the binary logic of a system" (EOC, 1983). Since many local authorities in those two countries depend on MEP for in-service training and advice in using computers in schools, such an emphasis will presumably be reflected in practice at the grass-roots level in the schools themselves.

The fact that computing studies tend to be taught, at least in the UK, by teachers of physics and mathematics reinforces the tendency to emphasize the theory and the electronics of the technology itself, and may contribute to the speed at which girls, who tend to have much less affinity with machines as a whole, often opt out of such courses. Moreover, the problems set for pupils to solve by using computer programs tend to be mathematically based, and may thus create gratuitous difficulties for girls who are insecure about their mathematical abilities in the first place.

Other possible reasons for girls' withdrawal from computers emerge from the responses given by girls in England who had chosen Computer Studies at the end of their third year in secondary school. EOC (1983) cited some typical answers to questions which the girls were asked:

Q Has the course been of use to you? Why?
A Yes, it helps me practise my typing.
Q Do you think the course was aimed mainly at boys, girls, or both equally? Explain why.
A Boys – all the teachers are men.
Q Has the course turned out as you expected? (Explain fully.)
A No. I expected to be taught more practical use of the computers; more lessons on actual programming.
Q Can you suggest any changes in the course which could have helped out?
A 1: More practical programming. 2: The present course is very dull. A more active lesson would create greater interest on the pupil's part.
Q Has the course been of use to you. Why?
A No, I have found the majority of the work uninteresting and the concepts difficult to understand and grasp.
Q Can you suggest any changes in the course which would help you?
A More explanation and practice of computer language and terms.

This sample of pupil responses draws unflattering attention to the effect of the quality of teaching in work on computer studies. Because computer studies form a new area of academic study – an area where in many cases teachers are not even a single step ahead of their more able pupils – it is perhaps inevitable that standards of presentation may not be as high as in more traditional subjects. There is now evidence to suggest, however, that this apparent lack of high quality does discourage more girls than boys.

Why? Here again there seems to be a variety of interlocking factors. In the first place, boys seem to have a much stronger motivation to engage with computers for their own sake and will, therefore, probably be more tolerant of difficulties placed in their path, such as poor quality teaching. Girls, with their stronger practical bent, will often wonder what the point of it all is, when, in many cases, the power of the computer is used to perform trivial tasks which could be carried out more efficiently by hand or by using a calculator. Indeed, as McClain (1983) has shown, while men are more interested in computer games and graphics, females tend to see the computer as a tool – a means to an end. Where they fail to find sufficient evidence of the efficacy of the computer as a tool, girls are likely to lose interest quickly.

Secondly, much of the material actually available to children in connection with computers is oriented primarily toward boys. Textbooks for Computer Studies in the UK tend to present a world in which computers are mainly for men and boys. The graphics in one textbook, for example, contained ten men to every woman, while those in another contained 11 men to the one woman, a barely clothed girl on a screen (EOC, 1983).

But children both at home and at school tend to use computer games far more than computer textbooks. And, as we have seen, those games tend to be for boys only. The noneducational games have titles like "Armageddon," "Dracula," "Space Invaders," or "War Games" (after the film of the same name in which an adolescent boy nearly destroys the world as a result of breaking into a computer defense system.) Nearly all girls are repelled by the violence in both the concept and the actuality of these games. Descriptions of two recent games from a review of them illustrate their typical characteristics:

Along with a nimble fire-button, you also need a keen sense of strategy, if you're to survive in its alien universe. You are a trader who will deal in anything in order to buy weapons and defenses to defend you from anything from galactic pirates to the police.

The atmosphere is created by the spoken start of the game when an evil voice welcomes you with the chilling words, "Another visitor, stay awhile, stay forever!" This voice belongs to [a man] . . . who will destroy the world unless you crack his security code, but to do that you will have to outwit the most fiendish robots." (Hetherington, 1984)

But much of the imagery used in educational programs is also either boring or unattractive to girls. Zimmerman (1983) reports on a game used to teach fractions to young children, which showed an arrow piercing a floating balloon when the pupil made a correct answer. "The girls, unlike the boys, did not care much about popping the balloons. When the reward image changed to a little puppy, girls' scores rose significantly."

A further difficulty often arises because most computer games foster a spirit of intense, often speed-ridden competitiveness either between the individual and the machine or between two individuals. There is a considerable body of evidence to suggest that females tend to view competitive success as dangerous (Whiting and Pope, 1973; Maccoby and Jacklin, 1974; Pollak and Gilligan, 1982; Gilligan, 1983; among many others). Games that appeal primarily to competitiveness rather than to the pleasures of interpersonal relationships may, therefore, tend to alienate girls and women.

Other social factors in girls' experience are also likely to alienate them from engaging with computers at school, as at home. It appears that many teachers and careers advisors still perceive science and technology, including computing, as subjects predominantly for boys. In the United States, for instance, women have consistently reported that the careers counseling which they received at school not only failed to encourage their participation in nontraditional fields but, in many cases, actually attempted to discourage them from study that would lead to mathematical and scientific careers (Luchins and Luchins, 1980). In the UK, concern about an analogous problem about careers counseling of girls led in 1984 to the establishment of the WISE (Women into Science and Engineering) campaign, designed to increase awareness of opportunities for girls in science and engineering, including the new information technologies.

All of these factors which contribute toward the alienation of girls from computers at school may also be found in the experiences of many women, with an even more pronounced adverse effect. Women have less money and less time to spend on themselves than men; many social factors conspire to make it more difficult for women to advance upwards in careers; the computer world itself tends to be composed primarily of young men rather than of middle-aged women. All of these factors make it unlikely that women will, of their own accord, contribute fully to the world of computing.

Does this relative exclusion matter? Well, there are compelling arguments that can be made about the need for our economies to use to the fullest the talents of both men and women. The moral arguments in favor of gender equality are becoming more generally accepted. But there are also specific reasons why the participation of women in the world of computing is necessary both for that world and for the economic position of women themselves. It is to these that I shall now turn, before considering some of the ways that have already been found to enable women to interact more fully with computers.

Redressing the gender imbalance

It is essential to encourage more women to engage in computers, both for their economic survival and for the ways in which their greater participation may help to make computers more responsive to human needs. Throughout most of the developed world, computerization seems to be having an apparently contradictory effect on employment: many new jobs are created in the new information technologies, at the same time as the demand for many older skills appears to be decreasing. To an even greater extent than men, women are trapped by this contradictory effect. The situation in Canada, as described by Menzies (1981), seems to be replicated in most other developed countries: "Informatics is creating new work and employment, but largely in the professional and technical ranks where men predominate and women are still in a minority." In particular, Menzies argues, there is likely to be an "alarmingly high rate of structural unemployment among female clerical workers . . . unless appropriate measures are taken by governments, employers, and women."

The same conclusion appears elsewhere in the growing literature of this field. Thus, Feldberg and Glenn (1982) find that "the expansion of computer-related occupations has increased the total number of jobs and created some new higher paid occupations. However, the workers displaced by automation do not appear to benefit: the new jobs are technical level and largely held by males." The finding is substantiated by Menzies, who cites the fact that, in the Canadian corporation which she examined, only two out of the 130 workers displaced from clerical work moved upwards to professional or managerial level.

The extent of the potential wastage of female staff may be seen in the fact that "in most industrialized countries . . . the reduction of staff predicted in offices and banks is in the region of 30 to 50 percent" (Trudel and Belanger, 1982). By far the vast majority of these workers are women, and, as Menzies bleakly notes, "the supply of clerical labour is projected to outstrip demand."

But it is not only the quantity of female jobs which are affected adversely by computerization. There is also evidence that the quality, particularly of the kinds of clerical work traditionally undertaken by women, may be suffering in the process. Examining four representative fields in which computerization has affected work – a large, broadly diversified corporation, an insurance company, banking, and supermarkets – Menzies concludes that:

The continuing standardization, streamlining, and fragmentation of work functions, which was observed in all of the case studies, suggests that clerical work is becoming more like an assembly line. . . . Monitoring tends to place quantity of output over sophistication of input, and thereby subtly degrades the scope of the work involved. . . . The operation of a word processor terminal does not require a great deal of skill on the part of the operator.

As a homely illustration, my word processor makes it possible for me no longer to need traditional typing skills: I can readily correct the many errors that arise from inaccurate typing before I print out a final version; I can, if I wish, use a spelling program to indicate to me words that I have unwittingly misspelled; indeed, the only loss may be stylistic, in that my computer cannot tactfully suggest where I have communicated unclearly in the way that a sympathetic typist might have done! The final result is to upgrade my incompetent typing skills and thereby to devalue the skills of a conventional typist, whose speed, accuracy, and neatness are largely redundant. Thus, Feldberg and Glenn (1982) conclude that "women have been differentially and more negatively affected than men by changes accompanying office automation." The clerical skills by which many women have earned their living, then, are no longer likely to ensure their economic survival.

But there are other reasons why women need to engage more readily with computers. The fact that some computing firms are actively recruiting and supporting their female staff is not altruistic. In certain respects, women tend to make better computer programmers than men. Women's traditional ability to master languages with apparent ease extends also to the mastery of computer languages, and women's tendency toward linear logic also stands them in good stead in this field. McClain (1983) has found that women are more likely to write good computer programs with the user in mind. Women's tendency to ignore extraneous factors and to concentrate on the task at hand also leads to good programming technique. Indeed, there is a considerable amount of evidence that, while males tend to be more curious and more likely to take risks, females are better able to screen out irrelevancies, carry out tasks, and be better problem-solvers under stress (Weizman, 1975; Safran, 1983; among others). All of these qualities again are conducive to good computer techniques.

The advantages that women bring to computing have also been spelled out by the course tutor in a computing school (Women's National Commission, 1984). She noted first that women provided a disproportionate share of the really able and most tenacious students and that they demonstrated an ability to serve industry well. In particular, she reported that women "frequently showed a clear advantage over men as project managers/systems analysts, as they communicated better with non-computing staff, an absolute requirement of the future."

Deakin (1984) notes that women are often as good as, or better than, men at selling computers. She analyzes her own experience as a sales consultant:

Now that I work as a sales consultant, I still feel that there are some ways in which I have something special to offer by being female. I think that I have been able to advise and assist the male customers particularly well because they do not feel threatened by me, because I have learned to communicate and because I am concerned with the practicalities of their needs rather than the beauty of any particular machine. As one person said, I am "into customer solutions." This may not be the preserve of women, but it is their very special contribution and one which the whole industry needs. This is one reason why it is as important for men as it is for women that women become more involved in computers and computing.

Although such comparisons are probably invidious, there are also snippets of evidence that women may be perceived as better than men in teaching computing to adults. Banks (1984) found that nearly half of the students whom he interviewed about their experiences of computing courses for adults did not consider their tutor to be a good teacher but that "generally students were less critical of female tutors than male." Salkeld (1983) has also suggested that the few female tutors on introductory computer courses for adults seemed to be particularly popular as teachers. Any rash hypothesis that most of the students were male and, therefore, preferred to have women tutors is nullified by the fact that nearly half of the students interviewed by Banks were female.

Finally, simply because of their traditional proficiency in clerical skills – especially in typing – women have a distinct advantage in using computer keyboards. Familiarity with the QWERTY keyboard and accuracy in pressing keys are practical skills, the lack of which are often disadvantageous to male users, particularly male users who wish to use computers for practical applications rather than to write programs or design computer architectures. It is largely for such male users that various devices such as the "mouse" have been designed, but, for sheer practical ease, using the keyboard remains the most efficient way to harness the power of a computer. And more women are better placed than most men to do so.

For their own economic good and for the economic good of the computer industry, then, there are clear advantages in a closer interaction between women and computers. Beyond these economic considerations, however, a more far-reaching case also exists for the need for more women to become involved in computing.

At least part of the world dominated by computers is pathological – obsessed by power and ruled by instrumental reason. There are many reasons why such characteristics have emerged. The relative scarcity of women in computing is probably only a minor factor in creating a situation where computers are used primarily for military purposes and commercial profit rather than to help to meet the real needs that people have to find out more about their local communities, to keep in touch with each other and their compassionate desires to help one another, and to nurture the young, the handicapped, and the frail. As later chapters will suggest, computer applications can provide valuable help in all of these traditionally "female" areas of concern. It may be, then, that when women play a substantially increased part in computing, greater attention will be given to ways in which computers can actively help people.

Many of the characteristics that women currently find so alienating about computers are not inevitable in the technology itself. There is no absolute reason why using computers has to be accompanied by smokescreens of jargon or delight in the machines themselves: women have used automatic washing machines for decades without feeling any need to worship the object which replaces unpleasant physical labor. Most women, too, bring to computers a hard core of common sense, based on a lack of time to waste. They tend to recognize that, just as there are many tasks which can be performed more efficiently and effectively on a computer, so there are many more which can be performed, but which are not worth performing. If women were to play an increased role in using computers, then, it is possible that a more humanly balanced view of the uses and nonuses of computers might result.

Despite these arguments for redressing the gender imbalance in using computers, however, strong counter-arguments have been advanced against any greater involvement by women. Some radical feminists in particular believe that technology is not simply a neutral means whereby individuals, groups, and societies can achieve their goals.

In the first place, the argument runs, women throughout the world are often exploited by computer technology, particularly in Third World countries where they tend to be employed in the production and assemblage of computer and microprocessor equipment. And there appear to be certain dangers to women's health when they are required to use computer terminals for long periods of time. In these ways, women are seriously disadvantaged by computer technology.

More broadly, radical feminists argue that:

Women must not forget that the range and nature of a society's technology is a reflection of the dominant socio-economic system. And in the Western culture that means that it is a process guided by the values of the various patriarchies and one which owes its very existence to the requirements of the military–industrial complex. At its furthest development their argument challenges the whole nature of technology and the societies that spawned it, asking the . . . question: can feminists use technology as it stands at all, or does using it involve fatal compromise and collusion with the forces of patriarchy? (Women and Computing, 1981)

Such a stance, however, involves the acceptance of premises that are not shared by all feminists. I should like to argue, more pragmatically, that women who exclude themselves from learning about and using computers risk experiencing even greater vulnerability in a world that is increasingly dependent on the power of computers and telecommunications. In a similar belief that education and training, rather than withdrawal from the world of technology, are more likely to empower women, many individuals and organizations are now responding to what they see as the need to help women to use computer technology for their own ends. During the 1980s, there has thus been a dramatic growth in the number of opportunities which have been created for women to learn about computers.

Women learning about computers

We have already seen that girls' mathematical and computer performance tends to increase when they are taught in single-sex settings. And women tend to use computers in greater numbers in women-only groups. Most of the opportunities currently being created for women to come to terms with computers, therefore, tend to be for women only and, more frequently than not, taught by women only. The one major exception to the general pattern – that of the BBC's Computer Literacy Project – appealed more or less equally to men and women, partly because it was careful to show that all ages and both sexes could use computers with equal facility and efficacy (Radcliffe and Salkeld, 1983), but also possibly because the television programs could be watched at home rather than in adult education classes composed predominantly of men.

The range of courses to enable women to learn about computers is wide, encompassing formal training courses, as well as formal courses in educational institutions and nonformal adult education classes. They seem clearly to be meeting a felt need: the demand for them almost invariably exceeds provision. Three case studies of courses in the UK, the United States, and New Zealand may illustrate the range and suggest some of the essential characteristics of successful courses of this type.

"Computers for Women" in New Zealand

In 1984 in Wellington, New Zealand, a course called "Computers for Women" was organized, according to one of the women course leaders,

To provide a "safe" environment where women can happily expose their ignorance and try things out and ask elementary questions without being or feeling put down. There has certainly been a lot of interest and a good response from a wide variety of women. We have pointed out to all enrolling that this is indeed a course for absolute beginners, and if they know *anything* about computers they are too advanced for the course. The usual response is "Oh good, that's just what I want – I've never even *seen* a computer" . . . We hope women who become interested through our courses will go on to take others in special fields of their own choosing. . . . Once they know a little, they can cope better with the "male expert" syndrome and feel less inadequate faced with all that jargon. (Else, 1984a)

The attractively elementary nature of the course would be very likely to appeal to women who feel uneasy about coming to terms with computers. Following the completion of the course, an analysis of completed questionnaires showed that participants

Appreciated the friendly supportive atmosphere and the availability of an all-women class. They liked feeling able to ask any questions at all without feeling threatened or put down. They liked the variety of speakers arranged and the exchange of ideas between course members and lecturers; also the chance to hear about others' problems with computers. They enjoyed the hands-on experience. . . . Three stated their approval/enjoyment of the way political issues to do with women, computers, and society were raised, as well as the technical points. . . . On the whole, the response was one of positive enjoyment and enhanced confidence. (Else, 1984b)

The difficulties experienced were largely those created by this being the first course of its kind in the country:

It was clear that we had not really broken down the initial instruction sessions into small or simple enough chunks for some people. We were still using too much jargon in places or moving too quickly over basic points, e.g., use of keyboard. We needed one more person to help the participants when all were present and using the computers, and should also have provided more written material as simple manuals and hand-outs. There were also some problems with the [computer equipment] breaking down. Not everyone liked politics being included — they would have preferred a straight technical approach. Time was a constant problem. (Else, 1984b)

The crucial element in this course was clearly the provision of an all-female environment in which women felt free to start from the very beginning. The second characteristic is that of utility, with an emphasis on what the computer can be used for rather than on the details of what exactly it is in itself. For many women, however, such a course may have created practical problems, both because it was relatively expensive, and because it made no provisions for the care of their children. Both of these issues have been directly addressed in Sheffield, UK, in a new scheme designed to introduce women to computing.

A Women's Technology Training Workshop in the UK

The purpose of this workshop, which is funded jointly by Sheffield City Council and the European Social Fund, is:

To provide basic and more advanced training in microelectronics and computing fields, where women are under-represented. The training . . . is intended for women over 25 who are unemployed, threatened with unemployment, or wishing to return to work after a period of child-rearing. The courses are specifically tailored to suit unskilled women who have been unable to take advantage of existing training facilities in the field. To this end . . . there are no formal entry requirements; the courses are part-time; child-care allowances are available; the courses are administered by, and taught by, women. (Sheffield City Council, 1984)

As soon as the course was advertised, despite the fact that its initial intake consisted only of 28 places, there were thousands of telephone enquiries which provided evidence of an unsuspected scale of demand for such training (Miller, 1984a). Over 500 women completed application forms, and trainees were selected primarily on a quota system of age, status, ethnic origin, and "social need." Over two-thirds of the women had no qualifications at all (Miller, 1984b).

The course which the women are following has four main components. The Return to Work component aims "to develop confidence and to provide support for the new training environment" and "to provide a critical appreciation of the social impact of New Technology." The Computing component aims to enable trainees "to gain familiarity and confidence in using both mini- and microcomputers, to gain an understanding of programming in a high-level language (BASIC), to gain skills in using software packages . . ., to become computer literate." The Microelectronics part of the course develops a range of technical knowledge and skills. Mathematics, ranging from basic numeracy to certificate standard, is also taught to enable the students to understand fully the technical course components (Miller, 1984b).

By late autumn of 1984, the response of the trainees, who began in March, was seen as "extremely encouraging. All the trainees, including those with small children, have not only shown considerable enthusiasm and dedication while attending the Workshop, but have also specifically requested that homework be set and assessed on a regular basis, despite the fact that this was not intended to be a requirement of the course" (Miller, 1984b).

However, an analysis of the course has indicated that, while lack of formal qualifications has been no bar to satisfactory performance, some women who lacked numeracy and literacy skills have been unable to grasp essential background concepts. The course organizer has accepted that "these basic skills cannot be taught concurrently with main courses. Moreover teaching of these skills is both a specialized and lengthy process and cannot always be done on an intensive basis. Accordingly, literacy and numeracy must figure in the criteria for admission to the course" (Miller, 1984b).

This problem is not dissimilar to that which emerged from the course in New Zealand, where the initial concepts were not simple enough for some people. Indeed, the Sheffield findings reflect elements in the experience of some girls in computer studies in schools, where they reported that "the concepts [were] difficult to understand and grasp" and that the course was "much more complicated, detailed and theoretical than I imagined" (EOC, 1983).

This issue of the interrelationships between computer literacy and more traditional forms of literacy and numeracy also arises in the use of computers in nonformal adult basic education, and is obviously a matter to which much more thought and research needs to be addressed. It is already clear, however, that women, disadvantaged as they often seem to be in numeracy, may also be disadvantaged in coming to terms with computers unless ways can be found of tackling the combined problem of computer illiteracy and general lack of numeracy.

Meanwhile, it appears as if the prospect of enhanced employment and training opportunities at the end of the course, together with the provision of child-care arrangements and the payment of training expenses to the trainees, have been significant factors in the overwhelming demand for the course. The Women's Technology Training Workshop appears to have demonstrated that, once socioeconomic factors are taken realistically and sensitively into account, women are very willing indeed to come to terms with computers.

The Women's Computer Literacy Project in the United States

This project to enable women to acquire computer literacy was set up as "an alternative to the computer classes many women found alienating" (Marohn, undated). As one of the organizers of the courses saw the situation, "many women have an approach-avoidance attitude toward computers, . . . and most men are not very good at teaching women. We've heard all kinds of horror stories about classes at city colleges and computer stores where smart women have been made to feel stupid and have been given the sense that they can't do it" (Marohn, undated).

The Project offers two-day, full-time, and four-week part-time courses in San Francisco and two-day courses in New York "for those who know nothing about computers and prefer to learn in a woman-centered environment." As is the course in New Zealand and that in Sheffield, it is highly practically oriented, as the leaflet proclaims:

At the end of the course you will know what microcomputers can and cannot do; you will be able to operate a microcomputer with confidence; and you will be able to read and understand most operations manuals for computer hardware and software systems. You will also understand the differences between various microcomputer systems so that you can shop for the correct system to meet your personal, business, or organizational needs.

Unlike the course in Sheffield, however, the American course, like most others in the United States, has to be self-financing; it is expensive, at least for women who do not have much money at their disposal. Clearly, however, it meets considerably more needs than the courses in programming in BASIC which formed the staple diet of computing courses for adults in the UK and other countries in the first years of using microcomputers (Gerver, 1984).

Other ways of encouraging women to use computers

Even where no computer is actually provided as part of an introduction to the new technologies, there is now substantial international evidence that women will respond in large numbers to events and material which are prepared specifically for them about computers. In Israel, NA'AMAT, the largest women's organization in the country, chose "Women and Technology" as the theme for its annual Status of Women Month in 1983. The movement designed a portfolio designed to give women a feeling of familiarity with computers, selected films showing high technology at work in various fields, and used both print and television media to reinforce its message about ways in which women could link up to the new technology. The result was that, even though they themselves were not providing computer experiences or training opportunities, they received more enquiries than they could handle (NA'AMAT, undated). The same experience of demand exceeding supply has been almost invariably repeated in other countries.

As well as burgeoning opportunities in education and training, there has also been a number of important developments in other ways for women to use computers. The WISE Campaign in the UK exemplifies campaigns designed to encourage girls to choose computing as a career; groups to support women in computing have mushroomed in the past few years throughout the developed world; and books and conferences are increasingly addressing the question of the under-representation of women in computing.

The WISE Campaign promoted by the Equal Opportunities Commission in the UK in 1984 aimed to encourage girls themselves to consider positively the opportunities for careers in science and technology, including particularly information technology. The EOC's (1984) booklet "Working with Computers" exemplifies the approach, in its careful selection of biographies of women who have achieved significant success in the world of the new technologies. Throughout, its approach is one of demystifying. It points out, for example, that for one girl, "the key to coping with computers for her was much more to do with being able to use the English language than to do with maths"; it draws attention to various cooperative ways of using computers and it highlights women who have come into the field from apparently unrelated disciplines and interests.

Such an approach to girls and women to help themselves in coming to terms with computers is likely, of course, to lead to only very limited change. WISE has placed great stress on what can be achieved "simply by a change to more positive attitudes by all concerned. . . . Girls leaving school simply need the interest and energy to find out and fully appreciate the many incentives and opportunities available in engineering and science" (WISE, 1984). As this present discussion has suggested, however, the matter cannot be resolved merely by altering the attitudes of girls, who, in many cases, are merely responding adversely to characteristics of the world of technology which are genuinely alienating.

Other organizations in Britain and the United States are trying to use the technology itself to offer more concrete help to those women and girls who feel they would like to use computers but are not sure how to go about it. One of the best examples of such supportive use of computers for women who feel that they may want to use computers may be seen in Microsyster, a London-based organization which was set up in 1982.

Microsyster "aims to encourage women to think about positive ways of making computers work for women. We are aware that many women feel alienated and excluded by new technology and are worried by the threat they do pose to our jobs and privacy. We not only want to provide a service for women, but also to open up these debates in the Women's Liberation Movement" (Microsyster, 1984). Microsyster, therefore, aims to "provide computing services to women and women's groups; make contact with and support other feminists working in computing; provide a feminist perspective on new technology; to introduce the skills and knowledge necessary for women to benefit from and critically assess new technology" (Microsyster, 1984).

As with the computer courses offered by women for women, so also the computer services offered by Microsyster are highly practical. They offer advice about whether a computer would really help an individual or a group; they help determine the system that would be most suitable and they even help with the writing out of the applications for grants to buy it. They also offer to help to set up systems and to teach women how to use the software packages which they have bought or acquired; the presentation of information in most computer manuals makes such informed help mandatory!

Support for women who want to use computers and for women who might want to use them if they were presented in a nonthreatening way has also come from an increasing number of books and conferences which, in the mid-1980s, have addressed the problem directly. In the UK in 1981, Simons' account of *Women in Computing* aimed "to encourage a search for constructive policies on the part of managers, employers, politicians, and others." Deakin's *Women and Computing: The Golden Opportunity* (1984) looks "first at the special benefits that exist for women in computing and then . . . at the ways in which the arrival of microcomputers can be a heaven-sent opportunity for them." Both books rely heavily on illuminating case studies of women who have successfully made careers for themselves in the world of computing.

Academic investigations of the problem of the under-representation of women in the new technologies generally and in computing in particular have multiplied during the 1980s. Work has been particularly concentrated on the adverse effects of computerization on the employment of women (Menzies, 1981; Rothschild, 1982; Werneke; 1983, among many others). The educational implications of the under-representation of women in computing are attracting European concern. In 1984, at least two European conferences devoted a substantial amount of time to the question of women and new technology, and there are plans to consider the subject in at least four conferences to be held in the UK in 1985. The awareness of the subject in the United States is also indicated by the growing numbers of academic publications on the topic (Gerver and Lewis, 1984). The International Council for Adult Education, which is based in Canada, also has plans to investigate the topic.

Those adult educators who feel that there is an overwhelming case for making it possible for more women to engage with computers are thus, at least in the mid-1980s, well supported. But much much more remains to be done, as the enormous over-subscription to the Women's Technology Training Workshops in Sheffield suggests.

One potentially worrying development is that the current pressures on higher and further education throughout most of the developed world are likely to exclude more and more women from formal study. One indicator of the full extent of the emerging problem may be seen in a report from the UK from the Computing School of Thames Polytechnic in London. In 1980–1, women formed 25 percent of the intake to courses in computing. In 1983–4, women formed only 16.9 percent of those admitted, and applications from women were down to 18 percent. The course tutor speculated that "the main reason was the increasingly competitive entry to courses . . . which activated women's diffidence, dislike of competition, and belief that a high-powered prestigious profession was 'for men only' " (Women's National Commission, 1984).

As places in higher education continue to be cut back in many developed countries, so one can safely predict that this pattern in London will be replicated many times. The onus will, therefore, lie even more heavily on those who provide informal education in the community. Adult educators need to become more aware of the extent of the problem, its main causes, and their possible solutions, so that they can offer greater gender equality than that which presently exists in most educational experiences involving computers.

References

Banks, David (1983), "Adult classes in computing: a survey," *Adult Education*, vol. 56, p. 1.

Banks, David (1984), "The effectiveness of introductory computing evening classes," *Adult Education*, vol. 57(3), pp. 255–61.

BBC (1983), "BBC's computer literacy project: an evaluation," unpublished BBC Broadcasting Research Special Report, London: British Broadcasting Corporation.

Bernstein, Danielle (1984), "The invisible woman," *Practical Computing, January*, p. 189.

Beyers, Charlotte (1983), "Growing sex gap shows up in computer tastes," *The Times Educational Supplement*, November 18, p. 15.

Chivers, G. E (1984), "A comparative international study of intervention studies to reduce girls' disadvantages in science and technology education and vocational training," paper presented to Conference on Interests in Science and Technology Education, 12th IPN Symposium in cooperation with UNESCO, Kiel, West Germany, April 2–6.

Deakin, Rose (1984), *Women and Computing: the Golden Opportunity,* London: Macmillan.

Else, Anne (1984a), Written communication to the author from Wellington, New Zealand, August 31.

Else, Anne (1984b), Written communication to the author from Wellington, New Zealand, November 29.

EOC (1983) *Information Technology in Schools: Guidelines of Good Practice for Teachers of IT,* produced by the London Borough of Croydon for the Equal Opportunities Commission, Manchester, UK.

EOC (1984), "Attract more girls to information technology," news release, Manchester, UK, January 19.

Feldberg, Roslyn and Glenn, Evelyn (1982), "Technology and work degradation: effects of office automation on women clerical workers," in Joan Rothschild (ed.), *Machina ex Dea: Feminist Perspectives on Technology,* New York: Pergamon Press.

Gerver, Elisabeth (1984), *Computers and Adult Learning,* Milton Keynes, UK: Open University Press.

Gerver, Elisabeth and Lewis, Linda (1984), "Women, computers, and adult education: liberation or oppression?" *Convergence,* vol. 17, p. 4.

Gilligan, C. (1983), *In a Different Voice,* Cambridge, MA: Harvard University Press.

Hetherington, Tony (1984), "Guy's games," *The Times Educational Supplement,* December 12, p. 40.

Luchins, E. H. and Luchins, A. S. (1980), "Female mathematicians: a contemporary appraisal," in L. H. Fox, L. Brody, and D. Tobin (eds), *Women and the Mathematical Mystique,* Baltimore, MD: Johns Hopkins University Press.

Maccoby, E. and Jacklin, C. (1974), *The Psychology of Sex Differences,* Stanford, CA: Stanford University Press.

Marohn, Stephanie (undated), "Computer age feminists," *Woman News,* San Francisco, CA.

McClain, E. (1983), "Do women resist computers?" *Popular Computing,* January.

Menzies, Heather (1981), *Women and the Chip: Case Studies of the Effects of Informatics on Employment in Canada,* Montreal: Institute for Research on Public Policy.

Microsyster (1984), Written communication to the author from London, November 13.

Miller, Wendy (1984a), Personal communication to the author at Women's Technology Training Workshop, Sheffield, May 8.

Miller, Wendy (1984b), "Women's Technology Training Workshop – Progress Report," report to Board of Directors, City Center Training Limited, October 24.

NA'AMAT (undated), "Working women and technology," leaflet produced by the Status of Women Division, Movement of Working Women and Volunteers, Tel Aviv.

National Science Foundation (undated), "Science and engineering education: data and information," prepared for the National Science Board Commission on Pre-college Education in Mathematics, Science and Technology by the Office of Scientific and Engineering Personnel and Education, Washington, DC.

PEER (1983), "Microcomputers in the classroom: are girls getting an even break?" Washington, DC: Project on Equal Education Rights for the NOW Legal Defense and Education Fund.

Pollak, S. and Gilligan, C. (1982), "Images of violence in thematic apperception test stories," *Journal of Personality and Social Psychology,* vol. 42, p. 1.

Radcliffe, John and Salkeld, Roberts (1983), *Towards Computer Literacy: The BBC Computer Literacy Project 1979-1983,* London: British Broadcasting Corporation.

Rogers, Rick (1983), "Pick a winning combination," *The Guardian,* August 16.

Rossen, P. (1982), "Do schools teach computer anxiety?" *Ms. Magazine,* December.

Rothschild, Joan (1982), (ed.), *Women, Technology, and Innovation,* Oxford: Pergamon Press.

Safran, C. (1983), "Hidden lessons," *New York Daily News,* October 9.

Salkeld, Roberts (1983), Personal communication at the British Broadcasting Corporation, London, on June 7.

Sheffield City Council (1984), "Report of the employment coordinator, Women's Technology Training Workshop," unpublished report for the Employment Program Committee, March 26.

Shotton, Margaret (1984), Personal communication at the University of Loughborough, June 15.

Simons, G. L. (1981), *Women in Computing*, Manchester, UK: National Computing Centre Limited, 1981.

Smith, Stuart (1984), "Single-sex setting," in Rosemary Deem (ed.), *Co-education Reconsidered*, Milton Keynes, UK: Open University Press.

Stanley, J. C. (1973), "Comparison of men's and women's behaviors in high school math classes," California: SRI International.

Trudel, Lina and Belanger, Paul (1982), "Computerization: for better and for worse," paper prepared for International Council of Adult Education Conference, Paris, October.

Weizenbaum, Joseph (1976), *Computer Power and Human Reason*, San Francisco: Freeman.

Weizman, Lenore (1975), "Sex-role socialization," in Jo Freedman (ed.), *Women: A Feminist Perspective*, Palo Alto, CA: Mayfield Publishing.

Werneke, Diane (1983), *Microelectronics and Office Jobs: The Impact of the Chip on Women's Employment*, Geneva: International Labour Office.

Whiting, B. and Pope, C. (1973), "A cross cultural analysis of sex differences in the behavior of children age three to eleven," *Journal of Social Psychology*, vol. 91.

Wider Opportunities for Women (1983), "Bridging the skills gap: women and jobs in a high tech world," Washington, DC: Wider Opportunities for Women, April.

WISE (Women into Science and Engineering) (1984), "When I chose engineering, my friends thought it was a joke . . ." Equal Opportunities Commission leaflet, Manchester, UK.

Women and Computing (1981), "Are computers feminist?" London.

Women's National Commission (1984) "The other half of our future," report of the WNC's Ad-Hoc Working Group on training opportunities for women, London: Cabinet Office.

Yeates, Robin (1982), *Prestel in the Public Library: Reaction of the General Public to Prestel and Its Potential for Conveying Local Information*, Library and Information Research Report 2, London: British Library.

Zimmerman, Jan (1983), cited in Charlotte Beyers, "Growing sex gap shows up in computer tastes," *The Times Educational Supplement*, November 18, 1983.

15 Global Issues

The Role of IT in Third World Development

Robert Schware and Ziauddin Choudhury

The transfer of computer technology to the Third World is a controversial issue. This article reports on the recent efforts of international aid agencies to foster the use of IT in developing countries and discusses the policy implications. Perhaps surprisingly, the authors conclude that it is still by no means clear what the potential of IT is for developing nations. Schware and Choudhury both work for the Washington-based World Bank and this article is adapted from a piece which appeared in Information Technology for Development, *June–July 1988.*

Information technology is defined as the combination of computer technology, micro-electronics applications, and information and communications techniques and methods. The importance of information systems and IT for national and institutional development has long been recognized by international and national aid organizations.[1] However, most of these organizations treat IT only as a tool that supports projects in other traditional sectors such as agriculture, energy, and health. A few of these organizations are beginning to recognize IT as an important sector in itself, and to subject it to integrated rather than piecemeal analysis and planning. In this article we report on some new initiatives by development organizations to help countries build and strengthen their information technology industries. The article also includes some of the results of research on the role of the World Bank in the application of information technology in development.

Potential benefits

One is hard pressed to name an area of national development that could not potentially benefit from the introduction of IT. Application areas, both potential and actual, include such diverse fields as financial planning and management, agriculture, transportation planning, water resource management, utilities, primary health care management, banking, geophysical computing, and the design and control of machinery.[2]

Other potential benefits of IT may not be easy to realize or to quantify, but it could relieve people of repetitive and tedious work, improve productivity within particular processes, as well as increase the accuracy and reliability of systems in place now that are fragmented, duplicate information, and produce internally inconsistent data. More importantly, the use of IT can help governments with scarce resources to deploy them more effectively and thereby contribute to the national economy.

The prospect of IT being used in private and public sector operations with consequent cost reductions and improvements in product qualities, productivity, and other ancillary operations is extremely attractive. Appropriately applied, the provision of IT and related information systems can improve management, for example, in the control of inventories, costs, finance, or marketing. In addition to improving these strategic and tactical functions, developing countries might consider entering the huge worldwide market for information technology. Although precise data are lacking, it is estimated that the market for software alone has increased by 30 percent annually.

So many applications of IT have emerged recently that no single company or group of companies can hope to cover them all. Markets are rapidly expanding and fragmenting, which means that new opportunities in IT are opening for software suppliers, particularly those with intimate knowledge of applications that are difficult to acquire by large centralized firms. The current scheme of some developing country firms – to build on unique strengths and fill market niches too narrow or specialized to attract large firms – works well at present. Joint venture arrangements hold certain advantages for other firms from the perspective of technology transfer of skills as well as software development tools at reduced costs.

International assistance

International development activities in projects involving IT are no recent phenomenon. For many years organizations like the US Agency for International Development, the UN Development Programme (UNDP), the World Health Organization, the Food and Agriculture Organization, the World Bank, the UN Industrial Development Organization (UNIDO), and UNESCO – to name just a few – have provided IT for projects in developing countries. For example, between 1975 and 1987 the UNDP supported some 1,500 projects with IT components – mostly hardware and training in using hardware.[3] UNESCO is one of the few agencies within the UN system with a sectoral unit responsible for "informatics." The Informatics Section sponsors small project activities such as postgraduate and short-term training courses in computer science and technology, and support for computer centers and for publication of journals, as well as other professional activities.[4] The Rome-based Intergovernmental Bureau for Informatics (IBI) was established in late 1974 to promote the development and utilization of informatics within its 35 member countries (of whom none is a major technical assistance donor), as well as the establishment of informatics authorities in countries where they do not exist. IBI organized the first world conference on transborder data flow policies in 1980.

However, support from aid organizations has tended to be sporadic and uncoordinated, and often creates great problems for countries in terms of compatibility and parts. For example, a tally (done in mid-1986) of microcomputers in Burma included 32 different models and brands, which ranged from Cromenco, IBM, Canon, Commodore, Sharp, Wang, Elbit and Daisy, to a whole host of other lesser-known machines from Presto and Comart to Logitech.[5]

Further, the lion's share of the support from the aid organizations has been in using IT for particular tasks – such as management information systems, project tracking, billing and payroll applications, surveys, projections and simulations, investment and financial planning, etc. – rather than in building and strengthening the capacity of these countries to develop their own information technology industries.

Few development organizations have policies concerning IT use in developing countries, and even fewer have units responsible for promoting IT applications.[6] In this respect most assistance agencies are lagging behind countries as varied in size, and economic and political systems as Mexico, India, Brazil, Korea, Colombia, and China, which are committing great human and capital resources to information technology development. These agencies must offer those countries with potential in IT development the means to fashion a strategy for medium- to long-range IT development, and help these countries make appropriate policies and institutional arrangements to get the job done.

However, it is encouraging to see the growth and scale of some new international development activities that have taken place in the past two years and that are joint efforts with Third World countries. This recent trend may be considered an unsurprising byproduct of the burgeoning global information industry. But, to no small degree this growth of activity reflects increasing concern by development analysts that south–north dependency will increase even further unless these countries can promote the development of their own microelectronic, computer, and/or software industries. Such interest has been fueled by increasing demand for technical advice and evaluation studies from international development agencies such as the Canadian International Development Agency, UNIDO, the United Nations University (UNU), and the World Bank. What follows is an examination of the directions taken by a few of these organizations. The trends they illustrate are those we consider to reflect an appropriate, though modest, role for aid agencies in this field.

Microelectronics and software: UNIDO

UNIDO is preparing an international project for the "Transfer of Microelectronics and Software Technology" which is designed to strengthen the technological capability of developing countries.[7] In cooperation with computer and software manufacturers, the center will do this by providing developing countries with: (1) technical services (advice on various problems, formulation of projects, documentation, and analyses); (2) knowledge (on worldwide microprocessor applications, and software production and marketing); (3) technology (in the form of software or readily applicable solutions); and (4) information (on available microprocessor applications and software, software development methods, marketing, and training).

UNIDO's primary purpose in creating this center is to strengthen the technological infrastructure and capabilities in microprocessor applications and software development at national and regional levels so that participating countries can apply the technology for their local needs and, where possible, for export of products. Because a number of developing countries do not have a core group or an institutional group of people to undertake work in the microelectronics/software field, or to select the right type of applications, equipment, and software, the center will serve as a kind of capability building venture for these countries.

The center offers potential advantages to developing countries that suffer from scant technical know-how in modern microprocessor applications and software production, little capital, limited choices in equipment, software, and services, and from foreign exchange problems that prevent the acquisition of modern technology and capital equipment.

These rather ambitious advantages may be realistically fulfilled by the center's specific activities, which will be to:

- Help developing country firms find companies in industrialized countries interested in setting up joint ventures in microelectronics applications.
- Provide technical assistance in hardware and software acquisition, maintenance, and the optimal utilization of existing computer facilities.
- Assist developing countries in negotiating the acquisition of hardware and software.
- Train people and develop a human resource base capable of designing software and microelectronic applications.
- Locate experts who can upgrade the skills of microprocessor and software designers, and to assist in the development and adaptation of software and products to meet local needs.
- Function as a central clearing-house for agencies and software firms for information about available microprocessor applications and software that could be developed by firms in developing countries.

Software development: UNU

The software industry is becoming an arena of worldwide competition in which many nations participate. Measured by revenues, by the number of firms engaged in software development, and by the variety of available software, industry performance the past six years has been extraordinary. The future looks bright for this area as well. For example, the European market for software and data services is estimated to grow at an annual rate of 20–30 percent during the next four years. By 1991, it is predicted to exceed US$50,000 million.

A number of analyses of the role Third World countries might play in the burgeoning global information industry have alluded to software development as an area that might grow rapidly. It has been shown that certain developing countries possess or can acquire the ability to compete in the international software marketplace.[8] Other developing countries can use and adapt software successfully, without ambitions of development and export.

Undoubtedly the single most important factor in the design, application, and marketing of software products is the people and the training and experience they bring with them. Software companies are built largely on the capabilities of skilled personnel with specialized knowledge of the analysis of useful, cost-justified software systems, the principles and practices of programming, methodologies for software design, supporting system software capabilities and limitations, and the methods of analyzing organizations and their information requirements. In general, a country needs its own expertise in the following areas: (1) developing and supporting applications software; (2) evaluating and modifying software packages, design methodologies, and productivity tools; (3) providing special consultancy and software support services; and (4) promoting products and services. To help meet these needs, the UN is studying the feasibility of a UNU-sponsored software development institute devoted to training and research in software development for Third World countries.[9]

Two major activities have been identified for the institute: research and training in software development and methodology, and research and training in software generation and adaptation for end-use applications. Specifically, the institute would conduct field research on application software needs particular to developing countries; acquire and test existing software for adaptation, allowing for cultural values embedded in software; develop courses in the use of new software; and train a large number of people in developing countries in software production methods necessary to set up local software houses that can either develop software for local needs or for export to regional or international markets.

World Bank efforts

Although a precise figure is lacking, a small survey we conducted ourselves identified over 260 projects which the World Bank has supported with IT components in 63 countries in the past 20 years.[10] This support ranges from a few microcomputers for data collection, processing, and analysis in a health and nutrition project to large mainframes for complex computing work in a petroleum exploration project. The cost of IT as a percentage of total project costs varies considerably, from less than 1 percent to a high of about 60 percent, or from US$200,000 to US$160 million. Size and cost notwithstanding, the most noticeable feature of Bank assistance is the growth in spending on IT since 1981. During the past six years there has been an average annual growth of nearly 30 percent, a dramatic increase from the average 15 percent annual increases in the previous five years.

Several factors have contributed to this growth. First, microcomputers have relatively recently joined the larger mainframe computer and smaller minicomputers in Bank assistance. Because of their small size relative to their computing capability, their low cost, ready availability and ease of use, microcomputers are either replacing or complementing larger computers in projects. Improvements in memory technology (increases in storage density and speed of operation, and decreases in energy consumption) and portability have further encouraged this trend. Microcomputers are also easy to use, especially by those who have little technical knowledge of computers. Further, in many cases the Bank has been eager to assist its member countries in automating their statistical and economic data bases, in the development of reliable management information systems, and in applying the computer to deeper and better analyses for effective management of an organization's operations.

Most projects fall into two categories: information systems and computer applications. Information systems include the provision of hardware and software (and technical assistance) with a view to developing a financial, payroll, personnel, or management information system. Some outstanding projects in this area are the Pakistan Railway Project (1982), the China Petroleum Project (1983), and the Morocco Agricultural Credit Project (1986). Computer applications refer to projects where the objective of IT assistance (hardware and software) has been to help borrowing institutions in quantitative analysis, modeling, or simulation, and in office automation. The China Karamay Petroleum Project (1984), the Malaysia Energy Efficiency Project (1986), the Brazil Electric Power System Coordination Project (1976), and the Peru Agricultural Extension Project (1982) are applications projects as defined here.

The remaining three categories – education and training, consultancy, and technology development – account for 30 percent of the projects. The education category includes projects that provided hardware and software to educational and research institutions, or to data processing units of the borrower for training of students and staff in computer operation, in software applications, and in information systems development. There are 21 projects of this type, such as the University Development Project in China (1980) and an education project in Algeria (1980). Most projects include some form of consultancy support. A separate consultancy category was therefore established to classify projects where the Bank has provided consultant assistance to identify and plan for the information needs of an institution, to computerize routine recording of transactions such as billing and post auditing tasks, to automate manual data collection systems, or to remodel existing information systems.

Conclusion

It is by no means clear what the potential of IT is for developing countries. Differences among countries in using and producing IT make comparisons complicated and they oversimplify generalizations. However, several newly industrialized countries already have introduced IT successfully in a number of economic and management activities, and certainly many other developing countries plan to do so.

The rapid expansion of markets for IT raises many questions. Do certain developing countries possess – or can they acquire in a reasonable time – a competitive advantage in the development of IT? What are the sources of such competitive advantage? How will new technologies and low-cost communications technologies affect the competitiveness of a country in IT applications? What human resource and technical foundations are necessary to effectively utilize and develop IT products? What are the trade-offs between capital expenditures and education, training, and social costs in the short and longer terms? What policy or institutional measures can be initiated by governments to increase the rate of adoption of information technologies?

These are among the many questions developing country policy-makers are asking in their search for appropriate policies to govern IT use and transfer. Given the extensive experience of many international aid agencies with projects involving IT in developing countries, with both appropriate and inappropriate applications of IT, with negotiating hardware and software agreements, and in education and training requirements, it seems that such agencies could be providing more direct assistance, research and planning in this area to developing countries. Greater assistance would help these countries learn from mistakes previously made elsewhere in the world, and begin to contribute to the successful development of IT in their own countries.

A starting point for the international aid organizations might be to address the following issues:

- How to balance their current investments in hardware in projects with the investment needed to develop the skills and systems to operate, use and maintain it.
- How to knowledgeably identify the potential and applicability of IT in projects, and the institution's absorption capacity.
- What the economic and policy implications are of the imbalance in investments between hardware and software systems/applications.

- How to strengthen and expand projects in developing countries in education and training in IT.
- How to develop and promote a national capability for the production and dissemination of indigenous information technologies.
- How a coordinated process may be developed among aid agencies for procuring and installing IT within different ministries and across different sectors, to minimize proliferation of dissimilar product lines, operating manpower overheads, and investments.
- How to facilitate the sharing of application software across national boundaries in order to avoid "re-inventing the wheel."

Notes

1 As far back as 1970, the UN wrote in its ten-year plan for developing countries: "Computers will play an increasingly important role in developing countries which intend to participate in the world economy in ways other than the supply of raw materials. Developing countries will find computers a necessary ticket of admission. The next decade should see developing countries even more active in closing the computer gap," United Nations, *The Application of Computer Technology for Development* (Department of Economic and Social Affairs, New York, 1971).

2 See BOSTID (Board on Science and Technology for International Development), *Microcomputers and Their Applications for Developing Countries* (National Research Council) (Westview Press, Boulder, CO, 1986); also J. Bessant and S. Cole, *Stacking the Chips – Information Technology and the Global Distribution of Income* (Frances Pinter, London, 1985).

3 UNDP, Information Center, Division of Management Information Services, New York, July 1987.

4 UNESCO, *Informatics: A Vital Factor in Development* (UNESCO, Paris, 1980); and Intergovernmental Committee for the Intergovernmental Informatics Programme, *Main Working Document*, SC. 86/CONF. 208/4, Paris, July 1986.

5 R. Schware and B. Render, "The Computerization of Burma," *Information Technology for Development*, vol. 2(3), July 1987, pp. 157–65.

6 M. Dow, "Review of Selected Donor Agency Policies on Computers and Informatics in Third World Countries," Third World Academy of Science International Study Group on Computers and Informatics for Development, Trieste, Italy, January 8–10, 1986. See also J. Bogod, *Aid Agency Development Policy Study Report* (UK Council for Computing Development, London, 1986).

7 UNIDO, "Initiation of International Mechanism for Microelectronics Infrastructure, Applications and Software," Transfer of Technology Programme Branch, Project Proposal, Vienna, Austria, March 13, 1987.

8 R. Schware, "Software Industry Development in the Third World: Policy Guidelines, Institutional Options, and Constraints," *World Development*, vol. 15 (10/11), October/November 1987, pp. 1249–67.

9 UNU, "Draft Proposal for the Establishment of the International Software Development Institute as a UNU Research and Training Centre," Tokyo, July 1987.

10 The number of Bank-supported projects with IT components (until 1986) is probably larger than the 260 projects that this research has identified since many projects may include some small amount of microcomputers or office automation equipment. The purpose of this research was to identify only those Bank-approved projects where the IT component was significant, either because of the cost of IT or the contribution of IT to the project objectives. The projects selected for this study were identified through a search of the Bank's Integrated Bibliographic Information System (IBIS). The estimated total number of Bank-supported projects with IT components includes those identified through IBIS as well as through the Information, Technology, and Facilities Department's Operations Consulting Services Unit.

Brazil's Independent Computer Strategy

Antonio José J. Botelho

Not all Third World countries have gone along the development path favored by the World Bank. Brazil has a policy of restricting IT imports and the US government fears that this model could be copied by other nations. In a spirited defense of Brazil's strategy, the author rejects most of the criticisms of it. Botelho is co-editor of The Computer Question in Brazil: High Technology in a Developing Country, *and this article first appeared in* Technology Review, *May–June 1987.*

When Brazil's National Informatics Law of 1984 reinforced a ban on the import of many computers, the move provoked instant controversy. Multinational computer producers had long claimed that this exclusion doomed Brazilian consumers to obsolescent and expensive equipment, and that it favored only a few local companies at consumers' expense. US officials denounced the move as prejudicial to American interests and contrary to the principles of free trade.

The Brazilians responded by proclaiming the critical importance of fostering a locally controlled computer industry. They asserted that Washington was merely seeking to protect the oligopolistic power of IBM and other major US corporations. US computer firms derive a significant share of their revenue abroad – over 50 percent for some of the largest manufacturers. These firms naturally want to continue to dominate international trade in the industry. Although the Brazilian computer market currently is just 3 percent that of the US one, it is growing by 35 percent annually. It is potentially one of the largest markets in the world.

The debate has drawn considerable attention as other countries strive to define their stance on similar questions. Some countries, such as Mexico and Argentina, have had ambitions to imitate Brazil's approach. For the past 10 years Mexico has had an on-and-off protectionist policy. In compliance with Mexico's 1981 foreign-investment laws regarding computers, Apple and Hewlett-Packard constructed plants there in which they held only minority ownership. However, pressed by the increasing burden of its foreign debt, Mexico is now trying to attract new outside investment. In 1985, in return for major concessions, the Mexican government accepted an IBM proposal to expand its Mexican operations and construct a 100 percent IBM-owned plant to manufacture PCs. IBM will establish a semiconductor development center for Mexican industry, purchase a variety of high-tech products from Mexican companies, and produce software for Latin America in Mexico.

India has taken a somewhat different line, seeking to expand exports, particularly of peripherals and software, and also to boost the domestic use of large computers. Like Brazil, India has a fast-growing – potentially one of the world's largest – computer market.

India subjects computers valued under about $10,000 to heavy import duties to protect its microcomputer industry. The duties will gradually be phased out as the Indian industry becomes more competitive. Low duties on imported parts and components for producing peripherals aim to develop a peripherals industry capable of rapidly gaining international competitiveness.

The manufacture of mainframes and superminis is restricted to government-owned firms, while tax and R&D incentives assist India's private hardware and software industries. However, 30 computer models valued at over $10,000 can be imported with lower duties. These allowed imports are intended to ensure that India will get the latest technology. For example, IBM mainframe computers have been authorized for use in oil and natural-gas exploration and railway reservation systems. Included in the list are models produced by companies that have service offices in India and show potential for producing equipment in partnership with Indian companies. This selective list of larger computers also encourages software development for a few standard systems. One of India's goals is to produce $100 million worth of software annually over the next five years. Software exports have been growing by 40 percent a year.

South Korea, a success story among the newly industrializing countries of Southeast Asia, has a computer policy that reflects the export strategy it has pursued for the past two decades. The country's computer policy is built around three or four major conglomerates with significant experience in manufacturing and exporting televisions and other consumer electronics products. Korea seeks to help these conglomerates acquire a similar export edge in low-end microcomputers and semiconductors.

Toward this end the government has an extremely selective policy of acquiring technology, and has prodded firms to establish joint ventures with foreign computer companies to learn their technology. This strategy has paid off handsomely. Korean firms have penetrated the low-end professional microcomputer market in the United States. Only recently, with declining export sales, has the Korean computer industry expanded into the domestic market.

While India, Korea, and, to a lesser extent, Mexico focus on exports, Brazil's policy aims primarily to foster Brazilian-owned firms that will serve a domestic computer market. The basic principles of this policy, laid out in the early 1970s, were institutionalized in the National Informatics Law approved in November 1984. Informatics is the word used in Brazil to cover the whole field of computing, including microelectronics, automation, software, and peripheral equipment. The National Informatics Law reserves the market for microcomputers, minicomputers, and peripherals for Brazilian "national" companies. It defines a national company as one with 70 percent Brazilian ownership, and Brazilians must control management and technological decisions. At the end of 1985 Congress enacted the first National Informatics Plan (PLANIN), which created mechanisms designed to promote the industry. The "market-reserve policy" will last until 1992, when Brazilian firms are expected to be internationally competitive.

The roots of Brazil's informatics policy

The origins of the National Informatics Law lie in the so-called "Brazilian miracle." This process of economic development, begun in the late 1960s, was characterized by gigantic government projects – such as the Trans Amazonic Highway – and by the modernization of the consumer durables industry. This effort demanded more than imported technology. Thousands of students were sent abroad for graduate study. Public support for university research and graduate training increased rapidly, and major state-owned companies established R&D labs.

Another early step toward the 1984 law was an unsuccessful attempt in the early 1970s to develop a minicomputer industry through joint ventures with non-Brazilian firms. Foreign companies were supposed to supply the technology, while the state and the Brazilian private sector would supply capital and marketing experience. However, all major US computer manufacturers refused to make deals, since Brazil's Technology Transfer and Intellectual Property Code restricted their royalties and the length of contracts. In 1973, after extensive international negotiations, the British firm Ferranti and the Japanese firm Fujitsu did agree to participate. But only the Ferranti joint venture, Cobra, became a reality, and it was plagued by financial and managerial problems and poor product decisions, in part because the partners were unable to agree on major issues. Cobra did not sell its first Ferranti-based industrial minicomputer until late 1976.

Meanwhile the Brazilian data-processing market grew rapidly in the early 1970s (30 percent a year versus 20 percent for the world market). The Brazilian government accounted for a fifth of such purchases, prompting it to establish the Commission for the Coordination of Electronic Activities (CAPRE) in 1972. CAPRE's general mission was to coordinate federal data processing activities and purchases.

After the first oil crisis drained Brazil's foreign exchange, CAPRE in 1976 imposed import quotas on data processing equipment – by then the third largest import. At the same time, policy struggles in Brazil had led to the abandonment of the joint-venture strategy. With the backing of the powerful National Bank for Economic Development (BNDE) and a large segment of the academic community, CAPRE began to promote licensing agreements between domestic and foreign firms.

Finally, CAPRE began preparing an overall policy to develop a broad Brazilian computer industry. In June 1976 the agency recommended that "when feasible, mini- and microcomputers and peripheral devices be reserved for the domestic industry" – thus beginning the market-reserve policy later embodied in the National Informatics Law.

A challenge to the policy came quickly. When Brazil first decided to protect the minicomputer and microcomputer markets, no foreign firms manufactured or assembled such equipment in the country. IBM of Brazil assembled some mainframes and peripherals, mostly for export. However, a few months later IBM announced it would start manufacturing its small business minicomputer, the System/32, in Brazil, apparently to undercut the domestic market being developed in minicomputers. Associations of computer professionals, backed by CAPRE, protested, charging that IBM's plans threatened the development of a national minicomputer industry since IBM would retain control of the operation.

IBM shelved its plans in January 1977 after the Council of Economic Development (CDE),

Brazil's highest body for economic policy, announced criteria for approving new computer industry projects. The criteria aimed to increase the amount of technology transferred to Brazilian engineers, the degree to which Brazilian firms produced the equipment, and the share of the company's equity that Brazilian stockholders controlled. The CDE also announced that it would look favorably upon projects that improved Brazil's international balance of payments.

CAPRE selected three Brazilian firms to manufacture minicomputers by licensing foreign technology. A 1975 act limited the licensing period to five years and royalty payments to 5 percent of net sales, and did not allow the license to be renewed. The three Brazilian firms eventually produced minicomputers with technology licensed from French, German, and Japanese manufacturers.

In 1979 the Special Secretariat of Informatics (SEI), under the National Security Council rather than civilian control, took over CAPRE's responsibilities but basically reaffirmed its policies. SEI restricted imports of minicomputers for an additional three years and applied the policy to microcomputers and a variety of peripheral equipment. SEI also restricted imports of most software, digital instrumentation, and superminis.

The Brazilian microcomputer industry actually required little assistance. The simple design of microcomputers and the wide availability of microprocessors allowed domestic firms to clone equipment such as the Tandy TRS-80, Apple II, and IBM-PC. By contrast, Brazilian minicomputer manufacturers faced difficult times by 1984, suffering from competition from IBM 4341s – the smallest mainframe IBM produced in Brazil. Production of Brazilian minicomputers declined about 30 percent between 1982 and 1983, while the number of competing 4341s produced almost doubled, reaching 600 units. Therefore, CAPRE blocked attempts by IBM and Burroughs to introduce new low-end mainframes that would have further competed with high-end Brazilian minicomputers.

Even this prohibition was insufficient. Brazilian firms argued that to compete with IBM

Table 15.1   Brazil's major computer companies

Rank	Company	Percent of Brazilian gross informatics revenues 1984
1	Cobra	13.6
2	SID	12.2
3	Itautec	7.7
4	Prologica	7.5
5	Digirede	6.4
6	Elebra Int.	5.3
7	Laba	4.4
8	Scopus	3.8
9	Sisco	3.6
10	Racimec	3.2

they needed products based on proven technology, tested in international markets, and having a large supply of software. In response, SEI took a pragmatic course and relaxed restrictions in this area. It has allowed six Brazilian firms to produce superminis with technology licensed from abroad.

In the first round of minicomputer licensing in 1977, all major US minicomputer manufacturers had refused to share their technology. This time Digital, Data General, Honeywell Bull (a French firm), and several other non-US companies agreed to do so. Two main reasons underlay the change. First, the importance of the domestic market had increased Brazilian firms' bargaining power. Second, the Brazilian government, in response to complaints from US firms, agreed to consider extending licensing agreements for another five years. It also agreed that transferred knowledge would be kept confidential for five years from the end of the licensing agreement rather than the beginning.

Thus, when the Brazilian Congress passed the National Informatics Law almost unanimously in October 1984, it simply reaffirmed a policy that had evolved over a decade or more. Professional and scientific associations, industrial associations, all political parties, and a wide variety of public-interest groups supported the law.

The policy in action

Both the popularity of the Informatics Law in Brazil and the concern abroad are due to the success of the market-reserve policy. When CAPRE first restricted imports of data-processing equipment in 1974, the Brazilian computer market was valued at about $700 million. All equipment was either imported or produced by subsidiaries of foreign firms. Today Brazilian-controlled firms collect 55 percent of total revenues. Between 1975 and 1986, the number of computers produced by Brazilian-controlled firms jumped from 5 percent to over 75 percent. In 1986, more than 270 Brazilian companies accounted for 55 percent of the $2.7 billion domestic market in superminis, minicomputers, microcomputers, peripherals, and services. Gross revenues in the domestic informatics industry grew at about 75 percent a year between 1979 and 1985. The industry currently employs 16,000 people, one-third of whom hold university degrees.

The largest growth has been in microcomputers. The number of national microcomputer firms has expanded dramatically – from two in 1979 to 33 in 1984. These firms have kept up with the latest technology. In 1986 Unitron introduced a copy of Apple's Macintosh. Scopus developed a supermicro capable of running both AT&T's UNIX operating system and the DOS operating system for IBM compatibles. Digirede, Brazil's major independent producer of banking automation systems, developed a computer based on Motorola's 68000 chip and tailored to financial, commercial, and administrative uses. Itautec introduced a microcomputer that is compatible with the IBM PC-AT but that runs faster.

Foreign firms continue to dominate the mainframe field, led by IBM with about 70 percent of the $881 million market in 1984. But IBM's share of the low-end mainframe/high-end minicomputer market has been steadily declining, following an international trend. By 1982 Brazilian firms controlled a tenth of the value of the installed base, represented mainly by the Cobra 500 series. The introduction in 1986 of Brazilian superminis based on technology licensed in 1984 will certainly accelerate this trend.

Some Brazilian firms have actually improved minicomputers that were based on previously licensed technology. Edisa used a Motorola chip to transform obsolete technology it had licensed from Fujitsu in 1978 into an efficient banking computer. Edisa's experience with this project allowed it to develop a new multi-user supermicro in 1984. One year later this machine accounted for 33 percent of the firm's revenues.

Computer and related exports have been growing rapidly in recent years – 100 percent in 1985 – but they still are far below exports by foreign companies operating in Brazil. In 1985, while foreign firms exported equipment valued at $193 million (mainly mainframes, parts, and peripherals) from Brazil, national firms exported just $11 million worth. IBM accounted for 80 percent of total computer exports. That company's recent selection of Brazil as the site for an international procurement office should increase its exports sharply, as an increasing number of parts and components for IBM equipment worldwide will be bought in Brazil.

Brazilian-controlled firms export primarily to Latin America. Three Brazilian firms have entered the Argentina market for banking automation after winning contracts in competition with major international companies. Digirede established a joint venture with an Argentina firm, while SID and Itautec are selling their technology. Racimec has also signed contracts totalling $20 million to export its unique lottery-processing technology to several countries.

The Brazilian informatics industry is investing heavily in R&D, although perhaps less than similar companies abroad. Brazilian firms invested $69 million in R&D in 1982; only three years later R&D expenses had risen to about $130 million, or 11 percent of gross revenues. (The US minicomputer industry invests about 12 to 14 percent of its revenues in R&D.) And the incentives recently established by PLANIN should further increase the amount of capital spent on R&D and training.

According to the country's technology-transfer laws, agreements on software imports, either for direct licensing or distribution, must be approved by the National Institute for Intellectual Property (INPI). Brazilian technology-transfer legislation does not allow restrictions – such as those forbidding R&D on the product licensed – to be imposed on the Brazilian licensee. Foreign firms also cannot restrict Brazilian use after the contract expires or restrict improvements on the original technology during the period of the contract. Moreover, all licensing agreements are limited to five years, royalties paid to foreign licensees cannot exceed 5 percent of net sales. Over 280 Brazilian software companies now compete with 580 foreign firms.

Criticism and reality

Opponents of Brazil's market-reserve policy – including some Brazilian politicians and industrialists as well as critics abroad – argue that the policy holds back development by artificially shielding domestic firms from international competition. They say the policy is leading Brazil's computer industry down a path of technological backwardness, and that domestic consumers must pay higher prices for inferior equipment. Yet the evidence shows that almost all these criticisms of Brazil's policy are weak. Moreover, Brazil is responding flexibly to those that are valid.

When in 1977 Cobra tried unsuccessfully to license minicomputer technology from Data General and Digital, the head of Data General's service office argued that Brazil's policy, if successful, would be a dangerous international precedent. Data General wanted Brazil to reduce import tariffs on minicomputers and remove limits on royalty payments and the length of licensing contracts. At that time the US trade representative took no action.

Six years later, Data General again asked the US government to negotiate a change in Brazil's technology-transfer laws. The company wanted the United States to pressure the International Monetary Fund, the World Bank, and other trade and aid programs to force concessions from developing countries, including Brazil. Data General called for bilateral talks between the United States and Brazil. It suggested that the General Agreement on Trade and Tariffs (GATT), the forum for international trade negotiations, was too cumbersome to deal properly with the issue.

As the representative of US industry, the US Department of Commerce has criticized a supposed inconsistency between policy and practice. Although the 1984 law prohibits joint ventures between Brazilian and foreign firms in some areas, Brazilian firms continue to encourage such partnerships, perhaps hedging their bets should the law change.

The Commerce Department also argues that the informatics policy hurts Brazilian consumers, because Brazilian firms do not supply state-of-the-art technology at competitive prices. Finally, the department claims that foreign software firms are discouraged from entering the Brazilian market because neither patent nor copyright protection is available. That Brazil did not allow software to be copyrighted was, until recently, a particularly sore point.

However, market-reserve policies are not unique to Brazil. Many nations use them to reduce their dependence on imports and ease their balance of payments. The United States adopted such policies in the nineteenth century to protect its textile-machinery industry from British competition. Japan has used them for 30 years to promote its consumer electronics, semiconductor, and other industries. NASA and the Defense Department restricted purchases of electronic components and equipment to US firms in the 1960s. The Defense Department is currently under pressure to avoid buying foreign equipment and technology on the grounds such purchases hurt national security. A recent US–Japan trade agreement that requires Japan to sell microchips at fair market value, and National Security Council proposals to shield the US microelectronics industry from Japanese competition, are similar protectionist moves.

Moreover, both Brazil and the United States are signatories of the General Agreement on Trade and Tariffs (GATT). According to this set of regulations, developing countries have the right to restrict imports in certain industries. GATT also recognizes these countries' right to subsidize infant industries.

Brazil's National Informatics Law does not even prohibit direct foreign investment, provided Brazilians retain 70 percent voting and managerial control. IBM recently took advantage of this opportunity by investing $20 million in a joint venture with the Brazilian group Gerdau to sell data processing and software services. (Brazilian firms fear that such arrangements may be the computer giant's attempt to gain a toehold for the day the market-reserve policy ends.)

The National Informatics Plan even *specifies* a large role for foreign firms, and US computer firms do a good business in Brazil. They have licensed technology to Brazilian firms for mainframes, superminis, minicomputers, peripherals, modems, computer-aided design, computer-aided manufacturing, computerized numerical control, programmable logic control, chromatography, and microdevelopment systems. Furthermore, almost 200 US firms export parts, modules, and components to Brazil. Between 1979 and 1985 the adjusted gross sales of US computer companies in Brazil increased from $533 million to almost $1 billion. Moreover, between 1974 and 1983, foreign computer firms (of which US companies are a clear majority) sent profits home of almost twice the value of their total direct investments.

Criticism of Brazil's lack of copyright protection for software is also misplaced. On the one hand, copyright law has never assured software confidentiality, not even in the United States, where illegal copying is common. More important, at least since June 1984, when it sponsored an international conference on software copyright laws, the Brazilian government has been making an effort to protect foreign software manufacturers. Finally, in October 1986, Brazil responded to criticisms and adopted international copyright law for software protection.

The objection that the market-reserve policy means higher prices for end-users is similarly questionable. In July 1982 an Apple II clone manufactured in Brazil was 2.2 times more expensive than the original, but less than two years later Brazilian-made equipment was 8 percent cheaper than its US counterpart. Brazilian clones of the TRS-80 showed the same pattern, and the current wave of IBM-PC and AT clones is expected to follow suit.

By contrast, the price of the central processing unit of a Hewlett-Packard HP-85 scientific microcomputer manufactured in Brazil is 1.36 times that of the one produced in the United States. If the cost of peripherals is added, the Hewlett-Packard system becomes 50 percent more expensive than its US equivalent. Between 1981 and 1983 the prices of Brazilian-produced minicomputers varied only 5 percent from equivalents sold in the United States.

Also weak is the argument that adopting old technology hurts the international competitiveness of Brazilian industry in general. The latest computer technology is not necessary for achieving international competitiveness. Manufacturing firms in central and northwestern Italy have successfully used modern technology, though not necessarily the most modern, to carve out niches in textiles, clothing, specialty chemicals, industrial instrumentation, and specialty steel – while increasing exports and local jobs. Conversely, US manufacturing has lost its competitiveness despite easy access to the most advanced computer technology.

Attempts to export the Brazilian model to other newly industrializing countries (NICs) would be problematic at best. The major Asian NICs – South Korea, India, Taiwan – already have computer policies that reflect their own development strategies and international alliances. All three are committed to exports, in contrast to Brazil's internal-market orientation. Countries such as Mexico and Argentina would face a host of unique problems in implementing a computer policy patterned after Brazil's, including a lack of economic and human resources, a weaker established role in the international economy, and relatively small domestic markets. Argentina's previous military government left a large foreign debt (although smaller than Brazil's) and a rather weak and de-industrialized economy. And Mexico's vast common border with the United States would nullify any attempts to isolate a domestic market. Over two-thirds of the microcomputers currently in use in Mexico have been smuggled across the border.

Future challenges

Not the least of Brazil's future problems stems from the United States. In September 1985, under pressure from Congress to halt the growing US trade deficit the Reagan administration began to investigate Brazil's informatics policy. The American Electronics Association (AEA) asked the US government to request Brazil to lift its market-reserve policy and end some restrictions on imports of high-tech products. The AEA has also asked for changes in Brazil's intellectual property laws. And the US Computer and Business Equipment Manufacturers Association, which has issued perhaps the most comprehensive critique of Brazil's informatics policies, has repeated Data General's earlier call for quick bilateral negotiations.

The American investigation, conducted through the US trade representative, aims to determine the extent to which the informatics policy restricts foreign participation in the Brazilian market. If the trade representative decides that Brazil's practices are unfair, the United States could retaliate. Brazil is especially vulnerable to such action since the United States buys a fourth of all the country's exports, especially steel, textiles, and shoes.

As a result of the charges that Brazil's policy hurt US interests, in early 1986 the White House Economic Policy Council formed a working trade group to suggest retaliatory actions against Brazil. Council members argued that Brazil's market-reserve policy had cost US computer and information technology manufacturers $1.5 billion in sales between 1980 and 1984.

As the United States has made clear in current GATT negotiations, removing restrictions on international high-tech trade remains a major US goal. Brazil and India have fought at least since 1982 to keep high-technology protectionism out of GATT talks. Under intense US pressure and the threat that GATT talks would be suspended, those countries finally agreed to discuss the issue.

A decision about what action the United States will take was due at the end of 1986, but has been postponed at least until July 1987. This seems to indicate that bilateral negotiations between the two countries have produced results, such as Brazil's decision to allow software to be copyrighted. The Reagan administration has lately asked Brazil to change the definition of national firm. It wants Brazil to allow joint ventures in which foreign suppliers of technology have a 50 percent interest, and to relax the requirement that Brazilians control management and technology.

The two key characteristics of the Brazilian informatics policies over the past 15 years have been pragmatism and flexibility. Brazil's approval of a copyright law for software is evidence of this. These characteristics should be preserved at any cost. The only serious menace to their survival would be an unnecessary and unjustified hardening of the US position.

How the Next War Will be Fought

Frank Barnaby

Computers are transforming the art of warfare. Sophisticated "smart" missiles are making tanks, combat aircraft, and warships obsolete, says the author, who is a former Director of the Stockholm International Peace Research Institute. But the new military technologies could also be used to create a safer, more effective and "non-provocative" defense system for Western Europe. This article is adapted from Barnaby's book, The Automated Battlefield *(Free Press, New York, 1986) and is reprinted from* Technology Review, *October 1986.*

The year is 1995. Two industrialized countries are at war. One side decides to invade and occupy the other. Its tanks, in regular columns, approach the no-man's land at the border between the two combatants.

Suddenly, without warning, small missiles silently attack the invading tanks. Each missile hovers momentarily above the tanks, selects one and attacks it by firing a high-speed projectile at the weakest part – the turret and engine cover. The deadly accurate missiles are very selective: they don't attack any tank that has been been selected for attack by another missile. These missiles are fired from 30 or 40 kilometers away, far beyond the range of the tanks' guns. Few survivors crawl out of the burning wrecks, since red-hot pieces of metal ricochet around inside and hot, suffocating gases spread rapidly throughout. Only three of the tanks survive. Their morale completely shattered, the crews decide to retreat.

This scenario is more than a fantasy in the minds of military planners in the Pentagon and the Kremlin. As recent conflicts in the Falkland Islands and the Middle East have shown, modern warfare relies increasingly on such smart missiles.

These weapons are becoming more sophisticated every day. A main aim of current military technology is to develop missiles that are effective under all the adverse conditions under which battles are fought: when the battlefield is covered with thick smoke and dust; in heavy rain and snow, thick fog, and haze; and against electronic jamming devices, decoys, and other enemy countermeasures designed to confuse radars. Strategists can now foresee the "brilliant" missile that can find its target and attack it without instructions from any external source.

Advanced missile technology is already beginning to transform warfare. Battle tanks, long-range combat aircraft, and warships are, or will soon become, obsolete now that they are faced with accurate, intelligent missiles. These missiles make it much cheaper to destroy the weapons of invasion than to buy them. Thus, defense can be made much more cost-effective than offense. This has important implications for NATO. The alliance can use the new technologies to provide an effective deterrent based on non-nuclear weapons against an attack by Warsaw Pact forces.

Developments in military technology are well illustrated by considering the development of anti-tank missiles. A typical anti-tank missile now in operation is the US TOW (tube-launched, optically tracked, wire-guided) missile, which was used extensively in the Vietnam War and in wars in the Middle East. Altogether some 400,000 TOWs have been produced.

TOW is popular because it destroys tanks very efficiently and because it is relatively cheap; each $15,000 missile has a high probability of destroying a main battle tank costing $3 million or more. (All of the prices in this article are in 1985 dollars.)

TOW is carried in a jeep, armored car, or helicopter. The operator of the missile looks through an optical sight and pinpoints an enemy tank. The operator then presses the trigger and a rocket motor propels the missile from the launch tube. As soon as the missile emerges from the tube, small wings unfold and an infrared flare in the missile's tail ignites.

The operator's viewing system tracks the position of the flare relative to the line of sight between the operator and the tank. If the missile strays from the line of sight, a computer sends a command to the missile along two fine wires attached to the missile; the wires unwind from bobbins on the missile as it flies. So long as the operator keeps the cross-hairs in the viewer on the target, the missile will follow the line of sight. A modern TOW, which has a range of nearly 4 kilometers, carries a warhead capable of penetrating the armor of all existing tanks.

The TOW missile is one of an international family of anti-tank missiles. Others include the Soviet Sagger, used by the Syrians against Israeli tanks in the 1973 Middle East War; the British Swingfire; and the European Milan system.

But anti-tank missiles such as these have their limitations. One is that the operator of a TOW-type missile must remain within range of enemy fire while the missile is in flight, and, the enemy can determine the spot from where the missile is fired. Another problem is that missiles guided by infrared can be easily decoyed by infrared flares or burning vehicles near the target.

Many of the disadvantages of wire-guided missiles are eliminated in the new generation of anti-tank missiles just entering the arsenals. An example is the US Hellfire (heliborne-launched fire-and-forget) missile, which is guided to an enemy tank by a laser beam projected toward the tank. A sensor detects the light reflected from the tank and the missile, as it were, rides down the beam to the target.

The person operating the laser does not need to be in the vehicle firing the missile. Normally, Hellfire missiles are carried on helicopters, and the laser operator can be on the ground or in another helicopter. This gives the missile a big advantage over systems such as TOW, since the enemy cannot pinpoint the operator by observing the missile's launch site.

Hellfire missiles are mainly carried on the US Apache AH-64 advanced attack helicopters. Each helicopter carries up to 16 missiles, which can be launched in salvo. Several lasers are used simultaneously, each using a different pulse frequency. Each missile responds to one of the frequencies and is guided individually to its target. The Hellfire carries a 175-millimeter warhead, effective against all existing battle tanks. A small squadron of Apache helicopters armed with Hellfires is therefore a formidable anti-tank force, able to knock out a relatively large number of attacking tanks. At $40,000, the Hellfire is more expensive than the TOW, but it is still relatively cheap since it stands an excellent chance of destroying a $3 million tank.

The third generation of anti-tank missiles now under development will use "sub-munitions," in which one missile contains a number of smaller missiles each able to attack an enemy tank separately. These warheads, which will be carried by, for example, the new Standoff Tactical Missile, could quickly attack many armored vehicles spread over a large area.

The system operates with radar carried in an aircraft or a remotely piloted vehicle (RPV), an unmanned plane controlled by radio. First, the radar seeks out and tracks moving targets such as tanks that may be far inside enemy territory. A signal sent from the aircraft or RPV launches the missiles. The radar guides them into the air above the tanks, where they release their sub-munitions to attack the enemy forces. Each sub-munition is a "smart" missile, capable of what is called "terminal guidance." Each scans the target area with its own sensor, homes in on a tank turret, and fires a high-speed projectile. Since each warhead may carry 20 sub-munitions, and it may take an average of two to destroy a tank, each missile could destroy ten tanks – making it a formidable anti-tank weapon.

An example of a sub-munition being developed for the Standoff Tactical Missile is the Skeet, a smart bomblet weighing about 2 kilograms and carrying a 0.5-kilogram warhead. The bomblet wobbles as it falls to enable the infrared sensor in its nose to scan the terrain under it. If the Skeet "sees" an armored vehicle, it fires a warhead. If it doesn't detect a target, Skeet is programmed to explode anyway, scattering a large number of metal targets to destroy soft-topped vehicles and kill people in the area.

An effective anti-tank defense would consist of obstacles and sophisticated mines to slow down advancing enemy armor, as well as intelligent warheads to destroy the armored vehicles. Tanks would find it very difficult to penetrate territory defended with such weapons. As anti-tank weapons become smarter, the difficulty of invading with tanks will increase.

Anti-aircraft missiles

Aircraft, like tanks, are becoming more vulnerable to successive generations of intelligent missiles. Air defenses are already difficult to penetrate. According to NATO estimates, at least half of the attacking aircraft would be lost in a raid on a heavily defended area in Warsaw Pact territory, such as a main military air base.

Modern radars allow air defenses to track many enemy aircraft at the same time, no matter at what altitudes the aircraft are flying, and to guide many surface-to-air missiles to their targets simultaneously. Advanced "phased-array" radar used by, for example, the American Patriot missile system gives early warning of an air attack and tracks the hostile aircraft. A central computer analyzes the data from the radars, fires surface-to-air missiles at the right moments, and guides the missiles accurately to their targets. An eight-missile Patriot battery can keep track of a hundred aircraft and fire on nine of them with nine different missiles at the same time. The missiles reach speeds six times the speed of sound, and can attack enemy aircraft at distances of about 70 kilometers and at altitudes up to 24 kilometers.

The Patriot is largely automated, the only manned equipment being the central control station containing the main computer and 12 people. Patriot missiles cost about $1.5 million each, but combat aircraft cost much more. A modern strategic bomber, for example, costs well over $200 million, and a multi-role combat aircraft such as the European-built Tornado costs about $30 million. The US Army plans to deploy 54 batteries of Patriot missiles in Central Europe by the early 1990s.

Patriot missiles are generally meant for use against high-flying aircraft. Smaller surface-to-air missiles are normally used to defend against low-flying aircraft. This family of missiles includes the Swedish Bofors RB-70, the British Blowpipe and Rapier, the Soviet SA-6 and SA-8, and the American Stinger. The RB-70, Blowpipe, and Stinger are portable, carried and fired by one person. The Rapier is more sophisticated than the hand-held types, with missiles loaded in a launcher and carried in an armored vehicle, ready to fire.

The Rapier launcher is equipped with a surveillance radar to detect aircraft, which it interrogates using an "identification friend or foe" (IFF) system. If the aircraft fails to give the correct coded response, the launcher automatically turns toward the aircraft and the crew is alerted. The operator views the target through an optical sight and fires a missile that is automatically guided to its target. In bad weather or at night, a radar tracker can be used instead of optical viewing, with commands transmitted to the missile by microwave radio signals.

Combat aircraft are threatened not just from the ground but from other aircraft as well, so they carry sophisticated air-to-air missiles. The US Air Force and Navy, for example, use the Sidewinder, the Sparrow, the Phoenix, and the new AMRAAM advanced medium-range air-to-air missile. AMRAAM is an all-weather missile with its own active radar that gives it a "fire-and-forget" capability: it can seek out an enemy aircraft, identify it, and attack it without any further instructions from the pilot. Other current medium-range air-to-air missiles are guided to their targets by the radar systems on board the aircraft that launches them. The aircraft must stay in the neighborhood until the missile arrives at the target, making the plane vulnerable to enemy air defenses.

An aircraft carrying several AMRAAM missiles will be able to engage several enemy aircraft. Each missile will be able to isolate its own target, skipping over targets already chosen by other missiles. However, the missile will be relatively expensive, costing about $2 million. The US Air Force and Navy plan to begin deploying AMRAAM soon.

Modern radar, surface-to-air missiles such as the Patriot, and air-to-air missiles such as the AMRAAM are making combat aircraft increasingly vulnerable. As intelligent missiles become even more sophisticated, it will be even harder for aircraft to survive in battle.

The war at sea

Of all major weapon systems, large warships are the most vulnerable. New propulsion units, more efficient fuels, improved guidance systems, and better warheads have revolutionized anti-ship missiles.

These missiles have a simpler job than anti-tank and anti-aircraft missiles because it is much easier to guide missiles accurately over sea than over land, and it is easier to locate and track enemy warships than hostile tanks and aircraft.

The use of both types in recent wars has brought home their effectiveness. As early as 1967,

---

Table 15.2   1985 price list: Major weapon systems and missiles

M-1 main battle tank (US)	$3 million
TOW anti-tank missile (US)	$15,000
Aircraft carrier (US)	3 billion
Frigate (UK)	$50 million*
Exocet anti-ship missile (Fr.)	$250,000
B-1B strategic bomber (US)	$210 million
Phoenix air-to-air missile (US)	$1.3 million

---

*Price for the HMS *Sheffield*, built in 1972.

the Israelis were shocked when their biggest naval ship, the *Elath*, was sunk by a Soviet-supplied anti-ship missile fired by the Egyptians at a range of about 20 kilometers. Air-launched, sea-skimming missiles became famous during the 1982 Falklands War when the Argentinians used the French-built Exocet missile to sink the UK frigate HMS *Sheffield*.

The Exocet was launched by an Argentinian Navy Super Etendard fighter bomber, also bought from France, 35 kilometers away from the *Sheffield*. The 4,000-ton warship, built in 1972 at a cost of $50 million, carried some of the world's best defenses, including Sea Dart ship-to-air missiles. Yet it was sunk with a $250,000 missile.

The Exocet missile, which carries a 160-kilogram high-explosive warhead, is powered by a two-stage rocket that can be launched from land, sea, or air. Its maximum range is about 70 kilometers. After the missile is launched, its radar homes in on the target and guides the missile so that the warhead penetrates the enemy ship and explodes inside it.

The missile that sank the *Sheffield* was one of six Exocets fired by the Argentinians during the Falklands War. Four of the six hit their targets – a good success rate considering that the Argentine forces had only recently acquired Exocets and were not familiar with them.

Anti-ship missiles are of two basic types: one fired by a ship against another, the other fired by an aircraft at a warship. A typical modern ship-to-ship missile is the American Harpoon, which can be fired from the standard torpedo tubes of American submarines and those of many other nations.

The Harpoon's computer-controlled guidance system is remarkably effective: it steers the missile toward the chosen target even if it is fired in the wrong direction. The parent ship's over-the-horizon radar can determine the locations of targets at the extreme of the missile's range.

Once fired, Harpoon is independent of its parent ship; it is a genuine fire-and-forget missile. When Harpoon gets close to the ship, a radar seeker searches the area, finds the target, and locks on it. The seeker commands the missile to gain height to outmaneuver the target ship's defenses and then dive down on it from above. The missile can also continue skimming the surface of the sea and strike the target just above the water line.

Intelligent anti-ship missiles such as Harpoon make large warships obsolete, at least against a sophisticated navy. Large warships are extremely expensive – a modern aircraft carrier costs about $3 billion and a destroyer or cruiser costs about $1 billion. Such warships can be destroyed by a Harpoon missile costing about $800,000. In fact, the only naval ships that make military sense today are submarines and fast, small (about 200 tons) patrol boats armed with missiles. It is a sobering thought that a small missile-armed patrol boat can carry as much firepower as a cruiser or destroyer of World War II.

Missile countermeasures

Recent military experience has confirmed the growing vulnerability of tanks, aircraft, and warships. The first dramatic demonstration of the new vulnerability of tanks came during the 1973 Middle East War, when more than 1,500 Arab and Israeli tanks were destroyed in a few days by anti-tank missiles and guns. The experience spurred the search for countermeasures against intelligent missiles, but the tank is still losing in the measure-versus-countermeasure race.

The pro-tank lobby is strong, however, and the world's major armies are still buying main battle tanks in large numbers. The United States wants to deploy about 7,500 M-1 tanks by the early 1990s, producing them at a rate of 70 a month. NATO already has some 20,000 tanks in active service, while the Warsaw Pact has about 50,000.

Today's tanks are faster, sleeker, and heavier than their counterparts of World War II. They also have much longer ranges and are much better armored. The front of the US M-1, for example, is protected by a shield up to half a meter thick. However, other parts of the tank are much less well protected, with the top and sides of the turret, the hatches, and rear portions carrying relatively little armor. These areas are lightly protected because the turret must be light enough so that its heavy gun can be rapidly rotated and the hatches must be opened and closed quickly.

The upshot is that the tank is very vulnerable to attack from the sides, rear, and air. Even the front of the tank is vulnerable, since the latest anti-tank warheads are capable of penetrating more than a meter of the best armor.

For example, the widely used HEAT (high-energy anti-tank) anti-tank warhead is much more able to penetrate thick armor than the more traditional kinetic-energy projectile, which relies on mass and velocity to force its way through the armor. On impact, a HEAT warhead produces a metal plug and a concentrated jet of molten metal. The plug penetrates the armor of the tank, and a stream of molten metal and hot vapor enters the hole and fills the space inside. This kills or disables the crew by setting the tank on fire or exploding its ammunition.

The most recent innovation to reduce the effectiveness of anti-tank warheads is "active armor." Bricks containing an explosive are attached to the front of the tank. Sensors detect an approaching missile and explode one or more bricks to destroy the warhead before it can significantly damage the tank. Israeli tanks use active armor, and it has been reported on Warsaw Pact tanks in East Germany.

Active armor can be overcome by fitting anti-tank missiles with two warheads timed to explode with a short delay. The first warhead sets off the explosives in the active armor, deactivating it so the second warhead can penetrate the tank's armor. Nevertheless, the development of active armor has decreased confidence in warheads aimed at the fronts of tanks, and has increased interest in weapons that attack tank turrets from above – such as submunitions.

Perhaps the most critical factor in judging the usefulness of the main battle tank versus the anti-tank missile is the range at which the two can engage targets. The best tank guns are not very effective beyond about two kilometers, yet even small anti-tank missiles such as TOW are effective at longer ranges.

A modern main battle tank may be sleeker and more difficult to spot by eye than older tanks. But its exhaust gases typically have temperatures above 800°C. The large amount of heat that a tank gives off makes it very "visible" to infrared sensors. Moreover, countermeasures such as flares, decoys, and electronic jamming are proving much less effective against missiles guided by lasers and millimeter waves than those guided by infrared. Thus, countermeasure technology is likely to lag behind new missile-sensor technology for the foreseeable future, with the relative cost-effectiveness of anti-tank warfare continuing to increase.

The tank enthusiast's adage that "the best anti-tank weapon is another tank" is no longer true. Just as the machine gun made the cavalry horse obsolete, modern anti-tank missiles have made the tank obsolete. The plain fact is that it is virtually impossible to hide some 60 tons of hot metal on the modern battlefield from the sensors of intelligent missiles.

Defending combat planes

Recent military conflicts point up the growing vulnerability of combat aircraft. During the Falklands War, 114 planes were shot down, the majority by smart missiles. More recently, the Israelis used air-to-air missiles to shoot down 90 Syrian warplanes during the war in Lebanon.

Both the United States and the Soviet Union are trying to make their planes less vulnerable to detection by enemy radar. The American B-1B strategic bomber, for example, is one-tenth as visible to radar than its predecessor, the B-52. Military scientists are working on producing a warplane with even lower radar visibility – the so-called "stealth" bomber. Stealth will probably be achieved by a combination of shaping to reduce highly reflective angles, new radar-absorbing materials, and electronic jamming devices and other countermeasures. Stealth aircraft will not, of course, become completely invisible. They are also likely to be extremely expensive. For many if not all important military purposes, remotely piloted vehicles are far more cost-effective than manned aircraft.

RPVs could be used to launch air-to-air and air-to-surface missiles. Because there is no need to defend a pilot, which requires a great deal of expensive electronic and other equipment, RPVs are relatively cheap. If we assume that an air attack on well-defended bombers would knock out 20 percent of them, then 244 aircraft would be lost if 500 make three sorties. At $25 million an aircraft, the loss would total more than $6 billion. That money would buy more than 20,000 RPVs.

Can warships be defended?

The US Navy is making a major effort to develop a credible defense for its warships. To try to make their defenses more effective, US warships normally sail the oceans in battle groups headed by an aircraft carrier. The group includes destroyers, cruisers, attack submarines, and logistical-support ships. The US Navy now operates 13 aircraft carriers and plans to increase that number to 15. It believes that it also needs 100 ships equipped with sophisticated anti-aircraft weapons; some of these vessels will cost over $1 billion.

Military planners recognize that anti-ship missiles are so effective that they can best be countered by detecting and attacking the enemy ships, submarines, and aircraft carrying them before they reach their launch positions. The navy's anti-air-warfare program is designed to intercept enemy bombers in an "outer zone" before US ships come within range of their missiles. The "outer-zone" protection is provided by Hawkeye early-warning aircraft and F-14 Tomcat fighter interceptors, equipped with Phoenix air-to-air missiles. But because of the enormous range of Soviet maritime bombers, these defenses must cover huge areas of the world's oceans – so huge, in fact, that they are impossible to monitor fully. For example, the Soviet Backfire bomber has a range of some 5,000 kilometers and carries long-range supersonic AS-4 anti-ship missiles with a range of about 300 kilometers. Even if the warships escape air and submarine attack, they can be destroyed by missiles fired from Soviet surface ships. Of course, the United States offers a similar spectrum of threats to Soviet warships.

Therefore, many anti-ship missiles are likely to get through the outer zone defenses in an attack. The US Navy is trying to develop "area" defenses to attack the incoming missiles themselves at long range. This second layer of protection consists of long-range ship-to-air missiles carried aboard cruisers and destroyers equipped with the complex Aegis system. This system uses the most sophisticated technologies to detect and intercept high-speed cruise missiles at sea.

Anti-ship missiles that get through both the outer zone and the area defenses are supposed to be attacked by "point" defenses at relatively short range. This third layer of defense includes short-range interceptor missiles and radar-controlled guns that fire 50 rounds a second.

Submarines pose another threat to warships. Modern submarines are so effective that, once again, the best way of neutralizing them is to attack them before they come within range. For this the US Navy relies mainly on its own attack submarines and long-range P-3 patrol aircraft supported by undersea surveillance systems. The most effective weapon system for detecting and attacking enemy submarines is the hunter-killer submarine. The hunter-killer is usually a nuclear-powered sub equipped with sonar and other sensors, underwater communications systems, and a computer to analyze data from the sensors and fire weapons. Hunter-killer submarines are very expensive: the US Navy is paying about $700 million for each. Nevertheless, it has 96 nuclear attack submarines and the Soviet Navy has about 65.

A significant fraction of the submarines attacking a US carrier battle group will evade the hunter-killers and the patrol planes. The carrier group will therefore use formations of surface ships carrying sonar systems and torpedo-armed helicopters for short-range protection. Anti-submarine warfare has become an exceedingly complicated and expensive operation.

But despite the enormous resources that the superpowers are investing in naval anti-air and anti-submarine systems, large warships are becoming increasingly vulnerable to anti-ship missile and submarine attack. Warships are also much more expensive than the weapon systems that can destroy them.

Given the vulnerability of large warships and the escalating costs of building them, why are the great powers still procuring them? Probably not for any wartime use but to project power abroad in peacetime. In the words of US Defense Secretary Caspar Weinberger, "Carrier battle groups, perhaps the most visible symbol of America's maritime capability, support our foreign policy through a series of routine overseas deployments." Both superpowers want to play this game. We must therefore expect the Soviet–US naval rivalry to continue.

Defensive deterrence for NATO

As we have seen, new military technologies increasingly favor defense over offense. This has raised considerable interest in the concept of a "non-provocative" defense for European NATO countries. Such a strategy would be based on the principle that military forces can provide an effective defense while having virtually no offensive capability.

In Western Europe, a non-provocative, non-nuclear defense would look something like the following. A defense zone some 50 kilometers deep would be maintained all along the 1,000-kilometer East–West border. This zone would be saturated with all kinds of ground-based sensors, a vast network of underground fiberoptic cables for secure communications, and positions for troops to take cover.

NATO could build many anti-tank obstacles in this area and seed it with smart anti-tank mines. These devices would delay enemy tanks and channel them into areas where they could be bombarded and destroyed.

The Alliance could arm its troops with a judicious mixture of anti-tank missiles and cannons, anti-aircraft missiles, and light anti-aircraft guns. Emphasis would be given to simply operated and expendable missiles, cheap to produce in large quantities.

Mobile squads armed with weapons of high firepower would be used to deal with enemy forces that broke through the forward defense zone. Troops dispersed throughout each NATO country would defend coastal areas and deter attacks by airborne forces.

The armed forces would not have main battle tanks, long-range combat aircraft, or large warships. Nor would they have long-range airlift capability. The ranges of missiles would be no more than required to bombard the defense zone – roughly 80 kilometers – and therefore they would not be provocative. Combat aircraft would be limited to single-role interceptors and close-support ground-attack aircraft. Naval forces would rely on missile-armed fast patrol boats equipped with anti-ship missiles and on small diesel-powered submarines, which are less expensive than their nuclear-powered counterparts.

The Alliance can use the new technologies to provide an effective deterrent based on non-nuclear weapons against an attack by Warsaw Pact forces. Of course, the West needs to be able to respond in kind to a Soviet nuclear attack, but that eventuality is not what NATO strategists are most concerned about. They worry about the Warsaw Pact tanks, aircraft, and troops that outnumber their Western counterparts. With the new defensive technologies, NATO could abandon its current policy of resorting to nuclear forces – and very likely escalating to all-out nuclear war – merely to defend against a large conventional attack by Soviet-bloc forces.

A conventional defensive deterrent would be consistent with the universally recognized right of self-defense and would therefore be morally acceptable and unambiguously legal. It would also be militarily credible. For these reasons, the people of Europe in general and the armed forces in particular should welcome it.

Selected Further Reading

IT and the economy

Balancing the National Interest: US National Security Export Controls and Global Economic Competition (National Academy Press, Washington, DC, 1987).

Information Technology R&D – Critical Trends and Issues, Office of Technology Assessment (OTA) report to the US Congress, Washington, DC, 1985.

Technology, Innovation and Regional Economic Development, OTA report to the US Congress, Washington, DC, 1984.

Herb Brody, "States Vie for a Slice of the Pie," *High Technology,* January 1985.

Dan Dimancescu and James Botkin, *The New Alliance: America's R&D Consortia* (Ballinger, Cambridge, MA, 1986).

Therese Engstrom, "Little Silicon Valleys," *High Technology,* January 1987.

Kenneth Flamm, *Targeting the Computer: Government Support and International Competition* (Brookings Institution, Washington, DC, 1987).

Peter Hall and Ann Markusen (eds), *Silicon Landscapes* (Allen and Unwin, London, 1985).

T. D. Mandeville, "A 'Multi-Function-Polis' for Australia," *Prometheus,* vol. 6(1), June 1988.

Magoroh Maruyama, "Report on a New Technological Community: The Making of a Technopolis in an International Context," *Technological Forecasting and Social Change,* vol. 27(1), February 1985.

Sheridan Tatsuno, *The Technopolis Strategy: Japan, High Technology and the Control of the Twenty-first Century* (Brady/Prentice-Hall, New York, 1986).

Dale Whittington (ed.), *High Hopes for High Tech* (North Carolina University Press, Chapel Hill, NC, 1986).

Social problems I: Crime and surveillance

Electronic Record Systems and Individual Privacy, Office of Technology Assessment (OTA) report to US Congress, Washington, DC, 1986.

The Electronic Supervisor: New Technology, New Tensions, OTA report to US Congress, Washington, DC, 1987.

Federal Government Information Technology: Electronic Surveillance and Civil Liberties, OTA report to US Congress, Washington, DC, 1985.

Government Information Technology: Management, Security and Congressional Oversight, OTA report to US Congress, Washington, DC, 1986.

August Bequai, *Technocrimes* (Lexington Books, Lexington, MA, 1987).

Duncan Campbell and Steve Connor, *On the Record: Surveillance, Computers and Privacy* (Michael Joseph, London, 1986).

Hugo Cornwall, *Datatheft* (Heinemann, London, 1987).

Hugo Cornwall, *The New Hacker's Handbook* (Century, London, 1986).

R. Doswell and G. L. Simons, *Fraud and Abuse of IT Systems* (NCC Publications, Manchester, UK, 1986).

Rebecca A. Grant, Christopher A. Higgins and Richard H. Irving, "Computerized Performance Monitors: Are They Costing You Customers?" *Sloan Management Review*, vol. 29(2), Spring 1988.

Katherine M. Hafner et al., "Is Your Computer Secure?" *Business Week* cover story, August 1, 1988.

Bill Landreth, *Out of the Inner Circle* (Microsoft Press, Bellvue, WA, 1985).

Kenneth C. Laudon, *Dossier Society: Value Choices in the Design of National Information Systems* (Columbia University Press, New York, 1986).

Steven Levy, *Hackers: Heroes of the Computer Revolution* (Doubleday, New York, 1985).

Gary T. Marx, "I'll Be Watching You: Reflections on the New Surveillance," *Dissent*, vol. 32(1), Winter 1985.

Michael W. Miller, "Computers Keep Eye on Workers and See If They Perform Well," *The Wall Street Journal*, Monday June 3, 1985, p. 1.

Reid H. Montgomery, Jr and Ellis C. MacDougal, "Curing Criminals: The High-tech Prisons of Tomorrow," *The Futurist*, vol. 20(1), January–February 1986.

Michael Rogers, "The Electronic Informer," *Newsweek*, April 15, 1985.

Social problems II: Politics and gender

Rose Deakin, *Women and Computing: The Golden Opportunity* (Macmillan, London, 1984).

William H. Dutton, "Decision-making in the Information Age: Computer Models and Public Policy," *Progress in Communication Sciences*, vol. 5, 1984.

Wendy Faulkner and Erik Arnold (eds), *Smothered by Invention: Technology in Women's Lives* (Pluto Press, London, 1985).

William E. Halal, *The New Capitalism* (John Wiley, New York, 1986).

Heidi I. Hartmann, Robert E. Kraut and Louise A. Tilly (eds), *Computer Chips and Paper Clips: Technology and Women's Employment*, vols I and II: *Case Studies and Policy Perspectives* (National Academy Press, Washington, DC, 1986 and 1987).

Richard S. Hollander, *Video-Democracy: The Vote-From-Home Revolution* (Lomond, Mt Airy, MD, 1985).

Irving Louis Horowitz, *Communicating Ideas: The Crisis of Publishing in a Post-Industrial Society* (Oxford University Press, New York, 1986).

Vincent Mosco and Janet Wasko (eds), *The Critical Communications Review Volume II: Changing Patterns of Communications Control* (Ablex, Norwood, NJ, 1984).

Marguerite Zientara, *Women, Technology and Power* (Amacom, New York, 1988).

Jan Zimmerman, *Once Upon a Future: A Women's Guide to Tomorrow's Technology* (Pandora Press, London and New York, 1986).

Global issues: the military, the Third World, national rivalries

"High-tech Trade," *Issues in Science and Technology*, vol. 2(3), Spring 1986.

"Science in Japan," special issue of *Science*, vol. 233(4761), July 18, 1986.

Erik Arnold and Ken Guy, *Parallel Convergence* (Frances Pinter, London, 1986).

C. Ballamy, *The Future of Land Warfare* (Croom Helm, Beckenham, UK, 1987).

John Bessant and Sam Cole, *Stacking the Chips: Information Technology and the Distribution of Income* (Frances Pinter, London, 1985).

Martin Binkin, *Military Technology and Defense Manpower* (Brookings Institution, Washington, DC, 1987).

David H. Brandin and Michael A. Harrison, *The Technology War: A Case for Competitiveness* (Wiley-Interscience, New York, 1987).

Wilson Dizard, "Mikhail Gorbachev's Computer Challenge," *The Washington Quarterly*, vol. 9(2), Spring 1986.

Arnold Gibbons, *Information, Ideology and Communication: The New Nations' Perspectives on an Intellectual Revolution* (University Press of America, Lanham, MD, 1985).

Gene Gregory, *The Japanese Electronics Industry* (John Wiley, Chichester, UK, 1986).

Bruce R. Guile and Harvey Brooks (eds), *Technology and Global Industry: Companies and Nations in the World Economy* (National Academy Press, Washington, DC, 1987).

Alan Johnston and Albert Sassoon (eds), *New Technologies and Development* (UNESCO, Paris, 1987).

Paul Jowett and Margaret Rothwell, *The Economics of Information Technology* (Macmillan, London, 1986).

Meheroo Jussawalla, Dan J. Wedemeyer, and Vijay Menon, *The Passing of Remoteness? Information Revolution in the Asia-Pacific Region* (Institute of Southeast Asian Studies, Singapore, 1986).

James Lardner, *Fast Forward: Hollywood, the Japanese and the VCR Wars* (W. W. Norton, New York, 1987).

Herbert Lin, "The Development of Software for Ballistic-Missile Defense," *Scientific American*, vol. 253(6), December 1985 (must be "right first time!").

Ian Mackintosh, *Sunrise Europe: The Dynamics of Information Technology* (Basil Blackwell, Oxford, 1986).

Brian M. Murphy, *The International Politics of New Information Technology* (Croom Helm, Beckenham, UK and St Martins Press, New York, 1986).

Simon Ramo, *The Business of Science: Winning and Losing in the High-Tech Age* (Hill and Wang, New York, 1988).

Robert Schware and Alice Trembour, "Rethinking Microcomputer Technology Transfer to Third World Countries," *Science and Public Policy*, vol. 12(1), February 1985.

Steven M. Shaker and Alan R. Wise, *War Without Men: Robots on the Future Battlefield* (Pergamon-Brassey, New York, 1987).

Merritt Roe Smith (ed.), *Military Enterprise and Technological Change* (MIT Press, Cambridge, MA, 1986).

John Tirman (ed.), *The Militarization of High Technology* (Ballinger, Cambridge, MA, 1984).

The future

"The Economy of the 1990s," a special report in *Fortune*, February 2, 1987.

Isaac Asimov (ed.), devised by Peter Nicholls, *Living in the Future* (Multimedia, London, and Beaufort Books, New York, 1985).

Burnham P. Beckwith, *Beyond Tomorrow, A Rational Utopia* (Beckwith, Palo Alto, CA, 1986).

Joseph J. Corn (ed.), *Imagining Tomorrow: History, Technology and the American Future* (MIT Press, Cambridge, MA, 1986).

Norman Macrae, *The 2024 Report: A Concise History of the Future 1974-2024* (Sidgwick and Jackson, London, and Collier-Macmillan, New York, 1984).

Michael Marien and Lane Jennings, *What I Have Learned: Thinking About the Future Then and Now* (Greenwood Press, Westport, CT, 1987).

Charles Maurice and Charles W. Smithson, *The Doomsday Myth: 10,000 Years of Economic Crises* (Hoover Institution Press, Stanford, CA, 1984).

Howard P. Segal, *Technological Utopianism in American Culture* (University of Chicago Press, Chicago, IL, 1985).

Brian Stableford and David Langford, *The Third Millenium: A History of the World AD 2000-3000* (Sidgwick and Jackson, London, and Knopf, New York, 1985).

Index

Compaq 10–11
compatibility of systems 169, 180–1
competition
  computerized banking 376, 381
  global 358–9
competitiveness, gender difference 489–90
"compunications" 66
Computer Abuse Research Bureau (CARB) 418
computer-aided design (CAD) 298–9, 316
computer-based automation in factories 291–300
computer games 73, 489–90
computer-integrated manufacturing systems (CIM) 9, 10, 273, 308–17, 362, 363
computer literacy 73
Computer Literacy Project, BBC 482, 494
computer numerical control (CNC) 292–5, 312
computer output, theft 418
computer revolution
  the myth 82–3
  in US 281–2, 288
Computer School 243–4
computer security, 169, 425–6
Computer Security Act, 1987 456
computer society: to whom the benefits? 88
computer staff
  as criminals 419–20
  and security 426
computer studies, as academic discipline 483–5
computer systems, user interface 167–8
computerization
  benefits 338
  impact 337–9
  losses 338, 369
  possible growth 8–9
computers
  as controllers 36–9
  and crime *see* crime and computers; security
  as defining technology 4, 33–40
  Fifth Generation 87, 136, 153, 201
  growth, in banks 282

history and origins 19
impact on society 34–5
manipulating symbols 129–31
miniaturization 25
monitoring people 397–406
role in change 23–4
sales to service industries 112
sexy *see* Minitel
theft of 416
Time's Man of the Year 83, 428
value 126
varieties used in Burma 503
versus humans 149
see also personal computers
computing infrastructure, desktop computers 346
conferencing, political 444, 448; *see also* teledemocracy
conflict, political 427–8
Congress and information control *see* US Government, information control
Congressional Research Service (CRS) 170
Connecticut 466, 467
Connecticut Mutual Life Insurance Company 322–3
construction work, safety 303
consultation, lack of in industry 311
consumer durables 222
consumer electronic products 198–9
continuists, on IT 2–3
continuous flow manufacturing 277–8
contracts, standard, for software 414
control
  crisis of *see* crisis of control
  definition 53–4
  over desktop computerization 347–8
  revolution in 52–4
Control Data Corporation 432, 479
control systems in factories 301–2
control technology
  evolution 48–70
  new 59–63
controls, improved, in the home 200
convergence in political economies 434
copyright 407–14

kiosk, le 232
Knight-Ridder Newspapers 219, 403
know-how, human 126–7
knowledge
  in AI 157–60
  intuitive 126, 127–9
  and power 90
  use of IT 44
knowledge society 6
Kollmorgan 428, 430
Korea, South
  computer policy 504, 510
  piracy 410

labor, division of, and computerization 343, 348
labor force *see* employment
laboratories, computers in 337
law
  increased employment in 12
  use of IT 43–4
  see also crime and computers
layout of information 178–80
leadership
  in new firms 476–7
  in teams 304 6
learning new technology 329
learning process
  in AMS 312
  in children 241
  in factories 304–5
  incentives 343–4
  office computers 270–1
ledgers 318–19
LEGO/LOGO 238–9, 241
leisure society 7
Le Monde 236
levers 185
Liberation 230
librarians, information control 452, 455
libraries
  computer use 484
  and information 89
Library of Congress 170–1
life-critical systems, design 172

lifestyles 224; *see also* home informatics; social roles, in factories
light pens 182, 185
Limited Stores 114
Linear Accelerator Conference 455
linguistic incompatibility 181
LOGO 141, 237–9, 245–6
Lotus 1-2-3 319, 322, 324, 326, 369
  copyright 407–8, 410, 412
Lyons, France 474

MIT
  and AI 130, 131, 240–1
  origin 473
MIT Media Lab 42, 240–1
machines, access to 344
machines and users 166–197
machinists 293, 296
  as programmers 292–3, 294
McKinsey & Co. 376
magnetic fields in VDTs 195
maintenance features, HI 208
maintenance work 297–8
Malaysia Energy Efficiency Project 506
man
  as clockwork 40
  and the environment 29, 37
management
  changes required 359, 361
  see also team structure in factories
management control 12, 314, 328
  over production 293, 294–5
Management Focus Inc. 369
managers
  changing role 330
  reduction 380
  and security 425
  as social leaders 430
Manhattan Project 160
manufacturing 5–6
  importance 97–103
  use of IT 272–80
  and wealth 103
  see also industry
Manufacturing Automation Protocol (MAP) 9

Index by J. D. Lee